C0-AVK-598

Pn
685
B7
1928
v. 1
(c.1)

# The
# Evolution of Arthurian Romance
## From the Beginnings
## Down to the Year 1300

by

### James Douglas Bruce, Ph. D.
Professor of the English Language and Literature
in the University of Tennessee.

### Second Edition
with a supplement by Alfons Hilka (Goettingen)

### Volume I

LIBRARY
NOV 3 1966
FAIRFIELD U.

GLOUCESTER, MASS.

PETER SMITH

1958 [c1928]

WITHDRAWN
FAIRFIELD UNIVERSITY
LIBRARY

SECOND EDITION, 1928

REPRINTED 1958 BY PERMISSION OF
THE JOHNS HOPKINS PRESS

ALL RIGHTS RESERVED

9-4-81

# Preface.

The present volumes are the outgrowth of a series of six lectures on the Arthurian Romances which I delivered before the graduate students of the Modern Language Departments of the Johns Hopkins University in December, 1912, and which I repeated in the Summer School of the University of Pennsylvania in 1915 as part of a general course on the Mediaeval Romances. It was only after the repetition, however, just mentioned that I decided to work these lectures out in a fuller form for publication. The task of putting this purpose into effect grew constantly upon my hands, so that the final result is a far bulkier treatment of the subject than I originally had in contemplation. On the other hand, the need of a guide through the mazes of mediaeval Arthurian romance and of the vast body of modern critical writings pertaining there-to has been long felt by students of mediaeval literature, and the book, in its present form, is offered as an attempt to meet that need.

I regret the necessity of fixing upon 1300 as the downward limit of the treatise. This regret applies less, to be sure, to the continental romances of the cycle — since, notwithstanding the popularity in its own day of such a work as *Le Petit Artus de Bretaigne*, for example, all really notable productions in this *genre* on the continent antedate that year — than to those written in English. For, except *Sir Tristrem* and *Arthour and Merlin*, neither of which rise above mediocrity, the extant English romances of the cycle were composed after the year 1300. Nevertheless, even as regards the English romances, the expressed regret was mitigated by the reflection that, after all, mediaeval English literature can boast of only four contributions of substantial importance to Arthurian romance, viz. *Sir Gawain and the Green Knight*, the alliterative *Morte Arthure*, the stanzaic

79122

*Morte Arthur,* and Malory's great compilation in prose. In any event, the determining factor in the limitation of time which has here been adopted was that to have attempted to carry on the work any further would have meant an indefinite postponement of its completion.

In a domain where almost everything is the subject of controversy, as is the case with Arthurian romance, it is difficult for the author of a general treatise, like the present one, who has strong convictions in regard to the questions under debate, not to seem frequently over-dogmatic or even unfair to his opponents in the expression of these convictions. In the notes and in the division of the book entitled "Discussions", I have endeavored to justify at length my own position in many of these matters, but, owing to considerations of space, it has been obviously impossible to do this in all instances, and so I have often been compelled to content myself with inserting into my presentation of the subject such qualifying clauses as "in my opinion" and the like. But since such clauses are apt to become tiresome by repetition, I have on many occasions ventured to omit them, without intending, of course, to claim infallibility in leaving the expression of my views thus unqualified. As an example of such controversial questions the age-long debate concerning the debt of the Arthurian romances to Celtic sources may be cited. Like Professors Foerster and Golther before me, I am convinced that this debt has been, generally speaking, greatly exaggerated and that personal invention was the most important factor in the creation of these romances — that we have, therefore, in this species of literature the products of a literary fashion steadily developed by successive generations of writers in an age when the sense of literary property was virtually non-existent and men did not hesitate to use their predecessors' compositions for any purpose they chose — not, in any essential degree, the reflection of a great body of oral tradition.[1] My presentation

---

[1] This is undeniably true of the prose romances. I believe, however, that if we deduct most of the lays and a few episodes (indicated *passim* below) in the earlier romances, the statement will also hold good of the metrical romances. After all, most of the extant

of the matter proceeds, accordingly, from this point of view, although I have, of course, tried to be fair to the scholars who espouse the opposite theory. Indeed, my position with regard to the whole general question concerning the folk-tale sources of the Arthurian romances will be found to be somewhat similar to that just indicated in the case of the Celtic problem. For, even apart from the question of specifically Celtic sources, in my opinion, the element of individual invention and of purely literary origins in the romances has been unduly minimized. The authors of these romances were primarily poets, not transcribers of folk-tales, and it seems strange that scholars should so often have imputed to them the strictest accuracy in following imaginary folk-tale sources when we know that even the professional collectors of folk-tales in modern times have rarely taken down such stories from oral recitation without introducing into their texts numerous unauthorized alterations.

A further word of explanation is, perhaps, due with regard to the inclusion of many romances that are mediocre or even worse in the division of Vol. II which is devoted to analyses. This has been done with an especial view to the students of stories, who are, of course, particularly numerous in the field of mediaeval studies. The more tedious the romance, the more grateful for such condensed synopses, doubtless, will be the specialist who is endeavoring to run down the history of some *motif* in fiction. In any event, as I hardly need observe, these analyses have been grouped together in a section by themselves, so that they do not interrupt the general narrative of the development of Arthurian romance, and, consequently, readers who may be interested in the remainder of the book will be able to omit without inconvenience such analyses in this section as do not attract them, or, indeed, the whole section.

In conclusion, I wish to express my gratitude to Professor James W. Bright for having offered to include this book in the

---

romances in verse were written after the composition of the prose romances had begun, and, obviously, there was no reason why the authors of the former and of the latter, respectively, should have drawn upon sources of a different character.

series, *Hesperia,* — also, to the authorities of the British Museum and Widener Library (Harvard University), to whose well-known liberality and courtesy I have been deeply indebted whilst prosecuting my Arthurian studies in those institutions.

University of Tennessee,
  Knoxville, Tennessee,                J. D. BRUCE.
  November 16, 1922.

# Contents of vol. I.

## Part I: Traditions, Chronicles, Lays, and Romances

## Part II: The Holy Grail

## Part III: The Prose Romances

# Abbreviations employed in the present treatise.

(Herrig's) *Archiv f. d. St. der n. Spr.* = Archiv für das Studium der neueren
      Sprachen.
LB     = Literaturblatt für Germanische und Romanische Philologie.
LZ     = Literarisches Zentralblatt für Deutschland.
MLN  = Modern Language Notes.
MLR  = Modern Language Review.
MPh  = Modern Philology.
PMLA = Publications of the Modern Language Association of America.
RR     = Romanic Review.
RTR   = Paulin Paris's Romans de la Table Ronde (5 vols., Paris,
      1868—1877).
Sommer = H. O. Sommer's The Vulgate Version of the Arthurian
      Romances (7 vols. plus Index, Washington, D. C., 1908—1916).
Vollmöller, JB = K. Vollmöllers Jahresbericht über die Fortschritte der
      Romanischen Philologie.
*Zs. f. celt. Ph.* = Zeitschrift für celtische Philologie.
*Zs. f. d. A.* = Zeitschrift für deutsches Altertum.
*Zs. f. d. Ph.* = Zeitschrift für deutsche Philologie.
*Zs. f. frz. Spr. u. Litt.* = Zeitschrift für französische Sprache und Litteratur.
*Zs. f. rom. Ph.* = Zeitschrift für romanische Philologie.

# PART I.

TRADITIONS, CHRONICLES, LAYS, AND ROMANCES.

# Chapter I.

## Early Traditions Concerning Arthur in the Chronicles and Elsewhere.

In the earliest recorded traditions concerning Arthur, he is represented as a victorious leader of the Britons — early in the sixth century, it would appear — in their desperate struggle against the Anglo-Saxon invaders. But did any such person ever actually exist? The candid historian must admit that the evidence on the subject (which we shall review in this chapter) is meagre, relatively late, and almost wholly fantastic, and that, consequently, an affirmative answer to this question is, by no means, inevitable. Nevertheless, we may say that under the conditions that prevailed in the wild years just referred to there is nothing unlikely in the supposition that some born leader of men may have emerged from the mass of the Britons and by his energy and valor have enabled them to win such signal, though temporary, successes over their enemies as to have secured for him a legendary fame with posterity. Moreover, strong confirmation of Arthur's historical character seems afforded by the fact that his name is, in its origin, not Celtic, but Roman, being derived from the name, *Artorius*,[1] which occurs in Tacitus[2] and Juvenal[3] and which is,

---

[1] Cp. Heinrich Zimmer, *Göttingische Gelehrte Anzeigen* for Oct. 10, 1890, p. 818. The German scholar cites *ibid.*, note 1, various Celts with Roman names, e. g. Constantinus and Aurelius (Conan) among the Celtic princes denounced by Gildas (first half of the sixth century). Even the names of some of the best-known characters that figure in Celtic tales were derived from the Romans, e. g. *Yvain-Owein* from *Eugenius*, *Geraint* from *Gerontius*, *Kei* (perhaps) from *Caius*. Similarly, R. Thurneysen, *Zs. f. deutsche Philologie*, XXVIII, 91, note 1, with reference to *Ywein*, and *ibid.*, 97, note 1, with reference to *Urien (Urbgen)* = *Urbigenus*. It was a curious fancy of A. Holtzmann's,

indeed, the name of a Roman *gens*. During the long centuries of Roman occupation of Britain (from the first century to the fifth), many Romans, from one circumstance or another, had settled in that country, and a still larger number of the native Celtic inhabitants had become Romanized. When the Anglo-Saxon onslaught came, such elements in the population shared, of course, the fortunes of the rest, and, owing to the superiority in education and wealth which they generally enjoyed, were, perhaps, even more likely than the pure Britons to produce a national hero. Certainly we know from Gildas (ch. 5) that one of the principal leaders of the Britons in their wars against the invaders was Ambrosius Aurelianus, "a man of Roman race." When the chroniclers, then, report that Arthur won the battle of Mons Badonis (Badon Hill) — an historical battle fought, undoubtedly, as we know, in the first part of the sixth century — it seems wiser to accept this statement as authentic and to recognize in him a man of Roman descent or a Romanized Celt, who, in these times of stress, attained the leadership of the British hosts. There is no need, therefore, of regarding him simply as a creature of the popular imagination or of vaporizing him into a hypothetical culture-divinity, as various scholars have done.[4]

---

Pfeiffer's *Germania*, XII, 279 (1867) that not only were Arthur and Vortimer, son of Vortigern and enemy of Hengist and Horsa, the same person, in British and Anglo-Saxon tradition, respectively, but that their names were, also, identical, *Vortimer* having become *Arthur*, as he surmises, in Welsh pronunciation.

[2] *Annals*, Book XV, ch. 71.

[3] *Satires*, III, 29 — here in the feminine form, as a woman's name, *Artoria Flaccilla*.

[4] So John Rhys, *Studies in the Arthurian Legend*, pp. 39 ff. (Oxford 1891). He acknowledges that the derivation of *Arthur* from *Artor, Artorius* is, phonetically, unobjectionable; nevertheless, with his customary weakness for the fanciful mythological interpretations of Max Müller and his school — once so popular, but now generally discredited — he endeavors to connect the name with the Aryan root, *ar* — (= to plough), and hence conjectures that Arthur was by origin a culture-divinity.

Among the interpretations of Arthur's name, I note, also, the following: In his article, "King Arthur and Gildas", *The Academy*, Oct.

Let us examine now in due order the testimony of the earliest records with respect to Arthur and his achievements.

It appears surprising, at first sight, that Gildas, the British historian, who is our earliest authority on the Anglo-Saxon conquest of Britain, in his *De Excidio et Conquestu Britanniae* —[5] written about 540, A. D. — should not mention Arthur, although he refers (ch. 26) to the battle of Badon Hill with which later chroniclers connected that hero's fame.[6] The explanation, however, may well lie in the fact that Gildas's "Epistle", as he calls it (ch. 1), is not a regular historical narrative — it was not composed as such — but rather a homily on the misfortunes of the Britons as due to their sins — a "tract for the times", as a modern editor has aptly called it —[7] and that it gives us, therefore, simply glimpses of persons and events rather than an orderly account of them. Indeed, a large part of the work consists of a mere cento of passages

---

12, 1895, E. W. B. Nicholson identifies with Arthur the personage referred to by Gildas, ch. 32, as "Ursus", and regards *Arthur* as made up of two old Celtic words, *artos* (= *bear*) and *viros* (= *man*). Hence, the name would mean *Bear-male* or *He-bear*. J. Pinkerton, I may remark, in his edition of Barbour's *Bruce*, I, 26 (London, 1790), had anticipated Nicholson's etymology, but had interpreted the combination as meaning simply "the great man". As a matter of fact, Celtic proper names with *artos* (= *bear*) in composition are numerous. Cp. A. Holder, *Alt-Celtischer Sprachschatz*, 226 f. (Leipzig 1891), although Holder, himself, suggests a probable connection of *Arthur* with Irish *art* (= *stone*).

[5] The standard text of this work is Theodor Mommsen's, in the *Monumenta Germaniae Historica, Auctorum Antiquissimorum*, vol. XIII, (Berlin, 1898). Hugh Williams has reprinted this text (with a few changes) in his edition, *Cymmrodorion Record Series*, No. 3 (London, 1899—1901). He gives, also, a translation and valuable notes. Among the older editions, San Marte's — *Nennius und Gildas*, (Berlin, 1844) — is still useful. For the critical literature on Gildas, cp. R. H. Fletcher, *The Arthurian Material of the Chronicles, especially those of Great Britain and France*, pp. 2 f., note, (Boston, 1906): [Harvard] *Studies and Notes in Philology and Literature*, X.

[6] According to the most acceptable construction of this same passage, indeed, he tells us in it, also, that he was born in the year of that battle. He wrote the *De Excidio* before 547. Cp. Mommsen's edition, p. 5.

[7] Hugh Williams, p. V.

from the Scriptures — especially, thunders of the Old Testament
prophets against the sins of the Jews — both people and rulers —
which Gildas here applies to his own fellow-countrymen.[8] From
the silence of such a work no inference can be drawn as to the
matter in hand. The first record[9] of the name, *Arthur,* occurs in
Adamnan's life of Saint Columba,[10] the famous Irish missionary,
who founded the monastery at Iona in the Hebrides. In a Latinized
form, *Arturius* — for Adamnan's work is in Latin · - it is there
found as the name of a young Irish prince who perished in a battle
at Tigernach (Ireland) in the year, 596. The father of this young
man, Aed mac Gabrain, was the ruler of an Irish state, Dalraida,
on the southwest coast of Scotland. Still further, in the seventh
century we find a Welsh prince,[11] a British prince[12] and an Irishman whose rank is unknown,[13] all bearing this name, and since
Arthur was not a common name among the Celts, perhaps, we are
justified in interpreting these instances of its occurrence as testimony to the existence of legends in the sixth and seventh centuries
concerning the person who was destined to render it so illustrious.[14]
The first direct mention, however, of the great sovereign of romance occurs in the account of his exploits in the *Historia Brit-*

---

[8] Virtually only Part I (ch. 1—26) gives any historical information.

[9] For the first three Arthurs here noted, cp. H. Zimmer. *Nennius
Vindicatus,* pp. 283 ff. (Berlin 1893).

[10] Book I, ch. 9. Cp. J. T. Fowler's second edition (Oxford, 1920).
Adamnan died in 704. His *Vita Columbae* was written before 697
and is preserved in a MS. not later than 714.

[11] Arthur map Petr, who was ruling in Dyfed (Southwest Wales)
in the first decade of the seventh century.

[12] Arthur, son of Bicuir, apparently a prince. He slew a famous
Ulster chieftain in Cantire (Southwest Scotland) in 625.

[13] Cp. Kuno Meyer in his article "Eine verschollene Artursage",
pp. 63 ff. of the *Festschrift für Ernst Windisch* (Leipzig, 1914). The
name occurs here in a list of ecclesiastics who stood security for the
execution of the law known as Cäin Adamnain. The list was compiled
in 697 and contains the name, *Faradach hōa Artur* — i. e. "Faradach,
grand-son of Arthur". This Arthur, then, must have lived in the early
part of the seventh century.

[14] So Zimmer, *loc. cit.*

*tonum* (ch. 56), which goes under the name of Nennius.[15] Here it is said that, after the death of Hengest, the Saxon chieftain, Arthur fought against the Saxons *cum regibus Brittonum, sed ipse dux erat bellorum* — that is to say, that he was not himself one of the British kings, although he commanded their forces in battle.[16] Then follows an enumeration of his twelve great victories,[17] concluding with that of Badon Hill, which we know from Gildas to be historical — only here in Nennius the narrative is already colored with legend, for it is said that Arthur alone slew 960 of the enemy in a single attack.[18]

---

[15] The standard edition of Nennius is T. Mommsen's. It is in the same volume as his edition of Gildas, mentioned above. San Marte, also, edited Nennius, in the same volume as his Gildas. Cp. p. 5, note 5, above. His notes are still useful. For bibliography of Nennius, cp. Fletcher, *op. cit.*, pp. 8 f., note.

[16] Richard Thurneysen, *Zs. f. deutsche Philologie*, XXVIII, 98, note 1 (1895), suggests that the term *dux* was applied to rulers who did not spring from the *hochadel* (higher nobility). It is evident, however, here that Arthur is not conceived of as a ruler.

[17] The variants in Mommsen's edition (p. 200) show great confusion in regard to the eleventh in the list of Arthur's battles, "bellum in monte qui dicitur Agned." We shall see below, Part IV, that Anscombe has argued that "Mons Badonis" is simply a corruption for "Mons Hagonis" ("Hill of Agon"). Except for one MS., however, all MSS. seem to have "Mons Badonis" for the twelfth. A. Wade-Evans, *Y Cymmrodor*, XXII, 155, contends that the name of this battle got into the list from "pseudo-Gildas" (i. e. Gildas, whose work he regards as spurious and late) and Bede; but the analyses of Zimmer and Thurneysen seem to establish the antiquity of the whole list. The entry in the *Annales Cambriae* (under 516), however, concerning Mons Badonis apparently possesses no value. The annalist, it seems, took it from Nennius and attached to it details which he found in Nennius connected with the eighth battle ("in castello Guinion"). Cp. on the subject A. de la Borderie, *Revue Celtique*, VI, 2, and W. H. Stevenson, *The English Historical Review*, XVII, 633, note 34. The most detailed effort to identify the sites of the twelve battles is Anscombe's *Zs. f. celt. Ph.*, V, 103 ff. (1905), but in no case can he be said to have attained assured results.

[18] Anscombe, in the article just cited (p. 116), interprets this 960 as due to some scribal blunder. The figure was originally 470, he says, and indicated, really, the date of the battle of Mons Hagonis (the

In the section of this work (ch. 73) called *De mirabilibus Britanniae*, we have still further mention of Arthur in connection with a marvel localized in the region called Buelt — the present Builth in South Wales. Here it is stated that there was in this place a heap of stones, which was crowned by one stone that bore the impress of the foot of Arthur's dog, Cabal. The stone had received this impress during Arthur's hunting of the boar Troynt — an adventure which is related fully in the mediaeval Welsh tale of *Kulhwch and Olwen*. Nennius says that, although one might remove this stone from the heap one day, it would always be found there the next. Immediately after this we find still another marvel connected with Arthur — the tomb of his son, *Anir*, who had fallen at the hands of his father. This tomb varied in length at every new measurement. At one time it might measure six feet, at another fifteen — "and I alone have tested it," says the veracious chronicler.

The work which bears the name of Nennius is composite in character, and the history of its growth seems to be as follows:[19]

---

name he gives to the great British victory over the Saxons which in our text of Gildas is called, in the genitive, "Badonici montis"). Geoffrey of Monmouth, Book IX, ch. 15, as Anscombe contends, preserves the correct figure, viz. 470, only Geoffrey, too, uses it of the number of men that Arthur killed in the battle of Mount Badon. Wade-Evans, also, adopts these views of Anscombe's. Cp. *Y Cymmrodor*, XXII, 128. The speculation, however, is anything but convincing.

[19] My account of this growth is based on the investigations of Heinrich Zimmer, in his *Nennius Vindicatus* (Berlin, 1893) and of Thurneysen, in his reviews of this work of Zimmer's in the *Zs. f. deutsche Philologie*, XXVIII, 80 ff. (1895) and of Mommsen's edition of Gildas and Nennius in *Zs. f. celt. Ph.*, I, 157 ff. (1896), respectively. Before the publication of Zimmer's work the value of the *Historia Brittorum* was underestimated and the connection of any one named Nennius with it was doubted. Moreover, no part of it was regarded as of so considerable an antiquity as now seems to have been actually the case. The best representative of this depreciatory tendency is Arthur de la Borderie: *L'Historia Britonum attribuée à Nennius et l'Historia Britannica avant Geoffroi de Monmouth* (Paris and London, 1883). Similarly, G. Heeger, *Über die Trojanersagen der Britten* Munich, 1886), and even later, W. W. Newell, "Doubts concerning

In the third decade of the ninth century a writer named Nennius, who lived in South Wales, re-edited and expanded an older *Historia Brittonum* that dated back to 679, or, perhaps, in part, to an even earlier period in the seventh century. Now, the passage cited above concerning Arthur and his twelve victories belongs to the oldest portion of the work and shows the vigorous development of legend about the hero's name within something like one hundred and fifty years of the time when he must have lived. The section which relates the marvels of Arthur's dog and of Anir's

---

the British History attributed to Nennius", PMLA, XX, 622 ff. (1905). Both Zimmer and Thurneysen accept the earlier *Historia Brittonum* (mentioned in the text above) as dating from 679 and as containing still older materials. Thurneysen, *Zs. f. d. Ph.*, XXVIII, 83 f., is inclined, still further, to ascribe to a Run (Rum) mab Urbgen (mentioned in Nennius, ch. 63) the compilation of a part of these older materials. Urbgen (a historical character who died between 572 and 579) seems to have been the Urien of the romances; Run would, therefore, be the brother of the Yvain (Ivain) of these romances.

Zimmer neglected the important Chartres MS. (ninth or tenth century) of the *Historia Brittonum,* which preserves us the work in a pre-Nennian form. L. Duchesne published the text of this MS. in the *Revue Celtique,* XV, 174 ff. (1894), "Nennius Retractatus", together with a discussion of Nennius problems. Thurneysen had the advantage over Zimmer of the use of the Chartres text, and, taken altogether, his conclusions concerning the origin and development of the *Historia Brittonum,* as stated *Zs. f. celt. Ph.,* I, 166 f. (1896), are to be preferred, viz. that in the neighborhood of Builth (in South Wales), in the year 826, Nennius (Nemnius), compiled the work in the full form, known as the Harleian recension. Immediately thereafter, on the advice of his teacher, Beulan (cp. ch. 10), he prepared an abbreviated edition of this Harleian recension. Later on, he entered additions and corrections in this abbreviated recension. Excerpts from the life of St. Germanus by Map Urbgen constitute the oldest elements of the work. For the MSS. of the different recensions, see Mommsen, pp. 119 ff. and Thurneysen, *Zs. f. celt. Ph.,* I, 158 f. — Windisch, *Das keltische Britannien,* etc., p. 41, speaks of the Harleian recension as "vornennianisch", which seems, however, an error.

In *Romania,* XXIII, 432 ff. (1894) César Boser, in his article, "Apropos de Nennius", had already (before Thurneysen) attacked the argument by which Zimmer had attempted to fix the date of Nennius. He suggests, however, no alternative date.

tomb is one of the later additions, as the manuscript tradition proves, but it testifies also to the continued growth of wonderful legends about the British chieftain. It does not surprise us then to find that in the year, 1113, stories concerning Arthur were firmly established both in Brittany and in Cornwall. In that year certain monks of Laon in Brittany were sent to England to beg money for the rebuilding of their cathedral which had recently been destroyed by fire. We have an account of their experiences preserved in a treatise by Hermann of Tournai.[20] From this account it appears that a servant of the monks got into a dispute with a Cornishman as to whether Arthur was still alive — "exactly in the same way" remarks the chronicler significantly, "as the inhabitants of Brittany dispute with the French over Arthur." The affair drew together a mob and there would have been bloodshed. if a local ecclesiastic had not intervened. The chronicler concludes naively that the man who started this brawl was punished for doing so — for he had a withered hand and had come there to be cured by the relics which the visiting monks had brought with them. The Holy Virgin, however, was evidently displeased with him, for the relics would not work a miracle on him that day.

Still further, in a life of the Cornish saint, St. Carantoc, also dating from about the beginning of the twelfth century, we find Arthur reigning in Cornwall and hunting a dragon which had devastated his dominions.[21]

---

[20] Cp. Migne's *Patrologia Latina*, Vol. 156, col. 973.

[21] Cp. F. Lot, *Romania*, XXX, pp. 2 ff. (1901). St. Carantoc, however, did not allow any one to kill the serpent. He led the monster about like a lamb. Lot identifies Dindraithov, where, according to the legend, Arthur was reigning, with the modern Castle an Dinas (about ten miles east of Crantock). He points out, moreover, that Arthur is represented in *Kulhwch and Olwen* (Loth's *Mabinogion*[2], I, 344) as chasing the marvellous boar, Twrch Trwyth, in Cornwall (Kernyw) and as having (Loth, *op. cit.*, I, 38, 331, 334 et passim) a royal residence at Kelliwic (Bodmin) in Cornwall. He commands troops from Cornwall and Devon in the *Vita Gildae*, ch. 10, and has among his retinue Gwynnhyvar (Loth, *op. cit.*, I. 277), who is a high officer in those kingdoms — a man who was, also, among the persons responsible for the battle of Camlan. Cornwall figures, furthermore. in the tale of Arthur's fight with the Cath Paluc; for the mother (the sow, Henwen)

We need not linger over the meagre borrowings from Nennius which are incorporated in certain chronicles of the two centuries or slightly upwards that followed the compilation of that work in its final form,[22] for they have no independent value. In these chronicles of the succeeding centuries, only one entry is of importance, namely, that which in the *Annales Cambriae,* under the year 537, records for the first time in the barest possible

---

of this monster was, according to a triad (Loth, *op. cit.*, II, 271), in a drove of swine kept at Glynn Dallwyr, in Cornwall. On Arthur's combat with the Cath Paluc, cp. E. Freymond's monograph, *Artus' Kampf mit dem Katzenungestüm* in the *Festgabe für Gustav Gröber* (Halle, 1899). — The discussion of Arthurian localities in Cornwall by W. H. Dickinson in his *Arthur in Cornwall* (London, 1900) has been superseded by that of J. Loth, in his *Contributions à l'étude des Romans de la Table Ronde* (Paris, 1912).

It should be remembered, too, that according to the Welsh tradition, Arthur's last battle took place at Camlan — doubtless, Camelford in Cornwall, with which it is still locally identified. Cp. F. Lot, *Romania,* XXX, pp. 16 ff. (1901) and my edition of the *Mort Artu,* pp. 291 ff. This Welsh tradition would naturally be of Cornish origin. On the improbable identification of Camelon in Scotland as the scene of Arthur's final battle, cp. the works named, p. 73, note 72, below.

[22] There are four such chronicles: 1. *Annales Cambriae,* compiled in Wales in the second half of the tenth century. 2. A brief *Chronicle of Mount St. Michael,* apparently, of Breton origin, and probably of the eleventh century. 3. Aethelweard's *Chronicle,* written by an Englishman, probably early in the eleventh century. 4. Henry of Huntingdon's *Historia Anglorum,* English, of course, and probably not long before 1133. For these chroniclers and their relations to Nennius, the various editions of their works, etc., cp. Fletcher, *op. cit.,* pp. 31 ff. The best editions of the four chronicles, respectively, are by, 1. E. Phillimore, *Y Cymmrodor,* IX, 141 ff. (1888), reprinted by J. Loth, *Mabinogion*[2], II, 370 ff. This gives the oldest (uninterpolated) version, which is the only one we need consider. 2. Migne, *Patrologia Latina,* vol. 202, cols. 1323 ff. Cp. first entry. 3. H. Petrie and J. Sharpe's *Monumenta Historica Britannica,* I, 499 ff. Aethelward uses Nennius, it seems, but does not mention Arthur. 4. Thomas Arnold in Rolls Series, vol. 74 (London, 1879). Cp. p. 48.

There is no need of conjecturing with Fletcher that nos. 3 and 4 may owe something, also, to popular tradition.

way[23] the final battle (here called of Camlann) between Arthur
and Mordred (Medraut).

The first indisputable indication that the fame which Arthur
enjoyed among the Celts had spread to other peoples is supplied
by the *Gesta Regum Anglorum* of William of Malmesbury, which
was completed in 1125. Besides the information concerning the
British chieftain which he derived from the above-mentioned passages in Nennius, this writer condemns (I—8) the idle tales which
the Britons circulate about their hero as detracting from, rather
than adding to, his real glory, and explains (III, 287) the belief
that this hero will return from the fact that no one has seen his
tomb, adding at the same time an account of the death and supposed tomb of his nephew, Gawain, in Wales. The same writer's
work on the antiquities of Glastonbury — *De Antiquitate Glastoniensis Ecclesiae* — contains more Arthurian material, but the
passages are, no doubt, late interpolations and will be dealt with
elsewhere.[24]

If we could accept the contention of some scholars, much the
most interesting evidence in regard to the diffusion of Arthurian
stories before Geoffrey of Monmouth, would be that which was
brought to light in the year, 1888, by the Italian scholar, Pio
Rajna.[25] In the articles referred to Rajna collected numerous examples of the names, *Artusius* and *Galvanus* (Walwanus, Wal-
quanus, etc.) — that is, Arthur and Gawain, as he interpreted
them[26] — from the historical records of Northern Italy, including
Tuscany and the Marches in the twelfth century. *Artusius* is
found as early as 1114 and *Galvanus* as early as 1136 — and,
in both cases, as the names of grown men — so that these names
must have been given many years earlier to the persons that bore

---

[23] Gueith Camlann (battle of Camlann) in qua Arthur et Medraut
corruerunt; et mortalitas in Britania et in Hibernia fuit. Cp. Loth's
*Mabinogion*², II, 372. The *Annales*, in their earliest form, belong
to the latter part of the tenth century. Cp. *op. cit.*, p. 370.

[24] Cp. Part II.

[25] See his articles entitled "Gli eroi Brettoni nell' onomastica Italiana", *Romania*, XVII, 161 ff., 355 ff. (1888).

[26] Even Foerster accepted Rajna's interpretations without question.
Cp. *Zs. f. rom. Ph.*, XX, 247.

them — in the case of *Artusius* not later than 1090. Here, then, in the closing years of the eleventh century the tales concerning Arthur, if we accept Rajna's interpretation, were so widespread and popular as to affect the nomenclature of Northern Italy. Moreover, the forms of these names would appear to make it evident that the stories in question reached Italy in French versions, for *Artusius* seems, at first sight, plainly a Latinization of *Artus*, the Old French nominative of *Arthur*, and *Galvanus* similarly the Latinization of Old French *Gauvain*.[27] It is to be observed, however, that even if Rajna's identifications of those names are correct, it does not follow necessarily that his inferences are equally so, for Arthur was a Breton name and may have been brought to Italy by actual Bretons or inhabitants of French districts contiguous to Brittany, independently of any specifically Arthurian traditions.[28] The correctness of the identifications in question, however, is not entirely assured, and the forms, *Artusius* and *Galvanus*, respectively, may be variants of other names than those proposed by the Italian scholar.[29]

---

[27] In Geoffrey of Monmouth, Arthur's name is Latinized as *Arthurus*, Gawain's as *Walgannus*, *Walgainus* — probably from French *Gauvain*. Cf. Lot, *Romania*, XXV ff. (1896).

[28] This objection was already, raised by Suchier in Suchier and Birch-Hirschfeld's, *Geschichte der Französischen Literatur*[1], p. 141 (Leipzig, 1900).

H. Zimmer, *Göttingische Gelehrte Anzeigen* for Oct. 1, 1890, p. 831, note, suggests that the names may have been brought to Northern Italy by Norman mercenaries, who are known to have been in the service of states in that part of the peninsula as early as the eleventh century. He recalls, too, the Norman conquest of Sicily by Robert Guiscard and his followers in the same century.

[29] In his *Recherches sur les sources latines des contes et romans courtois du moyen age*, pp. 396f. (Paris, 1913), Edmond Faral has suggested that *Artusius* may really be identical with Germanic *Hartewic* and *Galvanus (Galgano, Gualguano, Walwanus, Walquano, Valvanus)* with either *Galganus* (name of an Italian saint) or *Galbanus* (the Roman cognomen). Faral refers, p. 397, note 1, to studies of the question of these names undertaken by a student of F. Lot's and by Professor Bédier. As far as I am aware, however, these studies have not yet got into print.

Faral's criticism (pp. 393ff.) of Rajna's articles strikes me as the

Less open to dispute are the Arthurian names which are attached to certain *bas-reliefs* over the northeast portal (Porta della Pescheria) of the Cathedral of Modena,[30] representing the siege of

best that has appeared. Obviously, as he observes, Arthurian names in Italian documents of later date than 1200 have no significance, since by that time the French romances had made these names familiar all over Western Europe. In the above-mentioned articles Rajna cites many such names — *Galasso (= Galaad), Yvannus (= Yvain)*, etc., — for this later period. Besides, *Artusius* and *Galvanus* (with variants), he cites only *Seldina (= Iselt, Iseut)*, from the year, 1180, for the period before 1200. As Faral remarks, the paucity of the names from the earlier period which Rajna conjectures to be Arthurian is in striking contrast to the abundance of indisputably Arthurian names for the later period.

In the *Archiv für das Studium der neueren Sprachen*, CXLI, 235 (1921), F. Liebermann has noted the occurrence of *Arthur* as the name of a man born, at the latest, about 1140 — apparently, in Sussex. But he may have had Welsh or Breton connections of some sort or other.

[30] Wendelin Foerster was the first person to bring these figures into Arthurian discussion, viz. in his article, "Ein neues Artusdokument", *Zs. f. rom. Ph.*, XXII, 243—8 (1898). See, too, his supplementary article, "Das neue Artusdokument", *ibid.*, pp. 526—529 (1898). The archivolt and its figures, however, had been the subject of repeated discussion before this, in works on Italian architecture. Cp. *ibid.*, p. 526. Foerster accepted the usual dating of the bas-reliefs (first decades of the twelfth century). He thought the situation represented on the archivolt was not derived from any extant Arthurian romance and observes that it is nearer to the episode of Carados and the Dolerose Tor in the prose *Lancelot* (cp. Sommer's *Vulgate Version of the Arthurian Romances*, IV, 90 ff.) than to anything else in the surviving romances and was possibly derived from some lost romance, which was the source of that episode. Foerster makes no effort to reconcile the evidence of these bas-reliefs with his customary theory that Chrétien invented the *genre* of the Arthurian romance.

Foerster's reading of the names attached to the respective figures and his identifications of the same, where offered, are probably right. They are as follows (p. 244): 1. *Winlogee = Guinloie* or *Guenloie* (which occurs in two romances, viz. *Li Chevaliers as deus espees* and *Yder*). 2. *Mardoc (= Madoc*, or, as I believe, more likely, the common Arthurian *Mariadok*, etc.). 3. *Burmaitus*, or *Burmaltus* (cp. p. 526), not known elsewhere. 4. *Isdernus*, probably = *Yder* (name of four different Arthurian knights). 5. *Carrado = Caradoc* (the giant, rather than Briebraz). 6. *Galvayinus*, probably = *Gawain*. 7. *Galvarium* a castle by Arthur and his followers, with knights issuing there-from to attack the besiegers. These bas-reliefs have been gene-rally dated early in the twelfth century and they include labelled images of Arthur, Kay, Caradoc, etc., which prove, if the above dating is correct, that stories concerning Arthur and the cha-racters associated with him were current in Northern Italy in that period. The evidence of these figures, however, stands in such absolute isolation for so early a period that one is disposed to await further investigation of their date, before accepting finally the dating which has prevailed among authorities on the archi-tectural history of Lombardy up to the present time.[31] For the

<hr />

(unknown). Foerster observes that this name seems Norman, whereas G. Paris, *Romania*, XXVIII, 145 (1899), was inclined to connect it with *Galuron* in the *Chronique de Nantes*. 8. *Che = Kai* (Kay). — The castle is at the top of the archivolt, in the centre, and nos. 1 and 2 are inside its walls. On the left hand, no. 3 comes forth to attack Arthur, no. 4, and a third (unnamed) knight. On the right, no. 5 rides out against nos. 6, 7 and 8.

Pictures of the figures which we have been discussing will be found in many publications that deal with the history of Italian archi-tecture or the Modena cathedral, more specifically, e. g. M. G. Zimmer-mann, *Oberitalische Plastik im frühen und hohen Mittelalter* (Leipzig, 1897), Plate 18; A. Venturi, *Storia dell' Arte Italiana*, III (Milan, 1904), Plate 138: Giulio Bertoni, *Atlante Storico-Paleografico del Duomo di Modena*, Plate X (Modena, 1909); A. K. Porter, *Lombard Architecture*, Plate 144, (3 vols. New Haven and London, 1917). Among discussions of the figures, cp. B. Colfi, "Di una recente interpretazione [i. e. Foerster's] data alle sculture dell' archivolto nella porta setten-trionale del duomo di Modena", *Atti e Memorie della R. Deputazione di Storia Patria per le Provincie Modenesi*, Serie IV, vol. IX (1899) — also, Zimmermann, p. 44, Venturi, III; 160ff., and Porter, I, 436f., III, 44f.

[31] Faral, op. cit., p. 395, dates these bas-reliefs about 1200. Pos-sibly, he may have authority for this dating, but the writers whose works I have cited above place them in the first half of the twelfth century, and Foerster (pp. 244f.), on the basis of the costumes, gives the same date as the latter. Venturi, III, 160, remarks: "Si e molto discusso sull' etá della porta della Pescheria, che pure mostra ad evi-denza la mano di Niccolo, cooperatore di Wiligelmo, di lui piu giovane e meno arcaico etc." Wiligelmo, it should be remarked, worked on the cathedral at the beginning of the twelfth century. Porter, III, 48, says:

names attached to them suggest an Arthurian romance from the
period of the fullest development of the *genre*, viz., the late twelfth
or early thirteenth century,[32] and it accords with this dating
that the architecture of the same portal contains figures from the

---

"Between 1099 and 1106 were erected, of the existing cathedral, the
crypt and also part of the façade with its sculptures and the Porta
della Pescheria, but the crypt and the Porta della Pescheria were subsequently very materially altered." Later on, he again speaks of there
being "abundant contemporary evidence that alterations and additions
to the church were made constantly during the XIII and XIV centuries",
but he evidently does not include the Arthurian figures among these
later additions, for in his interesting section, I, 434—438, on "Secular
Subjects" (including romances) in Lombard church architecture, he dates
(p. 436) these Arthurian figures, "1099—1106". On the other hand,
quite recently, G. Bertoni, who has made a special study of these
figures, has expressed the opinion, *Zs. f. rom. Ph.*, XL, 363 (1920)
that they cannot be later than the second half of the twelfth century
and more probably belong to the middle of the century.

Both Venturi, III, 167 and Porter, I, 436f., emphasize the resemblance of these figures to those which are found on the southwestern
side-portal of S. Nicolo at Bari (cp. Venturi, Plate 140, at III, 163):
"From a central structure issue on foot four men, two on either side;
against them come a series of men on horseback" (Porter, I, 436). Ana-
logous, too, are figures at Bobbio, and Porter, *loc. cit.*, thinks that ex-
cavation of the pavement there will throw light on the Modena archivolt.

[32] Guenloie, with whom Foerster identifies Winlogee, first occurs
in *Yder*, among the extant romances, and that is dated by its editor
in the second decade of the thirteenth century. Cp. H. Gelzer, *Der
altfranzösische Yderroman*, p. LXXIX (Dresden, 1913). To be sure,
it is probably based on an older romance, but the character of the story
shows that even this last source did not go beyond the latter part of
the thirteenth century. If *Mardoc* is the same as *Meriadoc*, the same
applies here. Cp. the *Chevaliers as deus espees*, whose hero is named
*Meriadeus* (= *Meriadoc)*, and the Latin romance *Historia Meriadoci*,
edited by J. D. Bruce, *Historia Meriadoci and De Ortu Waluuanii*,
Göttingen and Baltimore, (1913). Both, probably, belong to the second
quarter of the thirteenth century. *Mariadok* is the name of Marc's
seneschal in Thomas' *Tristan* (third quarter of the twelfth century),
but the character is less prominent than would seem to be required by
the Modena *Mardoc*. Besides, the latter evidently has nothing to do
with the *Tristan* legend.

French beast-epic which flourished in that period.[33] Even if the early dating, however, is correct, here, as in the previous case, there is always the possibility to be reckoned with that these Arthurian names may have been derived from oral tradition through Bretons or Normans.[34]

Leaving now these scanty indications of what may possibly be merely precipitates, so to speak, of tales transmitted orally, we come to the later written records of Arthur that have been preserved. Whatever interpretation we may put upon the abovementioned indications, unquestionably the *matière de Bretagne*[35] entered upon a new phase of influence with the publication of

---

[33] Lucien Foulet, *Le Roman de Renard,* p. 60 (Paris, 1914) assigns to 1152 Nivard's Latin poem *Ysengrimus,* which he thinks started the whole French beast-epic. He takes (p. 115) 1165 as the earliest possible date for any part of the *Roman de Renard,* but he assigns all branches but the second to the period after 1170.

[34] The sculptors of the figures may themselves have been from Normandy or Brittany, for such workmen in the Middle Ages often found employment in foreign countries. In any event, the immediate source was French. This is proved by the French forms of some of the names, viz., 1. *Artus* (*Artus de Bretania* in the inscription), not *Artur* or *Arturus.* 2. *Galvaginus* (formed on *Galvagin*). 3. *Che* (= French *Ke*), not *Caius* (Geoffrey of Monmouth). 4. *Winlogee,* not *Winlogea,* as the Latin form would be. Cp. Foerster, *op. cit.,* p. 248. 5. *Mardoc,* without Latin -*us.*

It must be confessed, however, that *Isdernus* is closer to the Welsh *Edeyrn (Edern)* than to the French *Ider (Idier, Yder)* in our MSS. of *Erec, Yder,* etc. Cp. too, Geoffrey's *Hiderus.* (The first *s* is, no doubt, due to the sculptor's blunder). Foerster, *ibid.,* plausibly surmises that *Carrado* stands for *Carradocus* — only limitations of space, as an inspection of the archivolt shows, prevented the sculptor from completing the name.

[35] The term, now in general use for Arthurian traditions, is taken from the famous lines of Jean Bodel, *La Chanson des Saxons,* 11. 6 ff.:

"Ne sont que. iii. matieres a nul home antandant:
De France et de Bretaigne et de Rome la grant;
Et de ces. iij. matieres n'i a nule samblant.
Li conte de Bretaigne sont si vain et plaisant;
Cil de Rome sont sage et de san aprenant;
Cil de France de voir chascun jor apparant."
The poem was written in the middle of the thirteenth century.

Geoffrey of Monmouth's *Historia Regum Britanniae* about the
year 1137.[36] In the dedication to this work, the author remarks

[36] The date of Geoffrey's work, as was pointed out by Sir Frederick
Madden in his article, "The Historia Britonum of Geoffrey of Monmouth", *The Archaeological Journal*, XV, 299 ff. (1858), is determined
by the double dedication which is preserved in the Bern MS. of the
*Historia*. This MS., which dates from about 1160, still remains unpublished. Unlike the other MSS., it contains a double dedication to
King Stephen and Robert of Gloucester. King Stephen is here extolled
in almost the same words that we find applied to Robert of Gloucester
in the other MSS. Robert, himself, is addressed as *altera regni nostri
columna* and is eulogized at greater length in terms of the most exalted
flattery. The text of this important preface is given in full in W. L.
Jones' above-mentioned paper. Cp. *ibid.*, p. 65, note. Now, as Madden
remarks, this dedication, if genuine — and there is no reason to doubt
that it is so — must have been written between April, 1136 and
May 1138, for only during this period were Stephen and Robert
of Gloucester on friendly terms. From the last-named date down to
his death in 1147 Robert was the principal supporter of the cause of
Queen Matilda in her strife with Stephen, and it is, of course, out of
the question that under these circumstances Geoffrey should have coupled
his name with that of the king in a joint dedication. The fact that
Henry of Huntingdon, writing in January, 1139, was able to give a
summary of Geoffrey's *Historia* in his letter to Warinus gives us that
year — or better, 1138 — as the *terminus ad quem* for the work. Con-
firmatory of Madden's dating of the *Historia* is A. Leitzmann's observation, that Geoffrey, at the end of his dedication, refers to Henry I
as dead, the "alterum Henricum" of that passage being really that
monarch (who died on Dec. 1, 1135), and not Henry II, as has often
been thought. See Leitzmann's "Bemerkungen zu Galfrid von Monmouth", *Archiv für das Studium der neueren Sprachen*, vol. 134,
pp. 373 ff. (1916).

The Latinity of the Bern MS. is less polished than that of the
other MSS., but, according to Professor Jones, who has collated it with
San Marte's edition (Halle, 1854), it does not differ in any essential
from the current text.

Owing to differences in Henry of Huntingdon's summary, the idea
formerly prevailed that there was a (lost) earlier recension of Geoffrey's
*Historia*. R. H. Fletcher, however, in his "Two notes on the *Historia
Regum Britanniae* of Geoffrey of Monmouth," PMLA *(Publications
of the Modern Language Association of America)*, XVI, 461 ff. (1901),
has shown that this is incorrect. For the text of Henry's Letter to
Warinus see the edition of Robert de Torigni's chronicle by Leopold
Delisle, I, 97 ff. (2 vols. Rouen, 1872—3).

that he had often marvelled at the little that had been recorded of the kings that had dwelt in Britain before the Incarnation of Christ and even concerning Arthur and his successors who lived after the Incarnation. "Now whilst I was thus thinking upon such matters, Walter, Archdeacon of Oxford, a man learned not only in the art of eloquence, but in the histories of foreign lands, offered me a certain most ancient book in the British language (quendam Britannici sermonis librum vetustissimum) that did set forth the doings of them all in due succession and order from Brutus, the first king of the Britons, onward to Cadwallader, the son of Cadwallo, all told in stories of exceeding beauty." Geoffrey's own work purports to be his translation of this ancient book. It is divided into twelve books, of which Book VII is really an earlier work of the same author, — viz. the pretended prophecies of Merlin — — and it introduces into European literature a host of new characters such as Lear, Cymbeline, Locrine, etc., whom the poets of later ages were destined to render famous. Here in the *Historia* (Book VIII, ch. 14 to Book XI, ch. 2), then, for the first time, we have related in pseudo-historical form, the glories of Uther Pendragon and Arthur, his son, the latter's birth and fictitious conquests extending as far as Rome, on the one hand, and the Baltic, on the other, until his downfall in his last battle with Mordred and his translation to Avalon. Merlin's marvels of enchantment and prophecy, Gawain's valorous deeds, and Guinevere's (Guanhamara's) marital disloyalty all form, likewise, a part of the story. The author of this book, though born in Wales, was probably the son of a Breton — a member of the Norman garrison stationed at Monmouth.[37] Between the years 1129 and 1151 he was living in the neighborhood of Oxford — probably as a canon of St. George's in the Castle of Oxford.[38] Some time sub-

---

[37] A man named Geoffrey at this time would hardly be a Welshman. Cp. J. E. Lloyd's *History of Wales down to the Edwardian Conquest,* II, 524 (2 vols. Oxford, 1911). Geoffrey signed himself *Galfridus Artur* — so his father was named Arthur.

[38] For Geoffrey's connection with Oxford, cp. the documents in which he figures as a witness (some of them new) discussed by H. Salter, "Geoffrey of Monmouth and Oxford," *English Historical Review,* XXXIV, 382ff. (1919). The best summary of all that was previously known

sequent to 1140 he was appointed an archdeaconry in the diocese of Llandaff, and on Feb. 24, 1152, after having been ordained priest only eight days before, he was made bishop of St. Asaph in his native land, but died two years later, before he had actually assumed the duties of his office. To few works in the history of literature can the much-abused term, "epoch-making," be so justly applied as to Geoffrey's *Historia*. Under any supposition, it was indubitably the most notable production in the Arthurian field that had appeared up to that date, and, in all probability, it was owing to the influence of this book, direct and indirect, that the Arthurian stories leapt into general literary popularity just at this time. The conception of Arthur as a great mediaeval monarch, the ideal representative of chivalry — not a merely fairy-tale king — originated, we may say, entirely with Geoffrey of Monmouth . He succeeded in embodying this idea in his work in a truly imposing literary form, and the pretended historical character of the *Historia* gave a dignity to the theme which it had not hitherto possessed. We need not take very seriously the author's declaration in his dedication to Robert, Earl of Gloucester, that he was translating into Latin an old book in the British language furnished him by his friend Walter, Archdeacon of Oxford. There is no evidence that he had a more than superficial acquaintance with Welsh[39] and probably he knew Breton no better. As a matter of fact, in addition to some borrowings from oral traditions, not exclusively of the Celts,[40] he drew ma-

concerning Geoffrey of Monmouth is W. Lewis Jones' paper on him in the *Transactions of the Honourable Society of Cymmrodorion* for the session, 1898—99, pp. 52 ff. Cp. too, H. L. D. Ward's *Catalogue of Romances in the Department of MSS. in the British Museum*, I, 203 ff. (1883) and E. Windisch, *Das Keltische Britannien bis zu Kaiser Artur*, pp. 123 ff. (Leipzig, 1912).

[39] Cp. Ward's *Catalogue of Romances in the Department of MSS. in the British Museum*, I, 205.

[40] In his "Bretonische Elemente in der Arthursage des Gottfried von Monmouth", *Zs. f. frz. Spr. u. Lit.*, XII[1], 231 ff. (1890), H. Zimmer endeavors to prove from the forms of certain Arthurian names that Geoffrey used Armorican sources as well as Welsh — more specifically, that he derived such materials from men who were Bretons by race, but who spoke French exclusively, or, at least, were bilingual. The

terials from Gildas, Nennius, Bede, Livy and others — in fine, from any quarter he chose, added to these materials from his own

most important names are *Eventus (= Yvain)*, *Walgainus*, *Walguainus* (= *Gawain*, who in Welsh is called Gwalchmei), *Caliburnus* (= Arthur's sword, Excalibur, which in Old French is called *Calibor(e)*, *Escalibor(e)*, etc.). In the same journal, XIII[1], 41, note 1, (1891), he adds *Ritho* to the list of such names. F. Lot, however, has pointed out, *Romania*, XXV, 1 ff. (1896), that *Eweint*, of which *Eventus* is the Latinized form, occurs as early as the tenth century in Welsh genealogies and that *Caliburnus* is as difficult to explain on the hypothesis of Armorican origin as on that of Welsh origin. On the other hand, he acknowledges that *Walgainus* is based rather on French *Gauvain (Gaugain)* than on Welsh *Gwalchmei* or Breton *Walchmoe*. In that case, however, I may remark, Geoffrey could have derived it as well from a Frenchman or from a French book as from a Breton. Lot, moreover, cites the form *Walven* for *Gawain* in William of Malmesbury's description *(De gestis Regum Angliae*, III, under the date 1086) of Gawain's tomb in the Welsh province Ros. Here it is stated that Gawain was ruler over *Waluuithia (= Galloway)*, but was expelled from his kingdom by the brother and nephew of Hengist. *Walven*, however, probably rests on French *Walwains*, and Lot, *loc. cit.*, conjectures that the tomb in question was really that of Maelgwn, and that the new identification was suggested by the name of a neighboring district, viz., Castell Gwalchmai (= Gawain's Castle). In any event, as Brugger, *Zs. f. frz. Spr. u. Lit.*, XXXIII[2], 59 f. (including p. 60, note 3) (1908), remarks, the connection of Gawain with Walweitha (Walwithia) is, no doubt, "eine gelehrte Erfindung", and, although the Welsh called Geoffrey's *Walgainus* (French *Gauvain*) by the name of *Gwalchmei*, it still remains uncertain whether the former is of Welsh origin, although this is *a priori* probable. In "Arthurian Notes", MLN, XVII, cols. 277 f. (1902) W. W. Newell suggests that Gawain's name (cp. Walwen) is formed from *Walweitha*, just as Geoffrey formed *Locrin* from *Loegria* and that Geoffrey represented him as the son of Lot (Loth), because of the usual association of Lothian and Galloway. This theory, however, seems hardly admissible.

There is, of course, nothing surprising in Geoffrey's use of French sources. Apart from the Arthurian materials under discussion, Lot, *loc. cit.*, points out his use of such sources in the episodes of Gormond (XI, 8—10, XII, 2) and Mont St. Michel (X, 3). It is evident, too, from the same scholar's discussion, *Romania*, XXX, 11 ff. (1901) that among Geoffrey's Celtic sources some were Cornish. The names of the Cornish dukes, Cador and Gorlois, prove this. So, too, with the name *Modredus;* Cp. Lot, *Romania*, XXV, 2 and Loth's *Mabinogion*[2], II,

imagination — the most important element of all — and moulded
the whole into the pseudo-historical work which we know.[41] Indeed, it is hardly open to question that Geoffrey's narrative reflects, in many particulars, even actual historical events of the
eleventh and twelfth centuries[42] — more especially, events of Nor-

---

**238**, note 1. Zimmer argues, *Zs. f. frz. Spr. u. Lit.*, XII[1], 254 f. that
it might be also a Breton form of the twelfth or thirteenth century,
but that is too late for Geoffrey's source.

San Marte (edition of Geoffrey's *Historia*, pp. LXXII ff.), like some
other students of his time and of earlier times, believed that the Welsh
*Brut Tysilio* was one of the sources of Geoffrey's *Historia*. But the
reverse is undoubtedly true, as has been shown by F. Zarncke and
B. Ten Brink in Ebert's *Jahrbuch für englische und romanische
Philologie.* Cp. the former's article, "Über das Verhältnis des Brut y
Tysilio zu Galfrid's Hist. Reg. Brit.", V, 249 ff. (1863), and the latter's
"Wace und Galfrid von Monmouth", IX, 241 ff. (1868). For some
additional points see, too, G. Heeger: *Über die Trojanersage der Britten,*
79 f. (Munich, 1886).

Altogether, I agree with Brugger, *Zs. f. frz. Spr. u. Lit.*, XXXII[2],
127 (1908), that Geoffrey borrowed names from Welsh tradition, but
little else. There are, doubtless, some exceptions, like the story of
King Leir (Lear) and his ungrateful daughters (II, 11—15). This story,
too, has analogues, it is true, outside of Celtic territory. Cp. J. Bolte
and G. Polivka, *Anmerkungen zu den Kinder- und Hausmärchen
der Brüder Grimm,* II, 47 ff. (3 vols. Leipzig, 1913—1915), and
Miss C. A. Harper, "A King Lear Analogue", *The Nation,* (New York)
for Feb. 10, 1916 (Correspondence Supplement, p. 17). The first is a
German, the second an Indian folktale. The German is closer to Geoffrey. In the Indian tale — entitled *The Hireling Husband* and printed
by Shovona Devi in her collection, *The Orient Pearls* (London, 1815) —
the choleric old king has seven sons and the youngest fills the rôle of
Cordeilla (Cordelia).

E. G. Cox's "King Lear in Celtic Tradition", MLN, XXIV, 1 ff.
(1909), gives no parallels to this immortal story. On the legend in
general, cp. W. Perrett, *The Story of King Lear:* Palaestra, no. 35
(Berlin, 1904).

[41] On Geoffrey's sources, in general, see R. H. Fletcher, *Arthurian
Material in the Chronicles,* ch. 3, and PMLA, XVI, 469 ff. (1901).
His debt to Virgil has been investigated by H. Tausendfreund, *Vergil
und Gottfried von Monmouth,* Halle, 1913, and his debt to the Old
Testament by Paul Feuerherd, *Geoffrey of Monmouth und das Alte
Testament,* ibid., 1915.

[42] So Zimmer, *Gött. G. A.* for Oct. 1890, pp. 824 ff. According

man history — of the reigns of William the Conqueror and his successors. Thus he gives Arthur in the beginning of the latter's career an imaginary King Hoel of Brittany with 15,000 Bretons as allies, no doubt, because a large number of Breton troops aided William the Conqueror in his invasion of England — these troops being led by the nephews of Count Hoel, who was then ruler of Brittany. Similarly, the way in which Arthur parcels out Gaul among his followers was doubtless suggested by the Conqueror's distribution of English lands among his companions in arms. The prominence that Winchester and Carlisle have in the Arthurian narratives of Geoffrey is also plainly due to the importance which these cities possessed in Geoffrey's own time. The former, though no longer the capital of England, as in Anglo-Saxon days, was often the residence of the Norman kings, and Carlisle under William Rufus had become one of the strong places of the kingdom.

In writing his history, Geoffrey's aim was primarily to exalt his own race. Nothing is more striking about the Normans than the interest which they took in their past and a whole crop of chronicles was the result of this interest. Geoffrey opposes now to these Norman chronicles a chronicle of the Celts with Arthur as the great hero. In an age when even such a man as Lanfranc, the great Norman Archbishop of Canterbury, could connive at forgery it is not surprising that a Celtic ecclesiastic, with the lively fancy of his race, should palm off a hoax like the *Historia* on the public of his time. That public was, in the main, uncritical and swallowed this pretended history as it swallowed the Constitutions of Constantine, which were invented to justify the temporal claims of the papacy.[43] Moreover, it touched the vanity of the

---

to Fletcher (second citation in the previous note), the kernel of the Belinus and Brennius episode of the *Historia*, III, 1—10, was supplied by the feud between Harold, the last Anglo-Saxon king, and his brother, Tostig.

[43] Although most mediaeval readers accepted Geoffrey's *Historia* as authentic, there were writers already in the latter part of the twelfth century who voiced their scepticism — so William of Newburgh and Giraldus Cambrensis, especially, in passages that have been often quoted. See the editions of their respective works in the Rolls Series, Vol. I, of the *Chronicles* of Stephen, etc. (1884), William's *Prooemium*, and

Anglo-Norman nobility, who were now identified with Great Britain, that they could claim a hero who was the equal, if not the superior, of Charlemagne, the great hero of their Continental kinsmen. The consequence of all this was that Geoffrey's *Historia* had an instantaneous and prodigious success and it stimulated immensely whatever interest there may already have been in Arthur and his companions.

The first sign of Geoffrey's influence on the vernacular literature appears in the metrical chronicles. Between 1147 and 1151 Geffrei Gaimar had used Geoffrey of Monmouth in compiling a chronicle of Great Britain in French verse.[44] His own statement is that he followed "the good book of Oxford which belonged to Walter the Archdeacon", but it is safe to say that this really means Geoffrey's *Historia*. The work was undertaken at the instance of Constance, wife of Ralph Fitz-Gilbert, an Anglo-Norman noble to whom Gaimar was chaplain. Women rarely understood Latin in the Middle Ages, and so just as vernacular versions of Biblical books were often composed for their benefit in that period, so too with the chronicles.

---

Giraldus' *Opera*, VI, 57 f. (1868) — also, the summaries of these passages in Fletcher, *op. cit.*, pp. 101 f. and 180, respectively. Among modern scholars who have expressed a belief in the reality of Geoffrey's *liber* are H. L. D. Ward, "Postscript to the article upon Geoffrey in the Catalogue of Romances, Vol. I (1883)," *Anglia*, XXIV, 383 ff. (1901), E. Windisch, *Das Keltische Brittanien bis zu Kaiser Arthur*, pp. 126 ff., (1912), and A. Leitzmann, *op. cit.*, pp. 375 f. (1916). Ward conjectures that the *liber* consisted of an Old-Welsh MS. containing many British genealogies and several historical glosses, brought home from Brittany by Archdeacon Walter. Windisch and Leitzmann argue that Geoffrey would not have dared to pass off on Robert of Gloucester — the most powerful man in the kingdom — so audacious an invention. But the examples cited above show to what length mediaeval audacity might go in such matters, and, besides, Robert of Gloucester, though cognizant of the fraud, may not have taken the matter seriously, or may have even accepted the *Historia* gladly as a sort of national epos. As such it has been interpreted with some plausibility by Sebastian Evans in his translation of the *Historia*, pp. 357 ff. (London, 1904).

[44] *L'Estorie des Engles*, edited by T. D. Hardy and C. T. Martin for the Rolls Series, 2 vols., (London, 1889), is all that survives of it.

The MSS. of Gaimar's chronicle preserve only the later portion of the work, — *L'Estorie des Engles,* as it is called. To be sure, the so-called Munich *Brut,*[45] which appears to be of the same date, is by some eminent scholars supposed to be a fragment of the earlier portion. Even this fragment, however, ends before it reaches the reign of Arthur. The only part of the extant portion of Gaimar's Chronicle, then, that contains any mention of Arthur is the story of Havelock which he has inserted in his poem. The Arthurian allusions here accord substantially with Geoffrey of Monmouth.

Of far greater importance, however, was the paraphrase completed by Wace in 1155 — the poem which is commonly called the *Roman de Brut,* or simply, *Brut,*[46] although the author's own name for it was *Geste des Bretons.* There is no dedication of it preserved in the MSS., but the English poet, Layamon (11. 42ff.), tells us that Wace "gave it to the noble Eleanor, who was the

---

[45] Edited by K. Hoffmann and K. Vollmöller, Halle, 1877. There is still another fragmentary French version of Geoffrey of Monmouth in monorhymed *laisses* preserved in M. S. Harley, 1605 (British Museum). Cp. Ward, *Catalogue of Romances,* I, 272 ff. and Otto Wendeburg, *Ueber die Bearbeitung von Gottfried von Monmouths Historia Regum Britanniae in der HS. Brit. Mus. Harl. 1605.* Braunschweig, 1881 (Erlanger Diss.). H. Suchier, LB, III, 107 f. (1882), pronounces the dialect Picard and the date not much later than Wace. The fragments have no especial interest. The condition of this version and of the Munich *Brut* (both preserved in fragmentary and unique MSS.) shows, however, how easily the French original of Layamon could be lost.

[46] Edited by Le Roux de Lincy, 2 vols., Rouen, 1836—1838. F. M. Warren, MLN, XIV, 95, points out that the numbering in this edition is wrong — 130 lines too high. A new edition of this work based on all the MSS. is a great desideratum. *Brut* is the French form of *Brutus,* name of the first king of Britain, according to Geoffrey. For Wace's life, cp. especially, G. Paris, *Romania,* IX, 592 ff. (1880). He was born in the island of Jersey about 1100 — was a canon of Bayeux in the latter part of his life. He is also well characterized by G. Paris in his *Mélanges,* I, 85 f. For a full bibliography of Wace, cp. Annette B. Hopkins, *The Influence of Wace on the Arthurian Romances of Crestien de Troies,* University of Chicago dissertation, 1913, p. 10, note 24 a.

high King Henry's queen" — that is to say, the wife of Henry II
of England, who ascended the throne in 1154.

A detailed study of Wace's relation to Geoffrey[47] proves that
he followed his original closely, as far as the facts are concerned.[48]
Allusions which we shall consider later on in another connection show
that he knew of an oral tradition of Arthur outside of Geoffrey, but
he adds practically no new material to that which his original
offered and so the advantage which his work has over Geoffrey's
is merely in its superior vivacity and vividness. A French poem
in octosyllabic couplets was likely to be livelier than a pseudo-
chronicle in the artificial Latin prose of the Middle Ages, and
Wace's style, as it happens, is particularly lively, so that Geoffrey's
legends and fictions are now cast in the form which was really
appropriate to them — namely, that of a metrical romance.[49]
He substitutes direct for indirect discourse, is fond of rhetorical
questions and exclamations, and amplifies, especially, the descriptions of battles and festivities. Even in respect to style, then,
Wace is an important factor in the development of the Arthurian
romances. He accordingly contributed largely to the spread of interest
in the Arthurian stories, for in the Middle Ages, as well as now, more
people could enjoy a tale in the vernacular than in Latin. But he
influenced Arthurian literature in another way, also — that is to
say, the *genre* of the *Brut* —[50] the chronicle of British history

---

[47] Cp. Fletcher, *Arthurian Material in the Chronicles*, pp. 127 ff.,
Alfred Ulbrich's, "Ueber das Verhältnis von Wace's Roman de Brut zu
seiner Quelle, der Historia regum Britanniae des Gottfried von Monmouth", *Romanische Forschungen*, XXVI, 181 ff. (Erlangen, 1908),
and Leo Waldner, *Wace's Brut und seine Quellen*. Jena diss. (Karls-
ruhe, 1914).

[48] For the main additions made by Wace, cp. Waldner, pp. 120 ff.

[49] Substantially true is the remark of the Abbé de la Rue, who
calls Wace's *Brut* "incontestablement le premier Roman de la Table
Ronde." See his *Essais historiques sur les bardes, les jongleurs et
les trouvères normands et anglo-normands*, etc., I, 50 (3 vols., Caen,
1834). M. Wilmotte, *Le Moyen Age*, XXVII, 100 f. (1914), makes
the same observation.

[50] The term, *Brut*, in the sense of *chronicle*, was also adopted
from the French by the Welsh, and so we have in Welsh the *Brut
Tysilio*, Gwentian *Brut*, etc.

which follows the Geoffreyan tradition and makes a fabulous Brutus the founder of the kingdom — did not end with him. Curiously enough, the most important representatives of this *genre* actually preserved are not in French, but in English; nevertheless, the English poems undoubtedly are based on (lost) French originals. The poems in question are, 1. Layamon's paraphrase of Wace, which it is common to call, after Sir Frederick Madden's example, Layamon's *Brut* —[51] a poem which was finished not long before 1205. 2. The alliterative *Morte Arthure*[52] of the fourteenth century, which has often been ascribed —[53] wrongly, no doubt — to the Scotch poet, Huchown of the Awle Ryale. In both of these poems the principal interest is pseudo-historical. Indeed, the narrative of the second is almost wholly taken up with the continental wars of Arthur and his final conflict with Mordred — that is, selected episodes of some lost *Brut*. The spirit is, therefore, considerably nearer that of the *chansons de geste* or poems of the Charlemagne cycle than is the case with the Arthurian romances proper. Indeed, the encounter of Gawain and the Saracen prince, Priamus, together with the latter's conversion to Christianity in the *Morte Arthure*, is actually drawn from *Fierabras*,[54] one of the most famous of the *chansons de geste*. More-

---

[51] The only edition is Madden's, in 3 vols. (London, 1847), for the Society of Antiquaries of London. A complete bibliography of Layamon down to 1906 was published by B. S. Monroe, *Journal of English and Germanic Philology*, VII, no. 1, pp. 139 ff. (1908). For the critical literature since then, cp. J. E. Wells, *A Manual of the Writings in Middle English*, 1050—1400 (Yale University Press, 1916), and the supplements thereto. Layamon's *terminus a quo* is 1189, since he refers I, 3, to Henry II as dead; his *terminus ad quem* is 1205, date of the crisis over the collection of Peter's pence, which, contrary to Madden, seems in the allusion to this tax, III, 286, unknown to him.

[52] The latest and best edition is Erik Björkman's (Heidelberg and New York, 1915), in Morsbach and Holthausen's *Alt- und mittelenglische Texte*, no. 9. The Introduction contains a full bibliography.

[53] Cp., for example, G. Neilson, *Huchown of the Awle Ryale*, (Glasgow, 1902).

[54] Cp. R. H. Griffith, "Malory, Morte Arthure, and Fierabras", *Anglia*, XXXII, 389 ff. (1909).

over, the parts played in the story by Lancelot, Gawain, and others
show plainly the influence of the fully developed Arthurian romances; and there is nothing surprising in this, seeing that the
alliterative poem belongs to the fourteenth century. But in its
essentials the *Morte Arthure* is based on a lost *Brut*.[55]

Of far greater importance, however, in this connection is
Layamon's *Brut*, which is a specimen of a metrical chronicle preserved in its entirety. At the beginning of his poem Layamon
gives as his sources "the English book that Saint Bede made,
another, in Latin, that Saint Albin made and the fair Austin who
brought baptism in hither" (i. e. St. Augustine, the missionary),
and, lastly, Wace. It is of little importance that he has cited
here other books besides Wace. His poem does not show any use
of such books and there can be little doubt that he took over me-
chanically from his French original this citation of authorities.[56]
With regard to the question of his relations to Wace, Layamon's
poem is about double the length of Wace's: the one contains something upwards of 15000 lines, the other something upwards
of 32000.[57] Until quite recently it has been the common assump-

_____

[55] On its sources see P. Branscheid, "Ueber die Quellen des stab-
reimenden Morte Arthure", *Anglia, Anzeiger*, VIII, 179 ff. (1885) and,
especially, R. Imelmann's treatise, named in the next note. Branscheid's
idea that Layamon is a source of the poem is certainly wrong.

[56] In his treatise, *Layamon, Versuch über seine Quellen* (Berlin,
1906), p. 17, R. Imelmann has pointed out that this coupling of Wace
and Bede as authorities is found in other chronicles which relate the
history of Great Britain under Anglo-Saxon as well as Celtic rule. The
addition of Albin the abbot, who died at Canterbury in 732, and
St. Augustine to the list of authorities was also, no doubt, already in
Layamon's original. And this addition is not hard to explain — for
Bede incorporates in his work the long interrogatories which St. Augustine
addressed to Pope Gregory asking for instructions as to how he should
proceed in his mission of converting the Anglo-Saxons, and he still
further speaks of Abbot Albin in his Preface as *auctor ante omnes
atque adjutor opusculi hujus*. So Albin and Augustine were to a
certain degree part-authors of his Ecclesiastical History. It was an
easy blunder, of which the Middle Ages furnishes many examples, to
make them now the authors of a separate work, although Augustine
died, of course, before Albin was born.

[57] Wace's poem is written in octosyllabic couplets — which became

tion that the expansions of the English poem were due to Layamon himself and that its author, who was a priest at Arley-Regis
(modern Ernley) on the Severn in Worcestershire, not far from
the Welsh border, had derived the most remarkable of these expansions from Welsh oral tradition.[58] In the light of recent research, however, it is no longer open to doubt that this assumption
was mistaken and that Layamon was merely following an expanded (French) version of Wace, now lost.[59] As long as the

the regular form of the French Arthurian romances; Layamon's in alliterative verse, but in a somewhat disintegrated form and with frequent
admixture of rhyme.

[58] Such was the view enunciated by Sir Frederick Madden in
editing Layamon's poem and it has found especial advocates, also, in
R. Wuelcker, "Ueber die Quellen Layamon's", Paul and Braune's *Beiträge*, III, 524 ff. (1876) and in A. C. L. Brown, "Welsh Traditions
in Layamon's Brut", MPh., I, 95 ff. (1903).

[59] R. Imelmann, in the above-mentioned treatise, was the first
scholar to propose this view. See, too, J. D. Bruce, "Some proper
names in Layamon's *Brut,* not represented in Wace or Geoffrey of
Monmouth", MLN, XXVI, 65 ff. (1911). According to Imelmann, Layamon's original was an enlargement of Wace by combination with
material drawn from Gaimar. He imagines, moreover, that the text
which resulted from this combination still further underwent the influence of the Vulgate *Mort Artu*. But the latter was certainly later
than Layamon's source — later, indeed, probably than Layamon. It
is to be observed that other poems of Wace's underwent expansion in
the way that we are here assuming for his *Brut,* viz. his *Conception*
and *Assumption*. For a version of the former, expanded by the interpolation of passages from another French poem, *L'histoire de Marie et
de Jesus,* cp. P. Meyer, *Romania*, XVI, 232 ff. (1887).
    According to MS. 749 (fol. 132) of the Bibl. Nat., Robert de Boron
in his *Merlin,* refers to a *Brut* translated from the Latin by a certain
Martin of Rochester, who is otherwise unknown. The passage, which
is quoted from this MS. by P. Paris, RTR, II, 36, note, is not found
in most MSS. and may be merely a scribal invention. Besides, in the
MSS. where it does occur, we do not always find *rouecestre* (Rochester).
*Rouain* and other names occur, instead. Cp. W. E. Mead's *Merlin*
treatise, E. E. T. S., Original Series, no. 112, (1899), pp. CLI, CLIX,
CLXI, CLXXI. Some scholars have accepted this Martin as Robert's
chronicle-source, instead of Wace, e. g. Wechssler, *Sage vom Heiligen
Gral,* p. 124 (1898), Brugger, *Zs. f. frz. Spr. u. Lit.,* XXIX[1], 60,

forms of certain names in the French poet's *Brut* were known only through our sole printed edition of that work, which is based on an indifferent MS., it was possible to maintain that the greater similarity of these same names in Layamon to the corresponding Welsh names revealed a direct contact with Welsh Arthurian traditions on the part of the latter. But investigation has proved that the better MSS. of Wace's *Brut*, which its editor left unused, show no such divergence between the two poets in respect to the forms of these names, and the argument from such alleged differences has consequently collapsed. As a matter of fact, the whole nomenclature of Layamon's poem bears throughout the stamp of French origin and he was so ignorant of Welsh that he did not recognize what are often originally Welsh names in the French forms with which they were clothed in the manuscript that lay before him.[60]

Now the conclusion to which the unmistakably French character of the nomenclature points is borne out by other evidence. Above all, the circumstance that certain features which the English poem has in common with the Old French prose romance, the *Mort Artu*, are entirely absent from the Wace of our MSS., puts beyond dispute the fact that these two works, which were nearly contemporary[61] and quite independent of each other, had a common source, not identical with Wace's *Brut* in its original form.[62] The features here in question are: 1. Arthur learns from a messenger of Mordred's treason in usurping the throne, whilst the former is engaged in a war against Lancelot on the continent, and sees in

---

including note 8 (1905), XXX[1], 182 ff. (1906), XLIV[2], 13 ff. (1916), and elsewhere. If Martin's chronicle really existed, it may very well have been the expanded Wace.

Sommer, Introduction to his *Vulgate Version of the Arthurian Romances,* pp. XX ff., cites a number of passages in the prose *Lancelot* (to be found III, 3, 46, V, 130, 117, 144, respectively, in his series) as allusions to a lost *Brut,* which Brugger, *op. cit.* XLIV[2], 14, identifies with Martin's. None of these supposed allusions, however, are convincing. They are much more likely to be mere inventions for the nonce.

[60]　Cp. Bruce, *op. cit.,* pp. 67 ff.
[61]　For the date of the *Mort Artu,* cp. Part III.
[62]　Bruce, RR, IV, 451 ff. (1913).

this intelligence the realization of a prophetic dream.[63]  2. At the end of the final battle between Arthur and Mordred only the former and two of his knights are said to be left alive.[64]  3. Arthur is translated to Avalon by Morgan and her fairy ladies.[65].  4. One of Mordred's sons who seized the kingdom after Arthur's death. is given a definite name.[66]

Many other names and details which distinguish Layamon from Wace are found scattered through different French works or works of French origin.[67]  From these various circumstances the conclusion, then, is unescapable that the version of Wace which constitutes the basis of the English poem had received here and there additions of considerable significance. Some of these additions, perhaps, should be accredited ultimately to Celtic — most likely Armorican — sources, but, in any event, Layamon was not responsible for them.

The matters which have just been cited prove beyond reasonable doubt that Layamon in many instances drew from an expanded Wace. In the light of these instances, it is a pretty safe inference that all other additions to the story of the English poem of any considerable extent come from this same source. There are, for example, long passages in the former where, over against the concise and matter-of-fact account of Wace, we have a full and circumstantial narrative with free introduction of speeches

---

[63]  Bruce's edition of MA (the *Mort Artu*), p. 202 and Madden's edition of Layamon, III, 117 ff.  There are some differences between the two, for a discussion of which cp. Bruce, RR, IV, 451 f.

[64]  MA, p. 244, and Layamon, III, 143.

[65]  MA, pp. 250 ff., and Layamon, III, 144.

[66]  MA, p. 254, and Layamon, III, 150.

[67]  Cp. Imelmann, pp. 24 ff.  The chief works which he cites are, 1. The prose *Brut d'Angleterre* (unpublished), apparently of the fifteenth century.  According to Imelmann, it is the prose rendering of a lost Norman verse-chronicle, closely connected with Wace. 2. The Middle English alliterative *Morte Arthure*. 3. An unprinted French verse-chronicle preserved in the British Museum MS., Royal 13, A. XXI. This MS. is of the early fourteenth century. 4. The Munich *Brut*, which may well be a fragment of Gaimar's lost chronicle of the Britons. It was from such works, no doubt, that Layamon really derived the details noted by Fletcher in his article "Did Layamon make any use of Geoffrey's Historia?", PMLA, XVIII, 91 ff. (1903).

and dialogues — in fine, a leisurely breadth of narrative art that approaches that of the French Arthurian romances. To say that an English writer of about the year 1200 was capable of this genial amplification is contrary to all the evidence. Not only is there no other example in this early time of such amplification of his originals on the part of any English author, but one may extend the assertion to the entire Middle English period. There is nothing like this, for instance, in the relations of the whole body of the Middle English romances to their French sources, for here compression, not expansion, is the rule.

The amplified passages in question occur in all parts of the English poem,[68] but those pertaining to Arthur possess naturally the greatest interest. Thus it is the English poem which first tells us[69] of how the elves (fairies) conferred on the king their best gifts at his birth: "They enchanted the child with magic most strong; they gave him might to be the best of all knights; they gave him another thing, that he should be a rich king; they gave him the third that he should live long; they gave to him — that royal child — virtues very good, so that he was the most generous of all men alive." Still further, we have here among other novelties, detailed descriptions of Arthur's armor,[70] an account which we shall return to later on, in another connection, of how the Round Table was founded,[71] and an allegorical dream in which the monarch is warned of his impending destruction through Mordred. In this dream Arthur finds himself on top of a great hall from which he looks out over his dominions. Mordred comes and hews down the posts that hold up the hall and Guinevere aids the traitor in pulling down the building, so that Arthur and Gawain

---

[68] For a list of them cp. Sir F. Madden's Preface, pp. XIV ff.

[69] Madden, II, 384 f. Layamon here shows a serious discrepancy as compared with Wace which seems to prove that the MS. of the expanded version of that author which he was using was defective in this place; for when Arthur is next mentioned (after Uther's death), he is — in some unexplained manner — in Britanny. See on the passage, Bruce, MLN, XXVI, 69 f., note. Other examples of discrepancies like this in Arthurian literature, due to defective MSS., are there given.

[70] Ibid., 463, 576.          [71] Ibid., 531 ff.

had their arms broken in its fall. He rises, however, and slays Mordred and Guinevere. His followers had all fled and he wanders alone until a lion takes him into the sea, where he is rescued by a fish — but at this point he awakes.

Most justly celebrated of all the amplified passages, however, is the one which gives us the first vernacular description of Arthur's translation to Avalon (the Celtic Elysium).[72] Wace merely remarks (ll. 13683ff.) of this translation that Arthur caused himself to be carried to Avalon to have his wounds cured. He is still there and the Britons expect his return, as they say, — with a few more words in the same vein. Instead of these bald statements, however, we have in the English poem the following highly poetical lines, which open with Arthur's speech to his successor, Constantine, after he (Arthur) has been grievously wounded in his final battle with Mordred: "'I give thee here my kingdom, and defend thou my Britons ever in thy life, and maintain them all the laws that have stood in my days, and all the good laws that in Uther's days stood. And I will fare to Avalun, to the fairest of all maidens, to Argante the queen,[73] an elf most fair, and she shall make my wounds all sound, make me all whole with healing draughts. And afterwards I will come again to my kingdom and dwell among the Britons with great joy.' Even with these words there approached from the sea a little boat, floating with the waves; and two women therein wondrously formed; and they

---

[72] III, 144f. The one in Geoffrey's Latin poem, *Vita Merlini*, discussed below, is about 50 years earlier than Layamon.

[73] Miss Paton, *Fairy Mythology*, pp. 26f. has tried to show that Argante was a Celtic divinity, but we have here indisputably merely a corruption of *Morgan (Morgant)*, name of the famous fairy queen of Arthurian romance — Arthur's sister — whom Malory calls Morgan le Fay. Cp. on the subject, Bruce, MLN, XXVI, 65ff. and RR, III, 190f. In these places examples are given of corruptions of the character's name that involve the loss of initial *M* and change of *o* to *a* — especially, in *Roman de Troie*, l. 8024 (most MSS.), and in the Spanish romances, where the name becomes *Urganda*. This passage may have been suggested to the author of the expanded Wace by Geoffrey's poem *Vita Merlini* — for there, too, Morgan (Morgen) figures as the healer of Arthur's wounds — but, in my opinion, it was more probably drawn directly from Celtic tradition.

took Arthur anon and bare him quickly to the boat and laid him
softly down and forth they gan depart. Then was it accomplished
that Merlin formerly said that there should be great care on account of Arthur's departure. The Britons believe yet that he is
alive and dwelleth in Avalun with the fairest of all elves; and the
Britons yet expect when Arthur shall return."[74]

Although translating a French poem which constitutes a sort
of spacious antechamber to the vast new palace of Arthurian romance, Layamon is himself thoroughly under the dominion of
the old Germanic epic tradition. He inherits its metrical form
— although admitting into his verse many laxities — its stock
of epic formulae, and, above all, its ethical emphasis and its spirit
of staunch courage and devotion. His patriotism is so sturdy that
Arthur, the scourge of the English according to Celtic tradition,
becomes in his work, himself, an Englishman. Despite his diffuseness, which, by its insistent elaboration of detail, made a poem,
already long, intolerably longer, Layamon had a larger share of

---

[74] This account of Arthur's end accords, in general, with
Geoffrey's *Historia* and Wace — also, with the former's *Vita Merlini*.
There were other legends, however, about his death: 1. He is still
asleep with his warriors in a cave, whence he will issue some day to
restore the glory of his people. The earliest recorded forms of this
legend represent him as in Mount Aetna. Cp. Gervase of Tilbury in
his *Otia Imperialia* (composed about 1211), Secunda Decisio, cap. 12
(ed. F. Liebrecht, Hannover, 1856) and Caesarius of Heisterbach,
*Dialogus Miraculorum*, Distinctio XII, cap. 12, ed. Joseph Strange
(Cologne, 1851). Crusaders were, doubtless, responsible for this localization. There are similar legends connected with hills in England,
Scotland and Wales. 2. He is the Wild Huntsman of the storm-myth.
Cp. Index, below. 3. He was turned into a bird: (a) a chough. Cp. M. A.
Courtney's *Cornish Feasts and Folk-Lore*, p. 58 (Penzance, 1890)
and *Notes and Queries* (7th series), IV, 247. (b) a raven. This
superstition is first mentioned by Cervantes, *Don Quixote*, Part I,
ch. 13. See, too, for Cornwall, *Notes and Queries* (First Series) VII,
618, and for Brittany, Felix Bellamy's *Forêt de Bréchéliant*, I, 129
(Rennes, 1896). 4. He was killed by the Cath Paluc, a catlike
monster. Cp. p. 41, note 9, below. Nos. 1, 2, 3 are mere adaptations to
Arthur of widespread *motifs*. On everything relating to Arthur's end
cp. Bruce, *Mort Artu*, pp. 298 ff. (Halle, 1910). There, *inter alia*,
fuller details concerning the legends just enumerated are given.

the genuine poetic spirit than any other Englishman during the two centuries and a half that followed the Norman Conquest. He was connected, however, with a perishing tradition, and it was this circumstance rather than the defects of his work that caused him to pass away without leaving a trace of influence on English poetry. The author of his French original may seem, at first sight, to have been even more unfortunate, since not a single copy of his work has survived.[75] He bequeathed, however, to a man of greater genius than his own — the author of the Vulgate *Mort Artu* — the materials for one scene, at least, through which he has merited a reflected immortality — namely, the scene of Arthur's translation to Avalon near the end of that romance.

There is no profit in following the stream of the Geoffreyan tradition concerning Arthur — his achievements and his tragic end — further down than Layamon. As late as the sixteenth century and occasionally even beyond the pseudo-historical fables which had their fountain-head in Geoffrey found a place in all histories of Great Britain. It was through such channels that the story of *King Lear*, for example, reached Holinshed, and then Shakespeare. The later chroniclers, however, it is evident, contented themselves with copying and combining the accounts of their predecessors. If they made any additions to their sources, it was not from oral tradition that they did so, but from their own

---

[75] Of Layamon's poem only two copies have survived, one dating from the first part of the thirteenth century, the other from the latter part, or, perhaps, even from the first part of the fourteenth. Both are in the Cottonian collection of the British Museum. The second, which is much mutilated by fire is inferior to the first and represents a new recension of Layamon's work. Cp. Rudolf Seyger, *Beiträge zu Layamon's Brut* (Halle diss., 1912). — Layamon's immediate original, after all, was substantially identical with Wace. The ratio of the added lines to those in the original Wace could not have been large. Nevertheless, one has to make allowance for the fact that all apparent expansions in Layamon of any extent were already in his French original. This is neglected by Miss Frances Lytle Gillespy in her „Layamon's *Brut*: A. Comparative Study in Narrative Art", *University of California Publications in Modern Philology*, III, 361 ff. (1916).

fancies, mainly in the way of interpreting what seemed to them difficulties of their originals.[76]

---

[76] In his *Arthurian Material in the Chronicles,* to which I have already often referred, R. H. Fletcher has sifted this enormous mass of writings — in Latin, French and English, in verse and in prose — with an industry and judgment that leaves nothing to be desired. If the result for the period subsequent to Layamon is almost wholly negative, he has none the less earned the gratitude of all students of these subjects.

# Chapter II.

# Origin of the Lays and Romances.

The first French chronicles in verse, based on Geoffrey, which developed the Arthurian theme were somewhat earlier in date than any of the Arthurian romances that have come down to us, the earliest of the extant romances being the *Erec* of Chrétien de Troyes, which was composed, as was stated above, about 1168. The influence of the chronicles on the new *genre* is important, but it was not in supplying the latter with specific narrative *motifs* for development, but rather in giving *éclat* to Arthur and his court and turning the attention of the literary world of the time in the direction of the stories already connected with his name,[1] and in

---

[1] For the specific influence of Wace on Chrétien, the most important of the romancers and the one whose works are the earliest that have survived, cp. Annette B. Hopkins, *The Influence of Wace on the Arthurian Romances of Crestien de Troies* (Chicago diss., 1913). Even the rather modest claims which Miss Hopkins makes on behalf of Wace are somewhat exaggerated. Brugger, moreover, in his review of her study, *Zs. f. frz. Spr. u. Litt.* XLIV[2], 13 ff. (1916), criticizes her for attributing to Wace influences that may have been really due to the versions of Gaimar or Martin (of Rochester), to the Munich *Brut* or the version in *laisses monorimes*. The versions just named, as stated above, have all perished, except for fragments that are not pertinent to our inquiry, so that one cannot control the matter with certainty. Nevertheless, we know that Wace — though only *named* once in subsequent mediaeval literature, viz. in the prologue to *Guiron le Courtois* — was much read and we have seen that his *Brut*, in an expanded form, was used in two of the most important of Arthurian texts, whilst there is no indication at all that the other paraphrases of Geoffrey ever exercised the slightest influence. I cannot, therefore, regard Brugger's point as possessing any real importance.

stimulating the poets to still other inventions of the same nature. That is to say, their influence was the same as Geoffrey of Monmouth's — only more powerful, for, as has been already remarked, poems in the vernacular commanded a more extensive audience than pseudo-histories in Latin.

Since the metrical romances have only this general relation to the chronicles, we have to look elsewhere for their origin, and here we are brought back again to the question of those traditions of the Celtic races which gave the starting-point for the narratives of Geoffrey and his followers. This problem of the relations of the Arthurian romances to Celtic tradition has been hotly debated and some extremists have gone so far as to deny that the French writers owed practically anything to this tradition.[2]

---

[2] This is, virtually, the position of Adolf Holzmann in his very able article, *Artus*, Pfeiffer's *Germania*, XII, 257 ff. (1867). In most of his contentions with respect to fundamental questions of Arthurian discussion he agrees with the Anti-Celticists of later decades. Thus, pp. 262 ff., he regards the three Welsh tales, *Geraint, Owen* and *Peredur* as derived from the French; pp. 276 ff. he argues that the Arthurian passages in William of Malmesbury's *De Antiquitate Glastoniensis Ecclesiae* are late interpolations, and that the same thing is true of the passage concerning Gawain's tomb in that writer's *Gesta Anglorum*, III, 287, else, the author would have told of Arthur in his First Book; p. 282 he declares that the *Brut Tysilio* is based on Geoffrey, etc., etc. Foerster and Golther do not go to such extremes as Holtzmann, but the whole tendency of their work, as we shall see, throughout the present treatise, is, likewise, to minimize Celtic influences in the Arthurian romances. Perhaps, the best general statement of Golther's position in the matter is to be found in two articles which he contributed to the *Zs. für vergleichende Literaturgeschichte, Neue Folge,* III (1890), viz., pp. 211 ff., „Zur Frage nach der Entstehung der bretonischen oder Artus-Epen", and pp. 409 ff., „Beziehungen zwischen französischer und keltischer Literatur im Mittelalter". Golther distinguishes (pp. 212 ff.) three different successive forms in which the *matière de Bretagne* was embodied. 1. *Sagenbestandteile*, i. e. the episodes which constitute the materials of the Breton epics and which, also, occur independently of these, e. g. the chastity ordeal of Iseult in the Tristan poems. 2. *Sagendichtung*, i. e. oral tales which might combine and elaborate earlier independent incidents. 3. *Die vorhandenen altfranzösischen Epen aller Art,* i. e. the Old French romances. The Celts, he thinks, (p. 213) are impor-

The principal circumstance which renders a satisfactory judgment in the matter so difficult is that we have so little preserved of the early literature of the two Celtic peoples who are most directly concerned in the debate — namely, the Welsh and the Bretons. Indeed, nothing but names and glosses in the Breton language have survived from the Middle Ages.[3] The folk-songs which Th. H. de la Villemarqué published in 1839 under the title of *Barzaz-Breiz* and which related in some instances to the principal characters of the Arthurian legend — for example, the king himself and Merlin — being so late, would not have had very much value for our purpose, even if they had been genuine. As a matter of fact, however, these have been proved to be substantially forgeries and not songs taken down from oral recitation, as they pretended to be.[4] Indeed, they are, in a large measure, free inventions of their nineteenth century author — sometimes owing a mere suggestion to genuine folk-songs, but more frequently based on books. It is a case of the Macpherson forgeries over again — the fraud of a perfervid patriot — only the connection with actual tradition in this instance is even slighter than could be claimed for the Ossian and Fingal pieces.

The conditions are somewhat better with Welsh literature, for here we have in verse the poems of the *Four Ancient Books*

---

tant only for no. 1, and with regard even to no. 1, not all of the materials under this heading, by any means, are of Celtic origin. No. 2 is French (developed by itinerant and often bilingual *conteurs*), and we find combined here not only Celtic materials, but others drawn from the general fund of mediaeval stories. The Celtic names in the French romances of the Arthurian cycle are due, in a large measure, to fashion and caprice (p. 215), after the conquest of England had made the matter popular, and they no more imply necessarily Celtic origin for the stories in which they appear than Germanic names in the *chansons de geste* imply Germanic origin for the stories of those poems. Golther ascribes to the combinations and inventions of the authors a large share in no. 3.

[3] Cp. H. Zimmer, *Die romanischen Literaturen und Sprachen, mit Einschluß des Keltischen*, p. 133 (1909) in Paul Henneberg's series, *Kultur der Gegenwart*.

[4] Cp., especially, F. M. Luzel: *De l'authenticité des chants du Barzaz-Breiz de M. de la Villemarqué* (Paris, 1872).

*of Wales* —[5] The Black Book of Caermarthen, The Book of Aneurin, The Book of Taliessin, The Red Book of Hergest. These poems, although they purport to be the work of Welsh bards of the sixth century, are dated by modern scholars in a much later time — from the tenth to the twelfth centuries.[6] They relate in part to battles which fall in the period to which Arthur belonged — that is to say, the sixth century — and a few of them mention Arthur[7] and certain characters connected with him who play a

---

[5] Edited, with translation by W. F. Skene, under this title, in 2 vols. (Edinburgh, 1868.)

[6] Zimmer, op. cit., p. 116.

[7] English translations of the poems relating to Arthur in the four ancient books of Wales are given by Skene, I, 259—268. There are only four of such poems and of these four the first, entitled *The Chair of the Sovereign (Book of Taliessin,* XV), seems to mention Arthur only incidentally. The poem, it is true, is obscure to the last degree. In the second (*Black Book of Caermarthen,* XXXI) Arthur and Cai (Kay) are seeking entrance to a castle, but the porter, Glewlwyd Gavaelvawr (represented in the Welsh prose tales as one of Arthur's own porters), refuses until he knows more about the persons who wish to be admitted. Arthur eulogizes, then, his followers — particularly, Cai, to a description of whose exploits most of the poem is devoted. Thus, although Arthur is the speaker, the piece is really a glorification of Cai. In the fourth poem, *Geraint, son of Erbin (Black Book of Caermarthen,* XXII), Arthur is barely mentioned (Skene, I, 267) as "emperor, and conductor of the toil" in the battle of Llongborth (wherever that may be), in which Geraint, the hero of the poem, was slain. Only the third poem, *Preiddeu Annwvn (= The Harryings of Hades), Book of Taliessin,* XXX (Skene, I, 264 ff.) celebrates Arthur as the central character. I have quoted an extract from this poem in the text above. The piece, as will be seen, refers in an obscure manner to expeditions which Arthur and his men — in his ship, Prydwen — made against certain places, named in the poem, but not yet identified. Sir John Rhys, pp. XXIV f. of his preface to the edition (London, 1906) of Malory's *Morte Darthur* in Everyman's Library, says: "The poem evidently deals with expeditions conducted by Arthur by sea to the realms of twilight and darkness". He also compares the quest of the cauldron of the Head of Hades in the Welsh poem to a similar quest in *Kulhwch and Olwen,* only the cauldron in the latter is in Ireland, not Hades. The preface, just mentioned, contains the best discussion of Arthurian allusions in these Welsh poems that we have. Rhys, however, omits to comment on

large part in the French Arthurian romances — for instance, Gwalchmei[8] (Gawain) and Kay (Kei),[9] Arthur's seneschal

---

the passages (Skene I, 263, 295) about Llachau, son of Arthur. This son reappears in several of the French romances under the name of "Lohot". Cp. my discussion of the character in RR. III, 179 ff. (1912).

[8]) For Gwalchmei (Gawain of the French romances) in Welsh literature cp. Loth's *Mabinogion*[2], I, 288, note 1. *Ibid.* in *Kulhwch and Olwen* he is called son of Gwyar, and it is said of him: "He never returned from a mission without having achieved it; he was the best of footmen and the best of horsemen. He was Arthur's nephew, son of his sister and cousin". In a triad, Loth, II[2], 89, he is one of the "three goldentongued knights at Arthur's court"; but this last may have been written under French influence. Loth observes, I[2], 288, note 1, that *gwalch* means "male falcon" and *gwyar*, "blood". He does not explain *mei*. According to Rhys, *Arthurian Legend*, p. 13, *Gwalchmei* probably means "hawk or falcon of May".

As has just been stated, Gwalchmei's father in *Kulhwch and Olwen* is named Gwyar; in Geoffrey (Book VIII, ch. 21, *et. seq.*) and the French romances Gawain's father is named Lot (Loth). In his article, "Le roi Loth des romans de la Table Ronde", *Revue Celtique*, XVI, 67 (1895), J. Loth is inclined to identify this Loth with the Lloch Llawwynnyawc who figures among Arthur's warriors in *Kulhwch and Olwen* (Loth's *Mabinogion*[2], I, 264) and in the *Black Book of Caermarthen* (Skene, I, 262). It is to be observed, however, that further on in *Kulhwch and Olwen (op. cit.* p. 276) this Lloch (or Llwch, as the name is there spelt) is represented as the great-uncle of Arthur (on his mother's side), not his brother-in-law. Since Geoffrey's Lot (Loth), Book VIII, ch. 21, *et. seq.* is from Lothian (Londonesia), may not Geoffrey have fabricated this name from the name of the country with which he connects him, just as he fabricated (XII, 19) the name of his fictitious prince of Wales, Gualo, from Guallia (Wales) or Sabrina, (II, 5), name of the goldess of the river Severn, from Sabren? Loth, in the above-mentioned article, does not credit Geoffrey's invention, I believe, with its proper share in what that writer says in regard to Loth.

[9]) In these poems, as in Welsh literature, generally — excepting the pieces that betray French influence (cp. Loth's *Mabinogion*[2]), I, 256, note 1) — Cai (Kay) plays a heroic rôle — not that of a butt, as in the French romances. For instance, in the *Black Book of Caermarthen*, XXXI (Skene, I, 264) he slays the monster, Cath Palug or Cath Paluc (Capalu or Chapalu of the Old French), which, according to one line of Arthurian tradition, killed Arthur. Cp. on this subject E. Freymond's masterly monograph, mentioned above, viz.,

in the French romances. Indeed, Urien, a prince of the North,
who figures in the French romances as the husband of Morgan le
Fay and the father of Ivain, is even more frequently mentioned
than Arthur himself. The style of these poems, however, as of the
Bardic poetry generally, is obscure and oracular. They are, besides, lyrical, not epical, so that they could not in themselves con-
tribute to the transmission of legends concerning the heroes that
are mentioned in them. The following, for instance, is from one
of the poems concerning Arthur in the Book of Taliessin.[10] It

---

*Artus' Kampf mit dem Katzenungestüm: Sonderabzug aus: Beiträge
zur romanischen Philologie, Festgabe für Gustav Gröber* (Halle, 1899).
I have summarized the main points of this monograph in my edition
of the *Mort Artu,* pp. 304 f. The idea of Arthur's death through
this monstrous cat (water demon, according to Freymond) may be one
of the debts of French romance to Wales, although it is not found in
the extant Welsh texts. A similar tradition may have prevailed in
Brittany. Cp. *Galeran de Bretagne,* 5068 ff., where it is ascribed
to the Bretons. In any event, early in the thirteenth century we
find it localized at Lake Bourget in Savoy and J. Loth, *Romania,*
XXIX, 125 f. (1900) suggests that the story reached Savoy by way of
Champagne and Flanders-Alsace, whose princes (patrons of Chrétien
de Troyes) we know were interested in the materials of romance.
Freymond, to be sure, thinks that travellers crossing the Alps brought
the tale to Savoy. The earliest allusions to the killing of Arthur by
a monster cat occur in texts of the latter part of the twelfth century — not all of them romances. A lengthy account of this fight
will be found in the *Merlin* of the Vulgate cycle. Cp. Sommer's
*Vulgate Version of the Arthurian Romances,* II, 441 ff. Here, however, Arthur is victor. The episode is plainly connected with the
localization of the legend in Savoy, only in the *Merlin* the combat
is represented as taking place on Lake Lausanne (i. e. Geneva), and
not on Lake Bourget, where the Mont du Chat still preserves a trace
of the early localization.

For some corrections to Freymond's monograph, cp. Loth, *loc. cit.*
In "Arthurian Notes", MLN, XVII, 277, W. W. Newell identifies the
monster of no. 30 in Child's *English and Scottish Ballads* with
the Chapalu.

According to *Kulhwch and Olwen* (Loth, I², 275) Cai was slain
by Gwyddawc, son of Menestyr, who, in turn, was slain — and his
brothers, too — by Arthur in revenge for Cai. There is nothing to
correspond to this in the French romances.

[10] Skene, II, 264.

celebrates apparently some disastrous expedition by sea of the
great hero:

"Am I not a candidate for fame with the listened song
In Caer Pedryvan, in the isle of the strong door?
The twilight and pitchy darkness were mixed together.
Bright wine their liquor before their retinue.
Thrice enough to fill Prydwen (i. e. Britain) we went on the sea;
Except seven none returned from Caer Rigor.
I shall not deserve much from the ruler of literature.
Beyond Caer Wydyr they saw not the prowess of Arthur.
Three score Canhwr (i. e. centuries of men or a legion) stood on
        the wall;
Difficult was a conversation with its sentinel.
Thrice enough to fill Prydwen there went with Arthur.
Except seven, none returned from Caer Golud.

I shall not deserve much from those with long shields.
They know not what day, who the causer,
What hour in the serene day Cwy was born,
Who caused that he should not go to the dales of Devwy.
They know not the brindled ox, thick his head-band.
Seven score knobs in his collar.
And when we went with Arthur of anxious memory,
Except seven, none returned from Caer Vandwy."

To the uninitiated such a piece as this would not convey much
information concerning the events to which it relates, and the
rest are no better. The same is true of the dialogue between Arthur
and Guinevere,[11] the only Welsh poem in which these two characters appear together.

Besides the poems from which extracts have been given above,
we have the highly characteristic brief poems called *Triads*.[12] The
nature of these pieces will be sufficiently manifest from the following specimens,[13] which have reference to incidents and personages
in Arthurian saga:

"Three furious blows in the isle of Prydein [i. e. Britain].

"One was given by Matholwch the Gael to Branwen daughter

---

[11] Printed, with translation, by J. Rhys, *Studies in the Arthurian Legend,* pp. 57 f. (Oxford 1891). He gives it no date.

[12] The best translations are in French by J. Loth, *Les Mabinogion*², II, 223 ff. (Paris, 1913).

[13] Ibid., p. 246, and p. 247, respectively.

of Llyr, the second by Gwenhwyvach [ i. e. a sister of Guinevere's ]
to Gwenhwyvar[14] [ i. e. Guinevere], which led to the battle of
Kamlan [ i. e. Arthur's final battle with Mordred ]; the third by
Golyddan, the bard, to Kotwaladyr Vendigeit."

Or again:

"Three costly pillaging expeditions in the isle of Prydein
[ i. e. Britain ]. The first took place when Mordred went to Arthur's court at Kelliwic in Cornwall: He left neither food nor
drink in the court; he consumed everything; he drew Guinevere
from her royal chair ànd buffeted her. The second was when
Arthur went to Mordred's court; he left neither food nor drink
in the court nor in the district. The third was when Aeddan Vra-
dawc (the traitor) went to Alclut to the court of Rydderch Hael;
after him there was left neither drink nor beast alive.".

The triad-form seems to have originated in Ireland, but it
received its especial development in Wales, and Loth's collection
contains 153 of these pieces — only an insignificant portion, no
doubt, of those that once existed.   There are others besides the
ones just quoted that contain allusions to Arthurian matters and
we shall have occasion later on to return to them, but, after all,
the information we glean from them is scanty and it is obvious
that these little poems played virtually no part in the transmission
of Arthurian material to the French poets.[15]

---

[14] Sir John Rhys, *Studies in the Arthurian Legend*, pp. 35 ff.,
cites one of the Welsh triads as declaring that Arthur had three
wives of this name. But, according to the translation of J. Loth,
*Mabinogion*[2], II, 250, the three Gwenhwyvars there named are merely
called the "principal ladies of Arthur's court". To be sure, the third
of these Gwenhwyvars (the one whose father was Ocvran Gawr, the
giant) is Arthur's consort. Rhys's comparison, *loc. cit.*, with the Irish
Echaid Airem and the three Etains, therefore, falls to the ground.
   For Gwenhwyvar (Guinevere) in Welsh literature cp. Loth, *op. cit.*,
I, 259, note 3. She is always called the daughter of Gogrvan or Gogrvan
Gawr in Welsh ("Ocrvan" in the triad cited above being merely a
variant of that name). Loth cites from *Myvyrian Archaeology*, p. 863,
col. 1, a Welsh proverb, which says of her that "she was bad when
she was small, but worse, when she grew up." The name means
"white phantom" or „white fairy".

[15] One of the most interesting evidences in regard to the currency of Arthurian traditions in Wales occurs in the Code of Gwent

A much more important branch of Welsh literature for our present purpose are the prose tales called the *Mabinogion,* so well-known to the present generation through the reprints of Lady Charlotte Guest's translation, which appeared originally in 1838 and which is now almost an English classic.[16] The Welsh word *mabinogion* in the manuscripts of the collection is the plural of *mabinogi,* [17] which in turn seems to be a term applied to the tales

---

(South Wales). Cp. Aneurin Owen's *Ancient Laws and Institutes of Wales,* I, 678, (London, 1841). There it is said: "When the queen shall wish a song in her chamber, the bard will sing the song about Camlan [i. e. Arthur's last battle], bnt in a low voice, for fear lest it may cause trouble in the hall" [i. e. for fear lest the song may provoke quarrels in the hall]. The earliest MS. of the code dates from shortly before 1200, but Howel Dda, who is supposed to have compiled it in its original form, ruled in South Wales in the first half of the tenth century.

[16] For scientific study, however, the French translation by J. Loth, *Les Mabinogion,* 2 vols. (second edition, Paris, 1913) is the only one to be recommended.

[17] This interpretation of the word, however, seems to have originated in a scribal error. The proper meaning of *mabinogion* (plural of *mabinog,* and not of *mabinogi*) is really *disciples,* and this is the meaning given it in the Iolo MSS., p. 211. So, according to the most careful discussion of the sense of *mabinogi* and *mabinogion,* viz., J. Loth's *Contributions à l'Etude des Romans de la Table Ronde,* pp. 30 ff. (Paris, 1912) and *Les Mabinogion*[2], I, 11 ff. (Paris, 1913). Elsewhere in the Red Book, the four branches, *Pwyll, Branwen, Manawyddan, Math,* are spoken of as forming one *Mabinogi,* and this is, no doubt, correct.

J. Rhys, *The Text of the Red Book Mabinogion,* p. VIII (1887), interpreted *mabinog (mebinog)* as "a literary apprentice", one who aspired to be a bard, and the still obscurer word, *mabinogi,* as the literary baggage of such a bardic apprentice. So, too, H. Zimmer, *Göttingische Gelehrte Anzeigen* for June 10, 1890, pp. 513 f. and J. Loth in the passages cited above. These scholars reject specifically the old interpretation of the word *mabinogi,* to which Lady Charlotte Guest gave currency, viz. "a tale for children". On the other hand, in *The White Book Mabinogion, Welsh Tales & Romances reproduced from the Peniarth Manuscripts,* p. XXVI (Pwllheli, 1907 — published really in 1909, it would seem, since the preface is dated in that year), J. G. Evans takes *mabinogion* as the plural of *mabinogi* and denies that *mabinog* meant "literary apprentice"

that a *mabinog* or apprentice in the art of storytelling practised reciting. This term applies properly only to four tales in the collection that goes under the name of *Mabinogion* —[18] namely, "Pwyll, Prince of Dyfed", "Branwen, Daughter of Llyr", "Manawyddan, son of Llyr" and "Math, son of Mathonwy" — none of which contain Arthurian material. Nevertheless, the collection thus miscalled does contain some tales in which Arthur and other characters of his cycle appear. Three of these tales are, undoubtedly, derived from French romances — either the extant romances of Chrétien (as the present writer believes) or lost French versions of the same stories.[19] The tales in question are *Owen* or *The Lady of the Fountain*, corresponding to Chrétien's *Yvain (Chevalier au Lion), Peredur ab Evrawc*, corresponding to the same writer's *Perceval (Conte del Graal), Geraint* or *Geraint and Enid*, corresponding to his *Erec (Erec et Enide)*.

The French origin of the three Welsh tales just named is indicated unmistakably by their coherent structure and by the character of the life which they reflect and which in social spirit,

---

or "was a technical term belonging to the bardic system". In his view, "any narrative that treats of early life is a *mabinogi*". He cites in proof the title, *Mabinogi Jesu Crist* (as Rhys, *Arthurian Legends*, p. 2, note 2, indeed, had already done), which is a Welsh version of the Gospel of pseudo-Matthew, called *Liber de ortu beatae Mariae et Infantia Salvatoris*. (This Welsh version was edited by Miss Mary Williams, *Revue Celtique*, XXXIII, 184 ff., in 1912). Evans's interpretation of *mabinogi* is adopted by Miss Williams in her *Peredur* essay, p. IV, note 3 (1909) and by W. J. Gruffydd in his paper, "The Mabinogion", *Transactions of the Honourable Society of Cymmrodorion, Session 1912—1913,* ρp. 39 f. J. Loth, *Contributions,* pp. 30 f., has argued convincingly, however, that the sense which Evans ascribes to *mabinogi* did not belong to the word in its earlier history, but was a later (fourteenth century) development. For a review of the publication and discussion of the *Mabinogion* down to 1902, see Alfred Nutt's note, pp. 323 ff. of the edition of Lady Charlotte Guest's translation of these tales published by his firm in that year.

[18] This was pointed out by Zimmer, *Göttingische Gelehrte Anzeigen* for June 10, 1890, pp. 511 ff. Even J. Loth had failed to make the distinction in the first edition (1887) of his above-cited translation.

[19] For a full treatment of this question, cp. Part IV, below.

domestic custom, the usages of war — indeed, in every respect — was that of twelfth century France, as depicted by Chrétien and the other French poets. Here, moreover, instead of the precise localization of the genuine Welsh stories, which makes it possible even at the present day to follow with substantial exactness the movements of their heroes in Wales, everything is vague and shadowy.[20] On the other hand, there are two tales in the collection that represent genuine Welsh tradition about Arthur. One of these is without suspicion of contamination from French literature — namely, *Kulhwch and Olwen;* and the other, the *Dream of Rhonabwy,* although from allusions which it contains to Geoffrey's *Historia* it could not have been composed before the second half of the twelfth century, does not seem contaminated in any important respect. These stories are touched with much of the natural magic which ever since Matthew Arnold's famous essay we have associated with the Celtic genius, but, despite great beauty of detail, which illustrates the wild fancy and vivid sense of color that are features of the Celtic endowment, in reading them one cannot but be reminded of the proverbial saying that "A. Kymro [ i. e. Welshman ] has imagination enough for fifty poets without judgment enough for one." As in most Celtic stories, from the early Irish sagas down to the tales which J. F. Campbell collected in the nineteenth century in the Western Highlands of Scotland, the main impression left on the reader is one of diffuseness and incoherence. Let us glance rapidly at the narrative of *Kulhwch and Olwen*[21] for the light which it may throw on the subject of the relation of the Arthurian romances to the Welsh tales. Of all the ancient Welsh stories that have survived it is best suited to that purpose. Here we have a genuine, uncontaminated Welsh tale which we may compare with the French romances and thus gain a measure of the possible influence of the Welsh stories

---

[20] In *The Mabinogion,* pp. 347 ff. (London, 1902) A. Nutt has commented on some of these features of the three tales. He remarks that, as in the French biographical romances, in these tales" the centre of interest is less the incident than the hero whose personality is the chief, if not the sole, connecting link"

[21] Loth, *Mabinogion*[2], I, 243 ff.

on the latter. Like the other tales of the Red Book of Hergest, the fourteenth century manuscript which has preserved to us the so-called *Mabinogion, Kulhwch and Olwen* was probably written down about the end of the twelfth century — so shortly after the period in which the Arthurian romances in French appear to have begun — but it was manifestly older than this and had in all likelihood been current in substantially the same form for at least a century before.[22] It is possible that Foerster is right in contending that the interest in Arthur inspired by the French romances was the cause of the writing down of this tale, but it shows no trace of their influence, so, even if this is true, the circumstance is immaterial.

The hero, Kulhwch, is a cousin of Arthur's. He has fallen in love with Olwen, daughter of Yspaddaden Penkawr, merely from report, for he had never seen her. At his father's instigation he sets out for Arthur's court to ask him to cut his hair — that is, according to Welsh custom, to adopt him as his godson — and to assist him in winning the hand of his unseen lady-love. The journey is described with the most brilliant play of fancy. Take, for instance, the description of the dogs that accompanied the young prince: "Before him were two brindled, white-breasted greyhounds, having strong collars of rubies about their necks, reaching from the shoulder to the ear. And the one that was on the left side bounded across to the right side and the one on the right to the left, and like two sea-swallows they sported around him." And similarly it is said of the steed that "he cast up four sods with his four hoofs, like four swallows in the air, about his head, now above, now below. About him was a four-cornered cloth of purple, and an apple of gold was at each corner, and every one of the apples was of the value of an hundred kine upon his shoes, and upon his stirrups from his knee to the tip of his toe. And the blade of grass bent not beneath him, so light was his courser's tread as he journeyed towards the gate of Arthur's Palace."

---

[22] Loth, *ibid.*, p. 40, dates the first redaction of the tale in the second half of the eleventh century or beginning of the twelfth — so, too, *Revue Celtique,* XXXII, 436 (1911), after full discussion of the evidence.

He demands an interview with the king, but Glewlwyd Gavaelvawr, the porter who guards Arthur's gate on New Year's
Day — the day of the prince's arrival — will not admit him
within the precincts of the palace, where the king is engaged
in revelry — but he promises him suitable entertainment outside. "A lady shall smooth thy couch, and shall lull thee with
songs; and early to-morrow morning, when the gate is open for
the multitude that came hither today, for thee shall it be opened
first, and thou mayest sit in the place that thou shalt choose in
Arthur's hall." The young man, however, insists on admission
and threatens, if his request is not granted, that he will set up
three deadly shouts which will be heard throughout Great Britain
and Ireland and which will render the women of the palace barren
from that day on. The porter, then, informs Arthur of his arrival and lauds in extravagant terms his appearance, so that contrary to Kay's advice the king admits the stranger, who rides into
the hall on horseback in true mediaeval style. The young prince
then asks for a boon, accompanying his petition with threats.
Just as in the French romances, Arthur pledges himself to make
this *don*, before he has even learned what the stranger is going
to demand, provided only that he does not ask for his ship, his
mantle, his sword, Caledvwlch (i. e. Excalibur), his lance, his
shield, his dagger and his wife. Kulhwch then demands the assistance of Arthur and his warriors in obtaining Olwen as his bride.
He enumerates these warriors in a list six or seven pages long,
which doubtless in the course of tradition underwent expansion
from time to time, like the catalogue of the ships in *The Iliad*
or the lists of peoples and princes in the Anglo-Saxon *Widsith*.
The most familiar characters among them are Kay (Kai) and
Bedivere. But it is a different Kay from the butt of the French
romances, who is always the first to undertake every adventure
announced at Arthur's court and is always ignominiously overthrown. Not only is he a valiant warrior here as throughout Welsh
tradition, but, like everyone else in this fantastic tale, he has marvellous qualities: He had "this peculiarity that his breath lasted
nine nights and nine days under water, and he could exist nine
nights and nine days without sleep. A wound from Kay's sword

no physician could heal. Very subtle was Kay. When it pleased him, he could render himself as tall as the highest tree in the forest. And he had another peculiarity — so great was the heat of his nature, that, when it rained hardest, whatever he carried remained dry for a handbreadth above and a handbreadth below his hand; and when his companions were coldest, it was to them as fuel with which to light their fires."

Arthur is bound by his promise and sends forth messengers to every land within his dominions to seek for Olwen. For a year the search is vain and Kulhwch begins to reproach the king with the failure. Arthur now goes forth in person to remove the dishonor of an unfulfilled promise and he is accompanied by the young prince and a band of his followers, including a guide who was "as good a guide in a land he had never seen as he was in his own." They come to a beautiful castle, which proves to be that of Olwen's father. Near it is a flock of sheep which seemed endless and which was guarded by a mastiff, whose fiery breath was as devastating as that of a dragon. They go to the herdsman's house, and the herdsman's daughter runs out with joy to meet them and tries to throw her arms about Kay's neck. The uncanny mastiff, however, had probably made Kay suspicious, so that he had provided himself with a billet, and when she endeavored to embrace him, he thrust forward the log instead. It was lucky that he did so, for she squeezed it so hard that it became a twisted coil. "Oh woman," exclaimed Kay reproachfully, "if thou hadst squeezed me thus, none could ever again have set their affections on me."

By the assistance of this maiden they have an interview with Olwen, whose beauty is charmingly described, and Kulhwch obtains from her a promise of marriage, if he will fulfill the conditions which her father imposes. The father cannot see his future son-in-law until the latter has raised his eyebrows which have fallen over his eyes — these eyebrows being usually supported by forks. On the fourth day the father, after the manner of the fairy-tales, announces all sorts of extravagant conditions for the achievement of his daughter's hand. The lover is, of course, not deterred and insists that they will all prove easy. The crowning condition, however, is stated as follows: "Throughout the world there is not a comb or scissors with which I can arrange my hair, on account of its rankness, except the comb and scissors that are between the two ears of Twrch Trwyth, the son of Prince Tared. He will not give them of his own free will, and thou wilt not be able to compel him. This Twrch Trwyth turns out to be a marvellous wild boar — doubtless a parallel to the classical Minotaur —[23] with one parent a man and the other a beast — the same that we have heard of already in Nennius — the Tortain of the *Conte del Graal.*[24]

In the tale of *Kulhwch and Olwen,* as in Nennius, Arthur's dog, Caval or Cabal, also takes part in the chase of the boar. In order to catch Twrch Trwyth, still other extravagant conditions are stated. Suffice it to say, however, that in the end, by the help of Arthur and his hosts, the young prince overcomes all difficulties and wins the hand of his bride, although at the expense of her father's life, whose fate it was that he should die a violent death, as soon as all the above-mentioned conditions had been fulfilled.[25]

---

[23] Cp. G. Paris, *Romania,* XXVIII, 217, note.

[24] J. Rhys, *Celtic Folklore,* II, 521 (Oxford, 1901), identifies Twrch Trwyth with "Orc treith" in Cormac's *Irish Glossary.* The latter means "King's Boar". The hunting of Twrch Trwyth is described so exactly in *Kulhwch and Olwen* that it is possible to trace its course (in essentials) on a modern map of Wales. Cp. Rhys, *ibid.,* pp. 509 ff. On the local coloring of the *Mabinogion* and the local legends which they embody, see too, E. Anwyl, "The Four Branches of the Mabinogi", *Zs. f. celt. Ph.,* I, 277 ff. (1897). His "Notes on *Kulhwch and Olwen*" in the *Revue Celtique,* XXXIV, 132 ff. (1913) are purely textual in character.

[25] As regards the relations of the French romances to Welsh literature it is desirable to note that F. Lot has cited some names in the French romances as of specifically Welsh origin: Thus, in *Romania,* XXIV, 322, he points out that *Lis* in the name *Chateau de Lis* (first continuation to Chrétien's Perceval and elsewhere) is really Welsh *Llys* = castle, and *ibid.,* p. 326, he explains the personal name *Gorvain Cadrut* (in *Meraugis* and other romances) as a combination of Welsh *Gwrvan* and *Cadrod (Cadrawd).* For Welsh *din, dinas* (= fortified place), in the names *Dinas, Dinan* (Béroul's *Tristan)* cp. Lot, *Romania,* XXIV, 337, but cp., also, the glossary to Bédier's edition of Béroul under *Lidan.* So, too, with reference to *Dinas-*

We have taken now a hasty survey of mediaeval Welsh literature, as far as it bears on our subject, and we have only to
add that the literature of the Bretons of which, as was said above,
nothing has come down to us from this period did not probably
differ from it in essentials. Especially in the matter that most
concerns us, the form of epic narrative, there is no reason to doubt
that with the Bretons as with the other branches of the Celtic
race this was the prose tale and not narrative in verse, as was the
case with the Germanic tribes or the Greeks and the Italian races.
So, for instance, the Irish epic consists of the famous prose sagas
concerning Conchobar, Cuchullin, and the rest; and the only branch
of the Germanic race which shows, by way of exception, a highly
developed prose epic is that which at a comparatively early period
underwent Irish influence — namely, the Norsemen.[26] It will
be necessary in the following to remember this peculiarity of the
Celtic literatures.[27]

## 1. The Lays.

We have seen, then, what is the form of the narrative literature of the Celtic races, as it is actually preserved. Let us turn
now to the consideration of a more or less hypothetical *genre* of
this literature, about which Arthurian controversy has waged most
bitterly, since it has been regarded as most closely connected with the origin of the Arthurian romances. I refer to
the Celtic *lais*. The difficulty is that we have French *lais*
from the twelfth century down, like those of Marie de France
— *lais* that are often said to be based on *lais bretons* — but we
have no such pieces in extant Celtic literature, and leaving aside

diron *(Dinatiron)* of the *Roman de Troie* (son of Priam), as against
Lot, *Romania*, XXX, 195 (1901), G. Baist, *Romanische Forschungen*,
XXIX, 319 f. (1910), sees here the influence of *Dinas*, supposed name
of the penitent thief, who was crucified with Christ. But this is not probable.

[26] Cp. Andreas Heusler, "Die Anfänge der isländischen Saga"
in the *Abhandlungen* of the Berlin Academy, Philos.-Historische Klasse,
Jahrgang 1913, no. 9. He concludes that the Norse prose saga-form was
derived from the Irish, although we cannot point to specific borrowings.

[27] Zimmer, reviewing G. Paris's treatise on the Arthurian romances in verse *(Histoire littéraire de la France,* vol. 30) in the
*Göttingische G. A.* for Oct. 1, 1890, was the first scholar to lay
stress on this in Arthurian discussion.

for the moment the word, *Breton*, the very meaning of the word, *lai*, is the subject of debate.[28] Suffice it here to say that the most probable etymology so far suggested[29] identifies it with the Irish *loid* or *laid* — which seems to mean "song" — and so, no doubt, *lai* meant "song."

Before discussing, however, this question of the *lais*, it will be well to indicate briefly the character at least of the French poems so designated by giving an outline of one of them. We may remark, in passing, that they are all in octosyllabic couplets, but vary greatly in length. I will select for the purpose the first in the collection of Marie de France, and one of the longest, namely, *Guigemar*, a poem of 886 lines. Whatever theory we may hold as to the origin of the story, it is evident that in Marie's version it has been adapted to the conditions of twelfth century feudal society:

Guigemar[30] is the son of the lord of Liun (Leon) in Brittany and he serves his apprenticeship in knighthood at the court of Hoilas (Hoel), king of that country. After he is dubbed knight, he takes part in a military expedition in Flanders, and distinguishes himself in the highest degree. He has one fault, however: he is wholly insensible to love. After a time he goes home to his parents and whilst there engages in the chase. On one occasion, being separated from his companions, he sees a beautiful white doe which he shoots at. The arrow wounds the animal mortally,

---

[28] The history of the discussion of the word is given in Karl Warnke's second edition of the *Lais* of Marie de France, p. vi.

[29] Proposed by H. d'Arbois de Jubainville. Cp. *Romania*, VIII, 422 ff. (1879).

[30] The text stands first in Warnke's edition. The fullest discussion of the name is H. Zimmer's *Zs. f. frz. Spr. u. Litt.*, XIII[1], 7 ff. (1891). Zimmer identifies it — correctly, no doubt — with the Breton, *Guilhomar*. On the other hand, though granting that the *tale* is Breton, J. Loth maintains, *Annales de Bretagne*, XI, 479 (1895—6), that the *name*, *Guigemar*, can just as well be Cornish. It occurs, indeed, as *Wihumar* in Domesday Book.

Variant forms of this name, viz. *Guigamor (Guiagamar), Guiomar (Guionmar)*, appear elsewhere in Arthurian texts. On this subject, cp., besides Zimmer, *op. cit.*, E. Freymond, in the same journal, XVII[1], pp. 17 ff. (1895), and W. Hertz, *Spielmannsbuch*[2], p. 382.

but, strange to say, rebounds and wounds Guigemar also severely in the thigh, so that he has to descend from his horse. To his astonishment, the dying doe speaks to him and predicts that he will never recover, save through a lady whom he will love and who will love him in return, but this mutual passion will cause them unheard-of sorrow. Guigemar gets rid of his servant by sending him after the other huntsmen and he, himself, strikes through the forest until he arrives at the seashore. He sees there a beautifully appointed ship with no human being about it. He lays himself down in a magnificent bed in the ship, with the intention of resting, but before he is aware, the ship is out on the high sea, and it moves on until about evening he finds himself before an ancient city, which was the capital of the land. The lord of the city was an old man with a young wife whom he kept shut up in a castle, accessible by only one entrance and that from the sea. Her only companions were a niece and an old priest who was a eunuch. Now, the day of Guigemar's arrival the lady and her damsel were walking in the enclosed garden which was attached to the castle and they saw the strange boat approaching. When the boat has reached the castle, the damsel enters it, observes the wounded knight and returns to tell her mistress. They both go down now, Guigemar awakes and tells his story, and they take him to the damsel's room and keep him there. Soon his wound ceases to pain him, but he is pierced to the quick by the arrows of love. The damsel perceives that her lady and the stranger love each other and she exhorts the latter to disclose his love. This he does and the two live in happiness for a year and a half. But the lady has all along the feeling that their amour will be detected and that they will be doomed to separation. So she makes a knot in the shirt of her lover and compels him to promise that, if they are ever separated, he will love no woman who cannot untie this knot. He, on his part, gives her a girdle and requires of her a similar promise: She is never to love any man who cannot undo it.

The fears of the lady at last come true. That very day a chamberlain discovers her intrigue and informs his master. Guigemar, when caught, tells his story to the husband and puts on so bold a front that he is finally allowed to embark again in his boat. He reaches home again, but he remains melancholy and, among other things, refuses to entertain the idea of marriage, vowing always that he will wed no woman, unless she is able to untie the knot. Ladies come from all sides, but none are able to fulfill the condition.

In the meanwhile the lady of the castle is as full of sorrow as Guigemar, and this continues for two years. She resolves at last to drown herself in the sea at the point from which her lover had set forth. She goes to the spot and finds the boat there, but the thought comes over her that Guigemar perhaps is drowned and she falls into the boat in a swoon. The boat takes her to Brittany, to the castle of a lord, named Meriaduc, who soon falls in love with her. She rejects him, however, alleging as an excuse her vow about the girdle. This leads him to tell her of the strange knight in this land who has made a similar vow about the knot in his shirt. The news that her lover is so near causes her to swoon. After this one knight after another tries to unloose the girdle, but without success. Finally Meriaduc proclaims a tournament and summons Guigemar to fight on his side. He comes — he and his lady recognize each other, but hold back — then Meriaduc exhorts her to try the knot in Guigemar's shirt. She unties it at once. Her lover now learns that no one as yet has undone the girdle and he demands her of Meriaduc, who refuses. Thereupon Guigemar and the assembled knights declare themselves against Meriaduc. They besiege and capture his castle — they put to death Meriaduc and the garrison — and finally the two lovers are united for good and all.

This, then, is a specimen of the French *lais*. Even in such an abstract as this not all of the wild interest of the story is lost, but one must read the original to catch the charm of its naïveté, which effaces completely the boundaries between fairyland and actual life, and of the simple, direct story of passion, which, neither hasting nor lingering, goes straight to the mark. If one were asked to name the books which represent best the romantic charm of the Middle Ages, the wisest answer, perhaps, would be the *lais*[31] of Marie de France and Gottfried of Strassburg's *Tristan*.

Of this admirable poetess, whose naive grace cast its spell over Goethe in his old age, we know little more than her name, her nationality, and her works. We may safely affirm, however, that the unnamed king to whom she dedicates her lays in her prologue was Henry II of England (1154—1189). The designation, "de France," seems to show, moreover, that she was of royal blood.[32] Indeed, she has been plausibly identified[33] with an illegitimate half-sister of Henry II's, on the paternal side, who was abbess of Shaftesbury from as early as 1181 and was still alive as late as 1215.

Let us return now, however, to the question of the origin of the French *lais*.

Apart from other considerations, convincing testimony to the fact that stories concerning Arthur and his followers were current among the Normans both in England and on the Continent about the middle of the twelfth century is supplied by various passages

---

[31] The little that we can gather about Marie de France from her poems is best summarized by Miss Edith Rickert: *Marie de France: Seven of her Lays done into English*, pp. 137 ff., (New York, 1901). Emil Winkler in his *Marie de France, Sitzungsberichte* of the Vienna Academy, Philosoph.-Hist. Klasse, 188 Band, 3 Abhandlung (1918), endeavors to identify her with Marie de Champagne, patroness of Chrétien de Troyes. On this improbable theory, however, see Giulio Bertoni, "Maria di Francia", *Nuova Antologia* for Sept. 1, 1920, pp. 18 ff. Scholars differ as to whether her dialect is pure French or Franco-Norman. It seems most probable that she was from Normandy or from the part of the Isle de France that borders on Normandy. Cp. T. A. Jenkins's edition of her *L'Espurgatoire Seint Patriz*, pp. 21 ff. (Philadelphia, 1894) for a discussion of her language and for previous literature on the subject — also, Bertoni, *loc. cit.*

[32] Cp. Marguerite de France, daughter of Louis VII of France and wife of Prince Henry of England, Henry II's oldest son — Blanche de France, daughter of Louis IX, king of France and wife of the Infanta of Castile — and many other royal personages in later history. Elise Richter, *Zs. f. rom. Ph.* XL 728 ff. (in her review of Winkler), disputes, unconvincingly, that the designation was limited to royal personages.

[33] By John Charles Fox, "Marie de France" *English Historical Review*, XXV, 303 ff. (1910) and "Mary, Abbess of Shaftesbury", *ibid.*, XXVI, 317 ff. (1911).

in Wace's *Brut,* a work which, as we have seen, was finished in
1155. First the famous passage (11. 9994ff.) which contains the
earliest recorded mention of the Round Table:

> Por les nobles barons qu'il ot
> Dont cascuns mieldre estre quidot . . .
> Fist Artus la Roonde Table,
> Dont Breton dient mainte fable.
> Illoc seoient li vassal
> Tuit chievalment et tot ingal . . .
> Nus d'als ne se pooient vanter
> Qu'il seist plus halt de son per.

And then again (11. 10032ff.):

> En cele grant pais que jo di,
> Ne sai se vos l'aves oi,
> Furent les merveilles provees
> Et les aventures trovees
> Qui d'Artu sont tant racontees
> Que a fable sunt atornees:
> Ne tot menconge ne tot voir
> Ne tot folie ne tot savoir;
> Tant ont li conteor conte
> Et li fableor tant fable
> Pour lor contes ambeleter
> Que tout ont feit fables sanbler.

Among the followers of Arthur who perished in his last battle
Wace includes (11. 13675f.):

> cil de la Table Roonde
> Dont tex los fu par tot le monde [34]).

What was the form now of these Celtic stories — the term,
*Breton,* we shall see, is somewhat ambiguous — to which Wace
alludes?[35] In his treatise on the metrical romances,[36] mentioned

---

[34] "Those of the Round Table, of whom there was such praise
throughout the world."

[35] Besides the two passages just quoted, cp. too, Wace, 11.
10401ff. and 11. 10555f. (reference to the Round Table). G. Huet,
*Moyen Age,* XIX, 234f. (1916), "Notes d'histoire littéraire. I. Le
témoignage de Wace sur les fables arthuriennes", remarks that the
terms, "merveiller" and "aventures", correspond exactly to the contents of the French Arthurian romances and prove the existence of
such tales among the Celts before Chrétien and independently of
Geoffrey.

above, Gaston Paris interprets them as embracing both *lais* of the
French kind (short narrative poems) and informal prose tales
told by professional storytellers who haunted castle and inn. The
existence of the prose tales is beyond dispute, as is made clear
enough by the passages which Paris himself cites;[37] it is only a
question of the *lais*. That these, whatever their character, were
set to music is manifest from passages in the French *lais* — as
when it is said at the end of Guigemar:

> De cest cunte qu'oi avez
> Fu Guigemar li lais trovez
> Que hum dit en harpe e en rote
> Bone en est a oïr la note.

It is evident still further that the instruments to which they
were usually sung were the Celtic rote — a rude kind of violin —
and the harp, but especially the former. As we have already seen,
however, there is no epic narrative in verse in extant Welsh or
Irish literature and there is no reason to believe that the Bretons
differed from their Celtic kinsmen of the British Isles in this
matter; so what do the writers of the French *lais* mean by their
citation of *lais Bretons* in connection with their own poems?[38]
It would seem most probable that the Celtic lays referred to were
simply lyrical pieces set to music concerning the characters who
are told of in the *lais* of Marie de France and others. In singing

---

[36] *Histoire littéraire de la France.* XXX, 7 ff. (1888).

[37] *Op. cit.,* pp. 9 ff., from Thomas's *Tristan,* from Chrétien's
*Erec,* from the continuation of his *Perceval* by Wauchier de Denain
(Gaucher de Dourdan), and from still others.

[38] It was natural that Gaston Paris, who had no firsthand knowledge of Celtic literature, should have mistaken the force of these
allusions and assumed that they referred to narrative poems in a
Celtic language of the same character as the French *lais* themselves.
But, on the whole, the assumption seems unjustified. As Warnke has
pointed out, pp. XXVI ff., Marie de France, for instance, does not say
that she is translating or paraphrasing a *lai Bretun:* she says that
she is following the *cuntes* or tales from which the *lais* too, it seems,
sprang: So, for example, near the beginning of her collection she uses
the following words: "The tales which I know to be true, concerning
which the Britons have made the lays, I will relate to you quite
briefly."

such a piece, the singer would find it necessary to recite in prose the story to which the poem related. This would be the case especially, of course, if the Breton singer were singing before French-speaking audiences who did not know the legends of his race. There is, in all probability, then, no reason for trying to distinguish between epical and lyrical *lais*, as has sometimes been done. There were, we may assume, as a matter of fact, only lyrical *lais* in the Celtic language and the term was extended by Marie de France and her fellows to the short narrative poems in French which they composed; but this poetical *genre* had really nothing to correspond to it in the Celtic and was their own independent invention. In French literature, besides, the word, *lai*, continued often to designate brief lyrical pieces *(chansons)* as we have just assumed that it did in the Celtic. Indeed, *lai* in the sense of tale *(conte)* was never very popular in France and passed out of use altogether by the end of the thirteenth or first quarter of the fourteenth century.[39]

Granting that the French lays embody tales that came to their authors from Celtic sources — and this is certainly true of some of them, at least — it remains for us to inquire from what division of the Celts did the French poets derive these tales. Was it from the Celts of Great Britain or of Brittany (Armorica)? The answer to the question turns on the meaning of the term, *Breton*, which qualifies the word, *lai*, in the references of Marie de France and others to their sources. That the term, in some cases, is equivalent to Armorican is plain. For example, the names of two of Marie's lays — *Bisclavret (=Werewolf)* and *Laustic* (= *Nightingale*) — are somewhat distorted Breton words and could not come from the Welsh.[40] Furthermore, the name, *Guigemar*,

---

[39] In only five of her lays does Marie use *lai* as a synonym of *conte*. Cp. Foulet, *Zs. f. rom. Ph.*, XXIX, 303 f. He traces there her hesitating adoption of the term in this sense. He points out, p. 311, its very limited use in the anonymous lays. In Italian *lai* meant *lament*. Cp. O. M. Johnston, *Studj Medievali*, II, 554 ff. (1907).

[40] This was first pointed out by Zimmer in the *Göttingische Gelehrte Anzeigen* for Oct. 1, 1890, pp. 800 f. The article is of the first importance with reference to the origin of the lays. So, too, is the same writer's "Beiträge zur Namenforschung in den altfranzösischen Arthurepen", *Zs. f. frz. Spr. u. Litt.*, XIII [1], 1 ff. (1891).

occurs in numerous historical documents in Brittany from the early eleventh century down and not in Wales.[41] In the case of still other lays — *Equitan, Lanval, Les Dous Amanz, Eliduc* — geographical allusions connect them definitely with Brittany.[42] These observations afford irrefragable proof that in the particular cases the word, *Breton (Bretun)*, is synonomous with Armorican. Indeed, a comprehensive inquiry into the subject has shown that, in the general usage of the Middle Ages, the terms *Bretagne, Breton,* and their Latin equivalents[43] were employed only of contemporary Brittany and its inhabitants and language, or, retrospectively, of Great Britain before and during the period of the Anglo-Saxon conquest and of the ancient Celtic population that inhabited it.[44] Consequently, when Marie de France and her contemporaries refer to *lais Bretons* as their sources, they have Brittany in mind, and their own lays are, accordingly, based on Breton stories, as far as they are of Celtic origin at all. It is true that Marie and her fellows sometimes localize the plots of their lays in Great Britain. For example, *Chievrefueil (Honeysuckle),* in which Tristan sends down stream to Iseult messages carved on pieces of wood, is connected with Tintagel (in Cornwall); in *Yonec* (and in *L'Espine,* under the influence of *Yonec)*[45] Caerleon (in

---

[41] Cp. Zimmer's last named article, pp. 1 ff.

[42] Cp. Zimmer, *Gött. G. A.,* for October 1, 1890, pp. 797 ff.

[43] *Brito, Brittanicus, Britannia.*

[44] These are the conclusions of Brugger's article, "Über die Bedeutung von Bretagne, Breton in mittelalterlichen Texten", *Zs. f. frz. Spr. u. Litt.,* XX¹, 79 ff. (1898). One has to except *Britannia,* used as a name for Great Britain in learned writings. Still further, as Lot, *Romania,* XXIV, 508 ff. (1895), and in his reply to Brugger, entitled "La Patrie des lais bretons", *ibid.,* xxviii, 1 ff. (1899), has shown, these archaic terms, *Britones, lingua Britannica, Britannia* are, also, occasionally applied to contemporary Wales, its people and its language, respectively, in the Latin writings of Welshmen, (Geoffrey of Monmouth, Giraldus Cambrensis, etc.). For a full bibliography of the controversy over the meaning of *Breton,* etc., see Miss Hopkins's dissertation, pp. 114 ff. Brugger, like Zimmer, is an advocate of the Armorican origin of the stories told in the French lays.

[45] Cp. Foulet, *Zs. f. rom. Ph.,* XXIX., 36.

Wales) and St. Aaron's church in that city are mentioned.[46] But such localizations were merely innovations of the French poets, under the all-pervading influence of Geoffrey or Wace.[47]

Again, two of Marie's lays bear alternative titles, English and French, for the poetess says of *Chievrefueil* that the French call it by that name, but that the English call it *Gotelef (Honeysuckle)*, and of *Laüstic* that the French call it *Russignol*, but the English *Nihtegale (Nightingale)*.[48]

G. Paris drew[49] from this latter circumstance the far-reaching inference that even before the Norman Conquest Welsh musicians had spread among the Anglo-Saxons a knowledge of the stories with which the lays deal. But in this matter, also, as it turns out, we have merely another mark of Wace's influence — an imitation of his trick of giving names in different languages,[50] as, for in-

---

[46] In his articles, "De la provenance des lais dits bretons", *Romania*, XXIV, 513 ff. (1895) and "La patrie des lais bretons", *ibid.*, XXVIII, 321 ff. (1899), Lot tried to establish a Welsh or Cornish origin for some of the lays, such as *Yonec, Chievrefeuil, L'Espine, Le Cor.*

[47] This is Brugger's suggestion. Cp. his last-cited article, pp.147 ff. As he points out, this influence is patent in the case of Marie's *Milun,* where she says that her hero was known "in Ireland and in Norway and Guhtlande [i. e. the island of Gotland in the Baltic], in Loengres [i. e. Logres, name for England in the romances] and in Albania [i. e. Scotland]". This enumeration was taken indisputably from Geoffrey's list of Arthur's conquests, Book IX, ch. 10, or, possibly, Wace's diffuse paraphrase of the same, 11. 9900 ff. Especially significant is the occurrence of the Baltic island in both lists.

[48] Through a slip, G. Paris, *Hist. Litt.*, XXX, 7, cited, also, *Bisclavret* as an example, for Marie says that the Normans called this lay *Garulf (Garual)*. But this has nothing to do with English origins.

[49] *Loc. cit.*, and, before this, in *Romania*, XIV, 604 ff.

[50] So Lucien Foulet, "English Words in the *Lais* of Marie de France", MLN, XX, 109 ff. (1905). He points out the example here cited — also, another in the episode of Hengist's treachery towards Vortigern (11. 7409 ff.), where Wace explains (11. 7473 ff.) that the English call the knives which Hengist's men used *sexes* (= Anglo-Saxon *seaxas*), the French *costiax*. Foulet points out still other mannerisms of Wace which Marie imitates. — The trick just discussed

stance, when in speaking of the famous dolmens or prehistoric
temples at Stonehenge, on Salisbury Plains, in England, he says
(ll. 8383 ff.): "The Britons in the British language call them
*Karole as gaians* [ i. e. Giants' Dance or Round ]; in English they
are called *Senhange* [ i. e. *Stonehenge* ]; in French *Pierres Pandues*
[ i. e. Scattered Stones ]." We have here an exact parallel to the
*Laustic* of Marie de France, where the title of the poem is given
first in Breton, and next in French and English.

Although Marie, then, derived the materials for some of her
lays from Breton sources, there is no ground for supposing that
she, herself, ever came into personal contact with Bretons.[51] In
any event, she was certainly ignorant of the Breton language —
otherwise she would not have distorted Breton *bleiz lauaret* (i. e.

is not confined to Wace and Marie. It is found in other mediaeval
writers. Cp. Foulet, *Zs. f. rom. Ph.*, XXXII, 275 f. (1908).

Before Foulet, Warnke, in his second edition of Marie's lays,
p. XXI (1900), and Bédier, edition of Thomas's *Tristan*, II, 127 ff.
(1905), had both offered unsatisfactory explanations of the alternative
titles of the above-mentioned lays: Warnke suggests that, writing in
England after the Norman Conquest, Marie provided her poems with
the alternative titles to suit either a French or English audience as
the case might be. Similarly, Bédier — only he ascribes the double
naming to Breton *jongleurs* in England. For criticism of Bédier's
suggestion, cp. Foulet, *loc cit.*

[51] So L. Foulet, in his article, "Marie de France et les lais
bretons", *Zs. f. rom. Ph.*, XXIX, 319 ff. (1905). *Ibid.*, 315 ff., he
shows from *Guigemar*, 11. 22 ff. (compared with corresponding ex-
pressions in her *Fables*, which was, of course, certainly based on a
written source), that she used written sources — doubtless, French. He
has proved, too, "Thomas and Marie in their relation to the *conteurs*",
MLN, XXIII, 205 ff. (1908), that her occasional appeals to an oral
source is "a meaningless mannerism". In his "Marie de France et la
légende de Tristan", *Zs. f. rom. Ph.*, XXXII, 274, note 4 (1908),
the same scholar remarks pertinently: "Je ne trouve dans Marie aucun
texte où elle nous affirme avoir entendu *la même personne*, ou le
même groupe de personnes, chanter la 'note' et raconter le conte qu'elle
se propose de nous répéter en vers français — aucun texte où elle nous
affirme avoir entendu un *Breton* chanter ou raconter, quoique se soit. . . .
Ainsi le conteur Breton n'apparaît nulle part chez Marie. Les musi-
ciens qui faisaient en harpe et en rote le lai de *Guigemar* étaient-
ils bretons? C'est possible, voilà tout ce qu'on peut dire."

*talking wolf*) into *Bisclavret* — the name of her werewolf-hero — or have failed to see that the *L* of *Laüstic* — the title of another one of her lays — was merely the French article prefixed to *Aostic*, the Breton word for "nightingale."[52] It is evident, therefore, that she was entirely dependent on intermediate written versions in French for her knowledge of these Breton stories. And what was true of Marie was, no doubt, true of the other authors of French lays.

Even in Marie's collection of lays there are some which have no real connection with Brittany. Thus, she, herself, tells us that the incident on which her lay, *Les Dous Amanz (= The Two Lovers)*, is based occurred in Normandy. When she adds that the Bretons made it the subject of a lay, one begins to suspect that the term *lai Breton* is already becoming conventionalized[53] and may be applied to any short narrative poem of the kind which Marie had been composing on genuine Breton themes. One may say somewhat the same thing of *Le Fraisne (= The Ash)* — a tale with no distinctively Breton features, which the poetess localizes in Brittany, but which is found in variant forms in every part of the world. Above all, it has been immortalized by Chaucer in his *Patient Griselda (Clerk's Tale)*.[54] What we have suspected here in the case of these two lays by Marie is true, beyond question, of the lays of later authors in this *genre:* the term became a purely conventional one with the meaning just indicated

---

[52] Cp. Zimmer, *G. G. A.* for Oct. 10, 1890, pp. 800f. G. Cohen, *Zs. f. frz. Spr. u. Litt.*, XXIV², 3 (1902), suggests that the fusion of the article with the noun in *Laustic* may have been the work of a scribe, but the equating of the word with simple *russignol* and *nihtegale* (without articles) at the beginning of the lay shows that the suggestion is groundless.

[53] F. Lot, *Romania*, XXIV, 527f. (1895), makes this observation with regard to this lay and *Le Fraisne*. *Ibid.*, p. 525, however, he cites the fact that in *L'Espine* an Irishman is said to have sung a lay *(Aelis)*, as proof that the Irish took part in the propagation of lays, but the Irish had long before figured in the romances — especially since the appearance of the *Tristan* poems — so we doubtless have in this instance, too, a purely conventional use of the term, *lai*.

[54] With this story in *Le Fraisne* is combined the widespread popular notion that twins are always the offspring of different fathers.

and the Celtic coloring in such poems is, if not invariably, certainly more often than not, purely factitious.[55]

A main factor in rendering the use of the term, *lai Breton*, a popular literary artifice was Thomas's poem on Tristan, composed about 1170.[56] Here, probably under the influence of Marie de France, that writer makes his British hero an accomplished harper who charms audiences with his lays, and so it was the example of Tristan, the most popular figure in the literature of the time, that led subsequent poets to represent their characters as singing *lais bretons*, or even to designate their works by that title as in the case of the French versions of *Havelok* and *Horn*, which have, of course, no connection with Brittany.

Marie is the only author of genuine narrative lays[57] whose name has been preserved. We have, however, besides the collection which is unquestionably her work, a number of anonymous lays[58] of the same character, one or two of which may be also from her pen. Some of these pieces deal with the *matière de Bretagne* and have much the same charm of ,,faerie" — the charm of wild and delicate fancy — that we have noted in Marie's recognized works. So in the story of *Guingamor* (probably Marie's), where, after enjoying the love of a fay in the Otherworld for a hundred years, that passed like three days, the hero is allowed to return to his native land, but by disobeying the command of his mistress not to partake of mortal food, whilst there, loses both his apparent gift of immortal youth and the power to return to her — or, again, in *Tydorel*, where a king, the son of a water-

---

[55] In the opinion of the present writer, this has been clearly established by L. Foulet in his "Marie de France et les lais bretons", *Zs. f. rom. Ph.*, XXIX, 19 ff., 293 ff. (1905) and his subsequent articles on the *lais bretons* in the same journal, vols. XXX and XXXII.

[56] Cp., especially, Foulet, ,,Marie de France et la légende de Tristan", *Zs. f. rom. Ph.*, XXXII, 161 ff., 257 ff. (1908).

[57] *Le Cor* by Robert Biket (Biquet) in verses of six syllables, last edited by H. Dörner (Straßburg diss., 1907), is a fabliau, and *Ignaure* by Renaut, also, does not belong properly to the *genre*. We know nothing of these authors, save their names.

[58] For these lays and the critical literature relating to them see Part IV, below.

sprite and a mortal mother, on being taunted once with not being human, since, in consequence of his supernatural origin, he never sleeps, learns with mortification the true secret of his birth from his mother and plunges into his father's lake, never to be heard of again.

There is something suspicious in the fact that out of the seven anonymous lays that deal with the *matière de Bretagne* three constitute variants of themes which Marie has treated.[59] The choice of themes in such cases was, doubtless, determined by her example, and, as a matter of fact, these lays, in phrasing and other matters, also, betray her influence — so distinctly, indeed, that the question has been raised as to whether the authors of the pieces in question drew at all on Celtic tradition. This skepticism has included — and, justly, it would seem — even the beautiful *Franklin's Tale* of the *Canterbury Tales* in which a woman's honor is saved by the generosity of her lover, after she had placed herself in his power by promising him her favors, in case he performed a seemingly impossible task, which, however, he actually performs.[60] Nevertheless, *Tydorel*, at least — to say

---

[59] *Melion* is like *Bisclavret*; *Graelent* and *Desiré* are like *Lanval*. For the literature of these lays, cp. Part. V, below. Zimmer, *Zs. f. frz. Spr. u. Litt.*, XIII [1], 1 ff., has shown that the name *Graelent* is identical with *Gradlon mur*, name of a hero in early Armorican saga. Nevertheless, to my mind, Foulet, *op. cit.*, XXIX, 19 ff., has made out so strong a case for his thesis that *Graelent* is essentially a combination of Marie's *Lanval* and *Eliduc* that I hesitate to accept it as embodying an independent Celtic tradition.

[60] Chaucer describes it as a "Breton" lay, but cp. the article, "Le prologue du Franklin's Tale et les lais Bretons", *Zs. f. rom. Ph.*, XXX, 698 ff. (1906), by Foulet, who argued that the term is here conventional. On the other hand, the conclusions of Pio Rajna, "Le origini della novella narrata dal Frankeleyn nei *Canterbury Tales* del Chaucer", *Romania*, XXXII, 204 ff. (1903) — viz., that this tale is derived from Boccaccio's *Decameron*, X, 5 — are unconvincing. But one need not agree therefore with W. H. Schofield, "Chaucer's Franklin's Tale", *PMLA*, XVI, 405 ff. (1901), that Chaucer's source was a genuine Breton folk-tale. J. S. P. Tatlock has latterly, "The Scene of the Franklin's Tale Visited", *Publications of the Chaucer Society* (1914), even tried to determine the part of the coast of Brittany where the story is laid.

nothing of *Guingamor,* which is probably Marie's composition —
appears to the present writer to possess the natural magic of
Celtic fancy.

There is no convincing evidence that before Marie de France
narrative lays existed at all in French literature. She, was doubtless, the creator of the *genre*[61] and her genius seems to have
dominated it during the brief vogue which it enjoyed.[62]

----

[61] This is Foulet's conclusion, *Zs. f. rom. Ph.,* XXIX. 56, Apart
from the fact that *Le Cor* by Robert Biket is really a fabliau (cp.
already Brugger, *Zs. f. frz. Spr. u. Litt.,* XX[1], 140), there is no
valid ground for dating this poem earlier than Marie. Cp. the discussion of the subject by Foulet, *op. cit.,* p. 55, note 1. As the same
scholar observes, pp. 302 f., the *lais bretons* which are first mentioned
in the fabliau, *Richeut* (usually dated 1159, although it was in reality
probably composed considerably later. Cp. Foulet, ,,Le poème de
Richeut et le roman de Renard", *Romania,* XLII, 321 ff.), and to which
we have allusions in Chrétien, the *Roman de Troie, Horn,* etc., are
all lyrical, not narrative, and it was only by degrees that Marie,
herself, came to use the word in the new sense. — For views at
variance with the one here adopted, cp. Warnke's Introduction and
the literature there cited — also, H. Dörner's edition of *Le Cor,* cited
above, and Ezio Levi, "I lais brettoni e la leggenda di Tristano,",
*Studj romanzi editi a cura di E. Monaci,* XIV, 113—246 (Rome,
1917). The only original point which Levi tries to make is that he
finds in *canzoni* of the Countess of Dia (who died porbably in 1193)
and Guittone d'Arezzo echoes of the words "Isolt ma drue, Isolt ma
vie" in the Tristan *lai* (Thomas's *Tristan*). He assumes that these
*canzoni* were too early to be influenced by Marie. The dates of
both, as a matter of fact, are still uncertain. Above all, however, the
similarity is so general as to have no value.

[62] Interesting early testimony to the popularity of the *lais* is
supplied by Gautier d'Arras's *Ille et Galeron,* 11. 928 ff., composed
about 1167, or perhaps somewhat later. Cp. E. S. Sheldon, MPh.,
XVII, 383 ff. There, with reference to the fluctuations of love, it
is said.

> Mes s'autrement n'alast l'amors,
> Li lais ne fust pas si en cours,
> Nel prisaissent tot li baron.

Equally emphatic is the testimony on this subject in Denis Pyramus's
*La vie St. Edmund le rei,* 11. 35 ff. (ed. F. L. Ravenel, Philadelphia,
1906) — quoted by Warnke[2], p. XXXVI. Denis's poem dates, it
would seem, from the last decade of the twelfth century.

## 2. The Romances.

We have been dealing so far with the lays, but the problem of the origin of the romances[63] — more especially the question of their relation to Celtic tradition — is essentially the same, notwithstanding the position which has sometimes been taken that it is different. The fact, however, that most of the lays do not mention Arthur and his knights does not alter the case; for the most distinctive features of these romances still remain of the same general character as in the case of the lays. Take, for instance, the magic fountain at the beginning of Chrétien's *Yvain*, whose waters, if dropped on the neighboring stone, raise the storm, whereupon a strange knight rushes forth to encounter the offender, or the search of Lancelot for Guinevere in the land from which no one returns in the same writer's *Lancelot*, or Perceval's adventures at Arthur's court in the *Conte del Graal*. We move in the same world of romance and marvel in each *genre*[64] — only, in

---

[63] On the development of the meaning of the word, "romance", cp., especially, P. Voelker, "Die Bedeutungsentwickelung des Wortes Roman", *Zs. f. rom. Ph.*, X, 485 ff. (1887). It (OFr. "romanz") was used first in the sense of "a book in the vernacular" (earliest example noted is in Samson de Nanteuil's *Dits Salamon* — in the forties of the twelfth century) — but only of translations from the Latin. Wace, *Roman de Rou*, Part III, 11. 5331 f. (H. Andresen's edition), was the first writer, as far as we know, to drop this restriction. In the second half of the twelfth century, the term is applied to what we call "romances", but is, also, employed of chronicles, and continues to be employed of such works down into the fourteenth century. Nevertheless, the meaning "fictitious narrative" predominates from the thirteenth century on.

W. Meyer-Lübke, *Zs. f. frz. Spr. u. Litt.*, XLIV[1], pp. 131 f., (1916) draws attention to Chrétien's contrasted use of *conte* (short narrative) and *romanz* in *Cliges*, 11. 22 f. But the poet does not consistently maintain this distinction. Cp. the titles of his romances: *Conte de la Charette, Conte del Graal*.

[64] It has been maintained by certain Arthurian scholars — especially by G. Paris, *Histoire littéraire de la France*, XXX, 9 (1888), E. Brugger, *Zs. f. frz. Spr. u. Litt.*, XX[1], 151 (1898) and with unessential differences, J. L. Weston, *Legend of Sir Lancelot du Lac*, pp. 20, 66 ff. (1901) — that the romances were, in the first instance, made up of a combination of lays. The theory is similar to

the case of the romances, the Arthurization is not limited to a few
superficial details as in the Arthurized lays, but is thorough-going.
Similarly, the adaptation of these *motifs* to the conditions of
feudal society is even more drastic in the case of the romances.

Now, in view of what has been said about the lays there can be
no reasonable doubt that Brittany was one source of whatever
is Celtic in the romances of Chrétien and his followers. One may
go further and assert that the historical conditions render this
part of the Celtic territory a far more likely source of that element
in the romances than Great Britain could ever be. The emigration
to Armorica of the Britons who fled from Great Britain under
the pressure of Anglo-Saxon invasion was in progress during the
fifth and sixth centuries — so from this early period they were
in constant contact with their neighbors in Gaul. –Especially close
were their relations with Normandy. Indeed, from the first part
of the tenth century the Bretons were vassals of the Norman duke
and intermarriages between the reigning houses of the two states
testify to the intimacy of the intercourse which existed between
them. By the tenth century the portion of Brittany which was
closest to Normandy was thoroughly assimilated to Norman-French
civilization and there was a considerable zone in which, to a large
extent, the population was bilingual. Under these conditions, of

---

that which Paris maintained — e. g., in his *Histoire Poétique de
Charlemagne*[2], pp. 11 f., 69 ff. (Paris, 1905) — with regard to the
origin of the *chansons de geste*. These, too, he thought, sprang from
the combination of shorter pieces *(cantilenae)* — often, to be sure,
completely transformed. We have here, of course, the familiar theory
of epic origins which was first applied to the Homeric poems in the
latter part of the eighteenth century (the so-called Wolfian theory)
and afterwards to the mediaeval epics. This theory, as applied to the
latter, however, — to say nothing of the Greek — has latterly become
so generally discredited that there is no need of our discussing here
its application to the romances. Cp. Bédier's *Les Légendes Epiques,*
with reference to the *chansons de geste*. For supposed influence
of the Greek romances on the Arthurian romances — especially, in
structural matters — through the intermediation of the Crusaders,
cp. W. J. Courthope, "The Connexion between Ancient and Modern
Romance", *Proceedings of the British Academy for 1911—1912,*
pp. 245 ff. The theory, however, has no sound basis.

course, it was easy for the legends of the Bretons to penetrate into Normandy and the rest of France.[65]

How was it, on the other hand, with the insular Celts — the inhabitants of Wales and Cornwall and Scotland? We have seen already that the reasons advanced by Gaston Paris for supposing that even before the Norman Conquest Celtic tales were in circulation among the Anglo-Saxons are not sound. Moreover, in extant Anglo-Saxon literature there is no trace of such stories. We may say, in general, that the long and bitter hostility which prevailed between the two peoples was not favorable to the exchange of the materials of literature. In the main, the same thing is true of the relations that existed between the new Continental invaders and the old Celtic population of Great Britain in the decades that immediately followed the Norman Conquest. The Normans had utterly humiliated the hated Saxons, but the feeling of the Celts towards the conquerors was at first not so different from that which they had entertained towards their old enemies as might have been expected, for they found themselves engaged almost at once in a desperate struggle with the same foe. Nevertheless, during the reign of Henry I, South Wales was thoroughly subdued to Norman rule, and early in the twelfth century the conditions for peaceful intercourse between victors and vanquished were established.[66] Moreover, within such Celtic areas, there was one especial circumstance that doubtless facilitated the transmission of insular Celtic materials to the French-speaking invaders — namely, the part played by the Bretons in the conquest of England.[67] Except the Normans, themselves, no other people had so large a share in this enterprise or in the spoils that resulted from it. There is abundant documentary evidence of the gifts of land which

---

[65] In this connection it is significant that the names of the well-known Arthurian characters occur much oftener in the mediaeval documents of Brittany than of Wales. On this subject, cp. Franz Pütz's important article, "Zur Geschichte der Entwicklung der Artursage", *Zs. f. frz. Spr. u. Litt.*, XIV¹, 161 ff. (1892).

[66] Cp. J. E. Lloyd's *History of Wales from the Earliest Times to the Edwardian Conquest*, II, 433 ff. (London, 1911).

[67] So Zimmer, *Gött. G. A.* for Oct. 1, 1890, pp. 789 ff. The suggestion has found general acceptance.

they received in different parts of the conquered country, including Celtic Cornwall. Especially large were the holdings of the Breton prince, Alan Fergant,[68] in Yorkshire. But wherever there were large Norman garrisons, as in South Wales, there can be no doubt as to the presence of bilingual Bretons among them. Now, as we know from Giraldus Cambrensis, about the year 1200, say, the language of the Bretons was still so near to that of their Welsh and Cornish kinsmen that there was no difficulty in members of these different branches of the Celtic race understanding each other. So here was a ready channel for the diffusion of Welsh stories among the Normans and thence among the French. Since we have no direct testimony on the subject, the matter must remain more or less in the realm of conjecture, but the romances, themselves, furnish, to some degree, reasons for supposing that such a diffusion did take place, and it is accordingly highly probable that the Bretons did play some such rôle as we have indicated.

The problem of the relations of the romances to Celtic tradition — more particularly to Celtic insular tradition — would be simple, indeed, if we accepted, with some critics, the theory that the three Welsh tales, *Owen and Lunet* (or *The Lady of the Fountain*), *Peredur ab Evrawc*, and *Geraint and Enid* — all included in the *Mabinogion* — which deal with the same themes as Chrétien's *Yvain*, *Perceval* and *Erec*, respectively, were not mere adaptations of the latter, but went back independently to common Welsh sources. The differences, however, in style and construction between the three Welsh tales just named and the unquestionably native tales in the *Mabinogion*, such as *Kulhwch and Olwen* or *Branwen, Daughter of Llyr*, are too plain to deny. Instead of the incoherence and ineffectual rambling of the latter, we have here organization and order. Moreover, as far as he appears, Arthur in the three tales is the *roi fainéant* of the French romances, not the active hero of Welsh saga. These various differences, are, indeed, so manifest that it was obviously impossible to accept the above-mentioned hypothesis in an unqualified form. Consequently,

---

[68] Zimmer, however, was mistaken in representing this prince as taking part in the Norman Conquest of England. Cp. J. Loth, *Annales de Bretagne*, XI, 479 (1895—6).

nearly all scholars who have studied the problem have agreed that
the three tales were influenced by French originals, whether such
originals were the poems of Chrétien still extant, or those of some
other writer, now lost.[69] There seems really, however, no need
of calling into existence imaginary French sources: Chrétien will
suffice. For, although in the Welsh tales the narrative is more
condensed than in the corresponding romances of Chrétien, the
two concur in their incidents throughout, and, save for one exception
(in *The Lady of the Fountain*), in the order of these incidents.
Such divergences as we observe in comparing the two sets of narratives are, for the most part, not difficult to explain. The differences between Welsh and feudal French society at the end of the
twelfth century were enormous — in respect to custom, culture,
intellectual outlook — everything, indeed — and a Welsh adaptation of a French poem would, of course, inevitably, reflect these
differences. In these three Welsh tales of the *Mabinogion*, then,
we have, no doubt, the three above-mentioned poems of Chrétien
adapted, in part, to the conditions of contemporary Welsh society
and transmuted by that riotous fancy of the Celt which has never
had its equal — by some professional story-teller, we may say,
then, of twelfth or thirteenth century Wales, the representative
of a rude civilisation, to whose mind the marvellous was as familiar
as the real. After all, however, it is questionable whether the
transmutation in these cases is so great as that which was suffered
by the *Tale of Gamelyn*, as it passed through the hands of Lodge
and Shakespeare, becoming, in succession, the Euphuistic novel,
*Rosalynd*, and the loveliest of pastoral dramas, *As You Like It*,
or — to select an Arthurian example, — as that which befell
Malory's account of Arthur's last phase in Tennyson's *Guinevere*.[70]

---

[69] For recent writers who adopt the latter view, cp. Part IV,
below.

[70] As far as change of incident goes, there is, obviously, no
comparison — the modern writers are so much more drastic. But the
contrast in respect to sentiment is, in reality, equally striking.

For an admirable statement of the case for Chrétien as the source
of the three Welsh tales, cp. P. A. Becker, *Literaturblatt für germanische und romanische Philologie*, XXXIV, 19 ff. (Jan., 1913).

We have reviewed already above the scanty testimony of the chroniclers with respect to the existence of Arthurian traditions in Great Britain, and we have seen, moreover, that the sources of the extant lays were all continental. The question of these insular traditions will again arise when, in subsequent chapters, we endeavor to trace the history of the development of the legends concerning Merlin, Lancelot, Tristan, and the Holy Grail. With regard to these legends, we shall see that only for those that relate to Merlin and Tristan can it be claimed with certitude that they originated in Great Britain and that, even in the case of the former, the connection with Celtic popular tradition is of the slightest kind. Is there, now, any other evidence which would suggest that widespread traditions concerning Arthur and his companions were in circulation in Great Britain, or, indeed, in the British Isles — for we shall include Ireland in our examination — traditions which the authors of the Arthurian romances might draw upon directly or which, if not originally connected with the characters in question, have been actually applied to them by the romancers? The chief evidence that bears upon our inquiry would appear to be as follows:

1. Arthurian localizations.

Many localities in Great Britain bear Arthurian names — especially in those parts of the island where the Celtic element is strongest — that is to say, in Wales, Cornwall, and Somerset, and also in Scotland and Northern England.[71] It is to this circumstance that Tennyson refers in the well-known lines in the Epilogue to his *Idylls of the King,* when he speaks of

That *Peredur* is derived from Chrétien's *Perceval* and its continuations is now very generally conceded. Cp. Part. II, *Peredur* section, below. With regard to the two remaining tales, cp. Part IV, where a full history of the *Mabinogion* controversy is given and the evidence in the case examined.

[71] Full collections on the subject are given in J. S. Stuart-Glennie's *Arthurian Localities* — published as an introduction to Part III (1869) of the. E. E. T. S. edition of the Middle English prose *Merlin* (Original Series, no. 36). For Cornwall see, besides, W. H. Dickinson's *King Arthur in Cornwall* (London, 1900). Unfortunately, both writers are wholly uncritical.

> "that gray king whose name, a ghost,
> Streams like a cloud, man-shaped, from mountain peak,
> And cleaves to cairn and cromlech still."

Thus, "Arthur's Round Table" is a term applied to enclosures of one sort or another in various parts of Great Britain, — for instance, to what is really the remains of a Roman amphitheatre at Caerleon-on-Usk in Wales, — to a space surrounded by trenches on a hill at Cadbury in Somersetshire, and so on. This same Cadbury is identified locally with the Camelot of the French romances, the capital of Arthur's kingdom. In Cornwall, besides Tintagel, where the hero was born, and Camelford, where he fought his last battle with Mordred, we have King Arthur's Bed — a group of rocky hills — King Arthur's Cups and Saucers, rock basins in the slate of a promontory along the coast. But the localizations are especially numerous in Southern Scotland.[72] Every visitor to Edinburgh will remember the hill called Arthur's Seat which rises to the south of the city, but the same name is met with elsewhere in the south of Scotland. Further north at Meigle is Guinevere's grave — the queen, according to local tradition, having been tied to wild horses and torn to pieces as a punishment for marital infidelity. These are only a few well-known examples which might be increased almost indefinitely.

It is frequently taken for granted that this widespread Arthurian nomenclature furnishes indisputable proof of an equally widespread diffusion of early Arthurian traditions in Great Britain, those traditions being embodied, as it is conjectured, in fantastic tales of the same general character as the Welsh *Kulhwch and Olwen*. But the validity of this assumption depends entirely on the antiquity of the localizations, and, in default of a critical work on the subject, no one can affirm that such localizations

---

[72] On the basis of these frequent localizations, Skene, *Four Ancient Books of Wales,* I, 60, and Stuart-Glennie, p. LXI, have placed the scene of Arthur's last battle in Scotland at Camelon, on the south bank of the river, Carron, where there are remains of an old Roman town. W. H. Dickinson, pp. 82 f., also argues at length in favor of this view. All the conditions of sixth century Britain, however, point to the South as the scene of this last battle, if, indeed, it is not purely legendary.

were not really suggested, in the majority of instances, by the chronicles and romances. They would occur particularly in the regions named above — partly, because it was known that the severest conflict between the Celts and the Anglo-Saxon invaders did take place in just those regions, and, partly, because people of Celtic descent would naturally feel the greatest interest in connecting with objects in their own territory the names of these mythical characters of their race whom the chroniclers and romancers had made world-famous. It is significant that the parts of Great Britain where the localizations in question are most numerous of all — viz., Northern England and Southern Scotland — were also just those parts where Arthurian romance as a literary *genre* took deepest root. It was here (in Northern England), for example, that the finest of the English romances, *Sir Gawain and the Green Knight* and the alliterative *Morte Arthure*, were written, and the last of the species that was composed on British soil was a Scottish romance, *Lancelot of the Laik.* It will be observed, then, that the evidence of these place-names is inconclusive.[73]

2. Traditions concerning Arthur's death (journey to Avalon) and expected return.

In spite of their enthusiastic patriotism, native Welsh authorities are agreed that Arthur was a late-comer in the traditions of Wales.[74] Moreover, one of the most eminent of Celtic scholars

---

[73] Zimmer, however, maintains, *Gött. G. A.* for June 10, 1890, pp. 525 f., that the localization of Arthur's capital at Carlisle (Carduel), which occurs often in the French romances, is a genuine tradition inherited from an early period.

[74] The testimony of the native Welsh authorities on this subject is virtually unanimous. Cp., for instance, Thomas Stephens, *The Literature of the Kymry*, pp. 400 ff. (second ed., London, 1876). He regards (p. 406) Arthur as an Armorican creation. E. Anwyl, *Zs. f. celt. Ph.*, I, 293 (1897). declares that "in the legends of Gwynedd [Northwest Wales] and Dyfed [Southwest Wales] he [Arthur] had no place whatever", and W. J. Gruffydd in his paper "The Mabinogion", *Transactions of the Honorable Society of Cymmrodorion*, Session of 1912—1913 (London, 1914), says (p. 31) that to Cornwall and Devon "must be given the credit of cradling the superb mythology of Arthur", and (pp. 32 f.) that "whether he appears in the well-ordered tales of Chrétien de Troyes or in the chronicles of Geoffrey of Mon-

on the Continent, the late Professor Zimmer, even went so far as to
deny that there was any popular tradition at all among the Welsh
concerning Arthur's voyage to Avalon (the Celtic Elysium) and
expected return.[75] According to the German scholar, this was
a purely Armorican (Breton) conception and became known to
the Welsh only through the Bretons — after the appearance of
Geoffrey's *Historia* — whose passionate attachment to the idea
of the *espoir breton (hope of the Britons)*, as it was called, is

mouth and in others or in Malory, or, above all, in Welsh literature
he is clearly no dweller in Wales or in the Gogledd" [i. e., the old
Celtic territory in Northwest England and Southern Scotland]. Gruffydd
avers (p. 32) that even in *Kulhwch and Olwen* Arthur is "no necessary part of the romance", and with reference to the same tale,
J. Loth, *Revue Celtique*, XXXIV, 379 f. (1913), observes that, if Arthur
plays a preponderant part in a Welsh story, this is a sign of late date.
    Gruffydd, op. cit., p. 35, asserts that Arthur's tables, mounds, etc.,
in Wales are all of late origin. The little that is found concerning
Arthur in Welsh literature, he thinks, came in through Powis. The
Anglo-Saxon victory at Deorham (in 577) cut off henceforth the Celts
of Wales from those in Devon and Cornwall. Gruffydd suggests that
this event prevented the Welsh from absorbing the Arthurian traditions
which their Southern brethren had created.
    It seems significant that South Wales — the part of Wales
nearest Cornwall — should, among all divisions of Wales, best preserve the tradition of Arthur and his last battle (Camlan). Cp. F. Lot's
note, "La bataille de Camlan", *Romania*, XXX, 16 ff. (1901). As
Lot says, the people of Cornwall localized Camelford (twelve miles
east of Bodmin) as the scene of the battle and the river, Camel, as
the Cambula. In the Welsh *Mabinogion* and *Triads* we find also
the Cornish localization of Arthur's residence at Kelliwic, which Lot,
*ibid.*, pp. 13 f., identifies with Bodmin (capital of Cornwall).
    [76] In his article, "Bretonische Elemente in der Arthursage des
Gottfried von Monmouth", *Zs. f. frz. Spr. u. Litt.*, XII [1], 231 ff. (1891)
— especially, pp. 238 ff. In this same article Zimmer tried to draw
a distinction between a *historical* Arthurian tradition in Great Britain
(cp. Nennius) and a *romantic* tradition developed by the inhabitants
of Brittany in the course of the generations which followed their
separation from the actual scenes of his struggle and triumphs. But
the distinction is a fanciful one and has found no favor with scholars.
The popular imagination could have been just as active in full sight
of Badon Hill or on the field of Arthur's last battle as in far-away
Brittany.

well attested by contemporaries, such as Wace[76] and Alanus de Insulis. [77] The latter, for example, in his commentary on Geoffrey's *Prophecies of Merlin* (Book VII, of the *Historia*) avers that any one who in Brittany disputed the superstition concerning Arthur's return would be cursed and stoned. Geoffrey, himself, indeed, has only a brief phrase concerning the matter: *illinc ad sananda vulnera sua in insulam Avallonis advectus* (XI, 2). But, interest in the subject having been awakened by this statement, according to Zimmer's view, the Welsh later on drew a fuller account from the Bretons, by way, doubtless, of the French chroniclers and romancers.

As a matter of fact, the evidence of Welsh belief in this most famous of the conceptions that relate to Arthur is surprisingly meagre. Nennius, for instance, does not mention it, nor is it mentioned in the *Mabinogion*. In fact, only two texts have been cited that seem to furnish any evidence as to the currency of these conceptions in Wales: 1. a description of Wales in French octosyllabic verse which dates from the middle of the twelfth century and which is attached to Gaimar's chronicle in certain MSS. of that work. Describing the Norman invasion of Wales after the Conquest of England, the writer says that the Welsh recovered much of the ground which the invaders had taken from them and that they averred that they would recover it all in time through Arthur. 2. A Welsh poem of about the same date in the Black Book of Caermarthen. Here it is said in an enumeration of tombs:

A tomb for March, a tomb for Gwythyr,
A tomb for Gwgan of the red sword.
A tomb for Arthur would be foolish.

That is to say, of course, because he was still alive.[79]

[76] *Brut*, 11. 13683ff., quoted in part, p. 57, above. Wace, with Geoffrey, VII, 3, in mind, says that, according to Merlin, Arthur's end would be doubtful.

[77] For the words of Alanus in his *Prophetia Anglicana* cp. San Marte, *Sagen von Merlin*, p. 55 (Halle, 1853), and Zimmer, *op. cit.*, p. 240. They were written during the reign (1154—1189) of Henry II.

[78] By F. Lot, *Romania*, XXVIII, 16 f. (1899).

[79] W. J. Gruffydd, who maintains, as we have seen above (p. 74 note), that Arthur was an alien to genuine Welsh tradition, suggests,

Does not Giraldus Cambrensis, however, the famous Welsh ecclesiastic of the late twelfth and early thirteenth centuries, testify to a Welsh tradition of Arthur's expected return in the well-known passage of his *Speculum Ecclesiae* (II, 9)[80] which de-

p. 35 of the *Transactions of the Honorable Society of the Cymmrodorion*, Session, 1912—1913 (London, 1914), that the real meaning of the last line is: "His exploits were not performed in Welsh territory; his grave was unknown, simply because he was not buried in Wales." But even if Gruffydd's general theory about Arthur and Wales is correct, Lot's interpretation of the line strikes me as preferable.

Arthur's last battle (Camlann) is mentioned often in Welsh texts. See Index to Loth's *Mabinogion* under *Camlann*. The text above, however, is the only one in the Welsh language that even hints at the conception of Arthur's translation to Avalon, and there are none in Irish — for Irish literature is virtually entirely ignorant of Arthur. In my edition of the *Mort Artu*, pp. 300f., I have summarized and discussed the suggestions that have been made as to Irish parallels to the story of Arthur: *Death of Cuchullin* (cp. Eleanor Hull, *The Cuchullin Saga*, pp. XXVIIIff., London, 1898), the legend of Mongan (cp. A. Nutt, *The Voyage of Bran*, II, 23, London, 1897), and the legend of Finn (cp. A. Nutt, *Revue Celtique*, XII, 190). There is no real similarity, however, in any of the cases — least of all, in regard to the end of the respective heroes. J. F. Campbell. *Popular Tales of the West Highlands*, IV, 240ff. (London, 1893) was better inspired, when he cited as a parallel the Gaelic legend of Diarmaid and Grainne, a cognate, as we shall see below, of the Tristan-Iseult story. The parallel is closer, if we take (with Geoffrey) Mordred as the adulterer, instead of Lancelot, as Campbell does. Here, as in the stories of Tristan and Iseult and Arthur and Guinevere, we have the faithless wife who commits adultery with her husband's nephew. On the other hand, the legend in question does not end with an Otherworld voyage. Altogether, there is probably no historical connection between the stories.

The idea that only three men survived Arthur's last battle is known to Welsh literature. Cp. the triad in Loth's *Mabinogion*[2], II, 290, and *Kulhwch and Olwen, op. cit.*, I, 270. For a discussion of these passages see Bruce, *Mort Artu*, pp. 295f. and on Arthur's mythical end, in general, cp. pp. 298ff. Cp., too, Miss Paton, *op. cit.*, pp. 25ff.

[80] Giraldus, *loc. cit.*, erroneously states that it was in Henry II's reign, but Henry died in 1189. It occurred really in the reign of Richard I. Cp. J. S. Brewer's edition of Giraldus's works for the

scribes the pretended exhumation of Arthur and Guinevere at Glastonbury in 1191? To increase the importance of their monastery, which, according to their impudent assertions, was founded by King Arthur, the monks concocted this solemn farce of the exhumation, an account of which Giraldus received from an eyewitness. The bodies were found buried sixteen feet deep in the ground and when a monk seized a yellow lock of Guinevere's hair, it is said to have vanished away. The Welsh writer contrasts with the evidence of Arthur's real death which this affair supplied the absurd tales which are propagated by *fabulosi Britones et eorum cantatores;* for the latter were accustomed to relate, he says, how a certain fantastic goddess, Morganis — *Dea quaedam phantastica*—took Arthur to Avalon to be healed of his wounds and how, when they are cured, he will return to reign over the Britons. Giraldus comments still further on the likeness of this belief to that of the Jews in the coming of the Messiah.

Everything here turns on the disputed meaning of *Britones.* Is Giraldus referring to Armoricans or Welshmen? Despite contentions to the contrary,[81] Welsh writers in the Middle Ages do occasionally, though not often, use this term of contemporary Welshmen, as well as of the whole race of Britons combined — both continental and insular.[82] Consequently, the passage is open to varying constructions and throws no decisive light on the sub-

---

Rolls Series, IV, 48 ff. (London, 1873). A few sentences which are unintelligible in the Latin text, owing to mutilation of the unique MS. of the *Speculum,* have been preserved in the Welsh version of Giraldus's account edited by Timothy Lewis and J. D. Bruce, "The pretended exhumation of Arthur and Guinevere," *Revue Celtique,* XXXIII, 432 ff. (1912). The inscription on the cross over the tomb in Giraldus, p. 50, speaks of Guinevere as Arthur's second wife. In a Welsh triad, according to Rhys, *Arthurian Legend,* pp. 35 ff., he is said to have had three wives, all named Gwenhwyvar (Guinevere). Nowhere else in Arthurian literature, however, is he given more than one wife and, besides, as we have seen above, p. 44, note 14, Loth does not translate the Welsh in the same manner as Rhys. According to his translation, the triad does not speak of Arthur's three wives, but of the three principal ladies at his court.

[81] Zimmer, *Zs. f. frz. Spr. u. Litt.,* XII ¹, 241 ff. (1890).

[82] Cp. Lot's articles cited p. 60, note, 44, above.

ject of our inquiry. The form of Morgan's name in Giraldus, *Morganis* (instead of *Morgana*) seems determined, it is true, by the French nominative form, *Morgains*,[83] but even this detail cannot be taken as settling the whole question; for, in forming the Latin name, Giraldus might well have been influenced by the most popular works in which the character had appeared (the French romances) even though he knew, also, from Welsh sources of Arthur's *exitus dubius*.[84]

Morgan[85] and Avalon[86] being, of course, inseparable from

---

[83] Cp. Brugger, *op. cit.*, XX', 100 (1898). *Ibid.*, pp. 97 ff., he presents the strongest argument that has been offered for the interpretation of *Britones* as *Armoricans* in this passage.

[84] "Doubtful exit" — i. e. from life.

[85] For the name which, according to J. Rhys, *Arthurian Legends*, 348 f., must have been *Morgen* (as actually in Geoffrey's *Vita Merlini*) in mediaeval Welsh, cp. L. A. Paton, *Studies in the Fairy Mythology of Arthurian Romance*, pp. 9 ff.: Radcliffe College Monographs, no. 13 (Boston, 1903), and J. D. Bruce, MLN, XXVI, 67' note 16, where the opinions of the leading Celticists on the subject are assembled — in the latter, also, similar observations on the common Welsh man's name, *Morgan*. Miss Paton, *loc. cit.*, proposed to identify Morgan with Morrigan, an Irish battle-goddess, but this unlikely suggestion has won no adherents. — Rhys, *op. cit.*, p. 22, interprets Welsh *Morgen* as etymologically identical with *Muirgen*, meaning "sea-born", which actually occurs as a woman's name in Irish.

Morgan (Morgen) is first mentioned in Geoffrey's *Vita Merlini*, 11. 918 ff. (composed probably in 1149) — and here as the person who is to heal Arthur in the Isle of Apples (Celtic Elysium). She is next mentioned in the *Roman de Troie*, 1. 8024 (Constans' edition, I, 434), — composed about 1160 — as a fairy who hated Hector, because he did not return her love. The name here, it is true, is in most MSS. disguised by mutilation, as we have seen above, p. 33, note 73, that it was also in Layamon. Chrétien, in his *Erec*, 1. 1957, composed about 1165), mentions her as the mistress of Guigomar, lord of Avalon, and, 11. 4216 ff., as Arthur's sister and as highly skilled in healing. The two passages combined betray a knowledge of the part which she played in the story of Arthur's end. The poet, himself, however, doubtless, invented the idea that she was Arthur's sister, which was afterwards adopted, among others, by Robert de Boron in his *Merlin*. To be sure, it must be confessed that as early as about 1170, in the *Draco Normannicus* (a Latin metrical paraphrase of Geoffrey's *Historia*), the author (Etienne, a monk of Bec,

the myth of Arthur's end, the problem of their origin is simply a part of the general problem of the origin of that myth.

---

it seems), also, makes Morgan (Morgana) Arthur's sister. Cp. Fletcher's *Arthurian Material,* pp. 145 f. This is more likely, however, to be due to Chrétien's influence, direct or indirect, than to a misunderstanding of the bearing of the word, *sorores* (Morgan and her fairy companions), in the *Vita Merlini,* 1. 919, as Fletcher surmises.

Miss Paton's hypothesis, pp. 29, 33, that the conception of Arthur's translation to Avalon (in company with Morgan) is merely a fairy-mistress story transformed has no support whatever in the innumerable Arthurian texts. Cp. Bruce, *Mort Artu,* p. 300.

Miss Paton, *op. cit.,* has followed Morgan through the romances and her collection of material on this character and on the fairy mythology of the Arthurian romances in general is invaluable, but her work suffers from the fundamental error of assuming virtually always that the romancers in what they say concerning the great fairy are drawing on a body of popular tradition concerning her. As a matter of fact, their draughts on tradition are infinitesimal — they drew on their imaginations, instead.

In the course (p. 326) of his article "Morgue la Fee et Morgan Tud", *Romania,* XXVIII, 321 ff. (1899), F. Lot suggests that Geoffrey based his famous description of Arthur's end on an Irish tale, which probably reached him in a Welsh version. The grounds of the suggestion, however, are insufficient.

The name, "Morgan Tud", occurs only in the Welsh "Geraint and Enid" (Loth, *Mabinogion* [2], II 143, 174) — as the name of a wonderful male physician. Zimmer, Foerster's edition of Chrétien's *Erec,* pp. XXVII ff., argued that this otherwise unknown person was a blundering creation of the Welsh writer, which was due to his ignorance of the fairy-queen (Morgue, Morgain) of his French original (Chrétien's *Erec).* For a refutation of this hypothesis, cp. Miss Paton, *op. cit.,* pp. 259 ff., and J. Loth, *Contributions à l'étude des romans de la Table Ronde* (section entitled, *Morgan Tut),* pp. 51 ff. (Paris, 1912). For a refutation of the opposite theory, according to which the change of Morgan's sex was due to a misunderstanding on the part of Chrétien of what was originally a Welsh source, see Miss Paton, *loc. cit.* This latter theory was proposed by J. Loth, *Revue Celtique,* XIII, 496 f. (1892) and defended by F. Lot in his article just named. Miss Paton, herself, pp. 263 ff., urged that *Morgan Tud* of the Welsh text was merely a corruption of the Old Welsh proper name, *Morgetiud* (and variants) — modern *Meredith.* This seems to me the most probable explanation of all, but subsequently, Loth, *Contributions,* pp. 56 ff., has connected the Welsh *Tut (Tud)* with Old Irish *túath,* which

In the face of the scanty and, for the most part, ambiguous evidence, one is compelled to fall back on general considerations in order to reach a final decision in the case. Looking at the question from this point of view, we are forced to conclude that the above-mentioned conception must have already prevailed among the Bretons before their exodus from Great Britain; for there would seem to be no reason why such a conception should have sprung up among them, after they had left the land with which Arthur's. glory was associated, and, besides, we know that their kinsmen of Cornwall, who remained behind, were, at the beginning of the twelfth century, cherishing the faith in the hero's

---

sometimes means "magician". He supposes that this was translated by an Anglo-Norman "Morgan le Fe or le Fed" *(fée* being masculine in the Norman dialect) and that Chrétien misconstrued this as feminine. Cp. too Loth's recent article, *Revue Celtique,* (1920). To the present writer, however, all of this is unconvincing. Geoffrey of Monmouth, Benoit de St. Maure and the author of Layamon's original, not to look for others, all knew of Morgan as a supernatural female and there is no need of hazardous speculations, therefore, to explain how Chrétien conceived of her similarly.

[56] For a summary of discussions concerning Avalon (Avallon) or Avallach and the literature of the subject, see W. E. Mead's *Selections from Morte Darthur,* pp. 316f. (1897) and Bruce, *Mort Artu,* p. 273. Zimmer, *Zs. f. frz. Spr. u. Litt.,* XII [1], 238ff. (1890) and Brugger, *ibid.,* XXVII [1], 98ff. (1898) contended that Avalon, like everything relating to Arthur's translation, was unknown to the Welsh. On this subject, see still further pp. 74ff., above. Lot in his "Glastonbury et Avalon", *Romania,* XXVII, 553ff. (1897) attacked Zimmer's thesis, but, himself, advanced the improbable view that Avalon was originally the name of a man (or god) and not of a place and that the latter conception is due to French misunderstandings of the original Celtic form of the name, Avalloc. — F. M. Warren points out in "The Island of Avalon", MLN, XIV, 93f. (1899) that Avalon is already known to the author of *Le Couronnement de Louis,* who, 11. 1796, 1827, uses the expression, "tot l'or d'Avalon", as a hyperbole for riches. This poem was written in the Isle de France about the middle of the twelfth century. Warren regards it as earlier than Wace's *Brut.* This cannot be determined definitely, but the phrase at least shows no influence from the *Brut.*

For the identification of Avalon with Glastonbury, cp. Part II, below.

return with equal fervor — a faith which, of course, they must
have inherited from their ancestors of something like six centuries before. On the other hand, Arthur was certainly, also, a
character in Welsh saga in the first part of the ninth century (when
Nennius compiled his chronicle), near the end of the tenth (when
the *Annales Cambriae* were compiled), and, again, round about
1100 (when *Kulhwch and Olwen* was composed). There are even
numerous allusions, as we have seen,[87] in Welsh texts to his last
battle, although none to his voyage to Avalon and expected return,
save in the one obscure line which has been given above. It seems
strange, indeed, that, having been adopted, as we know from the
sources just indicated, as one of their national heroes by this
branch of the Celts, also — although, perhaps, with less ardor
and universality than was the case with his nearest kinsmen
(the Celts of Devon and Cornwall and Brittany) — the conception
of his apotheosis should have made no impression on them. Nevertheless, in view of the evidence that confronts us, we can only
conclude that the two passages cited above (one French and one
Welsh) do not express a general Welsh faith. The two writers
concerned doubtless knew of the "hope of the Britons" that prevailed in Brittany and in the old Celtic territory of Southwest
England and adopted it for the Welsh, although in Wales it was
no part of general popular tradition.[88]

The source, then, of the fine description of Arthur's translation to Avalon in Geoffrey of Monmouth's *Vita Merlini*, of
which we shall hear more anon, was, no doubt, also Armorican.[89]

### 3. The Origin of the Round Table and Some Other Questions of Celtic Origins.

1. The Round Table: (a) According to Wace's *Brut* (11.
9994 ff.)[90] the Round Table was instituted to prevent quarrels

[87] Cp. p. 77, note 79 above.

[88] As far as the French writer is concerned, he may have simply
invented the incident, or, if this is not so, the Welshmen, referred to,
may not have spoken in all seriousness.

[89] It is to be remembered that, apart from general knowledge
of Breton matters, Geoffrey had special sources of information on this
subject, if his father was a Breton, as seems most likely.

[90] Quoted below, in the chapter on Merlin.

in regard to precedence among Arthur's barons. Now we hear of similar brawls at the royal board in the Irish sagas[91] — for example, at Conchobar's table in Emain Macha, according to the *Tale of MacDatho's Pig*,[92] and at Bricriu's, according to *Bricriu's Feast*.[93] The following is an incident of this character which took place at Bricriu's table. He prepared a great feast for Conchobar, the renowned king of Irish saga, and the nobles of Ulster. Knowing that he would not be allowed to share in the feast because of his evil tongue, he caused to be built for himself a little chamber or balcony from which he could see all that went on. True to his character, he determines to stir up strife among his guests, and when they begin to arrive, he urges each secretly to demand at the banquet "the hero's portion", as it is called in the Irish sagas — that is, the biggest portion, which was supposed to go to the worthiest warrior at the table. In this way he approaches successively Loegaire, Conall, and Cuchulinn, the last-named being, so to speak, the Achilles of the Old Irish epic. The feast commences and Bricriu retires. Soon, however, the charioteers of the three champions get up and each demands the hero's portion for his master. A dispute arises over this, and arms begin to clash, but it is agreed after a while to divide the portion equally among the three claimants and to refer to King Ailill of Connaught the decision as to who is the greatest champion. Quiet is restored for the time being, but the dispute again breaks out and Ailill is urged to render his decision. To test the warriors' abilities he puts them through a series of adventures against strange

---

[91] Zimmer first called attention to these Irish parallels to the Round Table, in the *Göttingische G. A.* for June 10, 1890, pp. 518 ff. He says, too, p. 518, note 1, of the Pentecost festivals with which the Arthurian romances so often begin: "Die Maiversammlungen der Arthursage sind durchaus im keltischen Altertum begründet". He cites the May festivals held at Tara, according to Irish saga, to which the overlord of Ireland summoned all his men. Cp. on the subject of this note, also, Brown, "The Round Table before Wace", pp. 193 ff., including notes.

[92] D'Arbois de Jubainville, *Cours de littérature celtique*, V, 66 ff.

[93] *Ibid.*, pp. 120 ff. The Irish title is *Fled Bricrend*. *Bricriu* means "Poison Tongue".

monsters. Cuchullin fares best in these trials, but Ailill, who is
apparently afraid of offending the rest, gives each one privately
a goblet as a token of superiority. Cuchulinn's, however, is of gold,
whereas the others are of inferior metals. So when subsequently
at a feast the old dispute over precedence begins anew and each
presents his goblet, much bitterness is produced. The claimants
are again sent forth now on a fresh series of adventures to test
their worthiness, but at this point the MS. breaks off.

(b) Like these episodes of the Irish sagas is the account which
Layamon gives (11. 22736ff.) of how the Round Table came to
be instituted.[94] At a great feast on Yule-day which Arthur gave,
says Layamon, a sanguinary quarrel sprang up among the guests,
"because each, on account of his high lineage, wished to be within" (whatever that may mean). Several had lost their lives before the king succeeded in quelling it. Shortly after, when the
king was in Cornwall, a smith there offered to make him a table at
which 1600 and more people might sit, "all around about so that
none be left out without and within, man against man". Moreover, the king could carry it about with him anywhere. In four
weeks' time the work was completed and thereafter all was peace
and fraternity at Arthur's feasts.

This passage has nothing to correspond to it in the extant
text of Wace's *Brut*, but, in view of the Irish parallels, must be
accepted as undoubtedly derived ultimately from Celtic tradition.
It has been taken[95] as a proof that Layamon drew directly from

---

[94] The similarity was pointed out by A. C. L. Brown, "The Round
Table before Wace", Harvard *Studies and Notes in Philology and
Literature,* VII, 183ff. (1900).

[95] By A. C. L. Brown, *op. cit.,* and "Welsh Traditions in Layamon's *Brut*", MPh., I, 95ff. (1903). In his review of Brown's "Round
Table before Wace", in *Romania,* XXIX, 634 (1900), G. Paris, however,
differs from Brown, inasmuch as he supposes that the Welsh traditions
in question reached Layamon not directly, but through the English.
This is, of course, a corollary of Paris's very questionable theory concerning the Anglo-Norman origin of the Arthurian romances.
In the *Zs. f. frz. Spr. u. Litt.,* XXIX[2], 247, note 11 (1905),
Brugger has attacked, in particular, Brown's assumption that Layamon
derived his story of the Round Table from Wales. He points out very
aptly that in no writings of Welsh authorship (*Mabinogion,* Giraldus

the oral traditions of his neighbors, the Welsh. We have seen, however, that the English writer was, in all probability, wholly dependent on a French source (an expansion of Wace) for his so-called additions, so that the inference is unwarranted and we are left in the same state of doubt as to the Welsh or Armorican *provenance* of this incident as of the incidents of the Arthurian romances generally — with the usual balance of probabilities, however, in favour of the latter.

(c) It has also been proposed[96] to derive the Round Table from some Celtic feast, like the Beltane or May-day feasts of the Highlands of Scotland — a spring festival which descends no doubt from pagan times. According to an account of such a feast at Callender, recorded in the nineteenth century, the boys in that neighborhood on May-day cut a table in the green sod by digging around it a trench of sufficient circumference to hold the entire

---

Cambrensis etc.) is the Round Table mentioned. He suggests (pp. 245 ff.) that the name "Round Table" arose in Armorica and that Wace probably invented the idea that it was made round in order to *forestall* quarrels as to precedence. On the other hand, according to Layamon (or his source), who was modifying Wace, the purpose was to *put an end to* such quarrels. Like Ten Brink and Mott, Brugger believes, as against Brown, that the story about the Round Table which is told in Layamon originally was not connected with Arthur at all. This may well be so, but I see no reason to imagine that this connection was first made by the author of the expanded Wace (Layamon's French original) rather than in the sources (probably Armorican by origin) on which he drew. Similarly with the idea, which we find in Wace, that quarrels over precedence caused a *round* table to be constructed.

In this same article, p. 246, note 9, Brugger speaks of a similarity between the Round Table and the table of the Last Supper in the Gospels, which, he says, is not purely accidental, for the latter, too, is "ein Überrest altheidnischen Opferbrauches". But wherever any such similarity exists, it is under the influence of the Grail romances. The Grail Table was, of course, modeled by Robert de Boron directly after the table of the Last Supper.

[96] By Lewis F. Mott, "The Round Table", PMLA, XX, 231 ff. (1905). Brugger, *Zs. f. frz. Spr. u. Litt.*, XXIX[2], 238 ff. (1906), in reviewing this article, expresses substantial approval of its results. I agree, however, with F. Lot, *Étude sur le Lancelot en prose*, p. 245, note 5, in rejecting it.

company. Then after making a fire in the circle and cooking and eating certain prescribed things they put bits of cake into a bonnet and blindfolded draw them out. Whoever draws a certain black bit is to be sacrificed to Baal to induce him to render productive the year which has just begun. The sacrifice is now a joke, but, originally an actual human sacrifice was, very likely, involved in the ceremony.

There is a far cry, however, from this custom observed in a limited district of the Highlands to the Round Table of Arthurian romance — even in its most fantastic form, that of Layamon's *Brut*. Besides, it is a serious weakness of the theory that the part which disputes over precedence play in accounting for the form of the table is unjustifiably treated as an afterthought.

(d) Miss J. L. Weston[97] connects the Round Table with some hypothetical turning table of Celtic tradition of mythical significance. The only evidence for the Round Table as such a turning table — if evidence it can be called — is a single line in Béroul's *Tristan*, 1. 3384 (end of the twelfth century), where, in replying to a messenger of Iseult's who is inquiring about the king, a shepherd says:

> "Sire", fait il, "il sit au dois.
> Ja verroiz la Table Reonde,
> Qui tornoie come le monde:
> Sa mesnie sit anviron."

From the eighth century Irish text called *The Voyage of Maelduin* down, we have turning *castles* in Celtic tradition; but no mention is made of equally marvelous turning *tables* in this same tradition. Béroul's words may possibly refer to the vicissitudes of life to which the company gathered about the board, like the rest of the world, are subject, or, if construed literally, they may express a passing fancy of this particular poet — but, whatever the meaning of this obscure line may be, it does not justify us in jumping with Miss Weston to the conclusion that the Round Table is connected with some supposed solar ritual.

Whatever we may think of the theories just presented, there

---

[97] See her article "A hitherto unconsidered aspect of the Round Table", in the *Mélanges offerts à M. Maurice Wilmotte* (Paris, 1910).

is hardly room for doubt that Arthur's Round Table belongs to the paraphernalia which attached itself to him in Celtic tradition. We cannot regard the legends relating to it as a mere development out of the old stories concerning Charlemagne and his twelve peers, as has been suggested. The Irish parallels, moreover, render it probable that the conception obtained, also, among the insular Celts,[98] as we know from Wace that it did among the Bretons. Perhaps, after all, in seeking for an explanation of this most famous of tables and the customs which were connected with it, we need go no further than the account which is given of Celtic feasts by the Greek philosopher and traveller, Posidonius, who lived in the first century before Christ, his observations being made probably in Southern Gaul. He tells us[99] that at their feasts the Celts sit in a circle and that the bravest sits in the middle like the leader of a chorus. Moreover, primitive Celtic houses were often circular. It is quite possible that these actual customs may have determined the shape of the celebrated table of romance.

2. *Excalibur (Caliburnus* in Geoffrey's *Historia,* IX, 4), which is Arthur's sword in Geoffrey and commonly in the romances,[100] is certainly identical with the sword *Caladbolg* of the Irish prose epic *Tain bo Cualnge (The Cattle-Raid of Cooley),*[101] which is there the property of Fergus, the fugitive ruler of Ulster. It is said to have become of the size of the rainbow, whenever any

---

[98] Zimmer, *Gött. G. A.,* for June 10, 1890, p. 525, denies this.
[99] Quoted by A. C. L. Brown, "The Round Table before Wace", p. 195, note 3, from Carl Müller, *Fragmenta Historica Graecorum,* III, 260 (Paris, 1849).
[100] In the relatively late Vulgate *Merlin*-continuation Arthur presents it to young Gawain. Cp. Sommer, *Vulgate Version of the Arthurian Romances,* II, 253.
[101] The identification was first made by Zimmer, *Gött. G. A.,* for June 10, 1890, pp. 516 f. For Caladbolg, cp. Miss Winifred Faraday's translation of the Irish epic: *The Cattle-Raid of Cualnge,* London (Grimm Library, no. 16), 1904. Loth maintains, *Revue Celtique,* XIII, 495, that French *Calibor (= Caladbolg)* is drawn from a *written* Welsh form. See, too, F. Lot, *Romania,* XXV, 1 f., who contends that Geoffrey's *Caliburnus* does not necessarily come from the Breton.

one struck with it. Fergus cuts off the tops of three hills with this sword. Moreover, like Excalibur, it was made in fairy-land.

3. Miscellaneous Celtic folk-tale *motifs*, such as are found, for example, in the Tristan romances.[102] With regard to such *motifs*, it should be premised that even in instances where insular records appear to offer parallels to incidents in Arthurian romance, it may be that the same stories were current in Brittany and transmitted thence to the French writers — only the complete absence of all Breton records from the Middle Ages leaves us without the means of control. We may select for notice here, particularly: (a) the *motif* of the Turning Castle mentioned above, which is found in *La Mule sans Frein*, 11. 440ff., the Middle High German *Diu Krône*, 11. 12951ff., and other romances, both metrical and prose, and is, likewise, familiar to Irish saga, *Voyage of Maelduin*, etc.;[103] (b) the *motif* of the Beheading Game:[104] A strange visitor turns up at court and offers to submit himself to decapitation at the hands of a knight, provided that at the expiration of a given period the knight will, in turn, subject himself to the same test of courage. The knight naturally accepts this as a very easy test, but to his surprise the stranger picks up his head after decapitation and at the appointed time is ready to return the blow. This incident is found in several romances — earliest, perhaps, in the so-called *Livre de Caradoc (Livre de Karados)*,[105] which is an interpolation in the first continuation of Chrétien's *Perceval*. It is even better known, however, through the Middle English romance, *Sir Gawain and the Green Knight*,

---

[102] Cp. especially Gertrude Schoepperle: *Tristan and Isolt*, II, 267ff. (Frankfort and London, 1913).

[103] Cp. Gideon Huet, "Le chateau tournant dans la Suite du Merlin", *Romania*, XL, 235ff. (1911). Cp., too, W. E. Sypherd, *Studies in Chaucer's House of Fame*, pp. 114ff. (Publications of the Chaucer Society, London, 1907), where numerous Celtic examples of Whirling Houses are given, but, also, some from other sources.

[104] On this *motif* both in the romances and in folk-tales, cp. G. L. Kittredge, *A Study of Gawain and the Green Knight*, pp. 9ff., 147ff. (Cambridge, Mass., 1916).

[105] Cp. Potvin's *Perceval li Gallois*, III, 117—221. For the episode in question, cp. *ibid.*, pp. 125ff.

which certainly goes back substantially to a lost French original.
But we have this same incident also in the Irish saga, named
above, *Bricriu's Feast*,[106] of which a manuscript from *circa* 1100
has been preserved, but which is itself much older. One of the
tests of courage which the three champions Loegaire, Conall, and
Cuchullin, have to undergo in that tale is an adventure of this
nature with the giant Uath Mac Imomain (Fright, Son of Great
Fear). Cuchulinn, however, alone is equal to the test. When the
giant has been decapitated, he clasps his head to his breast and
jumps into the lake. The next day he returns and when Cuchulinn
exhibits no fear even when stretched out and ready to receive the
fatal blow, his enemy spares him, at the same time, declaring
him to be the first of Irish warriors.

4. The individual episode in the romances the insular Celtic
— apparently Scotch — origin of which appears best assured is
one that also occurs in the *Livre de Caradoc*,[107] just mentioned —
viz. the episode of Carados (Caradoc, Karados) and the serpent,
which occurs also as a Gaelic tale[108] and was still in oral circu-

---

[106] Cp. George Henderson, *Fled Bricrend*, pp. 116 ff. (London,
1899). Kittredge, *op. cit.*, pp. 10 ff., gives an analysis of the episode.

[107] Potvin, *op. cit.*, II, 191 ff. Secondary to this version is the
one in the *Roman de Renart le Contrefait*. See Miss C. A. Harper,
MLN, XIII, 422 f.

[108] Cp. J. F. Campbell's *Popular Tales of the West Highlands*,
IV, Introduction, pp. XCV f. Campbell took it down from a travelling
tinker. "The Queen of Scotland", no. 301 in Child's collection of
ballads, is, also, a variant of this Carados story.
It was Miss C. A. Harper, "Carados and the Serpent", XIII, 417 ff.
(1898), who first observed the resemblance of the episode in the
*Livre de Caradoc (Karados)* to the Highland tale. She discusses
there the relations of all the four versions which I have named.
G. Paris, "Caradoc et le Serpent", *Romania*, XXVIII, 214 ff.
(1899), following up Miss Harper's study, pointed out that this story
was also a part of Welsh, tradition in the Middle Ages, for a knowledge of it is implied in a Welsh triad (Loth, *Mabinogion*[2], II, 284 f.)
on three famous chaste young women of Britain. Here the heroine
is called, to be sure, not *Guinor* (in variant forms), as in the *Livre
de Karados*, but *Tegan Euron (Eurvron)*, i. e. Tegan of the Golden
Breast. Assuming that Caradoc Brechbras belonged to Armorican
tradition, Paris concluded that the tale reached Wales from Brittany.

lation in the nineteenth century in the Highlands of Scotland. The essential features of the story as we find it in the French are as follows:

Carados (Caradoc) is the son of the enchanter Eliaures and of Queen Ysaune who has been unfaithful to her husband. After he has grown up, he learns from his true father the secret of his birth, but he is indignant when he hears the story and repeats it to the king, whom he has hitherto supposed to be his father. The king then shuts Ysaune up in a tower, but her lover still manages to visit her, until they are detected by their son, who again informs on them. Ysaune appeals to Eliaures, who offers to punish Carados in this way: He will create a horrible serpent and shut him up in her cupboard. When Carados visits her, she is to send him there immediately for her mirror. As soon as he puts in his hand, the serpent will wind about his arm. His flesh will then waste away and in two years he will die. The mother agrees to this and carries out her part in the plot. The serpent winds about the arm of Carados and his mother Ysaune then tells him that he has got what he deserves and that the best thing for him to do is to go forth and repent of his sins during the two years of life left to him. Carados takes the advice and goes into an abbey. Here he is discovered after a long search by his friend Cador of Cornwall, who wishes to kill the serpent, but cannot, since his friend's life is bound up with that of the creature. Cador, however, induces Carados to go with him to Ysaune's tower, to see if something cannot be done for him, and, owing to his reproaches, she consults with her paramour, who prescribes the following procedure by which the unhappy Carados may be released from the serpent: Only a beautiful, well-born maiden who loves Carados loyally can effect the release. This maiden must prepare two caldrons and fill one with milk and the other with the sourest wine she can find. She must get into the caldron of milk

---

The story, however, he believed, was ultimately Irish and had nothing to do with Caradoc. In "Caradoc et Saint Paterne", *Romania*, XXVIII, 568 ff. (1899), however, F. Lot shows that Caradoc was really a hero of the Britons of Strathclyde and Cumberland, that the tale in question was Scotch, not Irish in origin, and passed into Wales by way of Northwest England, not Brittany.

and Carados must get into the caldron of wine. Then she must
show her breast over the edge of the caldron and pray to God to
cure Carados immediately. The serpent, disliking the wine and
tempted by the sweet milk, will then leave Carados and seize her
breast. On going home, Cador learns that his own sister loves
Carados, and when she hears of the condition of his release, she
agrees to sacrifice herself for her lover. Cador, however, is
to try to kill the serpent as he passes from the one to
the other. The serpent, however, actually seizes hold of the girl,
and Cador, to accomplish the release, has to cut off a part of the
breast to which it has attached itself. He then kills it between
the caldrons and Carados marries the girl. Later on, after a number
of strange adventures, Carados obtains from a knight named Alar-
din del Lac a shield-buckle which has a wonderful power of healing wounds. If a knight has lost half of his nose, a touch of
this buckle will make a golden nose just like the one he had before.
So with any other part of the body. Carados takes the buckle
home and touches his wife's breast with it. She is at once cured,
but henceforth has a golden breast. She is, later on, the only
lady at Arthur's court who can stand the test of chastity.

One may mention in conclusion that in this story Carados's
arm was said to have always remained smaller after this experience
with the serpent, so that he was known henceforth as Carados
Brisie Braz (Carados with the broken arm) or Briebraz (short-
armed). This rests on a curious misunderstanding of the Celtic
epithet of the hero — namely, Breichbras (*breich*-arm, *bras*-
strong), which really means virtually just the opposite of what
the French romancers (including the author of the *Livre de Caradoc)*, being misled by the similarity to words of their own language,
imagined.[109]

---

[109] It is a delicate question, however, whether F. Lot, *op. cit.*,
pp. 222 ff., is justified in assuming that the retention of *B* as the
initial sound of this epithet proves that the French authors used written
sources, the *b's* in their language, as he declares, being *pronounced*
like a *v* from the eighth century on, so that, if only heard, the French
would have written down *v, b*. Confusion in catching the spoken name
is too common to admit of a confident decision in this case. Cp.
too, W. Meyer-Lübke, *Zs. f. frz. Spr. u. Litt.*, XLIV¹, 164, on the
subject.

5. Arthur himself is virtually unknown to mediaeval Irish literature of purely native origin,[110] but, as will have been observed

[110] In his article, "Eine verschollene Artursage", pp. 63 ff. of the *Festschrift für Ernst Windisch* (1914), Kuno Meyer calls attention to an *Äigidecht Artūir* (= *Entertainment of Arthur*) in a list of Irish sagas in the Book of Leinster (twelfth century). Meyer conjectures on the analogy of the Middle Irish ballad, *Find and the Phantoms* (Book of Leinster), that the lost saga described how Arthur, whilst hunting a boar, came to a haunted house and had strange adventures with the spirits there.

In the *Revue Celtique*, X, 185 ff. (1889), Max Nettlau published from Stowe MS. 992 (Br. Museum) some excerpts from an Irish romance concerning the Holy Grail — so, too, F. N. Robinson, *Zs. f. celt. Ph.*, IV, 381 ff. (1903) fragments from a MS. in the Franciscan library at Dublin. In both cases, however, the Irish is not original, but based on the Old French prose romance, *Queste del Saint Graal*.

R. A. Stewart Macalister has published from MS. Egerton, 128 (B. M.), dated 1748, *The Story of the Crop-Eared Dog* and *The Story of Eagle-Boy* (Irish Texts Society, London, 1908). He entitles them *Two Irish Arthurian Romances*, and, as a matter of fact, King Arthur appears in both, and the principal character in the first bears the name of Sir Galahad. Nevertheless, Miss Weston, *Folk-Lore*, XX, 361 ff. (1909), very properly questions their right to be called Arthurian. The stories belong to the "Wonder-Voyage" type of tale, as their editor, himself, remarks, and the mere adoption of Arthurian names does not render them Arthurian. A. C. L. Brown, MPh., IX, 120 ff. (1911) has expressed an opinion similar to Miss Weston's. The first of the two stories is probably based on a French original, the second certainly. Cp. T. P. Cross, MPh., X, 229, note 1 (1913).

In his "Arthurian Motifs in Ghadelic Literature", *Miscellany presented to Kuno Meyer*, edited by Osborn Bergen and Carl Marstrander, pp. 18 ff. (Halle, 1912), George Henderson calls attention to another "Wonder Voyage" tale of which Lancelot and Galahad are the heroes, preserved in Rawlinson MS. B. 512 (Bodleian Library). This, however, is as little Arthurian as the two stories published by Macalister. Henderson observes that, apart from fragments about the Grail, Arthurian *motifs* may be traced in 1. *Eachdoaidh An Amadain Mhoir (Tale of the Great Fool)*. 2. *Am Brat (The Cloak)*. 3. *Am Bron Binn (The Melodious Sorrow)*. These are, however, all late and manifestly derived from the French romances. No. 3 is a Gaelic ballad which Henderson, himself, took down at Dalibrog, South Uist, in 1892, from oral recitation. The King of Britain dreams of a fair lady and falls in love with his vision of her. Gallomhai

from the preceding pages, this is not true of many of the *motifs* that occur in the Arthurian romances. We have seen above that mediaeval Breton literature is practically non-existent and that the bulk of extant works of the imagination in Welsh for the same period is not very large. On the other hand, an enormous quantity of Irish folk-tales and sagas has been preserved to us in MSS. of the eleventh and following centuries and of this body of narrative literature much was actually composed at a still earlier date. These sagas, etc., reflect, moreover, a more primitive state of society than the extant literature of any other branch of the European races, and hence they offer a store of material for the folk-lorist which is without parallel, as far as the Occident is concerned. Under these circumstances, it is natural that students of the romances who approach the subject from the folk-lorist's point of view should so frequently seek in Irish tradition the origin of the tales that make up the plots of the French romances. In cases where the theory of Irish origins is justified, it would seem most probable that the stories in question reached France by way of Wales and England. Nevertheless, difficult as navigation between Ireland and France might seem to be under mediaeval conditions, direct intercourse between the two countries was not unknown in the Middle Ages, and the late Professor Zimmer has even striven to prove that the usual trade-route between Ireland and the Continent in those centuries was across the sea from the Irish coast to the mouth of the Loire.[111] Inasmuch as all records

---

(Gawain) traverses the sea for weeks to find her. A "big man" (i. e. giant) keeps her captive in a tower. In collusion with Gawain, she lulls him to sleep with her harp. Gawain then cuts off the giant's head and they escape. In general, it should be said that Henderson was ignorant of Arthurian discussions and his observations on the subject are utterly confused and without value.

[111] For evidence regarding the intercourse between the Celts of Ireland and those of Great Britain by which the traditions of the former might have been diffused among the latter, cp. T. P. Cross, *Revue Celtique*, XXXI, 421 ff. (1910), where the earlier literature of the subject is given in the notes. For direct communication between Ireland and Gaul (France) cp. H. Zimmer, *Über direkte Handelsverbindungen Westgalliens mit Irland in Altertum und frühen Mittelalter* in the *Sitzungsberichte, Philos.-Hist. Klasse,* of the Berlin

of the sagas current in Brittany during the period under discussion have perished, we cannot say whether, after all, these same *motifs* and incidents which we find in the Irish sagas may not have been familiar also to the Bretons, and so have passed directly from them into France. Besides, the ancestors of the Bretons were brothers of the ancestors of the Welsh and so even where such tales are, indeed, Irish by origin, they may have been brought over from Ireland to Great Britain before the emigration to Armorica began. Waiving, however, these considerations, the debt of the French romances to Irish sources, in any event, seems to the present writer to have been greatly exaggerated. But it is best to let the reader judge for himself by putting before him the materials in a typical case — viz., the outlines, respectively, of a French romance, Chrétien's *Yvain*, and of an Irish saga, *Serglige Conculaind (Cuchulinn's Sick Bed)* — a version of the fairy-mistress theme — which, in some variant form, is supposed to be the source of this same romance:[112]

Academy of Sciences for 1905, pp. 363 ff., 430 ff., 543 ff., 582 ff. — for 1910, pp. 1031 ff. See, too, this scholar's *Auf welchem Wege kamen die Goidelen vom Kontinent nach Irland?* in the *Abhandlungen* of the same Academy for 1912 — especially, pp. 55 ff. As against D'Arbois de Jubainville, Rhys, etc., Zimmer (approved by Kuno Meyer) argues that the Gaels in their original settlement of Ireland did not reach that island by way of Great Britain, but direct from West Gaul, and, moreover, that down to the English conquest of Ireland (late twelfth century) the main intellectual as well as trade relations of Ireland were with West Gaul and not with Great Britain. The argument, on the whole, seems plausible but, as J. Vendryes has remarked in his review of the paper *(Rev. Celt.)*, Zimmer does not sufficiently consider the archaeological evidence.

[112] This is the thesis of A. C. L. Brown in his *Iwain, a Study in the Origins of Arthurian Romance:* Harvard *Studies and Notes in Philology and Literature*, vol. 8 (1903). Cp., too, his articles, "The Knight of the Lion", PMLA, XX, 673 ff. (1905) and "Chrétien's 'Yvain'", MPh., IX, 109 ff. (1911). In these articles Brown brings together from various Irish sagas parallels — frequently far-fetched, as it seems to me — to all the principal features of the *Yvain* — a parallel to one detail from one saga, a parallel to another detail from another saga, and so on. He concludes that all the motley incidents of the French poem are derived from a single Celtic *märchen*.

In *Yvain* the hero, incited by the report of another knight, Calogrenant, tries the adventure of the fountain in the Forest of Broceliande: If one pours water from this fountain on a stone nearby, a terrible storm arises which is followed by a calm. A knight then comes forth and jousts with the offender. On the way to the fountain Yvain (Ivain, Iwain), like Calogrenant, passes a flock of fierce fighting bulls guarded by a giant herdsman — a black creature with a head larger than that of a horse. He goes through the fountain adventure, but, unlike his predecessor, overthrows the knight and wounds him mortally. Yvain pursues his wounded adversary into the latter's castle. He finds himself caught between two iron gates, but he is recognized by Lunete, a damsel who attends the lady of the castle and who had once been befriended by him at King Arthur's court. This girl gives him a magic ring which will render the holder invisible at will. By the use of this talisman Yvain witnesses in safety the funeral of the knight he has slain and falls in love with the latter's widow, Laudine. Immediately afterwards he begins the courtship of the widow and with the help of the damsel gains her consent. He now becomes the lord of the castle and defender of the fountain.

---

I have given the two stories according to Brown's own analysis, with only slight compression here and there, so that whatever resemblance there may exist between the two loses nothing in my outlines. In his review, MLN, XIX, 80 ff., (1904) of Brown's *Iwain*, — which he describes as "more especially a contribution to the history of Celtic mythology than a monograph on the romance of Crestien de Troyes" — Nitze dissents from the author's hypothesis that the French poet was following "a clearly defined *conte*". Similarly, E. Windisch, *Das keltische Britannien bis zu Kaiser Arthur*, p. 181 (Leipzig, 1912). — Already Axel Ahlström, *Mélanges de philologie romane dédiés a Carl Wahlund*, p. 302 (Macon, 1896), expresses the opinion that Chrétien's sources for the *Yvain*, besides *contes* and popular legends (such as he supposes, gave rise to Marie's *lais)*, embraced, also, "de petits romans en prose" on the same subjects. But Chrétien knew only French (no Celtic), and there was no French prose so early as this. In his *Sage vom heiligen Gral*, pp. 138 ff. (Halle, 1898) Wechssler argues that there were already romances of chivalry among the Celts, but the works which he cites to prove this are, in reality, French, e. g., Chrétien's *Perceval*, the lays, *Milun* and *Doon* — and just how far they contain Celtic elements is a debated question.

In his new capacity, Yvain barely avoids an encounter with Arthur, but when the king departs, his wife gives Yvain permission to accompany him and to be absent for a year. He overstays his time, is reproached for it, goes mad in consequence, but is finally cured by an ointment of Morgan le Fay's. There are all sorts of disconnected adventures that follow upon this. He succors a lion who is fighting with a serpent and the lion henceforth follows him. With the beast's assistance he rescues Lunete, who is condemned to be burned to death on the false accusation of a wicked seneschal. In the midst of this affair, however, he combats a giant who is besieging a castle and threatening to kill the sons of the owner or carry off his daughter. Next he has an indecisive encounter with Gawain, without recognizing his identity, in the affair of two sisters, who are disputing over an inheritance. But this adventure is interrupted likewise by another in which the hero does away with an evil custom that requires thirty girls of the Isle of Maidens to be annually delivered over to two monsters. Lastly, Yvain returns to the fountain and stirs up a storm there. Lunete discovers who he is and brings about a reconciliation with Laudine.

Let us turn now to *Cuchulinn's Sick Bed:* [113]

Cuchulinn tries to kill two strange birds linked by a golden chain that appear at a lake in Ulster. Being unsuccessful, he sits down against an upright stone and falls asleep. In his sleep he sees two women, one clad in green, the other in red, who come up to him, laugh and keep striking him until he is almost dead. (As it turns out this is the fairy, Fand, and her sister.) He was carried into a house, where he lay till the end of a year without speaking to anyone. Then, as he lay in the bed, a man mysteriously appeared, who sang verses promising him health and strength, if he would accept the invitation of the daughters of Aed Abrat, one of whom, named Fand, wished to marry Cuchulinn. The man departed after that and they knew not whence he came or

---

[113] In connection with this tale, I will call the reader's attention to an interesting account of the Irish *fili* (professional story-tellers) and of the way in which Irish tales were handed down, which A. C. L. Brown gives, MPh., IX, 121 ff. (1911).

whither he went. Cuchulinn rose up and spoke and went back to the upright stone where he saw again the woman in the green cloak. From her he learned that Fand, deserted by her husband Manannan mac Lir (a Celtic divinity), had fallen in love with him. Her own name is Liban. She is sister to Fand and wife to Labraid, who has sent her to ask Cuchulinn for one day's assistance against Labraid's enemies, promising in return to give him Fand to wife.

Cuchulinn sent his charioteer, Loeg, to see the mysterious land from which she came. Liban and he went till they came to the place where Fand was waiting for them. Then, it is said, Liban took hold of Loeg by the shoulder. "O Loeg," said Fand, "thou wilt not come out alive today, unless a woman protect thee!" "I have not been much accustomed to woman's protection" was Loeg's reply. Then they came to the water's edge, where they entered a boat of bronze and crossed over to an island. Loeg saw Labraid and his palace and, returning, told his story to Cuchulinn and everyone else.

Again Liban came to invite Cuchulinn to Mag Mell. She sang to him in praise of the place where Labraid dwelt — evidently fairy-land. [114] "I will not go at a woman's invitation,"

---

[114] Otherworld journeys are frequent in Celtic literature. For an account of them cp. *The Voyage of Bran*, 2 vols. (London, 1895—1897), by A Nutt and K. Meyer, A. C. L. Brown's *Iwain*, 27 ff. (Boston, 1903), Josef Baudis, "The Mabinogion", *Folk-Lore*, XXVII, 31 ff. (1916) — particularly, pp. 35 ff. There seems to have been no distinction in the minds of the Celts between their "Land of the Dead" and their Elysium. So, lately, Baudis, *loc. cit.*, who, I believe, is right. Hence we include both in the term "Otherworld". For a discussion of the whole subject, cp. J. A. MacCulloch, *The Religion of the Ancient Celts*, pp. 362 ff. (Edinburgh, 1911), whose conclusions are different. MacCulloch (pp. 374) disputes the view held by D'Arbois de Jubainville, Baudis, etc., that the two Otherworlds were not distinguished. He deduces (p. 370) the idea of the Celtic Elysium from some early myth of a Golden Age. The literature concerning the descriptions of the Celtic Otherworld is given by T. P. Cross, *Revue Celtique*, XXXI, 461, note 3 (1910). In "Two Otherworld Stories", MLN, XXXII, 280 ff. (1917) John C. Hodges has compared with Celtic conceptions of the Otherworld two stories from the, *Arabian Nights*,

he declares; but he again consents to send his charioteer. Fand admonishes the latter that Cuchulinn must come with speed, for the battle is appointed for that day. Loeg returns with Fand and describes at even greater length the fairy palace of Labraid and the beauty of a woman there, who is, doubtless, Fand herself. Cuchulinn is now persuaded, mounts his chariot, and accompanies Loeg and Fand to Mag Mell. At early dawn he transfixes with his spear one of Labraid's chief enemies, as he was washing himself at a well. After that he slew still another and won a victory for Labraid. In return he received Fand, with whom he lived for a month. When he departed, she said to him: "I will meet thee in whatever place thou shalt appoint for me to come."

After Cuchulinn returned home, he revealed to his wife, Emer, the appointed place of meeting. The jealous queen lay in wait with knives to murder Fand. Cuchulinn rescued her, but when Manannan mac Lir heard of it, he suddenly appeared, visible to Fand alone. When she saw her husband, the sea-god, coming over the sea, she forsook her mortal lover and went away with him. When Cuchulinn perceived that she had gone, he sprang three leaps upward and three leaps to the right of Luacra, so that he was for a long time without drink and without food among the mountains and "tis there that he slept every night upon the road of Midluacra —" that is to say, he ran mad.

Emer persuaded Conchobar to send "poets and people of wisdom and druids of the Ulstermen" to heal Cuchulinn, but "he sought to murder the people of wisdom". However, they sang

---

(viz., *The Porter and the Three Ladies of Baghdad* and *The Man Who Never Laughed during the Rest of his Days.* Burton, I, 151 ff., VI, 160 ff., respectively), which seem to parallel the Celtic more closely than any others in that collection. In the Arabian tales the mortal, not the fairy mistress, takes the initiative. For the literature of the Fairy Mistress theme in Celtic cp. (besides Brown's *Iwain)* Cross, MPh., XII, 598, note 1, 594, note 2. For a contemporary Breton ballad on the fairy mistress theme, taken down by J. Loth, cp. "Le Comte et la Fee", *Annales de Bretagne,* XXVII, 199 ff. (1911) — also, a Welsh tale noted by G. Dottin, "Notes sur le Folklore Gallois, *ibid.,* XXIII, 462 ff. (1907—8).

their druidical charms over him till they captured his feet and
hands and till he recovered a little of his senses. He asked for
a drink then. They gave him a drink of forgetfulness. As he
drank the drink, there was no recollection to him of Fand nor
of anything that he had done. Manannan shook his cloak between Cuchulinn and Fand, so that they should never meet again.

Most readers, we believe, will agree with us, that it would
be impossible for the French poet to extract from such a story
the plot of *Yvain,* as we have recounted it above. Except that
in each the lover runs mad, on losing his mistress, the two stories
have virtually nothing in common. In the *Yvain,* besides, the
loss is only temporary.

# Chapter III.
## Chrétien de Troyes and his Successors.

We have now come to Chrétien de Troyes, who, even if he had predecessors, gave, as we may safely assert, a new value, and probably a new character, to the poems relating to Arthur and his knights. The fact that all poems devoted especially to Arthurian subjects before Chrétien — granting that such existed — have disappeared, shows that, on the whole, they could not have been marked by any great literary excellence.[1]

We know nothing positively of the life of the poet. The designation, "de Troyes", which he uses in the *Erec*, seems to prove that he was a native of Troyes in the province of Champagne, and that he was a herald has been conjectured[2] on the

---

[1] This is, of course, contrary to Brugger's view, *Zs. f. frz. Spr. u. Litt.*, XXXI[2], 143 f. that all the finer Arthurian romances have perished and that we possess only the productions of a period of decadence.

[2] By G. Paris, *Journal des Savants* for June, 1902, pp. 295 f. = pp. 251 f. of the reprint in the G. Paris-*Mélanges* (Paris, 1910). Owing to the logic-chopping debates between Fenice and Thessala in *Cliges* (ll. 3085 ff. and 4409 ff.) and Laudine and Lunete in *Yvain* (11. 1589 ff.), M. Wilmotte has suggested, p. 167 of the *Bulletin de la Classe des Lettres*, etc., for 1890 of the Académie Royale de Belgique that Chrètien was a jurist; but his scholastic training would sufficiently account for the character of the passages in question. Cp. the same scholar on Chrétien, *Le Moyen Age*, for 1914, pp. 102 ff. For various speculations concerning Chrétien's life and a very thorough sifting of such speculations see especially, G. Paris, *loc. cit.*, pp. 293 ff. and Foerster, Chrétien *Wörterbuch*, 22 ff., 39 ff.

Paris, *Mélanges*, I, 260, conjectures — and W. Meyer-Lübke, *Zs. f. frz. Spr. u. Litt.*, XLIV[1], 162, expresses his approval of the conjecture — that Chrétien visited England. The evidence to that effect is: 1. that in his *Cliges*, 11. 4579 ff., the poet makes the insignificant English town, Wallingford (Galinguefort), the scene of one

basis of the *Lancelot* (11. 5591 ff.), where the herald recognizes
Lancelot, who has come *incognito* to a tournament, and cries out:
*Or est venuz qui aunera* (i. e., the conqueror has come). Chrétien
adds that this was the first time the expression had been used:

> Nostre maistre en fu li hira
> Qui a dire le nos aprist,
> Car il premierement le dist.

In any event, his translations from Ovid prove that he had
the usual scholastic education of the time and even render it probable  that he shared the renewed ardor with which the study of
the classics, and, particularly, Ovid, was pursued in learned circles
toward the middle of the twelfth century. In a well-known passage at the beginning of *Cligés* the poet enumerates his works
up to that date (about 1168): *Erec and Enide,* a poem on King
Marc and Iseult, and translations of Ovid's *Ars Amandi (L'Art
d'Amors)* and *Remedia Amoris (Les Comandemenz Ovide),* with
two other pieces which appear to be derived from the same writer's
*Metamorphoses.*[3]

---

of Arthur's tourneys, as it had actually been the meeting-place of
Henry II and his barons. 2. that he gives, *Cliges,* 11. 276 ff., a rather
vivid description of sea-sickness. These matters are supposed to have
been drawn from his personal experience. Obviously, however, the
inference is not imperative. Cp., *contra,* Foerster, Chrétien *Wörterbuch,* Introduction, pp. 40 f.

[3] The *Cliges* begins as follows:

> Cil qui fist d'Erec et d'Enide
> Et les Comandemanz Ovide
> Et l'Art d'Amors an romanz mist
> Et le Mors de l'Espaule fist,
> Del roi Marc et d'Iseut la blonde,
> Et de la Hupe et de l'Aronde
> Et del Rossignol la Muance,
> Un novel conte recomance
> D'un vaslet qui an Grece fu
> Del lignage le roi Artu.

It is generally agreed that considerations of rhyme, not fact, dictated
the order in which these works are enumerated. Only Meyer-Lübke,
*Zs. f. frz. Spr. u. Litt.,* XLIV [1], 129 ff. objects.

   *Le Mors d'Espaule* has been taken to be a version of the
classical legend concerning Pelops's shoulder wich was devoured by

If we accept the *Philomena* episode of the *Ovide Moralisé* as one of these pieces,[4] our author would be identical with the enigmatical Crestiiens li Gois, the author of that work, but this is more or less doubtful. From the omission of the hero's name in the allusion, G. Paris argued[5] that Chrétien's poem concerning Marc and Iseult was episodical in its nature and not a genuine *Tristan* romance. The inference seems hardly justified, but, in any event, the work has completely disappeared. Of the extant romances, *Erec* (about 1168) is the first, and *Cliges* (about 1170) the second. Next come his three latest romances, with the following approximate dates:[6] *Lancelot*, 1172, *Yvain*,

---

Ceres. This legend receives only a passing mention in Ovid — though accessible, doubtless, to Chrétien in Hyginus, Fable 83 — and besides, *Mors* (bite) does not necessarily imply devouring. On these grounds, G. Paris, *Mélanges*, I, 248, objected to the above-mentioned identification of the story and suggested a Celtic origin. Nevertheless, the identification is, most likely, correct. The poem dealing with the *muance* (transformation) of the three birds was, of course, the story of Tereus, Procne and Philomela in the *Metamorphoses*. It is possible that both *L'Art d'Amors* and the *Comandemenz Ovide* refer to the *Ars Amandi*. — For Ovid's influence on Chrétien see F. E. Guyer's exhaustive study, "The Influence of Ovid on Crestien de Troyes", RR, XII, 97 ff., 216 ff. (1921). I regret that the article appeared too late for me to cite it in detail. It throws new light on many conceptions in Chrétien's poems — especially on those that relate to love. In his "Zum Text des Erec", *Zs. f. frz. Spr. u. Litt.*, XXXVIII[1], 97 f. (1911), G. Cohen has tried to show that the above lines of the *Erec* are spurious, but his argument is futile. As far as I know, no one has expressed approval of this suggestion, save W. Meyer-Lübke, "Crestien von Troyes Erec und Enide", *ibid.*, XLIV[1], 136. On the subject of the above lines, cp., too, Foerster, *Cliges*[3], pp. VI ff. (Halle, 1910).
    [4] So G. Paris, *loc. cit.*, and C. De Boer in his edition of the *Philomena* (Paris, 1909); but for an argument *contra*, cp. Foerster, *op. cit.*, p. VII, note 2.
    [5] *Op. cit.*, pp. 254 ff.
    [6] So G. Paris, *op. cit.*, pp. 262 ff. He dates the *Erec* about 1168. For discussions of the respective dates of Chrétien's romances, except *Perceval*, see Foerster's introductions to these romances in his editions. His maturest opinions on the dates of all (including the *Perceval*) will be found pp. 33 ff. of the Introduction to his Chrétien *Wörterbuch*. Ibid., p. 39, he expresses the opinion that Chrétien's

1173, *Perceval*, 1175. The *Perceval* remains a fragment. This was the last of the poet's works, its composition being broken off, it seems, by his death. We leave aside *Guillaume d'Angleterre*, since, even if it is Chrétien's,[7] the poem does not belong to the *genre* of Arthurian romance.

It is significant that at the very beginning of his career Chrétien should have been occupying himself with Ovid and with a subject which lay so close to the Arthurian cycle — namely, the story of Iseult. With the exception of the *Cliges*, whose connection with Arthur is wholly artificial, all the writings of our poet from the *Erec* down relate to the *matière de Bretagne* and they all, without exception, betray the influence of Ovid. It would appear that the course of his development was as follows: He first becomes interested in the love-poetry of Ovid (it may be in his school-days), then he is attracted by the theme of *Tristan*, which he knew through oral tradition, or, possibly, some earlier French poem on the subject. With a poem of some kind on this hero he makes his first essay in the *matière de Bretagne*. If we had this *Tristan* poem, we should probably find that in the analysis of love-moods the influence of Ovid and of the French romances of antiquity was already traceable in it. The charm of the Celtic stories has laid its hold on the author and in all of his succeeding works, with the single exception of the *Cliges*, he draws incidents from this source, though by no means exclusively. Since Geoffrey and Wace, however, the authority of Arthur is great,

---

production began slightly before 1160 and ended not so very long after 1170. He dates *Cliges* about 1164 (p. 38) and accepts the *Erec* as earlier, though he suggests no definite date for the latter. The *Lancelot* and *Yvain* he places (p. 33) between 1164 and 1173, the latter being the later. *Perceval* he dates not much later than *Yvain*. Paris and Foerster agree as to the order in which Chrétien's Arthurian works were written and we may indeed regard the question as settled. See further on the date 1170 as the upper limit of the date of the *Yvain* M. Mörner: *"Le 'terminus a quo' du Chevalier au Lion"*, *Archivium Romanicum*, III, 95 f. (Geneva, 1919).

[7] Cp. Introduction to Foerster's edition (Halle, 1911) for discussion of the question of its authorship. Foerster upholds the ascription to Chrétien.

and under the influence of these works a new standard of refinement is already, to a certain degree, associated with his court.
Chrétien avails himself of this prestige, which had more or less
historical validity in the eyes of his contemporaries, since perhaps the majority of them accepted as historical truth Geoffrey's
pictures of Arthur's glories, and makes Arthur's court the starting-point of the adventures of all his heroes. This conception,
it is safe to say, was his own invention — only the setting and,
in part, the incidents are Celtic. The ideas which his romances
embody are those of his own time and country, and even the incidents he has adapted in thorough-going fashion to the conditions of French feudal society in the second half of the twelfth
century. A comparison has often been made between Tennyson
and Chrétien, as regards their attitude towards their originals,
and it is, in many respects, just. The French poet probably ad-
hered less closely to a single original for each poem than Tennyson did — although, on the other hand, in the matter of incident,
he, no doubt, drew less from his own invention than the English
poet. Both, however, are alike in making the stories of an earlier
time the vehicle of the ideals and sentiment of their own age.
Chrétien's principal importance, then, lies in the fact that he is
the chief literary exponent of the feudal society of his age. Just
as the *Song of Roland* and the cycle of William of Orange reflect
the feudal life of the early twelfth century, so Chrétien's romances reflect more perfectly than any other works the life of
the aristocratic classes in the later twelfth century.

Now, before illustrating somewhat more in detail by reference
to the specific works the observations we have just made with
regard to Chrétien's development and his shaping of the Arthurian theme, we should recall briefly what were the distinctive
ideals of this society: Chrétien himself during the period of his
literary activity was connected mainly with the court of Marie,
Countess of Champagne, whose father was Louis VII of France
and whose mother was Eleanor of Poitiers, the latter (the Eleanor
of Shakespeare's *King John)* being successively the wife of Louis
VII of France and Henry II of England. At a later period he
found a patron in Philip of Alsace, Count of Flanders. The dif-

ference between the ideals of the society of such a court as Marie's
in the second half of the twelfth century and those of the earlier
time represented by the *chansons de geste* is connected, above all,
with the improved position of women. This accords with the general advance of civilization from the unrestricted reign of physical
force in the earlier Middle Ages and is manifest even in the
political arrangements of the time, since women were now permitted
to inherit the great fiefs. The centre from which this move-
ment radiated was the south of France — the land of Eleanor of
Poitiers and the land where all ideas of social and intellectual
liberty had so far received their highest development. The love
lyrics of Provence show the growing idealization of woman, and
the conception of the *amour courtois* is the product of this idealization.

The starting-point of this idealization, to be sure, was earthy
enough in its nature — for it was, first of all, the motive of self-
advancement that prompted these Provençal singers — the troubadours, as they are called — to confer a poetic exaltation on the
wives and daughters of the great barons of the South, and where
panegyric passed, apparently, into love-poetry, the love was, in
the vast majority of instances, a pure fiction,[8] just as in the
case of the amorous effusions with which the Elizabethan poets
were accustomed to tickle the vanity of their Virgin Queen. But
the very unreality of the theme of the troubadours, who, as a rule,
were separated by a social gulf from the objects of their pretended
adoration, drove these poets within themselves to an idealization
of the persons addressed.[9] For the poet who found himself in

---

[8] On the origins of the *amour courtois* (Middle High German
*Minne*) cp. E. Wechssler's "Frauendienst und Vassalität", *Zs. f. frz.
Spr. u. Litt.*, XXIV[1], 158ff., and, above all, his *Das Kulturproblem
des Minnesangs*: Band I, *Minnesang und Christentum*, Halle, 1909
— also K. Heyl: *Die Theorie der Minne in den ältesten Minne-
romanen Frankreichs: Marburger Beiträge zur romanischen Philologie*, IV (Marburg, 1911), and T. F. Crane, *Italian Social Customs
in the Sixteenth Century and their influence on the literatures of
Europe*, ch. 1 (New Haven, 1920).
[9] Cp. Wechssler's book, pp. 219ff. As appears from this same
work, there were other Christian elements that helped to shape the

this attitude of inward contemplation the doors were thrown wide
open to the spirit of mysticism which was at that time coloring
contemporary thought in all its higher forms and which, through
St. Bernard of Clairvaux and his fellows, in the same century,
had already imparted a new life to the Church. Thus woman
who had been, in the beginning of the Provençal lyric, merely the
object of a rhetorical lip-service, became in the course of its development the object of a cult, which varied in genuineness according
to the spiritual capacity of the individual singer. As all students of literature know, this half mystic and half philosophical
conception of woman and love passed from Provence into Italy
and after being still further developed there by Guido Guini-
celli and other Italian poets, attained immortal expression in
Dante's idealization of Beatrice Portinari in the *Vita Nuova* and
*Divina Commedia.* For the great mass of noblemen and noble
ladies, as well as writers, however, these conceptions remained,
no doubt, merely a convention which they adopted for the sake
of fashion or amusement, but they, at least, pretended to take
them seriously, and so from about the middle of the twelfth century the duties of the lover towards his mistress amount to a complicated code[10] — a code which was perhaps not very strictly
conformed to in real life, but which at least expressed an ideal.

Chrétien's patroness, Marie de Champagne, as is evident from

conception of the *amour courtois* — the worship of saints, the doctrine
of *Charitas,* the methods of scholastic philosophy — but mysticism
was much the most powerful single influence. Contrary, however, to
the view which has been often expressed, Wechssler points out, pp.
434 ff., that the worship of the Virgin Mary (mariolatry) was a consequence, not a cause, of the cult of woman that was developed in
Provence. It does not arise until about the end of the twelfth century.

[10] Cp. especially, the one embodied in Andreas Capellanus's *De
Amore Libri Tres,* edited by E. Trojel (Copenhagen, 1892). Andreas
was for a time, at least, in the service of Marie de Champagne, and
composed his treatise apparently before 1196.

It is improbable that there were ever any serious "courts of love"
(to decide points that might arise in the relations of lovers). On the
whole subject, cp. W. A. Neilson, "The Origins and Sources of the
Courts of Love", Harvard *Studies and Notes in Philology and Literature,* VI (Boston, 1899) and Crane, op. cit., ch. 1.

the poet's own statement in his *Lancelot,* played an important part in the development of the literary tradition relating to these things and his work is the very highest expression of such ideals. In contrast with the *chansons de geste,* pictures of courtesy and refinement of manners, still more than in the romances of antiquity, constitute one of the main sources of interest of the narrative and much space is given to the functions, the feasts and festivities, where these traits are exhibited or developed. Even fighting appears in a more civilized aspect. The tourney, with its formal regulations, takes the place of the rude combats of the *chansons de geste* and the somewhat similar descriptions in the romances of antiquity, and the valor of the knight is now mainly employed in the succor of distressed women. The whole modern conception of the relation of the sexes finds here its beginnings. An advance towards these conceptions, to be sure, had already been made in the romances of antiquity, and there can be little doubt that both in respect to form and sentiment these works — particularly the *Thèbes* and the *Eneas*[11] — were the true precursors and, in a large measure, the models of Chrétien's romances.

---

[11] Both were probably composed in the fifties of the twelfth century. On the relative date of the *Eneas* see, last, Faral, pp. 169 ff. There are the beginnings of a spirit of courtesy in the fragmentary Latin poem, *Ruodlieb,* (edited by F. Seiler as *Der älteste Roman des Mittelalters,* Halle, 1882), which has usually been regarded as of German origin (near Tegernsee) and dated about 1030, but which M. Wilmotte, "Rodlieb, notre premier roman courtois", *Romania,* XLIV, 373 ff. (1916—1917), now assigns to Northeastern Gaul (valley of the Meuse, between Liege and Namur) and the early twelfth century. The author is not so much interested in combats as in the manners, diversions, decorations, etc., of aristocratic society. Wilmotte sees in all this an early independent development in the North in the direction of the romances of antiquity and Chrétien. Wechssler, *Sage vom heiligen Gral,* p. 139 (Halle, 1898) and *Problem des Minnesangs,* p. 30 (Halle, 1911) had already mentioned *Ruodlieb* in this connection, but had distinguished between the pictures of courtly life here and the special ideal of courtesy which we find in the romances and which he derives, I believe, justly from Southern France. In any event, there is no evidence that the *Ruodlieb* exercised any influence on subsequent poetry.

It is important to recollect these distinctive traits of French feudal society in the latter part of the twelfth century when we come to consider the element of originality in Chrétien's works — when we come to determine what is Celtic in incident or manners in his poems and what is possibly of his own invention or at any rate of non-Celtic origin in these works. A greater contrast with the position and character of woman as depicted in these romances than that which is furnished by the Celtic sagas could hardly be imagined.[12] In the latter we have a conception of woman which is inferior not only to that of the Arthurian romances, but to that of the sagas of any other branch of the Indo-European races, even the earliest in date. The Irish heroines have strength and stature, but the abundant examples which Professor Zimmer has adduced from the Cuchulinn sagas amply justify the term *gemein* ("low-down") with which he stigmatizes these women. Indeed, the exploits of some of the most famous of them, like Medbh, wife of King Ailill of Connaught, do not bear repetition in modern polite society.[13]

Let us turn now to Chrétien's romances themselves. Of the romances which have come down to us the earliest is *Erec*. The Welsh tale of *Geraint and Enid,* which corresponds to Chrétien's

---

[12] Alfred Nutt, *The influence of Celtic on Mediaeval Romance* (London, 1904), and others, to be sure, have tried to establish the existence of chivalrous feeling towards the weaker sex in these sagas —, for instance, in that of Deirdre, the great heroine of Irish legend —, but, as it appears to me, without success. I will refer the reader for the proof of the contrary to the remarkable paper by the late Professor Zimmer, published , after his death in the *Sitzungsberichte der königlichen preußischen Akademie der Wissenschaften. Philosophisch-Historische Classe,* 1911, IX, 174 ff. entitled *Der Kulturhistorische Hintergrund in der altirischen Heldensage.*

[13] J. Vendryes, *Revue Celtique,* XXXII, 232 ff. (1911) in his review of Zimmer's paper, has tried, to be sure, to show that the inferences of the German scholar are unjust. J. Loth, too, has objected, *ibid.,* XXXIII, 260, note (1912), that we might as well judge the manners and morals of the women of early Greece from the conduct of the Homeric goddesses. But there is no such vulgar *abandon* in the case of these goddesses.

poem, is, doubtless, derived directly from the latter[14] and not *vice versa*, but evidence of Celtic elements in the *Erec*, itself, are not lacking. To begin with, the name *Erec* is Celtic, being an alteration of Breton *Weroc*.[15] The same seems true of some of the other principal names in the poem: Eurain, Mabonagrain, etc. Take, moreover, the episode (11. 5461 ff.) known as the *Joie de la Cour:*[16] There is an enchanted garden next to the palace of King Eurain. It is enclosed with a wall of air, which is, nevertheless, just as effective as a wall of iron, so that no one can enter it save by the will of the possessor. To overcome this enchantment now is the task of Erec. Stakes with human heads crowning them at the entrance of the garden confirm the warnings which the hero has received from Eurain and his companions against undertaking the adventure. In the garden under a sycamore he comes upon a beautiful girl reclining on a silver couch; but just at this moment the girl's lover appears — Mabonagrain, a giant knight — and threatens him. A combat follows in which Erec, of course, vanquishes his opponent and thereby dispels the enchantment of the garden. It turns out that Mabonagrain had promised his damsel that he would never leave the garden until he had been vanquished in combat.

Now Celtic parallels seem to establish the Celtic origin of the episode.[17] Similarly, the custom of hunting the white stag

[14] Cp. Part. IV, below.

[15] Cp. G. Paris, *Romania*, XX, 166, note 1 (1881), and J. Loth, *Revue Celtique*, XIII, 482 ff. (1892), who prove that Zimmer's derivation, *Zs. f. frz. Spr. u. Litt.*, XIII¹, 26 ff., is wrong.

[16] F. Lot, *Romania*, XXIV, 321 ff. (1895). *Evrain* is a mistake for *Euuain* (i. e. *Owen*). *Mabonograin* is a combination of *Mabon* and *Evrain* — names of two magicians in the *Bel Inconnu*. Cp., too, E. Philipot, "Un episode *d'Erec et Enide*, la Joie de la Cour", *Romania*, XXV, 258 ff. (1896) and W. H. Schofield, *Studies in the Libeaus Desconus*, pp. 124 ff.

[17] Cp. the examples of "druidic mist" (walls of air from which there is no exit) cited from Celtic stories by Miss Paton, *Fairy Mythology*, p. 84, note 3. Foerster, *Erec²*, p. XXIII (Halle, 1909), on the other hand, maintains that we have here merely a variant of the *märchenmotiv* diffused all over the continent of Europe of the deliverance of a maiden held in captivity by a giant. According to Foerster, Chrétien again used this *motif* in the *Yvain*.

at the beginning of the romance reminds one irresistibly of the marvellous white doe in *Guigemar*, which, as we have seen, is, no doubt, of Celtic origin. On the other hand, the principal *motif* of the poem, the *Verliegen* (to use a convenient German term) of the hero — that is, the way in which, through uxoriousness, Erec neglects deeds of valor and gives himself up to love, so that his decline in knightly prowess becomes a matter of general reproach, and, at length, of sorrow, even to the young wife herself — bears on its face the marks of its French origin. Spurred by the grief of his wife, the hero, though angry at the implied reproach, arouses himself from his sloth and redeems his reputation, just as a young French knight of the twelfth century doubtless would have done, when touched in the point of honour. The wife endures patiently the tribulations to which his wounded vanity subjects her and in the end her love triumphs — a *motif* that recalls the Patient Griselda of Chaucer's *Clerk's Tale*. There is nothing Celtic in the conception, and, considering that it is intimately interwoven with another *motif* that is manifestly French — namely, that of *Verliegen* — there seems to be no reason for ascribing to it a Celtic origin. The same is true of the sparrow-hawk incident in the earlier part of the romance, in which the bird is the prize of beauty which each knight endeavors to win for his lady — also, of the kiss of the most beautiful girl at Arthur's court, which is to reward success in the chase of the white stag. These incidents exhaust the *motifs* of the romance, for the combats with robbers and chance knights, like Guivret le Petit, of which there are many, have no significance.

If the above outline of the sources of *Erec et Enide* is correct, the poem owes little, after all, to Celtic models. It is merely the Arthurian setting, the nomenclature, the *Joie de la Cour* episode, and a detail here and there that we may ascribe to this origin. The novelty consists in the happy selection of incidents, in the elegance of style, in the idealized pictures of chivalry, with its refinement of manners and its courage enlisted in the service of beauty. But just as the direction of Shakespeare's art at the beginning of his career is determined in a considerable measure by Marlowe and Lyly, so Chrétien, too, has had his precursors —

in the authors of the romances on subjects of classical antiquity, as we have already said, the *Roman d'Alexandre, Roman de Thèbes, Eneas, Roman de Troie.* The dates of these works are not fixed precisely, but there can be no reasonable doubt that the composition of the last three fell within the ten or fifteen years preceding the composition of *Erec.* In this group of romances we already have the effort to depict the new ideals of courtesy and chivalry, so that Eneas and Dido, Achilles and Polyxena, are twelfth century knights and ladies. One can observe the influence of these works on Chrétien even in matters of phrasing and technique,[18] and besides, the length of his romances was, no doubt, approximately determined by the example of the *Thebes* and *Eneas.* But since, in questions of art, sentiment, form, and style are even more important than subject-matter, it is, after all, the debt of the French poet to these predecessors rather than his meagre and uncertain borrowings from Celtic tradition that needs to be emphasized. The full force of these models — the romances of antiquity — did not make itself felt, however, in the *Erec.* As far as the refinements of life are concerned — rich and brilliant externals, careful etiquette and polished manners — these are already given prominence in Chrétien's first extant romance; but he has not yet accepted love as the all-dominating factor in human life, in the spirit of the *amour courtois,* which had already touched the *Eneas* and *Troie,* in particular. In his subsequent romances this fashionable conception of the relations of the sexes — doubtless through the influence of his patroness — was destined to impose

---

[18] This has been convincingly set forth by M. Wilmotte, *L'évolution du roman français aux environs de 1150,* Brussels, 1903, and F. M. Warren, "Some Features of Style in Early French Narrative Poetry", MPh., III, 179 ff. (1905), 513 ff. (1906). IV, 655 ff. (1907). For the general influence of the romances of antiquity on subsequent literature, including Chrétien, see, besides Foerster's *Chrétien Wörterbuch,* pp. 33 ff., and Faral's oft-quoted book, the following Göttingen dissertations: R. Witte: *Der Einfluß von Benoits Roman de Troie auf die altfranzösische Literatur* (1904), A. Dreßler, *Der Einfluß des altfranzösischen Eneasromanes auf die altfranzösische Literatur* (1907) and G. Otto, *Der Einfluß des Roman de Thebes auf die altfranzösische Literatur* (1909).

itself upon the different love-stories that he dealt with, until in
the *Perceval* he set his hero a new aim, and sexual passion, now
subordinate in his scheme, strips itself again of ephemeral conventions.[19]

Let us examine now the manner in which Chrétien composed
his romances.[20]

The plan and the main idea of each romance are his own.
He makes up his narrative by combining *motifs* which he derived
from earlier sources, in some instances, using episodes drawn from
such sources to embellish or lengthen out the story which is the
basis of his work. One may question whether a single fundamental idea[21] runs through the whole of the *Erec* or the *Yvain* or
the *Perceval*, but otherwise the above is, probably, an accurate
statement of the manner in which these works were composed.

---

[19] Myrrha Borodine (now Mme. Lot-Borodine) in her important
study, *La femme et l'amour au XIIe siècle d'après les poèmes de
Chrétien de Troyes*, (Paris, 1909) distinguishes three stages in Chrétien's
development in his treatment of love: 1. *Erec:* the ideal of active
knighthood (*l'ideal chevaleresque*) is stronger than love. 2. *Cliges,
Lancelot, Yvain:* love is the sovereign power. 3. *Perceval:* the religious ideal is stronger than love. If one remembers that Chrétien's
religious feeling had no great depth, these divisions may be accepted
as valid.

Foerster, Chrétien WB, p. 55*, has observed that the *Erec*
resembles the *chansons de geste* not only in the view of woman's
subordination to man, but in literary technique and in its outbreak
against the *conteurs* — moreover, that it contains a number of allusions
to various heroes of these works.

[20] The views on this subject which I adopt in this place are,
in the main, those of W. Foerster, *Yvain*, pp. XXIff. (Halle, 1913).

[21] *Grundidee* is Foerster's word. He regards Chrétien's romances as *Thesenromane*. Cp. Chrétien *Wörterbuch*, pp. 43*ff.
Foerster, moreover, minimizes, perhaps, even more than is due the
Celtic element in the poet's works. To be sure, in my opinion, there
is no reason to believe that this element was at all large. For an
argument — in the main, correct — to the effect that Chrétien's
object in composing his romances was to interest by his narrative,
not to illustrate a thesis, see W. Küchler, „Über den sentimentalen Ge-
halt der Haupthandlung in Crestien's *Erec* und *Ivain*", *Zs. f. rom.
Ph.*, XL, 83ff. (1919).

That this was the mode of their composition, indeed, seems clear from the next of the series — namely, the *Cliges*, for here the principal element in the story is a familiar one and we can observe how the poet has united it with other material in order to secure the requisite length for his work. To elucidate his method, it will be necessary to outline briefly the narrative of the romance. The poem falls into two unequal divisions: 1. The story of the hero's parents. 2. The hero's own story. It contains 6784 lines, of which 2382 are given to the story of the parents, the remainder to the hero's, except about 300 lines, which serve as a connecting link between the two. As was said above, it is generally agreed that no part of this romance has any genuine connection with the *matière de Bretagne* and the Arthurian affiliation which Chrétien gives it is of the most artificial kind. First as to the story of the parents: The father, Alexander, is a prince of Constantinople, who, on account of Arthur's fame, journeys to Britain to receive from the great king the order of knighthood. Arthur goes to Brittany and leaves Count Engres regent of his kingdom. On the voyage he is accompanied by Alexander and his niece, Soredamors, who fall in love with one another, but fear to declare their mutual passion. But Engres, like Mordred in Geoffrey of Monmouth, from whom he is evidently imitated,[22] endeavors to seize the kingdom in Arthur's absence, so that Arthur is compelled to return. He besieges the faithless Engres at Windsor. Finally, it is Alexander who by a ruse gains possession of the castle for the king. In the meanwhile, he had often been thrown with his lady-love in the court-circle of Guinevere, who guesses the secret of the lovers. She brings about the long-delayed declaration, and they marry. Cliges, the hero of the story, is the fruit of their union. This ends the first division of the poem, and next comes the connecting link.

During the absence of Alexander from Constantinople his

---

[22] Cp. Bruce's edition of the *Mort Artu*, p. 287 (Halle, 1910). Cp. also, Annette B. Hopkins, *The Influence of Wace on the Arthurian Romances of Crestien de Troies*, p. 35 (University of Chicago dissertation, 1913). Curiously, Chrétien does not mention Mordred directly in any of his works.

father, the emperor, has died and a younger son, Alis, has ascended the throne, having received false intelligence of his brother's death. The latter now comes to Constantinople and makes a compact with Alis by which Alis is to retain the imperial title, but he is to be the real ruler. Moreover, Alis agrees not to marry, so that Cliges may inherit the throne. Before his death Cliges's father urges his son to test his knighthood at Arthur's court by encounters with the best knights there — especially Gawain. Both father and mother die. Now follows the second and main division of the poem.

Alis breaks his promise and carries off by force as his bride Fenice,[23] the daughter of the German emperor, who had been engaged to a Saxon prince. But Fenice and Cliges fall in love with one another. Fenice appeals for aid to her nurse, Thessala, who saves her from the consummation of her marriage with Alis by giving the husband a magic drink that deludes him into believing that he has consummated it, when he has not. On the way home Cliges confirms his hold on his lady-love's affections by defending her from the Saxon prince who tries to recover his betrothed.

The hero now carries out his promise to his father by going to Arthur's court and measuring himself there in tourneys with the greatest knights.[24] He distinguishes himself, but love in time drives him back to Constantinople. Here the lovers again avail themselves of Thessala's magic arts, and it is agreed that, to elude her husband, Fenice is to take a magic potion which will throw her into a death-like trance. According to their anticipations, she is carried out as dead to her grave. Certain skilled physicians from Salerno see through the deceit, but they are slain and the girl is buried. Her lover evades the watch and brings Fenice into

---

[23] This name is, doubtless, Greek *Phoinike,* although, G. Cohen, *Zs. f. frz. Spr. u. Litt.,* XXV [2], 146, derives it from Macedonian *Pherenike* (= *Berenike*). The Greek names in the romance are classical, rather than Byzantine in origin. Cp. Krumbacher's communication to Foerster in the latter's *Cliges* [3], p. XXXVII.

[24] We have here in the tournament, lasting four days, a variant of the widespread "three days' tournament motif".

a tower, where she is restored to life by her nurse. Here they
live for months tagether. A new trouble, however, awaits them, for
they are detected by a young knight, named Bertram. Nevertheless,
they escape to Arthur's court, and after a time, on the death of Alis,
they return to Constantinople and reign there for the rest of their
lives.

The kernel of this romance is the love-affair of Cliges and
Fenice, including the deceits which it involves to defeat the consummation of the latter's marriage with the uncle of Cliges and
to bring about the union of the lovers. All the rest is secondary
and, for the most part, as is obvious, added merely to give variety
to the poem. Now we have here in this main story merely an adaptation of the oriental *motif* of the wife who feigns death in order
to deceive her husband for the sake of her lover.[25] In what is,
perhaps, the earliest of its known forms, the Solomon and Marcolf
tale, it is the wife of Solomon who practises the deceit. Though
not of identical origin, the story is similar to that which is familiar to all the world in Shakespeare's *Romeo and Juliet*.

At the beginning of his romance Chrétien tells us that he
derived his story from a book which belonged to the library of
the church of Saint-Pierre de Beauvais. An allusion in the poem
itself shows that he was acquainted with the Solomon and Marcolf
tale, but his version of the *motif* bears so close a resemblance to
that which is preserved in the thirteenth century prose continuation of the *Seven Sages*, called *Marque de Rome*, that one may
reasonably conclude that the tale which he found in the above-
mentioned book had virtually this form.[26] The deluding of Alis
by Thessala's magic drink, however, has no parallel in the oriental

---

[25] Cp. Foerster, Introd. to small *Cliges* (second ed.), XXXII ff. and
G. Paris, *Mélanges*, 309 ff.

[26] So Foerster, *Cliges*[3], pp. XXXII ff. (as in his previous editions)
and G. Paris *Mélanges*, p. 312. W. Golther, *Zs. f. frz. Spr. u. Litt.*,
XIII[2], 7 (1891) and *ibid.*, XXIV[2], 7 ff. (1902), expresses the opinion
that the passage in the *Marque de Rome* is derived from *Cliges* and
not *vice versa*, but see on this subject Foerster, *Cliges*[3], p. XXXIV
(1910). Besides, in his *Tristan und Isolde*, p. 213 (Leipzig, 1907)
Golther seems to have retracted his earlier opinion.

tale. In this we have a *motif* imported from another source[27] —
namely, from the old *chanson de geste*, the *Enfances Guillaume*,
where the delusion is the effect of sorcery. That the magic drink
should be substituted for the sorcery of the old poem is plainly
due to the influence of the *Tristan* story, which was occupying
at this time so large a place in Chrétien's mind.

It has been pointed out by Professor Foerster and others[28]

---

[27] Cp. G. Paris, *Mélanges*, p. 293.

[28] Foerster was the first to advance the theory that *Cliges* was
composed as an *Anti-Tristan*, viz., in the Introduction to his small
*Cliges* (1901). He repeated it in subsequent editions. Cp. the third
(final) edition (1910), pp. XLVI ff. The theory was accepted by Golther,
*Zs. f. frz. Spr. u. Litt.*, XXIV², 7 ff. (1902) — see, also, his *Tristan
und Isolde*, pp. 211 ff. (Leipzig, 1907) and A. G. van Hamel, "Cliges
et Tristan", *Romania*, XXXIII, 465 ff. (1904). G. Paris also accepted
it, but with the modification indicated in the text above. See his
fourth *Cliges* article, *Journal des Savants* for August, 1902, pp. 442 ff.
(in the *Mélanges* reprint, pp. 288 ff.). For a reply to Paris, cp. Foerster,
*op. cit.*, p. LIII, note 2.

In his "Randglossen zum Athisroman", *Zs. f. rom. Ph.*, XXXVI,
727 ff. (1912), Foerster finds, also, strong resemblances between this
famous tale of friendship (especially, in Part II of the text of the
Tours MS.) and *Cliges*. He argues that *Athis et Prophilias* contains
no allusion to Arthur or Tristan, and no marks of the *Minne* spirit
— hence is older than *Cliges*. The reasoning, however, to my mind,
is, by no means, conclusive. The omission of allusions to Arthur and
Tristan is not surprising in a romance based on Oriental materials,
and, as a matter of fact, many passages in the romance betray the
new *Minne* ideal, e. g. 11. 2805 ff. (Athis and Gaite fall in love
with each other), 3360 ff. (Athis's monologue on his love-sickness).
Cp. A. Hilka's edition, I, 99, 118 (Dresden, 1912). — *Op. cit.*, p. 736,
Foerster thinks that Chrétien's *Perceval*, 1. 9336 (Baist's edition, l.
7926) shows, also, the influence of *Athis et Prophilias*, 11. 2936 ff.
In each we have a discourse extending through several lines on the
necessity of being on one's guard against catching cold after overheating.
Prophilias thinks that Athis, owing to his neglect of the requisite
precautions in such cases, has taken cold and is "sanmellez", and the
girl in the *Perceval* warns Gawain, "Que maint an sanc meslé an
sont", from the same cause. Foerster declares that he knows of no
other parallel to these passages in Old French literature and that only
in the *Athis and Prophilias* passage is the meaning of *sanmellez
(sanc mesle)* clear. The two passages are certainly very similar, but,

that the whole character of the *Cliges*, indeed, was determined by
the lost *Tristan* poem. Not only have we here the introductory romance of the hero's parents told in full, but the whole poem may
be regarded as an *Anti-Tristan*, or, in any event, as a pendant of
*Tristan*.[29] The manner in which Iseult in the older story yields
herself to the embraces of two men, her husband and her lover,
was shocking to the sentiment of the cultivated, though immoral,
society for which the poet was writing, so that the *Cliges* was
manifestly composed by way of polemic against the coarser views
of love which underlay that romance. It is hardly correct to assume[30] that our poet is here adopting the *bourgeois* ideal, which
permits the union of lovers only through the marriage ceremony.
Such an ideal would have had but little attraction for Chrétien's
aristocratic patrons of the twelfth century[31] — either women or
men — and, besides, the deceit which Fenice practised on Alis,
her legitimate husband, and her subsequent conduct are little con-

---

apart from the unsettled relative date of the two romances, the similarity may be due to the fact that both authors drew independently
from contemporary notions concerning the physiological process in
such attacks.

In his *L'évolution du roman français aux environs de 1150*,
p. 345, M. Wilmotte states that *Cliges* was composed manifestly under
the influence of Gautier d'Arras's *Eracle*, which, like Foerster, he dates
(p. 337) 1164. He even lists pp. 351 ff. (including notes) a number
of verbal coincidences in which, as he thinks, *Cliges* shows the influence of *Eracle*. It is difficult to say how far their common classical
sources account for the resemblances of situation and of phrasing, but
Wilmotte's argument is plausible. — W. M. Stevenson assumes in his
*Der Einfluß des Gautier d'Arras auf die altfranzösische Kunst-
epik, insbesondere auf den Abenteuerroman*, p. 102 (Göttingen diss.
1910), that Gautier and Chrétien mutually influenced each other. This
seems very likely.

[29] This last is the opinion of G. Paris, *Mélanges*, p. 293.

[30] So Foerster, *Cliges*[3], pp. XXIX ff.

[31] Andreas Capellanus ascribes to Chrétien's patroness, Marie de
Champagne, the sentiment "Amorem non posse suas inter duos conjugales
extendere vires", (Trojel's edition, p. 133). We know, too, from the
author of the *Eracle* that she suggested to him the story of Athenais's
adultery in Part II of that romance.

sonant with such an ideal. To be sure, the heroine frequently expresses a horror of being associated in the minds of the people with Iseult. She exhibits, however, no repulsion for Iseult's sin, but merely for the evil reputation which the detection of her guilt had given the latter throughout the world.[32]

This main story Chrétien has complicated and retarded by the episode of the hero's visit to Arthur's court, the most interesting feature of which is the well-known Three Tournament *motif* where the knight, *incognito*, wins the tournament on three successive days, appearing each day in a new colour — red, white, and black — still further, by the final episode, borrowed from the *Tristan,* in which Bertram detects the lovers together in an orchard — an incident which is common in tales of Eastern origin.

No less important, however, for an insight into our poet's methods of composition is the first division of the *Cliges* — the story of the love of the hero's parents. As already observed, it was obviously suggested by the corresponding division of Chré-tien's *Tristan* original — the story of the love of Rivalin and Blanchefleur, the parents of Tristan; but the correspondence does not extend to details — at least, to the more important features. Paris has justly noted the inferiority of the imitation to the ori-ginal in the essential matter of its connection with the main theme of the romance. The whole life of Tristan is determined by the tragical fate of Rivalin and Blanchefleur, whereas there is no such relation between the stories of Cliges and his parents. In this the *Cliges,* then, exhibits a manifest want of unity.

Altogether the connection between the first and second di-vision of the narrative is full of blunders in composition.[33] But the first division is, itself, also composite. For the rest, this first division contains a rather commonplace story of love between two young people of high rank. Doubtless, the fact that their love-affair begins at sea is a pale reflection of the same feature of the *Tristan* romance with the love potion left out; and similarly with some other features. The whole story, however, such as it

---

[32] So G. Paris, *loc. cit.*

[33] G. Paris has enumerated them, *Mélanges,* p. 285.

is, is interwoven with a supposed episode in Arthur's career, according to which the king goes abroad, appoints a regent in his absence, but is compelled to return, because of the treachery of this regent. There is an incident somewhat like this in the *Tristan* story, but, as I have noted above, there can be little doubt that the real original which Chrétien here had in mind was Mordred's treachery to Arthur, under similar circumstances, as related in Geoffrey of Monmouth's *Historia* and Wace's *Brut*. Apart from the incidents, the monologues on the subject of love constitute a marked feature of this first division of the *Cliges,* but these, too, have their originals; they were suggested by the monologues of the *Roman de Troie* and *Eneas* — especially the latter — and are ultimately descended from Ovid and Virgil[34] — for example, the monologues of Byblis and Myrrha in the *Metamorphoses* and Dido's speeches in the *Aeneid,* which, of course Chrétien also knew at first hand.[35]

It will be observed that virtually every incident even of this first division of the poem can be traced to its source. It approaches, however, close to invention — certainly as near to invention as we can expect of a poet of the Middle Ages or of most poets of modern times — that is to say, Chrétien, has taken widely separated details and brought them into a new combination, so as to produce the effect of originality. That the total impression in this case is not particularly striking is due to the fact that the

---

[34] Cp., especially, E. Faral: *Recherches sur les sources latines des contes et romans courtois du moyen age,* pp. 73 ff. (Paris, 1913).

[35] The Greek names of certain characters have led some scholars to imagine that Chrétien used a lost Greek source for this division of his romance. Cp. E. Herzog, *Literaturblatt,* XXV, 19 (1904). But these names, insofar as they are genuine. are derived from Ovid and the Old French romances of antiquity. Cp. Foerster's *Cliges*[3], p. XXXVIII (Halle, 1910). In his "Byzantinisch-Geschichtliches im *Cliges* und *Yvain",* *Zs. f. rom. Ph.,* XXXII, 400ff. (1908), F. Settegast sees in the Byzantine element of *Cliges* a reflex of the history of the Byzantine emperor Isaac I (1057—1059) and, especially, of his two nephews, Isaac and Alexios I. The latter reigned 1081—1118 and was well-known in the West, because of his relations to the First Crusade. On this fanciful hypothesis see Foerster, *op. cit.,* pp. XXXVIf.

elements combined do not individually possess any especial interest — far less, for instance, than attaches to the ancient story that underlies the second division.

It cannot be too strongly emphasized that the *Cliges* constitutes the proper starting-point for any study of Chrétien's relation to his sources.[36] We can analyze with certainty his principles of composition in the case of this poem, whose sources can be fixed, one may say, even in the minutest details. Now we may be reasonably sure that these principles were essentially the same in the poems whose sources we are unable to fix — at any rate, so exactly. And this is substantially true, whether we assume his originals to have been mainly Celtic or not. The analogy of *Cliges* then certainly tells against the theory[37] as to a uniform Celtic tale's forming the basis of the *Yvain*. The narrative of that romance is also obviously a composite one and it is impossible to fit it into the scheme of some hypothetical Irish analogue.

We have already considered the question of the sources of the *Yvain* in another connection and the same question in the case of the *Lancelot* and *Perceval* will be dealt with when we come to trace the history of these heroes in romance. In general, it is sufficient to say here that the sources are, in each instance, composite and that the writer exercises a certain amount of invention in combining originally disparate elements — moreover, that these elements are only partly Celtic.

Taken altogether, Chrétien is undoubtedly the best of the French authors of metrical romances that deal with the *matière*

[36] This has been stressed by A. G. van Hamel, *Romania*, XXXIII, 486 (1904), and in his "Bydrage tot de vergelijking van Cliges en Tristan", *Taal en Letteren*, XIV, 193 ff. (Leiden, 1904) — especially, p. 211. On the other hand, Nitze, *Romania*, XLIV, 33 (1915) objects that what is true of *Cliges* is not necessarily true of the rest — especially, since *Cliges* is a combination of an Oriental tale with an Arthurian theme, as the others are not. The last point, at least, however, is of no weight, for, as Faral, pp. 418 f., has observed, the division of the romances into four groups according to their subject-matter is largely artificial.

[37] A. C. L. Brown, "The Knight of the Lion", PMLA., XX, 673 ff. (1905).

*de Bretagne.* In saying this, however, we are making an acknowledgement of the limitations of what was achieved in this *genre* — at least, in France; for in the works of this writer there is no question of the higher imagination, of philosophical insight into the riddles of existence, of "the dower of spanning wisdom", with regard to either character or the conduct of life, or of the magic of diction and phrase, which have distinguished the representative poets of many other ages. His imagery is confined to a few similes — the majority of which are of a purely conventional kind — and to a restricted, though somewhat richer, store of metaphor. His "criticism of life" is merely that of a shrewd, alert, man of the world of his time. He was quite contented with the feudal society in which he moved and he delighted in the bustle and splendor of its festivities, its pageantry, and its tournaments. Within the bounds of this society, apart from the externals just mentioned, the code of chivalry and the problems of the relations of the sexes — the latter especially in the new form which these problems had assumed under the system of the *amour courtois* — were the things that most attracted him. Moreover, living in a naive age, when in the elementary interests and emotions the grown man was nearer to the child than at present, he was keenly susceptible to the spell of the marvellous, as were his contemporaries generally. Consequently, the setting which he gives to the life of chivalry and to his solution of the above-mentioned problems is taken largely from the folk-tales of Celtic regions and of the Orient, where such fancies most abounded, with occasional admixture of classical *motifs*. In the case of the *Perceval*, perhaps, he did not understand the full significance of the materials that he drew from his sources, but, in general, the combination of the various elements of content and setting in his poems produces on the reader an effect of harmonious unity, and the creation of this new world in which mediaeval barons and ladies jostle fairies and even stranger Otherworld figures is no mean achievement.

Since love is the dominant theme of Chrétien's romances, it is natural that he should display most knowledge of the human heart in his characterizations of women. We are wearied occasionally, it is true, with the hair-splitting analyses of amorous emo-

tions in the lovers' soliloquies of his romances and with the conceits
which such analyses engender, but the patient loyalty of Enid, the
sovereign haughtiness of Guinevere and the piquant fickleness of
Laudine in their relations with their lovers or husbands are depicted with much truth to nature and with no little charm, and,
in the last-named case, also, with an effective touch of *malice*.

It is particularly however, as a born *conteur* that Chrétien
can claim a notable place among the poets of the Middle Ages. In
telling a story his sparkling vivacity never fails him, and, as a
German critic has happily said, he makes the impression of a
juggler who can shake couplets out of his sleeve as long as he
pleases. He, himself, thoroughly enjoys telling his tale and his
enjoyment is consequently contagious. We have seen above that
his work is marred in some instances by serious faults of construction; but the same thing is true of *Marmion* and *Rokeby* — yet,
in spite of these defects, Scott is, perhaps, our greatest English
master of narrative poetry. Chrétien, of course, paints on no such
broad canvases and with no such variety of poetical resources as
the nineteenth century writer. With greater vividness and *agré-
ment,* nevertheless, than any other poet of the Middle Ages, he has
preserved for us, at least, the outward lineaments of the society
which Scott idealized. After all, however, his most memorable
services to the great cause of poetry, perhaps, were in stimulating
immeasurably the imagination of his contemporaries — for the vast
forest of mediaeval Arthurian romance sprang mainly from the
seeds of his sowing — and in enriching the whole poetic tradition
of Europe with new and beautiful themes on which greater men
than himself have exercised their genius, from the age immediately
succeeding his own down to that of Tennyson and Wagner.

During the life-time of Chrétien there were other romance-
writers like Gautier d'Arras, author of *Eracle* and *Ille and Galeron,*
which, though similar in the most essential respects, cannot be
classed as Arthurian romances, inasmuch as Arthur and his knights
do not figure in them. No one, however, but Chrétien, during
these years, as far as the extant works show, made it his object
to embody the ideals of contemporary feudal society in romances
connected with Arthur.[38]  Thomas's *Tristan* was written about

1170 and those critics are probably right who see in it here and there the influence of Chrétien rather than *vice versa*,[39] but, apart from its dependence on the lost *Tristan* romance, the spirit of this work is somewhat different from Chrétien's. The new ideals of chivalry occupy here a subordinate place in comparison with the passion of the lovers and the subterfuges to which they resort in the fulfilment of that passion. The Béroul *Tristan* fragments are, at least in the main, later than Chrétien, but they belong, besides, to the tradition of the popular minstrels and are on a different level from the poems we are dealing with.

It may be that the supremacy of Chrétien during his lifetime deterred others from trying their hand in a *genre* which he had made his own. In any event, he was the object of admiration for the generations that immediately succeeded him. The frequent allusions to his works prove this, but even more decisively the variety of influences which they exercised on subsequent literature. In the first place, we have from the closing years of the twelfth century and the first part of the thirteenth many biographical and episodical romances which continue the *genre*. So, for instance, *Li Biaus Descouneus (Le Bel Inconnu)*[40] by Renaud de Beaujeu, on the theme which has also been treated in the middle English romance, *Libeaus Desconus* — itself based, of course, on some lost French original — that is to say, the theme of the unknown young knight who claims the first adventure after his arrival at Arthur's court, astonishes the girl whose champion he has been made by his acts of prowess, visits the fairy isle, L'Ille d'Or, resists its temptations and abolishes its bad customs, delivers the enchanted princess who has been turned into a serpent by venturing the *fier baiser* (dangerous kiss). Similar are the works of Raoul de Houdenc, at the beginning of the thirteenth century, which show,

---

[38] On the probable mutual influence which Chrétien and Gautier exerted upon each other, cp. p. 117 note 28 above.

[39] Cp. M. Wilmotte, *L'évolution du roman français*, p. 67, and Foerster, Chrétien WB, pp. 65*f., as against G. Paris, *Mélanges*, p. 282.

[40] For editions of this and the other metrical romances mentioned in this chapter, cp. the Bibliography at the end of the present work.

to a marked degree, the influence of his great predecessor — the *Meraugis de Portlesguez,* where the heroine, Lidoine, exemplifies the idea that courtesy — the perfection of courtly breeding — is superior to mere beauty, and the *Vengeance de Raguidel,* which recounts the vengeance that Gawain took for a knight named Raguidel, who was slain before the action of the romance begins. These are only a few of those that have survived. The list drawn up by Gaston Paris[41] includes thirty-seven romances, and some additional ones have come to light since the publication of his treatise. Even now (1921) one of the very best of Paris's list remains unedited — namely, *Gliglois.* And so the Arthurian metrical romance drags on into the fourteenth century until it expires with the *Meliador* of Froissart in the second half of that century.[42]

The influence of this product of French genius outside of France is well-known to all the world. In Germany, before the end of the twelfth century, we have in the *Lanzelet* of Ulrich von Zatzikhoven an adaptation from a French romance, and, about the same time, the *Erec* and *Iwein* of Hartmann von der Aue — paraphrased, of course, from Chrétien's romances of the same names. Then come Gottfried von Strassburg's adaptation of Thomas's *Tristan* and Wolfram von Eschenbach's *Parzival,* based, according to his own statement, on the work of an enigmatical *Kyot* — a French poet, of course. Both of these illustrious writers belong to the early thirteenth century and there are others less illustrious of the same nation who about the same time drew likewise from the vast store-house of the French metrical romances. Especially to be noted is Heinrich von Türlin (about 1220) whose *Crône* preserves in German dress much lost French material which we know only from this poem. The same thing is true of the vast

---

[41] At the beginning of the *Histoire littéraire de la France,* XXX (1888).

[42] For references to Arthur in works outside of the Arthurian romances, cp. F. L. Critchlow, "Arthur in Old French Poetry not of the Breton Cycle", MPh., VI, 477 ff. (1909). The author's list, however, is by no means exhaustive. For analyses of these romances see Part V, below.

thirteenth century Dutch compilation in short-rhymed couplets called the *Lancelot*.[43] Its 87000 lines (and somewhat more) embraces, besides large portions of the prose-romances of the Arthurian cycle, more than one metrical romance which in its original French form has perished.

Owing to the special conditions which prevailed in England after the Norman Conquest, when the language of the patron-class was for many generations French, the English were slow in adapting in their language these most characteristic reflections of the life of the ruling classes in the Middle Ages. As long as the language of those classes was French, there was, of course, no incentive to produce English versions of the French originals, and when at last there was such an incentive in the growing decline of French in familiar use among the upper classes, these poems belonged to a past age and no longer represented, at least with such perfection, the spirit of contemporary society. Perhaps, this may account in part, at least, for the fact that the Middle English romances, on the whole, are inferior to German production in the same *genre;* for the latter, it will be recalled, fell at the end of the twelfth century and beginning of the thirteenth — that is to say, it was coincident with all but the first period of production in France itself and so was a vivid representation of actual contemporary ideals. It is significant that the best English Arthurian romances — those which seem addressed to the more cultured classes and not to rude popular audiences — belong to the north — the most backward part of the kingdom, where the old feudal ideals and the literary tastes corresponding were least changed. To this region belongs the gem of the English romances, *Sir Gawain and the Green Knight,* which was composed about the middle of the fourteenth century — at a time when the metrical romance on the continent was utterly decadent. Notwithstanding the impression of uncouthness which Middle English alliteration always makes on the modern reader, this romance, by the general verdict, belongs among the best productions of the Arthurian muse

---

[43] Edited by W. J. A. Jonckbloet, 2. vols. (The Hague, 1846 —1849).

in the Middle Ages. It is safe to say, too, that although derived from a lost French original, it contains a larger share of original invention than is the case with any other English specimen of the *genre*. A similar vigor and a similar uncouthness mark the alliterative *Morte Arthure*, which was produced in the same general region. It is a pity that the large proportion of words of French and Scandinavian origin in this romance and in *Sir Gawain and the Green Knight* that time has rendered obsolete should have rendered these fine poems sealed books to all but professional students at the present day.

The earliest Middle English metrical romance that has come down to us is the *King Horn*, which dates from the middle of the thirteenth century, and the earliest Middle English metrical romance connected with the Arthurian cycle is the *Sir Tristrem* which belongs to the close of that century. The latter is a rude poem in stanzas of eleven lines and it was composed in the Northwest of Midland England. It is based on Thomas's *Tristan*, but, like virtually all the Middle English romances, whether Arthurian or not, it condenses the original. The English audiences of the time were evidently unequal to the task of appreciating the refinements of the French romances and the poets themselves stood on a lower level of culture than the authors of their originals.[44]

To the following century, however, — the fourteenth — belong the great bulk of the English metrical romances, including those with Arthurian connections. One of the most important of these, the alliterative *Morte Arthure*, which is often assigned to the Scottish knight, Huchown of the Awle Ryale, although it more likely originated in Northern England, represents, as we have already seen, rather one of the later developments of the chronicles in verse than the metrical romance proper, as we have it in the works of Chrétien and his followers. Moreover, a large number of the Middle English metrical romances are derived from

---

[44]) It has been contended by Bossert, Kölbing etc. that the English poet was not following a written text, but was merely working up in his own language the narrative of Thomas, as he recollected it from a previous reading or from having heard it read. For a contrary view, cp. Bédier's edition of Thomas's *Tristan*, II, 87f.

French romances in prose and not in verse. This is the case with the stanzaic *Morte Arthur* of the end of the fourteenth century — a poem of much naive charm, whose ultimate original is the great French prose romance of the early thirteenth century, called the *Mort Artu, (Mort Artus, Mort d'Arthur)*.[45] It is also the case with the Middle English poems that deal with the Holy Grail theme — namely the alliterative *Joseph of Arimathie* (Midland dialect about 1350) and Lovelich's *Holy Grail* (South or South Midland, about 1480), both based on the thirteenth century *Estoire del Saint Graal (Grand St. Graal)* — one of the great French prose romances of the Vulgate cycle. It is the case, also, with the *Arthour and Merlin* (end of thirteenth century) and the *Merlin* of Lovelich, the fifteenth century poet, both of which are derived from the Old French prose *Merlin* in the same cycle of the prose romances as the *Estoire del Saint Graal*. So too with the Scotch *Lancelot of the Laik* of the late fifteenth century, which merely paraphrases an episode of the famous *Lancelot del Lac* — the prose romance of the early thirteenth century. This is interesting as the latest in date of all the metrical romances composed in Great Britain.

It must be confessed that with the exception of the stanzaic *Morte Arthur,* none of the English romances in verse that are based on French romances in prose rise above mediocrity. Lovelich's works, especially, are monuments of tediousness.

But, besides the English Arthurian romances in verse which are based on French romances in prose, we have, in addition to *Sir Tristrem,* a number of others which are based on French romances in verse and which are markedly superior in literary quality to the former. First, the *Sir Perceval of Galles* which is, probably, a mere adaptation of Chrétien's *Perceval* [46]) — then the *Libeaus Desconus,* mentioned above, whose lost French original was closely akin to the *Li Biaus Descouneus* of Renaud de Beaujeu — the *Yvain and Gawain,* an adaptation of Chrétien's *Yvain* — *Sir Gawain and the Green Knight* (already mentioned), whose French original is also lost — the *Aunters of Arthur,* made up,

---

[45] Cp. Part III, below.
[46] Cp. Part II, below.

it seems, from various French sources, which is also probably true
of the *Avowing of Arthur,* preserved in the same MS. and apparently of the same date. All of the romances just enumerated were
composed in the North Midland or Northern districts of England
during the fourteenth century. The Scotch *Gologrus and Gawain,*
the story of which is taken from the continuation of Chrétien's
*Perceval,* belongs to the fifteenth century. Still further, five brief
romances, hardly more than ballads, concerning Gawain have been
printed by Sir Frederick Madden in his great edition of the romances[47] relating to that hero published by the Bannatyne Club,
London, 1839. If we add in conclusion a version of Marie de
France's *Lanval*[48] and the brief fragment called *Arthur* which
Dr. Furnivall published in the second issue of the Early English
Text Society,[49] we have completed the list of the Middle English
Arthurian romances. This last piece is a very condensed narrative
based on Geoffrey's *Historia.*

[47] *Sir Gawayne: a collection of Ancient Romance-Poems by
Scottish and English Authors relating to that celebrated Knight
of the Round Table, with Introduction, notes and a glossary.*
London, 1839.

For everything relating to these poems — sources etc. — cp.
G. L. Kittredge, *A Study of Gawain and the Green Knight* (Boston,
1914). They are entitled respectively, (1) *The Green Knight* (fifteenth
century), which is derived from the English romance, *Sir Gawain
and the Green Knight.* (2) *The Turk and Gowin* (fifteenth century). (3) *The Jeaste of Syr Gawayne* (fifteenth century). (4) *Syre
Gawene and the Carle of Carelyle* (fifteenth century). (5) *The
Weddynge of Syr Gawen and Dame Ragnell* (fifteenth century).
Part IV, below, I have discussed the use which Miss Weston makes
of these poems in her hypothesis of a primitive "Gawain-complex".

[48] Last edited by Rudolf Zimmermann at Königsberg in Preußen,
1900. For previous editions and literature of the poem, see this edition
or Miss A. H. Billings's *A. Guide to the Middle English Metrical
Romances,* pp. 144 ff. (New York, 1900). The author was Thomas
Chestre and he wrote in the fourteenth century — probably the first half.

[49] *Arthur, a short sketch of his life and history in English
verse of the first half of the fifteenth century, copied and edited
from the Marquis of Bath's MS.* By F. J. Furnivall. E. E. T. S.
Original Series, no 2. London 1864. It was composed about 1400
in the Southern dialect. The fragmentary poem (only 642 four-stressed
lines) is based on one of the *Bruts.*

## Chapter IV.

# Merlin.

It is only in the writings of Welshmen that we find any trace of a character corresponding to Merlin before the Arthurian romances. As has been said above more than once, literary records from mediaeval Brittany are practically non-existent and the Breton ballads about Marzin or Merlin which in the last century La Villemarqué published in his *Barzaz-Breiz* and *Myrhddin*, (having collected them, as he pretended, from oral tradition) are now universally regarded as forgeries.[1] Indeed, the lady from the neighborhood of Molaix, whom he cites as an authority for these ballads, has been pronounced by one critic to be probably a sister of the imaginary Mrs. Harris in Dickens's *Martin Chuzzlewit*. Furthermore, Merlin, like the other characters of Arthurian romance, does not, of course, appear in the literature of the Gaels. Now, with regard to the Welsh evidence: In the body of ancient Welsh poetry[2] there are eight poems which purport to be the compositions of a bard named *Myrddin*. This is evidently the same name as the *Merlinus* of Geoffrey of Monmouth — only as Gaston Paris has remarked,[3] Geoffrey probably shrank from Latinizing the Welsh name in the natural way as *Merdinus*, owing to the similarity to a French word of unpleasant associations which would have resulted, and so changed the *d* to an *l*. But the value of these poems as evidence of traditions concerning Merlin among the Welsh is seriously impaired by the doubt which attaches to their antiquity. The result of the most authoritative

---

[1] Cp. pp. 39 ff. and notes.

[2] Edited by W. F. Skene, *Four Ancient Books of Wales*, 2 vols. (Edinburgh, 1868).

[3] *Romania*, XII, 376 (1883).

examination of this question that has been made[4] is that all the Welsh poems in question were really composed later than Geoffrey of Monmouth, with the single exception of the *Dialogue of Merlin and Taliesin*,[5] which is either contemporary with Geoffrey of Monmouth or perhaps slightly earlier.[6] Moreover, all of them, except the *Dialogue*, betray the use of Geoffrey's *Vita Merlini*.[7] Nevertheless, these poems give evidence as to the existence in Welsh tradition of Merlin and the personages associated with him in the *Vita Merlini* — only the few concrete allusions they contain bearing on the history of Merlin seem derived from Geoffrey. Besides, after all, they merely show that Merlin was a bard like Taliesin, who certainly enjoyed greater fame among the ancient Welsh than Merlin ever did. The *Dialogue*, which, as we have seen, is the least open to suspicion of the Welsh poems gives us a conversation between Myrddin (Merlin) and Taliesin concerning

---

[4] By F. Lot, "Études sur Merlin", *Annales de Bretagne*, XV, 324 ff., 505 ff. (1900).

[5] Skene, I, 368 ff. (translation), II, 3 ff. (Welsh text).

[6] In *Y Cymmrodor*, XI, 48 (1892), E. Phillimore, one of the best Welsh authorities, speaks of the Welsh Merlin-poems "following" Geoffrey's *Vita Merlini* in making the hero go out of his mind, in consequence of the battle of Arderydd, so that he, too, evidently regards these poems as subsequent to Geoffrey. In the same article ("Additional Notes" to J. E. Lloyd's "Welsh Place-Names", *ibid.*, pp. 15 ff.) this scholar interprets *Myrddin* (the Welsh name for Merlin) as a mere eponymus "derived from the place-name *Caerfyrddin* (= modern Carmarthen), like *Efrog* (Peredur's father in the *Peredur*) from *Caer Efrog* (Modern English *York*) or *Lleon Gawr* from *Caerleon* (Modern English *Chester*). And again, pp. 47 f., he remarks that, in changing the narrative of Nennius (his source) and putting "the fatherless boy" (Geoffrey's Merlin) at Carmarthen, "Geoffrey had here in his mind's eye the connection of *Myrddin* with *Caerfyrddin*" — that, moreover, Geoffrey in the *Vita Merlini* makes Merlin king of Dyfed (his mother in the *Historia* was already daughter of a king of Dyfed), because in those days (down to 1132) Dyfed included Carmarthen.

It would seem, however, from Lot's study that, even if the name *Myrddin* is derived from *Caerfyrddin*, the derivation is older than Geoffrey. May not, indeed, the latter name be derived from the former?

[7] Cp. Lot, *op. cit.*, p. 515.

the battle of Arderydd in which Merlin expresses sadness at the slaughter. This battle, it may be remarked, was fought at Arthuret, near Carlisle, about the year 575, between Rhydderch ap Tudwal, the friend of St. Columba, and another Celtic chieftain of the North, Gwenddoleu ap Ceidio, the former being victorious.[8] The poem, however, is so meagre and its meaning so dark, that we merely gather from it that Merlin is a bard. At the end of the *Dialogue* we have the obscure words:

> Since I, Myrddin, am next after Taliessin,
> Let my prediction become common.

This is the only hint in the poem that Merlin has prophetic gifts — indeed, the only thing in works not demonstrably dependent on Geoffrey that suggests the possession of prophetic powers on the part of Merlin in all Welsh literature. But, apart from the doubtful antiquity even of the *Dialogue*, this would be a slender basis for supposing that the Welsh regarded Merlin as a prophet, especially as, notwithstanding the words just quoted, there is actually no prediction in the poem — a fact which excites the suspicion[9] that these words may have been a later addition.

If the poems which we have been considering throw little light on the subject of Merlin's place in Welsh tradition, it is even worse with the remaining Welsh records — the *Triads* and the *Mabinogion*. Two of the former mention Merlin — the first of them as one of the three chief bards of Britain, the second in connection with his marvellous disappearance. But these triads are late[10] and, hence, worthless for our purpose. The *Mabinogion* do not mention Merlin by name at all and the only connection whatever between the tales in this book and the traditions concerning Merlin is that in one of them, *Lludd and Llevelys*, there is a story of a combat between a white and a red dragon which figures in the narrative of Merlin and Vortigern's tower in Geof-

---

[8] Cp. J. E. Lloyd's *History of Wales*, I, 166.

[9] Cp. Lot, *op. cit.*, p. 535, note 2.

[10] Cp. E. Phillimore's observations on the subject in the Early English Text Society's edition of the Middle English *Merlin*, Part IV, p. XCVIII, note 3.

frey's *Historia*. This same story, to be sure, appears in Nennius
connected with another name.

The conclusion to be drawn from extant Welsh literature,
then, is, evidently, that Merlin was of relatively little importance
in Welsh tradition, and, if we depended merely on the mention that
the above records make of him, we should say that he was known
to that tradition simply as a bard — not as a magician or prophet.

It will simplify subsequent discussion, if we state at once the
conclusion to which we are forced by all the evidence — namely,
that Merlin owes his fortune in the history of fiction and popular
tradition to Geoffrey of Monmouth. He is virtually the creation
of Geoffrey. Let us take up now the history of this wondrous
being.

In the *Historia Brittonum* of Nennius (ch. 40—42)[11] we
have the following story concerning the tower which Vortigern
tried to build on Mount Hereri or Snowdon as a refuge from the
Saxons:

Workmen begin to lay the foundations of the building, but on
three successive nights the work done during the preceding day is
destroyed. Vortigern's wise men inform him that, before the tower
can be built, the ground must be sprinkled with the blood of a
child born without a father. The king at once sends out messengers
in search of such a child. When they arrive at the field of Elleti
in Gleguissing they hear a boy jeer at a comrade, because he has
never had a father, and the boy's mother confirms the truth of
the taunt and asserts that the child is, indeed, the son of no mortal
man. The messengers accordingly take him to Vortigern whom
the boy proceeds to question shrewdly, until the king admits why
he has been brought thither. Then the child orders the wise men
to declare what there is beneath the spot where Vortigern wishes
to build. When they say that they do not know, he bids them
dig into the ground where they will find a pond in which there
are two vases; in the vases is a folded tent and in the tent are
two sleeping dragons, one white and the other red. The men dig
and find that the boy's words are true. Suddenly the dragons

---

[11] See Mommsen's edition, pp. 181ff., *Monumenta Germaniae
Historica*, 1904.

begin a terrible combat with each other, in which the red dragon succeeds in routing the white one. The boy proceeds to explain to the king that the pool signifies the world, the tent Britain, the red dragon the British nation, the white dragon the Saxons. Vortigern, he adds, must depart from this place, but he himself to whom fate has allotted it will remain there. The king asks him his name, and he replies: "I am called Ambrosius."[12] The king next asks as to his origin and he replies that he is the son of a Roman consul. This is, of course, a flat contradiction of what was said at the beginning of the episode. Vortigern obediently assigns the site of the stronghold to Ambrosius with all the other provinces of Britain and himself departs elsewhere. Later Nennius tells us that, after the death of Vortigern, his son, Pascentius, received two provinces from Ambrosius, "who was the great king among the kings of Britain."

Miss L. A. Paton has justly observed[13] that we evidently have here a reminiscence of the barbarous "custom of offering a human being to the deity of a selected site as a foundation sacrifice". Whether, as she maintains, the two dragons were originally two supernatural shape-shifters who had assumed for the time being the form of dragons is, I believe, much less certain. The part which Ambrosius plays in this affair[14] seems borrowed from one of the numerous Talmudic legends concerning Solomon in which the wise king by a ruse captures the demon Aschmedai (or Asmodeus, as we are accustomed to call him) and makes him

---

[12] Nennius's Ambrosius is identical, of course, with the Ambrosius Aurelianus who, according to the historian Gildas, led the Britons against the Anglo-Saxon invaders after the withdrawal of the Roman legions. E. Phillimore remarks, *Y Cymmrodor*, XI, 48 f. (1892), that the identity is proved by the gloss which is found in all the MSS. of Nennius after the words "Ambrosius vocor", in this passage, viz., "id est Embreis Guletic". Now, Gwledig *(Guletic)*, which is equivalent to the Latin *Princeps* or *Imperator*, could indicate here no one save the historical chieftain named by Gildas.

[13]) In her article on this episode, "The Story of Vortigern's Tower — an Analysis", *Radcliffe College Monographs*, no. 15, pp. 14 ff. (1910).

[14] Cp. Miss Paton, *op. cit.*, p. 18, note 1.

tell how he can obtain possession of a certain wonderful creature who is necessary in the building of the Temple of Jerusalem.

Now this story of Nennius was used by Geoffrey of Monmouth (Book VI, ch. 17—19) with certain differences of which the most important are as follows: He calls the boy without a father Merlin as well as Ambrosius.[15] Moreover, the messengers take Merlin's mother, who is the daughter of a king of Demetia, to Vortigern with the lad, and she gives the king a full account of Merlin's birth, explaining that his father was an incubus.[16] Just after this story Geoffrey inserts the famous prophecies of Merlin, which, as a matter of fact, in large part, refer to recent political events of the author's own time. They make up the entire Seventh Book of his *Historia,* but had already been in circulation as a separate work.[17] The next book begins with a pro-

---

[15] Cp. Geoffrey, Book VI, ch. 19: Tunc ait Merlinus, qui et Ambrosius dicebatur". Similarly, VII, 3.

In his "Merlin and Ambrosius", Kittredge *Anniversary Papers,* pp. 119 ff., G. H. Maynadier explains (p. 125) Geoffrey's identification of Merlin with Ambrosius as follows: Nennius says, ch. 41, that Ambrosius was found in the region Gleguissing, which, even if it did not actually include the vale of the river Towy, was, in any event, near that stream. Now, Caermarthen, which is connected by name with Merlin (Myrddin) — see p. 130, note 6 above — lies on the Towy. Hence, "nothing would be more natural than for Geoffrey to combine the two men". — Apart, however, from our ignorance as to the extent of Gleguissing, the vague geographical connection here assumed seems unnecessary for the identification. The inclusion of a great magician in his work was suggested to Geoffrey by Nennius's Ambrosius and the designation, *Ambrosius Merlinus,* testifies to this historical connection between the two characters, but Geoffrey's enchanter was to have an altogether different scope from Nennius's — as a matter of fact, he was destined to prove one of the greatest creations of the mediaeval imagination — and so he calls him, after a brief period of hesitation, exclusively by the new name.

[16] This notion of the sexual commerce of incubi with mortals was common in the Middle Ages.

[17] On Geoffrey's so-called *Libellus Merlini* and the numerous political phrophecies which were modelled after it in the Middle Ages, see San Marte, *Die Sagen von Merlin,* pp. 32 ff., (Halle, 1853) and Rupert Taylor, *The Political Prophecy in England,* (New York, 1911),

phecy of Merlin concerning the death of Vortigern and, later on, tells of his exploit of moving the stones of Stonehenge — or Giants' Dance, as it is called — from Mount Killaraus in Ireland to their present site. In this affair, which was probably invented by Geoffrey, Merlin appears as hardly more than a marvellous engineer. He reappears, however, (ch. 15), as interpreting to Uther Pendragon, the father of Arthur, a portent which betokens the death of Aurelius Ambrosius — the Ambrosius Aurelianus of Gildas — whose gallant deeds constitute a large part of the narrative of this Eighth Book. Then follows (ch. 19—20) the last and most famous of Merlin's achievements related by Geoffrey — his transformation of Uther into the likeness of Gorlois, Duke of Cornwall, so that he might have access to Igerna, the wife of Gorlois — on which occasion he begets Arthur. It has often been maintained, and no doubt correctly, that this episode is merely an adaptation of the well-known story of the conception of Hercules — how Jupiter assumed the appearance of Amphitruo and in the latter's absence deceived Alcmena and begot the famous hero.

Looking back over the Merlin material in Geoffrey's *Historia,* which I have just summarized, it seems in the highest degree unlikely that any of it was derived from oral tradition. Nennius, classical legend, and his own fancy seem to account for the whole. Things are not so plain — at first blush, at any rate — when we come to the next important Merlin document — namely, the poem in Latin hexameters called the *Vita Merlini* — which is also commonly ascribed to Geoffrey of Monmouth. To be sure, the correctness of this ascription which is found at the end of the poem itself, has at various times been disputed,[18] but the fact that

in Columbia University Studies in English. Despite the title of the latter, it contains also, ch. 6, a discussion of the Galfridian type of prophecy in other countries than England.

There is, in addition, a thirteenth-century French (prose) work entitled *Les Prophécies de Merlin,* which, notwithstanding its title, is very different from the *Libellus Merlini.* On this later work cp. Part III, below.

[18] Cp. San Marte's *Die Sagen von Merlin,* pp. 273 ff. and various scholars cited by H. L. D. Ward, *Catalogue of Romances in the De-*

in the concluding lines of the poem the *Historia* is spoken of as
celebrated throughout the world is no reason for doubting the
authenticity of the ascription. Modesty was certainly not the
strong point of the writer who tried to palm off the *Historia* as
an authentic narrative. Moreover, the prophecy of Ganieda found
in this poem (11. 1474 ff.) relates to actual political events during
the years 1139—1144,[19] and 1148—9 has been established as its
date.[20] These facts support the view that the work is really
Geoffrey's. It is, indeed, singular that a poem by so famous an
author should exist in only one complete MS. (Vespasian E. IV,
of the British Museum), and that of the late thirteenth century
— yet this does not justify us in rejecting it as spurious.

The *Vita Merlini* is the most original of all the works concerning Merlin which the Middle Ages have left us, and parts of
it are genuinely poetical — so that it will be necessary to consider
for a moment this curious production, the action of which is supposed to fall after the translation of Arthur to Avalon. Following
is a condensed analysis of its contents:

Merlin was a king and a prophet who had already lived an
indefinite age, when a war breaks out between the princes of
Britain, Peredur, King of Venedotia (North Wales), being the
leader on one side, and Guennolous, King of Scotland, on the
other. Merlin and Rodarchus, King of Cumberland, were with
Peredur. The Scots are routed, but Merlin loses three brothers in
the battle. This misfortune plunges him into grief and madness
and he flies to the desert. There he becomes a wild man *(silvester homo)*, lives on fruits, and fills the Caledonian forest with
his lamentations. Rodarchus, however, who had married Ganieda,
Merlin's sister, tried to bring back the fugitive to his court. At

---

*partment of Manuscripts in the British Museum,* I, 278 ff.　So
far as I know, however, Brugger is the only living scholar who denies
the poem to Geoffrey. For his views cf. *Zs. f. frz. Spr. u. Litt.,*
XX[1], 105 (1897) and *ibid.,* XXX[1], 217, note (1906). For an answer
to the objections which have been raised to Geoffrey's authorship of
the *Vita Merlini,* cp. Ward, *loc. cit.*

[19] Cp. Ward, *op. cit.,* pp. 282 ff.

[20] Cp. Ward, pp. 285 f. and F. Lot, *Annales de Bretagne,* XV, 333.

last, this is effected by a messenger, who finds Merlin seated by a spring in the forest and watching the play of the wild animals. This man sings to a "cithara" the woes of Merlin's wife, Gwendoloena, on account of her absent husband. The music heals Merlin of his madness and he allows himself to be led back to the court of Rodarchus. But there his madness soon returns on him and he is eager to return to the oaks and high mountains of the forest. To prevent his escape, Rodarchus has him put in bonds. Merlin falls into a profound melancholy and does not utter a word. One day the queen was traversing the hall, when her husband took her by the hand and made her sit down; but, as he leant over to kiss her, he observed a leaf in her hair. He took it and threw it on the ground. Merlin burst into laughter at this. Everyone was astonished, but the sage refused to explain his singular merriment, unless he was set at liberty. Rodarchus had him unbound and Merlin explains that the leaf which the king had just removed from his wife's hair had fallen there shortly before as she was passing through the thicket for a rendezvous with her lover. The queen tries to discredit Merlin's power of divination by putting him to a test. She has the same child brought in three times in different costumes, so as to deceive the enchanter as to his identity, and Merlin each time predicts a different kind of death for him: he will fall from a high rock — he will die on a tree — he will be drowned. The queen is exultant over the success of her ruse, but, as a matter of fact, Merlin's prophecies all come true; for the child, when he grew up, whilst chasing a stag, fell from a high rock and was drowned in a stream that flowed at its base, but his feet caught in a tree and there he was suspended.

Merlin returns to the forest and gives permission to Gwendoloena to marry another man, but the bridegroom must beware of letting Merlin see him. One bright night the seer reads in the stars that his wife has taken him at his word and is about to marry. He assembles a great herd of wild deer and goats and mounts a stag. Driving the remaining animals before him, he goes to his wife's house and calls her out to see the wedding presents he has brought her. She naturally smiles at the spectacle,

but the bridegroom puts his head out of the window and laughs.
Filled with rage, Merlin tears off the antlers of the stag he is
riding, hurls them at his unlucky rival and kills him on the spot.
He then flees, but is stopped by a torrent, made prisoner, and
brought back before his sister in chains. He falls into a sullen
dejection and refuses food. To distract him, his brother-in-law
has him taken out for a walk through the town, but at the palace
gate they meet a porter miserably clad, asking alms of the passers-
by. Merlin bursts out laughing and acts similarly when, a little
further on, in the market-place, he sees a young man buying shoes
and pieces of leather to repair them with. In both cases Merlin
refused to explain his laughter, unless his freedom was to be the
reward. Rodarchus at last consents, and Merlin explains that the
beggar had at that very time a hidden treasure under his feet
and the young man was drowned immediately after making his
purchases.

The enchanter returns again to the wilderness. His sister
wishes to follow him, but he prevents her — only, later on, he permits her to visit him and bring him food in the cold season.
He gets her, moreover, to build him a house in the forest with
70 doors and 70 windows, so that he can sit within and predict
the future by observation of the heavens. His prophecies are
taken down by 140 scribes. Here he foretells most of the calamities
which are to befall the Britons — including the death of Rodarchus,
after which event Ganieda resolves to fly from the world and live
with her brother.

Taliesin joins Merlin and gives a long description (11. 737 ff.)
of the universe,[21] winding up with the famous account (11. 908 ff.)
of the Happy Isle, where Morgan lives with her eight sisters.[22]

---

[21] The immediate source of this description, as of several other
similar descriptions (11. 827 ff., 859 ff., 1179 ff,, 1298 ff.), in the *Vita
Merlini,* is the *Etymologiae* of Isidore of Seville, who, in turn, derived
his information from Pliny's *Historia Naturalis.* Cp. F. Lot, *Romania,* XLV, 1 ff. (1918—1919).

[22] "Insula pomorum quae Fortunata vocatur,
Ex re nomen habet, quia per se singula profert:
Non opus est illi sulcantibus arva colonis;
Omnis abest cultus nisi quem natura ministrat:

Thither Taliesin in a boat, steered by Barinthus,[23] has taken Arthur

---

Ultro foecundas segetes producit et uvas,
Nataque poma suis praetonso germine silvis;
Omnia gignit humus vice graminis ultro redundans.
Annis centenis aut ultra vivitur illic,
Illic iura novem geniali lege sorores
Dant his qui veniunt nostris ex partibus ad se:
Quarum quae prior est fit doctior arte medendi,
Exceditque suas forma praestante sorores;
Morgen ei nomen, didicitque quid utilitatis
Gramina cuncta ferant, ut languida corpora curet;
Ars quoque nota sibi qua scit mutare figuram,
Et resecare novis quasi Daedalus aera pennis;
Cum vult est Bristi, Carnoti, sive Papiae
Cum vult in nostris ex aere labitur horis.
Hancque mathematicam dicunt didicisse sorores,
Moronoe, Mazoe, Gliten, Glitonea, Gliton,
Tironoe, Thiten, cithara notissima Thiten.
Illuc, post bellum Camblani, vulnere laesum
Duximus Arcturum, nos conducente Barintho,
Aequora cui fuerant et coeli sydera nota.
Hoc rectore ratis, cum principe venimus illuc,
Et nos quo decuit Morgen suscepit honore,
Inque suis talamis posuit super aurea regem
Strata [MS. has *stulta*] manuque sibi detexit vulnus honesta.
Inspexitque diu; tandemque redire salutem
Posse sibi dixit, si secum tempore longo
Esset, et ipsius vellet medicamine fungi.
Gaudentes igitur regem commisimus illi,
Et dedimus ventis redeundo vela secundis."

Only in this passage is Morgan represented as one of the nine sisters. For a plausible explanation of the names of these sisters see L. A. Paton's *Fairy Mythology,* p. 44, note 2. There is a similar description in the *Gesta Regum Britanniae* — a thirteenth century adaptation in verse of Geoffrey's *Historia.* The island, however, is unnamed and the healer is merely called *regia virgo.* For the text of this passage and a discussion of the same see Bruce, *Mort Artu,* p. 300.

[23] In the *Revue Celtique,* XXII, 339ff. (1901), A. C. L. Brown has pointed out that this character is really a seagod, who, like Manannan in the Welsh tales, conducted voyagers to the Celtic Otherworld. We have a similar Christian adaptation of this idea in the *Navigatio Brendani.*

after the battle with Mordred, in the hope that the fay might be able to bring him back to life.

Merlin then laments over the misfortunes which the Saxons are destined to inflict on the Britons; but no one now alive will see that time. Conan of Brittany and Cadwallader, however, will expel the invaders.

During the dialogue of the two friends an attendant announces that a fountain of pure water has sprung up in the valley. Merlin drinks of it, to quench his thirst, but it also restores him to reason. He thanks the creator, and Taliesin takes occasion (11. 1179 ff.) to describe the celebrated fountains of the world.

At the end of this conversation Merlin is again plunged into sadness by the sight of a madman who comes up and whom he recognizes as a friend of his youth. The madman had been a noble and worthy knight. He and some of his companions had gone hunting with Merlin. They came upon a spring with fruits lying about them. Merlin picked them up and distributed them so generously among his friends that there was not one left for himself. But the men who ate them were deprived of reason and ran away like wolves. The poisoned fruit had really been intended for Merlin by a quondam mistress of his whom he had abandoned (11. 1422 ff.). They take the poor madman now, compel him to drink of the spring, and he recovers his reason. He announces his purpose of remaining in the wilderness with Merlin. Taliesin sends home the kings who had assembled to hear Merlin's prophecies and the enchanter is left with his two friends and his sister. The latter, Ganieda, is, in her turn, seized with the prophetic gift and declares a number of marvels. With her speech the poem ends — only there is an epilogue in which Geoffrey bids the Britons weave a crown for him.

On first reading this strange narrative concerning the great enchanter of Celtic legend, as we are accustomed to call him, one is naturally inclined to take for granted that the materials on which it is based are Celtic — but a closer analysis of its elements reveals the fact that the sources are only to a very limited degree Celtic, in any proper sense, and that the Orient has supplied a far larger proportion of the *motifs*.[24] The longest step made in the analysis of the Merlin legend we owe to the late H. L. D. Ward, who published[25] in 1893 the so-called Lailoken fragments preserved in the British Museum MS., Titus A. XIX. Here we have the most important single source for the *Vita Merlini*. To be sure, Ward does not seem to have been fully aware of the importance of his own discovery.

There are two fragments in the manuscript just named. Both relate to a madman named Lailoken, but the second is later than the first, and its author seems to have been familiar with the first fragment. In the first fragment at one point Merlin is identified with Lailoken, but this sentence, as Ward has observed, is the addition of a later hand under the influence of Geoffrey. In the first of these fragments Lailoken gives the triple prediction of the death of one person (only the person is himself). In the second we have the incident of the leaf which betrays the queen's adultery. The fragments give these narratives in a more consistent and primitive form than the *Vita Merlini*, and there can be no question that Geoffrey made use of these Lailoken stories and possibly of others concerning the same personage that have not survived. The whole conception of Merlin in the Latin poem is borrowed from this earlier madman and prophet, and the one ranges the Caledonian forest, because the other had done so before him. In the words of Phillimore,[26] the eminent Welsh scholar, Merlin has simply stepped into the shoes of Lailoken.

---

[24] This has been proved by Ward and Lot in the discussions which I have already cited above.

[25] In "Lailoken or Merlin Silvester", *Romania*, XXII, 504 ff. (1893).

[26] Cp. *Y Cymmrodor*, XI, 45 f. (1892). He observes, also, (p. 48): "With Geoffrey the identification of Merlin and Lailoken was complete; but with the later Scottish writers it was still a matter of doubt." Phillimore says, *loc. cit.*, that Lailoken (Lailocen) "is mentioned in ch. XLV of Jocelyn of Furness' *Life of St. Kentigern* as Laloecen or Laloicen, a fool at the court of Rhydderch Hael, who possessed the gift of prophecy; in the Welsh Merlin poems this word (there used as a name or epithet of Merlin) is made into Llalogan, which has been explained as meaning 'twin-brother'; but there is plenty of evidence that it was a personal name." He then cites (p. 48) Lalocan in the Cartulaire de Redon, 125 (already cited by Ward) and the simpler form, Lalócc, as a woman's name, in Whitley Stokes' *Tripartite Life of St. Patrick*, pp. 82, 104, 317.

According to the first fragment of the Cottonian MS., Lailoken had an evil disposition and, like the Irish Bricriu, was constantly stirring up discord among his compatriots. As he was one day watching a battle, however, (localized, it would seem, in the neighborhood of Carlisle) which was due to his malicious efforts, a voice from heaven reproaches him with the responsibility and condemns him henceforth to a life among the beasts. He also saw a supernatural light and hosts of angels casting their lances at him. At this sight he loses his reason and flies to the desert. But he would often come to a rock in sight of Glasgow and utter predictions which people took down in writing. One day whilst Saint Kentigern, the famous Scottish saint, is celebrating mass, Lailoken disturbs the ceremony by howling and demanding communion. Kentigern sends a messenger to bid him be quiet — but without success. The messenger goes three times and each time the madman predicts that he is about to die — stating, however, in each instance a different mode of death. He adds also a prediction of the impending death of three eminent personages in Britain. After this he runs away, but the same day the triple prediction of his own death is fulfilled.

In the second fragment Lailoken is captured by king Meldred and kept in chains at Dunmeller. He will not gratify his captors, however, by uttering prophecies — on the contrary, for three days he will neither eat nor speak. Then comees the incident of the leaf, when, like Merlin, he bursts out laughing and will only explain his laughter on being promised his liberty. At the same time he gives directions as to his burial, for in a few days he is to die the triple death. On being released, he discloses the queen's adultery. She tries to discredit the prophet by pointing out the impossibility of the triple death. The king, however, will not believe her. On the other hand, the queen, later on, out of revenge, compasses the death of Lailoken, and he is buried, as he had requested, at the junction of the Pausayl with the Tweed.

The Lailoken legend, then, is the most important source for the *Vita Merlini*, but it is doubtful how far this legend itself represents oral tradition among the Celts. The *motif* of the prophecy of a triple death is found in the East — so, too, the revelation of adultery by the scornful laughter of a captive gifted with supernatural knowledge.[27] The same is true of the *motif* of the boy whose ignorance of his impending fate, when making provision for the repair of his shoes, causes the prophet to laugh. Parts of the remainder, like Ganieda's prophecy, are, no doubt, mere inventions of Geoffrey,[28] whilst the apples that cause madness and the wild story of Merlin's appearing at his wife's marriage riding a stag with whose antlers he slays the bridegroom are, in all probability, both drawn from oral tradition. The latter has every mark of a folk-tale, but there is no reason to suppose that it was originally told either of Merlin or Lailoken, and Geoffrey was, no doubt, the first to connect it with the former.

Before leaving the *Vita Merlini*, it should be remarked that Giraldus Cambrensis distinguishes two Merlins[29] — Merlin Ambrosius and Merlin Silvester — and this fictitious distinction has descended to our own time and confused some modern students of the Arthurian romances. But there is no reason whatever for such a distinction;[30] the Merlin of the *Historia* and the Merlin of the *Vita Merlini* differ in some respects, but, as we have seen, both are substantially the creations of Geoffrey and neither have any root in popular tradition. He himself identifies them by a specific reference in the *Vita Merlini* (11. 681ff.).

During the forty years or so that followed upon the composition of Geoffrey's Latin poem the fame of Merlin was spread far and wide, not only by Geoffrey's own writings, but by deri-

---

[27] Compare the Indian tales cited in another connection by Miss Paton, PMLA, XXII, 241 ff. (1907).

[28] Miss Paton, in her article, "Merlin, and Ganieda", MLN for June, 1903, has tried to prove that in the original form of the story Ganieda must have been the enchanter's fairy-mistress, not his sister. But this theory is a pure exercise of fancy, for there is no documentary evidence whatever to support it. Cp. this scholar's similar theory in regard to the original relations of Arthur and Morgan le Fay, in her *Fairy Mythology*, pp. 29, 33.

[29] Cp. *Itinerarium Kambriae*, Book II, ch. 8.

[30] This has been made clear by F. Lot, *Annales de Bretagne*, XV, pp. 333 ff.

vatives from those writings — especially, by extensions of Merlin's *Prophecies* and by paraphrases of the *Historia* in the verse
and prose chronicles. It was not until the appearance of the *Merlin*
of Robert de Boron, however, that the stories that centre about
the character received any material development. This poem —
which, for the most part, survives only in a prose version — falls
probably in the last fifteen years of the twelfth century. As
we shall see more fully later on, it constitutes the second member
of an intended series of poems and follows, in the main, the account of Merlin given by Geoffrey, whom Robert, however, probably knew only through Wace.[31] The most striking thing in
the poem — the story of Merlin's conception — is based on Geoffrey, but the original story is happily combined with a *motif* drawn
from popular notions concerning Anti-Christ in the Middle Ages.
We find here again some of the *motifs* of the *Vita Merlini* —
which reached the French poet, however, no doubt, through indirect
channels — viz., the triple prediction, the incident of the man
about to die who is so careful in regard to his future footwear.
Some variations in the account of Arthur's conception, as compared with Geoffrey and Wace, may be due to the lost chronicle
of a certain Martin of Rochester, which appears to have covered
these events.[32] In the account of Arthur's birth and childhood,
however, Robert makes a radical departure from his sources in
order to increase the importance of his hero, Merlin. In Geoffrey
(Book VIII, ch. 20), immediately after Uther Pendragon had be-

---

[31] In his Introduction to the *Huth-Merlin,* pp. X ff., G. Paris
has established, in essentials, the sources of Robert's *Merlin.* Note,
besides, that the incident of the man who so carefully provides himself
with foot-gear, although, as a matter of fact, in a few minutes he is
destined to die, occurs in Robert (*Huth-Merlin,* I, p. 48 f.), as well
as in the *Vita Merlini,* 11. 495 ff. — so, doubtless, the latter should,
also, be reckoned among Robert's sources. Cp. Lot, *Annales de Bretagne,* XV, 336, note 1.

[32] According to MS. 749, fol. 32 (Bibl. Nat.), as quoted by
P. Paris, RTR, II, 36, note, Robert used a chronicle by this person,
and some scholars, as we have seen, — e. g., Brugger, *Zs. f. frz.
Spr. u. Lit.,* XXX¹, 182 ff. (1906) — accept the statement as authentic.
With regard to this Martin cp. p. 29, note 59, above.

gotten Arthur upon Igerna, having assumed the form of her husband, Gorlois, through Merlin's magic art, Gorlois himself is killed
and Uther marries his widow. Thus when Arthur is born, there
is no scandal concerning his birth, only Uther and Merlin being
in the secret of his conception. But Robert puts the marriage
two months after the conception, so, to obviate scandal, Merlin
has the boy turned over to him, as soon as it is born, and entrusts
it to a good man named Antor (Auctor)[33] who does not know
the child's rank and whose wife gives it suck. Fifteen years afterwards Uther dies and Britain is without a king. The kingdom
is to go to the man who can draw a sword from a certain marvellous anvil. Arthur alone proves equal to the task.[34] The
barons murmur at the success of a person of apparently low rank,
but he soon convinces them that he possesses royal qualities, and
he is first knighted and then crowned king at the Feast of Pentecost. Here Robert's poem ends.

Finally, we should note that, in a passage[35] which occurs
before the account of Arthur's conception, Robert connects the
poem with an unnamed knight who is destined to achieve the adventures of the Grail.[36]    Merlin relates here the story of the

[33] This is, probably, a mere corruption of *Arthur*. Gawain and
Helyas (the Swan-Knight) were, also, named after their foster-fathers.
Cp. Bruce, *Mort Artu,* p. 288.

[34] This sword *motif* is found, also, in the legends of Theseus
and Sigmund. Cp. Bruce, *op. cit.,* pp. 297 f.

[35] Sommer, II, 53 ff.

[36] Scholars (e. g., G. Paris, *Huth-Merlin,* I, p. XVII) have been
accustomed to assume that this unnamed knight was Perceval. This,
is, however, by no means, certain, although I have no doubt that Robert
knew Chrétien's *Perceval*. The passage runs in the Huth MS. (cp.
*Huth-Merlin,* I, 98) as follows: "Tant te puis jou [i. e., Merlin, who
is speaking to Uther Pendragon] bien dire qu'il ne sera pas emplis
en ton tans. Et cil qui l'emplira naistera de celui qui engendrer
[Paris's emendation for MS. *emplir*] le doit. Et n'a point encore de
feme prise ne ne set riens qu'i[l] le doie engenrer. Et couverra
que cil qui emplir le doit acomplisse chelui [lieu] avant ou li vaissiaus
del graal siet, car cil qui le gardent ne le virent onques acomplir;
ne che ne sera jamais en ton tans, ains averra au tans le roi qui
apries toi verra."
In the MS followed by Sommer (II, 56) the second sentence in

two holy tables of Jesus and Joseph of Arimathea — the table of our Lord's last supper and the table which Joseph instituted in memory of our Lord's table — and he induces Uther to institute a third table at which there is to be a vacant seat as at the former tables. Merlin prophesies that this seat will only be filled in the reign of Uther's son and by a knight who will put an end to the adventure of the Grail. This idea, like most of Robert's inventions, had a great success with the prose romancers.

Robert de Boron's poems have no striking merit — they are far inferior to those of Chrétien de Troyes — but in the *genre* of the prose-romances their influence is of capital importance. He is, above all, responsible for three innovations in Arthurian romance: [37] he gave it both a religious and a pseudo-historical coloring and he cast his compositions in a cyclic form. His *Merlin*, with which we are now more especially concerned, was turned into prose, and this prose rendering, as we have seen, forms the first section of the various prose *Merlins* which were composed in the first half of the thirteenth century. These romances, accordingly, begin with Robert's story of Merlin's conception, whose elements we have indicated above. The devils hold council as to how they shall counteract the work of Christ. They agree that

---

the passage just quoted is represented by: "& cil qui l'acomplira nest encore mie engendres", whilst there is nothing at all corresponding to the third sentence.

If the reading of the Huth MS. is correct, the allusion certainly would not fit with anything that we learn about Perceval's father in Chrétien's poem. On the other hand, it seems to correspond rather with the allusion to the future heir of Alein (Hebron's son) in Robert's *Joseph*, 1. 3467:

"Et ques oirs de li peut issir",

where there is no hint that Perceval is intended. In any event, even if the unnamed knight in the passage under consideration is to be accepted as Perceval, to judge by Robert's extant works, he would have been a very different character from Chrétien's and his story would have differed accordingly. On this subject, see, still further, Part IV, below.

[37] This has been pointed out by Brugger, *Zs. f. frz. Spr. u. Litt.*, XXIX[1], 75 ff. (1905).

this can only be done by a man who is born of a virgin and one
of the devils undertakes to engender such a person. The narrative
of how this enterprise is executed is weird in the extreme and has
a real tragic force, but, fortunately, the innocence of the victim
defeats the object of the fiends and the child who is thus begotten
inherits his father's supernatural powers, but not his wickedness.
We have already seen how this being was destined to watch over
Arthur's infancy and childhood up to the coronation of the great
king with which Robert de Boron's poem ends. In the several
continuations of Robert's *Merlin*, the enchanter appears again from
time to time as a *deus ex machina*, but, after all, the Merlin material in these huge continuations — the Vulgate continuation,
for example, is more than four times the length of the de Boron
section — constitutes only a small portion of the whole romance.
Take, for instance, the continuation, just named, which is the
oldest of the three extant continuations. It is really, as we shall
see, a pseudo-history of Arthur's reign down to the appearance
of Lancelot on the scene — Arthur's wars with his rebellious
barons and with the Saxons, his marriage with Guinevere, and
what not. Most of this narrative is a patch-work of *motifs* derived from Wace or from the lost expanded version of that writer's
*Brut* or again from romances like the *Meraugis de Portlesguez*.
Only occasionally do we have a bit of genuine Celtic tradition
as in Arthur's fight with the Capalu, a monster-cat.[38] As far
as Merlin is concerned, there is no reason to believe that any of
the new incidents connected with his name in the Vulgate continuation (or *Livre d'Artus*, as it is also called) are of Celtic
origin.

The most distinctive of these are: 1. the Grisandole episode.
2. The episode of Merlin and Viviane, which ends in *l'enserrement
Merlin*, as the Old French romance calls it: he succumbs to Vi-

---

[38] See Sommer, II, 442 ff. Freymond (cp. p. 41, note 9, above),
in a masterly monograph, *Artus' Kampf mit dem Katzenungestüm*
(in the *Festgabe für G. Gröber,* Halle, 1899), has shown that the
Capalu is the Cath Paluc of Welsh saga, although in Welsh the creature
is not at all connected with Arthur.

viane's spell and is imprisoned forever in the forest of Brocé-liande.[39]

First, as to the Grisandole episode,[40] it is briefly as follows: Julius Caesar, emperor of Rome, is troubled by an incomprehensible dream. Merlin knows of it, assumes the form of a stag, comes to Caesar's palace, followed by a multitude of people, and tells him that only the wild man of the woods can interpret his dream. The enchanter then opens the palace gates by magic and vanishes. The emperor promises his daughter's hand as a reward for the capture of the wild man or the stag. Many knights go on the quest, but all later abandon it, save Grisandole, who is really a princess disguised as a man. The stag appears to Grisandole and tells how the wild man may be caught. She is to spread food for him in the forest as a snare. She does this, and when the creature, after gorging himself, lies down to sleep, she and her men capture him and take him back to court. We have now the *motif* of the sudden bursts of laughter, like those of Merlin in the *Vita Merlini*. There is no need of relating the three incidents — all significant, however, of the wild man's powers of divination. In the end he explains his laughter in each case, as Merlin does in the Latin poem. The main thing is that, on reaching the palace, he interprets Caesar's dream as signifying that the twelve ladies-in-honor to the queen are really twelve youths in disguise with whom she is leading an adulterous life. He further explains that he had laughed on looking at Grisandole, because a woman by her craft had taken him prisoner when no man could capture him. Grisandole's sex is thus revealed. As a result of it all, the queen and her paramours are burned, Grisandole marries the emperor and her brother the emperor's daughter.

The wild man refuses to reveal who the great stag is or his own name and leaves the hall abruptly, writing an inscription in Hebrew on one of the door-posts, as he passes out. Some time afterwards a messenger from Greece interprets the inscription, which explains that the wild man and the stag are one and the

---

[39] For this latter episode see Sommer, II, 208 ff., 280, 421.
[40] Cp. Sommer, II, 282 ff.

same being, named Merlin, Arthur's counsellor. Instantly thereafter the letters vanish.

The main *motifs* of the above episode are found combined,
already in a number of stories current both in Europe and the East
— that is to say, the story of the disguised girl who captures the
wild man or satyr, as he is sometimes called, this wild man being
endowed with the gift of divination by which he reveals his captor's sex and a queen's infidelity to her husband. We even have
in these tales the sudden outbursts of laughter.[41]   The stories
of Solomon and Aschmedai (Asmodeus), as we have seen, had
already furnished *motifs* to the *Vita Merlini*, and in the above
episode, no doubt, we have these same stories drawn on; for in
the Hebrew legend of Solomon Asmodeus plays exactly the same
rôle as the wild man does here. As regards Merlin's assumption
of the form of a stag, this seems a sort of confused recollection
of the passage in the *Vita Merlini*, where Merlin rides to the
palace on a stag. This preface of the Grisandole episode was
evidently introduced merely to connect with Merlin the piquant
tale of the disguised maiden, the faithless queen, and the marvellous wild man of the woods; but the connection is, after all,
of the most awkward kind.

The Grisandole episode, then, is not Celtic in origin. The
same thing is true of the story of Merlin and Viviane, immortalized

---

[41] In her paper on this episode, "The Story of Grisandole",
PMLA, XXII, 234 ff. (1907), Miss L. A. Paton tries to show that we
have here again the hard-worked fairy-mistress theme (see p. 256) in
disguise (Grisandole was originally a fairy and Merlin her lover) and
that the story is drawn from oral Celtic tradition. For my own part,
as I have already intimated, I am skeptical on principle as to virtually
every story of any importance in mediaeval romance being a variant
of the fairy-mistress theme. But, besides, as Miss Paton herself acknowledges, some features of the tale — to my mind the most essential —
are indisputably of Oriental origin — for example, the capture of the
laughing wild man who is compelled to exercise his powers of divination. Why not take this wide-spread story at its face value, instead
of reading into it the worn out fairy mistress *motif?* This explains
everything in the episode, except Merlin's part in it, and that is plainly
a clumsy addition, as anyone might have guessed, even if a comparison
with the cognate tales did not prove it.

by Tennyson, and here the case is even plainer than in the episode just examined. It was pointed out by Gaston Paris,[42] that the essential conception of this famous story — the only really pretty one in the whole *Merlin* continuation,[43] is first found in the prose *Lancelot*.[44] There Merlin betrays the magic spell to Viviane or Niniane (the MSS. vary as to the form of the name),[45] on her promising him her love, but, after obtaining the secret, she uses her magic power to make him believe that he has enjoyed her favours, though, in reality, he has not. At last she shuts him up forever in a cave in the forest of Darnantes. Viviane in this passage is identified with Lancelot's foster-mother, the Lady of the Lake. This story of Merlin and Viviane is, probably, an early interpolation in the *Lancelot*,[46] but, in any event, it is certainly the original of the more fully developed episode in the prose *Merlin*. Furthermore, it is unquestionable that, contrary to former views on the subject, the conception here involved was first attached to Merlin by the author of the above-mentioned passage in the prose *Lancelot* and has nothing Celtic about it; for, obviously, the Merlin-Viviane incident is merely a new adaptation of the old fabliau *motif* of the wise man deceived by a woman, which is ultimately of Oriental origin.[47] Aristotle,

---

[42] Cp. *Huth-Merlin*, I, p. XLVI.

[43] Cp. Brugger, *Zs. f. frz. Spr. u. Litt.*, XXXIII [1], 149 (1908).

[44] Sommer, III, 19 ff.

[45] The MSS. show still other variants. Cp. Sommer's *Index* to his *Vulgate Version* under *Viviane*. This is, most probably, the correct form of the name. It would be, then, the feminine, corresponding to the masculine *Vivian (Vivien)*, so well-known from the *chansons de geste*. Names, however, are subject to such corruption in mediaeval MSS. that, after all, *Diane (Diana)* may be the true etymon of *Viviane*. In her *Fairy Mythology*, ch. 4, Miss Paton treats at length Viviane's character, as well as her name, and concludes that both are Celtic. The episodes in the *Huth-Merlin*, etc., however, which she discusses, in reality, are all of purely literary manufacture. We shall see in our chapters on the prose romances that this was true, in general, of these works.

[46] In the *Zs. f. frz. Spr. u. Litt.*, XXX [1], 175 ff. (1906), Brugger seems to me to have proved this.

[47] A. Jeanroy was the first to point this out in his review of Miss Paton's *Fairy Mythology*. Cp. *Romania*, XXXIV, 120 (1905).

Hippocrates and Virgil, as we have seen above, figure successively in these tales as the butt of feminine deceit. Merlin's turn was sure to come. That this is the true derivation of the Merlin-Viviane story is so evident that no further argument on the subject is required. Even the detail noted in the *Lancelot* passage of the magical illusion under which Merlin labors as to his enjoyment of his lady's favors is found in the Solomon and Marcolf legend and had already been employed by Chrétien in *Cliges*, as was observed above. It is a noteworthy mediaeval feature of the Vulgate *Merlin* that Viviane was only twelve years old when Merlin fell in love with her. The author of the *Merlin* of. the so-called Robert de Boron prose cycle, best represented in the somewhat shortened form of the *Huth-Merlin*, took over this episode from the Vulgate romance and from his work [48]) it passed into Malory [49] and thence into Tennyson's *Idylls of the King*.[50] This episode and a general reputation for magic and prophetic powers are all that can be still called vital in the stories concerning Merlin which are found in the books that we have been passing in review.

---

Brugger had, independently, arrived at the same interpretation. Cp. his elaborate argument in *Zs. f. frz. Spr. u. Litt.*, XXX [1], 117 ff. (1906).

[48] II, 191 ff., in the edition of G. Paris and J. Ulrich.

[49] Book IV, ch. 1.

[50] *Merlin and Vivien.*

# Chapter V.

# Tristan.

In one important respect the study of the story of Tristan is easier than is the case with that of Lancelot: there is substantial agreement among authorities on the subject that all the mediaeval romances and shorter poems concerning this hero go back to a lost French romance[1] of a considerably earlier date

---

[1] Owing to its archaic character and, the (in many respects) rude civilization which it depicted Bédier, II, 314, dates this lost romance back "jusq' aux premiers temps de la conquête de l'Angleterre par les Normands", which must mean, at the latest, the early years of the twelfth century. Golther, p. 73, however, objects that the introduction of Arthur and his knights proves that it must have been written after Geoffrey's *Historia,* which dates from about 1136, had made these characters familiar figures — more specifically, between 1140 and 1150. Indeed, Golther, p. 34, was inclined to believe that the adultery of a nephew with his uncle's wife in this primitive *Tristan* was imitated from the similar relations of Mordred, Arthur, and Guinevere in Geoffrey's work, as Muret, *Romania,* XVI, 322 (1887) had already suggested. Miss Schoepperle, p. 183, dates the lost romance "very shortly" before the extant redactions, none of which, according to her, antedate the last decades of the twelfth century.

Bédier, II, 154f., accepts 1154 as the date of Bernart de Ventadour's lyric which contains the earliest allusion to Tristan and Iseult, and hence as the *terminus ad quem* of the primitive *Tristan,* but Miss Schoepperle, pp. 112ff., has shown that the true date of composition of this lyric is wholly uncertain, and, consequently, that it cannot be used for dating the lost archetype of our Tristan poems. Her own late dating of this archetype (pp. 120ff.) is based on the observation that it contained *motifs* that did not become current until the latter half of the twelfth century: 1. A girl who eludes an importunate lover (Kaherdin-Camille episode), imitated, according to Miss Schoepperle, from the *pastourelles;* 2. Two lovers deceive a jealous husband, despite all his precautions (Kaherdin-Gargeolain), imitated from

than any on the subject that is now in existence. The close relation of the incidents in the various extant versions of the story,
despite individual divergencies, was explained by scholars of the
last generation as due to the fact that the writers all drew from the
same body of lays or prose tales which were supposed to be current
orally,[2] but the conviction gradually forced itself on the minds
the *chansons de mal mariée.* 3. Notions that are rooted in the *amour
courtois* (cp., already, Muret, *Romania,* XVI, 360), such as the extravagant tests of humiliation to which a lady puts her lover and the
idea that a lover must do anything, if appealed to in the name of his
lady-love. 4. The stereotyped characters of Arthur, Kay and Gawain,
which show the influence of the Arthurian romances. In Eilhart ll. 5047ff.
especially, I may add, show unmistakably this influence. They describe
as accurately as possible the plan of the regular Arthurian romances.

F. Lot's criticism (*Romania,* XLIII, 128f.) of these points has
invalidated, I think, so late a dating of the primitive *Tristan* as Miss
Schoepperle's (which, besides, would be impossible, if Thomas' poem
were written about 1170), but it seems to me that the evidence, especially under the above heading, is sufficient to prove that this lost
archetype was not earlier than the romances of antiquity (1155—1165).
G. Huet, *Moyen Age,* 2e. série, XVIII, 380ff. (1914), has added
Iseult's love-monologue (Eilhart, 2398ff.) to Miss Schoepperle's illustrations of the *amour courtois.* The matter is not susceptible of
determination, but it seems most likely that ideas of the *amour courtois* were in the archetype, since they are found in all the extant
versions. The same thing applies to the Arthurian connections of these
versions. To be sure, in the case of Thomas, this connection is very
slender, consisting entirely of Arthur's encounters with two giants
(Bédier, I, 290ff., 307), which really stand outside of the Tristan
adventures and may very well have been borrowed directly from Geoffrey's *Historia,* Book X, ch. 3 or Wace's *Brut,* ll. 11634ff. In
Béroul, ll, 3706ff. *et passim,* and Eilhart, ll. 5231ff., Arthurian
characters are more intimately connected with the narrative, and Lot,
*op. cit.,* pp. 131f., argues that the episode in Eilhart was expressly
introduced by the author for the purpose of imparting novelty to the
story. This, of course, is possible.

In his "Tristan bei Cercamon ?", *Zs. f. rom. Ph.,* XLI, 219ff.
(1921), C. Appel, detects an allusion to Tristan in a poem of this
Provençal poet. He assigns the poem to the period, 1150—1160,
and contends that this is the earliest extant allusion to Tristan. The
evidence, however, is too uncertain.

[2] So R. Heinzel, *Zs. f. d. A.* XIV, 272ff. (1869), W. Golther,
*Die Sage von Tristan und Isolde,* pp. 30ff. *et passim* (Munich 1887).

of students of the *Tristan* romances that the resemblances in
question were really due to a common original — a definite romance, now lost.[3] This solution of the problem was given scientific

F. Novati, *Studj di filologia romanza*, II, 390 (1887), G. Paris,
*Manuel*, pp. 99 ff. (1888). For historical surveys of *Tristan* studies,
cp. Bédier, II, 168 ff. and Golther, 1 ff.

[3]) In his review of Röttiger's Program in *Romania*, XXVII, 608ff.
(1898), E. Muret makes Chrétien's lost poem and Thomas the sources
(one or the other) of all extant Tristan versions. E. Brugger, *Zs. f.
frz. Spr. u. Litt.* XX, 134, note (1898) suggested a single source
(undefined). Golther, however, *ibid.* XXII[1], 23 (1900), was the first
to work out a definite scheme, based substantially on the hypothesis
of a single source (Chrétien). In his later work Golther gives up
Chrétien as the author of the *Ur-Tristan.*

In the *Journal des Savants* for 1902, p. 301, note 2, G. Paris
expressed the belief that all French Tristan poems go back to a lost
English poem, itself incomplete. In that case, the story of Tristan
and Iseult would have passed from the Cornish (or Welsh) to the
English and from the English to the French. For a discussion of this
hypothesis and the reasons which led Paris to adopt it see Bédier II,
314 ff. In so far as these reasons are connected with Paris's general
theory of the Anglo-Norman origin of the Arthurian romances, I have
dealt with them elsewhere. For the rest, I will add to what Bédier
says on the subject that the testimony of the unpublished French poem
*Waldef* (eleventh or twelfth century) as to the existence of an early
English *Tristan (Tristram)* is, on the face of it, valueless, since in
the same line the author of this poem speaks of an early English
original for the French *Bruit (Brut).* The line of works entitled
*Brut,* however, all go back to Geoffrey of Monmouth (cf. Gaimar,
Wace etc.) and have, of course, nothing to do with any earlier English
works. Cp. on this subject Golther, *Zs. f. frz. Spr. u. Litt.* XXIX[2],
151 ff. (1906) and Brugger, ibid. XXXII[2], 136 ff. (1907), and, above
all, R. Immelmann in his edition of the fifteenth century Latin *Waldef*
romance, *Johannes Bramis' Historia Regis Waldei*, pp. XXX ff.
(Bonn, 1912). The argument from the *Waldef* which Paris had already cited, *Romania* XV, 597 (1886), XVIII, 510 (1889), in connection with the discussion of Tristan's origin, was adopted, also, by
W. Hertz, *Tristan und Isolde von Gottfried von Strassburg*, pp. 477 f.
— so, too, apparently by W. H. Schofield, *English Literature from
the Norman Conquest to Chaucer*, p. 202 (New York, 1906). Schofield
here goes so far as to connect the incident of Tristan's sending his
message to Iseult by the chips on the stream with the Anglo-Saxon
lyric which is usually entitled *"The Husband's Message."*

demonstration by Bédier in the Second Volume (1905) of his great edition of Thomas' *Tristan*,[4] and substantially the same results were reached independently by W. Golther in his *Tristan und Isolde* (1907), which, though published two years later, had been written before the appearance of Bédier's work. The conclusions of Bédier and Golther have been disputed by a few scholars, as will be observed from the notes below, but, in general, we may say that the existence of a single primitive Tristan romance (*Ur-Tristan*, as German scholars call it) from which all extant versions are ultimately derived is one of the few matters of Arthurian discussion on which students are definitely agreed.[5]

---

[4]) Also in a popular article in the now defunct *International Quarterly* (March-June, 1904).

[5] It would seem natural to identify this *Ur-Tristan* with the lost poem "del roi Marc et d' Iseut la blonde" which Chrétien, in the list of his works, *Cliges*, ll. 1 ff., tells us that he wrote, and, as a matter of fact, Foerster, *Cliges*[3], p. LXVIII, argues that the two are identical. But its connection in this list with Chrétien's tales from Ovid (certainly compositions of the poet's youth) shows that the lost poem was an early work. Now, the *Ur-Tristan* was evidently a masterpiece and superior in construction and in poetical content to even the maturest romances from Chrétien's pen, so that it is inconceivable that it was one of Chrétien's compositions. Golther, p. 74, very properly raises this objection to the theory of the identity and adds with less force that Chrétien is not likely to have had the knowledge of English conditions that the *Ur-Tristan* (as reconstructed by Bédier and himself, with a high degree of probability) implies. Foerster, *loc. cit.*, tries to meet Golther's objection, with the supposition that Chrétien had before him a still earlier *Tristan* poem (*Ururtristan*) and that the merits of construction may have come to him from his original.

In the *Journal des Savants* for 1902, pp. 299 ff., G. Paris has argued that Chrétien did not write a full poem on the story of Tristan and Iseult, but merely a brief one, dealing with some episode in which Marc and Iseult figured. Novati, *Studj di filologia romanza*, II, 411 and Röttiger, *Der heutige Stand der Tristanforschung*, pp. 28 f. (1897) had already discerned a significance in the absence of Tristan's name from Chrétien's allusion to his lost poem. Paris's hypothesis is based on the consideration that in all the literature of the Middle Ages there is no allusion to a Tristan poem by Chrétien. We have, however, no episodic poems from Chrétien's pen, and it seems to me more likely that he planned a long poem on Tristan and Iseult, but

Bédier has reconstructed the narrative of this primitive *Tristan* by the comparative method, and so has Golther. Their respective

failed to complete it, as he later failed to complete his *Lancelot* (to say nothing of the *Perceval*) — only in the case of this earlier composition he never put his work into circulation, recognizing it . as immature. — In Paul's *Grundriss der germanischen Philologie* II, 1, 459 (1890) J. te Winkel conjectures that there was a (lost) Dutch translation of Chrétien's *Tristan,* but gives no reasons for this conjecture.

In the *Roman de Renard,* Branch II, there is an allusion to a lost Tristan poem by a certain La Chievre and in a *conte dévot* (Foerster *Festschrift,* Halle, 1902) there is a similar allusion to this lost poem — only its author's name is here given in the Picard form, Li Kievres. The poem, of whose contents we know nothing, was probably composed in the twelfth century and its author should, doubtless, be identified with the lyric poet, Robert La Chievre of Rheims. On these subjects cp. Gröber's *Grundriss,* Band II, Abteilung I, pp. 494, 671, and G. Paris, *op. cit.* p. 299.

In l. 2119 of his *Tristan,* Thomas appeals to "Breri" as his authority for representing that Tristan sent Kaherdin, and not Governal, as his messenger to Iseult on a certain occasion. G. Paris, *Romania,* VIII, 425 ff. (1879) identified this "Breri" with "famosus ille fabulator Bledhericus, qui tempora nostra paulo praevenit", of Giraldus Cambrensis, *Descriptio Kambriae,* ch. XVII, in Vol. VI (London, 1868) of that writer's Works edited for the Rolls Series by J. F. Dimock. As Paris, himself, however, says, Thomas does not hereby imply that he is using a book by Breri, but is merely appealing to the authority of a person of that name who is said to know more about British history than anybody else. "Breri" and "Bledhericus" are, indeed, probably the same name and Paris's identification of the persons concerned is *a priori* admissible. The identification was favored, also, by H. Zimmer, *Göttingische Gelehrte Anzeigen* for Oct. 1, 1890, p. 805, note, and *Zs. f. frz. Spr. u. Litt.,* XIII [1], 84, (1891). Nevertheless, Thomas's appeal to Breri is, no doubt, merely one of the innumerable instances in mediaeval literature of a writer's bolstering up his narrative by the citation of fictitious authorities. He puts off on Breri the responsibility for innovations in the story which are really, his own. Cp. Muret, *Romania,* XVII, 608 f. For a full discussion of the Breri question cp. Bédier, II, 95 ff. He lists p. 95, note 1, the chief previous discussions of the subject. Add J. L. Weston, *Romania,* XXXIII, 334 ff. (1904), who identifies Thomas's Breri with the Bleheris (Blihos-Bleheris) of the additions made to Chrétien's *Perceval* — also, W. Golther, *Tristan und Isolde,* pp. 139 f.

reconstructions do not differ in essentials, so that the task of the Tristan student at the present time consists mainly in the study of the sources of this hypothetical romance, as reconstructed by these scholars.

The materials which form the basis of these reconstructions are. 1. The *Tristan*-poem of the Anglo-Norman poet, Thomas, composed somewhere between 1155 and 1170.[6] 2. The fragments

(Leipzig, 1907), who points out that Thomas, in the passage referred to above, cites Breri as a great authority on British history, yet, as a matter of fact, derives all his knowledge of that history from Wace. Very important is L. Foulet, "Thomas and Marie in their relation to the conteurs," MLN, XXIII, 205 ff. (1908). Foulet shows that Thomas's reference to the "conteurs", to whose varying accounts he opposes the authority of Breri, is really a "meaningless mannerism", copied from Marie de France, and does not imply any knowledge of oral traditions concerning Tristan.

We shall have to return to this mysterious Breri in the discussion of the continuations to Chrétien's *Perceval*.

[6] The upward limit is fixed by the author's use of Wace's *Brut*, the lower by his influence on Chrétien's *Cliges*. F. Lot, *Romania*, XXVII, 42 (1898), called attention to the first point, G. Paris, *Journal des Savants* for July, 1902, pp. 354 ff. to the latter. For a full discussion of the subject cp. Bédier, I, 37 ff. M. Wilmotte, *L'évolution du roman francais*, p. 67 (Brussels, 1903) and W. Foerster, *Cliges*[3], pp. LXVI ff. (Halle, 1910) have disputed Paris's proofs as to the priority of Thomas's *Tristan* over the *Cliges*, on the ground that Chrétien and Thomas may have been drawing from a common source (one of the lost Tristan poems), in the cases where Paris assumes imitation of the latter by the former. The question is difficult to decide, but it seems to me that Thomas would hardly have appropriated from a predecessor so distinctive a play on words as *amer: mer*. The limits of date would be still further narrowed, if we could accept S. Singer's contention, "Thomas, Tristan, und Benoit de Saint Maure," *Zs. f. rom. Phil.* XXXIII, 729 ff. (1909), that the *Roman de Troie* influenced Thomas's *Tristan;* for the former was written about 1165. Singer compares especially the description of the loves of Rivalen and Blanchefleur, Bédier, I, 12 ff., with those of Achilles and Polyxena, *R. de Troie*, 17554 ff. But the matter is too indefinite, and the passage in Thomas, just named, may be imitated from some other romance embodying the new spirit of the *amour courtois*. Singer, himself, compares, also, Gottfried, ll, 16478 ff. (which goes

of a French poem which is, at least in part, by a poet of Normandy
named Béroul,[7] coupled with the Middle High German poem

---

back, doubtless, to Thomas) with *Eneas*, 9885 ff. (eye belongs to love,
hand to grief).

Traces of the influence of the *Disciplina Clericalis* in Thomas
throw no light on the subject of date, since the author of that work,
Petrus Alfonsi, flourished in the early part of the twelfth century.
Cp., on this influence, A. Hilka, "Der Tristanroman des Thomas und
die Disciplina Clericalis," *Zs. f. frz. Spr. u. Litt.*, XLV[1], 38 ff. (1917).
That Thomas was not identical with the poet of the same name
who wrote *Horn et Rimenhild* has been shown by W. Söderhjelm,
"Sur l'identité du Thomas, auteur de Tristan, et du Thomas, auteur
de Horn", *Romania*, XV, 175 ff. (1886). The identification of our
Anglo-Norman Thomas with Thomas of Erceldoune is, of course, merely
the individual fancy of the author of the English *Sir Tristrem*.

Novati, *Studj di filologia romanza*, II, 403, note 3, conjectures
that Thomas, author of *Tristan*, was an ecclesiastic. There is no
means of deciding the matter, but the conjecture hardly seems probable.

[7] The poem has been preserved in the unique MS. 2171 of the
Bibliothèque Nationale and was edited by H. von der Hagen in Vol. II
of his edition of Gottfried von Strassburg (Breslau, 1823) and by
F. Michel in his edition of the Tristan fragments I, 1 ff. (London and
Paris, 1835). The authoritative editions, however, are E. Muret's 1.
*Le roman de Tristan par Béroul et un anonyme* (Paris, 1903, for
the Société des Anciens Textes Français) and 2. *Béroul, le roman
de Tristan, poème du XII*<sup>e</sup> *siècle* (Paris, 1913, in *Les Classiques
français du moyen age)*. Ll. 1268 and 1790, the poet calls himself
*Berox* (nominative form). Down to l. 2754 the narrative accords
closely with that of Eilhart. Not so with ll. 3028—4485 (end), nor
with ll. 2767—3031, which latter connects the two principal divisions
of the poem. In his first edition of Béroul (Paris, 1903) Muret, pp.
LXV ff., concluded with G. Paris and others that Béroul II (ll. 3028
—4485) was by a different hand from Béroul I (ll. 1—2754) and that
the two were connected by still a third hand. Beroul II, he observes,
is grosser and more barbarous, is not marked by the same literary knowledge or influences of chivalrous courtesy. In his second edition (Paris,
1913) he repeats this opinion, though with some hesitation (pp. VIII ff.),
being affected, it would seem, by Bédier's view *(Légendes Épiques,*
III, 399), that the whole of the Béroul fragment is by one person.
Heinzel *(Zs. f. d. Altertum,* XIV) had maintained, as no one would
now, that it consisted of nineteen different lays by different authors.
Bédier's view seems to me, the most likely. — The Béroul *Tristan*
was undoubtedly addressed to an audience of lower social position

on Tristan by Eilhart von Oberge.[8] Both belong to the closing years of the twelfth century and both draw evidently from the same source — a lost derivative of the primitive *Tristan*.[9] 3. Por-

than Thomas's poem. It is a jongleur's version. There is nothing, however, to support the view, formerly held, that it was older than Thomas.

The upward limit of date for Beroul II, is fixed by an allusion (l. 3853) to the epidemic of leprosy which raged among the crusaders at Acre, 1190—1. This part of the poem probably falls in the last decade of the twelfth century. Muret (p. LXIV of his first edition) assumes that Beroul I was not earlier than 1165 or 1170. There is no evidence, however, to prove that this part of the poem was not composed substantially at the same time as Béroul II, granting even that the two parts were by different authors.

[8] Edited by Franz Lichtenstein (Strassburg, 1877). In the extant MSS. Eilhart's poem has been subjected to changes. On this subject cp. especially E. Muret, "Eilhart d'Oberg et sa source française", *Romania*, XVI, 287 ff. (1887) and G. Schoepperle, II, 476 ff. Between these two discussions E. Gierach, "Zur Sprache von Eilhart's Tristrant", *Prager Deutsche Studien*, IV (1908), had shown that the Czech version of Eilhart did not have the importance for the reconstruction of Eilhart's text that Knieschek and Muret attributed to it. Knieschek translated the Czech version into German, *Zs. f. d. Altertum*, XXVIII, 261 ff.

Eilhart composed his poem probably between 1185 and 1189. Cp. Gierach, *op. cit.* pp. 254 f. When Muret, *Romania*, XVI, 361 f., suggests that the author of his source was Li Kievres, this is pure conjecture.

Recently a fragmentary twelfth century MS. of Eilhart's *Tristrant* — now in the (formerly) Royal Library at Berlin — has been discovered. It contains 461 lines, corresponding to ll. 7061 ff. of Lichtenstein's edition, and has been edited by H. Degering. "Neue Funde aus dem zwölften Jahrhundert: Ein Bruchstück der Urfassung von Eilharts Tristrant", PBB, XLI, 513 ff. (1916).

[9] Like Golther, p. 59, Miss Gertrude Schoepperle, *Romania*, XXXIX, 277 ff. (1910) and *Tristan and Isolt*, pp. 72 ff. (Frankfort and London, 1913), disputes the existence of this hypothetical intermediate derivative (the *y* of Bédier's stemma) and derives both Eilhart and Béroul direct from the primitive *Tristan* poem. In my review of her book, MLN, XXIX, 213 ff. (1914), however, I have pointed out the improbability of her derivation. So, too, Nitze, JEGc Ph. XIII, 444 ff. (1914). Muret, in his review of Golther's book, *Zs. f. frz. Spr. u. Litt.*, XXXVII², 167 ff. (1911), has adopted Golther's and Miss Schoepperle's conclusions in regard to this matter, but adds

tions of the French prose *Tristan* which, in its earliest form, is dated by Löseth (p. XXIV) between 1215 and 1230 and by Bédier (II, 309) about 1230.[10] 4. Two short French pòems each called *La Folie Tristan:* One (the Oxford version) was the production of an Anglo-Norman poet of the last quarter of the twelfth

no new arguments. *Ibid.* he contends that the author of the primitive *Tristan* merely combined Celtic (insular) traditions concerning Tristan.

Bédier's reconstruction has been criticised by Jakob Kelemina, *Untersuchungen zur Tristansage* (Leipzig, 1910), and by Muret and Miss Schoepperle *loc. cit.* — also, by R. Zenker in his "Zum Ursprung der Tristansage," *Zs. f. rom. Ph.*, XXXV, 715 ff. (1911) — especially, pp. 728 ff. — and again in *Romanische Forschungen,* XXIX, 328 ff. (1911). Kelemina and Miss Schoepperle complain that the French scholar does not sufficiently recognize cross influences between the extant versions, and Zenker offers the same criticism, though in milder terms Zenker, accordingly, does not accept the lost primitive *Tristan* poem as the sole source of Eilhart and the prose *Tristan.* What he says of the partial dependence of the prose on Béroul and Thomas is, doubtless, true. A romance on Tristan, written so late as the prose (circa 1220) could hardly escape such influences. — Kelemina, on the other hand, denies altogether the possibility of reconstructing an *Ur-Tristan* and takes the ground that already in the pre-literary period of the development of the *Tristan* legend there were two lines of tradition, corresponding roughly to the Béroul and Thomas forms of the story, respeetively. His theory, however, has found no adherents.

[10] The passages in question are preserved only in MS. 103 (Bibl. Nat.) and are printed by Bédier, II, 321 ff. See, also, his article, "La mort de Tristan et d'Iseut d'après le manuscrit fr. 103 de la Bibliothèque Nationale comparé au poème allemand d'Eilhart d'Oberg," *Romania,* XV, 481 ff. (1886). The relation of these passages, however, to the primitive *Tristan* is somewhat uncertain. They were late modifications, doubtless, of the prose *Tristan* under the influence of a poetic version — but of which one? According to W. Röttiger, *Der heutige Stand der Tristanforschung,* p. 26 (Hamburg, 1897), it was a compilation similar to the source of Eilhart and Béroul. Miss Schoepperle, I, 10, conjectures, on the other hand, that the episodes were drawn from the source of the primitive *Tristan,* which seems, however, very improbable.

It should be noted that G. Paris once held the opinion (cp. *Romania,* XV, 602), that an imitation (presumably in prose) of Chrétien's *Tristan* constituted the nucleus of the prose *Tristan.* His subsequent

century, the other (Berne version) of a poet of North-Eastern France, probably of the early thirteenth century.[11]

theory, however, that Chrétien composed only a brief episodic poem concerning Tristan implies a withdrawal of his earlier opinion. In his discussion of the subject Röttiger, *op. cit.*, pp. 28 f., had already expressed himself unfavorably as to the dependence of the prose romance on Chrétien. Löseth, in his analysis of the prose *Tristan*, p. XXV, regards that work as based largely on the lost poem of Chrétien. For the closeness of the prose-romance to Eilhart-Béroul cp. Heinzel, *Zs. f. d. Altertum*, XIV, 354, Brakelmann, *Zs. f. d. Phil.*, XVIII, 87, Muret, *Romania*, XVI, 292.

[11] The two *Folie Tristan's* have the same general design: Tristan gains access to Marc's court by disguising himself as a madman and in this disguise gradually reveals himself to Iseult by recalling the various incidents of their love-affair. Both poems were first edited by Francisque Michel in his *Tristan: recueil de ce qui reste des poèmes relatifs a ses aventures*, from the Berne MS. (No. 354 of the Berne Library), I, 215 ff., and the Bodleian MS. (Douce d 6) II, 89 ff. (1835). The second of these versions was, also, edited by H. Morf, *Romania*, XV. 558 ff. (1886). The standard edition of both poems now, however, is that of J. Bédier, *Les deux poèmes de la Folie Tristan*, 1 ff. (Paris, 1907, for the Société des Anciens Textes Français). The Oxford *Folie* is plainly dependent on Thomas; that of Berne is closely related to Béroul, but, according to Bédier, pp. 82 f. not directly dependent. On the subject see, still further, W. Lutoslawski, "Les Folies de Tristan," *Romania*, XV, 511 ff. (1886) and E. Hoepffner, "Das Verhältnis der Berner *Folie Tristan* zu Berols Tristandichtung," *Zs. f. rom. Ph.* XXXIX, 62 ff. (1917), and "Die Berner und die Oxforder Folie," *ibid.*, XXXIX, 551 ff. (1918), 672 ff. (1919). According to Hoepffner, the Berne version follows closely an hypothetical lost poem (X), derived from Béroul. On the other hand, the author of the Oxford version, he thinks, recast this, using very fully in the process Thomas's poem and aiming at the production of a romance in the courtly style. *Ibid.* XL, "Die Folie Tristan und die Odyssee", Hoepffner has discussed the *motif* in the French *Folies* as compared with the similar one in the Odyssey.

A similar episode to that of these two poems is found in the prose *Tristan* (cp. Bédier's edition of Thomas, I, 372 ff.), in Eilhart, ll. 8695 ff., in Ulrich von Turheim's and Heinrich von Freyberg's continuations to Gottfried von Strassburg.

For a discussion of the affiliations of all the various versions, see W. Lutoslawski's above-mentioned article and Bédier, II, 287 ff.

The problem of reconstruction was rendered more difficult by the fact that only fragments of Thomas's poem in its original French form have come down to modern times, and so this poem itself, in the missing portion, had first to be reconstructed from the versions in foreign languages which are known to be based upon it — viz: the Scandinavian prose *Tristan* saga, Gottfried von Strassburg's *Tristan,* the Middle English Sir *Tristrem,* the *Folie Tristan* of the Oxford MS., and the Italian *La Tavola Ritonda.*[12] This task has been accomplished in masterly fashion

Bédier's stemma (p. 296) is preferable to Lutoslawski's (p. 287). Somewhat different is W. Golther, p. 219, note 1.

Tristan appears elsewhere in other disguises—namely, as *1.* leper, Thomas, ll. 1773 ff. *2.* penitent, *ibid.,* ll, 2061 ff. *3.* minstrel, Gerbert's continuation to Chrétien's *Perceval, Romania,* XXXVI, 497 ff. *4.* monk, Middle High German poem (based, no doubt, on a lost French original), *Tristan als Mönch,* edited by H. Paul, *Sitzungsberichte der Münchener Akademie der Wissenschaften* for 1895, pp. 317 ff., from the two extant MSS. of the thirteenth century. The author, it seems, was an Alsatian.

As Golther, p. 29, has remarked, these stories of Tristan seeking his lady-love in various disguises were probably due, in the first instance, to the influence of the legend of Solomon.

[12] Of Thomas's French original only 3144 lines, all told, are extant. Following are the works on which reconstructions of the remainder of Thomas's poem have to be based: *1.* The Old Norse prose saga (dating from 1226), edited by Brynjulfson, *Saga af Tristram ok Isondar* (Copenhagen, 1878) and E. Kölbing *Tristrams Saga ok Isondar* (Heilbronn, 1878). *2.* Gottfried von Strassburg's poem, *Tristan* (early thirteenth century), which has been often edited (cp. list in Golther p. 165, note 1) — last by K. Marold (Leipzig, 1912). Marold furnishes the best text, but the commentary has not appeared. A. Bossert, *Tristan et Iseult, poème de Gotfrit de Strasbourg, comparé à d'autres poèmes sur le même sujet* (Paris, 1865), was the first to show that Gottfried's poem was based on Thomas. For the best studies of the relation of the German poet to his original see W. Hertz, *Tristan und Isolde,*[5] pp. 473 f. (Stuttgart and Berlin, 1907), F. Piquet, *L'originalité de Gottfried de Strasbourg* (Lille, 1905) and Bédier, II, 76 ff. (1905).

Of minor importance are the articles in a controversy on this subject in Pfeiffer's *Germania* between O. Glöde (who claims greater independence for Gottfried) and E. Kölbing: cp. that journal, Glöde XXXIII, 17 ff. (1888), XXXV, 344 f. (1890) and Kölbing, XXXIV,

by Bédier in the First Volume of his edition of Thomas's *Tristan*, so that we have here a solid basis for the reconstruction of the primitive poem.

In the discussion of the sources of this hypothetical romance, from which the whole mediaeval tradition concerning Tristan flows,[13] it will be necessary, as in previous cases, to indicate

---

187 ff. (1889). *3.* The English *Sir Tristrem* (probably, end of the thirteenth century) edited by E. Kölbing (Heilbronn, 1882) and by G. P. McNeill (Edinburgh, 1886, for the Scottish Text Society). *4. La Folie Tristan* (Oxford MS.), edited by Bédier (Paris, 1907). *5. La Tavola Ritonda* (thirteenth century), edited by F. L. Polidori, 2 vols. (Bologna, 1864—5). Chapters 63—67 are based on Thomas's poem for this part of the narrative (Marc spies upon Tristan and Iseult from the pine-tree, but is observed, etc.). On this subject see E. G. Parodi, *Il Tristano Riccardiano*, pp. LXXXII ff. (Bologna, 1896) and Bédier, II, 91. The text edited by Parodi is the chief source of *La Tavola Ritonda*.

[13] In the Middle Ages no branch of the *matière de Bretagne*, perhaps, won such popularity as the story of Tristan and Iseult. For allusions to the same in mediaeval literature cp. L. Sudre, "Les allusions à la légende de Tristan dans la littérature du moyen age," *Romania*, XV, 534 ff. (1886) and Bedier, II, 397 ff. For allusions in Italian literature cp., more particularly, A. Graf, "Appunti per la storia del ciclo brettone," *Giornale Storico della Letteratura Italiana*, V, 81 ff. and *Miti, leggende e superstizioni nel medio evo*, II, 339 ff. (Turin, 1893), and, above all, Elvira Sommer-Tolomei, „La leggenda di Tristano in Italia," *Rivista d'Italia* for July, 1910, pp. 73 ff. P. 127 of the last-named article, some additional minor contributions to the subject of Tristan and Iseult in Italy are named. The fourteenth century Italian poem, *La Morte di Tristano*, is still unpublished. For an account of it see G. Bertoni, *Fanfulla della Domenica*, nos. 43, 46, 48 (Rome, 1915). It is of popular origin. — For similar allusions in Spanish literature see A. Bonilla y San Martin, *Libro del esforçado cauallero Don Tristan de Leonis*, pp. XXVI ff. (Madrid, 1912).

For the literature of allusions to Tristan and Iseult in German writings of the Middle Ages cp. Golther p. 211, note 1.

The popularity of the Tristan romances (especially the Eilhart-Béroul tradition) is reflected, also, in the use which is made of them in the decorative arts (apart from miniatures in MSS.). Examples of such use are found in all the principal European countries, — particularly, from the fourteenth century. For the literature of this subject see Hertz, pp. 475 f., 541, Golther, pp. 408 ff. and, above all,

briefly the succession of episodes which made up the romance. The reconstructions of Bédier (II, 194 ff.) and Golther (pp.

R. S. Loomis in "A Sidelight on the *Tristan* of Thomas," *Modern Language Review*, X, 304 ff. (1915) — an article which corrects Bédier's reconstruction of Thomas in three minor details — and "Illustrations of Medieval Romance on Tiles from Chertsey Abbey," *University of Illinois Studies in Language and Literature*, Vol. II, No. 2 (1916). The tiles in question are both the earliest (circa 1270) and the finest specimens of decorative illustrations drawn from the *Tristan* romances. In the second of his above-mentioned studies, Loomis gives plates (with identifications and discussions) of the tiles (34, in all). They are based on Thomas. In this same study he gives, also, full indications of the very extensive literature on the subject of the *Tristan* romances in the decorative arts. Cp. now, also, the same scholar's articles: "The Tristran and Perceval Caskets," RR, VIII, 196 ff. (1917) and "Notes on the *Tristan* of Thomas," MLR, XIV, 38 ff. (1919). The first describes a *Tristan* casket in the Hermitage Museum at Petrograd; the second makes additions to the author's previous articles — also, some corrections.

Of especial interest is Pio Rajna's description of two coverlets (dating from about 1400), embroidered with figures from the legend of Tristan. See his article "Intorno a due antiche coperte con figurazioni tratte dalle storie di Tristano," *Romania*, XLII, 517 ff. (1913). The legends accompanying the figures are in the Sicilian dialect and the ultimate source of the scenes is the prose *Tristan,* the immediate source some Italian version of that romance. The plates in Rajna's article reproduce the figures in the coverlets.

Localizations from the Tristan poems in Dublin and its vicinity from as early as the twelfth century are noted in letters to *The Athenaeum* for Feb 21 and April 26, 1913. Cp., too, the issues for May 10 and 17, 1913. The writers naively cite these localizations as proofs of the actual existence of the characters concerned. "Chapelizod" (= Iseult's Chapel), as the name of a village near Dublin, persists even to this day.

From the romances, the name, *Tristan,* passed into the general nomenclature of France, England, etc. Students of the romances appear to have overlooked the fact that *Tristan* is recorded as a French surname as early as 1207. In that year a person of this name, whose Christian name seems to have been *Arnoul,* bought a property in the neighborhood of Soissons. More distinguished than himself was one of his sons, Pierre Tristan, (Tristran) — or in Latin, Petrus Tristanides — who saved the life of Philip Augustus in the battle of Bouvines (1214). Cp. *Oeuvres de Rigord et de Guillaume*

40 ff.) do not differ very materially.[14] The following succinct outline which is based on the former, represents, then, in essentials, with virtual certainty, the content of the lost French romance: *le Breton*, I, 282 (2 vols., Paris, 1882—1885), edited by H. F. Delaborde for the Société de l'Histoire de la France. We have, also, a record of Pierre's purchasing a piece of property in 1207 — from the convent of St. Magloire de Paris. On the other hand, he was still living in 1249. Since he was of age in 1207, he could hardly have been born later than 1185 and his father, who bore the same name, is not likely to have been born later than 1165. If he (Arnoul), in turn, inherited the surname from *his* father, we should have *Tristan* occurring as the proper name of an actual person in the first half of the twelfth century. I see no way, however, of determining which of Pierre's progenitors was the first to assume the surname. For abundant documentary evidence relating to this family cp. Henri Stein: „Pierre Tristan, chambellan de Philippe Auguste et sa famille," *Bibliothèque de l'École des Chartes,* LXXVII, 135 ff. (1918). Stein does not mention the legendary Tristan in connection with the family.

[14] For an enumeration of the differences cp. Golther, pp. 59 ff. I have given my reasons, MLN, XXIX, 214 ff. for not accepting with Golther (p. 59) and Miss Schoepperle (pp. 75 ff.) certain features of Eilhart and Béroul as belonging to the lost Tristan poem: In these poems (as against Thomas) there is an abatement in the influence of the love-potion after the lapse of three (Béroul) or four (Eilhart) years, whereupon the lovers confess to a hermit (Ogrin) in the forest and on his advice it is agreed that Iseult shall return to Marc. Marc takes her back, but banishes Tristan. In the earliest form of the story, however, the efficacy of the love-potion obviously could not have been limited as to time and it is not so limited in Thomas (nor in the prose *Tristan*), so that it is highly improbable that in the intermediate version (the primitive Tristan poem) there was any such limitation. It is principally on account of these views regarding this feature and the changes in the narrative that are corollary to it that Golther (p. 103) and Miss Schoepperle (pp. 72 ff.) consider the narrative of Eilhart as differing very slightly from that of the lost Tristan poem.

Another point in which Eilhart's narrative shows degradation is in dropping the *motif* of jealousy, which is necessary to explain the conduct of Iseult of Brittany at the end of the story, in the incident of the sails. Miss Schoepperle, pp. 96 ff. and in the *Zs. f. d. Ph.*, XLIII, 453 ff. (1911) "Isolde Weisshand am Sterbebette Tristan's," argues that she is jealous in Eilhart, too, but the argument does not convince.

Altogether, Bédier's stemma of the *Tristan* versions seems to me to be the soundest that has yet been offered.

Tristan was the son of Rivalen, King of Loenois (in some versions, Armonie or Parmanie) in Great Britain and of Blanchefleur, sister of Marc, King of Cornwall. Blanchefleur dies in the act of giving birth to Tristan, whose name[15] was suggested by the affliction that accompanies his birth. A knight, named Gorvenal, instructed the young Tristan in the accomplishments of knighthood, and when his charge was fifteen years old, they set out for Cornwall and arrive at Marc's court. Although Tristan does not disclose his identity, he becomes a favorite at court. In the course of time an opportunity arises which enables him to show his prowess. A great knight called Morholt, brother-in-law of the Irish king, comes from Ireland to exact the tribute of every third child of fifteen years old, but he was ready to settle the matter with any suitable Cornish champion. The Cornish knights hold back, but Tristan undertakes the combat, after having first had himself knighted. The duel takes place on the isle of Saint-Samson and only the combatants are present. Morholt is mortally wounded, but escapes to his boat with a fragment of Tristan's sword in his head. He expired before he could reach Ireland; nevertheless, his niece, Iseult, daughter of the Irish king, kept the fragment of Tristan's sword.

Tristan, too, had been wounded in the combat and his condition grows constantly worse. In despair, he finally has himself put in a boat which is pushed out to sea.[16] He carries his harp with him. The boat drifts to the Irish coast, and the king, hearing Tristan playing on his harp, takes him ashore, and Iseult, who is skilled in the healing art, cures him. He calls himself Tantris, and so eludes identification. He then returns to Cornwall.

King Marc had always refused to marry, but one day a swallow brings to his hall some strands of a woman's hair as beauti-

---

[15] Cp. French *triste* = sad.

[16] In the primitive *Tristan*, the hero, when he started on his voyage, evidently had no fixed destination in view. According to F. Piquet, *"L'originalité de Gottfried de Strasbourg,"* pp. 165 ff. (Lille, 1905), Thomas modified this and made Ireland his destination from the beginning. For a refutation of this opinion, however, cp. R. S. Loomis, MLR, XIV, 39 ff. (1919).

ful as gold. The king thought that he could rid himself of the
importunities of his courtiers by declaring that he was willing
to marry the woman to whom this hair belonged, but no one else.
Tristan goes forth to discover the unknown beauty and is borne
by chance to Ireland. The king's officer is sent to slay him, but
Tristan pretends that he is a merchant and secures a delay. A
dragon was then devastating Ireland and the king promises his
daughter's hand to any man that would kill the monster. Tristan
accomplishes this and cuts out the dragon's tongue as a token
of his victory. He falls afterwards into a swoon and the king's
seneschal, stealing the dragon's tongue, represents himself as the
victor.[17] Iseult knows, however, that the seneschal is a coward,
suspects some deceit, goes forth with her mother to look into the
matter and finds Tristan. Aided by her mother, she heals him,
but Tristan, perceiving her golden hair, sees that she is the woman
for whom he is looking. She, however, observes that the fragment taken from the dead Morholt's head fits exactly a gap in
Tristan's sword. She would have informed on him, despite his
prayers, but she knew that she would then be compelled to marry
the treacherous seneschal. The deceit of this man is disclosed
and the Irish king pardons Tristan, who asks for Iseult's hand
on behalf of his uncle. Iseult is sent to Marc under the charge
of Tristan. Then follows the incident of the fatal love-potion.
Iseult's mother had prepared it, to render perpetual the love of her
daughter and Marc, but, through an accident on the voyage, Bringvain (Brangien), Iseult's female attendant, gives it to Tristan and
Iseult, so that they are united in an undying passion.[18] Accor-

---

[17] For parallels in folk-tales to this incident of the false seneschal
cp. Bolte and Polivka's *"Anmerkungen zu den Kinder- und Hausmärchen der Brüder Grimm,"* I, 547 ff. (Leipzig, 1913).

[18] Miss Schoepperle, "The Love-Potion in Tristan and Isolt,"
*Romania*, XXXIX, 277 ff. (1910), tries to show that the *motif* of
the love-potion here is Celtic. I agree, however, with Bédier, II, 163 ff.
and Golther, p. 34, that it was introduced into the legend by a French
poet from classical sources.

For the variant forms of the name of Iseult's attendant in the
different mediaeval versions of the *Tristan* story, cp. W. Hertz's *Tristan
und Isolde von Gottfried von Straßburg*[5], p. 527 (Stuttgart and

dingly, on Iseult's wedding night, Bringvain takes her place with Marc and she remains with her lover.[19]

Fearing that Bringvain would betray the deception practised on Marc, Iseult engages two men to murder her. By a clever allegory the girl touches the hearts of these men and they spare her. They report to Iseult that they have executed their commission, but she exhibits such remorse that they tell her the truth.

One day an Irish harper plays at court on condition that Marc will grant anything he wishes. It turns out that he wishes Iseult, and Marc, though reluctant, is constrained to comply with his promise. The Irishman takes the queen to his ship, but Tristan returns at this moment from the forest and goes to seek Iseult. He tells her captor that he can quiet her distress with his rote.[20] He gains time in this way, wins the Irishman's confidence, and finally manages to carry off Iseult, flinging back the taunt, as he goes, that the Irishman has won her with his harp, but that he has won her back with his rote.[21]

---

Berlin, 1907). It is hardly open to doubt that *Bringvain* was the form used by Thomas, although in our extant MSS. of his poem, the name sometimes appears in an altered form. See on the subject W. Golther, *Zs. f. rom. Ph.* XII, 352. According to G. Paris, *Romania,* XVIII, 323, *Brenwain* was the form employed in the source (or sources) of the *Tristan* romances. This is, however, purely hypothetical, and I have thought it better to use in an outline even of the *Ur-Tristan* the form of the name which is virtually assured for Thomas. There is no agreement as yet in regard to the etymology of this name.

[19] For parallels to this *motif* in folk-tales and literature cp., especially, Hertz, *Tristan und Isolde*[5], pp. 533 ff., and P. Arferth, *Das Motiv von der untergeschobenen Braut* (Rostock Diss. 1897).

[20] The rote was a kind of violin, it seems.

[21] Miss Schoepperle, II, 417 ff., has shown that this incident, doubtless, formed a feature of the *Tristan* saga in its original Celtic form. In the *Archiv für das Studium der neueren Sprachen,* CXXIX, 375 ff. (1912), Brugger had already contended that the incident was of Celtic origin. He cites examples from the Welsh tales, *Kulhwch and Olwen* and *Pwyll Prince of Dyvet* — also, from the Irish story of Mongan, son of Manawyddan. It is very questionable, however, whether the *don-motif* in Arthurian romance is so exclusively of Celtic origin as Brugger believes.

The lovers now continue their intrigue, but Audret (Andret), another nephew of Marc's, who hates Tristan, spies on the pair, and, assisted by a wicked dwarf, endeavors to ruin them. Tristan communicates with his mistress by sending inscribed pieces of wood down a stream which flows through Iseult's chamber. They have all sorts of escapes. Once Marc is hidden in a tree above them, listening to them, but they observe his shadow in a spring and give their conversation such a turn that he is deceived. They are, however, finally detected. Tristan is sleeping in the same chamber with the king and queen. The king by design leaves the chamber and Tristan wishes to join Iseult. The dwarf has strewn the floor between them with meal, so that Tristan's tracks may be shown, but, seeing the snare, Tristan springs over to Iseult's bed. He had lately been wounded, however, and the exertion broke his wound. The blood accordingly stained both his bed and Iseult's and their guilt was divulged. Tristan escapes, but Marc, who at first had determined to burn his wife, later decides to give her up to a band of lepers. Her lover, however, rescues her from this fate and they fly to the forest and spend two years there in the enjoyment of each other's love. One day Marc, in hunting, came upon them asleep in their hut, but Tristan's sword lay between them, which convinced him of their innocence.[22] On awakening, the lovers observe signs that Marc had been there (his sword and his glove) and fly deeper into the forest.

The forest-life, however, becomes no longer bearable, and Tristan and Iseult agree to part. Tristan threw a letter into Marc's chamber, inquiring whether he would take her back. By another letter Marc signified his willingness to do so, provided Tristan left the kingdom.

Tristan now goes to Arthur's court, but with Gawain's help has another meeting with his mistress. Arthur hunts near Tintagel and Marc has to receive him and his followers, including Tristan. To guard Iseult from Tristan, he has sharp blades set near her bed. Tristan is wounded by them, but, in order to pro-

---

[22] For this common folk-tale *motif* cp. Hertz, *Tristan und Isolde*, pp. 551 ff., B. Heller, *Romania*, XXXVI, 36 ff., XXXVII, 162 f., and Bolte and Polivka, I, 554 f.

tect him, his companions feign a fight, get wounded with the same blades, and so it is impossible the next day to convict him. The king now compels Iseult to make a public declaration of her innocence. To confirm her veracity, she will have to endure the test of holding a red-hot iron in her hand. On the way to the place where the test is to be made Iseult is borne across a ford by Tristan disguised as a beggar. She swears afterwards that no one but the king and this man had touched her. The people do not see into the real significance of this oath, but it enables the queen to go through the test unharmed.[23]

Tristan next goes to Brittany and helps Duke Hoel of Carhaix in his war with a rival. The latter has a daughter named Iseult (Iseult of the White Hands she is called) and she is wedded to Tristan, but the marriage remains merely nominal, the husband's mind still dwelling on Iseult of Cornwall. The wife lets her brother Kaherdin know this. Tristan tells this brother of the love of Iseult of Cornwall for him and they go then to Cornwall together, where Tristan has a secret meeting with Iseult. Afterwards, however, through a misunderstanding, Iseult is out of humor with him because of a supposed act of cowardice on his part. Disguised as a leper, he seeks an interview with her to explain, but although she recognizes him, she has him beaten away. He returns, therefore, to Brittany and becomes really the husband of the other Iseult. Iseult of Cornwall now feels remorseful in regard to her lover and even puts on haircloth. On hearing the news of this, Tristan again comes from Brittany — meets her in secret — the

--------

[23] For numerous parallels in Oriental literature to this *motif* cp. J. J. Meyer's *Isolde's Gottesurteil in seiner erotischen Bedeutung,* (Berlin, 1914). For some additional examples see Golther's review of Meyer's book in the *Deutsche Literaturzeitung,* March 14, 1914, and Miss Schoepperle, pp. 223 ff. Miss Schoepperle gives references to articles and books on the *motif,* in general. Bédier II, 265, expresses some uncertainty as to whether this episode was in the *estoire.* He, also, rejects the beautiful incident, told in some of the versions, concerning the dog, Petitcrû, presented by the King of Scotland to Tristan and by him, in turn, to Iseult. The sound of a magic bell hung about the creature's neck had the power of dispelling grief, but Iseult would not be happy, whilst her lover was sorrowful, so she broke the bell.

next day bears off the prize in some sports, but is detected by accident and escapes. At a later time, however, having been much altered in appearance because of his sufferings from a wound which he had received in war, he goes back to Cornwall, disguised as a madman, and carries on his clandestine *amours* with Iseult, until he is finally detected and returns to Brittany.

Kaherdin carries on an intrigue with the wife of Bedenis. In the fight that follows on account of this affair he is killed and Tristan severely wounded. Tristan sends to Iseult of Cornwall to come and cure him. It is agreed that the ship on its return shall hoist a white sail, if it brings her — otherwise a black sail. She comes, but Tristan's wife is jealous and reports that the sail is black. At this the hero dies, and when Iseult of Cornwall arrives, she too expires upon his body. Marc at last learns how the lovers were bound together by the fatal potion and has them buried side by side. Rose-bushes spring up out of the two graves and intertwine their branches.

Now, the investigations of Miss Gertrude Schoepperle[24] have made it virtually certain that the starting-point of this long and romantic narrative is a Celtic *Aithed*[25] (elopement story), similar to the Old Irish story of *Diarmaid and Grainne*.[26] In this Irish story, too, the hero (Diarmaid), under the influence of passion, violates the obligations of friendship and loyalty and flies with the wife of his uncle and king to the forest. They are pursued from place to place and have to endure all sorts of hardships. *Diarmaid and Grainne* is preserved only in such varying fragmentary and

---

[24] Later Mrs. R. S. Loomis. See her fine study, *Tristan and Isolt, a Study of the Sources of the Romance,* 2 vols. Frankfort and London, 1913. The pagination of the volumes is continuous.

[25] For a list of this class of Celtic tales cp. Schoepperle, II, 393f. The *Aitheda* are not to be confounded with tales headed *Aided (Death),* which recount the deaths of heroes and heroines. Cp. the long list of the latter in G. Dottin's catalogue of Irish epic literature, *Revue Celtique,* XXXIII, 1 ff. (1912).

[26] J. F. Campbell identified the story of Tristan and Iseult with that of Diarmaid and Grainne in his *Popular Tales of the West Highlands,* IV, 240 (4 Vols. London, 1890—1893). Miss Schoepperle seems to have overlooked this.

corrupt versions[27] that it is difficult to compare the story with
that of Tristan in detail, and the difficulty is still further enhanced by the fact that these versions are so largely lyrical. The
central *motif*, however, is the same in the two stories, so that
the derivation of the latter from the former or some similar *Aithed*
seems to be an acceptable conclusion.[28] It is, doubtless, due to
this origin that the Tristan of the Old French poems still differs
so greatly from the conventional hero of the French romances
of chivalry — Gawain, for example, whose main function is to
exemplify the knightly virtues of prowess and courtesy in their
highest manifestations. Tristan's nimbleness of hand and foot, his
forest cunning, his skill in elementary feats of strength (leaping,
putting the stone) are all surviving traits of a more primitive type.
Apart, however, from the numerous accretions to the central theme
and the coloring of French chivalrous society which the whole
story has received, it must be acknowledged that the Celtic tale,
even in respect to this central theme, has undergone a transformation in the hands of the French romancers, who developed it
into what is, perhaps, the greatest love-story in literature. The
transformation, indeed, is so great that some scholars have been
disposed to deny any Celtic influence at all in the shaping of the
love-story. In particular, it has been objected that the conflict
of passion and law which constitutes the tragedy of the lovers
in the romance could not have been of Celtic origin, since the dis-

---

[27] For an account of these versions, which range from the tenth
century to the present time, see the two articles by J. H. Lloyd,
O. J. Bergin and G. Schoepperle in the *Revue Celtique:* "The Reproach of Diarmaid," XXXIII, 41 ff. (1912), and "The Death of
Diarmaid," *ibid.,* 157 ff. We have here, also, editions and translations
of some of the most important texts. Cp., also, on the subject Miss
Schoepperle's *Tristan and Isolt,* II, 395 ff.

[28] It must be confessed that in the *Diarmaid and Grainne* texts
the passion displayed is mainly on the part of the heroine. Cp. for
instance, *The Reproach of Diarmaid,* just cited, where the hero
bewails to the heroine the misfortunes which she has brought on him.
In still other versions (cp. *Revue Celtique,* XXXIII, 49 and Miss
Schoepperle, II, 402) he resists her advances for a long time. On
the other hand (cp. *Rev. Celt., loc. cit.),* in some of these versions
Grainne is unfaithful to Diarmaid with a stranger who visits their cave.

solution of the marriage tie was easy among the Celts[29] and the idea of womanly modesty and virtue had little force among the Celtic populations in the period with which we are concerned.[30] There is a measure of truth in the first of these objections, for the moral reprobation of adultery is not emphasized in these Celtic tales, which reflect a more primitive condition of society than the French romances, but the parallelism with *Diarmaid and Grainne*, or even with the more celebrated story of the love of Naisi and Deirdre, wife of Conchobar,[31] is too striking to be accidental. All three of these tales, with their forest setting to a drama of adultery, in which the principal actors are a hero, his uncle (a king), and the latter's wife, bear unmistakably, it would seem, the stamp of the same mint. A recognition of this fact, however, does not conflict with the view that, after all, the tragedy of Tristan and Iseult, which, through the romances, has impressed itself on the imagination of the modern world so deeply, owes its strength, mainly, to the changes which the French poets wrought in the Celtic tradition. Leaving aside the addition of the story of Iseult

---

[29] Cp. Bédier's edition of Thomas's *Tristan*, II. 163 ff. Bédier appeals especially to the Welsh law on the subject in the so-called Laws of Howel the Good (ninth and tenth centuries). In his reply to Bédier, *Revue Celtique*, XXX, 270 ff. (1909), Loth has attenuated, in some measure, the force of that scholar's argument.

[30] Cp. the posthumous article of H. Zimmer, cited above: "Der Kulturgeschichtliche Hintergrund in den Erzählungen der alten irischen Heldensage," *Sitzungsberichte der königlichen preussischen Akademie der Wissenschaften*," pp. 174 ff. (Berlin 1911), where he collects some extraordinary instances of shameless immodesty on the part of women in the Irish heroic sagas. Loth observes in reply, *Revue Celtique*, XXXIII, 260, note (1912), "Quant aux faits de divergondage qu'il cite ils ne prouvent pas plus contre les moeurs des Celtes que la conduite des personnages de l'Olympe contre les moeurs des anciens Grecs." Loth, *ibid.*, refutes Zimmer's idea that this supposed immodesty was a concomitant of the matriarchal system which was in vogue among the Picts.

[31] The *Aithed* of these two characters is preserved, in one of its versions, in the *Book of Leinster* (a MS. written before 1150). For editions and translations cp. Miss Schoepperle, II, 411, note 1. There are convenient English translations of this Irish saga in A. H. Leahy, *Heroic Romances of Ireland*, I, 95, (2 vols., London, 1905—6) and Eleanor Hull, *The Cuchullin Saga*, pp. 123 ff. (London, 1898).

of Brittany to the original *Aithed* and other accretions that
heighten, in a variety of ways, the interest of the legend, one may
note among these changes the discardal of the bizarre paganism
of the Old Irish tale with its duplicate *motifs* of the hero's love-
spot and the heroine's *geis*[32] — both based on forms of superstition that are too primitive to win the interest or sympathy of
modern society — and the substitution in the romances of the incident of the love-drink, shared by the two lovers, which has the
double advantage of a unified *motif* and of the hallowed famili-
arity of classical associations. But, above all, the power of the
story in the French romances is due to the initial scene of Tristan
and Iseult's love-story (the scene of the love-potion), with
its definite symbolism that dominates the rest of the narrative —
the symbolism of a passion against which no human convention
can stand — to the elaboration of the forest scenes, to the true
and vivid picture of the passion that constantly draws the hero
back to the heroine, contrary to the obligations of kinship
and personal loyalty, and, despite every variety of obstacle, not
permitting him to forget her even in the embraces of another
woman. The Celtic texts, such as *The Reproach of Diarmaid* and
*Death of Diarmaid*, have a beauty of their own that testifies to
a more intimate contact with the life of nature, but the French
romances are manifestly the products of a higher civilization[33]
and a more strongly sustained narrative art.

---

[32] Cp. Miss Schoepperle, II, 401f. on this subject. The "love-
spot" was a mark on a man's person that rendered him irresistible to
women. "The *geis* is a peculiarly Irish taboo which any individual
seems to have been at liberty to impose upon any other, and which,
if disregarded, entailed moral degradation and swift retribution." D'Arbois
de Jubainville observed, however, *Revue Celtique*, XV, 406, note 1
(1894), that the Irish *geis* differs from the spell which the love-potion
exercises in the French *Tristan* romances, inasmuch as one was free
to disregard the former — only the punishment inevitably followed.

[33] It has been remarked that the whole character of this great
love-story, with its *dreieckiges Verhältnis* (husband, wife and lover),
is manifestly French, and, consequently, could only have entered into
the Tristan tradition after the French writers began to handle the
theme. But adultery has been a favorite theme of romances, both
written and oral, in all parts of the world. The Irish *Aitheda* show
how common it was in Celtic romances. Nevertheless, as said above,

Granting, now, the Celtic origin[34] of this famous love-story of Tristan and Iseult of Cornwall, it remains to fix as far as pos-

---

the conflict of passion and law which is at the basis of the tragedy of Tristan and Iseult in the French romances is characteristic of a more advanced stage of civilisation than that which produced the Irish sagas. There are some admirable remarks on this subject by H. D'Arbois de Jubainville, *Revue Celtique*, XV, 407 f. (1894). It was the growing power of women in the twelfth century, who now inherited fiefs, that gave their quality to such heroines as Iseult.

I may remark, in passing, that, owing to the idea of fate, which the Tristan legend seems to show, Egidio Gorra has suggested that the primitive story concerning this hero was of classical origin. Cp. his article "Tristano," pp. 577 ff. of the *Studj letterari e linguistici dedicati a Pio Rajna, nel quarantesimo anno del suo insegnamento* (Milan, 1911). This is true, doubtless, of the love-potion feature of our extant texts, but one cannot make such an assertion of the story as a whole. Gorra's article is purely subjective throughout and adds nothing to our knowledge of the evolution of the legend.

[34] Bédier, II, 155 ff., has noted the following details in various Tristan poems as being too primitive for a French knight of the twelfth century, and hence, as of Celtic origin: *1.* In the Tristan episode, ll. 453—662 of the *Donnei des Amanz (Amorous dialogue of lovers)*, edited by G. Paris, *Romania*, XXV, 497 ff. (1896). According to Paris (pp. 531, 534), the poem, which is a mediaeval "debate", and not a romance, was written in England towards the end of the twelfth century. The lover (a cleric, it seems), urging his lady-love to yield to his suit cites the example of various heroines of romance — among others, Iseult — and, in connection therewith, tells a story not found elsewhere in the *Tristan* romances, viz. how Tristan, returning to Cornwall from Brittany, signaled his presence to Iseult from a garden near Marc's palace by imitating various birds. From childhood, the poet says (ll. 475 ff.), Tristan had been able to imitate any bird in the forest. The episode is one of the most vigorous things in the literature of the Tristan legend, and Paris is, no doubt, right in regarding it (p. 536) as based on an earlier short poem concerning Tristan. One may agree, too, with Bédier *(loc. cit.)* that the power of the hero to imitate birds exactly belongs to a different state of society from that which prevailed among the knights and barons of the twelfth century. But the episode, as is acknowledged even by G. Paris (p. 537), who is inclined to believe that it is essentially of Celtic origin, shows unmistakable dependence on Béroul, and so the trait in question is, in all probability, secondary. Besides, Miss Schoepperle, II, 288 ff., has shown that the power of imitating birds was a not

sible, the history of its growth before it reached the French romancers and the share which the different regions, inhabited by

uncommon accomplishment of French minstrels in the twelfth and
thirteenth century. It would be, then, quite natural for one of the guild
to attribrte to the hero of a poem he was composing this trick under
the circumstances of the above-mentioned episode, especially as we find
one of them in the *Folie Tristan*, ll. 184 f., ascribing to him other
juggler's tricks. Cp. Schoepperle, II, 290 ff. *2.* In Béroul, ll. 1752 f.
Tristan has a bow that never fails to hit the mark. For a similar
bow, however, in English tradition, much earlier than Béroul cp. the
example from Geffrai Gaimar, *Lestorie des Engles*, ll, 4409 ff. (edited
for the Rolls Series in 1888 by T. D. Hardy and E. Martin), cited
by E. Muret in his edition of Béroul, p. IX, and Miss Schoepperle, II,
316 f. The traitor, Eadric, is there said to have slain Edmund, King
of England, in 1016 with such a bow. *3.* Mark's horselike ears which
he has to conceal under his hair, Béroul, ll. 1306 ff. As stated above,
this is, doubtless, Celtic, although similar to the Midas legend. *4.* Tintagel, *Folie Tristan* ll. 129 ff. (Douce MS.), disappears twice a year.
Occurring in only one version, the detail may well be the fancy of
the individual poet.

There is nothing distinctively Celtic in vanishing castles, which
are common in fairy-tales the world over. I agree with Miss Schoepperle, II, 325, note 2, that the Irish parallels to this and the next
detail, No. 5, cited by D'Arbois de Jubainville, *Revue Celtique*, XXII,
133 (1901) and approved by Bédier, ll. 156 f., are really no parallels.
In the *Folie Tristan* (Douce MS.), ll. 301 ff., Tristan, playing the rôle
of a fool, says that he has a hall of glass up in the air. What I
have said of No. 4 applies here, too. On the subject of glass-houses
cp. W. O. Sypherd, *Studies in Chaucer's House of Fame*, pp. 85 f.
Publications of the Chaucer Society (London, 1907).

Besides these five features, Bédier has conjectured, also, a Celtic
origin for two others, though less positively: 1. In both Thomas (cp.
Bédier, I, 194 ff.) and Eilhart, ll. 3504 f., and hence, one may say,
certainly in their common (lost) source, Tristan communicates with
Iseult by writing on bits of wood which he drops into a stream that
flows through or past Iseult's chamber. Kuno Meyer, *Zs. f. rom. Ph.*
XXVI, 716 f. (1902) and XXVIII, 353 f. (1904), first cited indubitable parallels to this from Irish sagas, with examples of streams
flowing through houses in Wales and Southern Scotland even at the
present day. See, also, Miss Schoepperle, pp. 303 ff., for examples
drawn from the saga of Dairmaid and Grainne, which, as we have
seen, is so closely akin to that of Tristan and Iseult. It seems certain
that this detail descended to the Tristan poems from the original Celtic

the Celts, had in this process. The task is one which has long
enlisted the energies of the ablest students of the *matière de
Bretagne*.

As is customary in cases where the records are so scanty,
scholars have turned to the nomenclature[35] of the story in the

saga, although streams running through houses, despite K. Meyer, *Zs.
f. rom. Ph.* XXVIII, 353, note 2, are not confined to Celtic regions.
Cp. Miss Schoepperle, II, 302, notes 1 and 2. To the examples which
she discusses I may add one from the version of the Alexander saga
called *Historia de Preliis*, III, 22 (tenth century). It is cited by
A. Hilka, Vollmöller's *Jahrbuch*, Teil II, p. 86, note 89. Here a stream
flows under Candace's palace. 2. The incident of the blades which
Marc places by Iseult's bed and by which Tristan is wounded. Here
thirty or forty guests are represented as sleeping in the chamber of
their host. This trait belongs, as Bédier remarks, to a primitive state
of society. This is true, but that society need not have been Celtic,
for we find the same thing in the actual customs, as well as folk-
tales, of other regions too. — Cp. Schoepperle, I, 215 ff. The trick,
by which, Tristan, with the aid of Arthur's knights, evades detection
(they all wound themselves, so that no one can say who is really the
guilty person) is merely a variant of the tale of the Masterthief, which,
from Herodotus, Book II, Ch. 121, down, is found in innumerable variants.
For the literature of the subject see Schoepperle, I, 214, note 3. On
this particular episode, cp. G. Huet, "Sur un épisode du Tristan d'Eilhart
d'Oberg," *Romania*, XXXVI, 50 ff. (1907).

[35]) For variants of Tristan, Iseult, Marc and the other names in
the Tristan romances, cp. W. Hertz, *Tristan und Isolde*, pp. 479 ff.
Hertz, however, is mistaken (pp. 483 f.) in accepting the supposed dis-
covery of the name "Tristan" in a document of the year, 807 (from
Langenargen on Lake Constance). The name there is really "Cristan".
Cp. F. Lot, *Romania*, XXXV, 596 f. Hertz, *ibid.*, discusses there
(pp. 482 f.) other Tristans in mediaeval romances — likewise, other
Iseults (pp. 487 f.).

In his "Tristan on the Continent before 1066", MLN, XXIV,
37 f. (1909) F. M. Warren points out in early documents relating to
South Italy instances of the occurrence of names (of Normans) which
he identifies with *Tristan*, viz. *Trostayne* in *Ystoire de li Normant*
(early fourteenth century), translated from the lost chronicle (written
in Latin about 1075) of Amatus of Monte Cassino; *Torstainus, Tri-
stainus* (also, names of Normans in South Italy) in the part of the
Latin chronicle of Monte Cassino by Leo de Marsico (died 1115),
which ends towards the year 1075, *Trostenus (Tristaynus), Tro-
staynus*, in the continuation (carried down to 1139) of the same chro-

search for light regarding the question just mentioned. In his well-known studies of Arthurian names,[36] the late Professor Zimmer endeavored to establish the Pictish origin of the hero's name, and that scholar's identification[37] was all but universally accepted, even by those who had been engaged in the bitterest controversies with him.[38] In the Irish chronicles of the Picts we have in the eighth century a *Talorcan filius Drostan* and a *Drest filius Talorcan*.[39] Now, Celtic scholars are agreed that *Drostan* is the same as *Drest (Drust)*, with a common Celtic suffix added, and that *Tristan* is derived from *Drostan*.[40] It has been shown, however, that *Drust (Drest* and its derivatives) is not con-

---

nicle by Peter the Deacon. We may have here, however, MS. corruptions of the common Norman name *Turstin* (from Old Norse *Thorsstein),* which is found in Domesday Book and (as *Tursten)* in *Rotuli Scaccarii Normanniae,* p. LVII (2 vols., London, 1840). In Ordericus Vitalis's *Historiae Ecclesiasticae Libri Tredecim* we find twelve different men of this name *(Turstinus).* Cp. the edition by A. Le Prevost, V, 477 (5 vols., Paris, 1838—1855. Société de l'Histoire de France). It occurs many times as *Tosteins (Tostains)* in Wace's *Roman de Rou,* II, 166, *et passim* (edited by H. Andresen, 2 vols. Heilbronn, 1877—1879). In the form of *Toustain* the name is still met with in Normandy. The variant *Tristaynus* would then be due to the influence of the *Tristan* of our romances. Warren thinks that the forms which he has cited represent Celtic *Drostan* and that they reached Normandy through Brittany. As he remarks, however, this would not necessarily imply that the legend accompanied the name.

[36] *Zs. f. frz. Spr. u. Litt.* XIII[1], 1ff. (1891).

[37] *Ibid.* pp. 58ff.

[38] So by F. Lot, *Romania,* XXV, 15 (1896), who goes so far as to say that this is Zimmer's sole serious contribution to the question of the origin of the Arthurian romances.

[39] Cp. Zimmer, *op. cit,* p. 71.

[40] That is to say, by weakening of the radical vowel under conditions of light stress. The examples of *Tristan (Trystan)* from Celtic documents, cited by Zimmer, p. 72 of the above-mentioned article, show that there is no need of assuming the influence of French *triste,* as is sometimes done, to explain the change of form.

Zimmer still further maintained that the *Trystan mab Tallwch* of a Welsh triad, which we shall soon discuss, was merely a Welsh

fined to the Picts, as Zimmer maintained, but belongs to the general nomenclature of the Brythonic Celts, although commonest among the Picts.[41] As far, then, as the name alone is concerned, we could not infer anything positively as to the ultimate origin of the story. It might have belonged to any branch of the Brythonic Celts. Nevertheless, there are sufficient reasons, I believe, for regarding Tristan as, in the first instance, a Pict. First of all, the name, although not confined to the Picts, is much commoner among them than among the other Celts. Furthermore, all the chief versions of the story represent the hero's father as ruling *Loonois (Loenois)* and the region in which he and Iseult lead their forest-life as *Morois*. Now, despite mistaken identifications in the romances, themselves, it seems most probable that *Loonois*

rendering of a Pictish *Drostan mac Talorg.* J. Loth, however, the eminent Celtic authority, who argues, as we shall see, that the story of Tristan and Iseult is a Cornish legend, which reached the French poets through the Welsh, has proved, *Revue Celtique,* XXXII, 409 (1911), that there is no phonetic correspondence between *Tallwch* and *Talorg:* the names are not identical. On the other hand, as it seems to me, *Tallwch* is so close in sound to *Talorg* that we may reasonably accept it as an inexact rendering of the latter. It is significant that the name, *Tallwch,* is not found elsewhere in Welsh records.

[41] Loth further contends that *Dristan,* the form nearest to the French name, which is actually found in Welsh documents of about 1100, cannot even be Cornish, that it is only possible in Welsh and, still further, that, since in pronunciation this *i* had the sound of an umlauted *o*, the French must have derived the name from written and not oral sources. (On these subjects cp. *loc. cit.* and the reprint of the same in his *Contributions à l'étude des romans de la table ronde* pp. 16 ff. In *Romania,* XIX, 455 ff. he had already contended that Welsh (Cornish) *Drystan* was independent of the Gaelic and the French *Iseult* came from Welsh Essylt). I confess, however, that this distinction seems to me somewhat wire-drawn. It would be easy for anyone who was not familiar with the name to catch imperfectly the pronunciation, *Drostan* or *Trostan,* and write it down, *Tristan.* Indeed, there would be nothing very surprising if a person, hearing even the Cornish or Breton pronunciation of the name, *Drostan,* were to record it inaccurately as *Tristan.*

On the names, *Tristan* and *Iseult,* see, still further, E. Windisch, *Das Keltische Brittanien bis zu Kaiser Arthur,* pp. 213 ff. (Leipzig, 1912).

is the Scottish *Lothian* and *Morois (Morrois)* the Scottish *Murray* — so two districts that were undeniably inhabited by the Picts.[42] The fame of Tristan began, then, as we may assume, with the Picts, probably merely as a character in heroic saga, with no love-story attached; but did it pass through Wales[43] and, perhaps, Cornwall on its way to the French, and, if so, what accretions did it receive in those regions? The principal evidence bearing on the Welsh side of the question is that which is offered by the Triads. In one of these (Loth's *Mabinogion*, II, 231) Tristan is called one of the three chief diadem-wearers of Britain; in another (*ibid*, p. 238) he is one of the three machine-masters of Britain; in still another, (*ibid*, p. 260), he is one of the three lovers of Britain. Lastly, in a fourth triad (*ibid*, pp. 247 f.), he is one of the three great swine-herds of Britain, but he is, at the same time, the lover of Marc's wife, apparently. He keeps Marc's swine, whilst the regular swine-herd goes on a message to Essyllt, as she is here called; Arthur, Marc, Kay and Bedivere could not get a

---

[42] This interpretation was first proposed by F. Lot, *Romania*, XXV, 16 ff. (1896). J. Loth, *Revue Celtique*, XXXIII, 280 ff. (1912), identifies *Morois* with a manor in Cornwall named *Moresc* (now, St. Clement's), in the neighborhood of Truro; but, as A. Smirnov has pointed out in his excellent review of Loth's *Contributions à l'étude des romans de la table ronde*, *Romania*, XLIII, 121 (1914), Moresc, as a place-name, occurs frequently in other Celtic regions. Besides, as he says, the situation of the Cornish Moresc does not fit well with the requirements of the *Tristan* narrative. For my own part, I would add that Loonois and Morois evidently belong together and that they are both explained satisfactorily on Lot's theory, whereas Loth, *op. cit.*, pp. 286 f., is unable to explain the former at all, under his new theory. In the *Annales de Bretagne*, XI, 479 (1895—6) he had accepted the identification of *Loonois* with *Loonia (Lothian)*.

[43] The question would be hardly arguable, if the Welsh *Tristan* fragments from the Black Book of Carmarthen which J. Loth has edited and translated, *Revue Celtique*, XXXIII, 403 ff. (1912), really date from the first half of the twelfth century, as he thinks. These fragments are excessively obscure, but the second one would appear to relate to Kaherdin, brother of Iseult of Brittany. Now the story of Iseult of Brittany seems plainly a French addition to the Tristan romance, as set forth above, but the date assigned by Loth to these fragments would be too early for French influence.

single hog from him, whether by ruse, violence, or theft. Further-more, in the *Dream of Rhonabwy*, a prose tale of the *Mabinogion* collection, he appears *(Drystan mab Tallwch)* among Arthur's counsellors. This tale is certainly not earlier than the middle of the twelfth century and it may have been influenced by the French poems. The triads, enumerated above, are found only in a MS. of the fourteenth century, when the French romances had spread the fame of Tristan throughout Europe, and if we were dependent entirely on them, it would be impossible to say whether, in representing the hero as a lover of Marc's wife, they were really reflecting native tradition. After he became known through the French romances, it would be only natural that native writers should weave still other stories about him and his famous mistress. This seems certainly the origin of the pretty tale[44] in which Arthur is called on to judge between Marc and Tristan as to the

---

[44] Arthur decided that one should possess her, whilst the leaves were on the wood, the other, whilst they were off, the husband to have the choice. Mark chose the second alternative, because the nights are longer in that season, but Iseult joyfully pointed out that the holly, the ivy and the yew were never without leaves — hence Mark lost her forever.

This tale, the earliest MS. of which dates from about 1550, was first edited by J. Gwenogvryn Evans in the *Report on Manuscripts in the Welsh language* (Historical Manuscripts Commission), Vol. I, Part II, (London, 1899) and Vol. II, Part I (1902). It has since been edited (as *Ystoria Tristan*), with translation, by J. Loth, *Revue Celtique*, XXXV, 365 ff. (1913), and by T. P. Cross, under the title of "A Welsh Tristan Episode," [University of North Carolina] *Studies in Philology*, XVII, 93 ff. (1920). Cp., too, W. Golther, *Tristan und Isolde*, pp. 238 f. for an outline of the tale, which he quotes from I. B. John's paper on it in the *Transactions of the Guild of Graduates*, pp. 14 ff. (Cardiff, 1904). Loth gives, also, an account of the story in the *Comptes Rendus de l'Académie des Inscriptions et Belles-Lettres, Bulletin de Mars-Avril*, 1913, pp. 92 ff.

Bédier does not include this tale in his discussion (in his Intro-duction) of the different versions of the Tristan legend. Evans claimed that it was the story of Tristan in its earliest form and Windisch, *Das Keltische Brittanien bis zu Kaiser Arthur*, p. 285 (Leipzig, 1912), unwarily accepted this claim, but Loth has refuted it in his edition, pp. 377 ff.

possession of Iseult. It includes a metrical dialogue[45] of mutual compliment between Tristan and Gawain (Gwalchmai), the latter's object being to induce his friend to meet Arthur.

The following considerations, however, seem to show that the conception of Tristan as the lover of Iseult originated either in Wales or, more probably, in Cornwall. The mistress of Tristan is in all versions represented as the wife of Marc (Mark), King of Cornwall. Now *Mark* is common as a Germanic name, but it is also given as the name of a king of Cornwall in the sixth century in the life of the saint, Paulus Aurelianus. It is said of this saint in his Latin biography, which was written by Wrmonoc, a monk of Landevennec (in Brittany) in 884, that his fame reached the ears of King Marc — "otherwise Quonomorius".[46] Quonomorius, it may be observed, is a Celtic name occurring elsewhere. On the other hand, *Marc* means *horse* in the Celtic languages. In the *Tristan* poem by Béroul, King Marc is represented as having the ears of a horse, which he tries to conceal, and we have here, doubtless, a trait of Cornish tradition[47] which came to Béroul through the primitive *Tristan*. Moreover, Marc's seneschal, Dinas of Lidan, bears a name of Welsh[48] or Cornish[49] origin, which, to be sure, as it appears in the French poems, rests on a misunderstanding, since *Dinas Lidan* in these languages means "large fortress." In the poem the proper name (perhaps, *Dinan*) or title, which must have stood in the original Celtic source, has

---

[45] These verses, which belong to the species of poetry called *Englynion* (epigrams) in Welsh, were known to scholars long before the rest of the tale in which they occur. Cp. Golther, *op. cit.*, p. 239. Cross, p. 93, cites another Welsh dialogue between Tristan and Gwalchmai, similar to this.

[46] F. Lot, *Romania*, XXV, 19f. (1896), shows that Wrmonoc's sources were certainly insular, and he is probably right in regarding Marc (Quonomorius) as an actual person. For other occurrences of *Marc* as a Celtic name, cp. Miss Schoepperle, II, 271, note 3.

[47] In a note, however, to A. le Braz's *La Légende de la Mort*, II, 97 (new ed. Paris, 1902), G. Dottin derives it from the story of Midas and cites it as an instance of the adaptation of a classical legend by the Celts.

[48] Cp. F. Lot, *Romania*, XXIV, 337.

[49] Cp. J. Loth, *Revue Celtique*, XXXIII, 288f.

dropped out.[50] This character, it should be remembered, has an intimate connection with the legend and his name is, therefore, significant of the origin of the romance, or, at least, of the episodes in which he plays a part.

As regards the name of the heroine, Iseult, this has been usually regarded as of Germanic origin, and, accordingly, seemed to conflict with the theory of the Welsh or Cornish, or, indeed, Celtic origin of the love-story. *Iswalda, Ishild* (parallel to *Brunehild, Richild)* have been suggested as Germanic equivalents.[51] Zimmer disputed the Celtic character of the name, *Essylt,* which is given to Marc's wife in the Welsh triads, and derived it from the Anglo-Saxon *Ethylda.*[52] This accorded with his view that the triads about Tristan and Essylt do not reflect a native tradition.[53] The Cornish place-name, *Ryt-Eselt* ("Eselt's ford"), which is found in an Anglo-Saxon charter of the year 967,[54] proves, however, that this name could be Cornish as well as Welsh. The matter is too technical for a layman to pass judgment on, but, on the whole, the argument in favor of the Celtic origin of the name appears to carry with it the weight of probability, and it seems, furthermore, mere pedantry to lay stress on the fact that the French *Iselt (Iseut)* is not quite exact in its phonetic correspondence to Welsh *Essylt* or Cornish *Eselt.*[55] Foreign names are

---

[50] Loth, *loc cit.* p. 290, points out that "Dinas" cannot be Armorican. "Pendennis" (whence the name of Thackeray's hero), name of a place in Cornwall, was originally "Pen-dinas" — "chief fortress". On *Dinas* and its diminutive, *dinan,* cp., still further, E. Phillimore, *Y Cymmrodor,* XI, 38f., 42ff. (1892). The last is frequent as a suffix in place-names, though disguised in spelling as — *dinam,* — *dinham,* e. g. Cardinham in Cornwall, which Phillimore wrongly identifies with the Arthurian *Caradigan.* Cp. Lot, *Romania,* XXX, 19f.

[51] Cp. Muret, *Romania,* XVII, 606, and G. Paris, *ibid.* XVIII, 423.

[52] *Zs. f. frz. Spr. u. Litt.,* XIII[1], 73ff. (1891). F. Lot, *Romania,* XXV, 18f. (1896) was inclined to accept Zimmer's view.

[53] So, too, D'Arbois de Jubainville, *Revue Celtique,* XV, 408 (1894), and Golther, *Tristan und Isolde,* pp. 237ff. (1907).

[54] Cp. J. Loth, *Revue Celtique,* XXXII, 414ff. (1911). He argues that *Iseult (Iselt)* is Celtic in origin.

[55] Loth, *ibid.,* XXXII, 420, declares quite positively that Armorican participation in transmitting the name of Iseult to the French is, on phonetic grounds, out of the question.

seldom caught correctly and the difference, after all, is very slight. This difficulty seems, then, to offer no serious obstacle to the acceptance of the Welsh or Cornish origin of the love-saga.

As between Wales and Cornwall, the evidence would seem to point rather to the latter as the region in which the great love-story of Tristan and Iseult first took shape. Indeed, but for the rôle of an intermediary between Pictland and Cornwall — regions far apart — which we are compelled to assume, there would be no reason to attribute to Wales any part at all in the development of the legend. The wronged husband, as we have seen, bore a Cornish name, and was very likely an actual Cornish king. As Loth has pointed out,[56] his Lancien was identical with the *Lantien (Lantyan)* of our own day, a village on the river Fowey, and the parish in which this village is situated is still called Saint Sampson's — that is to say, still bears the same name as the church where, according to Béroul (l. 2977), Marc and Iseult performed their devotions.[57] In the neighborhood there is a place of the name of *Kilmarth,* a corruption for *Kilmarch* ("Marc's retreat"). Taking into consideration the evidence of these place-names, to say nothing of some others, suggested by Loth, which are more open to question,[58] and the fact that the *Tristan* poems distinctly

---

[56] Cp. *Revue Celtique*, XXXIII, 270f. (1912). It appears in Domesday Book as *Lantien (Lanthien)*. This name for Marc's capital is found only in Béroul, ll. 1155 *et passim*, and in Gerbert's continuation to Chrétien's *Perceval,* in the episode which Bédier and Miss Weston have published, *Romania* XXXV, 497ff. (1906), under the title of *Tristan menestrel*. The latter derived it from Béroul, no doubt. It is safe to assume that Béroul, in turn, derived it from the (lost) primitive Tristan poem.

In the *Comptes Rendus* of the Académie des Inscriptions et Belles-Lettres, *Bulletin de Decembre, 1916*, pp. 592f., Loth points out that a gate entering Lantyan Wood is still called Mark's Gate.

[57] According to the *Folie Tristan,* prose *Tristan* and Chrétien's *Erec,* Tristan and the Morholt fight on an island of St. Sampson, off the coast of Cornwall. In the *Bulletin* cited in the previous note, pp. 589ff., Loth cites a charter of May 20, 1301, to prove that an island once existed at the mouth of the Fawe. This isle he identifies with the Isle of St. Sampson.

[58] Namely, of *Tristan's Leap* with *Bodrigan's Leap* (south of Lantien), *Mal Pas* with *Malpas* (near Truro, on the Truro river),

locate the story in Cornwall, there can be no doubt that Cornwall had a main share in the formation of the legend. It would appear that the fame of a character, originally Pictish, had spread through Wales and Cornwall, and that in the latter, owing to circumstances over which time has drawn an impenetrable veil, that character became the hero of this crowning love-story of the Middle Ages.

Apart from the Pictish, Welsh and Cornish elements already noted, an analysis of the Tristan tradition[59] reveals still further Breton and French names, which point to the conclusion that both of these people likewise had a hand in the final shaping of the story, before it reached the author of the lost romance which was the common source of the extant Tristan poems. For instance,

---

*Blanche Lande* with *Blauncheloimd* (not far from Malpas and recorded as early as 1306), now called *Nansavallan.* Cp. *Revue Celtique,* XXXIII, 274 ff. (1912) and the above-cited *Bulletin,* 590. The first of these identifications, however, is hardly more than a guess. As for the last two, A. Smirnov, *Romania,* XLIII, 121 ff., has raised objections which appear to me worthy of serious attention: The two names are common in the Middle Ages; Arthur, coming to Lantien from Wales, would not pass by Blanche Lande; and, besides, the names occur in episodes that do not appear to belong to the story of Tristan in its original form.

Loth, *Revue Celtique,* XXXIII, 287 f. (1912) also proposes to emend *Parmenie* (name of the kingdom of Tristan's father in Gottfried) to *Hermenie* and identify it with the manor named in Domesday Book *Hoimenen* (now *Harmony*). But it is not likely that a manor should be called a kingdom. The alternative identification which he suggests, viz. with *Hen-moniu,* is not open to the same objection, but this, too, is pure speculation.

It is to be observed, finally, that the Cornish names, *Malpas; Blanche Lande, Mark's Gate,* may be due to attempts at localization of the Tristan story, suggested by the romances. As early as the twelfth century such localizations of the story as we have seen, were made about Dublin, and one of them, *Chapelizod* (name of a village near Dublin), has persisted to this day. Cp. letters on the subject in *The Athenaeum* Feb. 21 (p. 26), May 10, 17, 1913. The writers naively cite these localizations as proofs of the actual existence of the characters concerned, but they are, of course, like the localizations of the Romeo and Juliet story at Verona, which are all recent and based on Shakespeare's play.

[59] Cp. Bédier, II, 122 f.

the names of Rivalin, Tristan's father, and Hoel, his father-in-law, are ummistakably Breton, whereas Blanchefleur, the name of his mother, and Petitcru, that of his marvellous dog, are evidently French. It is plain, then, that the Bretons acted as intermediaries in the transmission of the story from Great Britain to the French. The fact that one of the hero's parents bears a French name, the other a Breton name, is especially significant.[60] The inventor of this part of the legend must have been familiar with both languages and he was, doubtless, a Breton from the bi-lingual zone. According to Bédier, it was the Breton jongleurs who were drawn to Great Britain by the Norman occupation that brought the story of the lovers home with him across the channel, but since the researches of Loth have shown that there was certainly, to say the least of it, an early localization of this story in Cornwall, it would seem likely that it was transmitted directly from Cornwall to Brittany by the ordinary processes of oral tradition.[61]

Accepting, in general, the theory that the essential feature

---

[60] I am assuming here that *Riwelin (Riwelen)* — which is Breton (cp. Zimmer, *Zs. f. frz. Spr. u. Litt.*, XIII[1], 58 ff.) — was the name of Tristan's father in the legend in the form in which it first became known to the French. This is the name of the hero's father in Eilhart and Gottfried. The early part of Thomas's *Tristan* is lost, but, doubtless, Gottfried derived the name from Thomas. In the prose romance, the character is called *Meliadus*. This, however, is certainly a late substitution. He is surnamed, still further, *Kanelangres* by Thomas. Brugger, in his article, "Zum Tristan-Roman", *Archiv für das Studium der neueren Sprachen*, CXXIX, 134 ff. (1912) tries to prove that *Kanelangres* is a mere corruption of *Talergen* (diminutive of *Talorch*, the name of the eighth century Pictish king, whose son was named *Drust-Tristan*), but his argument is not convincing. The name still awaits a satisfactory explanation. Cp. Bédier, I, 2, note 2.

[61] This is, on the whole, the most likely hypothesis, and Golther (p. 70) has accepted it as such. But he believes that the Tristan legend was among both Welsh and Bretons, mere heroic saga, not a love-story and that the love *motif* was first introduced by the French. Indeed, he sees in the Tristan story the influence of Geoffrey of Monmouth and the narrative of the infidelity of Arthur's wife with his nephew, Mordred. But, as I have observed above, the balance of probabilities seems against this supposition.

of the Tristan legend — the love-motif — was Celtic, and that it reached the French poets in the manner that has been described, I will conclude with an examination of those elements in the story which we may regard as later accretions.

It has always been recognized that the various stratagems by which the lovers elude the vigilance of King Marc were not characteristically Celtic and were probably brought into the story at a comparatively late stage. Thus the incident of the blades by which Tristan is wounded, with the subsequent trick to deceive the husband, has been shown to be a modification of a story as old as Herodatus — the tale of the thief who robs a king's treasury.[62] Iseult's oath that no one has touched her save Marc and the beggar (really the disguised Tristan) is likewise a wide-spread folk-lore *motif*. For instance there is a close parallel to the incident in the Icelandic Grettissaga (end of thirteenth century).[63] Take also the episode in which Marc, concealed in a tree, listens to the lovers, who, becoming aware of his presence, change their conversation so as to deceive him. This was manifestly suggested by the pear-tree story, so well known to folklorists and immortalized by Chaucer in the *Merchant's Tale*. The *motifs*, to be sure, are not the same, for in the pear-tree tale the lovers persuade the husband that the disgraceful scene which he has witnessed was the result of optical illusion. Nevertheless, the situation is so similar — the husband hidden in the tree and the lovers beneath — that we may safely accept the *Tristan* episode as a mild adaptation of that story.

More important than these matters is the question of the origin of the opening and concluding divisions of the romance — Tristan's birth and childhood, on the one hand, and the story of Iseult of Brittany, on the other. There is no indication of these features of the romance in the scanty Welsh tradition, and there can be hardly a doubt that both episodes are later developments in the story — doubtless, inventions of the author of the lost primitive French *Tristan*. In the *chansons de geste*, nearly all

---

[62] Cp. G. Huet, "Sur un épisode du Tristan d'Eilhart d'Oberg" *Romania*, XXXVI, 50ff. (1907) and G. Schoepperle, I, 213ff. (1913). The latter gives, p. 214, note 3, the previous literature of the subject.
[63] Cp. Golther, p. 28.

the great heroes had *enfances,* including occasionally some romantic narrative concerning their parents, so that when the legend
of Tristan passed into the hands of a poet familiar with French
epical tradition, Tristan, too, was provided with a set of youthful
adventures. The name, for which the hero's tragical fate suggested a connection with French *triste,* set the poet's imagination
to work, and we have as a result the sorrowful birth of the character. Then for the last division of the romance — the elements
here also seem plain. The man loved by two wives was one of the
common themes of mediaeval romance, *Eliduc,* the lay by Marie
de France, being perhaps the most famous example of it. Combine
with this, now, the classical legend of *Oenone,* the jealous wife
of Paris, who is skilled in the healing art, but refuses to save
her wounded husband, from jealousy of her rival Helen, and we
have the essentials of the concluding episode in our romance,[64]
beginning with the expulsion of Tristan after his second detection
with Iseult.

To be sure, Iseult of Cornwall retains the knowledge of the
healing art which she had evidently possessed already in the Celtic
legend, so in this respect the conditions required that she, rather
than her rival, should resemble the nymph of the classical legend,
but the general situation is obviously the same, and I see no reason
for rejecting Golther's identification of the stories. On the other
hand, with equal confidence we may accept the *motif* of the white
and black sails as derived from the legend of Theseus, in which
the hero's father, Aegeus, perished in consequence of his son's
forgetfulness in regard to this same signal. Servius's commentary
on the *Aeneid,* doubtless, made this incident the common property
of the Middle Ages.[65]

[64] The author of the primitive French *Tristan* poem, doubtless,
transferred to Iseult of Brittany some traits that originally belonged
to Iseult of Cornwall. Cp., especially, the incident of the water which
splashes up under the latter's dress and which, she says, is bolder
than Tristan has been. Miss Schoepperle, II, 415, points out that this
incident occurs, also, in the Diarmaid and Grainne saga — so that
we may accept it as attached to the original of Iseult of Cornwall
in the Celtic *Aithed.*

[65] This was pointed out by Bédier, II, 138f. To be sure, Brugger,
*Archiv für das Studium der neueren Sprachen,* CXXX, 124 ff. (1913),

It will be observed that even the central theme of the primitive French *Tristan*, as outlined above, is a much more complex affair than the Irish *Aitheda* (*Diarmaid und Grainne* etc.), from which we have derived it. We have, in addition to the *motifs* of the *Aitheda*, the combat with Morholt, the two voyages to Ireland, the first of which involves the hero's healing at the hands of an enemy and the second his quest for the princess of the beautiful hair, the part played by Bringvain, besides the series of incidents, in which the lovers evade detection. Now, the combat with the Irish champion, Morholt, and the voyage for healing manifestly belong together, and, inasmuch as the name of this strange champion seems Celtic,[66] we may accept both combat[67] and voyage as of Celtic origin, although the idea of a wound which can be

---

disputes Bédier's conclusion. He cites especially (pp. 132 ff.) a Gaelic parallel (a tale written down by J. G. Campbell) as proving the Celtic origin of the incident. But the Gaelic story is not recorded before the nineteenth century and may very well be, itself, derived from the Theseus legend. Miss Schoepperle, *Revue Celtique*, XXXII, 185 f., and in her *Tristan* book, II, 437 f. (1913) is more cautious than Brugger. The fact that the white and black sail *motif* is here combined with a classical *motif* (that of Paris and Oenone) points strongly, in my judgment, to the conclusion that it, too, is of classical origin.

[66] The question one must acknowledge, is doubtful, since the name is not found in Celtic, nor in exactly this form, indeed, anywhere outside of the *Tristan* poems. *Mor*, however, means "sea" in the Celtic languages, and Loth, *Revue Celtique*, XXXII, 420, note 1, (1011) has derived *Morholt* tentatively from an hypothetical Old Celtic *morispolto* = "sea-splitter". Miss Schoepperle, II, 331, note 1, seems to me to have misunderstood Muret, *Romania*, XVII, 606 (1888) when she imputes to him the idea (which is really Golther's, p. 17) that Morholt's name was connected with that of the Fomori (giants or marine monsters in Irish saga). Muret merely means that originally Morholt was one of these Celtic giants. Like Miss Schoepperle, *loc. cit.*, I cannot regard the story from the Cuchullin saga (Cuchullin frees a princess who has been offered as a tribute to the Fomorians) which Deutschbein, *Beiblatt zu Anglia*, XV, 16 ff. (1904) and *Studien zur Sagengeschichte Englands*, 172 f. (Cöthen, 1906) cites, as having any historical connection with the Morholt episode.

*Morhold* occurs as a Germanic name in eighth century documents (Cp. E. Foerstemann, *Altdeutsches Namenbuch*, col. 1118), but the similarity is probably accidental.

healed only by an enemy is by no means confined to the Celts.[68]
It has been suggested that this episode reflects early historical
conditions, when the Pictish population of Scotland were being
subjugated by Irish invaders.[69] This would seem to be a plausible conjecture, and if Tristan was, indeed, in the beginning, a
Pictish hero, no incident is so likely to have belonged to him in
that character as that of this combat and its sequel. The second
voyage in which Tristan goes forth on his indeterminate search
for the unknown golden-haired princess, owes its suggestion, too,
no doubt, to a favorite class of Celtic tales—the *Imrama* (tales of
fantastic voyages),[70] one of which in its Christianized form, the
legend of St. Brendan, enjoyed a wide-spread popularity in the
Middle Ages throughout Western Europe. In the episode of the
*Tristan* under consideration, however, the object of the voyage
has no parallel in these Celtic tales,[71] and the *imram motif* seems
plainly combined with that of a hero's quest of a bride for a king,[72]
and in a specific form which is apparently unknown to the Celts —
the search for the girl, the strands of whose hair have been brought
to the king by a bird.[73] A distinguished scholar, indeed, once
regarded this adaptation of the well-known fairy-tale of the Fair
Maid with the Golden Locks as the fundamental theme of the

----

[67] That the combat should take place on an island was once
regarded as a Scandinavian (Viking) feature of the story, another
example of the *holmgang*. Cp. Golther, p. 16. Miss Schoepperle,
however, has shown that island-combats were stock features of the
Old French romances and that the combat in the *Tristan* does not
conform to the rules of the *holmgang*. Cp. her paper in the Radcliffe College Monographs, No. 15, (1910) and her *Tristan and Isolt*,
II, 338 ff.

[68] For examples from different parts of the world see Schoepperle,
II, 377 ff.

[69] Golther, *Tristan und Isolde*, pp. 15 f. (1907).

[70] For a discussion of the *Imrama* see A. C. L. Brown, *Iwain*,
566 ff. For MSS. and editions cp. G. Dottin, *Revue Celtique*, XXXIII,
26 (1912).

[71] Cp. Schoepperle, I, 188 ff.

[72] Miss Schoepperle, I, 188, note 3, gives a very full list of such
stories in the various literatures.

[73] Miss Schoepperle's list, just cited, contains no Celtic tale with
this particular feature.

Tristan legend,[74] but the fairy tale in question, beautiful as it is, is too gossamerlike ever to have suggested the most passionate love-story in literature, and, since the publication of Miss Schoepperle's researches, we may safely regard this adaptation as merely a later embellishment — introduced, no doubt, by a French poet — of what is, in itself, a secondary element in the legend, the second voyage to Ireland.[75]

[74] Cp. W. Golther, "Die Jungfrau mit den goldenen Haaren", *Studien zur Litteraturgeschichte, Michael Bernays gewidmet von Schülern und Freunden,* p. 173 (Hamburg and Leipzig, 1893) — also, Reinhold Köhler, "Tristan und Isolde und das Märchen von der goldhaarigen Jungfrau und von den Wassern des Todes und des Lebens", *Germania,* XI, 389 ff. (1866) — reprinted in Köhler, *Kleinere Schriften,* II, 328 ff. (Berlin, 1900). For additional notes on the theme cp. Felix Liebrecht, *Germania,* XII (1867), and Köhlers *Kleinere Schriften,* I, 511.

[75] This ends our discussion of the *Tristan* romances; for the endeavor of Zenker to connect the saga of this hero with the Persian epic of Wis and Ramin has been generally pronounced a failure. Cp. his *Die Tristansage und das persische Epos von Wis und Ramin* (Erlangen, 1910) — also, *Zs. f. rom. Ph.,* XXXV, 715 ff. (1912). Zenker, p. 326, cites Hermann Ethe, *Die höfische und romantische Poesie der Perser,* p. 38 (Hamburg, 1887), as the first to call attention to the resemblance of the stories. So, too, W. Hertz, *Tristan und Isolde von Gottfried von Strassburg,* p. 478 (Stuttgart and Berlin, 1907).

On other Tristans, besides the famous hero, see W. Hertz, ibid. pp. 482 ff. Of most interest, perhaps, is the "Tristanz qui onques ne rist," who figures in a number of romances, cited, *loc. cit.,* by Hertz — first of all, in Chrétien's *Erec,* 1, 1713, in the well-known list of Arthur's knights. It has been customary to regard this character as drawn from oral tradition, but he was, unquestionably, the invention of a Frenchman — no doubt, a French poet — to whom the similarity of *Tristan* and *triste* suggested the nickname. It occurred to the author of *L'Atre Perillos* to make him play the part of a host (cp. l. 5392) in a brief episode of that poem — otherwise (in Chrétien and the other romancers), he is a mere name. My own belief is that the character is an invention for the nonce of Chrétien's, who was put to it to make out the long list of knights in the above-mentioned passage and who, consequently, fabricated this new character, like some other characters in the list. He derived the name primarily, of course, from the renowned lover of Iseult, and the accompanying nickname was supplied to him, partly, by an obvious play on words, and, partly, by the necessity of finding a rhyme to *sist.*

## Chapter VI.
## Lancelot.

With no character of the Arthurian cycle, except Arthur and Guinevere, is the modern reader so familiar as with Lancelot. He does not appear, however, in the earliest Arthurian texts and he is in everything but name purely a literary creation — more clearly so, perhaps, than any other character of Arthurian romance. He is not mentioned in Welsh literature or in Geoffrey of Monmouth and his derivatives; he does not figure in the basreliefs of the cathedral at Modena. Indeed, the first we hear of him is in Chrétien's *Erec*, (1. 1694) in the well-known list of Round Table knights. As is always the case in the verse-romances, Chrétien in this passage gives Gawain the first place. The second place he awards to Erec, because that character is the hero of this particular romance. The third he gives to Lancelot del Lac. Now we have not a trace of Lancelot in Celtic saga or earlier Arthurian texts, and Chrétien himself does not allude to the character again in this poem, so that it seems surprising that he should in this off-hand way assign Lancelot so high a place among Arthurian heroes.

In view of the circumstances just mentioned, however, this *Erec* passage would hardly seem to justify the inference that Lancelot really occupied any very high place in Celtic tradition. In fact, when Welshmen came to translate the Arthurian romances, they thought that in Perceval they recognized their native Peredur and they accordingly substituted the latter's name for Perceval; similarly they substituted Gwalchmei for Gawain, Llacheu for Lohot, etc. But they knew nothing of Lancelot, and consequently, they kept the French form of his name in Welsh orthography: *Lawnselot*.[1] As a matter of fact, there is no ground for believing that

---

[1] Cp. Foerster, *Lancelot*, pp. XXXIXf.

the name is Welsh; more likely, it is a mere French adaptation of Breton *Lancelin,* which is, itself, ultimately of Germanic origin.[2] The most probable explanation of the character's prominence in the above-mentioned list is that Chrétien was already planning to make him the hero of a poem: the name had taken his fancy or he was influenced by some chance circumstance in this determination. In any event, a few years later he did make him the hero of his well-known poem, *Lancelot.*

In the *Cliges,* which comes immediately after *Erec* in order of composition, Lancelot still holds (by implication) the third place,[3] but Perceval, who was not mentioned in the *Erec* list, now holds the second place — for the same reason, perhaps, as that which has just been suggested in the case of Lancelot; for Perceval, too, was later on made the hero of one of Chrétien's romances. In the passage of the *Cliges* just referred to Lancelot is overcome by Cliges in a tournament — otherwise he does not appear in the romance. He is, however, the hero of the next poem composed by Chrétien — the *Conte de la Charrete,* or *Lancelot*[4] — and it was this romance which ultimately established his fame.

Now the main theme of this poem is the abduction of Guinevere by an evil prince named Meleagant and her rescue by Lancelot. We may summarize it briefly as follows:

Meleagant appears at Arthur's court and boasts that he holds many of the king's subjects in captivity. Arthur, however, can free them if he will commit Guinevere to the care of a knight who will fight a single combat with him. If Meleagant loses, the prisoners are to be freed; if he is victorious, Guinevere will remain his captive. Just then Kay, the seneschal, threatens to leave the court and Arthur can only keep him by the inconsiderate pro-

---

[2] Cp. H. Zimmer, *Zs. f. frz. Spr. u. Litt.,* XIII¹, 43 ff. (1891).

[3] Cp. 11. 4765 ff.

[4] Chrétien, 11. 24 f. says: "Del Chevalier de la Charrete romance Crestiiens son livre," but, for convenience' sake, recent scholars have been accustomed to cite the romance after its hero's name, and I shall follow their example.

mise that he will grant him any request he may proffer. To the
king's dismay, Kay demands that he shall be the queen's escort.
Nevertheless, Arthur is bound by his promise and so permits Kay
to ride off with Meleagant and Guinevere. He, himself, and his
knights follow later on. Gawain meets first the seneschal's horse
riderless and bloody and somewhat further on Lancelot (not named
yet, however). Lancelot's horse is tired out and Gawain lends
him a fresh one. Shortly after, Gawain finds his horse dead and
all the signs of a fierce combat about the spot — then, he comes
again upon Lancelot who, in his hurry to get forward after the
loss of his steed, had got into a cart — with some hesitation, it
is true, because that was contrary to the rules of chivalry. This
cart was driven by a dwarf. Now, Meleagant was the son of
a good king, Baudemagus, whose land was surrounded by a deep
water, and this water could be crossed by only two bridges —
one a sword, with the edge turned upwards, the other under the
water. Lancelot chooses the first. No account is given of his
crossing in the poem, but he gets over in safety, fights with
Meleagant, and delivers Guinevere, who, nevertheless, receives him
coldly, being offended at his momentary hesitation before moun-
ting the cart. Lancelot, in despair, tries to commit suicide; Guinevere, hearing a rumour of his death, is overwhelmed with grief,
and on his next appearance receives him with the greatest favour.
They pass the night together, Lancelot gaining access to the queen's
chamber by means of a heavily barred window and severely wounding his hands in wrenching asunder the bars. The traces of blood
on the bed-clothes causes the queen to be accused of a *liaison* with
Kay, who, severely wounded, is sleeping in the ante-chamber.
Lancelot undertakes to prove Guinevere's innocence by a combat
with Meleagant, which shall take place at Arthur's court; but
having set out to seek Gawain, he is treacherously decoyed into
prison by his foe. Meleagant, by means of forged letters, persuades the queen that Lancelot has returned to court, whither
Guinevere repairs, escorted by Gawain, who has meanwhile arrived on the scene. Lancelot, who has been released on parole by his
jailor's wife, to attend a tourney, and who acts there successively

the part of a coward and a hero, according to the queen's injunction, is subsequently walled up in a tower by Meleagant. Here Chrétien's portion of the poem ends, but it was continued with his approval and under his direction for about 1000 lines more by a certain Godefroi de Lagny (Leigni).[5] According to this continuation, he was released from prison by Meleagant's sister, and, reaching court at the last moment, overcomes and slays Meleagant.

Although in the subsequent history of literature it became the most influential of Chrétien's poems, with the exception of the *Perceval*, critics generally have agreed that the *Lancelot* is the poorest in construction of all the works of this author. He tells us at the beginning of the romance (ll. 26ff.) that his patroness, Marie de Champagne, gave him the *matiere et san*[6] (matter and meaning) of the poem and that he took pains to put into it nothing but *sa painne et s'antancion* (labor and thought). Of the defects[7] just referred to the most notable perhaps are the following: 1. Why should not Meleagant fight out at Arthur's court the question as to the possession of the queen, instead of going off with his adversary to settle it at some indefinite time later? The explanation, no doubt, is that the abduction originally took place in a wood and the author here is simply making an awkward attempt to connect the adventure with the court, which

---

[5] Foerster, Chrétien *Wörterbuch*, pp. 72*f., owing to linguistic considerations, identifies this place with Lagny in the department of Seine-et-Marne. Nothing is known of Godefroi, himself.

[6] For the interpretation of these words see, particularly, W. A. Nitze, "*San et matiere* dans les oeuvres de Chrétien de Troyes", *Romania*, XLIV, 14ff. (1915). *San* is derived from Latin *sensus*, which was used as a synonym of *sapientia* and *scientia*, when the wisdom or knowledge was given by God. Nitze traces *sensus* with this meaning back to the apocryphal *Liber Sapientiae* (accepted as canonical during the Middle Ages), e. g., VII, 7. Chrétien adopted it from the scholastic usage of his time, in which it was applied to interpretation — especially, the allegorical interpretation of the scriptures.

[7] In her *Legend of Sir Lancelot du Lac*, pp. 43f. (London, 1901), Miss Weston has given a full summary of the defects of construction in the romance.

is the customary starting-point of his Arthurian tales.[8] 2. We are told that the kingdom of Gorre — that is, the kingdom of Meleagant's father — is surrounded by water which no one can pass save by means of the two seemingly impossible bridges — the sword bridge and the subaqueous bridge. Lancelot is said to have chosen the former, but we hear no more of this striking conception, and as if no explanation were necessary, we find the hero next already in the kingdom of Gorre and pursuing his adventures there. One might add that it is strange that the cart which Lancelot gets into should disappear from the story. It may be that Marie's own knowledge of the tradition of Guinevere's abduction was imperfect and that Chrétien followed his mistress too literally, without attempting to supply the deficiencies.

The *matière* of Chrétien's poem is simply the abduction and rescue of the queen — the tradition to that effect being certainly anterior to his *Lancelot*. Everything else in the romance, we may confidently assert, is subsidiary to this theme. Some of the documentary evidence in regard to this tradition is independent of Chrétien, beyond question. There is even a fourteenth century Welsh dialogue between Arthur and his queen[9] that seems to hint at an incident of this kind in which Kay plays the rôle of abductor, but the piece is too obscure to be of much use. We have indisputably, however, a record of Celtic tradition on the subject in the *Vita Gildae,* attributed (rightly, it would seem) to Caradoc of Lancarvan and written probably about 1150.[10] Here it is said

---

[8] So Miss Weston, *loc. cit.*

[9] See the translation in J. Rhys's *Arthurian Legend,* pp. 57 f.

[10] See the passages in Mommsen's edition of Gildas and Nennius, *Monumenta Germaniae Historica* (1894), p. 109 — also, G. Paris's article, *Romania,* X, 491, note (1881). In his *Mélanges d'Histoire Bretonne,* pp. 267 ff. (Paris, 1907), F. Lot has discussed the date, authorship and sources of this (insular) *Vita Gildae.* The author, (Caradoc, most likely) came originally from Nantcarvan (in South Wales), it would seem, and afterwards was a monk at Glastonbury. The work was anterior to 1166; for a MS. of it from that year is extant. J. A. Herbert would place the *Vita* in the "middle of the twelfth century, perhaps even a little earlier." Cp. his letter quoted by Lot, *op. cit.,* pp. 275 f., note 2.

that Gildas, having been stripped of his possessions by pirates, came to Glastonbury, whilst Melvas (Melwas) was ruling in Somerset (aestiva regio).[11] This wicked king carried off Guinevere (Guennuvar) to Glastonbury, which was a difficult place to take,

---

[11] Cp. on the subject of Melwas, especially, F. Lot, *Romania*, XXIV, 327 ff. (1895), XXVII, 553 (1898).

As Lot remarks in the first of these articles ("Melvas, roi des morts et l'ile de verre"), the author of the *Vita Gildae* makes Melwas King of Somerset, simply because Glastonbury was in Somerset. For a similar reason (the chief city of this shire being Bath), according to Lot, Godefroi de Leigni, who doubtless knew in some form or other the story concerning Melwas in the *Vita Gildae,* in his continuation of Chrétien's *Lancelot* (l. 6255), made Bade (Bath) the capital of the kingdom of Meleagant's (Melwas's) father (Baudemagus). This conflicts, of course, with his acceptance of Gorre as Melwas's land, for whatever region Gorre is to be identified with (cp. the next note), it was certainly not Somerset. Consistency, however is not to be expected of a romancer.

Melwas is, doubtless, identical with Geoffrey of Monmouth's *Melga* (V, 16 and VI, 3) and *Malvasius, rex Islandiae* (IX, 12, probably for *Irlandiae.* Cp. Zimmer, *Zs. f. frz. Spr. u. Litt.,* XII[1], 253) — according to Rhys (*Studies in the Arthurian Legend,* p. 344), also, with Maelwys, son of Baeddan in *Kulhwch and Olwen* (*Loth's Mabinogion*[2], I, 261), Baeddan being the same, according to this scholar, as the Bademagus of Chrétien's *Lancelot.* He regards both Maelwys and Bademagus as ultimately of Irish origin. H. L. D. Ward had already expressed this view in regard to Melwas. Cp. *Romania,* XII, 512 (1883). More plausible, to my mind, is Lot's derivation *(loc. cit.)* of *Melwas* from *Maelvas* (= Prince of Death). Brugger, *Zs. f. frz. Spr. u. Litt.,* XXVIII[1], 6, note 10, thinks that Ward's hypothetical Irish prince may have been confounded with Lot's Maelwas, "Prince of Death". All of this about an Irish Melwas, however, is pure speculation. So, too, with Brugger's attempt to prove (*ibid.,* pp. 15 ff., 26 ff.) that Bademagus is of Pictish origin, which is a corollary of his theory (see next note) that Gorre was in Northern Scotland.

The story of Guinevere's abduction has been compared by Rhys and others with the Irish *Wooing of Etain.* For the literature of the subject, cp. Miss Schoepperle's *Tristan and Isolt,* II, 528, note 3. I do not believe, however, that there is any historical connection between the two.

owing to the river and marsh that protected it. Arthur besieged
it with an immense host, and a great conflict was about to ensue,
when the Abbot of Glastonbury and Gildas intervened and, on
their advice, Melwas restored the queen to Arthur. The two kings
then gave much land to the abbey. In this text — the *Vita
Gildae* — Glastonbury is represented as a rendering of the British
name for the place — *Ynys witryn (Ynisgutrin)* or City of Glass
but this absurd etymology was invented by some monk of the
local abbey about the middle of the twelfth century — doubtless,
by the author of the *Vita Gildae*, himself.[12] The name is really

------

[12] The passage (p. 110 of Mommsen's edition) runs as follows:
"Ynisgutrin nominata fuit antiquitus Glastonia et adhuc nominatur a
Britannis indigenis; ynis in Britannico sermone insula Latine; gutrin
vero vitrea.  Sed post adventum Angligenarum et expulsis Britannis,
scilicet Walensibus, revocata est Glastigberi ex ordine primi vocabuli,
scilicet glas Anglice vitrum Latine, beria civitas, inde Glastiberia id
est Vitrea Civitas."

In the *De Antiquitate Glastoniensis Ecclesiae* of William of
Malmesbury (*Migne, Patrologia Latina,* vol. 179, cols. 1682ff.)
"Ynisgutrin" again appears as a name for Glastonbury, along with
"insula Avalloniae".  Following is the text of this oft-quoted passage:

"Legitur in antiquis Britonum gestis, quod a Boreali Britanniae
parte venerunt in occidentem duodecim fratres, et tenuerunt plurimas
regiones.  Venedociam, Demetiam, Buthir [for *Guhir*], Kedweli, quas
proavus eorum Cuneda tenuerunt: nomina eorum fratrum inferius anno-
tantur Ludnerth [for *Iudnerth*], Morgen, Catgur, Cathmor, Merguid,
Morvined, Morehel, Morcant, Boten, Morgen, Mortineil [for *Mormeil*],
Glasteing [for *Glastenig*].  Hic est ille Glasteing [for *Glastenig*],
qui per mediterraneos Anglos, secus villam quae dicitur *Escebtiorne,*
scrofam suam usque ad Wellis, et a Wellis per inviam et aquosam
viam quae *Sugewege,* id est Scrofae via, dicitur, sequens porcellos
suos, juxta ecclesiam de qua nobis sermo est, lactentem sub malo
invenit, unde usque ad nos emanavit, quod mala mali illius *Eald-
eyrcenes epple,* id est Veteris Ecclesiae poma vocantur: sus quoque
*ealdcyre (sic) suge* idcirco nominabatur, quae cum ceterae sues quatuor
pedes habeant, mirum dictu, ista habuit octo.  Hic igitur Glasteing,
postquam insulam illam ingressus, eam multimodis bonis vidit affluentem,
cum omni familia sua in ea venit habitare, cursumque vitae suae ibidem
peregit.  Ex ejus progenie et familia ei succedente locus ille primitus
dicitur populatus, haec de antiquis Britonum libris sunt.

Anglo-Saxon and means the "city of the Glaestings" — Glaesting being, of course, a family name. Nevertheless, Gaston Paris has

"Haec itaque insula primo Yniswitrin, a Britonibus dicta, demum ab Anglis, terram sibi subjugantibus, interpretato priore vocabulo, dicta est sua lingua Glastinbiry; vel de Glasteing, de quo praemisimus. Etiam insula Avalloniae celebriter nominatur, cujus vocabuli haec fuit origo. Supradictum est, quod Glasteing scrofam suam sub arbore pomifera juxta vetustam ecclesiam invenit, ubi quia primum adveniens poma in partibus illis rarissima reperit, insulam Avalloniae sua lingua, id est insulam pomorum nominavit. Avalla enim Britonice poma interpretatur Latine; vel cognominatur de quodam Avalloc, qui ibidem cum suis filiabus, propter loci secretum, fertur inhabitasse."

W. W. Newell, however has shown, PMLA, XVIII, 474 ff., 492 f. (1903), that, like all other Arthurian passages in the *De Antiquitate*, this passage is due to an interpolator. His results are accepted by F. Lot, *Mélanges d'histoire bretonne*, pp. 277 ff. (Paris, 1907), although the latter previously in his "Glastonbury et Avalon", *Romania*, XXVII, 564 ff. (1898), had regarded it as genuine. Moreover, Lot is disposed (*Mélanges*, p. 283) to identify this interpolator with the author of the insular *Vita Gildae*. Since the publication of Newell's paper, however, it is hardly open to question that the identification of Glastonbury with Avalon was simply the consequence of the fraud of 1191, when the monks of Glastonbury pretended that they had discovered there the tomb of Arthur and his consort. The interpolator, accordingly, used the *Vita Gildae*, but was not its author.

In "Zu Wilhelm von Malmesbury", *Zs. f. rom. Ph.* XX, 316 ff. (1896), R. Thurneysen has pointed out that the story of Glasteing and his son is of Irish origin, being developed out of an incident in the legend of St. Patrick, and Newell, *op. cit.*, p. 476, notes that the incident of the pigs and appletree, which guide the founder to the site of the new city, is imitated from Virgil's *Aeneid*, (story of Aeneas and the founding of Alba Longa). The fanciful etymology which connects Avalon with the Welsh word for apple, "aval (afal)", is, at least, as old as the *Vita Merlini* (middle of the twelfth century), ascribed to Geoffrey of Monmouth; for there (l. 908) the island (Celtic Elysium) to which the wounded Arthur is borne is called "Insula Pomorum". Hence Glastonbury, having been identified with Avalon, is here also called "insula pomorum".

The alternative derivation of Avalon, suggested by the interpolator, viz., from a supposed Avalloc, who once lived at Glastonbury with his daughters, was accepted as correct by F. Lot, *Romania*, XXIV, 327 ff. (1895). Lot expresses there the belief that this Avalloc was argued justly, no doubt, in his classical articles on Lancelot,[13] that the narrative of the *Vita Gildae* here preserves a bit of Celtic mythology, though the localization is arbitrary. The author of that work, being a Celt, would naturally be familiar with the Celtic conception of the Otherworld as a Tower of Glass, and having hit upon the etymology for Glastonbury, just cited, and being essentially a romancer, he might very easily locate at Glastonbury this story of an Otherworld king. "Isle de Voirre" — the name of the kingdom of this same Melwas (Maheloas), according to Chrétien's *Erec*, ll. 1940 ff. — represents a confusion of two Celtic conceptions of the Otherworld — first, as the Island of Avalon, secondly, as a Tower of Glass.[14] In this passage of the *Erec*, Maheloas (Melwas) is represented as king of an ideal land — plainly, the Celtic Elysium — where there is no winter, yet where it is never too warm — an *aestiva regio*, in short, beyond the bounds of mortal ken. It is still further obvious that

---

a god and that his daughters were the women of the Celtic Elysium. (Cp. too, J. Rhys, *Arthurian Legend*, p. 335). The derivation, however, from Avalloc is, doubtless, just as fanciful as the derivation from "aval". In any event, the placing of Avalloc at Glastonbury is simply another consequence of the arbitrary identification of that locality with Avalon.

For the origin of Cuneda and his descendants see Thurneysen and Newell in the passages referred to above. J. Rhys, *Arthurian Legend*, ch. 14, has discussed all the matters dealt with in this note, but he goes on the erroneous assumption that the Arthuriana in the *De Antiquitate* are really by William of Malmesbury.

The passage about Glastonbury in the *Speculum Ecclesiae*, II, 9 (Rolls edition, pp. 49 f.) of Gerald of Wales is paraphrased from the above-quoted passage of the *De Antiquitate* — only it is that author's own invention when he suggests that the name, Inis Gutrin (so he divides it), came from the color of the stream nearby.

[13] *Romania*, X, 491 (1882), XII, 512 (1884).

[14] On the Irish Tower of Glass, cp. F. Lot, *Romania*, XXIV, 328 (1895). The Otherworld is often imagined as a Mountain of Glass in the myths of the most widely separated races. Cp. Léon Pineau, *Les vieux chants populaires Scandinaves*, II, 272 (Paris, 1901). For the conception in German folktales see, especially, Hans Siuts, *Jenseitsmotive im deutschen Volksmärchen*, p. 43 (Leipzig, 1911).

the Melwas of the *Vita Gildae* and the Maheloas of the *Erec* are
identical with the Meleagant[15] of the *Lancelot*, whose chief city
is Bath (in Somerset), and the Otherworld character of the abductor's realm[16] is plainest of all in the last-named work, for
in the *Lancelot* (ll. 645 ff.) it is called the country from which
no one returns. Moreover, the conception of the strange bridges as
the only means of access to Meleagant's land is found far and
wide in the mythology of various peoples connected with the king-

---

[15] In Foerster's edition of Chrétien's *Lancelot*, pp. xxxiii ff. (1899),
he and Zimmer dispute the identity. Their criticism of the supposed
Welsh sources for the Melwas-Guinevere story which G. Paris had
cited is searching and shows that the passages in question did not
have the value that the French scholar ascribed to them. It is idle,
however, to deny that the Melwas of the *Vita Gildae* is identical
with Maheloas and Meleagant.

In *Romania*, XII, 499 ff., G. Paris notes differences between the
accounts of the Rape of Guinevere by Meleagant (Mellyagraunce) in
Chrétien's and Malory, respectively, and explains them as due to independent Welsh (ultimate) sources of Malory. Foerster (edition of
Chrétien's *Lancelot*, pp. xxx ff.), however, rightly disputes this.

[16] The name of this realm "Gorre" ("Goirre") occurs twice
(ll. 643, 6141) in Chrétien's *Lancelot*. (Brugger, *Zs. f. frz. Spr. u.
Litt.*, XXVIII[1], ascribes the second instance to Godefroi de Leigni,
but cp. Foerster's edition of *Lancelot*, pp. XV f.) In the first passage
it is described as the kingdom "Don nus estranges ne retorne" (l. 645).
It is evidently in Great Britain, but no wholly satisfactory identification of it with any specific part of that island has ever been
proposed. Rhys, *Studies in the Arthurian Legend*, pp. 329 f. (1891)
believes that it is the peninsula of Gower (Modern Welsh *Gwyr,
Goer*) in Southwest Wales and that Bath (Bade) is made its capital
through confusion. One need not assume with Rhys that this confusion
is due to the contamination of two different Celtic conceptions concerning
the realm of the dead. It is sufficient to observe that the single
mention (l. 6255) of Bath (Bade), as the capital of Gorre, occurs in
the continuation of Chrétien's poem by Godefroi de Leigni. Now,
whatever one may think concerning Chrétien's sources, there is no
reason to believe that Godefroi was drawing upon any Celtic traditions,
and, as Brugger remarks, *Zs. f. frz. Spr. u. Litt.*, XXVIII[1], 7 (1905)
(although he fails to observe that this name occurs only in Godefroi's
portion of the poem), the name (Bade = Bath), of King Bdaemagus's

dom of the dead.[17]   We may accept, then, the conception of Meleagant's abduction of Guinevere as of Celtic origin, although there

capital was, no doubt, suggested to the poet by the name of the king
himself.

In *Romania*, XXIV, 332 (1895), F. Lot conjectures that *Gorre*
may not have been a place-name, originally, but derived simply from
Old Welsh *gutr* (= glass), the kingdom of Gorre being then merely
the "Isle of Glass" (Celtic Elysium). *Ibid.*, 327 ff., he had been
inclined to accept Rhys's views.

In Brugger's long article on Gorre, just cited, he concludes that
it is to be identified with *Strathmore* (a name which he would extend,
it seems, to the whole of ancient Scotland, north of the Clyde and
the Forth). For the stages which he supposes *Strathmore* to have
traversed in becoming *Gorre,* cp. *loc. cit.,* pp. 63 ff.   He reaches his
conclusions, however, through such a maze of hazardous speculations
that his results inspire little confidence. I may say, in general, that
it is highly improbable that the romancers in their fantastic compositions have preserved geographical accuracy, as Brugger's hypothesis
assumes. P. Paris *(Romans de la Table Ronde,* II, 111), says with
truth: "On ne peut trop répéter que nos romanciers ne se rendaient
pas compte des localités: ils n'inventaient pas les noms, mais ils n'en
recherchaient pas la valeur exacte." In other words, they made about
the same use of place-names (and, I might add, of other kinds of
names, as well) as, according to Brugger, himself, *Zs. f. frz. Spr.
u. Litt.,* XXXII[2], 127 (1908), Geoffrey of Monmouth did with the
names which he derived from Welsh traditions, viz. attach to them
any fiction he chose. Brugger (op. cit., XXVIII[1], 14) acknowledges
the correctness of P. Paris's observation, but proceeds on the opposite
principle.

In the consideration of names in the romances, one has to keep
in mind always the possibilities of manuscript corruption. The number
of apparently new names in these works that have come into existence
in this manner is enormous.

   [17] Cp. G. Paris, *Romania,* XII, 508.   The literature concerning
these bridges by which, in the myths and legends of various peoples,
the Otherworld must be reached is truly immense, and for publications
on the subject I will refer the reader, above all, to the notes to Miss
Laura Hibbard's article, "The Sword Bridge of Chrétien de Troyes
and its Celtic Original", RR, IV, 166 ff. (1913) — also, to H. R.
Patch's "Some Elements in Mediaeval Descriptions of the Otherworld",
PMLA, XXXIII, 601 ff. (1918), more particularly, the notes to pp. 635 ff.
For instances in German folktales, not mentioned by these scholars,

is no similar incident in extant Celtic stories of the Otherworld, but in Chrétien's description this conception appears to have been profoundly influenced by classical and oriental myths concerning the kingdom of the dead. The translator of Ovid would, of course, have been familiar with the stories of Proserpine and Eurydice and with Hercules's rescue of Alcestis from Hades.[18] On the other hand, the idea of the sword-bridge, doubtless, came to him ultima-

---

cp. Hans Siuts's *Jenseitsmotive im deutschen Volksmärchen*, pp. 41 f. (Leipzig, 1911). Although taking Chrétien's sword-bridge as Celtic in origin, Miss Hibbard denies (p. 184) that it ever had mythological significance. She regards it (cp. *loc. cit.*, pp. 177 ff. and notes) as simply one of the marvellous bridges that appear in the narratives of fantastic exploits performed by Celtic heroes — narratives that are without mythological connections. If the sword-bridge were really Celtic, Miss Hibbard's derivation would be preferable, for, as Patch has observed (p. 637), there is no real place for a bridge in the Celtic scheme of the Otherworld. An ocean voyage is there the essential thing. Patch, himself, regards it as derived from the Otherworld bridge either of Norse mythology (e. g. *Gylfaginning*, ch. 49) or Oriental vision. Marvellous Otherworld bridges (derived from the East, no doubt) are common in the vision literature of Western Europe in the Middle Ages. Cp. the examples cited by Miss Hibbard in her article, notes 14—21, from the *Dialogues* of Gregory the Great, the *Visio S. Pauli*, etc. It did not require any great invention to add a sword-bridge to this collection of wonderful bridges. For the human automata that often guard such bridges in the romances, cp. J. D. Bruce "Human Automata in Classical Tradition and Mediaeval Romance", MPh., X, 511 ff. (1913) and M. B. Ogle, "The Perilous Bridge and Human Automata", MLN, XXXV, 129 f. (1920). Ogle cites from William of Malmesbury's *Gesta Regum Anglorum*, II, 170 (Stubbs's edition in the Rolls Series, 1887) an example of the *motif* earlier than any reference to it in Celtic tales.

[18] Foerster, *Lancelot*, p. LXXI, goes so far as to contend that these classical myths were Chrétien's sole source for the abduction-story. Even more radical is G. Baist, *ibid.*, LXXII ff., who denies that this story contains any mythical elements at all. For example, he quotes striking parallels to Chrétien's description, *Erec*, 11. 1946 ff., of Maheloas's ideal kingdom from a description of Ireland in the *Topographia Hiberniae* of Giraldus Canibrensis. But Giraldus here is probably merely ascribing to Ireland characteristics of climate, etc., that are really derived from Otherworld conceptions.

tely from some Eastern source, for this feature of his description
of the mysterious realm, too, is not found in Celtic texts, save
those of ecclesiastical origin — Christian visions of the Otherworld, like the *Visio Tnugdali,* etc.[19] — which probably, likewise,
derived it from the Orient. Lastly, the bridge under the water
is probably Chrétien's own invention, to provide for Gawain's passage to the land of the captor.[20]

It may be observed that this abduction story had doubtless
already gained entrance into Arthurian literature in the episode
of Geoffrey's *Historia* (Book X, ch. 13), where Mordred, who
had been left regent during his uncle's absence on the continent,
violated his troth — had himself crowned and took possession of
Guinevere. To be sure, according to Geoffrey, Guinevere is a
partner in his guilt, but that is probably an innovation of Geoffrey's own. Now, there are no valid grounds for believing that
Lancelot was ever thought of as the rescuer of the queen until
Chrétien wrote his poem,[21] and so there can be no reasonable doubt
that it is either he or his patroness, Marie de Champagne, that
first assigned this part to the character. Indeed, in all likelihood,

---

[19] Chrétien's immediate source for this detail belonged, I believe,
to this class of literature.

[20] Cp. Foerster, *Lancelot,* p. LXIX.

[21] On the controversy as to the priority of the French original
of the Middle High German *Lanzelet,* see pp. 213 ff., below. Golther,
*Zs. f. frz. Spr. u. Litt.,* XXII², 2 (1900), expresses the belief that
the Bretons introduced Lancelot into the Welsh saga of Melwas and
that Lancelot already was the hero of an independent saga with them.
The first of these opinions, however, is unsupported by any evidence
and the second is of little importance, as far as the sources of Chrétien's
poem are concerned; for, *ibid.,* Golther ascribes rightly the spirit of
the *amour courtois* which distinguishes it to the influence of Marie
de Champagne and the following features to Chrétien himself: the cart,
Gawain's rôle, the kingdom of the dead (probably drawn from ancient
mythology, since Chrétien knew Ovid), Lancelot's love and Guinevere's
adultery. Finally the relations between Lancelot, Guinevere and Arthur are imitated, even in detail, from those of Tristan, Iseult and
Mark to each other. If we subtract these elements from Chrétien's
story, there is little left for the Bretons.

Arthur was the original rescuer,[22] as in the *Vita Gildae.* At the
court of Champagne, however, permeated with the ideas of love
which had been recently developed in Provence, it would not do
for the husband to play this rôle — only a lover could fill it —
hence Lancelot has taken the part of the king. Moreover, his
relations with the woman whom he has rescued must be regulat-
ed according to the rules of the *amour courtois,* or *Minnedienst,* as
it is called by the Middle High German poets, and so we have
the preposterous servitude of Lancelot to the queen which was
destined to have such success — especially, after it was adopted
into the prose *Lancelot.* He swoons almost when he sees a comb
with some of his mistress's hair in it; when she appears indifferent, he is ready to commit suicide; in the tourney he acts the
part either of a coward or of the invincible champion, in obe-
dience to her nod. In fact, his humility is grovelling.[23]

In framing this story there can be no doubt that the poet
or the countess, if it was really she that invented it, was consciously
ordering it, so that it might present a direct contrast to the loves
of Tristan and Iseult. The love-conventions which we associate
with the fictitious Courts of Love — *Minnedienst,* in short —
were to take the place of the natural passion which is the soul
of the earlier story. In *Cliges* Chrétien had already composed
what was, in a sense, an *Anti-Tristan,* but in his *Lancelot* we
have something to which the title applies far more exactly. A
just retribution has followed on this attempt to exalt convention
above nature, for the *Lancelot* leaves us cold, whilst the *Tristan*
poems embody one of the immortal love-stories of literature. In
fact, it was not until the author of the *Mort Artu* breathed his
genius into the new conception that these later lovers secured
something of the immortality which was assured for the old. The
source of the Lancelot-Guinevere story was evident to the author
of the prose-romance, and in composing his narrative of their
love-affairs in its last phase he constantly reverted to this source
— the *Tristan* poems — and exploited them even in detail.[24]

---

[22] Cp. G. Paris, *Romania,* XII, 513ff. (1883).
[23] Cp. Miss Weston, *Legend of Sir Lancelot du Lac,* p. 112.
[24] Cp. Bruce, *Mort Artu,* pp. 282f. and 286.

There was, however, another thirteenth century romance besides Chrétien's with Lancelot as its hero.  The French original
has been lost, but the poem survives in the form of the German
paraphrase by Ulrich von Zatzikhoven, called the *Lanzelet*,[25] and
in order to determine the true position of Chrétien in the develop-

---

[25] Whilst arguing, *Romania*, XII, 507, that Chrétien was the
first to make Lancelot Guinevere's lover, G. Paris, *Romania*, X, 493ff.
endeavors to prove that there are French romances, or works based on
French romances, that reflect an earlier form of his story, when his
name was not connected with the queen's, and still others that connect
his name with Guinevere's, but not as a lover — in other words, that
there were French romances concerning Lancelot before Chrétien de
Troyes.  But there are no convincing instances of the former and at
the end of his discussion of two of the romances in question (all of
them later) — viz: the tale of the stag with the white foot in the
Dutch version of the prose *Lancelot* and *Rigomer* he has to acknowledge himself that the argument has little force.  It is really no better
with his other two instances — *Durmart* and the *Crône (Krône)* of
Heinrich von dem Türlin, — for, if Durmart and not Lancelot is made
the rescuer of Guinevere in the romance of that name, it is simply
because he is the hero of that particular romance.  In the *Crône* we
have the episode of Lancelot's rescue of Guinevere from Meleagant, but
there are some other passages concerning him in which Guinevere does
not appear — he was accustomed to read concerning adventures —
his strength, like Gawain's grew with the growth of the day — his
*amie* cannot stand the test of chastity.  But the *Crône,* as is universally recognized, belongs to the period when the Arthurian romances
had begun to decline and these are simply old *motifs* attached now
to Lancelot.

Doubtless, in later life Paris would not himself have attributed
any importance to these passages.  It is different, however, with the
other set of romances — those that connect Lancelot und Guinevere
but not as lovers.  The romances that he takes here into consideration
are the Middle High German *Lanzelet* by Ulrich von Zatzikhoven and
the abduction episode of the *Crône.*  Now, the first of these, as will
be seen below, presents a real problem, but the *Crône* episode has
little force.  The point which Paris makes is that the *Crône* and
Malory's *Morte Darthur,* Book XIX, show in the narrative of this
affair certain coincidences which distinguish them from Chrétien's *Lancelot* and which go back to their common source, a hypothetical *Chevalier du Chariot* (Chrétien's source, too).  As Foerster, however, has

ment of the Lancelot tradition, we shall have to consider this German poem.

According to its author's own statement, it is a translation of a French book brought to Germany by Hugo de Morville, one of the hostages who in 1194 replaced Richard Coeur de Lion in the prison of Leopold of Austria.[26] In view of the methods of most Middle High German poets in handling French material, there can be little doubt that we have here substantially a faithful rendering of the lost French original. Scholars are of one mind as to the poor quality of Ulrich's poem, its immature construction, etc., which, no doubt, reflect the same defects in its source. It is on the question of whether this source was late or early that

observed in his Introduction to the *Lancelot,* p. LIX, none of these matters are important — for instance, the *Crône* and Malory make Lancelot ascend the cart, because he was tired, which, however, is a detail that might easily have occurred to any number of poets independently. In general, one may say that a writer like Malory who wrote some three hundred years after Chrétien and nearly three hundred years after the authors of the prose romances can be used only with the greatest caution in the study of Arthurian sources. His work is based largely on late modifications of the old standard romances, and, as far as has been shown, it is not available in a single instance for the study of early Arthurian sources.

[26] He was, also, one of the slayers of Thomas à Becket. I agree with Golther, *Zs. f. frz. Spr. u. Litt.*, XXII[2], 1 (1900) that the *Lanzelet* shows the influence of Chrétien's *Yvain* and *Perceval*, and, hence, that it was, doubtless, written after 1180. Ulrich is probably to be identified with the priest "Uolricus de Cecinhoven plebanus Lonmeissae [i. e. Lommis in Thurgau (Switzerland)]", who is named in a Latin document (dated March 29, 1214) from the monastery of St. Peterzell in Toggenburg. The document in question has been printed by J. Baechtold, Pfeiffer's *Germania*, XIX, 424 ff. (1874). That a churchman should concern himself with romances in an age when those works were universally popular is not strange.

Hugues de Morville and his fellow-hostages arrived in Austria in February, 1194, and left that country in December of the same year. Hence Lot, *Étude sur le Lancelot en prose*, p. 166, note 3, says that Ulrich must have written his *Lanzelet* between these dates; but Hugues may have made a present of the book to Ulrich, or the latter may have copied it then and executed his paraphrase later.

the doctors disagree. Let us glance hastily, however, at the contents of the romance:

Lancelot is the son of King Pant of Gennewis and his wife Clarine. By a revolt of his people Pant was driven from his kingdom with his wife and child. He died during the flight, and a water-fairy stole his infant boy from the mother and carried him away to Maidenland (the Celtic Otherworld). He is brought up there ignorant of his name and rank and of knightly accomplishments. The fairy, however, finally lets him go forth to try his valor. She will not tell him, however, of his name and parentage until he has overcome the strongest knight in the world, Iweret of Beforet.[27] Though provided with the best equipment, when he starts out, he does not know how to use it, until in the course of time he meets a knight, Johfrit de Liez, who gives him proper instruction in these matters.

He next comes with two knights to the castle of a certain Galagandreiz, who has condemned his daughter to perpetual virginity. She manages, however, to offer her love to each of the three knights. Lancelot accepts, slays the father, and weds the girl. Wandering forth on adventure, he is attacked at a castle named Limors and would have been killed, but for the intervention of Ade, niece of the lord of the castle. He is thrown into prison, but escapes after fighting successively with a giant, two lions, and the lord of the castle. He now becomes the lover of Ade. Whether he marries her is not said, but, at any rate, his wife, the daughter of Galagandreiz, drops out of the story.

Lancelot is now famous and Arthur sends Gawain to bring him to court. They meet (not knowing each other's identity), fight an undecided combat, which is terminated by news of an impending tournament between King Lot and Gurnemanz. Lance-

---

[27] This witholding of the hero's name, which is so common a *motif* in the romances, is connected ultimately, no doubt, with the widespread superstition among primitive peoples to the effect that to disclose one's name puts one in the power of another. Cp. on the subject Edward Clodd's interesting book, *Magic in Names and in Other Things* (London, 1920).

lot betakes himself thither, fights three days, and each day in armor of a different color, overthrows many knights including Lot, whom he sets free out of friendship for Gawain, and still *incognito*, rides away to Ade and her brother.

They come to a castle, Schatel le Mort (Castle of Death), the master of which is Mabuz, a magician — the son of the fairy who brought Lancelot up. Lancelot rides to the castle, which has this property that whoever crosses its drawbridge at once loses all courage. He falls under the spell and is made prisoner. His *amie*, Ade, rides off in dismay with her brother and disappears from the story. The territory of Mabuz is often raided by his neighbor, Iweret of Beforet. The magician is, himself, a coward, but makes Lancelot his champion — has him carried outside the castle-walls, so that he may again be free from the spell. Lancelot rides to a fountain beside which hangs a brazen cymbal on which he must strike three times with a hammer to summon his foe. In the meanwhile, Iblis, daughter of Iweret, has a dream of an unknown knight. She finds this dream realized in Lancelot and she wishes him to fly with her, but he first slays the father and then marries the girl, becoming master of Beforet.

At this point a messenger from Lancelot's fairy foster-mother informs him of his name and parentage, and it turns out that she stole him in the original instance to raise up a deliverer for her son, Mabuz.

Lancelot now decides to seek Gawain. On his way he meets a squire, who informs him that King Valerin (Falerin) has appeared at Arthur's court and laid claim to Guinevere, on the ground that she had been betrothed to him, previous to her marriage with Arthur. If no champion offers, he will carry off the queen. Lancelot undertakes the combat and defeats Valerin.

Following this, Lancelot has another adventure at a castle named Pluris — defeats in succession one hundred knights, and, forgetful of Iblis, marries the queen of the castle. During his absence from court Iblis successfully stands the chastity test (by means of a mantle). Gawain, Karyet (Gaheriet) Erec and Tristan go in search of Lancelot and by a ruse succeed in delivering him from the castle of Pluris, whose queen, like Lancelot's previous wives, now vanishes from the story.

But on their way back to court the knights hear that Valerin has carried off Guinevere and imprisoned her in a castle surrounded by serpents — in a magic slumber, as it turns out. At Tristan's suggestion they seek the aid of the enchanter, Malduc, in liberating the queen. Erec and Gawain, however, have to be given up to Malduc, who has a grudge against them, before he will render assistance. The two knights themselves consent to this and Malduc, by his magical powers, rescues the queen.[28] Lancelot and a giant now free Erec and Gawain from Malduc and they all return to Arthur's court. Here Iblis tells him of a knight who had recently been confronted with the adventure of the *fier baiser* — he is solicited for a kiss by a dragon, who speaks with a human voice. Lancelot undertakes the adventure and the seeming dragon is transformed into a woman. She has been put under a spell, because she had transgressed the laws of *Minne* — that is the conventions of the *amour courtois*.

In conclusion, Lancelot wins back his father's kingdom and retires with Iblis to Beforet, where they entertain Arthur and his consort. The pair are blessed with four children. They live to old age and die on the same day.

Now, there are different views held in regard to the relations of Chrétien's *Lancelot* and Ulrich's original. On the one hand, we have what to the present writer seems the true view — namely, that this latter romance was a biographical romance of the weakest sort, comparatively late and built up in a considerable measure on *motifs* derived from Chrétien's poems.[29] On the other hand, Gaston Paris and others have regarded Ulrich's original as derived

---

[28] Miss Weston points out, *Legend of Sir Lancelot du Lac*, pp. 15 ff. that, contrary to the statement of both G. Paris and Foerster, Lancelot has nothing to do with the rescue, his name even not being mentioned.

[29] Such is the view defended by Foerster, *Lancelot*, pp. XLV ff., and by Golther in his review of Foerster's edition of the *Lancelot*, *Zs. f. frz. Spr. u. Litt.*, XXII [2], 1 ff. (1900). Golther calls the *Lanzelet* "geradezu eine Ergänzung der Karre" (i. e. of Chrétien's *Lanclot*).

from the same source as Chrétien's *Lancelot* — that is, from a
biographical romance concerning Lancelot — only the great French
scholar thought that Ulrich's original was more primitive than
Chrétien and reflected better their common source.[30]

In an effort to answer the question at issue, let us examine now
more closely some of the *motifs* of Ulrich's *Lanzelet* which are
found also in Chrétien's poems or other early romances.

1. The trait of Lancelot's being brought up in the wilderness, ignorant of his name, parentage and all knightly accomplishments. For the source of this feature of the *Lanzelet* there
is no need of seeking any further than the story of Perceval's
youth as related in Chrétien's poem on that hero. So, too, with
the instruction which Johfrit de Liez gives Lancelot.

2. The Three Days' Tournament *motif*. We have a similar
episode in Chrétien's *Cliges*, ll. 4575 ff., and certain scholars[31]
contend that the *motif* in the *Lanzelet* is derived from that source.
Chrétien, however, makes Cliges fight four days (each day in armour
of a different colour), which is an expansion of the *motif* as we
find it not only in the German poem, but in a great number of

---

[30] Cp. *Romania*, X, 472 (1881). Miss Weston's view, *Legend
of Sir Lancelot du Lac*, pp. 17 ff., of the matter is akin to that of
G. Paris — except that she regards Ulrich's original as drawn not
from a biographical romance, but from a number of floating lays concerning Lancelot. Most of the episodes, however, which Miss Weston
supposes to be based on hypothetical "floating lays" have parallels
elsewhere, and there is no reason to believe that Lancelot ever had
any monopoly of these *motifs* in oral tradition — so her theory is,
in the opinion of the present writer, untenable — and, similarly, that
of G. Paris, in so far as it assumes a basis of Lancelot lays for his
hypothetical common source of Chrétien and Ulrich's original.

Similar to Miss Weston's theory is A. C. L. Brown's (in his "The
Grail and the English *Sir Perceval*", MPh. XVI, 559 ff. (1919), XVII,
361 ff. (1919). He supports this theory by an endeavor to prove
that *Sir Perceval* and the *Lanzelet* draw upon a "body of tradition"
older than Chrétien (p. 563). Brown's method in these discussions,
however, is open to the same criticism that I have expressed elsewhere.

[31] Foerster and Golther.

folktales. Accordingly, it has been urged,[32] on the other side, that the passage in Ulrich came from oral tradition and not from *Cliges*. There remains, however, the possibility that Chrétien's example may have led the author of Ulrich's original to employ the *motif*, although in a form nearer to that which it assumes in the folktales. But it seems even more likely that the author of this original was imitating here the romance of *Ipomedon*, which contains the *motif* in the same form as Ulrich's poem.[33] As we have seen, Hugh of Morville brought the French book to Austria in 1194, but it may have been then quite new — possibly the latest sensation.[34] If it was composed after 1190, it was certainly later than *Ipomedon*, for we know that this romance was written before that date.

3. Lancelot's challenging of Iweret by striking on the brazen cymbal at the fountain may very well have been suggested by the episode of Yvain and the fountain in Chrétien's *Yvain* (ll. 800 ff.).

4. The folk-tale motif of the *fier baiser* — a knight, by a kiss, undoes the spell which has transformed a beautiful woman into a serpent — here attached to Lancelot, is generally attached to Gawain's son in the Arthurian romances, and seems as distinctive of that character as the features of Perceval's youth, enumerated above, are of Perceval. The earliest of the romances dealing with

[32] By Miss Weston in her *The Three Days' Tournament* (London, 1902). A much better discussion of the *motif* in its manifold occurrences will be found in C. H. Carter's article on *Ipomedon, Haverford Essays*, pp. 248 ff. (Haverford, Pa., 1909).

[33] Miss Weston, *op. cit.*, pp. 3 ff., notes this herself.

In her treatise, named above, Miss Weston has entered into a long argument — to the present writer unconvincing — that this three tournament *motif* belonged to Lancelot in oral tradition. Neither she, however, nor Carter have taken into account the fact that Ulrich's original may very well have been later in date than *Ipomedon* and, consequently, may have drawn from it. There is no way of settling the question of whence the author of Ulrich's original derived this incident, but, in any event, there is, *pace* Miss Weston, no reason for believing that its connection with Lancelot belonged to oral tradition.

[34] Cp. Foerster's *Lancelot*, p. XLVI.

Gawain's son, viz. *Li Biaus Descouneus,* dates from the latter part of the twelfth century.[35]

5. The episode of Guinevere's abduction, which constitutes the main *crux* of the whole controversy. Is Ulrich's account of this affair more primitive than Chrétien's? Miss Weston thinks that it is.[36] The description of Guinevere's prison, she remarks, her magic slumber in a fair dwelling, surrounded by a dense thicket infested with serpents, is the sleeping beauty story in its oldest Otherworld form. The identification with the sleeping beauty *motif* is admissible; but who can say that this *motif* was not imported into the story of Guinevere's abduction by the author of the lost French romance which Ulrich was following? In any case, the element in question is no more Celtic in character than Chrétien's description of Guinevere's captivity, for in the numerous descriptions of the Celtic Otherworld there is none that represents it in this light.

That Ulrich's original was independent of Chrétien's *Lancelot* seems at first blush manifest, since here Lancelot is not the lover of Guinevere. He has four love affairs in the course of the poem — three of them ending in marriage — but none of them are with her. If he had known Chrétien's *Lancelot,* would the author of the poem have ventured to discard the conception of the love-affair which is embodied in that work? Considering the renown to which this love-affair has since attained, one is inclined to answer "no".

---

[35] According to Miss G. P. Williams, — see her edition (Oxford, 1915) of the romance, p. XXXVIII — it was written between 1185 and 1190. The *fier baiser* episode will be found, ll. 3114ff., in Miss Williams's edition. For an analysis of the episode in the various romances of the cycle, cp. W. H. Schofield, *Studies on the Libeaus Desconus,* pp. 47 ff., Harvard *Studies and Notes in Philology and Literature,* no. 4 (Boston, 1895). For the *fier baiser motif* in the literature of folktales, in general, cp. Bolte and Polivka, II, 271 ff. In "La légende de la fille d'Hippocrate", *Bibliothèque de l'École des Chartes,* vol. 79, pp. 45 ff. (1918), G. Huet defends the antiquity of the localization of this *motif* on the island of Cos in the Aegean Sea — the birth-place of the great physician, Hippocrates — which is found in *The Travels of Sir John Mandeville,* ch. 4.

[36] Cp. her *Legend of Sir Lancelot du Lac,* p. 19.

But it is to be remembered that for Chrétien's contemporaries this feature of Guinevere's story was a new thing — a quite recent innovation — and did not possess the authority that it now possesses. So, if a writer wished to introduce into a romance about Lancelot the abduction incident, in which the queen had long figured, he would not feel it necessary, as a modern poet, doubtless, would, to connect the episode with Lancelot as the lover and rescuer. Above all, however, it is to be observed that the narratives of their predecessors had no sanctity for the mediaeval romancers. If the author of the *Queste del Saint Graal* could displace Perceval by Galahad as the Grail hero and still retain the former as a prominent actor in the story, there is, surely, no reason why the author of the French original of the *Lanzelet* should not have displaced Guinevere by Iblis (the most prominent of Lancelot's lady-loves in the *Lanzelet*), say, and still have kept the hero as the queen's rescuer, although he is no longer her lover. An adequate motive for the change would be that the romances regularly end with the marriage of the hero and the heroine, yet this, of course, would have been impossible, if Arthur's consort had continued to be Lancelot's lady-love.[37] Thus, the French poet whom Ulrich translated may, after all, have been attracted to Lancelot by Chrétien's poem, although he chose to ascribe to him a new set of adventures, gathered, for the most part, here and there, from traditions or contemporary romances relating to other heroes. In any event, there is only one feature of Lancelot's story, as we find it in the various Arthurian romances, of which we can assert that it was

---

[37] The considerations here advanced meet sufficiently, I believe, Brown's criticism, MPh. XVII, 363. Important in this connection, also, are the instances of violent departure from Arthurian tradition which I have cited elsewhere in the present work. Furthermore, despite Brown's objection, *loc. cit.*, I cannot regard the parallel of *Escanor*, for example, as without value. The author of this poem uses as one of his sources the prose *Lancelot*, in which the great theme is the hero's passion for the queen, yet he not only ignores that famous love-story, though retaining Lancelot as a minor character in his poem, but says explicitly, l. 7344, that Guinevere loved *Gawain* most of all men, except her husband.

unquestionably connected with him in oral tradition — namely, the one according to which he was stolen when a child and brought up by a water-fairy. This account is first found in an explicit form in Ulrich's *Lanzelet*, but the name given the character in Chrétien's poems — *Lancelot del Lac* — presupposes this feature. From the French source of the *Lanzelet* it passed into the great *Lancelot* in prose,[38] and thence into general tradition.

It was through this prose *Lancelot* — composed in its earliest form, it would seem, near the end of the twelfth century — that the fame of Lancelot was spread far and wide. Although so important in the development of the history of the character, Chrétien's poem does not seem to have been much read, if we are to judge by the paucity of allusions to it in mediaeval literature.[39] It was otherwise, however, with the prose-romance, which, as we shall see, was destined to exercise a profound influence on the prose-fiction of Europe. To separate this romance, as it was originally written, from the additions and interpolations with which it has been overloaded in our relatively late cyclic MSS. is a difficult task.[40] Nevertheless, it is virtually certain that even in its unencumbered form the prose work was based, to a considerable ex-

---

[38] Cp. Sommer, III, 14. Foerster, *Lancelot*, p. XXXIX, ascribes to Lancelot, also, in popular tradition the rôle of Guinevere's rescuer, but as Miss Weston, pp. 15f., has shown, this is due to an erroneous interpretation of Ulrich's poem. The German scholar has remarked, moreover, that the temporary release of Lancelot from captivity, in order that he may attend a tourney, occurring in both Chrétien and Ulrich, was probably in the oral tradition; but one cannot shut out the suspicion that Ulrich's original was here borrowing from Chrétien.

Miss L. A. Paton, *Studies in the Fairy Mythology of Arthurian Romance*, pp. 188f. (Boston, 1903) suggested that the lake-fairy was, doubtless, originally not Lancelot's foster-mother, but his *amie*. A. C. L. Brown, MPh. XVII, 361ff., adopts this hypothesis, which figures largely in his discussion of the *Lanzelet*. It has, however, no support whatever in the extant texts and, in my own opinion, should be rejected.

[39] Cp. Foerster, *Lancelot*, pp. XLVIIIff.

[40] The present writer has attempted this in his study, "The Composition of the Old French prose *Lancelot*". *Romanic Review*, vols. IX, (1918) and X, (1919).

tent, on earlier romances in verse[41] — most of them lost — and there is no reason to believe that it drew at all from oral tradition. We shall return, however, to the prose *Lancelot* in a later chapter of the present treatise.

---

[41] Miss Weston's assumption (cp. her *Legend of Sir Lancelot du Lac*, pp. 89 ff.) that her hypothetical body of oral tradition concerning Lancelot affected independently the Arthurian romances like the prose *Merlin* and *Tristan* is baseless. The romances, just named, know nothing about this hero, except what they derive from the prose *Lancelot.* Equally groundless is the notion, first advanced in her book on *The Legend of Sir Gawain* (London, 1897) and repeated here, that Gawain was originally Guinevere's lover in Celtic tradition and that features of his story have descended to Lancelot. In the scores of Arthurian texts there is not a trace of any such relation between Gawain and Guinevere.

# PART II.

## THE HOLY GRAIL.

# Chapter I.
## Chrétien, Robert de Boron, and the Theory of Christian Origin.

It would materially facilitate the investigation of the origin of the legend of the Grail, if we could fix indisputably the relative dates of the various mediaeval romances that deal with the theme. Unfortunately here, as so often in Arthurian matters, the data are meagre, and even those who are most convinced of the correctness of any particular theory as to the chronological order of these works must acknowledge that an uncertainty which cannot be wholly dispelled must still hang over their conclusions. The two earliest romances that treat of the Grail are the *Conte del Graal* of Chrétien de Troyes and the *Joseph* of Robert de Boron. Let us look at the evidence regarding the date of composition in each case. First, as regards the *Conte del Graal*, as Chrétien named it, or the *Perceval*, as, following the example of modern scholars, it will be more convenient for us to call it. At the beginning of his poem Chrétien eulogizes Count Philip of Flanders, at whose command he was composing the romance — his source being a book given him for the purpose by this same Count Philip.[1] The

---

[1] The eulogy takes the form of an argument to prove that his patron, Philip, is superior to Alexander the Great. Despite this artificial form, his praise of Philip's justice, liberality, and charity produces an impression of greater sincerity than is usual in such cases. But, after all, the impression is probably due merely to Chrétien's art, for these encomiums are hardly borne out by the historical evidences as to Philip's life. With such a patron the poet continues in the oft-quoted lines (62 ff.):

Donc avra bien sauve sa peine
Crestiens qui antant et peine
A rimoier le meillor conte,

nobleman in question was Philip of Alsace, who was born about 1143 and who succeeded his father as Count of Flanders in 1168. In 1190 he went to the Holy Land and died there the following year. So the only positive limits within which Chrétien may be said to have written his poem are 1168—1190, i.e. the limits of the rule of Philip of Alsace before his departure for Palestine, which would surely have been mentioned by Chrétien, had he already gone. At the same time there are certain considerations which make the earlier part of this period more probable than the latter. In the first place, the romance which, according to general agreement, must have immediately preceded the *Perceval* in order of composition, i.e. the *Yvain*, was written, as seems manifest from an allusion in it, not later than 1174. Now, *Perceval* was the only one of Chrétien's works of later date than this. Is it likely that this romance was separated from the *Yvain* by any wide interval of years, so that its composition would fall, say in the eighties of the twelfth century? It is possible, of course, but his previous works, *Erec, Cligès, Lancelot, Yvain*, had followed each other in fairly close succession; consequently, the weight of probability, on the whole, would seem to lie on the other side. In any event, *Perceval* was the last poem from Chrétien's pen, for one of his continuators, Gerbert, tells us that he died whilst he was composing it, and this accounts, of course, for his leaving it a fragment, tempting others to continuations.

Let us now examine the evidence as to Robert de Boron's *Joseph*. The question is somewhat complicated by the fact that Robert's poem is preserved to us in what some scholars regard, though wrongly, I believe, as only a second redaction. The epilogue at the end of the *Joseph* in our unique MS. was plainly a late addition to the original poem, and, according to these scho-

---

> Par le comandement le conte,
> Qui soit contez an cort real;
> Ce est li contes del graal,
> Don li cuens li baille le livre,
> S'orroiz comant il s'an delivre.

Then begins the story of Perceval.

lars, in adding the epilogue the author made changes in the poem, itself. In this epilogue the poet remarks that it would be desirable to know the subsequent adventures of the principal characters in his poem and declares his intention of treating these subjects, if he can ever discover a book which might tell of them. But no one, he says, can assemble such a narrative who has not heard told the most high history of the Holy Grail (i.e. the *Joseph*) which is without doubt entirely true. Then, in this connection he makes the following statement, which bears on the question of date: "At the time that I treated it (i.e. the story of the Grail) in peace, (when) with my lord, Gautier, who was of Mont-Belyal, the great history of the Holy Grail had never been treated by any man that was mortal." Now, this Gautier of Montbéliard went to Palestine in 1199, became Constable of Jerusalem there, then Regent of Cyprus, and died in 1212. Inasmuch as Gautier's elder brother (Richard of Montbeliard) died so late as 1237, it it not likely that Gautier himself was born before 1150, or more probably 1160.[2] On the other hand, Gautier's father, Amadeus, died in 1183 and the same year Gautier became independent for the first time on receiving the county of Montfaucon. The probabilities are that he would hardly have become the patron of a poet that year. In any event, he must have been a grown man, so that Robert's connection with him could not have begun before about 1180.

It will be seen that the evidence as to the upward limit for the date of Robert de Boron's romance does not enable us to fix upon a precise year. But the range is not great; it was in the early eighties of the twelfth century. As regards the downward limit, we are better off. Robert states that he was with Gautier when he first composed his poem. Now, Gautier took his departure for Italy in 1199 and thence for Palestine in 1201, so that the composition of the *Joseph* in its original form, it is virtually certain, must have antedated 1199. With regard to the existing form, which, of course, may have undergone changes, as compared

---

[2] For these dates cp., respectively, Birch-Hirschfeld, p. 239, and G. Paris, *Huth-Merlin*, p. 18, note 1

with the original form, this would seem at first sight to date
from a period subsequent to Gautier's death, i.e. subsequent to
1212, since the author speaks here of Gautier as one "who was
of Montbéliard."[3] But I agree with Professor Heinzel that these

---

[3] This was Gaston Paris's interpretation, *Huth-Merlin*, vol. I,
p. IX, note 1. On the other hand, Heinzel, pp. 113f., suggests that
we have the past, *estoit* (1. 3491, *Qui de Mont-Belyal estoit)*,
because *retreis* (1. 3489, *A ce tens que je la retreis* — i. e. "at
the time that I related the history of the Grail") was in the past.
I believe that this is the correct explanation, and that we have here
simply a case of grammatical subordination. So, too, Brugger, *Zs.
f. frz. Spr. u. Litt.*, XXIX [1], 65, note 13. That this form of expression might give rise to misunderstandings would, of course, never
occur to so careless a writer as Robert de Boron. And, after all,
when I say: "At the time that I wrote my book in 1910, I was
closely associated with John Johnson, who was the professor of history
in the University of Chicago," I do not imply that Professor Johnson
is no longer professor in the University of Chicago or that he is now
dead. Moreover, if G. Paris's interpretation is the true one, Robert,
after an interval of at least thirteen years (1199—1212) — in all
probability, more — took up his work to continue it and apparently
on a very large scale (although we have no reason to believe that he
ever carried out the full plan). But this seems incredible. More likely
it would be an interval of not half that duration. On the other hand,
I see no reason for believing with Heinzel that the epilogue (or the
hypothetical redaction of the original *Joseph*) was composed after 1201.
Heinzel is evidently influenced by his identification of *Dou Graal la
plus grant estoire* (1. 3487) with the so called *Grand St. Graal
(Estoire del saint Graal)* of the Walter Map cycle, which, owing
to an erroneous interpretation of the well-known passage in the Chronicle of Helinandus, he placed some years before 1204.

Birch-Hirschfeld, p. 239, interpreted 1. 3491 as referring to the
time when Gautier was merely of Montbéliard and before he became
Count of Montfaucon in 1183. But this is not satisfactory, since he
was called Gautier de Montbéliard long after he became Count of Montfaucon. See on the subject Foerster, *Wörterbuch*, p. 173.*

G. Paris, *Mélanges*, p. 45, speaks of Robert as standing in relations, not only of friendship with Gautier, but of "collaboration",
whilst F. Lot says, *Bibliothèque de l'Ecole des Chartes,* LXX, 565,
note 4 (1909), "Je n'accorde, au surplus, aucune créance à l'assertion
de Robert qui n'invoque l'autorité de Gautier de Montbéliard que parce

words do not necessarily imply that Gautier was dead. The poet used the past tense simply because he was speaking of a connection which at the time that he composed his epilogue belonged to the past.

To sum up, then, Chrétien's *Perceval* was written between 1174 and 1190 and Robert de Boron's *Joseph* between 1180, say, and 1199. For Chrétien, the years from 1174 to 1180, as we have seen, seem more probable, though not certain. As regards Robert de Boron, there is no evidence that would enable us to draw the limits more narrowly.

I will now give an analysis of each of these poems — the earliest works concerning the Holy Grail, so that we may have the materials for determining their relations, as far as possible, and for settling the question of priority which the external data are insufficient to settle.

And first for Chrétien's *Perceval*.[4] After the dedicatory prologue which I have already indicated, the narrative begins:

It was in the spring when the son (Perceval, as he is subsequently called) of the widowed lady went forth to the hunt in the Waste Forest. He hears the rattling of weapons and believes that the sounds are caused by devils, from whom his mother had warned him to protect himself by making the sign of the cross. But he

---

qu'il est mort et en Terre-Sainte." But the text does not warrant either of these extreme views.

The words *en peis* (l. 3490, *O mon seigneur Gautier en peis*) have been interpreted as equivalent to *in pace*, i. e. dead, but this is not a necessary interpretation.

[4] I use Baist's *Crestien's von Troyes Contes del Graal (Percevaus li galois): Abdruck der Handschrift Paris, français 794, mit Anmerkungen und Glossar* (Freiburg i. B). This publication, which appeared in 1912, is undated, like the earlier impression, which did not bear Baist's name. The earlier impression (printed for private circulation in 1909) is very incorrect. Cp. R. Weeks' review of it, *Romanic Review*, II, 101 ff. (1911).

The only other edition of the poem is C. Potvin's in vols. 1 and 2 (Part 2) of his *Perceval le Gallois ou le Conte du Graal* (6 vols., 1866—1871). The Mons MS, which constitutes the basis of Potvin's edition, is inferior. Cp. P. Meyer, *Revue Critique*, Sept. 1, 1866.

decides that he will not do this, rather he will wait and strike down the strongest of them with a dart, so that the rest will not venture to attack him. Soon, certain knights, in brilliant harness, come into sight and the young man is so filled with admiration at their appearance that he concludes that the first of them is God and the others angels. A dialogue follows in which Perceval learns from the strangers that they are knights, that King Arthur confers knighthood — moreover, in reply to his eager questions, they tell him the use of each piece of their equipment. It is an amusing feature of this dialogue that, instead of answering the inquiries of the strange knights, the forest-bred youth seeks the gratification of his own curiosity by counter-questions as to their armor and other matters which his native war-like instincts suggest. He goes back home and relates his encounter with the knights to his mother. She falls into a swoon at the recital, for his father and brothers had fallen in combat and she had endeavored to keep the boy ignorant of deeds of war. He insists, however, on becoming a knight and on the third day after the encounter he departs for Arthur's court. Before he leaves, she gives him good advice, viz. to aid and do service to ladies, and as a reward of service to ask for a kiss or a jewel — moreover, always to seek the name of the companions whom he might join on the road, to keep company only with worthy men, and to pray, whenever he came to a church. Clad like a Welsh peasant and armed with a dart, he rides forth to obtain knighthood at Arthur's court. On the way he comes to a splendid tent which he mistakes for a church. There is a girl asleep inside, and he snatches from her a kiss and a ring, thinking that he is thereby fulfilling his mother's injunction. Before the gate of the king's castle he meets a knight in red armor with a golden cup. He now rides into the hall. Everybody there takes him for a fool, although they are struck with his beauty. Arthur sits in dejection, his principal knights being away and the Red Knight having just carried off the cup. Perceval acts like a rustic, but the king treats him kindly — and he now asks to be made a knight, demanding also the red armor which he had just seen. The seneschal, Kay (Kai) laughs at him and bids him seek it himself from the Red Knight, which Perceval hastens to do. As he rides out, a damsel who is present predicts his future prowess, which so enrages Kay that he knocks her down (1. 1030) and kicks into the fire a fool who had been wont to repeat that the damsel would not laugh until she beheld the best of knights. Perceval follows the Red Knight and bids him give up his arms and armour. They fight and Perceval slays his adversary with a dart.[5] Yonès who has followed him finds him put to it to remove the knight's armour. He is preparing to burn the dead body in order to get this armour, when Yonès shows him how to disarm the dead man and to arm himself. Perceval sends the cup back to the king and also a message to the effect that he would return to avenge the blow which Kay had given the damsel. He goes on and reaches a castle whose lord is an old knight named Gornemant of Gohorz. Gornemant entertains him and teaches him the use of arms and all knightly practices. In especial, he is to avoid over-readiness in speaking and in asking questions and to give up his habit of always quoting his mother's counsels. Gornemant then dubs him knight and sends him forth to return to his mother. After a day's journey he comes to Beaurepaire, a town defended by a castle, and, on entering it, finds it deserted. The lady of the castle, who is a damsel of surpassing beauty, welcomes him and bids him to her table. Being mindful of Gornemant's counsels, he remains silent and she must speak to him first. The girl turns out to be Gornemant's niece, Blanchefleur. That night she comes in distress to Perceval's bedside, and, in reply to his questions, tells him how the forces of King Clama-

---

[5] Ll. 1090 ff. In "The Death of the Red Knight in the Story of Perceval", MLN, XXXI, 53—55 (1916), R. B. Pace calls attention to the fact that in the corresponding passages of *Sir Perceval, Peredur* and Wolfram's *Parzival* there is nothing to represent the line, "Le sanc et la cervelle espant" (1. 1095) in Chrétien's account of the killing. He argues from this that the three versions are not based on Chrétien, but on a common source. The works in question, however, are, on no theory, literal translations of Chrétien; consequently I cannot ascribe to this omission the importance that Pace does. Pace cites other instances of the same phrase in Chrétien's romances.

deus encompass the castle and how on the morrow she must yield, but rather than be Clamadeus's she will slay herself. He promises her help, and they spend the night together.[6] The next day he vanquishes Clamadeus's seneschal and sends him to Arthur's court. Clamadeus presses the siege without success and then challenges Perceval to single combat. Perceval vanquishes him, also, and sends him to Arthur's court. Clamadeus and his seneschal relate wonders there of the Red Knight (Perceval). After remaining awhile with Blanchefleur, Perceval takes leave of her, as he longs to see his mother again. Now comes the Grail episode. On his journey the young knight comes to a river upon which there is a boat with two men in it. One of them, in reply to his questions, directs him for a night's shelter to his own castle hard by. Perceval starts for it, and, being at first unable to find it, reproaches the fisher. Suddenly he perceives the castle before him, enters it, is disarmed, clad in a scarlet mantle and led into a great hall. Therein is a couch upon which lies an old man; near him is a fire around which some four hundred men are sitting. Perceval tells his host that he has come from Beaurepaire. A squire enters, bearing a sword, and on it is written that it will never break save in one peril, and that known only to the maker of it. It is a present from the host's niece to be bestowed where it will be well employed. The host gives it to Perceval, "to whom it was adjudged and destined." Hereupon enters another squire, bearing in his hand a lance, from the head of which a drop of blood runs down on the squire's hand. Perceval would have asked concerning this wonder, but he remembers Gornemant's counsel not to speak or inquire too much. Two more squires enter holding each a ten-branched candlestick, and with them a damsel, a[7] "graal" in her hands. The Grail (to use the English form of the word)

---

[6] It has been sometimes maintained that the relations of the pair during the night they spend together (cp. Baist's edition, ll. 2030 ff.) are wholly innocent, but there is not the slightest suggestion of asceticism in the description and the language is like that of other descriptions of similar situations in the romances.

[7] Observe that the indefinite, not the definite, article is used in the passage.

shines so that it puts out the light of the candles as the sun does that of the stars. Thereafter follows a damsel holding a (silver) plate. All defile past between the fire and the couch, but Perceval does not venture to ask wherefore the Grail is used. Supper follows and the Grail is again brought in with each course and Perceval was curious to know the use of the vessel, but he again refrains from inquiring when he thinks of Gornemant and finally puts off his questions till the morrow. After supper Perceval is led to his chamber and, on the morrow, awakening, finds the castle deserted. No one answers his calls. Issuing forth, he sees his horse saddled and the drawbridge down. Thinking to find the inhabitants of the castle in the forest, he rides forth, but the drawbridge closes so suddenly behind him that, had not the horse leapt quickly forward, it would have gone hard with both steed and rider.[8] In vain Perceval calls: no one answers. He proceeds on his way and comes to an oak, beneath which there is a girl sitting who is holding a dead knight in her arms and lamenting over him. She asks him where he has passed the night, and on learning it tells him the fisher who had directed him to the castle and his host were one and the same person. Wounded by a spear thrust through both thighs, his only solace is in fishing, whence he is called the Fisher King. She asks Perceval whether he had seen the bleeding lance, the Grail and the silver plate and whether he had asked their meaning. He replies, no. She asks him his name and, according to the strange statement of Chrétien's poem, he answers (l. 3537) rightly that it was *Percevax li galois* (Perceval the Welshman), although he really did not know his own name and this was a mere guess. She replies that it ought to have been *Perceval the Caitiff*, for had he asked concerning what he saw, the good king would have been made whole again, and great good would have sprung therefrom.

---

[8] In "The Drawbridge of the Grail Castle", MLN, XXXIII, 399 ff. (1918), Esther C. Dunn cites a perilous bridge from the Irish saga, *The Wooing of Emer*, as a parallel. Both authors, however, were describing fairy-tale adventures and the similarity — such as it is — between the two passages is, doubtless, purely accidental.

She tells him too that he has been guilty of his mother's death, for she had died of grief after he left her — moreover, that she herself is his cousin and had been brought up with him. Perceval offers to revenge the death of her lover upon his slayer. She warns him, however, about the sword which he wears and which one of the nieces of his host at the Grail Castle had sent him the evening before. This sword easily flies to pieces, but, to mend it, he should take it to the smith, Trabuchet, who made it and who lives near the lake, Cotovatre. Next follows an encounter between Perceval and Orgellous de la Lande, the jealous husband of the lady of the tent from whom Perceval had snatched a kiss and a ring. The young knight overcomes this adversary, too, and sends him to Arthur's court with the same message as his predecessors. When he hears of Perceval's exploits, Arthur sets forth with his whole court to seek him. They come upon him plunged in meditation under the following circumstances: Snow had fallen, and a flock of geese blinded by it had one of its number wounded by a falcon. Three blood drops had fallen upon the snow and Perceval beholding them was plunged in deep thought on the red and white in his love's face. Sagremor addresses him and bids him come, and when he does not answer, tilts against him, but is overthrown. Kay fares even worse, for he has an arm and a leg broken. Thus Perceval's vow to take vengeance on him has been unconsciously fulfilled. Gawain guesses that love must be mastering the strange knight's thoughts. Accordingly, he approaches Perceval courteously and the latter is brought to Arthur and received by him with honour. On the morrow he returns to the court at Caerleon (Carlion) with Arthur and his train. The next day at noon a hideous damsel appears at court, riding on a yellow mule. She curses Perceval for having omitted to ask concerning the lance and the Grail; if he had done so, the king would have been healed of his wound and ruled his land in peace; now maidens will be put to shame, many will be made orphans and widows, and many knights slain. She then tells of the adventures to be achieved at the Castel Orgellous where there are 566 knights, each with his lady — all ready to joust, with the best estate in the world as the prize — still further, of the adventure of Montesclaire, where there is a captive maiden awaiting deliverance. Whoever liberates her will receive not only praise but *l'espée as estranges ranges*[9] (l. 4674), which was destined to play an important part in the later Grail romances. Gawain undertakes this last adventure, Gifflet (Gifles) undertakes that of the Castel Orgellous, and Perceval vows that he will not rest two nights in the same place until he has learned the meaning of the Grail and the spear. — The next 1466 lines (4709—6175) are devoted to adventures of Gawain; but despite the literary excellence of the episode of the *dameisele as petites mances* (the damsel with the small sleeves), this part of the poem has nothing to do with the Grail theme, save that at the end Gawain is released from a dangerous situation in Guigambresil's castle, on condition that he will bring back the bleeding lance within a year's time (6160). — The tale next returns to Perceval who has wandered about for five years without thinking of God, yet performing many feats. He meets three knights accompanied by ladies, all clad in penitents' dress. Perceval did not know it, but the day was Good Friday and the eldest knight rebukes him for riding fully armed on such a day. He must confess himself to a holy hermit who lives hard by. Perceval goes thither and accuses himself of having forgotten God through his great grief at not having learned the use of the Grail. The hermit reveals himself to the penitent as his uncle — tells him that he is in sin as having caused his mother's death and that for that reason he could not ask concerning lance and Grail — indeed, that but for her prayers he would not have lived till now. Perceval remains two days with his uncle, receives absolution, and rides forth. The remainder of Chrétien's poem (6476—9198)[10]

---

[9] Sword with the Strange Hangings.

[10] In *Ein Namenbuch zu den altfranzösischen Artusepen. Teil I*, pp. 25 ff. (Greifswald diss. 1882) Fritz Seiffert has made a futile effort to prove that Chrétien's division of the *Conte del Graal* only stops with l. 34934 (generally regarded as the end of Wauchier's section of the poem). He admits, it is true, that there are some interpolations in this division. No one, however, has accepted his arguments.

deals exclusively with adventures of Gawain that are independent
of the Grail story.

Now for the analysis of Robert de Boron's *Joseph*:[11] Before
the coming of Christ everbody, including the patriarchs and prophets, went to hell, but He, born of the Virgin Mary, like a rose
from the rose-bush, came in order that He might deliver them
from hell. Christ was incarnated when Judaea was subject to
Rome and Pilate governed a part of it. Now, a soldier of Pilate's,
Joseph of Arimathea, loved Christ, but dared not show it for
fear of the Jews. Of Christ's disciples one — his seneschal, Judas
— was bad, and he betrayed him to the Jews, according to a
bargain concluded at the house of Caiphas. Joseph of Arimathea
was there and grieved at the bargain. On Thursday Jesus gathers
his disciples together at the house of Simon and tells them that
He is to be betrayed. Then we have Judas' question as to who
was to betray Him; next, our Lord's washing of His disciples'
feet and His betrayal by Judas. When the Jews carry off Jesus,
one of them discovers in Simon's house the vessel in which He
made His sacrament, and after judgment had been passed on Jesus,
gave it to Pilate, who kept it until he learns of Jesus' death.
Joseph is angry at this and claims from Pilate pay for the five
years' service of himself and his five knights. Pilate says that
he will give Joseph whatever he desires and Joseph then asks for
Christ's body. Pilate thinks it insignificant payment and grants
it him, and Joseph hastens to the cross, but the guards will not
surrender the body to him, whereupon he complains to Pilate,
who sends Nicodemus to see that he obtains it. At the same time,
Pilate also gives Joseph the vessel, for he does not wish to have
anything pertaining to Jesus about him, for fear of accusation.
Joseph and Nicodemus take down the body and the former washes

---

[11] Edited by Francisque Michel, *Le Roman du Saint Graal*
(Bordeaux, 1841). M. le comte de Douhet reprinted Michel's edition
of Robert's *Joseph* and *Merlin* in the *Dictionnaire des légendes du
christianisme*, cols 454 ff. (Paris, 1855), published by Abbé Migne.
There is a Modern French (prose) paraphrase of the *Joseph* in
P. Paris's *Les romans de la table ronde*, I, 123 ff. Paris, 1868).

it, which makes the blood flow afresh from the wounds. Joseph brings the vessel and catches the blood in it, wraps the body in a fine cloth and entombs it. Then follow the descent into Hell (with the liberation of the saints there) and the Resurrection. The Jews are frightened by the report of the Resurrection and they are particularly incensed against Joseph and Nicodemus as responsible for the disappearance of Christ's body; the latter escapes, but Joseph is beaten and thrust into a horrible and dark dungeon. To him Christ appears with His vessel in a great light, and a long dialogue ensues. He tells Joseph that God had permitted him to serve Pilate, in order that he might (after the crucifixion) care for His body. He tells Joseph, moreover, that because of his love to Him he shall have the symbol of His death and give it for keeping to whom he would. He then gives Joseph the great, precious, vessel, in which was His most holy blood. Joseph wonders how it came there, for he had hidden the vessel in his house. Joseph is to entrust the vessel to three persons only, who are to take it in the name of the Trinity. [By the "three persons" Robert really means Joseph, Bron, and Bron's grandson. The mode of expression is clumsy, beyond measure.] No sacrament shall ever be celebrated but that Joseph shall be remembered. At Joseph's request, Christ instructs him concerning the Sacrament: repeats what He had said at Simon's house, viz. that the bread and wine were His flesh and blood, then adds that the tomb is the altar, the grave-cloth the corporal [i.e. the "cloth, usually of linen, upon which the consecrated elements are placed during the celebration of the mass, and with which the elements or the remnants of them, are covered after the celebration": New English Dictionary]; the vessel in which the blood was put shall be called the chalice and the paten signifies the tombstone. All who see Joseph's vessel shall be of Christ's company and have fulfillment of their heart's desire and joy eternal. Those who shall be able to understand these words cannot be made the victims of false judgment in court or be cheated out of their rights or be vanquished "en court de bataille", if they are in the right. [The author adds: I dare not, nor could not,

tell this even if I would, had I not the great book wherein are
written the histories made and related by the great clerks; therein
are the great secrets written that are named and called the Grail."]
Christ gives the vessel to Joseph and leaves him. Joseph remains
in prison, no man heeding him, until, when Vespasian, the emperor's son, was a leper, a pilgrim who had been a witness of Christ's
miracles, comes to Rome and, hearing of Vespasian's affliction,
tells his inn-keeper of Our Lord's marvellous cures. The inn-
keeper tells the emperor, who summons the pilgrim before him.
The latter pledges his head that Vespasian could be healed, if only
something of Christ's could be brought to Rome. The Emperor
sends messengers, who hear Pilate's story of the Crucifixion and
of Joseph. The Jews, being called together, confirm Pilate's story
and take the blame for Christ's death upon themselves. When
the messengers inquire whether there is any one who possesses
something belonging to Christ, they are told of Verrine [i.e. Ve-
ronica], who is brought before them and she finally relates how
at the request of the Jews she wiped Christ's face as he was being
led forth bound, and thus got the likeness of Him. They take her
to Rome, and the pilgrim and Verrine are both richly rewarded.
The emperor and his son now set forth for Judaea, in order to
revenge Christ's death. On their arrival there, Pilate suggests
a trick by which the Jews, believing that they are pleasing Vespasian, make full confession of their guilt in putting Christ to
death. Vespasian consequently kills many Jews and proclaims that
he will kill them all, if they are not able to produce Jesus alive.
One Jew, to save his own life, offers to bring Vespasian to Joseph,
and tells the story of why the latter was imprisoned. Vespasian
is let down into the prison and finds Joseph alive, although for
so many years he had had neither food nor drink. To his amaze-
ment, Joseph welcomes him by name and expounds to him the
history of the fall of the evil angels and of our first parents and
of the redemption of man by Christ. Vespasian is converted to
Christianity and sells the Jews at the rate of thirty for a penny.
Joseph proclaims salvation to all who believe in Christ and in-
vites those who accept his word to leave their possessions and go

with him into exile. Among those who go are his sister Enygeus and her husband, Hebron (Bron). He sets off with his company and they dwell for a long time in far-off lands. For a while things go well, but then all that they do turns to naught — on account of carnal sin. The host complains to Hebron that they and their children are dying of hunger. Hebron reports this to Joseph, who, weeping, goes and kneels before the vessel and asks Christ, in prayer, why his followers suffer. A voice from the Holy Ghost answers that Joseph is not at fault, but that he is to set the vessel which contains the blood of Christ quite openly before the people and to recollect how He had been betrayed and beaten and how at the Last Supper the false disciple, perceiving that he was detected, withdrew and left a seat vacant. No one will occupy it before Joseph. In the name of the table at which Christ last ate, Joseph is to prepare another, and then to call his brother-in-law, Bron[12] (as Hebron is henceforth generally called) and make him go into the water to catch a fish, and the first he catches Joseph is to put it on the table and then to take the vessel, set it in the middle of the table, cover it with a towel and then place Bron's fish opposite it. The people are now to be called, and they will soon see whose sin has caused these calamities to befall them. Joseph is to sit where Christ sat at the Last Supper, with Bron at his right hand. And Bron is to draw back the space of one seat, to signify the seat of Judas, and the place thus left empty is not to be filled until Enygeus shall have a child by Bron, her husband, and when the child in question is born, that shall be his seat. Let Joseph then bid all the people who have faith in the Trinity and have kept the commandments of Christ to sit down to the grace of Our Lord. Joseph does all this. Part of the people sit down, part do not. The sitters are so filled with sweetness and the desire of their heart that they forget their companions; the others feel nothing. One of the sitters, Petrus, asks the latter if they feel nothing, and when they answer that they do not, tells them that it is because they are defiled with sin. The sinners then depart, but Joseph bids them come back

---

[12] The nominative form is, of course, Brons.

each day. Thus Joseph detects the sinners and thus is the vessel first proved. The fortunate ones tell the others of the delight and joy which fills them and inform them that the vessel severs them from those that sin, as it holds no company with and bears no love towards any sinner. The sinners ask the name of the vessel. The reply is that it is called the *Graal*, for it is agreeable to all who see it. [ This is, of course, a rough-and-ready etymology — *Graal* and *agreer* — such as mediaeval literature abounds in. ] A few lines further down (ll. 2671 ff.) the author again rings the change on this etymology. Since all this is true, says the poet, "we call it the story of the Grail and it will bear the name of the Grail everywhere."

One sinner does not depart with the rest. He is Moyses by name, a hypocrite, and with much weeping begs the people to intercede with Joseph, so that he may share the delights of the Grail table. Joseph says that Moyses must be a hypocrite and undeserving, since he could not sit at the table. — At this point there is a lacuna in the MS.; the sequel, however, shows that Moyses tried to occupy the empty seat, but the earth opened and swallowed him up. — Joseph prays to Christ to show him what has become of Moyses. The voice tells Joseph again about the empty seat and how the one at Joseph's table was not to be filled until the third man, who will be of Joseph's line, should come — the son of Bron and Enygeus — and that *his* son should fill the seat. [ So Alain here is "the third man." This is, however, a blunder, for l. 3375, it is Alain's son, as is required by the whole plan of the poem. ] Moyses had stayed behind only to deceive; he had got his deserts and no more should be heard of him until the man who was destined to fill the empty seat should come. Joseph repeats to Bron what the Holy Spirit had said of Moyses. — In the course of time, Bron and Enygeus have twelve sons and are greatly troubled about them and, on the advice of his wife, Bron asks Joseph what should be done with them. Joseph prays before the vessel for enlightenment. God sends an angel to tell him that they will all be dedicated to God's service, and that eleven will marry, if they wish to, but one of them, the twelfth, named

Alain (Alein),[13] will remain single. Joseph must bid Bron and his wife bring him this son, who is to obey Joseph. Furthermore, when Joseph consults the vessel about Alain, the voice directs him to relate to his nephew all about Christ's sufferings, and death, and about his [Joseph's] imprisonment and the vessel and to show him the vessel and the blood therein, to give him also religious instruction, which he must impart to others, and to tell him that from him shall issue an heir who is to keep the vessel; Alain is to take charge of his brethren and sisters and go westwards to the furthest point possible, preaching Christ. An angel will bring a letter for Petrus to read, directing him to go whither he lists. Petrus will say, that he wishes to go to the vales of Avaron [a mistake, doubtless, for Avalon). [Here again, l. 3112, a blunder; for ll. 3132, 3193 ff., it is to remain unread until Alain's son reads it to him.] Thither shall he go and wait for the son of Alain, (who is here, l. 3128, first named) and he shall not pass away until the one shall come who will read him his letter and teach him the power

---

[13] In the prose-rendering of *Joseph* in one passage (Weidner's ed., p. 127), the epithet, "li gros" is attached to Alain's name, for what reasons no one can say. Inasmuch, however, as Alain was a common name in the ruling house of Brittany and that circumstance may very well have suggested to Robert the name for the character in the first instance, as Heinzel, p. 99, remarks, it is most likely (as Heinzel, p. 122, has still further suggested) that the author of the prose redaction derived his epithet from the same source — more particularly, from the Breton prince of the ninth century called Alan Mor (in French histories, Alain le Grand). Heinzel's alternative conjecture that the epithet originated with the *Grand St. Graal* (really a later romance) is not admissible. To be sure, the prose-rendering of Robert's *Merlin* shows contamination with the *Grand St. Graal,* e. g. Sommer, II, 19, where Nascien, who belongs to the Galahad Early History, usually takes the place of Alain in the MSS., it seems. But "Alain li Gros" is apparently the authorized reading at p. 127 of the prose *Merlin,* and the *Grand St. Graal* (like the *Didot-Perceval, Perlesvaus,* etc.), no doubt, borrowed from it. After all, the question has little importance, since the epithet does not occur in Robert. Brugger's discussion of Alain, *Morf Festschrift,* consists so entirely of a chain of hazardous speculations that it seems to me valueless.

of the vessel and tell him the fate of Moyses. After that he will die. All these things Joseph must repeat to his nephews. This Joseph does and tells Bron and Enygeus that Alain is to govern his brothers and sisters. — The next day, whilst they are at the Grail service, a heavenly letter appears. Joseph gives it to Petrus, who declares his intention of departing for the vales of Avaron and awaiting there God's grace. Bron calls his children and again warns them to be obedient to Alain. So Alain goes forth with his brothers into distant lands and preaches everywhere the name of Christ. Petrus wishes to depart also, but he is petitioned to stay, and, inasmuch as this is the will of Heaven, as is declared by an angel, he consents. He is to see something more of the vessel. The angel continues: "The Lord knows Bron for a worthy man and it was therefore his will that he should go fishing. He is to keep the vessel after Joseph, who must instruct him properly, especially concerning the holy words which God spake to Joseph in the prison, which are sweet and precious, gracious and merciful, and which are properly called the Secrets of the Grail." Joseph must then give the vessel to Bron and warn him to hold it in high regard — else he will pay dearly for it. Hereafter, Bron's right name is to be "The Rich Fisher." His honor will continue to increase on account of the fish which he caught when this grace began. Bron, too, is to go westward and dwell where he pleases. There he must wait for his son's son, and when the latter has arrived, the vessel and the grace (that accompanies it) are to be given to him. Then the meaning and significance of the blessed Trinity will have been fulfilled by the division among the three. With the third one [ here, l. 3373, Alain's son, not Alain, himself, as in l. 2790 ] Christ will deal as it pleases him. After the vessel has been given to Bron, Petrus is to go, as he may then truly say that he has seen Bron, the Rich Fisher, put in possession of the vessel, and God will have him in his keeping. When all this is done, Joseph is to go to perfect joy and life everlasting. His descendants will be safe. On the morrow Joseph at the service transfers the Grail to the Rich Fisher, and repeats to the people everything, as the voice commanded, save the words spoken to him by Christ in the prison. These he confides to the Rich Fisher alone. He committed them to him in writing, also, and expounded to him the secrets. The people were touched at the sight. They knew that Joseph had surrendered his authority, but did not exactly know how. Amid weeping and prayer, the Good Fisher left the assembly. He stayed three days longer with Joseph and then went forth. Joseph, however, remained in the land where he was born. — The poet adds now that it will be fitting to tell the subsequent fortunes of Alain, Petrus, Moyses, and the Rich Fisher. As already stated, he expresses, moreover, the intention to treat these themes, if he can find them in a book. For the present, however, he will leave aside these four branches and take up a fifth — that is to say, the *Merlin* which follows immediately after, but of which only a fragment in its original verse-form has been preserved. The object of the *Merlin*, of course, was to attach the story of the Grail to the popular Arthurian cycle.

Now, in discussing the origin of the Grail legend, whatever conclusions we may reach ultimately concerning this question, it seems advisable to take up first the sources of Robert de Boron's *Joseph*, for Birch-Hirschfeld[14] has, in my judgment, fixed these sources in the essentials beyond reasonable doubt, whereas the matter is not so clear in the case of Chrétien's *Perceval*. To be sure, eminent Celticists have endeavored to prove a Celtic connection for Robert's poem, but, as it seems to me, in vain.

First, as for Robert's idea of the Grail, it is to be noted that the Grail, in his conception, is not a vessel to which appertains the marvellous power of supplying food and drink, youth, health, and strength. Such a conception of its power is found in some Grail romances later than his. With Robert, however, it is a vessel of "grace" in whose service only the good and pure can remain. The delights which the Grail imparts to those that sit at the Grail table are purely spiritual. Sinners are excluded from these delights, and the hypocrite, like Moyses (Moses), who tries to partake of

---

[14] *Sage vom Gral*, pp. 215 ff. See further on this subject the interpretation of the Grail wanderings in Robert's *Joseph* which I offer, Part IV, below.

them is stricken with punishment. This last idea was suggested
by Judas's connection with the Last Supper in *St. Matthew,*
XXVI, 21ff: "21. And as they did eat, he said, Verily I say
unto you that one of you shall betray me. 22. And they were
exceeding sorrowful and began every one of them to say unto him,
Lord, is it I? 23. And he answered and said, He that dippeth
his hand with me in the dish, the same shall betray me. 24. The
Son of man goeth as it is written of him: but woe unto that man
by whom the Son of man is betrayed! it had been good for that
man if he had not been born. 25. Then Judas which betrayed him
answered and said, Master, is it I? He said unto him, Thou
hast said."

When Joseph in Robert's poem founds the Grail table, it
is modelled completely after the table of the Last Supper — only
here the Fish, the symbol of Christ, takes the place of Christ. The
sinners who sit down undeservingly at the sacred table suffer the
punishment which their prototype, Judas, suffered. But how did
the dish of the Last Supper become connected with Joseph of
Arimathea? This did not happen in any oral tradition. It was
the invention of Robert, who took here as his starting-point various hints in certain uncanonical writings of Early Christianity,
viz. the *Vindicta Salvatoris,* which contains the legend of St. Veronica — furthermore, a Latin composition on Pilate *(Narratio
Josephi),* and the famous apocryphal *Evangelium Nicodemi,*
more especially, the First Part, called the *Gesta Pilati.* From
the first of these Robert learned of Vespasian's supposed expedition to Judaea to revenge on the Jews the death of our Saviour.
To be sure, Tiberius is represented here as the Roman emperor and
Vespasian merely as a general. But Joseph of Arimathea appears in the *Vindicta* as a contemporary of Vespasian's — that is
to say, as still living some forty years after the death of Christ —
for in that work he tells the messenger of the Emperor Tiberius
of his former imprisonment from which Christ had delivered him.
Robert learned from the Latin poem on Pilate that Vespasian was
emperor. He makes him also Joseph's deliverer. This last feature may have been purely of Robert's invention; on the other ha~ '

it may possibly have been suggested by a passage in Suetonius's life of Vespasian (Ch. 5), where it is said that "one of the noble captives, named Joseph, when he was put in chains, kept affirming that he would soon be freed by Vespasian." What Robert owed to the Gospel of Nicodemus was the fuller information regarding the imprisonment of Joseph of Arimathea and Christ's visiting him in the dungeon. He preferred, however, to interweave the legend of St. Veronica with that of Joseph and so postpone the liberation of the latter until the time of Vespasian. So all that Robert tells about Vespasian's connection with Joseph and Christ's visit to Joseph in the prison was derived from or suggested by these sources.

Now, in the history of the Holy Grail, as given in Robert's poem, we have an undeniable parallelism with the history of Christ in his closing days. The Grail is present with Christ at the Last Supper; like Christ it is brought to Pilate; Joseph of Arimathea receives it, as he receives the body of our Lord; it is present at the entombment, remains then concealed and at last reappears with the risen Christ. It is plain, then, that we have in Robert's history of the Holy Grail a characteristic piece of mediaeval symbolism. The Grail is the symbol of Christ's body. A passage in the *Gesta Pilati,* ch. 15, which describes the visit of Jesus to Joseph in the prison, furnishes the basis for still further symbolism in Robert's poem. In the *Gesta* after describing the appearance of Jesus to him in the prison, his consternation, and the manner in which Jesus revived him, Joseph is made to say: "Rabbi, thou art Elias?" And he replied: "I am Jesus, whose body thou didst seek from Pilate and didst wrap it in clean linen and thou didst put a napkin over my face and didst place me in thy new monument and didst roll a stone to the door of the monument. Then I said to him who was speaking to me: Show me, O Lord, where I placed thee! And he led me and showed me the place where I had laid him and the cloth which I put upon him, and the napkin which I wrapped his face with, and I recognized that it was Jesus."

Now, all the chief points of this passage recur in Robert's poem, in some respects amplified. But when Jesus comes to men-

tion the Last Supper we have the following symbolical identification of the Eucharist with the Entombment, Christ saying to
Joseph: "When you took me down from the cross and laid me in
the sepulchre, that is the altar on which those who will sacrifice
me will put me;[15] the cloth in which I was wrapped will be called
the *corporal;* the vessel in which you put my blood, when you
received it from my body, will be called the *chalice;* the paten
which will go on top, will mean the *stone* which was placed over
me, when thou hadst laid me in the sepulchre." The detailed identification here of the different objects that figure in the interment
of Christ is found elsewhere in the Middle Ages[16] — only in these

---

[15] The mass, it is to be recollected, is, according to the Catholic
conception, a sacrifice.

[16] Cp. Heinzel, p. 103, for a list of mediaeval writers who offer
such allegorical interpretations of the objects used in the mass. Hertz,
p. 425, points to the Greek treatise of doubtful authorship, printed by
Migne in vol. 98 of his *Patrologia Graeca,* cols. 383 ff., among the
writings of Germanos, Archbishop of Constantinople (who died in 733),
as the earliest allusion to a vessel in which the blood that flowed
from Christ's side was received. The work is entitled (in Migne's
Latin translation) *Historia ecclesiastica et mystica contemplatio* and
is certainly not later than the tenth century. The allusion occurs
cols. 400 B and 421 D, and the vessel is identified with the cup of
the Eucharist. In these passages, and, also, in 397 A and B, the
other objects used in the Byzantine mass are, likewise, interpreted in
allegorical fashion. Hertz does not note what, however, is well worth
observing, that in 397 B the author of this treatise interprets the
paten [Greek *diskos*] which bore the holy bread in the mass as "the
bed [*kline*] in which the body of the Lord is prepared by the priest
and deacon, who are [i. e. represent] Joseph and Nicodemus." These
two names are again connected with the allegorical interpretation of
the *diskos* at 421 D, as, indeed, they occur in the Eucharistic liturgy
of the Eastern Church.

For the symbolical interpretations in Robert, especially, see Birch-
Hirschfeld, pp. 219 ff., and W. W. Newell, *Journal of American Folk-
Lore,* X, 22 ff. As a very instructive example of these allegorical
interpretations of the mass and the objects connected therewith I would
add Durandus, *Rationale Divinorum Officiorum,* Book IV, Ch. 51
(Naples, 1859). He was the leading writer on Christian ritual in the
twelfth century.

other interpretations the *chalice* is said to be the *tomb* (sepulchrum), whereas here it is said to be the vessel of the Last Supper which Joseph had used to collect the blood of Jesus in. It would seem, then, that by a confused symbolism this vessel — i.e. the Holy Grail — is taken as the tomb in which Christ was laid. In the *Gesta*, as we have seen, Jesus took Joseph to the tomb and showed him the objects which have just been interpreted symbolically. In the poem he simply gives him the Grail, which he expressly declares is the symbol of his death as well as of the Eucharist. Just as the Mediaeval Church commonly interpreted the Last Supper in terms of the Burial of Christ, Robert took now the vessel of the Last Supper (the Grail) as the symbol of both the Burial and the Eucharist. In fine, Joseph, who laid Christ's body in the gave, is the natural guardian of the symbol which commemorates that event; thus, too, the Grail is the natural centre of all the symbolism of mass and sacrament, and we have, consequently, the intimate union of the Joseph legend with the story of the Grail.

Furthermore, as we have endeavored to prove elsewhere in this work,[17] Robert, in the last division of his poem, which deals with the peregrinations of the Grail and its company, through a new act of symbolism, has expressed in narrative form what Jesus himself insisted on as the object of his mission on earth and the very foundation of the Christian Church — namely, the establishment of the New Covenant, symbolized by the cup of the Holy Communion (that is to say, the Grail in Robert's conception), to take the place of the Old Covenant.

The interpretation of the events of the Old Testament as a sort of allegorical adumbration of those of the New Testament[18] was still a vital element in the Biblical exegesis of the age, and so there was no new departure in Robert's employment of this method. It is to be observed, too, that in no other period of the Church has the doctrine of transubstantiation been so immediately

---

[17] Cp. Part IV.

[18] According to the well-known doctrine of types.

the centre of theological interest and discussion as in the latter part of the twelfth century and the early decades of the thirteenth.[19] It became so, especially, through the mystical writings of Hugh of St. Victor, Bonaventura, and others, and in 1215 was finally adopted, on the initiative of Pope Innocent III, by the Fourth Lateran Council of the Church as a part of the orthodox Christian faith, being directly attached to the mysteries of the Trinity and Incarnation in the canons which promulgated it, very much as

---

[19] This has been emphasized especially by M. Gaster, *Folk-Lore*, II, 55 (1891) and by Miss L. A. Fisher, *The Mystic Vision in the Grail Legend and in the Divine Comedy*, pp. 9 ff., Columbia Studies in English and Comparative Literature (New York, 1917). As far as the Grail is concerned, the main thesis of Miss Fisher's book — a study that deserves the careful attention of all Grail students — may be stated in the author's own words (p. 55): "that the Celtic vessel of increase and plenty, adapted to Christian purposes, became the symbol of the miracle of transubstantiation and that any accessory of the mass (i. e. ciborium, chalice, paten, or even altar-stone) intimately connected with the miracle, might be described as that symbol, in other words, might be the Grail."

Miss Fisher starts out by accepting, without argument, the theory that the Grail is ultimately of Celtic origin, but, as she goes on, her faith in this theory evidently weakens. Cp. pp. 74, 81, 123 f. I would like to call attention, especially, to Miss Fisher's refutation, pp. 63 ff. (including notes), of what Miss Weston had said, *Legend of Sir Perceval*, II, 232 f. in regard to the "secrets" of the Grail (cp. the *Joseph*, ll. 935, 3336). Miss Weston objected to interpreting (as, for example, Heinzel, p. 87, does) the term as referring to the words which the priest speaks in consecrating the bread and wine and which were supposed to convert them into bread and wine, respectively, on the ground that "the formula of consecration is not and never has been secret." But Miss Fisher shows by examples that in mediaeval usage these words were actually called "secret" — no doubt, because in that period, as in other periods, "secret" was applied not only to what is not known, but to what is not understood. Miss Fisher has been equally successful, pp. 63, note 1, in refuting by quotation from a contemporary writer Miss Weston's idea (I, 333) that between Robert and the *Queste* the interest had shifted "from *contenu* to container" — i. e. from the holy blood to the Grail. It is really a mere question of metonomy.

we see this done in the looser form of a narrative in Robert's *Joseph*.[20]

The relation of Robert to Chrétien will probably always remain a subject of debate. The advocates of a non-Christian origin for the Grail legend assume that both were drawing independently from lost sources.[21] As a matter of fact, the only feature which these two poems on the Grail have unmistakably in common is the term "The Rich Fisher" (Robert, l. 3387) or "Good Fisher" (l. 3456) as applied to the keeper of the Grail.[22] To be sure, that feature is a very distinctive one. Neither the lance nor the *tailleor* (paten),[23] however, of Chrétien's procession appear in the *Joseph*, and the whole interest is centred on the Grail. But, after all, there is nothing inconsistent in these facts with the view that Robert derived the suggestion of his poem from Chrétien and not from any

---

[20] In the light of the canons of 1215, it is interesting to read what Heinzel remarks, pp. 87f., on the close association of the Trinity and the Grail in Robert's *Joseph*. It may be that Robert had some definite treatise as the source of his ideas about the intimate association of the Trinity and the Eucharist which was taking shape in the theological thought of the time.

[21] This was, also, in part, the opinion of Heinzel (pp. 92ff.), one of the most eminent advocates of the Christian origin of the Grail legend. Birch-Hirschfeld (pp. 195ff.), who imagined — wrongly, as I have tried to prove — that the *Didot-Perceval* was a prose rendering of a lost poem by Robert de Boron, regarded that romance as the source of Chrétien's *Perceval*. More recently, Foerster in his Chrétien *Wörterbuch* (pp. 158*ff.) has tried to identify the "livre" given to Chrétien by Count Philip with Robert's *Joseph*. Neither of these theories, however, have attracted any adherents.

[22] One might be inclined to add the quality of luminosity, which Robert, ll. 719, 2032, as well as Chrétien, l. 3188, ascribes to the Grail. Apart from the fact, however. that this is a common feature of talismans in folk-lore, Robert may very well be transferring to the Grail here the dazzling light which in one of his sources, the *Evangelium Nicodemi* (Part I, ch. 15), marked the appearance of Jesus in Joseph's prison. See *Evangelia Aprocrypha*, pp. 359f. (Leipzig, 1853), edited by C. Tischendorf.

[23] The paten is mentioned in Christ's speech quoted p. 231, above, but it does not figure in the story.

hypothetical lost sources concerning the Grail.[24] It was not necessary that he should have any intimate knowledge of the *Perceval*. It was sufficient if he knew of the Grail and the Fisher King.[25] Just as romances relating the adventures of a mature hero in the Middle Ages awakened curiosity about his early history, and so stimulated the poets to the production of narratives concerning his youthful exploits *(enfances)*, so it may well have been in regard to the Grail. Chrétien's *Perceval* had, undoubtedly, created a widespread interest in this mysterious vessel, [26] and yet, being unfinished, it left the field open to the invention of other poets who might handle the theme. The only thing which his poem had fixed was that the Grail, since it contained the host (sacramental wafer), was the vessel so used in the eucharistic ritual — the ciborium, as it is called. But in the Middle Ages there was not a clear distinction in form nor in part (from doctrinal motives) even in function between the vessel that contained the wine in the Eucharist and the one that contained the holy wafer.[27] The latter, as

---

[24] This is true, too, I believe, of the apparent contradiction, when it is said in Robert, 1. 3032, that none of the Grail people, if sinless, can be maimed, although in Chrétien both the Grail keeper (Fisher King) and his father are maimed.

[25] Newell, who also believed that Robert derived the suggestion for his poem from Chrétien, remarks, *Journal of American Folk-Lore*, X, 225 (1897): "He may have been acquainted with the poem of Chrestien only by rumor, and have had no distinct idea, either of its contents or of Arthurian history." This, however, I think, is going too far.

[26] This is sufficiently attested by the continuations of Chrétien's *Perceval*. Newell, *ibid.*, 220 f. interprets, also, as referring to Chrétien's poem, the "meintes paroles contées, ki ne sunt pas foles," which, according to Robert, ll. 3457 f., were told of the Good Fisher (Rich Fisher), after he went westward.

[27] Miss Fisher has made this plain in her *The Mystic Vision in the Grail Legend and in the Divine Comedy*, pp. 58 ff. (New York, 1917).

The commixture of the elements (bread and wine) in the Holy Communion seems universal in the Eastern Church even to-day. Cp. Hastings's *Encyclopaedia of Religion and Ethics* under *Eastern Church*.

well as the former, had the shape of a cup, as it still has in the
Catholic Church of today, and it was also not infrequently called
the "chalice" (calix) — indeed, down into the eighteenth century. As to function, Durandus (Guillaume Durand, Bishop of
Mendo), the leading writer of the twelfth century on matters
of ritual, expressly directs that the host in the sacramental service shall be broken over the real chalice, (i.e. the chalice, containing the wine which typified the blood of Christ) and a portion
of it be dropped into that vessel, "primo ad notandum quod Christi
corpus non fuit sine sanguine nec sanguis sine corpore. Secundo
ad designandum quod unum sacramentum conficitur ex speciebus
panis et vini. Tertio, corporis et sanguinis post trinum crucis
signum permixtio est animae ad corpus reditio." [28]

These conditions perhaps help to explain why Robert (ll.
395 ff., 433 ff., 507 ff., 563 ff.) identifies the Grail, on the one
hand, with the dish of the Last Supper (which would naturally
correspond with the ciborium) and, on the other, with the chalice
of the sacrament (ll. 907 ff.).

---

[28] I owe the reference to Miss Fisher, p. 58, note 3. I quote
from the edition of the *Rationale Divinorum Officiorum* which was
published at Naples in 1859. The passage will be found at p. 304
of that edition, Book IV, Ch. 51 *(De fractione hostiae)*. According
to this quotation and other evidence which Miss Fisher adduces, as
she remarks, "both species contain the whole Christ." Consequently,
either could symbolize Christ and either of the containing vessels
indifferently could be identified with the Grail. Cf. her remarks, also,
p. 62.

A similar stress on the unity of the functions of the two elements
of the sacrament seems to me intended in the lines which Miss Fisher
quotes, in another connection, p. 75, note 4, from *Versus de Mysterio
Missae*, Migne, *Patrologia Latina*, vol. 171, col. 1180, especially,
in the following:

Oblati panis dextra tenet calicem
In cruce pendentis quoniam latus Omnipotentis
Dextrum sanguineam vulnere fudit aquam.

"Callicem" here, it will be observed, means the ciborium. Even the
paten (small flat dish covering the chalice), Miss Fisher *(ibid.)* thinks,
might have been taken as the symbolical vessel (the Grail), since, at
least, in the earlier periods the host was broken over it and Innocent
III identifies it with the dish of the paschal lamb.

Having once conceived the idea of relating the early history of the Grail, which he recognized as identical with a vessel of the eucharistic ritual in Chrétien, he would, of course, turn to Biblical and legendary materials that would furnish him with hints to give body to this conception. We have seen what these materials were and how he has used them.

As regards the *Merlin*, which follows upon the *Joseph*, this is mainly drawn from Geoffrey of Monmouth or Wace — or, possibly, some other verse-chronicle derived from Geoffrey — and shows no connection with Chrétien. In the Didot and Modena MSS. a *Perceval* in prose follows prose renderings of Robert's *Joseph* and *Merlin*, and, if it were really the work of Robert, this would show that he used Chrétien; but, despite the contentions of some scholars, we shall see later on[29] that the work is not his. So, altogether, Chrétien is only in a limited sense a source of Robert. Besides, Robert's poem, as will have been obvious from the analyses given above, is in a wholly different style from Chrétien's *Perceval*. Compared with the latter, the style is homely, awkward and often obscure, without colour or spirit. As regards the incidents, furthermore, we are moving here in the atmosphere of Christian legend *(Joseph)* or pseudo-chronicle *(Merlin)*, not of folk-tale and romance, such as is found in Chrétien's poem.

Let us turn now to an investigation of Chrétien's sources and endeavor to isolate, as far as we can, the Grail theme from the other elements which he may have chosen to interweave with it after the manner which had distinguished his methods of composition in earlier works.

In the beginning of his *Perceval* Chrétien speaks of exerting himself to "put in rime the best tale . . . that was ever related in a royal court" ("a rimoiier le meillor conte . . . qui soit contez an cort real"). "That is the story of the Grail of which the Count gave him the book." At first blush, it would seem, then, that he was merely putting into verse a prose-romance that the Count gave him. But this is impossible, for there were no prose-romances so early as this. They first began about 1200, or not

---

[29] Cp. Part IV, below.

long before. Some of the writers of romances, it is true, like Hugh of Rotelande in his *Ipomedon*, refer to Latin books as their sources, but this was simply a trick to impart an air of authority to their works, and certainly no Latin romances from this early time are extant. Indeed, as far as the Grail is concerned, Helinand of Froidmont, in a well-known passage written early in the thirteenth century, declares expressly that he had been unable to discover any Latin version of the Grail story.

Still further, the other productions of Chrétien afford no example of his merely working over in verse some tale that he had before him, whether in prose or in verse. He always makes up his romances by combining elements drawn from different sources. As we have seen before, this is particularly clear in the case of the *Cligès*, where (as in the *Perceval*) he similarly declares in the opening of his romance that he had found the story in a book in the cathedral library at Beauvais. He means by this simply the main theme, and with this theme he unites other elements at pleasure. Now, what are the main elements of the *Perceval?*

1. The Grail *motif*, to which the *motif* of removing a spell by putting a question is attached.

2. What is known in the study of folk-tales as the Great Fool *motif* [30] — the Great Fool (i.e. rustic or simpleton, who proves himself more than a match for the most renowned warriors), in this instance, being identified with the hero of the Grail-Quest.

3. The Arthurian setting of the whole.

Through this last element the Great Fool, who is also the Grail-quester, becomes a knight of Arthur's court and is brought

---

[30] Brugger, *Zs. f. frz. Spr. u. Litt.*, XLIV [2], 145 ff. (1917), cites an Icelandic tale as parallel to that of Perceval. We have, however, in this tale six "Great Fools" (brothers), instead of one, and, altogether, I do not think that the parallel in question throws any new light on the subject. *Ibid.* pp. 183 ff., Brugger disposes effectively of G. B. Wood's theory, "A Reclassification of the Perceval Romances," PMLA, XXVII 524 ff. (1912), that the Perceval story is merely a combination of two other types of fairy-tales, viz. *The Fated Prince* and *The Male Cinderella*.

into contrast with the famous knights of that court—especially with Gawain, the model of worldly courtesy and prowess. This gives an opportunity for variety, and, as a matter of fact, in the *Perceval*, as far as Chrétien carried it out, the number of lines given to Gawain's adventures is not so very much smaller than the number of those given to Perceval's.

What, then, did the book which Chrétien refers to contain? Certainly, the Grail *motif* — for Chrétien expressly terms it the *Story of the Grail*. But how about the two remaining *motifs?* If we trust to the analogy of his other romances, there is no probability that these additional *motifs* were associated with the Grail story in his book. That analogy would suggest to us that he, himself, was the first to combine these other *motifs* with the *motif* of the Grail. As far as the Arthurian setting is concerned, this is obvious on the face of it. In making Arthur's court the centre from which the action radiates, he would be merely doing precisely the same thing that he had done in all of his previous romances — notably, in the *Cligès*, where no one has ever pretended that the story had any connection originally with Arthurian tradition. Geoffrey of Monmouth and Wace had established the fame of Arthur's court, and in his *Perceval*, as in his other romances, Chrétien was simply availing himself of the fame of that court to give *éclat* to his own heroes and their exploits. There can be very little doubt that the same thing is true of the Great Fool *motif*. In virtually every country and tribe in the world we have these stories of the apparent simpleton or rustic who is able to achieve adventures that have baffled the most celebrated warriors or knights, very much as in our present-day circuses the clown usually turns out to be the most skilful acrobat of all. But nowhere else is the Great Fool the hero of a Grail quest — so that the probabilities are that Chrétien was the first to combine the two *motifs*.[31]

---

[31] In his review of Nutt's *Studies on the Legend of the Holy Grail* in the *Göttingische Gelehrte Anzeigen* for June 10, 1890, H. Zimmer says (p. 520) of Cuchullin's first adventures in the Old Irish epic, *Tain bo Cualnge:* "Die Aehnlichkeit mit Percevals Jugend-

Apart from these general considerations, the numerous *motifs* which Chrétien repeats in the *Perceval* from his previous romances show how large a part of this romance is due to his invention and not to his source.[32] Most obvious among these examples of repeated *motifs* is the rôle that Gawain plays. This is found in every one of the author's works without exception. In Geoffrey of Monmouth and Wace this nephew of Arthur figures as the best knight at his uncle's court, so that in Chrétien's romances, which celebrate the exploits of other heroes — Erec, Cliges, Yvain, Lancelot — Gawain always plays a part — an increasingly important one in the successive romances. In the *Erec*, his rôle is smaller, although he is even there spoken of as the best of Arthur's knights (ll. 2288ff.). In the *Cliges* (ll. 4916ff.) and *Yvain* (ll. 6106ff.) he is used as the touchstone of the hero's prowess. In the *Lancelot* his adventures rival those of Lancelot, himself. In the *Perceval*, we have him filling the same function as in the *Lancelot*

---

geschichte springt in die Augen." Cuchullin, too, is brought up by his mother far from the court of Conchobar (his uncle), hears of the life there, and, despite his mother's warnings, insists on going to Conchobar and distinguishes himself at once. The two stories, however, are alike only in the general *motifs*, and I do not believe that they have any actual historical connection with one another.

In his article, "The Aryan Expulsion- and Return-Formula," *Folk-Lore Record*, IV, pp. 1ff. (1881), A. Nutt pointed out some general resemblances between the story of Perceval in the Middle English *Sir Perceval of Gales* and the Irish *Boyish Exploits of Finn*. In "Sir Perceval, and *The Boyish Exploits of Finn*.", PMLA, XXXII, 598ff. (1917), R. B. Pace has listed systematically the points in question, but they amount to nothing, even if we allow that the English poem is independent of Chrétien. The Irish tale was formerly assigned by scholars to the fifteenth century, but latterly to the tenth (John Macneill) or the twelfth (Kuno Meyer).

In the same year (1897) a comparison between the story of the youthful Perceval and *Barlaam and Josaphat* was made independently by W. W. Newell, *Journal of American Folk-Lore*, X, 131, and L. Clédat, *Revue de Philologie Française et de Littérature*, XI, 14, note. Clédat, however, wisely regarded the resemblance as accidental.

[32] Cp. W. Foerster's list, *Kristian von Troyes: Wörterbuch zu seinen sämtlichen Werken*, Introduction, pp. 163ff.

— only he occupies an even larger place here, and he is a foil to Perceval: that is to say, he is the type of the perfection of worldly knighthood, devoted to arms and ladies, as contrasted with the knight who has a mystic function to perform.

More important, however, among these repeated *motifs* than the rôle of Gawain even is the quest *motif*. Just as in the novels of Le Sage, Fielding and Smollett, the author starts his hero on a journey, the adventures of which make up the materials of the story, so, from the *Erec* on, a quest was the main device which Chrétien employed for the development of his romances. In the *Erec*, we have first the search for the strange knight with the dwarf, etc. (2576 ff.); later the hero sallies forth in quest of adventures, in general, to re-establish his reputation for valour. This last *motif* is found again in *Yvain* (ll. 2539 ff.). In the *Lancelot*, Lancelot and Gawain have the more definite purpose of rescuing Guinevere from her captor, Meleagant. In *Perceval* it is again an indefinite search for adventure, although one incident of this quest is destined to assume an importance above all the rest — namely, the visit to the Grail Castle.[33]

Besides the two points just discussed, the *Perceval* possesses many minor features in common with Chrétien's earlier poems which considerations of space prevent us from enumerating here.[34]

Finally as another indication of Chrétien's free treatment of his theme — an indication that he is not merely versifying a story that lay before him — it is to be observed that he plunges *in medias res* here with his narrative, as he does in his other poems. He does not begin with the history of the misfortunes of Perceval's mother and how she was led to seek refuge in the forest. He simply speaks of her as the widowed lady, takes the previous

---

[33] In his *A Study of Gawain and the Green Knight*, p. 80 (Harvard University Press, 1916), G, L. Kittredge calls attention to a class of popular tales in which the hero can only escape death or disgrace by meeting certain tests, but "does not know in what the tests consist", or, perhaps "does not know there is any test at all". He puts the Grail - question in this category. This feature of the Grail story is, undoubtedly, of folk-lore origin.

[34] Cp. Foerster's list, just cited.

history of his hero for granted, and starts off at once with this hero's adventures.

It seems plain from this discussion, therefore, that the book which Chrétien refers to merely gave him the conception of the Grail, but that the character of the Grail knight and the conception of the quest are Chrétien's additions. What was it that determined him in the choice of Perceval as the Knight of the Quest? Naturally, the hero of the quest had to be an Arthurian knight. Apart from the general fame of Arthur, this was, of course, a necessity with Chrétien, the Arthurian poet. It was not desirable, however, to use for this purpose any of the well-known Arthurian knights. Their characters would not have suited the new theme — the quest of a holy, mystic vessel — but, in any event, in the interests of novelty a new knight was required. Furthermore, in the interests of novelty he confers on this new knight the character of the hero of the Great Fool tale. In the *chansons de geste*, as in the only one of Chrétien's own romances where he had related the *enfances* of his hero — viz. *Cligès* — the knight is always brought up in the familiar environment of feudal society. It was a happy thought now to vary the theme — to introduce a hero who, though of noble origin, had grown up in the wilderness, outside of the conventional life of the noble classes of the time, and whose consequent awkwardness and naiveté would render his prowess only the more piquant. It mattered very little what name was given him. The one, actually selected, was "Perceval li Galois" which we find already in the list of Arthurian knights in the *Erec* (l. 1526). There is no reason, however, to think that before Chrétien any definite story had ever been attached to his name any more than to that of Lancelot. Indeed, the name, "Perceval" is, on the face of it, French, and the epithet, "li Galois" was added, merely to give it the Arthurian colouring.[35]

---

[35] The fullest discussion of the name "Perceval", its variants in the different languages and the derivations which have been proposed for it, is to be found in W. Hertz's *Parzival von Wolfram von Eschenbach, neu bearbeitet*, pp. 490 ff. It is, as he says, an "Imperativname" ("Pierce the valley" "Press on through the valley") like German "Springinsfeld." We have a parallel formation in "Percehaie" ("Pierce-

From the Catalogue of the Ships in the Iliad down, the epic has always delighted in such lists of names, and the immediate model for those of the *Erec* may very well have been similar lists in the

---

hedge"), the name given to a son of Reynard the Fox (E. Martin, *Le Roman de Renart*, Supplément, Strasbourg, 1887, 118). The same name appears in the eleventh century as that of a Norman (Radulf Percehaie) in the Doomsday Book, the well-known register of English landholders which William the Conqueror had prepared. Cp. F. Hildebrand: "Über das französische Sprachelement im Liber Censualis," *Zs. f. rom. Ph.*, VIII, 341 (1884). *Ibid.*, II, 309 (1878), K. Bartsch had already cited as a parallel, "Perceforest," name of the hero of the romance, *Perceforest* (fourteenth century); but this was, no doubt, a mere imitation of "Perceval." Another parallel formation, "Passelande", is cited by Golther, *Zs. f. vergleichende Litteraturgeschichte und Renaissance-Litteratur, Neue Folge*, III. Hertz takes the name "Perceval," 420 (1890) (p. 493), as an "Umdeutung" of Welsh "Peredur," whilst Wechssler (*Sage vom Gral*, p. 135) and J. Loth (*Les Mabinogion*, I, 56, 2 nd ed. Paris, 1913) regard it as substituted for "Peredur." It is much more likely, however, that "Peredur" (the Welsh tale of that name, as we have seen elsewhere being a mere adaptation of the French *Conte del Graal*) is substituted for Perceval." This very substitution shows that "Perceval" was unknown to the Welsh, in whose records, for the rest, the name does not occur. Inasmuch as "Perceval," then, is plainly a French name, one cannot feel sure that the epithet, "li Gallois," which Chrétien attaches to it already from its first recorded occurrence (*Erec*, l. 1536), is not an invention of the French poet, who desires to give everything in his poem a Celtic coloring. W. W. Newell, *Journal of American Folk-Lore*, X, 125 (1897), interprets it as meaning "rude and rustic," since Welshmen were regarded by the Anglo-Normans in that light or even worse, and as applied here to Perceval with reference to his rusticity at the beginning of the tale. This interpretation, however, is, no doubt, erroneous. The name "Perceval," according to Foerster, Chrétien *Wörterbuch*, p. 162*, is Chrétien's own invention; according to Brugger, *Zs. f. frz. Spr. u. Litt.*, XXXI², 145, note 32, it was originally an epithet which later supplanted the hero's real name. We have no data for deciding the question, but it seems to me most likely that the name came to Chrétien from some lost French tale that embodied the Great Fool *motif*.

Hertz, p. 483, 486, cites parallels to show that in his attire and equipment Chrétien's Perceval was a genuine Welsh peasant of the day. There is nothing, however, really distinctive about the details

Celtic tales which gave their first impulse to the Arthurian romances — such a list, for example, as that in the Welsh tale, *Kulhwch and Olwen*, or, perhaps, similar lists in the *chansons de geste* or romances of antiquity.

Chrétien's book gave him, then, merely the materials for his conception of the Grail. What was the nature of this book? Did it belong to the literature of Christian legend, was it a Celtic tale, or was it of some other origin still? In other words, what was the origin of the conception of the Holy Grail? There are three theories on the subject: 1. that this conception originated in Christian legend; 2. that it was originally a Celtic conception which has been imperfectly Christianized by the French poets; 3. that it sprang from some ritual of the Vegetation Spirit, which survived the fall of the ancient world of paganism and continued down into the Middle Ages. The first two theories have confronted each other for seventy years or more — the third, though suggested by Simrock as far back as 1842, has only appeared in the field as a formidable rival since the beginning of the twentieth century.

In discussing this question of the origin of the Grail, naturally, the first step to take is to consider the etymology of the

---

in question, although Chrétien (ll. 1694, 1796) speaks of the lad's being appareled in the Welsh manner.

The French poets, probably, as a rule, interpreted "Perceval" as made up of "perce + val." In the oft-quoted passage (cp. Foerster's large edition of Chrètien's *Cligès*, p. xx), from the metrical prologue to a prose version of the *Vie des Pères*, where the author warns his readers against reading romances, he uses a play on words: "Laissiez Cliges et Perceval, Qui les cuers perce et trait a val." So, too, Wolfram 140, 15: "der nam is rehte enmitten durch." The author of the prose romance, *Perlesvaus*, likewise, plays (pp. 19, 87, 105) with the etymology of the name. This had, no doubt, become traditional.

On French names formed in this manner *(Brise-fer* etc.*)*, which are also found in French folktales, cp. E. Brugger, *Zs. f. frz. Spr. u. Litt.*, XLIV², 149, note 9 (1917). *Ibid.* in the text Brugger offers speculations as to when the name *Percevaus* became attached to the hero — i. e. at what stage in the development of the Perceval tradition.

word itself — *graal* or *greal* (the later form), as it is written in
the Old French — *grazal* in Provençal. According to some philo-
logists, it is derived from an hypothetical Low Latin word, *cratalis*, which, in turn, was a derivative of Greek *crater* (bowl). According to others, it is derived from a Low Latin *\*gradalis* or
*\*gradale*, which is actually recorded in a Spanish will as early
as 1010, and, again, in the early part of the thirteenth century
in the Chronicle of Helinand of Froidmont in the passage where
he alludes to the Grail romances.³⁶ This passage is a famous
one in many ways and so is worth translating in part. Under the
years 717—719 Helinand says: "At this time a wonderful vision
was shown to a certain hermit by an angel — a vision concerning
a noble decurion, Joseph, who took down the body of our
Lord from the cross, and concerning the bowl or dish ("de catino
illo vel paropside") in which the Lord supped with his disciples,
in regard to which a history which is called the Grail has been
written by the same hermit. [We have here an allusion to the
Old French prose-romance, called the *Estoire del Saint Graal* or
*Grand St. Graal.*] The Grail [*Gradalis* autem vel *gradale*] is the
French name for a broad and rather deep dish in which precious
viands are accustomed to be set before the rich in different rows
(gradatim), one piece after the other on different levels. It is
also called by the vulgar name *greal*, because it is grateful and
acceptable to the person who eats in it, both on account of the
containing vessel, because, perchance, it is of silver or some other
valuable material, and on account of the contents — that is, the
various order of the precious viands."

The wild etymological guess in this last sentence is quite in
the mediaeval style and is really identical with the one which
Robert had already offered on the subject. At the present day,

---

³⁶ W. Golther, it is true, in a private communication (dated
5 January, 1920) which I have received from him, has expressed the
opinion that this passage is a late thirteenth century interpolation.
He acknowledges, however, that he has "keine unmittelbaren Beweise
dafür." In the meanwhile, until such proofs are adduced, it seems
to me desirable to take the passage as genuine, as has hitherto been
done by scholars of all shades of opinion.

the word is still current in Provence and in Southeastern France, but there is no reason why in the Middle Ages its use may not have extended to Northern France — where Chrétien, for instance, resided. On the other hand, for phonetic reasons, the forms *graal* and *greal*, which we find in the French romances, could not have been drawn from the French of Western France or of England. As far as immediate derivation, then, is concerned, the word is apparently of Latin origin, but its etymology throws no light on the origin of the legend.[37]

If only Robert's poem were involved, there could be no doubt about the question: the Grail there, as we have seen, is the vessel of the Last Supper which was also used to catch the blood of the dead Christ in, and its subsequent history grew out of a combi-

---

[37] For the etymology of the word *graal (greal)* see, especially, Foerster, Chrétien *Wörterbuch*, p. 174* and Nitze's article, "Concerning the Word *Graal, Greal*," *Modern Philology*, XIII, 681 ff. (1916). In the latter the various etymologies that have been proposed are tested critically. The etymon suggested by Diez, viz. *\*cratalis*, as Nitze concludes, has most in its favor. Helinand's attempt to connect *greal* with *agreer* is obviously a mere guess, and, no doubt, as Baist (quoted by Nitze) surmises, his attempt to connect *gradalis* with *gradatim* is equally valueless. Nitze, too, is, doubtless, right (p. 188) in regarding *gradalis* as a mere variant of *\*cratalis*. — The word is still in use in parts of France (south, southeast) — also, in Portugal (*gral* = wooden mortar). For the Portuguese cp. A. Bonilla y San Martin, *Las leyendas de Wagner en la literatura espanol a*, p. 67 (Madrid, 1913).

"Saint Greal" (Holy Grail) in the later development of the romances (fifteenth century), owing to a false division of the two words, came to be misunderstood as "Sang Real" — i. e. "Blood Royal," meaning the Blood of Christ, which the Grail was supposed to contain. For the French, cp. Godefroi, *Complément*, under *Sang*, and for the English the *New English Dictionary* under *Sangrail* and *Sang royal*. We find in English sometimes the spelling, *Sank(e) royall*.

After what I have said elsewhere in this volume, it is hardly necessary for me to add that I do not admit, with Nitze, the existence of a Latin book on the Grail to which Helinand, Robert de Boron, and the respective authors of the *Grand St. Graal* and *Perlesvaus* may have had access. To be sure, Nitze seems latterly to have receded from his former position on this subject. Cp. *MPh.*, XVII, 162f. (1919).

nation of uncanonical writings with certain passages in the Bible — especially, the passage in St. Matthew's Gospel that describes the Last Supper. According to Robert, then, the Grail is of Christian origin and its wonder-working powers are like those that were ascribed to many relics in the Middle Ages. But even in Chrétien is not the Grail really again merely a Christian relic? The trouble here is that the *Perceval* is unfinished. Consequently, we have not the early history of the sacred vessel told. That was reserved for the portion which was never composed. All that Chrétien actually gives us, then, is the account of the procession in the Grail-castle (ll. 4391 ff.). The Grail is borne through the brightly illuminated hall where Perceval sits at the table. A damsel, splendidly clad, bears the vessel, which is ornamented with jewels and which sends forth a light that eclipses the lights of the hall. There follow then a silver platter (paten) and the lance. The Grail is expressly declared to be a holy thing in the passage (l. 7793) where it is said that the Fisher King maintained his life merely with a holy wafer in the Grail. The words are as follows: "Such a holy thing is the Grail and so completely spiritual that for his [ i.e. the Fisher King'. ] life nothing more is necessary than the holy wafer which comes in the Grail."[38] So here, too, we

---

[38] The lines (6384 ff.) run as follows:

> D'une seule oiste ce savons
> Que l'an an ce graal aporte
> Sa vie sostient et conforte:
> Tant sainte chose est li graax
> Et tant par est espiritax
> Qu'a sa vie plus ne sostient
> Que l'oiste qui el graal vient.

*Oiste* here is Latin *hostia* = host, eucharist. The passage leaves no doubt that in Chrétien's conception the Grail was a Christian relic — indeed, for my own part, I would say boldly, the plate of the eucharist. Even Brugger, *Zs. f. frz. Spr. u. Litt.*, XXIX [1], 58f. (1905), XXXI [2], 137 (1907) and Miss Weston, *Legend of Sir Perceval*, I, 154 (1906), although they believe that the Grail is of non-Christian origin, acknowledge that in Chrétien it is a Christian relic, and the former, *ibid.* XXXVI [2], 187 (1910), justly criticises Brown (PMLA, XXV, 7) and Baist (*Parzival und der Gral*, p. 41) for denying this.

have a Christian relic and the whole procession seems a Christian ceremonial — the procession of the Eucharist. The lance is the lance of the Roman soldier who pierced the side of Christ with his spear (*St. John*, XIX, 34), and for whom the name Longinus (from the Greek λόγχη = spear) was invented by early Christian legend. The Grail being the dish which received the blood that flowed from the wound made by that spear, it was natural that Chrétien should have added it to the Grail procession, and, in accordance with the general conception,[39] made the blood flow down to the hand of the bearer. The wounded Rich Fisher who is sustained by the marvellous food contained in the Grail — that is, the dish of the Last Supper — is naturally Christ. Indeed, the various objects[40] in the Grail procession all figure in the ceremonial of the Byzantine mass, and, accordingly, the most eminent advocates of the Christian origin of the Grail, adopting a suggestion of Konrad Burdach's,[41] have latterly been inclined to take

---

[39] Cp. R. J. Peebles, *The Legend of Longinus*, Bryn Mawr College Monographs. Monograph Series, IX, 185 ff. (1911).

[40] One of these objects, the *tailleor d'argent* (l. 3193), which a girl bore after the Grail, no doubt represented the paten. It was misunderstood by Wolfram von Eschenbach, who translated it wrongly by *messer* (knife), though it means *platter*. It was comparatively insignificant in the Grail procession, and so does not appear at all in Pseudo-Wauchier and Wauchier, nor in the narrative of the Grail castle episode in Gerbert, although he mentions it at another point (Potvin, VI, 177, 243). Manessier, however, restored it (ll. 44 700, 45 243 ff.) to a place among the talismans of the Grail procession. He borrowed it, of course, from Chrétien.

[41] See especially *Deutsche Literaturzeitung*, XXIV, cols. 3050 ff. (Dec. 12, 1903). The article is a review of Willy Staerck's *Über den Ursprung der Grallegende* (Tübingen, 1903), but presents new views as to the origin of the Grail legend. Burdach had already given some indications of his theory in the *Archiv für das Studium der neueren Sprachen*, vol. 108, p. 31 (1902), and in the article mentioned above, he speaks of having in preparation a comprehensive work on the origin of the Grail, but up to date no such work has appeared. — Heinzel, p. 9, had noted the use of the spear in the Byzantine mass, but did not draw the same inference therefrom as Burdach. So, too, Paulus Cassel, *Der Gral und sein Name*, p. 10 (second edition,

this as the model of Chrétien's procession. There was, as we know, constant intercourse between Constantinople and the West in the twelfth century — especially owing to the conditions which the crusades produced—and Chrétien's source may well have contained a description of the Byzantine mass which some crusader had brought home. In this form of the mass, along with the candles and, of course, the chalice and the paten, appears the lance which is used to pierce the bread with. To be sure, this lance has been reduced now to the form of a knife with a lance-like blade, but it retains its original name of the lance (λόγχη). Moreover, in the allegorical interpretation of the objects that figure in the mass which we find in writers of the Eastern Church we have it expressly identi-

---

Berlin 1878), identifies Wolfram's *Messer* with the *hagia logche* of the Byzantine mass. Throughout this little book (28 pages) Cassel constantly appeals to the rites of the Greek church for analogies to the Grail rites.

It is from Christian liturgy — more specifically, of the Eastern Church — and not from Christian legend, according to Burdach, that the Grail legend sprang. He thinks that it assumed literary form during the period of the Crusades in Provence or nearby. There is no evidence, however, to support this view. As Burdach points out, in the Byzantine mass which goes under the name of St. John Chrysostom, in the Introitus the lance gives the symbolical wound in the eucharistic bread; it is borne about with the cup and the paten; it is present at the symbolical entombment; and in the consecration and "conversion" of the bread it is used again to heal and resurrect.

The Greek text of the liturgy of Chrysostom is accessible in C. A. Swainson's *The Greek Liturgies,* 101 ff. (Cambridge, 1884). Cp. especially, pp. 104 ff. A picture of the lance (holy spear) will be found in J. M. Neale's *History of the Holy Eastern Church,* I, 342 (London, 1850). It is hardly a knife, but merely a shortened spear, with a cross-piece on the handle to suggest a crucifix.

Burdach sees a similarity between the scenes in the hall of the Grail Castle in the romances and the adoration of the holy spear described by Constantinus Porphyrogenitus, Migne, *Patrologia Graeca,* vol. 112, col. 421, as taking place in Constantinople. But the ceremony in the latter case is, evidently, in a church, and the lance is a definite relic which was regarded as the actual spear with which Christ's side was pierced.

fied with the spear of the Roman soldier and interpreted accordingly.[42]

It has been objected, however, to the theory of the Eucharistic origin of Chrétien's Grail procession that it takes place in a castle and not in a church — moreover, that the bearer of the Grail is a damsel, not a priest. Such things, it is argued, would have seemed blasphemous to the Middle Ages in the highest degree. On the other hand, as a matter of fact, such processions are not confined in Catholic countries to the churches — and, besides, it is to be remembered that we are dealing with poetry and not with a theological work. Chrétien is fitting a religious conception into a romance of chivalrous adventure. The general tone of his works is thoroughly mundane, and there is no reason to believe that he would have shrunk from making use of a Christian theme in the manner that we find the Grail used in the *Perceval*. As regards the second point, it was, of course, irregular in Western Europe for a woman to bear the eucharist, but it was allowed in the East and the custom was brought thence to Ireland and Brittany.[43] A ninth century instance in the reign of Louis the Pious has also been cited.[44] It is not necessary to assume that this feature of Chrétien's Grail procession was derived directly from some such heterodox usage.[45] That may have been the case, but, in any event, the fact that such usages are recorded sporadically in the Middle Ages proves that the conception of a girl bearing the

---

[42] Cp., for example, the Greek treatise attributed to Germanos which I have quoted above. *Ibid.*, 397, A—C, we find the "lance' of the mass, the plate *(diskos)* that contained the *corpus domini* and the chalice that contained the wine, all explained in this succession' one immediately after the other. The "lance" is said to represent "the spear that pierced the side of the Lord," and "to be purified by the lance means [the same thing as] 'As a sheep he was led to the slaughter'" etc.

Heinzel, pp. 9 f., cites from Martène, *De antiquis ritibus,* IV, 443, the description of a procession of a Western church (Fleury-sur-Loire) in which the lance also figures.

[43] Cp. Miss Peebles, p. 209.

[44] By B. Fehr, *Beiblatt zu Anglia,* XXIV, 295 (1913).

[45] So Miss Peebles, *loc. cit.*

eucharist was not out of the question for a mediaeval writer —
especially, for the author of such fantastic compositions as the
Arthurian romances. This adaptation of sacred materials to the
purposes of romance would not be more profane than similar adaptations which we find in the prose romances. For example, we
have in the prose *Lancelot* the conception of Christ, the most
sacred of all subjects, parodied in the account of Galahad's conception, and in the *Queste* and *Estoire del Saint Graal* the same
knight is supplied with ancestors taken from the genealogy of
Christ.[46] If the identifications which we have adopted are correct,
viz., of the lance of the Grail procession with the lance which
was thrust into the side of Christ on the cross, the Grail with a
vessel of the eucharist and the *tailleor* (platter) with the paten,
it is plain that the Rich Fisher or Fisher King, who has been
wounded through both thighs by a dart in battle and who, consequently, has to resort to fishing in a boat for diversion  (ll.
3471 ff.) is the crucified Christ, himself, who is present at the
eucharistic celebration (his symbolical feast).

In the allegorical exegesis of the Middle Ages the commentators regularly interpret the scenes in the Gospels where the apostles are engaged in fishing on the basis of Christ's words to Peter
and Andrew, *St. Matthew*, IV, 19, when he summoned them from
their nets to become his disciples: "Follow me, and I will make
you fishers of men." Accordingly, the fish in these scenes are
men, the commentators declare, those that are caught by the
apostles being Christians and the remainder heathen.[47]  It was natural that the epithet, "fisher," in this allegorical sense of

---

[46] See, respectively, my articles in RR, IX, 368 f. (1918) and
MLN, XXXIII, 129 ff. (1918).   Miss Fisher, pp, 124 f., cites in this
connection the procession of the hermits in the *Perlesvaus,* who mar-
ched into the hall in white garments with a red cross on their breasts
and then "annorerent Deu nostre Seingnor et batirent lor coupes," as
if they were before an altar.   The romancer, she observes, had no
feeling of irreverence here.

[47] On this subject, cp. Hans Achelis: *Das Symbol des Fisches
und die Fischdenkmäler der römischen Katakomben,* p. 8 (Marburg, 1888).

"one who saves the souls of men" should be applied not only to the apostles, but to Christ, *the* Saviour, *par eminence*. And so we actually find Christ called the Fisher by Early Christian Fathers — especially, it would seem, in the East.[48] Far more common, it is true, is the symbolization of Christ under the image of a fish,[49] which persists even today, as the fish symbols that often appear in the decoration of our churches still testify. This latter piece of symbolism would always render a transition to the related conception of Our Lord as the "Fisherman" easy, and, doubtless, we have such a shifting of the conception in the Fisher King of Chrétien. Doubtless, it was a fancy of Chrétien's that this Fisher King who was lame should be represented as seeking diversion in fishing.[50]

The father, or "double," of the Fisher King in Chrétien's poem, the mysterious king who is likewise lame and who has not

---

[48] Cp. Achelis, *ibid.*, pp. 8f. He cites Clement of Alexandria, Gregory of Nazianzene and Nilus. Jerome, however, remarks (to *Habakkuk*, I, 15) that the Devil and heretics can also be fishermen.

[49] For numerous examples of this from the early Christian era down see J. B. Pitra, *Spicelegium Solesmense*, III, 522ff. (Paris, 1855). This was due, in part, to the fact that the initials of the Greek words, Ἰησοῦς Χριστὸς Θεοῦ υἱὸς σωτήρ (= Jesus Christ, Son of God, the Saviour), make up ἰχθύς (= fish), in part, perhaps, to the place filled by the fish in earlier Asiatic religions. On the subject of the fish in these religions see Miss Weston's *From Ritual to Romance*, ch. 9 (Cambridge, 1920), where, in the notes, the authorities on the question are cited.

[50] This is suggested by Heinzel who says (p. 13) that we must assume "Crestien oder seine Quelle . . . habe entwęder, da er den Namen *riche pêcheur* nicht verstand, wohl aber von der Krankheit dieses Mannes wusste, die Tätigkeit des Fischens aus freier Erfindung mit der Krankheit in ursächlichen Zusammenhang gebracht — oder die Vorstellung von der Krankheit des Fischerkönigs aus dem unverstandenen Ausdruck *roi pêcheur* abgeleitet. Er ist ein Fischerkönig, weil er fischt, und er fischt weil er krank ist." The first of these alternative suggestions, however, seems to me preferable. The wounds which Jesus suffered on the cross would account for the conception of his representative in the legend as maimed or sick. It is the fishing activities of the character that require explanation.

left his room for fifteen years, being sustained exclusively by the holy wafer, would, under this interpretation, be the Holy Ghost.[51]

It is most convenient to discuss in connection with the origin of the Grail legend the theory which has been often advanced that this legend first took shape in Glastonbury Abbey (in England). The only item of evidence that might furnish an argument for such a notion is a passage in William of Malmesbury's *De Antiquitate Glastoniensis Ecclesiae,* where it is said that the apostle Philip "duodecim ex suis discipulis . . . misit in Britanniam, quibus, ut ferunt, charissimum amicum suum Joseph ab Aramathia, qui et Dominum sepulivit, praefecit." [52]

With regard to this passage, it should be observed that the story of St. Philip's having founded Christianity in Britain was virtually an invention of William's, who was desirous of establishing for the English a direct apostolic origin and a consequent independence of Rome. The desired result he achieved by drawing a convenient inference from a statement in the ninth century chronicle of Freculf, that St. Philip had converted the Gauls and neighboring peoples, and combining it with a fiction of Geoffrey of Monmouth's concerning the conversion of Britain.[53] Even if the allusion to Joseph in the above-quoted passage was really inserted by William of Malmesbury, himself, it would not prove the existence of any legend that would connect Joseph with Glastonbury. As a matter of fact, however, there is the strongest reason for believing that the words are a late interpolation, made under the influence of the French Grail romances, which had rendered Joseph, as a converter of the heathen, famous. William

---

[51] The character, which is as difficult to interpret under one theory of Grail origins as another, may have sprung, after all, from some misunderstanding of his original, on Chrétien's part. In any event, it is not fundamental in the Grail story, as is shown by the circumstance that it was dropped by all the continuators of Chrétien's *Perceval.*

[52] Migne's *Patrologia Latina,* vol. 179, col. 1683 (Paris, 1855).

[53] This has been proved clearly by F. Zarncke, PBB, III, 327 ff. (1876).

nowhere else mentions him and he does not fit in with the account of the conversion of Britain which this writer gives. According to his narrative elsewhere, it is twelve of St. Philip's disciples that effect the conversion. The theory of interpolation is strengthned by the fact that there was no Grail legend among the local legends of Glastonbury. Only the late prose-romance, *Perlesvaus,* pretended to be based on a Latin book at Glastonbury.[54] There

---

[54] When W. A. Nitze wrote his "Glastonbury and the Holy Grail", *Modern Philology,* I, 247 ff., he believed in the Latin book to which the author of the *Perlesvaus,* Potvin, I, 306, 348, appeals as his authority, but recently, in *Studies in Philology,* XV, 12, note 12 (University of North Carolina, 1918), he appears to renounce this idea. G. Baist, however, supposes this hypothetical Latin book to have been written by a Glastonbury monk, about the time of the pretended discovery (in 1191) there of Arthur's and Guinevere's bodies, and it is the cornerstone, so to speak, of his theory of the evolution of Grail conceptions. Through this book (written after Chrétien), as Baist thinks, the stories of Perceval and Joseph of Arimathea were woven together for the first time. Robert de Boron wrote his *Joseph* (later) as a *Vorgeschichte* to this *liber Glastoniensis,* and the other writers concerning the Grail, also, drew their matter partly from the hypothetical Latin romance and partly from Chrétien. For these views of Baist, cp. *Literaturblatt,* XIII, col. 160 (1892), "Zu Robert de Boron," *Zs. f. rom. Ph.,* XXXII, 231 (1908), and *Parzival und der Gral,* p. 39, (Freiburg in Br., 1909). In none of these places (or anywhere else), however, has the author supported his views by evidence. There is, in fact, every reason for rejecting the hypothesis. In the last-named reference Baist assumes that the legend about the founding of Glastonbury abbey by Joseph of Arimathea was a genuine early tradition at Glastonbury, but Newell, as we shall see, has proved that this is not so. The Latin book, moreover, (written, it is declared, by Josephus) which the author of the *Perlesvaus* invokes as his source, it is safe to say, never existed. The only Arthurian romances in Latin that we know of — the *Historia Meriadoci* and *De Ortu Waluuanii* — are not earlier than the second quarter of the thirteenth century. See my edition of these romances, pp. XVI ff. *Arthur and Gorlagon,* edited by Kittredge from the unique MS., Rawlinson B 149 (end of the fourteenth century, at the earliest), is merely a Welsh folk-tale in Latin dress, but we have no ground for dating that (in its Latin form), either, earlier than the two romances I have named. — Still further, it is, in the highest degree, questionable whether Robert de Boron

was an attempt to connect the abbey with Arthur, but this was separate from the Grail legend, and, likewise, of late origin. The motive for this attempt was political: On the one hand, the monks had no objection to their abbey being glorified by being connected with so renowned a hero as Arthur, and, on the other, the early Plantagenets were anxious to obtain a hold on the Celtic population. Consequently, Glastonbury was identified with Avalon, the place to which Arthur was reported to have been taken after receiving his fatal wound. Avalon was, of course, an island, and Glastonbury was not — but this discrepancy was explained on the ground that marshes lay about the place, so that, after all, it might be called an island. A comedy was then arranged in the year 1191, when it was announced that the tombs of Arthur and Guinevere had been discovered at the abbey. The supposed coffins were dug up and then reinterred before the altar in the church in solemn fashion. This pious fraud had the effect of weakening the inconvenient Celtic tradition that Arthur would one day return to rule over his people and of fixing on English soil the most precious relic of the Celtic race. Accounts of the transaction are given by Giraldus Cambrensis in two of his works, *Speculum Ecclesiae*, II, 8—10, and *De Principis Instructione*, I.[55] The fraudulent

ever intended to introduce Perceval into the cycle of romances which he outlines at the end of the *Joseph*. On this subject and the authorship of the Didot *Perceval* see, Part IV, below.

In this connection I will say that, whatever one may think in regard to the Wolfram-Kyot question, Nutt is undoubtedly right when, in reviewing Baist's *Parzival und der Gral*, in his article, "Recent Grail Literature," in *The Academy* for May 7, 1910, he condemns (p. 446) the view to which the author inclines and which is, indeed, the inevitable conclusion of his preceding criticism of the respective theories of Christian and heathen origin of the Grail — the view which is summed up in his words (p. 43); "dass der Gral in seiner ersten Gestalt ohne jede wunderbare Eigenschaft war und nur die Regel exemplifizieren half, dass unter Umständen auch Reden Gold sei." That the whole Grail story should be as meaningless as this is impossible.

[55] There is a mediaeval Welsh version of the transaction based primarily on the *Speculum Ecclesiae*, but with some sentences taken from the *De Principis Instructione*. The text has been edited with translation and notes by Timothy Lewis and J. D. Bruce, "The Pre-

tradition which was thus started was buttressed still further by the falsification of William of Malmesbury's treatise on the antiquity of the Glastonbury abbey — *De Antiquitate Ecclesiae Glastoniensis*. This treatise, composed in the first half of the twelfth century, did not originally contain the passages which in the existing text connect Glastonbury with Arthur. These passages were interpolated at the end of the twelfth or beginning of the thirteenth century as a part of the fraud which the monks of Glastonbury were then engaged in foisting upon the world.[56] The forging of

tended Exhumation of Arthur and Guinevere", *Revue Celtique*, XXXIII, 432 ff. (1912). The Welsh preserves a few sentences which have been lost in the unique (defective) MS. of the *Speculum*.

[56] In *Germania*, XII, 276 ff. (1867), A. Holtzmann maintained that the Arthurian passages in the *De Antiquitate Glastoniensis Ecclesiae* (composed between 1125 and 1139) of William of Malmesbury were late interpolations and drawn from Geoffrey of Monmouth and the French romances, and this was the view of F. Zarncke in his "Zur Geschichte der Gralsage," PBB, III, 331 ff. (1876), with reference to the passage about Joseph of Arimathea. G. Baist, however, in "Arthur und der Graal," *Zs. f. rom. Ph.*, XIX, 326 ff. (1895), with supplement, XX, 320 f. (1896), presented an elaborate defense of the authenticity of these passages, which seemed convincing to G. Paris, *Romania*, XXIV, 611 (1895). Baist admitted (pp. 328 f.) that the work contained interpolations, but denied that these Arthuriana belonged in that category. F. Lot, in his article "Glastonbury et Avalon," *Romania*, XXVII, 529 ff. (1898), also accepted the Arthurian passages as genuine and believed (pp. 567 ff.) that they were invented by Caradoc of Llancarvan, author of a *Vita Gildae*, which is likewise full of fabrications, and that they were communicated by him to William of Malmesbury, who adopted them without suspicion. W. W. Newell, however, in "William of Malmesbury on the Antiquity of Glastonbury," PMLA, XVIII, 459 ff. (1903), subjected the whole question to reexamination, and proved conclusively that the Arthuriana in the *De Antiquitate* were certainly late interpolations. F. Lot has accepted Newell's results in his *Mélanges d'Histoire Bretonne*, pp. 277 ff. (1907). So, too, Nitze, it would seem, in "The Glastonbury Passages in the *Perlesvaus*," *Studies in Philology*, XV, 7 ff. (University of North Carolina, 1918), who in a previous article, "Glastonbury and the Holy Grail," I, 254 ff., had assumed the authenticity of the Arthurian materials in the *De Antiquitate*. In a communication to Nitze, summarized by the latter in *Modern Philology*, I, 248, note 2,

documents for the purpose of securing wealth or prestige for a monastery was one of the most ordinary transactions of the Middle Ages — and there is no occasion for surprise at these so-called pious frauds of religious men, when it is remembered that the Papacy itself had set an example to the whole church by making the forged *Constitutions of Constantine,* as they are called, the basis of its claims to the possession of the Papal States.

The whole connection of Joseph of Arimathea with Glastonbury, then, is a late invention — a localization which may be compared with the localization of the Tristan romance at Dublin as early as the twelfth century,[57] only that in the latter case there is no reason to believe that any fraudulent purpose was involved in the localization. The identification of a village on the outskirts of Dublin with the site of a chapel of Iseult — the village is still called "Chapelizod" — was, doubtless, simply the fancy of some high-born lover of the old romance. As regards the connection of Joseph, and hence of the Grail, with Glastonbury, none of the early romancers know anything of it. In Chrétien's *Perceval,* of course, neither Joseph nor Glastonbury appear. In Robert de Boron, Joseph never comes to Britain, and he is consequently never brought into any sort of relations either with Arthur or with Glastonbury. Indeed, the only allusion in this poem to anything in Arthurian tradition is where it is said that Bron, the second guardian of the Grail is to go to the West (l. 3219), or, more specifically, the "vaus d'Avaron" (3123, 3221) — i.e. the vale of Avalon. But in the interpolated treatise of William of Malmesbury *(De Antiquitate)* Glastonbury is called "insula Avallonia" (in the British language it was called, it is said, Yniswitrin — i.e.

---

Baist called attention to a passage in Johannes Glastoniensis (fifteenth century) which is supposed to prove the existence of early Arthurian traditions at Glastonbury, but the passage is late and evidently compounded from details in the chronicles and romances.

R. Thurneysen, *Zs. f. rom. Ph.,* XX, 316 ff. (1896), "Zu William von Malmesbury", pointed out some important Irish sources for certain of the interpolations in the *De Antiquitate,* but they do not affect the question with which this note is concerned.

[57] Cp. *The Athenaeum,* Feb. 21 and April 26, 1913.

"isle of glass"). It has been, accordingly, suggested that Robert's "vaus d'Avaron" reflects the influence of the revised *De Antiquitate* and that the term is, therefore, intended to apply to Glastonbury.[58] But, apart from the uncertainty of the relative dates of the two works — Robert's was probably written in the eighties, whereas the revised *De Antiquitate* in all likelihood dates after 1191 — the terms "vaus d'Avaron" and "insula Avallonia" do not coincide. The one is a vale, the other is an isle. Very likely, Robert merely used Avalon as an indefinite expression for the West, — the Avalon of Celtic legend being indefinitely placed in the Western Seas. If he refers to this Otherworld of Celtic belief as a vale, instead of an isle, we may pardon this to a poet, whether it is due to confusion or to intentional change. In any event, his words do not offer the slightest justification for assuming that he was here alluding to Glastonbury.[59]

---

[58] Cp. Newell, *op. cit.*, p. 510.

[59] Inasmuch as the connection of Joseph of Arimathea with Glastonbury has been shown to be a late invention based on the romances, there is no need of discussing Nutt's hypothesis as to the origin of Robert de Boron's *Joseph* and the part that Bron plays in it, viz., that "Borron, or rather the sources he followed became acquainted with a *Bran* conversion legend, and fused it with the better-known *Joseph* one" (*The Legends of the Holy Grail*, p. 65, London, 1902). He had already advocated this theory in his *Studies*, pp. 218 ff., and A. C. L. Brown seems still to accept it. Cp. the latter's article "From Cauldron of Plenty to Grail," *Modern Philology*, XIV, 385 ff. (1916). Bran here, it should be explained, is the son of Llyr in the Welsh tale, *Branwen, Daughter of Llyr*. There he is represented as possessing a cauldron of healing and rejuvenation, which, Nutt thinks, may have developed in tradition into a talisman of increase and plenty. Nutt's idea that this Bran was a hero of a legend concerning the conversion of Britain, itself, rests on a slender foundation, viz., a Welsh triad of which there is no trace prior to the late thirteenth century. According to this triad he was "one of the three blissful Rulers of the Island of Britain, who first brought the faith of Christ to the nation of the Cymry from Rome, where he was seven years a hostage for his son Caradawc." For this triad see Loth's *Mobinogion*[2], II, 308 f. and for the character in Welsh literature, in general, *ibid.*, I, 119, note 2, — also Rhys: *Studies in the Arthurian Legend*, pp. 306 ff. Moreover, Bran is called "the Blessed" in the Welsh tale cited above.

These materials, however, are too slight to show that there ever existed
an actual narrative about Bran as the original converter of Britain.
In any event, the implication of the triad has nothing in common
with the story of Robert's Bron. Nutt regards the epithet "Blessed"
here as "originally pagan" and acknowledges that the triad may be
"a reflex of thè Grail romances," though he believes otherwise. Rhys,
*loc. cit.*, advocates strongly Nutt's theory, but unfortunately, since he
had no first-hand knowledge of the French romances, his opinions in
such a matter carry little weight. He confesses (p. 311) that the
extant Welsh texts do not support the theory. Before Nutt some
scholars had already derived the name of Bron in Robert's *Joseph*
from Celtic *Bran,* and identified the two characters. So, explicitly,
G. A. Heinrich, *Le Parcival de Wolfram d'Eschenbach et la Légende
du Saint Graal,* p. 59 (Paris, 1855). Cp., too, E. Martin, *Zur Gralsage,* p. 37 (Strassburg, 1880). I have tried to show in Part IV
the true origin of Robert's Bron.

# Chapter II.
## The Theory of Celtic Origin.

I have so far presented the theory which appears to me to offer the most acceptable explanation of the origin of the Grail. We have, however, the rival theory of Celtic origin to consider, the most important advocates of which have been the late Alfred Nutt,[1] and, among living scholars, A. C. L. Brown.[2] Nutt was primarily a folk-lorist and he accordingly approaches the subject

---

[1] In his chief work, *Studies on the Legend of the Holy Grail* (London, 1888) — also, in the *Legends of the Holy Grail* (No. 14 of *Popular Studies in Mythology, Romance, and Folk-Lore*, London, 1902), and other minor publications.

[2] In various papers, to be named as occasion arises. — So, too Rhys in Ch. 13, "Origins of the Holy Grail," and Ch. 14, "Glastonbury and Gower," of his work, cited in the next to the last note. For the reasons there stated, however, despite his eminence as a Welsh scholar, Rhys's contributions to the present subject are not profitable reading. Indeed, they strike me as fantastic to the last degree. Ch. 15, "Isles of the Dead," on the other hand, has an independent value for its discussion of such conceptions in the Celtic world.

In his review of Nutt's *Studies, Romania*, XVIII, 588 ff. (1889) G. Paris thinks that Nutt has proved "l'origine celtique d'une grande partie des élements qui figurent dans les romans du saint graal." He commends, especially, in this connection, the Gaelic tale of the Great Fool, which the English scholar adduces as a parallel to the accounts of Perceval's youth in the Arthurian romances. On the other hand, he speaks of Nutt's parallels to the Grail itself as merely plausible and of his hypothesis "sur l'origine britannique de la 'préhistoire' du graal" as wanting in solidity. But after Zimmer, *Göttingische Gelehrte Anzeigen*, June 10, 1890, objected to the Great Fool parallel as too modern, Nutt, *Folk-Lore*, III, 401 f. withdrew that parallel, "for the present, at least," and, as far as I am aware, never brought it forward again in his discussions of the Grail.

from that point of view. He says[3]: "Leaving subsidiary details out of account, we may bring all the instances in which the Grail appears under two formulas: that of the kinsman avenging a blood feud by the means of the three magic talismans, sword and lance and vessel; and that of the visit to the Bespelled Castle, the inmates of which enjoy, thanks to the magic vessel, a supernaturally prolonged life, from which they are released by the hero's question concerning that vessel. The one we may call the feud quest, the other the unspelling quest." "The castle to which the avenger must penetrate to win the talismans [ i.e. vessel, sword, etc. ] and that to which the hero comes with the intent of freeing its lords are both symbols of the otherworld" (p. 183). He finds the original of the Grail, then, in certain magic vessels that had the power of supplying food to an unlimited extent. He cites the cauldron of the Dagda (the good god) in the Irish legend of the Tuatha de Danann (a race of fairies and wizards who possessed Ireland before the Milesian invasion). There is considerable doubt, however, about the antiquity of this tradition. Less open to suspicion on this score is the next saga of *The Battle of Magh Rath,* which relates to events that took place in the seventh century and which seems to have been written down in the latter half of the twelfth century (p. 185). Here we are told how the sons of the King of Alba sought to obtain from their father the 'Caire Ainsicen' — so called, because it was the *caire* or cauldron which was used to return his own proper share to each and no party ever went away from it unsatisfied; for whatever quantity was put into it there was never boiled of it but what was sufficient for the company according to their grade or rank. "The [ Irish ] writer then goes on to instance similar cauldrons te be met with in the older history of Ireland. These may nearly all be referred to the oldest Irish heroic cycle, the Ultonian, of which Cuchullain is the most prominent figure" (p. 185). Two of the instances in question are cited from two of the most celebrated tales of this cycle — viz. the *Toghail Bruighne da Derga* and the *Tale of Mac Datho's Pig.*

---

[3] *Studies,* p. 181.

Nutt cited, also (p. 186), the cauldron of Bran in the Welsh tale of Branwen, the daughter of Llyr, which dates from the end of the twelfth century or beginning of the thirteenth.[4] Here, however, the vessel is not food-producing,[5] but it has (like Medea's cauldron) the power of bringing the dead to life again. As is said in the tale: "The property of it is that if one of thy men be slain to-day and be cast therein, the morrow he will be as well as ever he was at his best, except that he will not regain his speech." There is also a vessel of balsam in various Gaelic tales that has this revivifying power.[6]

A. C. L. Brown has similarly identified the Bleeding Lance of Chrétien with the Luin of Celtchar of Irish saga — a marvellous spear.[7] In the *Bruden Da Derga (= Destruction of Da Derga's Palace)* it is said of this lance that "a cauldron full of poison is needed to quench it when a deed of manslaying is expected. Unless this come to the lance, it flames on its haft and will go through its bearer or the master of the palace wherein it is. If it is to be a blow that is to given thereby, it will kill a man at every blow, when it is at that feat from one hour to another, though it may not reach him. And if it be a cast, it will kill nine men at every cast, and one of the nine will be a king or crown prince or chieftain of the reavers" (Brown, p. 18). In another Irish saga, the *Mesca Ulad (= Intoxication of the Ultonians)*, the cauldron which was

---

[4] Cp. Loth's *Mabinogion*[2], I, 30.

[5] Rhys, *Arthurian Legend*, pp. 305 ff., however, has cited food-producing vessels from Welsh tradition. He thinks (p. 312) that the *Mwys* (basket) of Gwyddno Garanhir, described in *Kulhwch and Olwen* (Loth's *Mabinogion*[2], I, 305) is more nearly "the pagan prototype of the Grail of Christian romance" than anything else in Welsh. Although the whole world, in groups of thrice nine men, should present themselves, every man would find food to his taste in this basket.

[6] A. C. L. Brown argues, Kittredge *Anniversary Papers*, p. 244, note 2, for a connection between the regenerating Celtic cauldron and the cauldron of plenty. All that one can legitimately say on the subject, however, is that they are both fairy-tale fancies of a kindred order. So, too, it seems to me, with the cauldron of inspiration in the Welsh story of Gwion, cited by Nutt, pp. 210f.

[7] Cp. his article, "The Bleeding Lance", PMLA, XXV, 1 ff. (1910).

needed to quench the ardour of the wondrous spear is described as "a blood-black cauldron of horrid, noxious liquid . . . composed through sorcery of the blood of dogs, cats and Druids" (p. 22). Brown, himself, however, acknowledges (p. 23) that perpetual bleeding is not mentioned in the Irish sagas as one of the marvellous properties of the Luin, and the same is true of all other wonderful weapons in Irish and Welsh saga. A spear dipped into a cauldron of blood to render it innocuous to its owner and those nearby is, certainly, a very different affair from the lance of Chrétien's procession. As Miss Peebles (p. 194) very sensibly remarks: "With the Christian lance [ i.e. lance of Longinus ] so obviously and suitably at hand, in literature, which, as writers of romances, themselves, they must have known, in art productions which they must have seen, and in the drama with which they must have been familiar, why should the Grail romancers seek a bleeding lance in the Luin of Celtchar, which after all does not bleed."[8]

Professor Brown cites (pp. 42ff.) also in this connection the story of Balin and the Dolorous Stroke which is found in the *Huth-Merlin*, I, 231ff.: In the palace of King Pellehan, pursued by its lord, Balin comes to a room filled with the fragrance of spices with a great silver bowl on a table in the centre and within this basin stood a lance perpendicularly pointing downward, "and any one looking at it would have marvelled because it was not inserted nor supported, nor fastened anywhere." Balin was on the point of taking it and a voice said to him: "Do not take it, sinner."

---

[8] Brugger, *Zs. f. frz. Spr. u. Litt.*, XXXVI[2], 189 f., in reviewing Brown's study, also, denies any connection of the spear of the Grail procession with this Luin of Celtechar, although he, like Brown, believes in the Celtic origin of the Grail legend.

In his article, "An Old Irish Parallel to the Motive of the Bleeding Lance," *Eriu*, VI, 156f. (1912) Kuno Meyer has printed an Irish poem which is supposed to offer a parallel to the lance of the Grail story: A chieftain pollutes the hall of Tara by secretly and mischievously bringing into it a bloody head on a pole or lance of the quicken-tree, while the king was holding a feast. Meyer thinks that the text is probably of the tenth century. Obviously, however, we have here again merely a *bloody*, not a *bleeding* lance.

But he did not refrain on this account from taking it with both hands and he struck with it Pellehan who was coming against him so vehemently that he thrust it through both of his thighs." The king fell to the earth and the knight returned the lance to the place from which he had taken it, and when he had replaced it, it stood as before. This was the Dolorous Stroke which Merlin had prophesied (I, 231) would put the kingdom in distress for twenty-two years and would wound the most holy man there was in the world." And so, as a matter of fact, desolation does overtake the land. Later on Balin is slain in a duel with his brother — an unnatural combat which has been made the subject of poems by both Tennyson *(Balin and Balan)* and Swinburne *(The Tale of Balen)*.[9] The *Huth-Merlin,* however, is a late prose-romance, and, like all the prose-romances, it is not based directly on Celtic sources — on the contrary, it is made up mainly by rehashing episodes in previous romances, and this very story of Balin and the Dolorous Stroke is plainly an invention that combines features of the Grail Castle episodes of the earlier romances with other features that are drawn from the prose *Lancelot,* the episode of Gawain and the Perilous Bed.[10]

Altogether Professor Brown (p. 57) takes the Grail, Lance, and Sword of Chrétien's Grail Procession as going back to the shining talismans of the Tuatha Da Danaan, viz. the Stone of Destiny, the Cauldron of the Dagda,[11] the Spear of Lug and the

---

[9] The development of the various versions from the Middle Ages down has been discussed by E. Vettermann, *Die Balendichtungen und ihre Quellen* (Halle, 1918). The book has no original value, however, for the affiliation of the mediaeval versions.

[10] In the review of Brown's paper on the Bleeding Lance, Brugger, p. 190, expresses the same view that I have here expressed. He points to the following romances as sources of the Balaain episodes in the *Huth-Merlin: Meriadeuc, Meraugis,* the first continuation to Chrétien's Perceval (or its source), *Grand Saint Graal.* On this subject see also Heinzel, p. 31, and Brugger, *ibid.,* XXXI[2], pp. 132 ff.

[11] In his "From Cauldron of Plenty to Grail," *Modern Philology,* XIV, 385 ff. (1916) Brown has collected from Irish literature — more especially from the *imrama* — examples which are intended to illustrate the supposed derivation of the Grail from a Celtic cauldron

Sword of Lug.[12] But the sole authority on which this grouping of talismans rests is the seventeenth century Irish historian, Keating. He usually draws from old sources — but in this instance, no one can say how old or how late. Moreover, Keating does not define the nature of these talismans, or "treasures" merely, as he calls them. He expressly identifies the Stone of Destiny with the stone brought by Edward I from Scone in Scotland, which to-day rests in Westminster Abbey and is occupied by the English kings on the occasion of their coronation. Perhaps, the sword and spear of the same list were as little marvellous as the stone. All this is obviously too vague to form the basis for conclusions of any value. And it is to be remembered still further that this late list of objects which we know nothing about is Irish, and we have not a scrap of evidence to prove that it was known to the only Celtic peoples from whom a writer of Northern France would with any probability have drawn his materials, viz. the Welsh and the Bretons.

Finally, in regard to these supposed evidences of the Celtic origin of the Grail, it has been argued[13] that the position of the fireplace in the hall of the Grail castle as described by Chrétien,

---

of plenty, just as his previous article was intended to illustrate the derivation of the Grail spear from a marvellous Celtic spear. But to me these illustrations are as little convincing as the others. The passages quoted by Brown contain some instances of miraculous feeding and some examples of the syncretism of Christian and pagan elements, but there is really no distinctly marvellous vessel in them, and the accompanying incidents are about as different from those which we find in the Grail romances as one could imagine.

Already in "Notes on Celtic Cauldrons of Plenty and the Land-Beneath-The-Waves", Kittredge *Anniversary Papers,* pp. 235 ff. (Boston and London, 1913), Brown had tried to prove that these cauldrons were connected with the Celtic under-sea Elysium and that the Grail castle was also connected with the sea — hence that the Grail was in origin such a Celtic cauldron, this feature, which the two have in common, confirming the evidence of other features of similarity.

[12] Nutt, *op. cit.,* p. 184, had already made this identification.

[13] By W. A. Nitze, in an important article, "The Castle of the Grail — an Irish Analogue," *Studies in Honor of A. Marshall Elliott,* I, 19 ff. (issued in 1911 at Baltimore, though undated).

11. 3055 ff. betrays Celtic origin. It is said that the fire before which the Grail-King sat was between four columns and that four hundred men could conveniently sit about this fire. The columns that held up the chimney were strong and made of brass. Now, the chimneys of French mediaeval castles were the same as at present, whereas the fire here is in the open hearth in the centre of the hall, like the one in the palace at Tara, as described in the Irish sagas. We are dealing, however, with a romance — with a narrative of a fantastic kind like that of a folk-tale, and it is questionable whether we should expect in such a work literal conformity with the actual customs of the time, even granting that no such primitive hearth may have really existed by way of survival in some French castles of the twelfth century. Moving in the atmosphere of a folktale, the poet may have purposely made his description archaic. In any event, there is no sufficient certainty about the matter for this detail to turn definitely the scales in favor of the Celtic theory.

In conclusion, it is obvious from this discussion, that the theory that in Celtic folk-tales the Grail legend found its origin is not satisfactory. No one has as yet brought forward a folk-tale, Celtic or otherwise, corresponding in incident and setting to the Grail story.[14] Parallels (not very satisfactory in themselves) to the individual features of it have to be collected from widely separated sources — sources, too, of uncertain date. This being the case, there is no need of considering a still further objection:[15] namely, the improbability that a purely folk-lore, food-providing vessel should be identified with the most sacred objects of the Christian faith, the Blood of the Redeemer, the Chalice of the Eucharist — and that not in stories of popular origin, but in the long romances of educated men. As will have been seen above, the food-producing quality of the Grail does not appear in the earliest versions of the legend — Chrétien's and Robert's. It is a later development, being found first in Pseudo-Wauchier (ll. 20114 ff.), and the very fact that a poet did attach to the vessel

---

[14] So Miss J. L. Weston, *Quest of the Holy Grail*, p. 70.
[15] Raised by Miss Weston, *op. cit.*, p. 68.

this quality, although his predecessors had described it as holy, tends to prove that the mediaeval romancers did not have the scruples that some scholars have imputed to them. But the reasons already advanced for rejecting the Celtic theory are, we believe, sufficient.[16]

---

[16] Celtic traces in certain names which we find in the Grail romances have no force in sustaining the theory of Celtic origins. For example, in *Romania*, XXIV, 322, F. Lot calls attention to the place name, "Chateau de Lis" in the first continuation to Chrétien's *Perceval*. *Lis*, as he points out, is *llys*, the Welsh word for "castle." But the writer is here probably adopting *Lis* as a place-name from Chrétien's *Perceval*, where we have a character named "Meliant de Liz (or *Lis*)." We have considered Chrétien's relation to supposed Celtic sources above. There is no doubt that in any event he would try to give a Celtic coloring to whatever romance he might write.

# Chapter III.
## The Ritual Theory.

The third theory of the origin of the Grail legend is one which was suggested by Simrock as far back as 1842 in the notes to his translation of Wolfram von Eschenbach[1] — namely, that the conception of the Grail sprang from the ritual of some cult of the Vegetation Spirit, or "the slain God", as he is called very often in the history of religion, as typified, for example, in Adonis and Osiris.[2] This particular theory, however, has only assumed importance in the last ten years or so through the publication of W. A. Nitze's *"The Fisher King in the Grail Romances"*,[3] and

---

[1] For a convenient summary of Simrock's views, cp. Nutt's *Studies on the Legend of the Holy Grail*, pp. 100 f.

[2] It lies, also, at the bottom of E. Martin's identification of the sick Grail King with the wounded Arthur, *Zur Gralsage*, pp. 31 ff. (Strassburg, 1880), and in his edition of Wolfram, pp. LVIII ff.; for he interprets (p. 32) the wounded Arthur, who is borne to Avalon, but is destined to return healed, as a representative of the Vegetation God. The best refutation, I may add, of Martin's identification is the fact that we find Arthur in all the romances in which the Grail King appears, except Robert's *Joseph*, and yet the two are never identified. In the *Joseph*, the action of which, besides, does not lie in Britain, sickness or lameness is not an attribute of the Grail King. We have, of course, stories (some of which are cited by Martin) in which Arthur is pictured as living in fairy-land style (especially in mountains) and as subsisting, presumably, in a miraculous manner, and in these respects there are points of contact between his legend and that of the Grail King, but these are, obviously, merely general folklore motifs. — For a criticism of Martin's theory, cp. Heinzel, pp. 67 f. — Cp. with Martin's theory the story about the imprisonment of Cronos on an isle near Britain, which Rhys, pp. 367 f, quotes from Plutarch.

[3] It was published in PMLA., XXIV, 365 ff. (1909).

Miss J. L. Weston's *Legend of Sir Perceval*, Vol. 2 (1909).[4]
Although these two scholars worked out the theory independently
of each other, their results agree in the most essential respects.
It was obviously under the influence of Frazer's *Golden Bough*
that both were led to adopt this theory.

First, as regards Professor Nitze, he takes for comparison the
Eleusinian mysteries of Greece which was a Demeter cult — that is,
a cult of the Vegetation Spirit. The Grail procession is, then,
by origin, a vegetation ceremony, and "The Holy Grail, by the
mediaeval romancers often conceived in terms of a quest, is *au fond*
an initiation, the purpose of which is to ensure the life of the
vegetation spirit, always in danger of extinction and to admit the
'qualified' mortal into its mystery" (p. 394). Professor Nitze
thinks that, like the Eleusinian, the Grail rites may have been

---

[4] Already in Vol. I (1906) of this work (pp. 329 ff.) Miss Weston
had put forward her theory. She developed it more fully in a paper,
"The Grail and the Rites of Adonis," which she read before the Folk-
Lore Society on December 19, 1906, and which was published in
*Folk-Lore*, XVIII, 283 ff. (Sept. 1907). Vol. II of her *Legend of
Sir Perceval*, however, contains the completest exposition of her theory,
although the essentials are more clearly presented in her *Folk-Lore*
paper, just mentioned, and in a more recent book, *The Quest of the
Holy Grail*, pp. 75 ff. (London, 1913). In her latest Grail treatise,
*From Ritual to Romance*, (Cambridge, 1920), she tries, still further,
to bring together parallels to each feature of the Grail story from the
records of the pagan mystery cults and to show the intimate union
that once existed between the latter and Christianity. It is characteristic of her method of work, when she declares (p. 5 of the last-
named treatise) that her aim is "to determine the *origin*, not to discuss the *provenance* and interrelation of the different versions."'"I do
not believe this latter task can be satisfactorily achieved unless and
until we are of one accord as to the character of the subject matter.
When we have made up our minds as to what the Grail really was,
and what it stood for, we shall be able to analyze the romances; to
decide which of them contains more, which less of the original matter,
and to group them accordingly." But to approach the texts with
preconceived notions, instead of making them, in due historical order,
as far as that can be ascertained, the primary basis of the whole investigation is, obviously, the reverse of all sound scientific method.

both agrarian and mystic from the start. On this basis, then, he interprets the three essential figures and the three essential symbols of the Grail theme in the following manner.

I.   The Fisher King. He is "an intermediary between the two planes of existence, the present and the hereafter; himself the symbol of the creative, fructifying force in nature, specifically associated with water or 'moisture'. The representative of the otherworld, he is also the guide to it, perhaps, as Nutt has suggested, the Dis or Pluto of the Celtic Hades. Hence he is described as fishing on the water, as directing the Arthurian knight to the Grail castle, as officiating as Perceval's host, as presiding at the Grail repast, as the person of whom the question must be asked, as being succeeded by the Grail knight. And his weakness or infirmity agrees with Nature's declining strength; thus, his land lies waste or is under the ban of enchantment."

II.   "The Grail Knight... is the initiate. As such he must qualify specially and is responsible for the success of the Grail service, since, if he fails, the crops fail and the springs run dry. Having succeeded, he is not only ἐπόπτης in the sense that he beholds the vision... but he shares in the secrets of the Grail and becomes the Fisher King's successor."

III.   The Fisher King's father or "double". This character, which occurs only in Chrétien and in certain prose romances, that all derive it directly or indirectly from him,[5] is, we may remark, about as difficult to explain under one theory as another. It may be due to some misunderstanding of his source, on Chrétien's part. In any event, it is a "double" and is not fundamental in the Grail legend, as its omission from so many versions proves. In Nitze's view, he stands for the life-god himself, like Adonis

---

[5] The *Queste* adopted it from Chrétien, and from the *Queste* (mainly) it passed into the other prose romances. Cp. on the subject my articles, "Pelles, Pellinor und Pellean," MPh., XV, 113 ff., 331 ff. (1918) and "The Composition of the Old French Prose Lancelot," RR, IX, 360, including note 72 (1918). Miss Weston, *From Ritual to Romance*, pp. 115 ff., regards this double as of purely literary origin and as having had no place in the original Grail ritual of her theory.

or Osiris.  If we interpret the Grail as of Christian origin, he may
well represent the Holy Spirit.

IV.  The Grail is paralleled in the [ Eleusinian ] Mysteries
by the "κίστη or Holy Box" [ a ritualistic vessel of which nothing
definite is known, but it seems to have contained bread as a symbol of the life-giving god, p. 388] and "is the receptacle for the
divine food (wafer or blood) by partaking of which the mortal
establishes a blood-bond with the god.  Thus the Grail comes
naturally to possess talismanic properties, primarily providing food,
but also preserving from disease and decay, distinguishing the
faithful from the sinners, and even ensuring victory in battle.  This
leads by easy stages to its identification in the twelfth century,
through the medium of a holy blood legend, with the relic of Cal-
vary, and thence with the cup of the Last Supper."  The avenue
of transmission, Nitze thinks, was possibly Glastonbury (in England) or Fécamp (in France).  It seems, he observes, that, at
least, in the twelfth century the monks at Fécamp laid claim to
the possession of a Holy Blood relic.  The same thing was true
of Glastonbury in the fifteenth century,[6] but the date is so late
that it affords no justification for Nitze's assumption.

V.  "The Lance... is a symbol like the Sword of Light of
Celtic fairy tales and probably identical in origin with it." — I
may remark, incidentally, however, that in the tales of which this
sword is a feature the weapon is merely a marvellous one, but no
definite characteristics are given it.[7]

Nitze concludes, then, that the Grail theme is based on an
agrarian cult with its ritual.  But he leaves it an open question
as to what part of the world we should localize this cult in.  He
had endeavored to show that the Grail ceremonies have the same
*leit-motiv* (p. 411) as the ancient mysteries — for instance, the
Eleusinian — but he thinks it possible that the Grail romances
may have derived it from a similar cult among the Celts — connected ultimately, it may be, with the Mediterranean cults.  He
even attempts to supply Celtic parallels to some of the essential
characters and objects of the Grail theme — e.g. Manannan mac

---

⁶ Cp. Heinzel, p. 42.

⁷ Cp. G. L. Kittredge, *Arthur and Gorlagon*, pp. 213 ff.

Lir, the shape-shifting supernatural being of Irish romance (p. 397), he compares with the Fisher King, the Lance with one in the Welsh Mabinogi, *Math, Son of Mathonwy*, the Sword, as we have seen, with the Sword of Light. But if our knowledge of the ancient mysteries and their ritual was meagre, our knowledge of any Celtic agrarian cult is simply *nil*. So the way is barred to any progress in that direction.

The objections to Nitze's theory are plain from what has already been said. To start with, our information in regard to the ancient mysteries is too fragmentary and vague to furnish a basis for any trustworthy conclusion.[8] Moreover, there is a gap of more than a thousand years between such records as we have of these mysteries and the appearance of the Grail theme in literature. Taken together with the indefinite character of such information as we do possess about them, we see that this leaves the whole matter hanging in the air. As regards the supposed origin from Celtic agrarian cults, here we have no basis whatever for discussion, since data on the subject are completely wanting.[9]

---

[8] The best authority for what is known concerning the details of the Eleusinian ritual is Paul Foucart's *Les Mystères d'Eleusis* (Paris, 1914). The author, however, sums up (pp. 368 f.): "Nous possédons donc peu de renseignements sur les rites et les cerémonies qui s'accomplissaient dans le télestèrion [i. e. place for initiation], et encore, chacun d'eux, comme on le verra, a donné lieu aux interprétations les plus diverses; si bien qu'en lisant tout ce qui a été écrit sur les Mystères, le lecteur se trouve plongé dans l'obscurité la plus complète." He rejects, pp. 59 ff., the interpretation of Greek agrarian cults put forth by the school of Mannhardt and Frazer.

[9] In a later Grail article, entitled, "The Sister's Son and the Conte del Graal," MPh., IX, 291. ff. (1912), Nitze takes the ground that "the success of the grail ceremony and the welfare of its two kings depend on Perceval's conduct towards his parent" (p. 295), i. e. his mother. "The fact that he deserted her sealed his lips in the presence of the grail" (p. 294). But there is no support for this view in Chrétien's text. There (ll. 3166 ff.) it is stated explicitly that Perceval did not ask the meaning of the first of the Grail objects — the bleeding lance — because of Gornemant's warning (ll. 1624 ff.) that he should not talk too much, and the same thing, of course, applies to the other objects. If his mother later dies through his sin

As has been already remarked, the theory of Miss Weston is, in the most essential respects, identical with that of Nitze. As I have intimated above, instead of seeking analogies to the Grail legend in the Eleusinian mysteries, she seeks them in the Adonis cult. This ancient cult she supposes to have persisted down to the twelfth century through the agency of occult sects — such as we have even at the present day — and thence to have passed into the Grail romances. The Adonis cult, however, forms an even less favorable starting-point than the Eleusinian mysteries for an explanation of the Grail legend; for, if we know little of the latter, we know even less of the former. The twelfth idyll of Theocritus and other sources show us, of course, the slain god stretched out on a bed with women wailing about him, but they give us no detail of the ritual which should correspond to the Grail procession. This slain god Miss Weston identifies with the Maimed King of the Grail Castle. Both, in the euphemistic language of the respective accounts, have been wounded in the thigh — i.e. both (according to Miss Weston) have been deprived of their procreative organs or reproductive powers — and are waiting for a resurrection. For evidence as to the perpetuation of the cult of the Vegetation Spirit down even to the present time in the form of various popular festivals Miss Weston refers the reader to such works as Mannhardt's *Baum- und Feld-Kultus*, and Frazer's *Golden Bough*.[10] On this theory, the wasting of the land —

in neglecting to ask the question (ll. 3555 ff.), this is simply one of the many misfortunes which his failure to do so brought about. — Nitze, *ibid.*, thinks that the Grail story came to the French romancers from the Celts and that the (supposed) mystic bond between Perceval and his mother in respect to the Grail reflects the spirit of the matriarchal system which he argues (pp. 304 ff.) prevailed among the primitive Celts.

Brugger, *Zs. f. frz. Spr. u. Litt.* XXXVI[2], 18 (1910), lays stress on the fact that in all the versions of the Grail story, except Robert's *Joseph* (and the *Didot-Perceval,* dependent thereon), the Grail-hero is related to the Grail-keeper on the mother's side. This fact, however, has no significance, for they are all merely following Chrétien, directly or indirectly.

[10] See, especially, her *From Ritual to Romance,* ch. 5 (Cambridge, 1920), for examples of such survivals drawn from these and

which, I may remark, is first found in Pseudo-Wauchier, not in Chrétien — is connected with the death or infirmity of the King, because the King represents the Vegetation Spirit. Similarly, the achievement of the quest, by restoring the King to health, restores the waste lands to verdure (pp. 80 f.). Miss Weston, however, strains her point to an unreasonable degree, as when she explains the situation of the Grail castle on the sea-coast or a river from the fact that the figure representing the Spirit of Vegetation in popular cults is often thrown into the sea. The Grail itself and the Bleeding Lance she interprets as phallic symbols, representing respectively the female and male organs or elements in the act of generation. These being the most important objects in the Grail rites, this interpretation constitutes the most important variation of Miss Weston's theory from that of Nitze.

The hypothetical ceremonies from which she derives the Grail legend Miss Weston assumes to have had both a general and an esoteric meaning. The main body of worshippers would "regard the whole celebration simply as a means of securing fruitfulness" (*Quest*, p. 85), but for the "elect who desired to penetrate beneath the outer symbolism of the ritual to its inner and hidden meaning the Grail, the Source and Food of Life" assumed a different form. "The aspirant would first be initiated into the mystery of the origin of physical life" (p. 88). At this stage the Grail would be merely a food-supplying dish. Then there would be two esoteric stages of initiation to pass as a symbol of the female element in the generation of life. Secondly (and lastly) he would be initiated into "the higher Secret of the Mysteries, that of regeneration and spiritual life" (p. 90). The experience here must "pass on a higher, a non-material plane and the source of spiritual life must be other than a material food-supplying vessel" (p. 91). "The Grail at this stage is wrought of no material substance." " The

---

similar authorities. Of particular interest are those (pp. 54 ff.) which illustrate the superstition that the fertility of the land is connected with the health of the king. We encounter this idea in the *Odyssey*, XIX, 109 ff. and it still prevails among fhe African tribe, the Shilluk, whose capital is Fashoda.

test here [ = at this stage] demanded of the Quester is that he shall ask concerning the nature and use of this mysterious vessel; but . . . he does not ask." It would be wearisome to follow out Miss Weston's discussion in greater detail. Suffice it to say that she concludes that "Regarded from the ritual point of view, it seems clear that the Grail Quest should be viewed primarily as an initiation story, as a search into the secret and mystery of life; it is the record of an initiation *manqué*" (p. 95). Miss Weston finds a proof of the correctness of her theory in the testimony of occultists among her friends as to the similarity of the Grail rites with rites of their sects.[11] One may remark on this subject, however, that scientific accuracy is not likely to be a virtue of the devotees of occultism, and, in any event, no mere hearsay testimony can be accepted as proof. The way in which Miss Weston herself misstated (unintentionally, of course) Ferdinand Lot's opinion concerning her theory that the *Didot-Perceval* was a prose-rendering of a hypothetical lost poem by Robert de Boron shows the danger of accepting such testimony.[12]

---

[11] Chrétien gives no specific name to Perceval's mother, and even the name of Perceval, himself, is not disclosed until 1. 3535. Accordingly, when the hero is first introduced to the reader, the poet merely calls him (1. 74) "li filz a la veve dame" ("the son of the widow lady"). Miss Weston, *Legend of Sir Perceval,* II, 306 f. sees in this simple descriptive appellation — the simplest conceivable — a deep mystical meaning. Having consulted an occultist friend, she writes: *"Sons of the Widow* is a very wide-spread synonym for Initiates. The Grail story was, as we have seen, an initiation story." But if Chrétien (as is not infrequently done in folk-tales and romances) chooses to hold back for the present the hero's name — doubtless, to pique the reader's curiosity — what other designation could he use?

[12] In *From Ritual to Romance* ch. 11, Miss Weston lays much stress on a Naassene (Gnostic) document of the second century as proving her theory concerning the ritual origin of the Grail legend. We have here, it seems, an originally pagan ritual that has absorbed Christian elements. But, in this case, again we are dealing with a matter that antedates our earliest Grail text by a thousand years and is consequently too remote for any direct bearing on the problem of Grail origins. Besides, there is no similarity between the Naassene document and the descriptions of the Grail procession in our texts.

Miss Weston is very positive that Gawain (and not Perceval) was "the original progatonist of the Quest in its primitive, pre-Christian form" (pp. 118f.). But she is alone in holding this opinion and there is no evidence whatever to support it. She is led to it by her assumption that the earliest form of the Grail story, "so far as the subject-matter is concerned is . . . that embodied by Wauchier de Denain in his continuation of [ Chrétien's ] *Perceval*" (p. 31). Wauchier (quoted *Legend of Sir Perceval*, I, 288), in an episode which has no connection with the Grail, cites as his authority a certain Bleheris, a native of Wales, who related the story to the Count of Poitiers.[13] The appeal might

_____

[13] Only one MS., Add. 36614 (British Museum) contains the name, Bleheris. Miss Weston printed it first in her article, "Wauchier de Denain and Bleheris (Bledhericus)," *Romania*, XXXIV (1905), 100 ff, giving, at the same time, the reading's of the other MSS. in a note. The passage runs thus:

> Deviser vos voel sa faiture,
> Si com le conte Bleheris
> Qui fu nes e engenuis
> En Gales dont je cont le conte,
> Et qui si le contoit au conte
> De Poitiers qui amoit l'estoire
> Et le tenoit en grant memoire
> Plus que nul autre ne faisoit.

The reading of Add. 36614, just reproduced, is clearer than the readings of the other MSS., but it is possible that this may be the result of an emendation on the part of a scribe who remembered the appeal made in Pseudo-Wauchier, l. 19434, to Bleheris (Bleobleheris). In any event, that appeal is probably the source of the present one. I shall have occasion to return to the subject in trying to establish the separate existence of Pseudo-Wauchier in a note below.

Brugger, *Zs. f. frz. Spr. u. Litt.*, XXXI[2] (1907), pp. 151 ff., XXXVI[2] (1910), 187, I believe, is the only scholar, besides Miss Weston, who has accepted this Bleheris as a real person. On the other hand, ibid., pp. 136 ff., he rejects as a hoax the appeal to a *conte*, written at Fécamp, which Miss Weston, I, 155, has also unearthed in the MSS. of Wauchier. There is really, however, nothing to choose between the two appeals. He identifies, (p. 158) the Count of Poitiers here spoken of with the count who was afterwards Henry II of England, and dates the composition of Bleheris' supposed poem in the years 1151—1154. Miss Weston (pp. 291 ff.)

be a genuine one and still prove nothing in regard to the origin
of the Grail legend, for it occurs in an episode that is not connected with the Grail and relates to a minor character of the poem —
viz. the Little Knight who guards the magic shield won by Gawain.
As a matter of fact, it is, in all probability, merely one of the
customary fabrications of the mediaeval poets, and Wauchier was
here no doubt imitating the equally valueless appeal at the beginning of Thomas' *Tristan* to an authority whose name, Bréri,
is a variant of this name. So Wauchier's appeal, even in regard
to this matter, is, in the opinion of most scholars (see Bédier, Lot,
Loth, Smirnov, etc.), a mere hoax, and he had no access to any
early independent source for the Grail theme. He was continuing
Chrétien's unfinished work and his version of the story was, no
doubt, the product of his own invention. The term, "invention",
does not exclude, of course, the application to the Grail theme of
*motifs* drawn from folk-tales and romances which stood outside
of that cycle.

Miss Weston thinks that the first step towards the Christianization of the originally pagan theme was the identification of the

---

had identified him with a Bishop of Llandaff, who filled that office
983—1023.    Assuming that Wauchier's Bleheris was a real person,
Brugger's dating would be preferable, but, for my own part, I regard
him as a myth. — Since the publication of Miss Weston's and Brugger's
discussions of the subject, Edward Owen has proposed still another
Bledri for identification with Wauchier's Bleheris, viz. Bledri ap Cadivor,
a Welsh chieftain of the early twelfth century, who seems to have
been favorable to the Normans in Wales.    Cp. "A note on the identification of Bleheris," *Revue Celtique,* XXXII, 5 ff. (1911).    In her
brief comment at the end of her article, p. 16, Miss Weston says that
the arguments are not decisive.    *Ibid.* XXXIII, 180 ff. (1912), in his
"Bledhericus, Bleddri, Breri," W. J. Gruffyd upholds the same thesis
as Owen. — It is to be observed that the name *Bleri* occurs also,
in Cornwall: J. Loth cites, *Annales de Bretagne,* XI, 480, from
Domesday Book a place named *Tre-Bleri.*

Among scholars who have expressed disbelief in the reality of
Bleheris, cp. J. Bédier, edition of *Tristan* poems, II, 98, J. Loth,
*Les Mabinogion*[2], I, 74 f., F. Lot, *Bibliothèque de l'École des Chartes,*
LXX, 572, A. Smirnov, *Romania,* XLIII, 126.

lance of the Grail ritual with the lance of Longinus, and that the next was the connection of the Grail as a feeding-vessel with Christian tradition through the personality of Joseph of Arimathea (p. 117). She believes that this connection was effected at Glastonbury, where, according to her theory, Joseph was accepted in tradition as Apostle of Britain and presumably a founder of Glastonbury. Here then the Grail was first definitely associated with Joseph. But the effort to connect Joseph with a relic of the Sacred Blood was inspired, she thinks, by the example of the abbey of Fécamp in Northern France, where a similar relic was associated with Nicodemus, whose apocryphal gospel was the principal source for the legend of Joseph. We have in all this, however, a mere deluge of hypotheses. As we have seen, there is no reason to believe that Joseph was ever connected with Glastonbury until after 1191. When the notion was first originated about the presence of a Sacred Blood relic at Fécamp[14] is not known, and there is no proof whatever that the French monastery had any influence on the English one — and so with the rest of it.

---

[14] Brugger, *Zs. f. frz. Spr. u. Litt.*, XXXI², 135 ff. (1907), rejects Miss Weston's theory of the connection of Fécamp with the development of the Grail legend and commends Heinzel who mentioned the Fécamp blood-relic in commenting on a passage in Wolfram which Miss Weston (p. 162) misuses, *(Über Wolfram von Eschenbach's Parzival*, p. 14, and *Über die französischen Gralromane*, p. 40)*, but did not draw the conclusion from its existence that Miss Weston does. The mediaeval documents concerning the blood-relic at Fécamp do not allude to such a connection, and the general resemblance between the Grail (which by this time was conceived of as a blood-relic) and this blood-relic at Fécamp was sufficient, Brugger thinks, to suggest to Wauchier an appeal to an imaginary book at Fécamp as the source of his Grail romance. This appeal, on which Miss Weston's whole theory is based, is found in two lines, which are not in the Mons MS., and, consequently, not in Potvin's edition of the *Conte del Graal,* but which occur in four MSS. and with a manifest error *(Trescamp* for *Fescamp)* in a fifth. They are given as follows in Miss Weston's *Legend of Sir Perceval*, I, 155:

si com le conte nus affiche
qui a Fescans est tos escris.

The allusion here to Fécamp, though it does not appear in four of the MSS., is probably genuine. In the two lines the author is appealing

Apart from the points specifically touched on already, one may say in general that Miss Weston's theory is open to the same objections as Professor Nitze's and to some additional ones, besides. The gap in the historical tradition between the latest records of the Adonis rites and the first Grail romances is, of course, virtually the same as the gap between the latest records of the Eleusinian mysteries and these same romances. Moreover, students of the Holy Grail do not know what are the rites of the occult sects of our own day, much less those of the Middle Ages, if such practices did, indeed, persist through that period, so that it is impossible to control the theory. The interpretation of the lance and Grail as phallic symbols seems especially fantastic. Al-

---

to the *conte* composed at Fécamp as his authority for thé story of Perceval's adventure at Mont Dolerous, ll. 33 900 ff.

Miss Weston (p. 156) imagines that this *conte* was a real book — "a fully developed Christian-Grail romance". For my own part, I have no doubt that Brugger is right in regarding the *conte* as imaginary and on a par with the other mediaeval hoaxes of this kind that he cites; but, even if it were genuine, the lines would not justify Miss Weston's large inference, for the Mont Dolerous adventure has nothing to do with the Grail, except that the hero is Perceval, and the appeal is made with reference merely to this adventure, not to Wauchier's poem, as a whole. It was suggested, doubtless, by the fact that, through the confraternity of jongleurs there, Fécamp was actually a centre for the production of *contes*. See Miss Weston, p. 167, and especially, J. Bédier, *Romanic Review*, I, 122 ff. In this article (pp. 113 ff.), "Richard de Normandie dans les Chansons de Geste", Bédier has shown how the jongleurs at Fécamp were responsible for the part played by Richard in the Old French epic.

In connecting the Fécamp blood-relic with the Grail, Miss Weston had been anticipated by Le Roux de Lincy, *Essai sur l'abbaye de Fécamp*, 137 f. (Rouen, 1840) and, secondarily, by G. A. Heinrich, *Le Parceval de W. d'Eschenbach et la Legende du Saint Graal*, 77 ff. (Paris, 1855). Blood-relics (vials that are supposed to contain the blood of Christ) are very numerous in Europe. Cp. Hertz: *Parzival*, p. 454, and Wechssler, *Sage vom Gral*, pp. 115 f. Heinzel, p. 48, names a number of books on the subject of such relics.

For an argument against Miss Weston's Fécamp theory, cp. also F. Lot, *Bibliothèque de l'École des Chartes*, LXX, 572 f. (including note 1 on p. 573).

together, of the two kindred theories, Nitze's appears the more acceptable, although, in the opinion of the present writer, even this does not get beyond the realm of ingenious conjecture.

Such similarities as may exist between the Grail rites and those of the agrarian cults of the ancients do not conflict, after all, with the theory that the former were made up of Christian elements — for the rites of the Christian church itself, as is well-known, developed under the influence of the old pagan mysteries,[15] just as the leading Christian festivals are definitely traceable to festivals of the old pagan religions. This is true, for instance, of Christmas, Easter and the Feast of the Assumption of the Virgin. Accordingly features of the Grail theme which offer analogies to these agrarian cults are found also in Christian legend, which derived them no doubt from those cults. For instance, just as vegetation dies with Adonis, so in some Christian legends it is said to have died as the result of the death of our Lord. Similarly the lance of Longinus in Christian legend is not only a symbol of peace, but, like the lance of the Grail romances, a symbol of destruction.[16] Altogether, however, where we have such features common to Christian legend and the ancient cults, it is much more likely that the Grail romances derived them from the former than from any supposed underground perpetuation of the latter. Certainly, as regards the Grail procession, the procession of talismans, we can find parallels to all of these in Christian ritual,[17] whereas we really know nothing definite about the objects that figured in the rites of the agrarian divinities of antiquity. So Christian ritual is far more likely to have been the immediate source.

---

[15] Miss Peebles, pp. 200f. rightly stresses this fact. Nitze, PMLA, XXIV, 372, note 1, and Brugger, *Zs. f. frz. Spr. u. Litt.,* XXXVI[2], 69, recognize it, but do not give it. I believe, its due weight in its bearing on the eucharistic origin of the Grail legend.

[16] Cp. Miss Peebles, p. 192 and note.

[17] Cp. Heinzel, pp. 7ff.

# Chapter IV.

# Continuations of Chrétien.

Chrétien's unfinished *Perceval* was carried on by later poets, and these continuations[1] combined are about five times as long as the original poem. The poets who are responsible for the continuations are as follows. 1. An anonymous writer, usually called in discussions of these matters Pseudo-Gautier or Pseudo-Wauchier. His work which relates Gawain's adventures extends through l. 21916. 2. Wauchier de Denain[2] (to employ

---

[1] For a study of the MSS. of the continuations see Hugo Waitz, *Die Fortsetzungen von Chrétien's Perceval le Gallois nach den Pariser Handschriften* (Straßburg, 1890), and J. L. Weston, *Legend of Sir Perceval*, II. 27 ff. et passim, (London, 1906). The MSS. vary considerably. For differences of view between Waitz and Miss Weston as to the priority of the redactions see the latter, pp. 47 f.

[2] His work was formerly cited generally under the name of Gaucher de Dourdan or Gautier de Doulens, but P. Meyer, *Romania*, XXXII, 583 ff. (1903), has established Wauchier de Denain as the correct form. For MS. variants of the name see Potvin's *Perceval le Gallois*, V, 109, note 2, Birch-Hirschfeld, pp. 88 f., and P. Meyer, *loc. cit.*, p. 585. For Wauchier's literary activities see P. Meyer, *Histoire Littéraire de la France*, XXXIII, 258 ff. (1906).

Birch-Hirschfeld, pp. 89 ff., and Miss Weston, *Legend of Sir Perceval*, II, 235 et passim, regard the first continuation of Chrétien, which I have ascribed above to Pseudo-Wauchier, as really by Wauchier. Miss Weston excepts apparently (cp. p. 214, note) ll. 10602—11596 (Chastel Merveilleus episode), as the work of "the copyists". It seems to me more likely, however, that Wauchier's work only begins with the narrative of Perceval's adventures — that is to say, with l. 21917. This view has been held by G. Paris, *Histoire Littéraire de la France*, XXX, 27, and *Manuel*, p. 98, Nutt, pp. 70 ff., Schorbach, edition of Wisse-Colin's Low German fourteenth century version of the *Perceval*. (Strassburg, 1888), pp. XXXV, XXXVIII f., W. Golther, *Zs. f. ver-*

the form of the name which is now common), who continues it
through l. 34934. He appears to have been at one time in the

---

*gleichende Litteraturgeschichte*, Neue Folge, III, 419 (1890), R.
Heinzel, *Über die französischen Gralromane*, p. 58 (good summary
of the argument therefor) and A. Jeanroy, *Revue des Langues Romanes*,
L, 542, note (1907). It is borne out by the Berne MS., which, after
an introduction of 13 lines, begins at this point. See A. Rochat:
*Über einen bisher unbekannten Percheval li Galois* (Zürich, 1855).
Interpolations, too, are much more frequent in Pseudo-Wauchier. Besides
those printed as such by Potvin in appendices, III, 369 ff. and IV,
343 ff., the description of the tournament, ll. 13481—14943 (not in
the Mons MS.), which is one of the feeblest things in Arthurian
romance, certainly belongs in this category. It is to be observed,
moreover, that Wauchier and Pseudo-Wauchier conflict in their conceptions of the Grail castle, and scarcely harmonize in their use of
the *Bel Inconnu* tale. Cp. particularly 20380 ff. and 38401 ff., respectively, where Wauchier takes no account of what Pseudo-Wauchier had
said of this son of Gawain. G. Paris, *Manuel*, p. 105, believed, indeed,
that Wauchier was unacquainted with Pseudo-Wauchier's work. But
this is refuted by the undeniable dependence of the account, ll. 33440 ff.
which Gawain gives to his son, Guinglain, of his visit to the Grail
Castle (including the circumstances that led up to it) on the account
(ll. 19664 ff.) of the same episode in Pseudo-Wauchier. Cp. Heinzel,
pp. 52 f.

The only reasons which Miss Weston gives, I, 235, for discarding
Pseudo-Wauchier are: 1. that the Gawain adventures in the two parts
are of the same kind; 2. both refer to the same authority (Bleheris).
The first statement, however, is not quite exact, for in Wauchier we
have no adventure imputed to Gawain like the visit of this character
to the Grail castle in Pseudo-Wauchier, ll. 19991 ff., and, in general,
the adventures in the Arthurian romances are so much alike in kind
that obviously the similarity would afford no criterion of authorship.
The second point has been found convincing by Brugger, *Zs. f. frz.
Spr. u. Litt.*, XXXI[2], 141. But granting that the citation of "Bleheris"
as an authority (instead of the corresponding "li escris" of the Mons
MS., printed by Potvin, l. 31675), which occurs only in the British
Museum Add. 36, 614 (for the readings of this and the other MSS.
cp. Miss Weston in *Romania*, XXXIV, 100 f.), is really due to Wauchier,
and is not simply a scribe's emendation of a passage that had become
corrupt in the MS. tradition, it may have been very well suggested
to him by Pseudo-Wauchier's citation of this same authority in l. 19434,
where the Mons MS. (printed by Potvin, III, 344) has "Brandelis",

service of the Countess Jeanne of Flanders, who ruled from 1206 to 1244, but the composition of his part of the *Conte del Graal* probably falls in the twelfth century. Wauchier's work was itself continued by two different writers, who each take up the narrative at the point where he left off. These writers are named respectively Manessier (Manecier) and Gerbert. 3. Manessier, who wrote at the command of the Countess Jeanne of Flanders, mentioned above, carries it on to l. 45379. 4. Gerbert, who seems identical with Gerbert de Montreuil, author of the *Roman de la Violette*,[3] inserts 15,000 lines between Wauchier and Manessier. To this day, Gerbert's intercalation has been printed only in part, viz. Potvin, VI, 161 ff. and *Romania*, XXXV, 501 ff. (the episode which Bédier calls *Tristan Ménestrel*).

As regards the dates of these continuators, we have no precise evidence on the subject.[4] We know that Wauchier was writing

---

but the other MSS. have "Bleheris" or "Bleobleheris", as Miss Weston (I, 241, including note) has pointed out. From what has just been observed in the preceding paragraph, it is established beyond question that Wauchier was acquainted with Pseudo-Wauchier's work.

[3] The identity, first suggested by Francisque Michel, in his edition of the *Tristan* poems, I, p. civ, note 75, has been generally accepted since. Cp. Birch-Hirschfeld, *Die Sage vom Graal*, pp. 110 ff., G. Paris, *Manuel*, p. 106, Kraus, *Über Girbert de Montreuil und seine Werke* (Würzburg diss., Erlangen, 1897), Maurice Wilmotte, in the proceedings of the Académie Royale de Belgique for 1900: *Bulletin de la Classe des Lettres*, etc., pp. 166—189. The last-named is much the most important discussion of the subject. Wilmotte lays particular stress on the abundance of leonine rhymes which distinguish the two among the poems of the time, and decides that there are "de sérieuses probabilités" in favor of the identity.

The *Roman de la Violette* is based on the same *motif* as Shakespeare's *Cymbeline* — the foolish wager about a woman's chastity that has such serious consequences.

[4] The most careful examination of the question is by E. Brugger, *Zs. f. frz. Spr. u. Litt.*, XXXVI[2], 45 ff. (1910). Brugger, however, takes no account of Wilmotte's paper on Gerbert which I have cited in the previous note. In this paper the author has pointed out that in the "lutte de Tristan" episode (Tristan prevails in succession over Gifflet, Lancelot, Yvain and Gawain), which occupies about 1500

at some time between 1190 and 1212 (limits of the rule of Philip, Marquis of Namur, for whom he executed a translation of the *Vitae Patrum*), how much earlier or how much later there is no means of determining. It is most probable, however, that his addition to Chrétien's *Perceval* belongs to the latter years of the

---

lines in Gerbert's continuation, though it hardly figures at all in Potvin's analysis, Gerbert had in mind the prose *Tristan*. There is no reason to believe that that work was in existence before 1220, at the earliest, so that this would give us a new *terminus a quo* for Gerbert's addition to Chrétien's poem.

In *Romania*, XXXV, 497 ff. (1906) Bédier has edited this "lutte de Tristan" episode and Miss Weston has added notes. She regards it as an interpolation embodying lost materials: 1. a Perceval poem, 2. a short episodic Tristan poem. The names, however, in the episode betray the lateness of its composition: "Meraugis" from *Meraugis de Portlesguez*, "Roi des C. Chevaliers" and "Claudas de la Deserte" from the prose *Lancelot*. So too probably "Bruns sans Pitie" is taken from the prose *Lancelot.*" Besides, Tristan, as a conventional knight, derives plainly from the prose *Tristan* (cp. Löseth, pp. 256 f.), not from any old tradition. — Golther, *Tristan und Isolde*, p. 226 ff. is inclined to accept the existence of no. 2.

Gerbert states, Potvin, VI, 212 f. that he has taken up the work (i. e. of continuing Chrétien's *Perceval*), "Quant chascuns trovere le laisse." Brugger, *loc. cit.*, p. 52, interprets this as implying that he did not know of Manessier's continuation, and, consequently, that he wrote contemporaneously with the latter or immediately thereafter. This interpretation, to be sure, is not necessary, and the fact overlooked by Brugger that Gerbert wrote after the prose *Tristan* tells against his conclusion. G. Paris, *Histoire Littéraire de la France,* XXX, 42, believes that Gerbert is unacquainted with Manessier. Heinzel, on the other hand, pp. 75 f., has argued that Gerbert knew all the continuations of Chrétien's *Perceval*. All the points of distinctive agreement between Gerbert and Manessier which he cites (p. 76) are unsatisfactory. The first of the three, indeed, is cited by Heinzel through an error, for the passage (ll. 29682 ff.) really occurs in Wauchier, not Manessier. It concerns the adventure of a knight in a tomb. The second (the breaking of Perceval's sword) is too commonplace to possess any weight, and the third (temptation of Perceval by a devil in woman's shape) may very well have been borrowed by Gerbert from the *Grand S. Graal*. On the whole, there is no proof that Gerbert knew Manessier.

twelfth century. The limits of Manessier's date are 1211—1244, with the probabilities in favor of the first half of this period. Gerbert's work should, doubtless, be, also, assigned to this period.

In discussions of the origins of the Grail legend, the greatest mischief, in the judgment of the present writer, has resulted from the use of these continuations, as if they were original authorities that drew directly from Chrétien's source, independently of him, or perhaps from sources that he did not know. This has been the fault even of some advocates of the theory of Christian origins (e.g. Heinzel), but still more of the opponents of that theory. Miss Weston, indeed, takes Wauchier as the best authority on the subject of the Grail. She believes that he, too, had access to the *livre* that Count Philip gave to Chrétien, only she thinks that Wauchier preserves better the character of the book in question than Chrétien did.[5] But we have seen that she also believes in Breri, who is, in all probability, merely one of the innumerable hoaxes of the writers of the Middle Ages, when a bold citation of authority was sufficient to quell all doubters, save perhaps a few invincible skeptics. As a matter of fact, one may safely affirm that Wauchier knew nothing of the Grail, except what he found in Chrétien's fragmentary poem, and Manessier and Gerbert were in the same case[6] — only they had Wauchier's and Pseudo-Wauchier's continuations, besides, to furnish suggestions to their imaginations.

As regards the contents of these continuations, Wauchier's work, like Chrétien's, offers us in alternation adventures of Perceval and adventures of Gawain. But the adventures of the latter here, besides being of the most commonplace character, make up not quite a fourth of the whole, and they are subordinated to the adventures of the former, as they are not in Chrétien's *Perceval*, for in Wauchier they are all incidents in a quest of Gawain for Perceval. On the other hand, the continuation of Pseudo-Wauchier

---

[5] Cp. her *Legend of Sir Perceval*, I, 323 ff.

[6] This accords, of course, with Golther's opinion. Cp. especially, p. 420 of his article, "Beziehungen zwischen französischer und keltischer Litteratur im Mittelalter", *Zs. f. vergleichende Litteraturgeschichte.* Neue Folge, III, 409 ff. (1890). Similarly, Foerster, Chrétien *Wörterbuch*, p. 185* (1914).

relates wholly to adventures of Gawain, including one at the Grail castle. The poet, however, makes it plain that Gawain is not the destined Grail Winner, for he cannot put together the pieces of the broken sword, and, besides omitting to ask about the Grail, he falls asleep before he has received an explanation of any of the other objects, save the lance.

In order to introduce the Grail episode into his narrative, the author has used an incident in Chrétien's *Perceval* (ll. 4380 ff.) which in that poem had had no connection with it — viz. the one in which Gawain by his courtesy brings Perceval to Arthur, after the latter (Perceval) had unhorsed Kay for rudely interrupting him in his revery about his lady-love. In Pseudo-Wauchier the unnamed knight who is brought back to Guinevere turns out to be mortally wounded with a dart and dies as he reaches the queen's tent. Equipped in the dead man's armor, Gawain goes forth to avenge him on the unknown slayer and in the course of his wanderings stumbles by chance on the Grail castle[7] to which the slain knight, it seems, belonged. Despite some clumsiness and inconsistency in detail, the air of mystery and the suggestion of the supernatural are well maintained throughout the whole episode, — as, for example, in the incident of the forest chapel upon which Gawain comes in the depths of the night and whose brilliant lights he sees extinguished by a bodiless black hand and in that of the elusive light which finally guides his horse through the darkness to the Grail castle. So, too, with the scenes in the hall of the Grail castle — the people's mistaking Gawain for the slain knight whose return they are expecting and whose armor Gawain has on, the procession of the canons and their service over the mysterious dead man, whose bier lies in the hall, with the cross

---

[7] The castle is out in the sea and is reached by a long causeway, which it took Gawain from nightfall to midnight to traverse. Consequently Brown observes, Kittredge *Anniversary Papers*, p. 247, that "the castle of the Grail was, in a more original form of the story, an under-wave-abode". But this is, surely, a far-fetched inference. Mediaeval castles were often thus situated, for better protection, and, as far as the length of the causeway is concerned, the whole conception of the Grail castle belongs, of course, to fairy-land.

and the fragment of a sword on the body, the moments that follow, when Gawain, with his face in his hands, sits alone in the hall, with the corpse — then, the return of the throng, with the Grail King, who wears a crown of gold and who, unlike Chrétien's Grail King, is able to walk. The poet has undoubtedly caught here the spirit of a folk-tale more distinctively than Chrétien in his corresponding description, only in the legitimate endeavor to gain the effect of mystery he commits some blunders and leaves the narrative in certain particulars unnecessarily obscure. But these obscurities are, no doubt, due mainly to the fact that, like Chrétien and Wauchier, Pseudo-Wauchier did not finish his tale. Just as in the episode which follows upon this one and which is strikingly similar to it in the central *motif* — the unknown dead man who lies on a bier in the hall with a broken weapon (the truncheon of the spear still in his body) and whose death calls for vengeance — he wraps the initial scene in the utmost mystery. He does, however, complete this later episode, and so what at first seemed to be an impenetrable mystery is in the end satisfactorily cleared up. We should, doubtless, have had the same result in the case of the earlier episode, if the author had not left it unfinished. Perhaps the most fateful innovation which marks this description of the Grail castle in Pseudo-Wauchier is the conception of the broken sword. In Chrétien (ll. 3092ff.), when Perceval visited the Grail castle, the Grail King (Fisher King) presented him with the *espee as estranges renges* (l. 4674) which had been given him by his niece, *la sore pucele* (l. 3107). It was there said that this sword would break in only one peril, and nobody knew what that was, save the person who forged the weapon. Later (ll. 3622 ff.) Perceval's cousin warns him that the sword will fly in pieces when Perceval enters a combat, but that the smith who forged it (Trebuchet) can mend it again.[8] Manifestly

---

[8] For the MS. readings of the passages in question cp. Miss Weston, *Legend of Sir Perceval*, I, 1-33 ff. The interpolations, found in certain MSS., which she discusses, pp. 137 ff., have no importance. They originated, obviously, in efforts on the part of the scribes to harmonize Chrétien and Pseudo-Wauchier.

Chrétien was preparing the way here for an intended episode in his *Perceval* which he never reached. Pseudo-Wauchier, however, adopted the hint and exploited this sword of the Grail castle for his own narrative.[9] Half of it lay on the corpse in the hall, the other half of it had been in the possession of the knight who was killed so mysteriously near the queen's tent and whose death Gawain had set forth to avenge. Gawain had carried it to the Grail castle, it would seem, as a part of the dead knight's equipment, which he was wearing, and when he laid aside this equipment on his arrival there, the lord of the Grail castle took the sword and brought it in for the test of Gawain's fitness to undo the spell which rested on the land of the Grail. This conception of the broken sword, as thus developed by Pseudo-Wauchier, had a great success, and with various modifications of setting, etc. turns up in all subsequent romances of the Grail cycle, and in the other continuations of Chrétien eclipses the question concerning the Grail in importance.

Not so successful, however, were certain other innovations of this writer — for example, his discarding of the Grail procession and of the epithets of the lord of the Grail castle, "Fisher King" and "Rich Fisher". The imposing procession and these romantic titles of the Grail lord proved, naturally, too attractive to later romancers. In Pseudo-Wauchier we have Chrétien's feast in the hall of the Grail castle (ll. 3237 ff.), but without his procession. On the other hand, the author has the unlucky idea of making the Grail supply the food and wine at this banquet.[10] So the table

---

[9] There is no need of resorting to the constantly recurring theory of lost sources here. The mediaeval romancers did not feel the awe of the Grail that some modern scholars seem to feel. The author of *Sone de Nausay* (late thirteenth century) added (ll. 17065 ff.) to the Grail relics a piece of the true cross and a candlestick which had done duty at the birth of Christ. What this writer did, a writer of a somewhat earlier time surely would not have shrunk from doing.

[10] The idea that the Grail possessed the magical quality of supplying unending sustenance is met with first in Pseudo-Wauchier. In Robert's *Joseph* the conception is somewhat different. There Joseph of Arimathea lives for years in prison without food or drink, and, at

is set in regular fashion, and yet the Grail, in some unexplained manner, furnishes the courses. Nothing could be more awkward. The author wanted to vary the scene in the Grail castle, but he fails to give the marvellous vessel any organic connection with the incidents that surround it. The way in which he disposes of

-----

the same time, he has the Grail with him, but Robert does not ascribe his hero's preservation to any sustenance furnished by this sacred vessel. It is merely said that that was due to the help of God (ll. 731 ff.) or Jesus (ll. 2620 ff.). Furthermore, in the passage about the Grail table, it is really the fish, caught by Bron (cp. ll. 2495 ff.), which (as in the Bible account of Christ's miracle of the loaves and fishes) supplies miraculous subsistence to the people. The Grail is present, so to speak, merely as the representative of Christ, through whom the miracle is wrought.

The conception of a magical object (table, vessel, or what not) with food-producing powers is common in folk-lore. For innumerable examples from every part of the world see *Anmerkungen zu den Kinder- und Hausmärchen der Brüder Grimm, neu bearbeitet von Johannes Bolte und Georg Polivka,* I, 346 ff. (Leipzig, 1912).

Pseudo - Wauchier, who was continuing Chrétien's work, like Chrétien, of course, identified the Grail with the vessel that contained the bread of the sacrament, and it is easy to imagine that the sacrament which afforded sustenance to the spirit could also afford miraculous sustenance to the body. Miss L. A. Fisher has cited an actual example of this from Caesarius of Heisterbach's *Dialogus Miraculorum,* Distinctio IX, exemplum XLVII (not XLVI, as she gives it), in her *The Mystic Vision in the Grail Legend and the Divine Comedy,* p. 81 (New York, 1917), and investigation would, doubtless, reveal still other instances. In any event, as Miss Fisher, *loc. cit.,* observes, the constant connection in Christian literature (beginning with *St. John,* VI, 49 f.) of the eucharist with the Old Testament manna miracle, and, still further, with the miracle of the loaves and fishes and with that of Cana in the New Testament makes this conception of the life-sustaining power of the sacrament the most natural thing in the world.

Chrétien (ll. 3187 ff.) had already attached a fairytale motif to the Grail — viz. its marvellous luminosity. This is one of the commonest qualities of marvellous objects in folk-tales. To be sure, this quality was sometimes ascribed to the eucharist in mediaeval writers. Cp. Miss Fisher, pp. 77 f. It is ascribed to the Grail, also, by Robert de Boron, *Joseph,* ll. 719, 2031 f.; but, as stated above, this was probably suggested by the *Gesta Pilati.*

the lance is equally unhappy. Having abandoned the idea of the procession, he represents the lance as resting in a lance-holder in the hall and the blood as running down the shaft from the steel head and through a golden tube, fixed to the handle, into a silver vessel, whence it flowed still further through a tube of silver — into what is not stated. This lance, as the Grail King tells Gawain expressly (ll. 20259 ff.), is the one with which the side of the Son of God was pierced (on the cross). So to the writer it was a Christian relic, as was, doubtless, the Grail, though in the author's fragmentary narrative the latter is left undefined.

New, too, in Pseudo-Wauchier is the conception of the blighted land. In Chrétien there is nothing of this kind. There, to be sure, Perceval's failure to ask the question which would have healed the wound of the lame Grail King will have, also, the effect of bringing unmeasured calamities upon the realm of the Grail castle (ll. 4637 ff.), but, apart from the fact that these calamities lie in the future, there is nothing supernatural about them. Here, however, the land goes to waste under an evil spell, which is partly undone by Gawain's question concerning the lance, the sword and the bier. Accordingly, the following day the waters ran again, the forests regained their verdure and the people blessed him, as he passed, for having brought them such relief. At the same time, they blamed him for not asking concerning the Grail, which would have completed the restoration of the "roiaume destruit". This conception of the land that becomes a desert under a spell which a certain question will undo is, of course, derived from folklore, but it does not appear in Chrétien, and there is no reason to doubt that, like the revenge *motif*, it was an original contribution of Pseudo-Wauchier's to the development of the Grail legend.[11]

---

[11] Nutt regards the revenge *motif* as already connected in popular tradition with a Grail-quest. Indeed, in his view (pp. 181 ff.), all stories about the Grail quest fall into two classes, whose essential *motifs* are respectively: 1. the avenging of a kinsman in a blood feud by means of sword, lance and vessel, 2. the bespelled castle *motif*. But two of the Grail stories of the first category, Manessier's and *Peredur*, derive from Pseudo-Wauchier. The third, *Sir Percyvelle*,

There are still other striking episodes in this first continuation to Chrétien's *Perceval* — for example, the one which I have already mentioned above and which shows contamination with the tale of the Swan Knight, viz. that of the dead man who was brought over the sea to Camelot in a ship, drawn by a swan. It is a night of heat and storm, and Arthur, who is seated by a window, seeing the strange vessel, goes down and, on entering it, finds there the dead body of a handsome knight, richly dressed and embalmed, with a spear still fixed in it. A letter in the dead man's hand contains the request that Arthur should permit the body to rest in his hall and refuse to let any body remove the spear from the wound for a year, if necessary, unless some one should appear to avenge the slain man on certain fantastic conditions, that seem impossible of fulfilment. Kahares (Guerehes), a brother of Gawain, however, achieves the adventure.

Among the most interesting stories in this continuation are those that are attached to the name of the Celtic hero, Caradoc, and which constitute the so-called *Livre de Caradoc* in this division of the *Conte del Graal*. There can be little doubt, however, that this group of stories is interpolated and that it is not by the same hand as the bulk of the first continuation. The *Livre de Caradoc* contains three well known *motifs*:

1. The arrival of a mysterious stranger with a head-cutting challenge (as in the Middle English romance *Sir Gawain and the Green Knight*) — he will submit to decapitation now, if the knight who accepts the challenge will submit to the same process a year hence.

2. A variant of *The Faithless Mother* folk-tale, involving an account of how Caradoc was relieved through the devotion of his

---

probably adopted it from the Bliocadrans-prologue; but this romance does not connect it with the Grail, for it omits the Grail altogether. I have discussed the sources of these romances in the appropriate places. It is misleading when Heinzel, pp. 52, 75, says that Gautier and Gerbert show this revenge *motif*. We have such a *motif* in their works, but it has no immediate connection with the achievement of the Grail adventure.

wife, Guimier, from the affliction of a serpent that had fastened itself on his arm.[12]

3. The chastity test by means of the drinking-horn, which proves that only Caradoc, of all the knights at Arthur's court, could boast of a chaste wife.

These famous *motifs* were all ultimately derived from folk-tales, as, indeed, the folk-tale stamp of its incidents is the distinguishing characteristic of the *Livre de Caradoc*.

The continuation of Pseudo-Wauchier cannot claim, of course, to be a very highly developed work of art, but, if we exclude obvious interpolations, such as the description of the tourney, ll 13481 ff., what remains is, in my opinion, the most readable of the French metrical romances of the Arthurian cycle, with the exception of Chrétien's works and the *Tristan* fragments. It is hard to parallel in these romances such a range of power as is exhibited here, on the one hand, in the vigorous duel of Gawain and Brandelis[13] (ll. 17729 ff.), which the sister of the latter ends by bringing in the child of herself and Gawain and appealing on its behalf to the compassion of the combatants, on the other, in the charming scene (ll. 19595 ff.) where the ladies,[14] preparing to meet Gawain's "amie", who has just arrived at court, pass judgment on each other's appearance, before going into her presence.

---

[12] See pp. 89 ff., above.

[13] Brugger, *Zs. f. frz. Spr. u. Litt.*, XXXI[2], 144, well characterizes this as one of the grandest passages in Old French literature.

[14]   Adont les veissies pinier
       Par cest castel et aplanier
       Ces dames et ces damoiseles,
       La roinne et les puceles.
       L'une faisoit son cief trecier,
       Et l'autre son coste lacier;
       La tierce dist: "Sour, suis-je bien?"
       "A vous, fait-ele, ne faut rien;
       Et a moi, coment en est pris?"
       "Vos iestes bien, ce m'est avis."
       Li quarte si dist d'autre part:
       "Damoisele, se Diex vous gart,
       Sui-jou ore bien coulouree?"
       "Oïl, plus que riens qui soit nee."

Wauchier is as thoroughly mundane as Chrétien or Pseudo-Wauchier. He has the same *joie de vivre*, and his hero's amours[15] and the occasional ironical comments in his work on sexual matters[16] are even more licentious in tendency than anything in Chrétien. Here, as in Pseudo-Wauchier, the Grail occupies really a very small part in the narrative, but, after a fashion, it gives unity to the whole, for at the conclusion the hero has at last reached the Grail castle. Unfortunately, Wauchier's continuation breaks off in the middle of this crowning scene. Unlike modern scholars, however, our poet did not take the Grail quest very seriously, for he makes his hero turn aside from it on any provocation. Look, for instance, at the absurd complex of adventures, concerning the magic chessboard, the stag-head and tomb-knight (ll. 22393 ff.).[17] The girl who owns the magic chessboard will

---

[15] Cp. ll. 25017 ff., 30449 ff., etc.

[16] Cp. ll. 28763 ff., 34011 ff., etc.

[17] The magic chessboard (self-playing chessmen) *motif* had a great success and from Wauchier (apparently) it passed into the *Didot-Perceval* (J. L. Weston's *Legend of Sir Perceval*, II, 31 ff.), the Welsh *Peredur* (Loth's *Mabinogion*[2], II, 114 ff.), the prose *Lancelot* (Sommer's *Vulgate Version*, etc., V, 151 ff.), the *Perlesvaus* (Potvin ed. p. 89) and Dutch *Lancelot* (ll. 1839 ff.). Cp. J. D. Bruce, *Romanic Review*, IX, 375 f. (1918), where the earlier literature on the subject of the relations of the different versions is given.

The second tomb-knight episode in Wauchier (ll. 29680 ff.) is probably nearer to the (as yet, unidentified) folk-tale of which both episodes are variants. In this second episode Perceval comes upon a marble tomb under a tree and a knight confined in it. In compliance with the knight's petition, Perceval cuts off a limb of the tree and prizes open the tomb, thereby freeing the knight. No sooner is the imprisoned man out than he knocks his liberator over into the tomb and shuts down the lid. He seizes still further Perceval's mule, but the animal, being enchanted, will not move, so that the ungrateful knight finally has to return, liberate Perceval, and resume his old place in the tomb, the lid of which now falls with such force that it shakes the earth.

In her *Studies in the Fairy Mythology of Arthurian Romance*, p. 223, note 5 (Boston, 1903) Miss Paton includes in a list of supposed parallels to this story an episode in the Welsh tale, *Pwyll, Prince of Dyved* (Loth's *Mabinogion*[2], I, 99 ff.), where Pwyll, following the

not grant Perceval her love, unless he will bring her the head
of the white stag in the park nearby. He takes her hound along
with him, kills the stag, and is cutting it up, when the ill-con-
ditioned owner of the stag, a girl, seizes the hound and will not
give it up, unless Perceval will challenge a knight who lives in
a tomb. The pursuit of the hound leads thus to a variety of extravagant adventures, which end in Perceval's enjoying the promised favors of its mistress. It has an almost comic effect that the
hero should be deflected from the quest of the Holy Grail by
such a series of achievements, the object of which, after all, is
the gratification of a merely sensual passion. This hero, in fact,
had made the pursuit of the hound the excuse for what in actual life
would be regarded as an act of much greater moral obliquity —
namely, the abandonment of Blanchefleur, whom, after lying with
her, he had promised to marry. But Wauchier was no ascetic, and
he was exploiting the story of the Grail by new inventions simply
for the entertainment of his high-born patrons, and, except in
so far as it contributed to that purpose, it had no more interest
for him than the materials of chivalrous and amorous adventure
which make up the greater part of his poem. Although inferior
to the work of his anonymous predecessor, Wauchier's continuation
contains some happily told episodes — for instance, the story of
Perceval's return to his old home and the scene of recognition there
with his sister[18] — also, his subsequent visit to his hermit uncle.

---

advice of the fay, Rhiannon, manages to entrap Gwawl in a sack. The
differences, however, are too great, and I agree with Josef Baudis,
*Folk-Lore*, XXVII, 44 f. (1916), that there is no connection between
the two stories. He compares with the Wauchier episode a trick in
the Irish *Naked Hangman* (*Eriu*, VII, 201) and the tale of *The
Three Gifts*, in which the hero, imprisoned in the magical bag, is a
devil or Death. "He gets a sound hammering" in the bag. It seems
to me, however, that the true original of Wauchier's tomb-knight incidents must be some ghost story concerning a haunted tomb, such
as abound in all parts of the world.

[18] This character, who figures also in the *Queste del Saint Graal*,
is, no doubt, the invention of Wauchier. Cp. Brugger, *Zs. f. frz.
Spi. u. Litt.*, XXXI[2], 126.

Coming next to Manessier, we have here an even more rambling romance of adventure than in the case of Wauchier's continuation, and in a much duller style. Episodes concerning Gawain and Sagremor, for example, that have nothing to do with the main action are introduced. Manessier's work is mainly a compilation of the mustiest commonplaces of Arthurian romance — knights vanquishing their adversaries and sending them to Arthur's court, etc. The only episodes of any interest are the variant of the Black Hand episode (ll. 39790ff.) and Perceval's visits to the Grail castle (ll. 44591ff.), the first really invented by Pseudo-Wauchier, as we have seen above, the latter modelled on Wauchier and Chrétien. Besides Chrétien, Wauchier and Pseudo-Wauchier, Manessier makes use of the prose romances of the so-called Walter Map cycle.[19]

Let us look, however, more closely at the Grail incidents in Manessier.

In Manessier we have two visits to the Grail castle. The first is merely a completion of the visit which Wauchier had begun to describe. Manessier here simply takes up the narrative where Wauchier left off. On this visit Perceval asks all the questions which he had failed to ask on his original visit — with such disastrous consequences to the land. The Fisher King gives him the most ample information on each of the points concerned, so that the real Grail problem would seem to be solved. But it turns out now that, according to a conception which the writer borrowed from the prose Grail romances, the Fisher King had received his wound from the fragments of a sword with which his brother, Goon Desert, had been slain, and it will never heal until an unknown knight has slain the murderer (Partinal). So this gives the author the excuse for several thousand lines of disconnected adventures, with the usual complement of damsels, hermits, etc. At last, Perceval kills Partinal and returns to the Grail castle with the head hanging at his saddle-bow. As soon as the king learns of this, he leaps to his feet and is straightway made whole. There is a repetition that night of the Grail procession at supper, and after-

---

[19] Cp. Heinzel, p. 73.

wards, on Perceval's disclosing his name to the king, it is discovered that the young knight is his own sister's son. The king
wishes to hand over his crown at once to his nephew, but the latter
refuses to take it, so long as his uncle is living. Perceval returns
now to Arthur's court — has, of course, new adventures on the
way — and when he arrives there, Arthur has a record of his
achievements written down and kept in a box at Sàlisbury. We
have here an imitation of the conclusion of the prose *Queste del
Saint Graal,* where the story of the deeds of the Quest-knights
is said to have been preserved in the same manner. The Grail
damsel now appears and tells Perceval that his uncle is dead. Perceval goes to the Grail castle, accompanied by all the court, who
assist at his crowning and remain with him a month, during
which time the Grail feeds all with the costliest foods. He marries
his cousins, the two Grail-bearers, to two valiant kings and reigns
in peace for seven years, after which time he follows a hermit
into the wilderness, accompanied by Grail, lance, and holy dish.
He serves the Lord for ten years, and, when he dies, Grail, lance
and dish were, doubtless, carried up to heaven, for since that day
no man has seen them.

There is no need of pointing out the numerous differences of
conception in matters of detail which Manessier exhibits as compared with his predecessors;[20] for these differences simply mean
that he has chosen to modify or add to the narrative according
to his own pleasure. There is no ground for assuming that he
had access to any sources for the legend of the Grail other than the
romances in verse and prose on this theme that we still possess.[21]

The same thing (*pace* Brugger and Miss Weston) applies to
the last writer of the series, viz. Gerbert.[22] He is acquainted with

---

[20] Heinzel, pp. 59 ff., has done this for Manessier and, 74 ff., for
Gerbert.

[21] Nutt, p. 182, is so possessed with the prejudices of a folk-
lorist that he not only believes that Manessier drew from oral Grail
traditions, but thinks that he represents them more closely than Chrétien.

[22] Miss Weston in her *Legend of Sir Perceval,* I, 140 ff. takes
Gerbert's account of Perceval's experience with the sword which he
received at the Grail castle, as evidence that he was using not merely

all the writers who have thus far been discussed and with the Grail prose-romances as well.[23]

Chrétien, but "the source of Chrétien's sword story, and that source was an elaborate and well-thought-on poem" (p. 145). But she, herself, says (p. 144) that this account is "thoroughly consistent with the indications given by Chrétien", and her only reason for refusing to accept it as Gerbert's own invention is that he does not develop the episode of Perceval's marriage with the same consistency. I need not point out how purely subjective this reasoning is. Besides, I may remark that the defects of the marriage episode are due to Gerbert's introduction of a didactic, moral, aim into the narrative. That has often brought better poets than Gerbert to grief. The conception of the sword, which we have already in Chrétien, may be ultimately derived from the Wieland saga, as Miss Weston, pp. 149 ff., contends, but that circumstance would have no bearing on the present question.

Brugger, *Zs. f. frz. Spr. u. Litt.*, XXXI[2], 130 (1907), says: "Ich bin auch der Meinung, dass Gerbert ausser Chrétien's *Perceval* mit Fortsetzung noch einen Perceval-Roman gekannt hat. Die Connection Percevals mit dem Schwanritter bei Gerbert und Wolfram beweist, dass jener Roman entweder Kiot's *Perceval* oder die gemeinsame Quelle von Chrétien und Kiot (das Buch des Grafen Philipp?) war." Later (p. 131) he thinks this romance, used by Gerbert, was probably Kiot's (Guiot's). Somewhat similarly before him, E. Martin in his edition of Wolfram, Strassburg, 1900—1903, II, Einleitung, p. XLII, says that Wolfram and Gerbert, who, independently of each other, show the combination of the Swan-knight and Grail stories, may have both drawn on "ältere französische Überlieferung". This hypothesis, however, is not necessary. At the time that Wolfram and Gerbert wrote, both stories were, so to speak, household words in Western Europe, and in Gerbert's case, especially, the suggestion to combine the two lay very near, for Pseudo-Wauchier, whose work he had before him, had already exploited the Swan-knight story in the incident of the swan-drawn boat, ll. 20857 ff. It is indifferent for the present inquiry whether we believe that the Swan-knight legend had a separate existence, before it became attached to the house of Bouillon or not. W. Golther, *Romanische Forschungen*, II, 103 ff. (1889), and G. Paris, *Romania*, XXVI, 580 ff. (1897), for example, affirm that it had, but J. F. D. Blöte *Zs. f. roman. Ph.*, XXI, 176 ff. (1897), XXV, 1 ff. (1901), XXVI, 1 ff. (1903), denies this. The former are, doubtless, right.

[23] Cp. Heinzel, 75 f. He shares with Chrétien's other continuators, as distinguished from Chrétien, himself, the revenge motive, and, like them, he discards the father of the Fisher King. His knowledge of

He connects his continuation[24] with Perceval's visit to the Grail castle at the end of Wauchier's division of the *Conte del Graal* (l. 34934). Wauchier, doubtless, intended that Perceval should finally achieve the Grail adventure at this point, and that would have ended the story; but Gerbert, who wished to make his own contribution to the Grail theme, does not complete in that sense the episode which Wauchier left unfinished. In the new poet's conception Perceval is still unable to join together the pieces of the broken sword, owing to his sin, in being indirectly the cause of his mother's death (VI, 163), when he insisted on leaving home against her will. Having thus made his own work possible, Gerbert launches out into a narrative of fantastic and chivalrous adventures of the ordinary kind, the best of which, perhaps, relate to the mysterious sword of the Grail castle. His hero has to expiate still further, however, his sin in respect to Blanchefleur, whom he had promised to marry. In this connection we have a precious bit of mediaevalism in the description (VI, 199ff.) of how the lovers pass the night before their wedding in bed together, yet abstain from carnal intercourse and mutually laud the virtues of chastity. Indeed, they practise this doctrine of continence until Perceval has achieved the Grail adventure, and would have done so to the end, had not a celestial voice on their wedding night

---

Pseudo-Wauchier is plain from his adoption (Potvin, IV, 166ff.) of the *motif* that, immediately after Perceval asks about the Grail, the blight which rested on the land was lifted, and of the further *motif*, VI, 249, of the swan-drawn boat. From Wauchier, too, he borrows, among other things, the character of Perceval's sister, invented by that writer, and he follows both Wauchier and Pseudo-Wauchier in conceiving of the Grail King as not disabled.

[24] Potvin, VI, 259, speaks of Gerbert's portion of the *Conte del Graal*, as an interpolation, but, as I have stated above, there is no convincing evidence that he knew Manessier's continuation, so that it is better to regard it with Nutt, p. 22, note, as an "independent finish" to the poem.

R. H. Griffith, "The Magic Balm of Gerbert and *Fierabras* and a Query", MLN, XXV, 102f. (1910), suggests that in the passage concerning the magic balm, Potvin, VI, 183ff., Gerbert is imitating *Fierabras*. The resemblance, however, may be accidental.

(VI, 209), instructed Perceval that the "delit carnel" was permissible in marriage, for the begetting of issue and avoidance of sin, and predicted that among his posterity would be the Swan-Knight and the three conquerors of Jerusalem. This allusion to Godefroi de Bouillon, the hero of the first Crusade, and his brothers, Eustace and Baldwin, as connected with the Swan-Knight, is imitated from the metrical romance, *Le Chevalier au Cygne*, which derives the house of Bouillon from that character. In the end (VI, 256ff.) Perceval again reaches the Grail castle, is welcomed by the Fisher King, witnesses the Grail procession, unites the broken sword — in short, brings to a conclusion the adventures of the Holy Grail.

None of these continuators of Chrétien, however, except Pseudo-Wauchier, rose above mediocrity, and, inasmuch as they are entirely secondary, being, in the present writer's opinion, without access to any independent sources for the conception of the Grail, it is needless to dwell longer upon their additions.[25]

---

[25] The Berne MS. of Wauchier, which is summarized by A. Rochat, *Über einen bisher unbekannten Percheval li Galois* (Zürich, 1855), adds (pp. 90 ff.) a brief conclusion of 56 lines to Wauchier's unfinished work. Perceval here ends the Grail quest by asking the necessary question. He is said to be the son of Alains li Gros and Enigeus. As Nutt remarks, p. 19, this shows use of Robert's *Joseph*. Heinzel, p. 59, objects that in Robert's poem Alain is not called "li Gros". See, however, the prose version, p. 127.

# Chapter V.

# Sir Perceval of Galles.

Besides the great *Conte del Graal* of Chrétien and his successors, there are three other important works that deal with the story of Perceval or the Grail, viz. the Middle English metrical romance, *Sir Perceval of Galles* (composed about 1370), the *Parzival* of Wolfram von Eschenbach, composed early in the thirteenth century, and the Welsh tale, *Peredur*, which was probably written somewhere about the year 1300. The fiercest controversies have raged in regard to these works, but, in the present writer's opinion, this is due to the baleful assumption that has come down from the Romantic Era to the effect that mediaeval poets were incapable of inventing anything themselves — they were always merely transcribing hypothetical sources. But nobody has ever explained why, if the authors of hypothetical sources were so gifted with invention, the authors of the works actually preserved should be so destitute of this faculty.

Let us take first the *Sir Perceval of Galles*. The peculiarity of this romance is that it contains nothing about the Grail, though it strongly resembles Chrétien's *Perceval* in other respects. The authority of Gaston Paris[1] gave currency to the view that this poem stood closest of all extant works to the primitive form of the story of Perceval, which, he supposed, belonged to Welsh oral

---

[1] *Histoire Littéraire de la France*, XXX, 259ff. G. Paris here expresses strong approval of W. Hertz's discussion of the subject, which antedated his own. The essay on the Grail by the latter is now easily accessible in his *Parzival von Wolfram von Eschenbach, neu bearbeitet*, pp. 413ff. For the English poem, see pp. 435ff.

tradition, so that it represents best the versions of that story which was used both by Chrétien and by the author of the Welsh *Peredur*. Miss Weston[2] and others have laid stress on some points of supposed agreement even between the English poem and Wolfram's *Parzival*, which, they argue, go back to a common source. The whole subject has been most fully discussed by R. H. Griffith in his treatise, *Sir Perceval of Galles* (Chicago, 1919),[3] and by A. C. L. Brown in his study, "The Grail and the English *Sir Perceval*."[4] Griffith endeavors to adduce parallels to the Middle English romance from various Celtic folk-tales, and his conclusion is that the English poem is not only wholly independent of Chrétien, but is merely "an English singer's versification of a folktale that was known in his district of Northwest England."[5] His parallels, however, are forced, in the extreme, and, in most cases, bear no essential resemblance to the Middle English poem. This

---

[2] *Legend of Sir Perceval*, I, 319, Cp. too, A. C. L. Brown, *"The Grail* and the English *Sir Perceval"* MPh., XVI, 553 ff. (1919).

[3] Cp. end of next chapter (note).

[4] MPh. XVI, 553 ff. (1919), XVII, 361 ff. (1919), XVIII, 661 ff. (1921). For comment on Brown's attempt in the first two sections of his study to connect the English poem with Wolfram and the *Lanzelet* cp. note just cited. The third section consists of a collection of supposed Irish parallels — to me, unconvincing — to incidents in *Sir Perceval*, cited to prove that the English romance has an Irish source. As I have stated in the text above, however, I see no necessity of looking further than Chrétien for a source.

[5] This conclusion is manifestly untenable. Cp. my review of Griffith's book in RR., IV, 125 ff. (1913). So, too, Brugger, *Zs. f. frz. Spr. u. Litt.*. XLIV[2], 170 ff. (1917); in other respects, he finds much to commend in Griffith's book. The complete agreement in the order of incidents between Chrétien and the English romance and the French nomenclature of the latter prove conclusively that *Sir Perceval of Galles* is based on a French original. *Acheflour*, the name of the heroine in *Sir Perceval*, is, I may remark, in passing, merely a MS corruption of *Blancheflor (Blanchefleur)*, the name of Chrétien's heroine. Nothing is commoner in mediaeval MSS. than the dropping of initial letters in proper names and the loss of *n* in the same. The latter error is, of course, due to neglect of the stroke (over the preceding vowel), which is so often used in these MSS. to denote *n*.

poem, however, seems to me plainly a mere adaptation of Chrétien's *Perceval* with the Grail left out. Moreover, the author had before him not only Chrétien's genuine work, but a spurious prologue, known as the Bliocadrans-prologue, which is found in two MSS. This spurious composition contains an account of the manner in which Perceval's father died and also of his youth. Accordingly, we have in the English *Sir Perceval* the story of Perceval's childhood given as well as the incidents of his career after he sets out for Arthur's court.[6] There is in the English poem an episode, not represented in Chrétien, in which the hero rescues a besieged lady and marries her. There are somewhat similar stories in the Latin prose romance of the thirteenth century, *De Ortu Waluuanii* and in *Yder*, a French romance in verse of the same century — and, no doubt, the English poet drew on some source of this kind for the particular episode.[7] As he approaches the episode of the Grail castle in Chrétien, he abandons his source, describes how, on hearing news of his mother, the hero sought her, found her demented, and going with her to the dwelling of a giant whom he had slain, cured her of insanity by a magic drink. With his mother he returns to his queen and his realm. Afterward he went to the Holy Land and there he was killed.

The motive that actuated the English poet in omitting the Grail incidents from his poem is probably the fact that they differed altogether from the usual material of the romances. The mystery of it all may well have puzzled him. The writer is by

---

[6] Hertz, *Parzival*, p. 438, cites as evidence that the English *Sir Perceval* drew from a more primitive source than Chrétien's poem, an approximate agreement between the former and the Italian poem *Carduino* (second half of the fourteenth century) a romance of the *Bel Inconnu* type, in a certain detail: In both the hero is a rustic simpleton, brought up in the forest, and in both he begins his martial experience with javelins (in *Carduino* he has two, in *Sir Perceval* one). The last detail is not very important, but, most likely, Carduino derived it from a version of the Perceval tale. This is, probably, true, likewise, of the simpleton *motif*.

[7] Cp. my *Historia Meriadoci and De Ortu Waluuanii*, p. LIX, Baltimore, 1913.

no means devoid of constructive skill, but there is no ground for believing that he, any more than the authors of the other Middle English romances, was very highly educated or that he had a brain for subtleties. These works deal, as a rule, with stock themes — fighting, especially with pagans and giants, witches, etc. — and it is quite likely that the author of the present poem balked at so unfamiliar a theme as the Grail. This would be particularly true, if he merely had before him Chrétien's poem with the spurious Bliocadrans-prologue, but none of the continuations. In view of the length of Chrétien's *Perceval* plus these continuations, and the consequent paucity of copies in circulation, all the probabilities are that such was the case. But Chrétien's work, being unfinished, leaves the Grail unexplained, and one can easily comprehend, then, why the English author should have shirked so difficult a subject. Moreover, it is to be remembered that the English romance was already fairly long (according to English standards), before it reached the Grail episode in Chrétien, and the writer may have concluded, very naturally, that his work was long enough. Surely, in view of all these reasonable considerations we have no cause to be surprised, if we find the Grail theme omitted in this poem alone of all the romances of which Perceval is the hero.[8]

---

[8] Cp. my review of Griffith's book in RR., IV, 125 ff. (Jan.-March, 1913).

It is worth noting that in a romance which was, in reality, a sort of continuation of Chrétien's *Perceval* and in which the hero was a son of Perceval, the Grail was omitted. I refer to the *Morien*, which only survives in the Dutch version, *Moriaen*. Cp. p. 331, note 33, below. G. Paris, *Hist. Litt. de la France*, XXX, 252 f., observed these peculiarities of the *Morien*.

# Chapter VI.
# Wolfram's Parzival.

No problem of the Grail literature has excited more active discussion than that of the sources of Wolfram von Eschenbach's *Parzival*.[1] Chrétien's poem is represented in its entirety in Wolfram, but the German poet has prefixed to the main narrative an

---

[1] As is customary, my *Parzival* references will be to Lachmann's divisions of the text, each containing 30 lines. These divisions are indicated in all editions of the poem.

Wolfram was a Bavarian knight (cp. the *Parzival*, 115, 11 and 121, 7) and the *Parzival* was composed in the first decade of the thirteenth century. At 379,19 there is a reference to an event that took place in 1203—1204, viz. the siege of Erfurt by Wolfram's patron, the Landgrave, Hermann von Thüringen. From the nature of the allusion it appears that that event was comparatively recent. On the other hand, Hermann von Thüringen, who died April 25, 1217, was still alive when Wolfram, at 297, 16 ff., addressed him, personally. So this part of the *Parzival* was certainly composed before the date just given. For other indications respecting the date of the *Parzival*, cp. R. Lück, *Über die Abfassungszeit des Parzival* (Halle diss. 1878).

It is nowadays generally agreed that Wolfram's *Titurel*, which deals with an episode of Chrétien's *Perceval*, 11, 3390 ff. — namely the one in which Perceval, after leaving the Grail castle, comes upon his cousin (called *Sigune* by the German poet), supporting the dead body of her slain lover in her lap — was written after the *Parzival* not improbably, even after the *Willehalm*. Cp., especially, A. Leitzmann, "Untersuchungen über Wolfram's Titurel," PBB, XXVI, 93 ff. (1901) — particularly, pp. 145 ff. The poem was left a fragment — doubtless, on account of the author's death.

As regards the *Willehalm* (also incomplete), which is based on *Aliscans*, an Old French *chanson de geste* of the Guillaume d'Orange cycle, Book IX, at least, must have been composed after April 25, 1217, the date of the death of Hermann von Thüringen, as stated above, for in that book (417,12) Wolfram alludes to Hermann as dead.

account (Books I—II) of the life of Perceval's father and he has
completed (Books XIV—XVI) the account of the quest of the
Grail which Chrétien left unfinished. Moreover, in these additions, both at the beginning and at the end, we are made acquainted with an elder half-brother of Percival's, named Feirefiz,[2]
who does not appear in Chrétien. There would be nothing strange
in it, if Wolfram had supplied these additions from his own imagination. His continuation of Chrétien's poem is wholly independent of the continuation by the French poets discussed above, but
the tantalizing condition in which Chrétien left the Grail-quest,
even the nature of the sacred vessel being unexplained, would
naturally stimulate him, as it did the first (anonymous) continuator
of his *Perceval*, Wauchier, and the rest, to develop the story to a

---

[2] I. e. Old French "vairs fiz" = "party-colored son", his father
being white and his mother black. With respect to the variegated
coloring of his skin and hair, Wolfram (57, 27) compares him to a
magpie. Cp., too, 758, 17 ff. The poet, doubtless, hit upon this bizarre
name, *vairs fiz*, because in Chrétien's *Perceval* (ll. 336, 537, *et
passim*) Perceval, the character's half-brother, is often addressed as
"biax fi(l)z" = "beautiful son." Surely, no French-speaking person
would have invented such a name as "vairs fiz." In Wolfram the
father of Parzïval and Feirefiz is named *Gahmuret*. Rochat, *Germania*, III, 114 (1858), identified this name rightly with *Gomeret*,
name of a kingdom in Chrétien's *Erec*, l. 1775, and in other romances,
which is, also, occasionally a personal name in these romances. Cp.
W. Hertz, *Parzival*, p. 469, (Stuttgart, 1898). Brugger's identification,
however, of *Gomeret* with *Sagremor*, Morf-*Festschrift*, pp. 55 ff., is
forced, in the extreme. On his attempt to connect the story of Gahmuret
with a passage in the *Livre d'Artus* of MS. 337 cp. p. 331, note 33,
below. Perceval's mother is named *Herzeloyde* in Wolfram, i. e. Old
French, *Herselot*.

In his important study, *Wolfram's Stil und der Stoff des Parzival*,
pp. 63 f. (Wien, 1918, in the *Sitzungsberichte* of the Vienna Academy
of Sciences, Band 180, Abhandlung 4) — which, in the rest of this
chapter, I shall refer to merely as "Singer" — S. Singer denies the
identity of *Gahmuret (Gamuret)* and the *Gomeret* of the romances.
But the names in the *Parzival* — as far as they are comprehensible
— are all either drawn from the romances or fabricated on the model
of the names in these works, so that there is no good reason for
questioning the identity.

conclusion. Similarly, the addition of the preliminary narrative, which tells of the hero's parentage, the adventures and marriages of his father, was quite natural, in view of the models with which Thomas's *Tristan* and Chrétien's *Cliges* supplied him.[3] We have seen that a French poet was also inspired — no doubt, by these same models (especially, Thomas's *Tristan*) — to prefix an early history of the hero's parents to the *Perceval*. But a difficulty is created by Wolfram's appeal to an unknown Kyot (Kiot) as the source of his poem. This Kyot is first mentioned, l. 12469 (416, 20, of Lachmann's text), that is to say, near the middle of the *Parzival*, and in a quite informal fashion. Contrary to the custom of the romance-writers, the German poet cites no authority here at the beginning of his poem, where the citation of a genuine authority would naturally belong, but at the point just noted he observes off-hand, at the end of a speech (416, 17), that a king's follower, named Liddamus, came forward. Kyot, he says, calls him thus. He also says here that Kyot is a Provençal, but curiously adds that, using a source in a heathen language,[4] he (Kyot) wrote his work in French. He refers to this same Kyot in other places,[5] only two of which, however, possess any importance. In

---

[3] Cp. the story of Tristan's parents in Thomas's *Tristan*, of Cliges's parents in Chrétien's *Cliges*, To be sure, there is no evidence that Wolfram knew Thomas's poem. In Eilhart's *Tristan*, which he knew well (cp. Lichtenstein's edition of Eilhart, pp. CXCIII ff.), the love-affairs of Tristan's parents are treated very succinctly. But he was certainly familiar with the *Cliges*. See his references thereto, 334, 11, 586, 27, 712, 8. The last two are to the love-story of Cliges' parents.

[4] The lines (416, 25 ff.) run:

Kiot ist ein Provenzal,
der dise aventiur von Parzival
heidensch geschriben sach.
Swaz er en franzoys da von gesprach,
bin ich niht der witze laz,
das sage ich tiuschen fürbaz.

So the story of Perceval was originally a heathen tale! The same statement is made, with different wording, 453, 11 ff.

[5] The passages are: 431, 2 (ich sage iu als Kiot las), 453, 5 ff. — 455, 22, 776, 10 (ob Kyot die wârheit sprach), 805, 10 (op der

one of these (453, 11ff.) the poet is describing what purports
to be Kyot's source, — namely, the pretended work of a half-Jew,
Flegetanis, on the history of the Grail, which Kyot found, cast
aside in the city of Toledo (in Spain). This Flegetanis, whose
father was a pagan and who must, therefore, have owed his descent from Solomon to his mother, is here said to have been a
great astronomer and he had read the name of the Grail in the
stars and had declared that a host of angels had brought the
sacred object down to earth, where only the chaste and the good
of the Christian faith might guard it. Through application, combined with knowledge of necromancy, Kyot was able to decipher
the strange characters in which this heathen (Arabic) book was
written and the virtues of Christian baptism enabled him, still
further, to understand its contents, which, as a matter of fact,
however, Flegetanis, who penned it, seems to have understood very
well. He (Kyot) now began to seek the story of the Grail in Latin
books, in order to discover where there was a people suitable to
cherish the Grail. He read chronicles of the various countries,
Britain, France, Ireland, and elsewhere, and he found at last (455,
12) in a chronicle of "Anschow"[6] — doubtless, Anjou (in France)
— the story which he sought. In this story he read concerning
Mazadan[7] and how the Grail descended in succession to Titurel,[8]

---

Provenzal die wârheit las), 827, 1ff. (at the end of the poem). It
will be observed that the first, third and fourth passages have no
value — are, indeed, merely phrases to make out the rhyme.

There is another Kyot in Wolfram's poem — viz. Sigune's father.
He is a minor character in the narrative, and, of course, is not to
be confounded with the Kyot (Kiot) to whom Wolfram appeals as his
source. For this other Kyot, who is a duke and the paternal uncle
of Condwiramurs (Parzival's wife), cp. 190, 6, 477, 4, 797, 4 etc.

[6] The coupling of *Anschowe* in the poem with Wales (103, 7)
and with Great Britain, Ireland and France, (455, 10ff.) leaves no
room for doubt that Wolfram's *Anschowe* is primarily Anjou. On the
Austrian *Ansowe (Antschau)* see p. 321, note 16, below.

[7] The interpretation of *Mazadan* as derived from an Irish *Mac
Adam* — "sons of Adam" (cp. Martin's edition II, 64) is, I believe,
purely fanciful. So, too, with Singer's interpretation (p. 49) of the
name as equivalent to "Macedonian" — i. e. Alexander the Great —

to his son Frimutel, and to Frimutel's son, Anfortas (Amfortas),[9] who was Perceval's maternal uncle and keeper of the Grail at the time that Perceval visited the Grail castle. Thus the Grail Kings, like their kinsman, Perceval's father, are Angevins. — Again, in the concluding paragraph of his poem (827, 1ff.), Wolfram says that if Chrétien de Troyes has not told the story of the Grail correctly, that may well arouse the anger of Kyot,

on the basis of later mediaeval conceptions of that hero's union with a fay. Wolfram had already (56, 17ff.) mentioned Mazadan as an ancestor of Gahmuret (as well as Uther Pendragon) by a fay, named Terdelaschoye (Tere de la joie), who had carried him off to Feimurgân (Fee Morgan). Through a blunder he has here — as elsewhere (400, 8, 496, 8, 585, 14f.) — given the name of the fay to the land and *vice versa*. I cannot agree, however, with Singer's estimate, p. 49, of the decisive value of this blunder in proving the existence of Kyot. It sprang, no doubt, from the poet's misunderstanding of some French text, but his French reading was not confined to poems on Perceval. It is one of the proper names in Wolfram which still await a satisfactory explanation.

⁸ In Wolfram's poem, 240, 24, Parzival, on his first visit to the Grail castle, saw this beautiful old man lying on a bed in a chamber apart. Afterwards, Trevrizent, 501, 22, explains that this was Titurel, the first person to whom the Grail was committed (first Grail King). The name, which Wolfram, doubtless, took from Hartmann von Aue's *Erec*, (l. 1650), is, probably, derived from French *Tydorel*, the name of the hero af a Breton *lai*. The stories of the two characters, however, are not connected.

Titurel corresponds to the Grail King's (Fisher King's) father, who is described in Chrétien's *Perceval*, ll. 6378—6393, as being sustained solely by a sacred wafer, which was brought to him in the Grail, and as not having left his room for fifteen years. It will be noted, however, that Titurel is grandfather, not father, of the actual Grail King, as in Chrétien. The French poet, indeed, does not mention the Grail King's grandfather, nor does he give definite names either to the Grail King or his father. The conferring of definite names on persons who are left unnamed in Chrétien is found all through the *Parzival*. This tendency is not confined to Wolfram. We find it throughout Arthurian romance. The later a romance is, the more liberal it is with names.

⁹ OFr. *Enfertez (Enfermetez)* = "Infirmity". In such Old French words *an-*, *am-*, instead of *en-*, was a common variant in the spelling.

who has given us the correct version. In this passage he speaks
of Kyot again as a, Provençal. The name is, doubtless, identical
with French *Guiot* and we know of two writers of that name in
mediaeval French literature. One of these was Guiot de Provins
(a contemporary of Wolfram's), who composed some lyrics in the
style of the *amour courtois,* but is best known as author of the
so-called *Bible,*[10] which is a satirical work on contemporary society. Some critics have been inclined to accept this writer as
Wolfram's Kyot and to explain the German poet's designation
of him as a Provencal as due to a misunderstanding of the French
place-name, Provins, for the name of the famous country, Provence.[11] But Guiot's extant works are of a totally different cha-

[10] The works of Guiot de Provins have been recently (1915)
reedited by John Orr in the Manchester University Studies.

[11] The most recent argument for the identification is E. Brugger's,
*Archiv für das Studium der neueren Sprachen,* CXVIII, 233f.
(1907). Brugger, of course, assumes a French original (by Guiot de
Provins) as Chrétien's source, and ascribes Wolfram's *Provenzal* to
an error on the part of the German poet. — For earlier arguments
in favor of the identification (which K. Wackernagel, *Altfranzösische
Lieder und Leiche,* p. 191, Basel, 1846, was the first to suggest)
see, especially, San Marte (A. Schulz), "Wolfram von Eschenbach und
Guiot von Provins", *Germania,* III, 445 ff. (1858) and *Parzivalstudien,* I, (Halle, 1861).

In his "Wolfram und Kiot", *Zs. f. deutsche Philologie,* XXXVIIIff.
198ff. (1906), Paul Hagen argues that Wolfram follows his (hypothetical lost) original in the closest manner. But this view of the
German poet's relation to his source adds new difficulties to the
acceptance of the work of a Provençal lyric poet as that source; for,
according to the *Parzival,* 158, 13ff., this source states ("Als uns
diu aventiure giht") that no painter from Köln or Maastricht (well-
known art-centers in those days) could have designed a more perfect
figure than Parzival's was, as he appeared on horseback, when he met
Iwanet. A Provençal surely, would never have hit upon such an
image. Hagen, consequently, ascribes Wolfram's citation of Kyot to
an error and proposes as the real author of the sources of the *Parzival*
Philip of Poitiers, later Bishop of Durham, who accompanied Richard
Coeur de Lion to Steiermark, on the latter's return from Palestine
in 1192. His main reasons for doing so are that Trevrezent's expedition, 496, 1 ff., follows nearly the same course as Richard's journey,

racter from Wolfram's poem and there is no reason to believe that he ever wrote a romance.[12] There was, apparently, another Guiot of the same period who is only known from an allusion in a poem of the thirteenth century as the author of a (lost) tale of incest.[13]

that Philip was deeply attached to the House of Anjou (which the *Parzival* was supposed to glorify and to which Richard I belonged), and that he knew the cities above-mentioned, for he attended the election of Otto IV, Emperor of Germany, at Köln (Cologne) in 1198.

This wild theory, as far as I know, has not gained a single adherent. — Hagen is so loath to grant Wolfram any imaginative capacity whatever that he even regards the *Titurel* as adopted from another work by the same person who wrote the (supposed) source of the *Parzival*. In respect to this theory, too, I believe, he stands alone.

[12] The fact that the extant works of Guiot de Provins are so different from Wolfram's *Parzival* should be given greater weight than Brugger is willing to admit. None of them, it will be noted, are narrative poems, and there is no evidence at all that he ever wrote a narrative poem. Moreover, what ground do his extant works afford us for expecting from the author's pen a narrative of the most bizarre quality, like the Gāhmuret and Feirefiz episodes in the *Parzival?* The distinctive quality of the best of these works — the *Bible* — is its shrewd common sense, enlivened by a racy vein of satirical humor. But whatever may be his merits, the author's muse is pedestrian, indeed, as compared with Wolfram's. Moreover, Singer, p. 43, aptly points out that there is not a trace of Wolfram's obscurity in Guiot de Provins and that the latter, instead of idealizing the Knights Templars, speaks disparagingly of them. Against such considerations, the few details of parallelism between Guiot's genuine writings and the *Parzival* have no weight. The point has sometimes been made, that in his *Willehalm* Wolfram renders the French place-name *Provins* correctly by *Provis* (which would be its regular equivalent in Middle High German) and hence that he would not have confounded *Provins* and *Provence* in his *Parzival*. *Willehalm*, however, is later than *Parzival*, and, hence, as Brugger *op. cit.* p. 233, note 1, observes, Wolfram might have become better informed in the interval as to the differences between the two.

[13] G. Gröber, who first printed the extract that concerns us, in his *Grundriss*, I, 430, note 2, speaks of the poem as a *miracle* of the thirteenth century from a MS. of the Arsenal library, but gives it no nearer dating. The passage is reproduced somewhat more fully in W. Foerster's large edition (1890) of Chrétien's *Cliges*, p. XIII.

But in this same passage — a list of authors of the twelfth century — Chrétien is spoken of as author of the *Perceval,* and if
the Guiot in question had written a poem on the Grail, no doubt,
the fact would have been mentioned.[14]

Nevertheless, it is argued that Kyot must have been a real person, for only a Frenchman — indeed, only an Angevin or one

---

The writer is contrasting the low estate of poetry in his own day with
the different conditions that prevailed in the former age.   In this
connection he gives a list of the poetical celebrities of this former age
(the twelfth century), which comprises the names of Gautier d'Arras,
Chrétien and our Guiot, among others.   He says of Guiot:

> "Et Guios qui maint bel *miracle*
> Traita de cele damoisele
> Qui sen pere enfante pucele,"

and eleven lines further down:

> "Mais d'aus tous me tieg a Wiot,
> Por ce c'ainc ne vol rimer mot
> Por qu'il i eust faussete, etc."

Brugger, *loc. cit.* p. 233 (including notes 2 and 3) endeavors to
prove that this Guiot, too, is identical with Guiot de Provins and
Wolfram's Kyot, but the thread of his argument is tenuous to the last
degree, especially as regards Kyot.   Even if the *miracle* referred to
in the above-quoted extract did not belong to the literary *genre* of
that name, it must have been a religious poem of a quite limited
scope — which would certainly not bring the author, whether he was
Guiot de Provins or not, very close to a poem like Wolfram's *Parzival.*
Brugger observes that composers of lyrics (Cp. Wolfram's *la schantiure,*
416, 21) like Chrétien, also, often wrote romances.   On the other hand,
however, this was, of course, frequently not the case.

[14] This point is made by W. Foerster, p. 201 of the Introduction
to his Chrétien *Wörterbuch* (Halle, 1914).   The section of this Introduction (pp. 187 ff.) entitled *Wolfram und sein Kyot* and W. Golther's
address, *Parzival und der Gral in deutscher Sage des Mittelalters
und der Neuzeit* (Rostock, 1910), along with Lichtenstein's article,
give the strongest presentation of the case against the reality of
Wolfram's Kyot.   Golther's address is easily accessible in his *Zur
deutschen Sage und Dichtung,* pp. 154 ff. (Leipzig, 1911).

The couplet in the anonymous *miracle* about Chrétien runs as
follows:

> "Et Crestiens qui mout bel dist
> Quant Cleget et Percheval fist."

whose patron was of the house of Anjou — would have been interested in magnifying the Angevin dynasty by connecting the herc
of the poem and the Grail Kings generally with that house.[15] But
there is more than one possible explanation of this. First, it is
to be observed that there is no personal allusion or note in these
passages about Anjou. It is said (6, 26), that "Anschowe"
(presumably, Anjou) is Gahmuret's country and that Kyot found
the story of the Grail in a chronicle of that land, but we hear
nothing more about it. In Wolfram's time the rulers of Anjou,
being also kings of England, were — or had been a short time
before — the most powerful reigning house in Europe. Moreover,
they were closely connected with the great family of Guelphs in
North Germany, whose influence extended to the court of Wolfram's patron, Hermann of Thüringen. If Wolfram, then, wished
to exalt his hero, by connecting him with some actual dynasty
of the time, none would more naturally suggest itself to him than
the dynasty of Anjou. It is even more likely, however, that the
poet's relations with the Austrian noble family of "Anschowe" are
responsible for his fancy of making his hero belong to the world-
famous house of the same name.[16]

---

[15] In his edition of the *Parzival*, pp. XLff., Martin even goes
so far as to identify the hero of Wolfram's poem with a definite Count
of Anjou, viz. Fulco (Fouques), paternal grandfather of Henry II of
England. He was a Templar and King of Jerusalem, 1131—1143.
The parallel which Martin draws is throughout extremely forced. For
similar speculations before Martin, cp. Wechssler, *Sage vom heiligen
Gral*, pp. 174f., and J. F. D. Blöte's criticism of the same, *Anzeiger
f. d. Altertum*, XLIII, 350ff. According to Wechssler, Wolfram was
inspired to connect the house of Anjou with Perceval by the fact that
the house of Bouillon had been connected with the Swan-Knight.

In connection with these matters, it has been observed that no
Frenchman would have made Anjou a kingdom, as Wolfram (5,25) does.
The heraldic figure in the escutcheon of England, in the early thirteenth
century, which Martin mentions, viz. a black leopard, does not accord
very exactly, after all, with the panther, Perceval's crest.

[16] "Ansowe", "Antschau", was in the Austrian province of Steiermark, with which, according to many indications, Wolfram had some
intimate connection. Note the following details bearing on the subject:
Gandin's crest is a panther, (101, 7). This figure was, also, the crest

It is most probable, then, that in these appeals to Kyot Wolfram was merely indulging in the common mediaeval trick of bolstering up his own inventions with an imaginary authority.[17] Nobody disputes that, for the part of his poem which corresponds to Chrétien, he stands close to the latter — I would, myself, say, follows him closely, for at times they agree word for word.[18] On the other

on the escutcheon of Steiermark. Now, from early in the thirteenth century, the burgraves of Steyer were united by marriage with a noble family that took its name from Antschau. Moreover, in 1216, we find a nobleman of this neighborhood, Ulrich von Stubenberg, on an expedition to the Holy Land, using precisely the same heraldic device as Gahmuret (*Parzival*, 14, 27 ff.), viz. a silver anchor with a gold rope wrapped around it. Furthermore, Gandin, Gahmuret's father, as we are told by Trevrezent in the *Parzival* (498, 25), was named after Gandine (Gandein) in Steiermark. — On all these matters see more fully A. von Siegenfeld, *Das Landeswappen Steiermarks*, pp. 296 ff. (Graz, 1901), and A. Schönbach, *Anzeiger für deutsches Altertum,* XXVII, 149 ff. (1903).

[17] This practice of mediaeval writers is well-known. For a valuable article on the subject, with special reference to the Kyot problem (and denying Kyot's existence), see F. Wilhelm, "Über fabulistische Quellenangaben", PBB, XXXIII, 286 ff. (1908). Such fictions did not carry with them the stigma then that they now do. It has been urged, however, that Wolfram's whole poem shows that he was particularly honest and that he must have been, consequently, incapable of such fraudulent statements. But, after all, every man is the creature of his age, and a "Schalk", like Wolfram, would be under peculiar temptation to avail himself of the general license in this regard. Besides, as we shall see below, we know that he did falsely attribute the original of his *Willehalm* to Chrétien de Troyes.

[18] For more or less systematic comparisons of Wolfram's text with Chrétien's cp. Alfred Rochat, Wolfram von Eschenbach und Chrétien's de Troyes", *Germania,* III, 81 ff. (1858), Otto Küpp, "Die unmittelbaren Quellen des Parzival von Wolfram von Eschenbach", *Zs. f. deutsche Philologie,* XVII, 1 ff. (1885), and, especially, J. Lichtenstein, "Zur Parzivalfrage", PBB, XXII, 1 ff. (1897). The last-named article deals with the *Parzival* from almost every point of view, and, in my opinion, nothing better has been written about the poem. See, too, A. Birch-Hirschfeld, *Die Sage vom Gral,* pp. 243 ff. (Leipzig, 1877) for a very important comparison of the portions of the two poems that relate to Grail matters.

In Wolfram there are many misunderstandings of Chrétien's text

hand, that the additions are Wolfram's own is shown by their character. There is nothing similar to them in the literature of the French romances.[19] We have in the *Parzival* a pure Arthurian romance introduced by what appears almost as a travesty on the stock situations in the French Arthurian romances. Just as the heroes of the latter, attracted by Arthur's fame, usually go to his court, enroll themselves among his knights, and from this court as a centre set forth on adventures, here we find the hero of the preliminary episodes, Gahmuret, drawn by the same motives to the court of the Caliph of Bagdad, who, as Wolfram is careful to explain, corresponds in the heathen world to the Christian Pope at Rome. Then comes this same hero's championship and rescue of the black pagan heroine, Belacane, queen of Zazamanc in Africa, when she is besieged by a Christian (Scottish) army, and their subsequent marriage. This situation has, of course, numerous parallels in the French Arthurian romances — only the heroine in such cases is always white and a Christian. Perhaps, a remembrance of the loves of Guillaume d'Orange and Orable — who, to be sure, receives baptism — or of some other Christian knight and fair Saracen princess has influenced this latter episode. Especially bizarre is the impression which is produced by the piebald Feirefiz — as variegated in his color as a magpie, says Wolfram — the offspring of the union of the white hero and the black heroine.

As regards, still further, the books (XIV—XVI) at the end of the *Parzival*, which carry the narrative beyond the limits of Chrétien's *Perceval*, it is to be observed that Book XVI, in which the hero finally achieves the quest of the Grail, is indissolubly

---

which show that he used Chrétien directly. Cp. Lichtenstein, *op. cit.*, p. 57, notes 1 and 2. If Kyot really existed, his text in these places must have been identical with Chrétien's.

[19] This remains true of the coloring which is given to such additions and of the general conceptions by which they are inspired, even if one accepts at the same value as Singer the interesting list of parallels between Wolfram, on the one hand, and French and Provençal writers, on the other, in respect to phrase and imagery, which he has collected. pp. 15 ff.

connected with the characteristic conceptions of the Grail which had already been developed in the earlier books of the poem — especially the Fifth and Ninth. Now, since even the adherents of Kyot generally acknowledge that these conceptions originated with Wolfram and constitute his chief glory, as far as the *Parzival* is concerned, there is no valid ground for denying to him the sole responsibility for this part of his poem. And, after all, why should we refuse to concede to Wolfram any power of invention? In respect to originality of style,[20] of moral conceptions, and of ideas,

---

[20] Singer, pp. 5 ff., it is true, contends that this style (really Kyot's according to his theory) — tortuous, barock, but never failing in strength — was formed on the *trobar clus* (style purposely obscure) of certain Provençal lyrical poets, and, in proof thereof, assembles the parallels referred to in the last note. Many of these phrases and images, however, are such as might suggest themselves independently to contemporary authors in different lands. On the other hand, a considerable proportion of them did, no doubt, come to Wolfram, directly or indirectly, from the French. But, to say nothing of those elements which may have reached him from that quarter through German channels, he was, of course, acquainted with other French books, besides the source of the *Parzival*. He translated a *chanson de geste*, and it is purely gratuitous to set down to Kyot's account, and not to his, the knowledge of the two romances of antiquity, the *Roman de Troie* and the *Roman de Thebes*, which his work evinces (cp. Singer, pp. 22 f., 104 f.).

The style of the *Parzival* — one of the most individual in mediaeval literature — is substantially the same as that of the *Willehalm* and *Titurel*. Surely, the natural inference from this state of things is that the style in question was the expression of the author's own personality, not (as Singer, p. 126, supposes) that he acquired it from Kyot and that it stuck to him later in his *Willehalm* (to say nothing of the *Titurel*), although there was no suggestion of it in the French source of this poem.

In a far-fetched manner, Singer, p. 10, seeks still further support for his theory as to the existence of a French poem, in the obscure style, on Perceval from a supposed allusion to such a poem in the late metrical romance, *Escanor*, ll. 325 ff. (latter part of the thirteenth century). Kay is here charging Perceval unjustifiably with obscurity of speech; but this is, plainly, merely a sarcastic thrust at Perceval as a Welshman, for the stupidity of the Welsh was proverbial in the romances.

in general, he is recognized as superior to all of his predecessors in mediaeval poetry and unequalled among romance-writers even to the end of the period. He impresses his personality on almost every line of his poem and gives a subjective coloring to every part of his work. Why, then, should we deny him every spark of *narrative* originality? After all, the mere incidents in these additions require no great creative gift, e. g. a young knight's service at the court of a famous monarch, his rescue of a besieged lady,[21] a fight between friends or relatives that do not recognize each other. These are all commonplaces of the romances. It is the new setting, however, which is given these incidents, the originality of conception with which such incidents are invested and the grotesque and vivid detail with which they are set forth that count. Now, these latter features are certainly Wolfram's own, so that there is no ground for depriving him of the very moderate credit which is his due for the former. The creative act here is insignificant as compared with that which is involved in the sublime invention of the world-wide Grail community, which is indisputably his.

Moreover, we have the splendid *Titurel* fragments before us — the finest of all of Wolfram's compositions — to emphasize the falsity of the view that, where narrative elements are concerned, he was unable to rise above the level of a slavish reproduction of his originals. Aside from the superb lyrical passion of these fragments, they offer a train of incidents which none but the most extravagant adherents of Kyot[22] have denied to Wolfram's invention. They are not provided with the novel setting of the books of the *Parzival* in which Gahmuret is the principal figure, but otherwise they show an equal capacity for new combinations of old *motifs*.

---

[21] G. A. Heinrich, *Le Parcival de Wolfram d'Eschenbach et la légende du Saint-Graal,* p. 192 (Paris, 1855) has plausibly suggested that the siege of Patelamunt and the deliverance of Belacane were imitated from the similar siege of Pelrapeire and deliverance of Condwiramurs.

[22] For example, P. Hagen, "Wolfram und Kiot", *Zs. f. d. Ph.*, XXXVIII, 1 ff. (1906).

In view of the considerations which I have just presented,
it seems most likely that Wolfram had no other story concerning
Perceval and the Grail than Chrétien's before him and that he
deliberately tried to conceal his obligations to Chrétien by the
invention of an imaginary authority whom he arrays against the
French poet.[23] It has been suggested that he put forward this hoax,

---

[23] All the scholars cited p. 322 note 18, above, except Küpp, conclude that Wolfram's Kyot was a .fiction. The same opinion has been
held, also, by the following, among others: K. Simrock (in the later
editions of his translations of Wolfram's *Parzival* and *Titurel*, of
which the fifth appeared at Stuttgart in 1876), F. Zarncke (see pp. 317 ff.
of his *"Zur Geschichte der Gralsage"*, PBB., III, 304 ff. 1876), G.
Paris, (Société Historique et Cercle Saint-Simon, Bulletin 2, p. 100,
Paris 1883, and *Romania*, XXII, 166), O. Behaghel, *Literaturblatt*
for 1898, Cols. 115, 263, W. Golther in the address cited above (as
against his earlier belief in Kyot's existence, *Romanische Forschungen*,
V. 115 ff.), W. Foerster, pp. 187 ff. of the Introduction to his Chrétien
*Wörterbuch* (Halle, 1914).

Besides Küpp, the following are some of the scholars who have
expressed a belief in the reality of Kyot: San Marte, *Germania*, III,
445 ff., (1858) and elsewhere, K. Bartsch, in his successive editions of
the *Parzival* and *Titurel*, T. Urbach, *Über den Stand der Frage
nach den Quellen des Parzival*, Programm, Zwickau, 1872, R. Heinzel,
"Über Wolframs von Eschenbach *Parzival*," *Sitzungsberichte der
Kaiserlichen Akademie der Wissenschaften in Wien: philosophisch-
historische Classe*, Band 130, Wien, 1894, W. Hertz, in the successive
editions of his translation of the *Parzival*, E. Wechssler, *Die Sage
vom heiligen Gral*, pp. 164 ff., Halle, 1898, where there is the best
summary of arguments on the subject, Paul Hagen, *Der Gral*, Strassburg, 1900, and in various articles.  Add to the above Miss J. L.
Weston, *Legend of Sir Perceval*, I, 72, 93, *et passim*, London, 1906,
E. Brugger in the article quoted above and elsewhere, and S. Singer,
"Über die Quelle von Wolframs Parzival," *Zs. f. d. A.*, XLIV, 321 ff.
(1900) and in his *Wolframs Stil und der Stoff des Parzival*.  Singer
concludes that there were three important French Grail romances,
now lost: 1. The oldest of all, in which the hero was Gawain, not
Perceval.  2. The common source of Chrétien and Kyot.  3. Kyot.
Wolfram's immediate source, according to this scholar, was Kyot, who,
in turn, derived his obscure style from the Provençal poets.  For a
good refutation of this artificial system of Singer's cp. W. Golther,
*Literaturblatt*, March-April, 1918, cols. 86 ff.

According to W. Golther, *Zur deutschen Sage und Dichtung*,

so as not to seem on a level with the rival poet, Hartmann von Aue, who had also translated a romance of Chrétien's.[24] Besides, Wolfram had a strong sense of humor, and in an age when no moral discredit attached to the citation of fictitious authorities, he might well take pleasure in laughing at his readers in his sleeve, in palming off his own inventions on the public as drawn from a poem that no one had ever heard of.[25] In any event, a Provençal poet who wrote in French and not in his native tongue was in the Middle Ages a most improbable person, and the improbability is increased when Wolfram calls him (416, 21) *la schantiure* (= *chanteur*, incorrectly feminine), for this term would apply to a writer of songs, not of romances.[26] Note, too, that through some blunder Wolfram (469, 2ff.) conceives of the Grail as a stone.[27] But no Provençal would have made this mistake; for the word for the Grail, Provençal *grazal*, was especially well-known in Provence

p. 167, Wolfram, on purpose, wrongly ascribed Chrétien's poem to Guiot de Provins. This particular poet, he thinks, was suggested to him, very likely, because the MS. of Chrétien's *Perceval* which he used was written by a scribe, Guiot, whose name was recorded at the end of the copy. This is the name of the copyist of the *Yvain* in MS. 794 (Bibl. Nat.). — Golther's conjecture is plausible, but some other chance circumstance might have led equally well to Wolfram's adopting just this name.

[24] Cp. Foerster, Chrétien *Wörterbuch*, p. 198*.

[25] This is F. Zarncke's view, who speaks of Wolfram as a "Schalk". Cp. PBB., III, 324.

[26] For the arguments of the Kyot advocates in regard to these matters, especially Brugger, see above, pp. 318ff. notes. Singer, p. 43, adopts the view that the MS. *lascantiure* should be devided *l'ascantiure* and that this means *l'enchanteur*. There is no reason, however, as far as one can see, why Kyot should be called an "enchanter", and the older interpretation is, doubtless, correct.

[27] The stone is called, he says (469, 7), *lapsit exillis* — which is probably a corruption of *lapis de celis*. For a discussion of the various interpretations of the term cp. J. F. D. Blöte, *Zs. f. d. A.*, XLVII, 101ff. (1903). Some scholars (cp. Wechssler, p. 167) contend that, after all, Wolfram meant by *stein* a vessel, but there is no evidence of this in the text. He was probably puzzled by the word, *Graal*, like the authors of the Norwegian saga and the *Peredur*, respectively, and ended by interpreting it as a stone, since in the

(its meaning being "dish") and it is in use there to this day.
Take, too, the word *tailleor* (= carving dish or board) which
Wolfram mis-translates *messer* (= knife). If he really had a
completed French story of the Grail before him, he would not
have fallen into this error.[28] Equally conclusive as to the hoax,
it would seem, is the fact[29] that in the first passage (416, 19 ff.)
where Wolfram cites Kyot as his authority he is really following
Heinrich von Veldeke (*Eneide*, ll. 8633 ff.).[30]

There is other evidence that Wolfram did not shrink from
false statements where they served his purpose. So, in his *Wille-*

---

Middle Ages (as even now) marvellous properties were so often imputed
to precious stones.

Singer, pp. 83 ff., still maintains that the Grail was originally
conceived of as a stone and that Kyot preserved this conception, from
whom it passed to Wolfram. The most elaborate defence of this point
of view is Paul Hagen's *Der Gral* (Strassburg, 1900). Cp. p. 335,
below.

[28] For these arguments see Foerster, Chrétien *Wörterbuch*, p. 201.
As an explanation of the misunderstanding by which Wolfram
cenceived of the Grail as a precious stone, Foerster here suggests
that he erroneously connected it with French *grais* (gres) =
sandstone. — *Tailleor* is found in Chrétien's description of the
Grail procession in his *Perceval* twice, viz., ll. 3193, 3249. In the
first line it is applied to the *tailleor* (the meaning of which is much
debated), borne in the procession by one of the Grail maidens; in the
second line it is used of a dish on which an attendant does carving at
the table of the Grail King. There is a difference of opinion as to
whether the *tailleors* of these two lines are the same. Wolfram regarded
them as different — hence his two *Messer* (234, 18, 490, 21 f.).

Miss Weston, *Sir Perceval*, I, 162, and Singer, pp. 88 f., stand
alone, I believe, in denying any connection between Wolfram's *Messer*
and Chrétien's *tailleor*. Adopting, it would seem, a suggestion of
Heinzel's (in his Grail treatise, p. 40), Miss Weston tries to bring the
former into relations with the Fécamp blood-relic which plays so important a part in her theory of Grail origins. But we know of no
knives being among the relics at Fécamp. For a refutation of this
point (about the *Messer*) of Miss Weston's cp. J. F. D. Blöte, *Anzeiger
für deutsches Altertum*, XXXII, 24 ff. (1908).

[29] Cp. Behaghel, *Literaturblatt* for 1898, cols. 115, 263.

[30] *Literaturblatt* for 1898, cols. 115, 263.

*halm* (125, 20), which, as stated above, is based on the Old French
*chanson de geste, Aliscans,* he pretends that his authority was
Chrétien de Troyes. So, too, with his assertion (*Parzival*, 115, 25)
that he did not know how to read or write. This assertion, which
occurs in a passage that is wholly humorous in its character, was
widely accepted at its face value, as long as the old romantic
notions about the origins of epic poetry were held, and some scholars still take it literally, but it seems obvious that we are confronted here with a falsehood. The writer knew French and paraphrased a French poem (Chrétien's) of more than 10,000 lines.
Add to this that his work, which runs to nearly 25,000 lines, is
singularly free from contradictions and inequalities. There is not
an authenticated case in history of an uneducated man's composing
a work of anything approaching the *Parzival* in extent, to say
nothing of its quality, whether with or without the aid of aman-
uenses, and this fact, of itself, justifies an attitude of skepticism,
The knowledge of French which he possessed, the varied learning
which he displays,[31] the closeness, with which he follows Chrétien

---

[31] Cp. his liberal use of Solinus as pointed out by E. Martin,
*Zur Gralsage,* pp. 5 ff. — also, *ibid.* pp. 9 ff., the great quantity of
names, drawn from different sources. Martin accepts Wolfram's statement concerning Kyot, but believes that he introduced these names,
himself, into his poem from a great variety of other sources. P. Hagen
in his *Der Gral* (Strassburg, 1900) and "Untersuchungen über Kiot",
*Zs. f. d. A.,* XLV, 187 ff. has, also, shown the use which is made in
the *Parzival* of the Bible, (ultimately) Oriental sources, the so-called
*Letter of Prester John,* etc. He imagines, it is true, that Kyot, not
Wolfram, is responsible for all this; but, unless we accept the German
poet's assertion as to his illiteracy, there is no ground for that assumption.

It is to be observed that the strange nomenclature (drawn from
Solinus, etc.) of Wolfram's poem which I have noted above is found
mainly in those parts that have nothing corresponding in Chrétien's
*Perceval.* These names have been the subject of much special study.
Besides Martin, cp. San Marte, "Über die Eigennamen im Parzival
des Wolfram von Eschenbach", *Germania,* II, 385 ff. (1857), K. Bartsch,
"Die Eigennamen in Wolframs Parzival und Titurel," *Germanistische
Studien* II, 114 ff. (Wien, 1875), G. Paris, *Romania,* IV, 148 ff.
(1875), the notes to Hertz's translation of the *Parzival.* The Arabic
names of the planets (782) and the lines about precious stones (791)

and the power of his style, which German critics declare to be the finest of the Middle Ages in their language, — these things all prove that Wolfram was far removed from illiteracy. His statement on the subject was, most likely, merely a humorous mystification, with a covert hit at the pretensions to learning of some contemporary poets — perhaps, above all, as we have seen, Hartmann von Aue.[32]

Let us review somewhat more systematically, though briefly, the contents of Wolfram's *Parzival*, parts of which I have had occasion to refer to in the discussion above.

In the portion which he has prefixed to Chrétien's narrative, the poet represents that Perceval's father was a prince of Anjou, named Gahmuret. In a manner which, as we have seen, has no parallel in the French romances he makes this Christian knight enter the service of the Caliph of Bagdad (the Baruc, as he is

and the men who were learned in regard to the same (773, 22 ff.) came, of course, from learned sources, the latter from Arnoldus Saxo.

For Wolfram's reading in French literature and, probably, Provençal, also, see, still further, Singer's above-cited treatise. He interprets, it is true, such evidences of wide reading in the *Parzival* as proofs of Kyot's existence. Among other things, he points out interesting borrowings from the *Roman de Thebes* (cp. Antigone and Antikonie) in the German poem.

[32] Even Bartsch (see note to 115, 27 in his edition of the *Parzival*), although accepting Wolfram's statement concerning his illiteracy at its face value, sees in this statement a hit at Hartmann. Wolfram's position is somewhat like that of Burns, as expressed in the "Epistle to John Lapraik": he upholds nature and depreciates learning. Wolfram, on the other hand, owes much, of course, to Hartmann in respect to narrative method. He has, besides, in the opinion of most scholars, borrowed from him a large number of names. To be sure, this is denied by Singer, pp. 56 ff., who acknowledges that Wolfram was well acquainted with Hartmann's *Erec*, but argues that, in such cases, it was Kyot who drew these names direct from the French and that the list in Hartmann, indeed, contains spurious late additions derived from the *Parzival*. Granting, however, that Singer's views as to the sources of these names in the *Parzival* and Hartmann are correct there is no reason why Wolfram, himself, should not have drawn, them from Chrétien.

called). He becomes famous among the Saracens and weds a Moorish queen, Belacane, whose noble character in her lover's eyes more than offsets her heathen faith.[33] Later, however, as he longs

[33] Brugger, Heinrich Morf *Festschrift*, 59 ff., has argued that Wolfram used for this prologue the same source that the author of the *Livre d'Artus* of MS. 337 used in his Baruch-Sagremor-Sebile episode (Sommer's *Vulgate Version of the Arthurian Romances*, VII, 280 ff.). This common source he supposes to be a lost romance. But the episode in the *Livre d'Artus* is a mere variation of the Clamedex-Perceval-Blanchefleur episode in Chrétien's *Perceval*, ll. 1921 ff., the author substituting for Blanchefleur the heathen widow, Sebile, of the *Chanson de Saisnes*. This accounts for the *chanson de geste* features of the episode, which Brugger remarks on. In the *Saisnes*, too, in the approved style, Sebile is baptized before being married to her Christian lover, Baudouin. *Sarmenie*, in the *Livre d'Artus*, is probably a corrupt or wilful variant of *Parmenie* of the *Tristan* poems. As far as Baruch in this romance is concerned, Brugger speaks of him as a Christian, but this is not certain. Indeed, inasmuch as he is called Li Noirs Cheualiers, he is very likely a dark-skinned pagan, like Sebile, whom he persecutes. The author gave him accordingly a pagan (Oriental) name. *Baruch* is still a common name among the Jews. Sommer lists it in the Index of his Vulgate Version as the name of a person in the *Estoire del Saint Gral*, I, 193, viz., as the name of one of Mordred's sons. This, however, is a mistake. It is the name of a castle that belongs to one of these sons.

The differences between Wolfram and the *Livre d'Artus* episode are, after all, very marked.

Brugger, ibid., 65 ff., like Martin, *Zur Gralsage*, p. 18, and Singer, *Zs. f. d. A.*, XLIV, 323 ff., before him, and Miss Weston, *Morien*, p. 15 (New York, 1901), since, has inferred from certain resemblances between the tale of Feirefiz and the Dutch poem *Moriaen*, that the two drew on a common source — a lost French poem. The latter is embedded in the vast Dutch (metrical) *Lancelot*, which was edited by W. J. Jonckbloet (The Hague, 1846—1849). It has since been edited separately by Jan Te Winkel, *Roman van Moriaen* (Bibliotheek van Middelnederlandsche Letterkunde, XX, Groningen, 1878). Despite the contrary opinion of the editors, Gaston Paris is, doubtless, right in regarding this poem not as an original Dutch composition, but as a translation of a French poem. Cp. *Histoire Littéraire de la France*, XXX, 254. According to the story, Agloval, Perceval's brother, being in the land of the Moors, had an amour with a princess there, but abandoned her, whilst she was *enceinte*, on the pretext that he had

for a more active life, he makes this difference of religion a pretext for leaving her, declaring at the same time that he will come back to her, if she will turn Christian. After his departure Belacane gives birth to a son, named Feirefiz. Gahmuret returns to Europe by way of Spain and in a tourney in Wales wins Herzeloyde, queen of Wales and Anjou and Norgales (i. e. really, North Wales). He marries her, despite some compunctions which the memory of Balacane causes him. In the course of time he hears that the Baruc, his former lord in the East, is pressed by enemies. So, under the influence of loyalty, he goes to this monarch's assistance, but not long after his arrival falls a victim to treachery — a heathen broke his helmet of adamant by throwing goat's blood on it — hence he was exposed to the fatal wound (105, 17ff.). Herzeloyde gives birth to Perceval fourteen days after his father's death. On hearing the ill news, she retires to the forest with

---

to go in search of Lancelot. The child of this intrigue, Moriaen, when he is a lad, goes forth to find his father and compel him to right this wrong to his mother, by marrying her. He comes to Arthur's kingdom, makes the acquaintance of Gawain and others, and, in the end, achieves his object. There is satisfactory internal evidence that Perceval, and not Agloval, was the father of the hero in the French original. Apart from the fact that Perceval in this hypothetical French romance was, as stated, father, and not brother, of the character concerned (as in Wolfram), G. Paris (p. 253) points out that this *motif* of a son seeking out a faithless father and compelling him to marry his mother occurs in other romances of the period and is here linked with one of the commonplaces of mediaeval romance — the love of a Saracen princess for a Christian knight. He, therefore, — rightly, in my opinion, — denies any connection between *Moriaen* and *Parzival*. Paris, however, should, not have included "le roman latin de Meriadoc" among the works that exhibit the *motif* just mentioned. In that romance *(Historia Meriadoci)* the hero's parents die at the beginning of the story. Cp. my edition, *Historia Meriadoci and de Ortu Waluuanii*, pp. 4f.

In *Romania*, XXIV, 336f. (1895), Lot ascribes a Celtic origin to Morien — identifies him with Mor of the Black Book of Caermarthen and Book of Taliessin. But "Mor" sounded like *Maure* (= Moor) — hence, says Lot, the Dutch or French author conceived of the character as black. "Moryen", he observes, also, means "sea-born" in Welsh. Lot's derivation of *Morien* from *Mor,* who is a mere name in the Welsh texts, is to me unconvincing.

her infant son, as intimated at the beginning of Chrétien's poem.[34] Even this brief summary brings out one fine feature of Wolfram's poem — namely, that he exhibits a universal tolerance. Pagan and Christian with him stand on the same plane of nobility. The fact, indeed, that he gives his Christian hero a pagan brother (Feirefiz), is symbolical of this broad humanity.

For the next 16000 lines, approximately, the poet, in general, follows Chrétien pretty exactly. He often amplifies his original in detail, it is true, developing sometimes descriptions of the external splendors of feudal life or giving a more individual stamp to the characters.[35] By slight additions, too, he endeavors to render more plausible incidents and actions and to weld into closer unity all parts of the narrative.[36] It is in the portion of his poem, how-

---

[34] Among the knights whom Gahmuret vanquished in the tourney, at the time that he won Herzeloyde, was Orilus's brother, Lähelin (i. e. Llewellyn). He conceived a great hatred of Gahmuret (79, 12 ff.) and after Gahmuret's death robbed his widow (128, 4 ff., 141, 7 ff.) of two of her dominions, Wales and Norgales. He appears also in one or two later passages of the poem. Some scholars (cp. Wechssler, p. 170) have seen a great significance in the brevity of the passages about this character in the *Parzival:* Wolfram must have been drawing on a longer narrative about him. But it is not necessary to assume this. He was first introduced to render more dramatic the scene of the tourney and, later, the isolation of the widow, but he was not needed in the part of the narrative where Wolfram no longer had to rely on his own invention, and the poet, merely in that part, refers to him occasionally, in order to keep up the connection between Book I—II and the rest. But even granting that what is said about Lähelin in the *Parzival* came from a longer poem, Wolfram could have drawn on such a poem just as well as Kyot.

[35] There are also some transpositions, the most important of which is the story of Sigune. Here an episode in Chrétien (ll. 3390 ff.) is divided into two parts (138, 9 ff., 249, 11 ff.) and the first part is put much earlier in the narrative — just after the conclusion of the episode of the tent-lady (called Jeschute by Wolfram) in Chrétien (l. 811). As Lichtenstein, p. 15, suggests, Wolfram's reason for the earlier introduction of this episode is, that he did not want his hero to remain unnamed any longer, yet, according to Chrétien (ll. 3535 ff.), it was in the dialogue with his cousin (Sigune) that Perceval first learns his name.

[36] This aim probably accounts, in a large measure, for the fact that all the characters of any importance in the *Parzival* are related

ever, in which the author expounds his conception of the Grail
(Books V and IX) that the expansion becomes really considerable—
especially, in the Ninth Book, where Perceval visits his hermit
uncle, Trevrezent, confesses to him his religious doubts and other
sins, and is absolved by this lay confessor, after having been first
enlightened by him with respect to the relations of God to man
and the true nature of sin as well (462, 11) as with respect to the
history and qualities of the Grail and its attendants.[37] Here something less than two hundred lines of Chrétien have been expanded
into upwards of fifteen hundred by Wolfram. More important
however, than the mere fact of amplification is the difference of
spirit which distinguishes the German poet's treatment of his
theme; for, whereas Chrétien moves in the ordinary grooves of the
conventional and orthodox theology and ecclesiastical practice of
his age, Wolfram, who had already revealed a saner morality than
the French poet in his exaltation of constancy of character and
rational chastity and in his putting the relations of his heroes
and heroines (Parzival and Condwiramurs, Orilus and Jeschute,
etc.) on the basis of marriage, deepens immeasurably in this
remarkable episode the moral import of the Grail conception, by
treating it in a profoundly mystical spirit.[38] .

and so constitute one great family. There was a beginning of this
in Chrétien's *Perceval,* but Wolfram, so to speak, makes it thoroughgoing.
The spirit of universal brotherhood which inspired the German poet's
conception of the Elect of the Grail was, also, probably a factor.
German critics have sometimes taken the matter we are commenting on
as especially characteristic of the Germans. Cp. for example, Lichtenstein, PBB, XXII, 69.

[37] See for a comparison of Book IX with Chrétien, A. Nolte "Die
Composition der Trevrezentscenen", *Zs. f. d. A.,* XLIV, 241 ff. (1900).
The additions, he concludes, are wholly Wolfram's, not Kyot's. In
his "The Ninth Book of Wolfram's Parzival", MPh., I, 275 ff. (1903),
A. B. Faust has defended this book from the charges of incoherence,
etc. which had been brought against it, especially by G. Bötticher,
*Das Hohelied vom Rittertum, eine Beleuchtung des Parzival nach
Wolframs eigenen Andeutungen* (Berlin, 1886).

[38] In some points, it is true, Wolfram's changes involve a loss
as well as a gain. For example, the wound of the Grail King of
Chrétien's poem (ll. 3470 ff.) is no longer impressive, when we learn

As we have seen, through some misunderstanding of his
French original, our author conceives of the Grail as a precious
stone somewhat like the Kaaba at Mecca. It would seem that it
had fallen from the heavens like the Kaaba. In one place (471, 15)
he says that the noble and worthy among the angels who remained
neutral at the time of the first great conflict between the Trinity
(God) and Lucifer were its guardians.[39] Afterwards, its defence
was committed to the Templeise[40] — that is to say, a company
of knights whose name and function recall the actual Knights
Templars of the time. In fact, it was obviously the order of
Knights Templars that suggested to Wolfram the brotherhood of
the Grail, just as it suggested to his contemporary,[41] the author
of the famous French prose romance, the *Queste del Saint Graal*,
the character of Galahad. The crusades, both in practical life and
in literature, had brought about the union of the two great ideals
that distinguish the Middle Ages — the ideal of chivalry and the
ideal of the Christian Church — but in the French romance the
ideal of chivalry, in a spirit of the narrowest asceticism, is completely subordinated to that of the Church, whilst in the German
poem, with a sane recognition of their respective values, the two
are combined in perfect harmony.

---

from Wolfram (479, 2 ff.) that it was received in the pursuit of the
usual adventures of a knight-errant, who was endeavoring to win the
favor of his lady by prowess. To be sure, Wolfram explains the misfortune as a punishment for Amfortas's pride and unchastity, as displayed in this pursuit. Similarly, according to Wolfram (501, 25),
the mysterious illness of the Grail King's grandfather (cp. Chrétien,
ll. 6391 ff.) is the gout.

[39] Later (798, 11 ff.) he retracts this.

[40] From Latin *Templenses*. Singer objects, pp. 93 ff., that a
German would have used a German term (*templaere* or another), instead of this French form, for the Knights Templars. But it did not
require any great knowledge of French to invent the word, *templeis*,
even if our author did not actually pick it up from some French
source. He might prefer it to the ordinary German terms, because
he did not want to identify too absolutely his ideal order with the
contemporary order that suggested it.

[41] The *Queste*, too, was, apparently, written in the first decade
of the thirteenth century.

The Grail, then, which is entrusted to the keeping of this new order of spiritual knighthood is a symbol of redemption and of eternal life. It renders immortal and ever-youthful those that dwell near it and look upon it. The place where it is preserved is called *Munsalvaesche* (doubtless, *Mont Salvage*)[42] and its guardians prevent any one from approaching the mystic castle, save those that are called to its service. These chosen servants, who are of both sexes, are summoned in their youth from all lands and from the ranks of the poor and the rich alike. They must renounce profane love *(minne)*, yet marriage is not forbidden them, since their children are to be dedicated to the same holy service as themselves. Among the men, however, this privilege is restricted to the Grail King and to those who (like Lohengrin) are sent forth

---

[42] It is to be noted that the name which Wolfram gives to the Grail castle is simply the French equivalent of the name of his own home, *Wildenberc* (Cp. *Parzival*, 230, 12 f.). This can hardly be an accident. In PBB, XXIV, 409 (1899), A. Gebhardt regards *Wildenberc* as a jesting translation of *Munsalvaesche;* but this is extremely improbable. The passage concerning Wildenberc occurs before Munsalvaesche has been named (251, 2), and the joke would, accordingly, have been lost on the reader. On the other hand, I believe with Golther, *Zur deutschen Sage und Dichtung,* p. 161, that Wolfram humorously named his Grail castle after his own home. In that event, there would be no need of considering — with Foerster, *Chrétien Wörterbuch,* p. 201\*, — the possible influence of *Montserrat* on the name of Wolfram's Grail castle.

It has been also suggested that *Munsalvaesche* is derived from *Montem Salvationis,* but this derivation is not phonologically unobjectionable, like the derivation which I have given above and which is now generally accepted — except by Singer, p. 90, who believes that Wolfram's French source had here *Mont Salvation.*

Wildenberc, Wolfram's home, is usually identified with modern Wehlenberg (formerly named *Wildenbergen*) near Ansbach. In his review of Panzer's Wolfram bibliography, *Anzeiger für deutsches Altertum,* XXIV, 316 ff., E. Schröder, however, has proposed, instead of Wehlenberg, Wildenberg on the eastern edge of the Odenwald. The older identification, nevertheless, is probably correct. Cp., especially, Johann Baptist Kurz, *Heimat und Geschlecht Wolframs von Eschenbach* (Ansbach, 1916).

to take charge of lands without a lord.[43] The Grail community, furthermore, has no concern in regard to subsistence, for on Good Friday a dove descends from the heavens and lays a sacred wafer on the stone, which is thereby endowed with the power to supply its votaries with food and drink.

Thus the Grail King, it will be seen, is the sovereign of a spiritual realm which is coextensive with mankind. His office, indeed, is more exalted even than that of the Pope, for its authority, resting wholly on a basis of spiritual and moral aspiration, is untrammelled by dogma and unsullied by worldly interests. If this was to be the ultimate development of the Grail legend, no wonder that the mediaeval Church was chary of lending it countenance!

It is to this unparalleled dignity that Perceval is appointed, after expiating nis sins through humility and human sympathy. As has been remarked by more than one scholar, the depth of Wolfram's conception in all this comes out plainly, if we contrast him with his contemporary, Hartmann von Aue. For the latter (compare his *Gregorius*) the only unpardonable sin is religious doubt. For Wolfram it is inconstancy of character, the want of a fixed purpose. To obtain salvation, then, one must be constant and loyal. Wolfram's hero shows these qualities in his relations to his wife and in his relations to the Grail.[44] We have in the poem the story of his sin and of his purification.[45] The poet's treatment of Perceval's failure to ask the fateful question at the Grail castle is particularly noteworthy. In Chrétien this failure has no moral significance — the whole incident is simply one of a fairy-tale spell which the question will undo. But with Wolfram it is otherwise. It betrays a want of sympathy with his fellow-

---

[43] Moreover, the marriage of the men had to be secret, whilst that of the women was public (494, 13 ff.).

[44] It is significant that Wolfram always makes his hero speak of them (wife and Grail) together, as determining the aims of his life.

[45] Noteworthy is Wolfram's independence of contemporary ideas as to how one should attain grace — that is to say, through penance, intercession of the Virgin Mary or the saints etc. There is not a trace of Mariolatry in his work.

man (255, 17; 484, 24), when Perceval omits to ask the question, and therein he has sinned. It is true that he is restrained by the injunctions of Gornemanz, but those injunctions were merely the formulas of a conventional etiquette, and etiquette has in the crisis proved stronger with the hero than compassion. He only frees himself from sin later on, when by asking the neglected question, he exhibits the sympathy which he had failed in before.

So, too, with the contrast of Perceval and Gawain as types, respectively, of the knight who pursues the ideal and the knight who is merely the perfect embodiment of conventional courtesy and wordly accomplishments. The antithesis is already found in Chrétien, but the French poet is purely a courtier and a man of the world, with a gift for depicting the externals of life — light, graceful, and endlessly fluent — whereas Wolfram has profound emotion and an original ideal which he wishes to express through his work.

So far for the portion of his narrative which Wolfram borrowed from Chrétien. It only remains to outline briefly the conclusion which he added to Chrétien's unfinished poem: The French poem had ended at the point where Arthur's mother and the other queens appear imprisoned in a magic castle.[46] The lord of this castle is called Clinschor by Wolfram, and he is said to be the nephew of Virgil, who, as is well-known, was regarded in the Middle Ages as an incomparable magician. Gawain overcomes the magician and releases the captives — later he has a fight with Perceval, neither being aware of the other's identity. After many minor adventures Perceval meets his half-brother, the heathen Feirefiz, and sustains with him the hardest of all his fights. They recognize each other, however, embrace, and repair to Arthur's court. Cundrie, a Grail damsel, learned in starlore, comes and tells Perceval that his wife and twin sons, Lohengrin and Kardeiz, have been summoned to the Grail castle and that the question will now free Amfortas and his land. With Cundrie and Feirefiz Perceval rides to the Grail castle, meets his wife,

---

[46] Owing to the fact that Chrétien had left this episode unfinished, Wolfram has remodeled it with great freedom.

and together they all behold the talismans, save Feirefiz, to whom as a heathen the sight of the Grail is denied. But soon, under the influence of the charms of the Grail damsel — as Wolfram intimates, with some happy strokes of humor — rather than from religious conviction, Feirefiz becomes a convert to Christianity, is baptized, and weds the damsel (Repanse de Schoie); the two then go to India, and from them is born Prester John. On the other hand, Perceval rules henceforth over his Grail kingdom. Lastly, it is told of his (Perceval's) son, Lohengrin,[47] how he was led to the aid of the Duchess of Brabant by a swan, how he marries her on condition that she shall not inquire as to his origin and how on her breaking his command the swan carries him away from her. — This introduction of the Swan-Knight into the Grail story was, of course, an innovation of Wolfram's, for the two legends had so far developed separately. So, too, with the idea that the lord of the magic castle where the queens were held in duress was a nephew of Virgil. Virgil — and the same thing is true of Prester John — had been well-known figures in mediaeval legend, before Wolfram composed his poem, but they had had no connection with the Holy Grail.

The conclusion just outlined calls for no particular remark. Like the corresponding prologue, it is, in the judgment of the present writer, plainly the invention of Wolfram.[48]

---

[47] Probably = *Loherenc Garin,* that is, Garin of Lorraine, with reference to Garin, a well-known character in the Old French *chansons de geste.* The Swan-Knight story had already been connected with the House of Lorraine. For its influence on an episode in Pseudo-Wauchier, cp. p. 300, above. That episode, however, is not directly connected with the Grail, so that the assertion which I make in the next sentence above is valid.

[48] In his "Parzivalstudien", *Germania,* XXXVII, 74 ff. (1892), P. Hagen studies the relations of Chrétien, Wolfram, and *Peredur,* and finds in certain supposed agreements between the last two, as against the first, proof that they are independent of Chrétien. *Peredur,* however, is certainly derived directly from Chrétien. On this subject scholars of virtually every school are nowadays agreed. Cp. p. 344 note 3, below.

R. H. Griffith has made the same sort of comparison as Hagen, but on a more elaborate scale, in his *Sir Perceval of Galles* (Chicago,

1911), laying especial stress on agreements with the English *Sir Perceval*. But on the subject of such supposed agreements cp. my review of Griffith's book in the *Romanic Review*, IV, 125 ff. (1913). What I have said there applies, in general, also, to similar comparisons in Carsten Struck's Münster dissertation, *Der junge Parzival in Wolframs von Eschenbach Parzival, etc.* (Boma-Leipzig, 1910) and A. C. L. Brown's "The Grail and the English *Sir Perceval*", MPh., XVI, 553 ff. (1919). Brown stresses, as the most important, five points of agreement (so he considers them) between Wolfram and the English poem, as against Chrétien, viz.: In both 1. Perceval meets three knights in the 'forest in the opening episode of the story, not five, as in Chrétien 2. had a bad mount 3. lives near "a natural source of water", — i. e., according to the English poem "He dranke water of the welle"; according to Wolfram, bathed every morning in a river nearby, 4. is connected with a vengeance *motif*, 5. his father in his marriage tournament "made an enemy", who is later to do battle against the son.

Now as regards these five points: No. 1 is not accurately stated, for in Wolfram there are really four knights. First three knights appear, and then, immediately afterwards, a fourth knight, who is lord of the rest. Besides, only the last of these in Wolfram has a name, viz. Karnahkarnanz, whereas in the English poem the three knights are Yvain, Gawain and Kay. — No. 2. The idea that the young rustic's mount should be more or less ridiculous springs naturally out of the situation. Otherwise, there is no similarity between the two poems. In Wolfram Perceval's mother, when he first leaves home, purposely gives him a poor horse, to protect his life, since, if so mounted, the knights would not take him seriously. Nothing is said of this in the English poem in the only passage where the matter is mentioned (one much later in the narrative, viz. at the point where Perceval has just slain the Red Knight). There (ll. 718 ff.) it is stated, merely in passing, that Perceval was riding a mare that was with foal. — No. 3. Here, on the face of it, there is obviously no real resemblance between the two. Besides, "He dranke water of the welle And yitt was he wyghte," (11. 6 f.) is introduced to emphasize the hero's sober bringing up, with which, of course, Wolfram's river has nothing to do. — No. 4. In the English poem the revenge *motif* (taken, doubtless, from the spurious Bliocadrans prologue to Chrétien) is one of the most important *motifs* of the romance and justifies Perceval's enmity to the Red Knight. In so far as there is any revenge *motif* at all in Wolfram, the object of it is Lähelin, who does not correspond to the Red Knight, in any way. Moreover, in Wolfram the matter has no importance. I called attention to these differences in *Romanic Review,* IV, 127, note 6 (1913). — No. 5. In Wolfram (unlike *Sir Perceval)* the knight overthrown (*not* killed) in the later encounter (Orilus) is not identical with the knight who was overthrown in the first encounter (Lähelin). One would have to read, however, the long and altogether different narrative in Wolfram to see how ill-supported this last point is.

# Chapter VII.

## Peredur, Diu Crône, and Sone de Nausay.

Different views have been expressed in regard to the relations of the French *Conte del Graal* (Chrétien's *Perceval* plus its continuations) and the Welsh tale, called *Peredur*, which is contained in the collection of Welsh tales, known generally as the *Mabinogion*.[1] This tale has been frequently taken by advocates of Celtic

---

[1] The best discussions of this question are by 1. W. Golther, "Chrestiens Conte del Graal in seinem Verhältniss zum wälschen Peredur und zum englischen Sir Perceval," *Sitzungsberichte der philosophisch-philologischen und historischen Classe der K. b. Akademie der Wissenschaften zu München*, 1890, Band I, Heft I, pp. 174 ff., and, 2. R. Thurneysen, in his review of Miss Williams's *Peredur* essay in the *Zeitschrift für Celtische Philologie*, VIII, 185 ff. (1912). Thurneysen's discussion of the evolution of the Welsh tale is convincing. As he points out, Miss Williams, like previous scholars, fails to observe that the Red Book of Hergest indicates that the *Peredur* really consists of three separate stories, each beginning on a new page and with large initial letters. To be sure, on other grounds, Miss Williams recognized the third of these stories as a later addition to the original text, but, according to Thurneysen, so is the second (II). Still further, the first of the stories, which ends at the point where Peredur is reconciled to Angharat Law Eurawc, is itself composite, and consists of two parts designated by Thurneysen, Ia (ending at the point where, after the incident of the drops of the blood in the snow, Peredur is found by Arthur's knights) and Ib. This Ia is a free paraphrase of the corresponding portion of Chrétien, with little admixture of native Welsh materials. On the other hand, Ib and II are free inventions of Welsh story-tellers, independent of each other, but both writing under the influence of Ia, which first introduced Peredur as a knight errant into Welsh literature. The author of Part III follows Chrétien, as far as his fragmentary narrative permitted, but adds to it from some other non-Welsh source, terminating the whole with his

origins for the French romances as evidence of the existence in
Wales of a Perceval legend embodying incidents that gave rise
to the legend of the Holy Grail. Few, however, latterly have denied
that it had some sort of connection with the French romances.
Nutt[2] speaks of it as "exhibiting . . . what is, on the whole, the
oldest form of a sequence of incidents found in the most diverse
shapes in the French Grail romances. It is practically a Grail
Quest before the introduction of Christian symbolism has transformed both the Grail itself and the Quest for it." In his *Studies
on the Holy Grail* (p. 145) he thinks that the extant *Peredur*
must be an amplification of an earlier Welsh tale, and that the
author of the story in its revised form was strongly influenced
by Chrétien and drew upon him also for materials. In a special
thesis on the subject, *Essai sur la composition du roman gallois de
Peredur* (Paris, 1909), Miss Mary R. Williams maintains that
only the final section (third, according to her division) is copied
from the French (*not* Chrétien) — the section which begins with
Peredur's return to Caerleon after his visit to the Grail castle
(pp. 13 f.), — although there was also a French poem corresponding to Section I. J. Loth, *Les Mabinogion,* I, 53 (Paris, 1913),
accepts *Peredur,* like *The Lady of the·Fountain* and *Geraint the*

own inventions, but on the basis of suggestions, which he found in Ia.
This Part III, as said above, begins with Peredur's return to Caerleon
after his visit to the Grail castle.

   [2] *The Mabinogion,* p. 354 (New York, 1902).

   In his *Studies in the Arthurian Legend,* Ch. 4—6, J. Rhys
discusses Peredur in Welsh literature, and tries to connect him with
the stories of Yvain and Lancelot, but, as far as I am aware, has
convinced no one. — To prove that Peredur was "early known" as
a Grail hero in Wales, Evans cites the Black Book of Caermarthen,
65, 7—9 (of the twelfth century, it seems), where we have Peredur
called *penwelic.* He interprets this as *pen-vedig = chief physician*
i. e. who healed the Grail king, and remarks: "Thus an independent
source of genuine antiquity reveals Percdur to us as the Welsh hero
of the Grail quest." Cp. *The White Book Mabinogion, Welsh Tales
Romances reproduced from the Peniarth Manuscripts, edited by
J. Gwenogvryn Evans,* p. 14 (Pwllheli, 1907 — really issued, however, in 1909, it appears, since the Preface is dated in the latter year).

*Son of Erbin,* as derived from the French — strange to say, however, not from Chrétien, but from hypothetical Anglo-Norman poems (now lost) which dealt with subjects of Welsh origin. In this he is following Gaston Paris. E. Windisch alone, *Das Keltische Britannien bis zu Kaiser Arthur,* p. 221 (Leipzig, 1912), appears to deny altogether any connection with the French. — But one is tempted to say, however, that only the obsession of Celtic origins could lead one to deny the derivation of *Peredur* from Chrétien.[3] The oldest MS. of the Welsh tale (fragmentary) dates from the thirteenth century (cp. Loth[2] I, 18) and the tale itself certainly dates from a period when the French romances had already developed — that is, not earlier than the latter half of the twelfth century, or, more probably, the beginning of the thirteenth. Welsh scholars have cited no evidence that would place them so early. The author shows no knowledge of anything concerning the Perceval legend which is not in Chrétien. His account of Perceval ends where Chrétien ends.

The construction of the tale bears testimony to its French origin. As compared with the Welsh tales of the native tradition, such as *Kulhwch and Olwen, Peredur* and its companions, *Owein (The Lady of the Fountain)* and *Geraint, Son of Erbin*[4] ex-

---

[3] Although an advocate of the Celtic origin of the Grail legend Brugger regards the *Peredur* as a mere derivative of Chrétien and his continuators. Cp. his review of Miss Williams's thesis, Herrig's *Archiv,* CXXV, 450 ff. (1910). So, too, W. A. Nitze, *Modern Language Notes,* XXV, 246 ff. (1910) and W. Golther, *Literaturblatt für germanische und romanische Philologie,* XXXI, 286 f. (1910) in their reviews of the same thesis. G. Paris, on the other hand, had advocated the certainly erroneous view that a lost Anglo-Norman poem was the common source of *Peredur* and Chrétien's *Perceval.* Cp. p. 99 of his *Perceval et la légende du Saint Gral: Société Historique et Cercle Saint-Simon, Bulletin no. 2* (Paris, 1883). He says, *ibid.* p. 98, that the Perceval story is Welsh in origin, and regards the Middle English *Sir Perceval* as preserving it in its most authentic form.

[4] J. Gwenogvryn Evans remarks that *Peredur* is more Welsh than the last two and "less influenced by the prevailing tone of the Romances of chivalry." See his *The White Book Mabinogion,* etc.

hibit, as has already been said, a different art. We have here, it is true, as in the mediaeval romances, generally, not a logically developed plot, but a series of episodes with hardly any thread of connection, save that the same character is the hero of each of the episodes. Nevertheless, the individual episodes are in themselves coherent, whereas in the native Welsh tales there is no coherence, and the fantastic narrative (with a multitude of beautiful details, to be sure), like a wild vine, strikes out in any direction it pleases. The structure of *Peredur* is, then, essentially the structure of *Perceval*. Indeed, the actual order of the incidents through the two works is the same — only that the hero's visit to Blanchefleur, owing, perhaps, to some disarrangement of leaves in the French MS. which the Welshman had before him, has been put later, and hence has produced an obvious confusion in the Welsh narrative. In parts there is, indeed, for a long stretch of narrative a verbal correspondence between the Welsh and the French, as in the passage which follows on the incident of Perceval's unhorsing Kay (Chrétien, ll. 5698 ff.). Elsewhere there are manifest errors, which are due to the fact that the Welshman has misunderstood his original. For example, Perceval's exclamation on first seeing knights: "They are angels," is transferred to his mother, in whose mouth they have no sense. Two nuns appear strangely as waitresses in Blanchefleur's castle, probably because, on approaching this castle, Perceval is said by Chrétien to have seen "II Abéies".[5] — On the other hand, the Welsh has some merits of style which are wanting in the French. As Nutt has remarked,[6] the narrative in the former is "direct and vivid, bathed in colour, bringing into high relief with an artistic instinct almost uncanny in its rightness those traits and features, which produce a picturesque, a romantic effect."

---

pp. XIII, XXIV. This is true, but is explained by the composite character of the work. Cp. p. 342, note 1, above. Evans believes that *Peredur* had undergone repeated redaction before the days of Chrétien and that it is older than *Owein* and *Gereint*.

[5] Cp. Nutt, *Studies*, p. 135.

[6] *Mabinogion*, p. 352.

Apart from the confusions, just noted, the main differences which distinguish *Peredur* are as follows: 1. Gawain's adventures are greatly abbreviated; 2. Descriptions pertaining to the life of chivalry are largely left out; 3. The Grail, as such, does not appear in the Welsh tale. Instead of the sacred vessel, we have simply a dish with a bleeding head on it. This is a talisman intended to incite the hero to avenge the death of the cousin, whose head is on the dish, and the harming of an uncle. The cause of this difference is that the Welsh author could make nothing out of the mysterious Grail in Chrétien's unfinished poem, so that he substituted the *motif* of vengeance which he found in Manessier's continuation and which was familiar to him already. Even the idea of curing the Fisher King by the execution of vengeance, employed by Manessier, would be well-known to him, for this is found among the Celts, and in Old Irish the same word meant to "pay" and to "cure".[7] All that the Welsh author did then was to put on the dish, instead of the wafer, the head of Manessier's Goon Desert, which here serves as a warning, not a token of victory. As an illustration of how impossible it was for foreign translators of Chrétien to fathom the meaning of the Grail, Golther[8] has cited the Norwegian translator, who betrays his despair by offering the reader a choice of translations of the word Grail, all equally nonsensical. This translator queries whether the term means *web* or *progressive alleviation* or *assistance!* The Welshman did better, inasmuch as he adopted from Manessier something that he could understand. 4. The Welsh author has introduced into the story some *motifs* drawn from native Welsh folk-tales. The principal instances are in the Witches of Gloucester episode. Peredur subdues one of these witches, who had been troubling a noble lady, and afterwards at the court of the witches he learns the arts of chivalry. By the aid of a precious stone that renders the bearer invisible the hero slays a great serpent that dwells in a lake and ravages the surrounding country. 5. He has substituted for the French name, *Perceval*, the familiar Welsh

---

[7] Cp. J. Loth, *Mabinogion*[2], I, 63, note.
[8] Cp. *op. cit.*, p. 194.

name, *Peredur.* The Welsh tale, then, is substantially merely an adaptation of Chrétien with some use of Wauchier and Manessier and probably the Bliocadrans-prologue.[9] Like the mediaeval translators, generally, the author does not usually follow his original *verbatim*, but paraphrases and shortens at will, and, most important of all, gives the style the colouring of the native tales. As we have seen, he has also made some additions, but these are not numerous. There is no need, then, of assuming the very improbable sequence: 1. a Welsh tale about Perceval. 2. a French version of this tale. 3. Chrétien's *Perceval*, based on the French version. 4. the extant Welsh *Peredur*, which is a modification of (1) under the influence of (2) or (3). Instead of this complicated scheme, we simply have 1. Chrétien + his continuators. 2. the extant *Peredur* based on the same.

Besides the three works which I have just considered and which have loomed so large in Grail discussions, there are two others which are of less importance, but which should not be passed over entirely in silence in a survey of the development of the legend of the Holy Grail. They are as follows:

1. *Diu Crône (Krône)*.[10] Gawain is the hero of this German poem of 30,041 lines, which was written about 1220 by Heinrich von dem Türlin, probably of Steiermark. In the *genre* to which it belongs it has few rivals in respect to the number and extravagance of the adventures that it offers. We find here specimens of almost every fantastic object that went to make up the treasure of mediaeval romance — drinking cups that test the chastity of knights and ladies, magic girdles that render the wearer invisible, images, the sight of which induce an irresistible sleep, etc. — and, of course, the incidents that are necessary to demonstrate the power of these objects. The final adventure of the

---

[9] Cp. Golther, pp. 197f.

[10] Edited by G. H. F. Scholl as vol. 27 in the Bibliothek des Litterarischen Vereins in Stuttgart (Stuttgart, 1852). Miss Weston has translated the Grail episode in her *Sir Gawain at the Grail Castle*, 33 ff. (London, 1903). Gawain reaches the Grail castle at l. 29 153 of the original poem.

romance is Gawain's visit to the Grail castle, on which occasion
he is accompanied by Lancelot and Calogreant. When the knights
arrive, they find in the hall of the Grail castle simply a cheerful,
pleasant scene, such as might have been witnessed almost daily
in a castle of the time — two youths of noble birth playing
chess and jesting, as they play, whilst the Grail lord, who, as in
the continuators of Chrétien (except Manessier), is not lame, looks
on at the game. So, too, with the feast in the evening, in describing which the author emphasizes the splendor of the service,
and the courtesy of the host, and the minstrels' music. Before
the Grail procession enters, a fair youth brings in a sword which
we recognize as the sword that was destined for the Grail knight
in previous Grail romances. As in the corresponding scene in
Chrétien, however, here it is not broken. Heeding the admonition
which he had received from a goddess beforehand, Gawain refrains
from drinking at the feast, but his companions succumb to thirst,
fall into a deep slumber,[11] and so do not share in Gawain's sight
of the Grail procession. The most distinctive feature of the Grail
procession in *Diu Crône* is that the Grail is brought in by a
crowned damsel (the fairest that God had ever created), on a
cloth of samite and resting on a jewel as its base, being, itself,
like a reliquary on an altar, and that the spear dripped three
drops of blood into a salver which the host at once took.[12] Gawain

---

[11] This inopportune slumber was doubtless suggested by Pseudo-
Wauchier, ll. 20299 ff., where Gawain is the victim. From the same
passage, probably, are derived (1) the conception of the Grail lord
as not lame, (2) the rather artless idea that Gawain is warned beforehand that he must ask the question.

[12] The Christian symbolism of this is obvious, and shows that
the author recognizes the whole Grail conception as Christian. The
King says that only he is nourished by the blood. This, however,
is the German poet's own innovation.

Miss Weston, *op. cit.*, p. 82, speaks of the rôle of the weeping
maidens in the Grail procession as being "never clear." In her theory
of Grail origins she derives this feature of the Grail procession (which
is not universal in the Grail romances) from the Weeping Women of
the ancient Adonis festival. But in a scene of mysterious sorrow, why
should one seek outside of the situation itself the suggestion of women

recognizes at once in the Grail-bearer the goddess whom he had met on his way to the Grail castle and who had warned him as to what he should do there (ll. 28345ff.). He now recalls another of her admonitions — namely, that when he saw her again with five maidens in her company, he should not fail to ask what they were doing. Gawain, accordingly, asks the unspelling question, and the Grail people rejoice at the freedom which, through this act of Gawain's, they have regained. Strangest of all, however, the old lord of the Grail castle now tells Gawain that he and his company are, in reality, dead. They had been doomed to this life-in-death as a penance for sin which they had committed in the form of strife among kinsmen, and nothing but the unspelling question could deliver them. Only the maidens of the Grail procession were not spirits. After this pronouncement he and his company vanish. Thus Gawain, as nowhere else in the Grail romances, is permitted to achieve the quest of the sacred vessel.

It has been generally assumed, and rightly, no doubt, that Heinrich von dem Türlin derived much of his material from French romances that are no longer extant, but there is no compelling reason for adopting this hypothesis in regard to the episode of the Grail castle. As was inevitable, every romancer that dealt with this theme introduced some variations into his description of the scene, and the variations which we find in the present instance, including the striking folk-tale conception of the phantom king and courtiers, are such as a German poet could have imagined just as well as a French one.[13] We need not suppose, either, with

---

uttering laments? Of course, after one writer had started this innovation, other writers would imitate him. If one is to seek for an original of this feature in some external source, the Gospels, of course, furnish the example which is nearest to hand, in the women who lament at the grave of Our Lord. And it is to be remembered that in every extant version of the Grail theme, the Grail is regarded as Christian.

[13] The idea that the Grail maiden was a goddess is, of course, not French. It is more natural, however, in a German poet who was doubtless as interested in Frau Saelde, Frau Venus, etc., as other countrymen of his in that age were.

Gaston Paris,[14] that Heinrich made Gawain the hero of the Grail adventure, because he misunderstood the intentions of Chrétien in his *Perceval*. If the author of the *Queste*, a few years before, supplanted Perceval as the Grail Winner by Galahad, an entirely new creation, it would be, to say the least of it, just as easy for the German poet to divert this honor to the credit of Gawain, who was already the most famous figure among the knights of Arthur's court.

2. *Sone de Nausay*.[15] This is a French romance of the latter part of the thirteenth century, a tedious poem of 21,321 lines, which in its incidents is often similar to the Arthurian romances, but is not really connected with Arthur and his knights — not even in its Grail episodes, which alone concern us here.

After various adventures in England, Scotland, and Ireland, Sone, the hero of the romance, goes to Norway with Alain, king of that country. He is taken (ll. 4339ff.) from the mainland to the Grail castle, which is a monastery situated on an isle, not far from the shore. One is surprised at the flora and fauna which Sone finds in Norway — almond and olive trees, camels, griffins and what not.[16] The island of the Grail castle is square, with

[14] *Histoire littéraire de la France*, XXX, 44. *Ibid.*, 43, he thinks that Heinrich, alone, is responsible for the incidents of the episode.

[15] Edited by Moritz Goldschmidt as vol. 216 of the *Bibliothek des Litterarischen Vereins in Stuttgart* (Tübingen, 1899). He says nothing as to the date. A. Scheler, *Le Bibliophile Belge*, p. 253 (1866), puts it in the thirteenth century, although he does not say in which half. The romance, however, evidently belongs to the latter half.

[16] In his "Sone de Nansai et la Norvège," *Romania*, XXXV, 555, (1906), K. Nyrop, whilst recognizing these fantastic features of the descriptions, argues that in certain matters of custom, fauna, etc., the author displays a knowledge of Norway which he could only have acquired by actual travel in the country. I do not, however, feel convinced. As far as custom is concerned, it seems to me that the romancer is much more likely to be adapting materials here which originally related to the Saxons and which he drew from Wace's *Roman de Brut* or some later *Brut*. Moreover, the name of the Grail castle, *Galoche(s)*, *Galoces*, is, surely, not a corruption of *Kastala-Klaustr* (name of one of the old Norwegian monasteries), as Nyrop (p. 568, note) is inclined to think, but of Old French *Galesche*,

a tower at each corner of the square and the Grail castle in the middle. The place is ideally beautiful, with sculptured marble walls enclosing the adjacent lawn and with springs and almond and olive groves nearby. On the walk there were images of leopards, which, when the wind struck their open mouths, emitted the loveliest music. Sone learns from the abbot of the Grail castle that Joseph of Arimathea, having arrived from Ascalon (in Palestine), equipped with arms, had expelled the Saracens from Norway (l. 475f.), converted the people, and made himself king. Joseph loved the daughter of the pagan king whom he had slain, had her baptized, married her, and begot a son upon her, and the son was, likewise, crowned. Nevertheless, his wife continued to hate him for killing her father and many of her friends. God afflicted Joseph for this foolish marriage, so that he was unable to feed or help himself, and a physical blight fell on his land, now called Lorgres (Logres) on account of its sorrows. Fishing was his main solace, whilst he was in this crippled condition, and he came to be known as the Fisher King (l. 4823). At last, a knight cured him and he confounded the misbelievers. Joseph's son, Adam, died first, and his body was placed in a shrine in the Grail castle. Later Joseph, himself, passed away, but, before dying, he provided for the foundation of the Grail castle or monastery. It was inhabited by thirteen monks (typifying Christ and his twelve apostles). The abbot, then (ll. 4885 ff.), produces the Grail, a relic of the true cross, and the bleeding lance. The people kneel and exclaim, "*mea culpa*", as this is done. The abbot next shows them the respective shrines, where Joseph and his son lay. A feast follows, and Alain and Sone, after that, quit the island. We hear later on of a sword which Joseph had guarded his realm with and which the abbot had given to Sone for the latter's combat with a giant King of Scotland. This sword, however, was to be returned to the abbot after the

---

*Galesce* (= Welsh). The Grail castle, being situated in Gales (= Wales) was a "castiax galesches". Owing to some misunderstanding or to the corruption of his source, the author of the *Sone de Nausay* mistook the adjective for a proper name.

combat — an agreement, however, which Sone was tardy in fulfilling.

After the death of Alain (ll. 11778 ff.), his daughter, Odee, inherits the kingdom. She had long been in love with Sone, and ultimately marries him. They go to the Grail castle to be crowned (ll. 16914 ff.) and after the coronation there is a religious service in which the Grail and the relics exhibited on the hero's previous visit to the isle are brought forth, with the addition of a candlestick that was borne by an angel, when the Virgin Mary gave birth to Jesus. It may be remarked that in this passage the last vestige of secrecy about the Grail has disappeared. The Grail service is conducted in the sight of the whole people (ll. 17055 ff.) and after the ceremony is over, the abbot puts the sacred vessel into an ivory box (ll. 17103 ff.), exactly as a priest of the period, after the sacramental service, would restore the chalice to its appointed receptacle. Indeed, the main interest of these Grail episodes of the *Sone de Nausay* lies in the fact that we see here the old veil of mystery that had surrounded the holy vessel in the earlier treatments of the theme finally thrown aside and the identity of the Grail with a vessel of the eucharist acknowledged without disguise.[17]

---

[17] In his edition of the poem Goldschmidt, p. 556, assumes that its author used lost sources that Wolfram also used. His reasons for this assumption are: 1. that in both "verbotene Minne" is the cause of the wounding of the Grail King—Joseph in *Sone de Nausay*, Anfortas in the *Parzival*, 2. that both show a connection with the Swan-knight story. S. Singer and Miss Weston have adopted Goldschmidt's suggestions enthusiastically — the former in "Über die Quelle von Wolfram's Parzival", *Zs. f. d. A.*, XLIV, 330 (1900), the latter in "Notes on the Grail Romances", *Romania*, XLIII, 403 ff. (1914). Singer goes so far as to accept the points which Goldschmidt urges as definitive proof that Wolfram used a different source from Chrétien's *Perceval*. "Nur ein voreingenommener," he declares, "kann noch behaupten, dass Wolfram Chrestien benützt hat." But the two scholars, just named, are blinded by their enthusiasm. Take the first of the two points. There is, in reality, hardly any resemblance at all between the cases of the crippled Grail Kings in the two romances. As we have seen in the *Sone de Nausay*, Joseph became infatuated with

the heathen princess, and had her baptized — though she did not accept Christianity in her heart and hated him for perfectly natural reasons — and then married her. It was a foolish match for him to make, but the marriage was an entirely legimitate one. On the other hand, Wolfram, 472, l. 26, stresses the fact that it was pride ("hochvart") that brought about Anfortas's misfortune and caused him to seek love "ûzerhalp der kiusche sinne", l. 30. His *liaison* was not with the heathen princess, Secundille, as Miss Weston, p. 412, states, but with Orgeluse, who is a "lady of Logres", and not a heathen. As to her relations with Anfortas, see what Orgeluse herself says, *Parzival*, 616, 11ff. Equally without warrant is Miss Weston's assertion, *ibid.*, p. 412, that the *Sone de Nausay* contains a Templar element.

As regards the combination in the French romance of the Grail with the Swan-knight story, the only trace of this in the poem is to be found in the four lines, 20807—20811, where it is said that Sone's son, Houdyans, married Matabrune, a cruel lady from the big and fertile island (sic) of Bohemia. This has, however, no significance whatever. The author is merely doing here what he does elsewhere in the romance, viz. bringing in as minor actors in the story characters who were well known in contemporary romance. Cp. Meleagant, ll. 17151 ff., Orson, 18017 ff., Madoc, 18162 ff. On the other hand, in the prose introduction (pp. 552 ff.), which furnishes a summary of the events of the poem and is obviously by a different hand, we have the Swan-knight tale epitomized in eight or nine lines at the point where Matabrune is mentioned in the poem. There is nothing singular in this, however, since the author of this introduction (like the author of the poem), doubtless, lived in the Netherlands or in the contiguous territory — that is to say, in the region where the Swan-knight legend was most widely current.

As far as the supposed resemblances between our romance and the *Perlesvaus* (cp. Miss Weston, p. 411) are concerned, these stand the test of an examination about as poorly as the matters I have just dealt with; but, if they were real, what difference would that make? The *Perlesvaus*, like virtually all other Arthurian romances of any importance, had been in circulation long before the *Sone de Nausay* was written, and its pages were open to anybody who chose to read them.

For the description of the square island. ll. 17131 ff., (which lies not far from the Grail castle), and its parallel in the Latin romance, *Historia Meriadoci*, pp. 43 f., see the discussion, pp. XXXIV f., in my edition of the *Historia Meriadoci and De Ortu Waluuanii.*

## Chapter VIII.

# Other Theories concerning the Origin of the Grail.

For the sake of completeness I will summarize very briefly certain theories of minor importance that have been advanced to explain the legend of the Holy Grail.

1. Attempts have been made to derive the conception of the Grail from late Jewish, Syrian, and Arabic legends, which are supposed to have reached Western Europe in the Middle Ages. The authors of such theories have none of them been especial students of the Old French romances, in which, of course, the legend was first developed. With the exception of Wesselofsky, they all start from Wolfram's *Parzival* in which (alone of all the Grail texts) the Grail is not a vessel of any kind, but merely a stone. As we have seen, however, this conception of Wolfram's is indisputably the result of some misunderstanding, on his part, of his French original, and so the whole basis of these oriental theories is false.

The authors of these speculations and the essential features of the respective theories are as follows:

(a) M. Gaster, "The Legend of the Holy Grail," *Folk-Lore*, II, 50ff., 198ff., (1891): The Grail quest sprang from an episode of the legend of Alexander the Great, viz. the *Iter ad Paradisum*, or journey to the Earthly Paradise and the marvellous castle or temple of the sun. The Grail, itself, was a certain sacred stone of the temple at Jerusalem, which is still preserved in the so-called Temple of the Rock of that city. A very severe criticism of Gaster's theory which Alfred Nutt appended to the second instalment of Gaster's study seems to have discouraged him from ever publishing the promised continuation. Nutt pointed out that the idea of connecting the Grail story with the *Iter ad Paradisum* had already been advanced by Weismann in his edition (1850) of the Middle High German *Alexander* by Lamprecht, II, 212, note — moreover, that the description of the temple of the sun in the French *Alexander* romances, which alone Chrétien and the authors of the other Grail romances would have consulted, bears no resemblance to the story of the Grail in these latter works. The conception of the Grail as a stone, he observes, too, is peculiar to Wolfram.

(b) Paul Hagen, *Der Gral* (Strassburg, 1900): Wolfram-Guiot represents the legend in its primitive form in many respects better than Chrétien, and he may have had an Arabic source. It developed from the worship of baetyli (holy stones) in the East. The author tries to connect it particularly with the legend of Prester John. Hagen's work is important for Wolfram, but not for the Grail legend, in general.

(c) Willy Staerk, *Über den Ursprung der Grallegende*, (Tübingen and Leipzig, 1903): The Grail legend is simply another form of the legend of an Earthly Paradise, which is found in all parts of the world and, especially, in the East. The author gives an interesting collection of examples of the latter idea, but presents no evidence to establish an historical connection between the two legends.

(d) A. N. Wesselofsky, "Zur Frage über die Heimath der Legende vom heiligen Gral," *Archiv für slavische Philologie,* XXIII, 321ff. (1901). For a list of Wesselofsky's earlier writings on the Grail theme (mostly in Russian) cp. *ibid.,* p. 321, note. The author, who is an advocate of the Christian origin of the Grail, concentrates his attention on the legend of Joseph of Arimathea — and, hence, among the Grail romances, on those in which Joseph plays a leading part, viz. Robert's *Joseph* and the *Grand St. Graal (Estoire del Saint Graal).*[1] In these ro-

---

[1] The oriental Joseph legend which he outlines, pp. 325ff. is now accessible in a German translation by A. Harnack: "Ein in georgischer Sprache überliefertes Apokryphon des Joseph von Aramathia," *Sitzungsberichte der königlich preussischen Akademie der Wissenschaften,* Jahrgang 1901, pp. 920ff. The only part of it which is of interest at all to Grail students, however, is a mere version of the Gospel of

mances, of course, the Grail is, as in the other French romances, a vessel of the sacrament. Wesselofsky's theory involves
all sorts of inadmissible assumptions, e. g. that the passages about
Joseph and Glastonbury in the *De Antiquitate Ecclesiae Glastoniensis* are genuine, that the author of the *Grand St. Graal* drew
(independently of Robert de Boron) on an oriental Christian-
Jewish legend for his conceptions of the Grail. The object of his
article is, as he says (p. 322), to prove "dass in den Quellen
der Romane vom heil. Gral sich Legenden einer christlich-jü-
dischen Diaspora in Palastina, Syrien und Athiopien abspiegeln
und daß ihre Anpassung an das Abendland sich auf dem Wege der
Übertragung vollzogen habe, wobei es augenscheinlich ganz me-
chanisch herging." In order to establish a connection of the
Grail romances with the East — especially with localities in Syria
and Mesopotamia — the author indulges, *inter alia*, in the most
fantastic Oriental derivations of the names of places and persons
in the Grail romances — above all, in the *Grand St. Graal.*[2]

(e) Theodor Sterzenbach, *Ursprung und Entwickelung der
Sage vom heiligen Gral* (Münster dissertation, 1908). He identifies the Grail with a "missorium" (portable altar-stone, according to Sterzenbach) which the Roman general, Aetius (fifth cen-

---

Pseudo-Nicodemus. To be sure, it offers some variants, but the main
one which represents Joseph as receiving the blood of Jesus in a head-
cloth and a large cloth (p. 923), is irreconcilable with the conceptions
of the Grail romances.

[2] Precisely the same criticism applies to Miss M. A. Murray's
attempt to establish an Egyptian origin for the Grail legend. See her
"Egypt in the Grail Romance," in the organ of Egyptian research,
edited by Flinders Petrie and entitled *Ancient Egypt*—volume for
1916, Part I, pp. 1 ff., Part II, 54 ff. She takes the *Estoire* as the
basis of her studies and in Part I offers fanciful Egyptian derivations
for some of its names. In Part II, she gives some illustrations of the
Eucharistic ritual of the Coptic churches. These illustrations are interesting in themselves, but throw no additional light on Grail problems.
Outside of the *Estoire*, the author evidently has little or no acquaintance with the long and intricate Old French texts, which must constitute the true basis for all study of Grail origins. She, accordingly,
makes no allowance for invention on the part of the authors of these
texts, the possibility of one developing suggestions from the other, etc.

tury) is said to have presented to Thorismund, King of the West-goths. He still further identifies it with a "tabula Salomonis" that was captured by the Arabs in their invasion of Spain in 711, and King Roderick, the Spanish monarch, who was slain on that occasion, is the Fisher King. This is all, really, too flimsy for discussion.

(f) Ludwig Emil Iselin: *Der morgenländische Ursprung der Grallegende* (Halle, 1909). The author argues that a Syriac book of sagas, *Book of the Cavern of Treasures*, is the source of the Grail legend. This book dates from the fifth or sixth century. It is one of the numerous Oriental works that pretend to give a complete and edifying history of Adam and his earliest de-scendants, filling out gaps in the Scriptures. The only tolerable analogue to the Grail conceptions, however, which the book offers is in the story of Melchisidek, who guarded the tomb of Adam (this tomb being unapproachable by the profane) and obtained strength and nourishment in a supernatural manner, and on whose offerings the Holy Spirit descended. But the similarity here is of too vague a nature to count for anything and the theory has gained virtually no adherents.[3]

2. Leopold von Schroeder, the eminent Sanskrit scholar, in his treatise *Die Wurzeln der Sage vom heiligen Gral,*[4] has endeav-ored to prove that the Grail legend is simply a variant of the

---

[3] See the very good review of Iselin's book by E. Brugger, *Zs. f. frz. Spr. u. Litt.*, XXXVI[2], 74 ff. (1910). A. Nutt, in *The Aca-demy* for May 7, 1910, though rejecting the theory of the origin of the Grail legend advocated by Iselin, commends his book as "the most convincing plea for the purely Christian origin of the bulk of the Grail cycle with which I am acquainted." But, as I have said above, Iselin proceeds on the assumption that the Grail, according to the primary conception of it, was a stone. Now, that assumption is indisputably false, and, consequently, his solution of the "psychological problem in-volved," as to how the sacrament of the Eucharist came "to be adapted for the purpose of secular entertainment," which Nutt finds "plausible", is without any real basis.

[4] *Sitzungsberichte der Kaiserlichen Akademie der Wissen-schaften. Philosophisch-Historische Classe*, Band 166, 2. Abhand-lung. Wien, 1910.

sun-myth. He seeks analogies in the *Rig-Veda*, which some scholars have dated as far back as 1500 B. C. In the *Rig-Veda*, the
sun is conceived of as a vessel containing hot milk or broth.
Schroeder thinks that the same thing is true of the moon, though
here the matter is not so clear. He cites (pp. 34 ff.) parallels
also from the mythological conceptions of other Indo-European
races and believes (although there is no extant evidence to that
effect) that similar conceptions prevailed among the Celts and
passed from them into the Grail romances. Altogether Schroeder
ransacks mediaeval legend for parallels to various features of the
Grail legend. He shows no knowledge of the Old French romances and the Indian analogues are so remote in time (some
2,000 years) and in space that they are really of no value. One
may remark that at one time or another, it has been the fate of
virtually every great saga to be reduced to the condition of a mere
variant of the sun-myth. The turn of the Grail-legend was bound
to come.[5] Another Austrian scholar, Victor Junk, in his *Gralsage und Graldichtung des Mittelalters*,[6] accepts Schroeder's
theory of the ultimate derivation of the Grail-legend, but regards
as the immediate source the Breton tale of *Peronnik l'idiote*, which
he takes as the myth reduced to the form of a fairy-tale. This tale
however, was first written down by Emil Souvestre in 1845—6,
so that no one can say whether it was in existence in the twelfth
century, or, if so, whether it may not have been modified in
the course of subsequent centuries directly or indirectly by the
Old French romances concerning Perceval, or finally whether the
suspicion expressed by some scholars may not be well-grounded
— viz. that Souvestre "cooked" the story as it was current in
oral form. But, after all, the story resembles the Grail-romances

---

[5] For a refutation of Schröder's theory, see the reviews of his
work by E. Brugger, *Zs. f. frz. Spr. u. Litt.*, XXXVII [2], 163 ff. (1911)
and A. C. L. Brown, *Journal of English and Germanic Philology*
for Jan. 1913 — also, E. Windisch, *Das Keltische Britannien bis
zu Kaiser Arthur*, pp. 119 ff.

[6] *Ibid.*, Band 168, 4. Abhandlung, Wien, 1911. — W. Hertz,
*Sage vom Parzival und dem Gral*, p. 25, (Breslau, 1882), had already
spoken of *Peronnik l'idiote* as plainly connected with the Perceval story.

in so few respects that it could not possibly be regarded as the source of these romances, even if we waived the objections just enumerated. W. Golther, in his review of Junk's treatise (see *Literaturblatt* for Dec. 1912) has pointed out that *Peronnik* is rather a variant of another well-known fairy-tale, *The Journey for the Water of Life.*

Vienna, of recent years, has been particularly fertile in wild theories respecting Arthurian themes. Julius Pokorny, the well-known grammarian (Old Irish) has attained the *ne plus ultra* in this line when he undertook to prove (*Der Ursprung der Arthursage: Mitteilungen der anthropologischen Gesellschaft in Wien,* vol. 39, 1909) that the whole Arthurian story is simply a cuckoo-saga in disguise. This writer derives the Grail legend from the Irish saga of Cuchullin (see above *Mittheilungen,* vol. 42, 1912), which in turn he derives from the same Indo-European myth as von Schroeder.[7]

_____

[7] One might include among these minor theories concerning the origin of the Grail legend the one which G. Baist has briefly outlined in his *Parzival und der Gral* (Freiburg, 1909), pp. 39 ff., and which in certain of its aspects, I have discussed above, p. 264, note 54, and p. 266, note 56. As we have seen, Baist assumes that the Grail originally (i. e. as set forth in the "livre" which Count Philip of Alsace gave to Chrétien) had no marvellous properties of any kind, (religious or otherwise), and that the whole incident of the Grail procession is simply intended to exemplify the rule that silence is not always golden. Any other object would have done just as well. The question (in Chrétien), "Whom does the Grail serve?" is merely the question that serves to undo a spell, which is a frequent *motif* in saga and fairy tales. Chrétien purposely surrounds the matter with a factitious mystery. Furthermore, the poet introduces the bleeding lance with reference to tne meeting of Gawain and Perceval, which he planned for the end of his poem. Chrétien represents the Grail king as nourished by the "ostie" (host), not because of any miraculous qualities of the Grail, but because he was a holy man. Count Philip's book, he thinks, belonged to the Latin "Unterhaltungsliteratur" of the early Middle Ages, and "Weisheitslehren" (e. g. silence is not always golden) were, doubtless, emphasized in it.

Baist brings forward no evidence to support the points which he makes, and as far as I am aware, has won no adherents for his theory.

3. In concluding this chapter on the legend of the Holy Grail, mention should be made of the hexagonal dish or basin,[8] called the Sacro (Sagro) Catino in the cathedral of San Lorenzo at Genoa, which was long accepted as the Holy Grail, not only locally, but by learned men elsewhere.[9] This vessel, which was prized by the Genoese beyond measure as early as the twelfth century, was regarded down to the first decade of the last century as of emerald and was generally identified with the dish of the Last Supper. In the eighteenth century, Fra Gaetano da Teresa produced a book of 335 pages on the subject, entitled *Il Catino di Smeraldo Orientale, Gemma consagrata da N. S. Gesu Cristo nell' Ultima Cena degli Azimi,* etc. (Genoa, 1726). This is a work of enormous industry and nearly everything that modern scholars have said about the Sacro Catino is drawn from it directly or indirectly.[10] It is needless to say that the author has the firmest faith that this is the veritable dish which was used by Our Lord at the Last Supper.

The first mention of this relic occurs in the *Bellum Sacrum*[11] of William of Tyre — a chronicle of the Crusades — in the latter

------

[8] There is a picture of it in C. Rohault de Fleury's *Mémoire sur les Instruments de la Passion,* Plate 23 (Paris, 1870).

[9] Cp. the article, *Graal,* in J. B. B. Roquefort's *Dictionnaire de la langue Romane,* (Paris, 1808). P. Paris, of course, did not share this belief, but he thought that this very vessel might have given the first impulse to the composition of the Grail romances. See his edition of the Old French (thirteenth century) translation of William of Tyre, *Guillaume de Tyr et ses Continuateurs,* I, 353, note 3 (Paris, 1879), where he says: "Mais peut-être l'auteur des deux fameux *Romans du Saint Graal,* devenus l'introduction et le dénoûment d'anciennes légendes bretonnes d'un ordre tout différent, était-il parti de ce vase de Césarée [i. e. the Sacro Catino] pour donner carrière à ses mystiques imaginations."

[10] This and Roquefort's article, *Graal,* just cited, are the main sources of the best modern treatment of the subject, viz., the one in W. Hertz's *Parzival,* pp. 456 ff. Hertz is discussing here blood relics, in general.

[11] Book X, ch. 16.

part of the twelfth century. There is no mention made here of
the identification of the vessel with the dish of the Last Supper,
although the chronicle tells us that the Genoese estimated its value
so highly that they accepted it as their sole share of the booty
on the fall of Caesarea. On the other hand, William already
intimates a doubt as to its being really of emerald, and from the
vehemence with which Jacobus de Voragine, archbishop of Genoa
and author of the famous *Legenda Aurea*, a hundred years later,
defends the venerated relic[12] as a genuine emerald, questionings
on this head must have become louder and louder in the interval.
Nearly five hundred years later we find Fra Gaetano still endeavoring to silence scepticism on this point.[13] The believers were finally discomfited, however, when in 1806 Napoleon I took the
Sacro Catino to Paris. There it was tested by a commission of
the French Institute and declared to be merely coloured glass.
It was restored to Genoa in 1814.

The earliest passage in which the identity of the Genoese
relic with the dish of the Last Supper is assumed is the one from
the Chronicle of Genoa by Jacobus de Voragine[14] to which I have
already referred. He says there that in certain English books
it is told how Nicodemus, when he took the body of Christ down
from the Cross, collected the blood of Our Lord in an emerald
vessel, "et illud vas dicti Angli in libris suis Sanguinalia[15] appel-
lant". This passage was written manifestly under the influence
of the Grail romances — only Jacobus forgets that it was Joseph
of Arimathea in the romances, and not Nicodemus, who collected
the sacred blood. The Sacro Catino he identifies with this vessel.

There are two traditions[16] as to how the supposed emerald
relic came to Genoa. According to one, as has been intimated

---

[12] In his *Chronicon Januense*, ch. 18. Cp. the edition of Muratori, *Rerum Italicarum Scriptores*, IX, 32 f. (Milan, 1726).

[13] Cp. Fra Gaetano, pp. XII ff.

[14] See the passage cited above.

[15] Fra Gaetano, p. 138, quoting the passage, has here *Sangreal*,
Muratori's text, however, gives, no doubt, the original reading.

[16] Cp. Fra Gaetano, pp. 1 ff. and 250 ff., respectively. He de-
clines, pp. 272 f., to decide between them.

above, it was a part of the Genoese booty on the capture of Caesarea in 1101, during the first Crusade; according to the other, it came into their possession in 1147, on the fall of Almeria in Spain. The Genoese had assisted King Alfonso in the siege of the city. The testimony of William of Tyre, however, seems to prove beyond question that the first of these traditions is the correct one.

# PART III.

## THE PROSE ROMANCES.

# Chapter I.
# Beginnings of the Prose-Romances.

As we have seen above, the production of the metrical romances was proceeding vigorously in the closing years of the twelfth
century and the opening years of the thirteenth, but it was just
in this period that the new *genre* of the prose romance began —
the *genre* which long before the end of the Middle Ages was destined to eclipse the metrical romances completely in popular favor.
The composition of romances in prose is simply one feature of the
general rise of French prose in the latter part of the twelfth
century, which, in turn, was favored, no doubt, by the more general knowledge of reading that was characteristic of the time. The
author of the Old French prose romance, the *Mort Artu*, thought
it worth while recording of Arthur that he knew enough of letters
to understand a writing.[1] We see, therefore, that even royal personages were not very learned in the period under consideration.
According to Wauchier de Denain,[2] Perceval was still worse off,
for he could not read at all. As long as facility in reading was
confined to a few and even members of the higher classes were
mainly dependent on being read aloud to,[3] the traditional form

---

[1] Bruce's *Mort Artu*, p. 50.

[2] Cp. his continuation to Chrétien's *Perceval*, l. 33957, "Mais
Pierchevaus ne savoit lire" (Potvin's edition). — The line occurs in
the description of Perceval's adventure at Mont Dolerous. On top of
the mountain there was a pillar with an inscription on it, declaring
that the achievement of the adventure was reserved for the best knight
in the world, but Perceval was unable to read it. — In the prose
*Lancelot* (Sommer, III, 154) we are told that Lancelot could read,
but Gawain could not.

[3] In the *Lancelot* (Sommer, III, 106) it is said that Lancelot's
mother used to make her chaplain read saints' lives aloud to her. This,
to be sure, does not necessarily imply that she could not read herself.
Even in antiquity reading aloud and in company was much commoner
than nowadays. In his *Confessions*, Book VI, ch. 3, St. Augustine
speaks of St. Ambrose's habit of silent reading, as if it were unusual.

of narrative — namely, verse — was not likely to yield ground; but as soon as a knowledge of reading became more general and people were no longer dependent on professional reciters, the superior attraction of prose for many who were interested in these stories of love and adventure would be sure to make itself felt. What is here said applies, of course, especially to women, who must have constituted the majority of the romance-writer's *clientèle*.

Owing to the causes just indicated, the production of the Arthurian prose-romances began about the end of the twelfth century, and, to judge merely by the bulk of what has survived, it must have been truly prodigious in the course of the next forty to fifty years, to say nothing of the later period.

Probably, the earliest prose-romance was the prose-rendering of Robert de Boron's *Joseph* which, doubtless, owed this distinction to its quasi-religious character. Down to this time virtually the only French prose consisted of brief saints' lives, and a work of the nature of the *Joseph*, so closely akin to that species of composition, would furnish a suitable transition from what was substantially religious fiction to purely secular romance. The *Merlin* which comes immediately after the *Joseph* in Robert's scheme, would naturally be the next of the romances to receive a prose dress[4] — not unlikely, from the same hand — and after

---

[4] This prose-rendering of Robert's *Merlin* begins, of course, the *Merlin* branches in the so-called Walter Map and Robert de Boron cycles of the prose romances. Cp. Sommer, II, 3—88 and Huth-Merlin, I, 1—146, respectively. In each of these cycles there are continuations far longer than the prose-Robert, itself.

Brugger, *Zs. f. frz. Spr. u. Litt.*, XXIX[1], 75 f. (1905), thinks, too, that the prose-renderings of Robert's *Joseph* and *Merlin* were the earliest prose-romances, and suggests that their author adopted this form, in order to accentuate the historical character of Robert's narratives the better. The reason for this adoption given above, however, seems more satisfactory.

On the other hand, G. Paris, *Mélanges de littérature française du moyen age*, I, 50, expresses the opinion that the *Lancelot* (in an earlier form than that which we possess) was the first prose romance.

these would follow the longer prose romances which have come down to us, also, in cyclic form and which, as we may safely assert, were composed in prose from the start.[5]

Having already dealt with the brief prose-renderings of Robert's *Joseph* and *Merlin*,[6] we shall begin our consideration of the prose romances in this place with the great cyclic romances in prose, which, as has just been said, never existed in metrical form.

---

He supports this opinion, however. with no evidence. The comparative brevity of the prose *Joseph* and *Merlin*, also, makes their priority more likely.

[5] It is possible that there existed, earlier than our cyclic romances, prose-renderings of metrical romances other than Robert's, but there is no evidence to that effect. Gröber, *Grundriss*, II, I, 1004, assumes that the adaptation of Chrétien's *Lancelot*, which we find in the prose *Lancelot*, was originally a separate work. Brugger, too, conjectures, *Zs. f. frz. Spr. u. Litt.*, XXXI[2], 276, that our prose *Lancelot* is simply an adaptation of an earlier poem. Neither conjecture, however, is supported by any evidence.

[6] Cp. pp. 144 ff., above.

## Chapter II.
## The Prose Cycles.

There are two great cycles of Arthurian romances in prose:
(1) That which is known as the Vulgate or Walter Map Cycle.
(2) That which is known as the Pseudo-Robert-de-Boron Cycle.
The former is not only infinitely more important than the latter,
in every respect, but it is earlier in date,[1] and it will, therefore,
first claim our attention.

The Vulgate Cycle is so called, because it became the most
popular redaction of the romances in the Middle Ages, almost
completely displacing all other versions. It is made up of the
five great romances, *L'Estoire del Saint Graal* (or *Grand St. Graal*,
as scholars have often called it, although this title is not found
in the MSS.), *L'Estoire de Merlin* (prose rendering of Robert's
*Merlin* plus a continuation), *Li Livres (L'Estoire) de Lancelot*, *La
Queste del Saint Graal* and *La Mort Artu*, and it exists either
complete or in part in a large number of MSS. — probably not
far from a hundred. The name of Map is, also, given to this
cycle, because the MSS. regularly ascribe to him the composition
of the last three members of the cycle.[2] This attribution, how-

---

[1] The contrary opinion which has been entertained by some
scholars will be considered below.

[2] The facts are correctly stated by Brugger, *Zs. f. frz. Spr.
u. Litt.*, XXIX [1], 90, note 47, — only, as regards the *Queste* and
*Mort Artu*, he should have expressed himself more strongly; for the
ascription occurs regularly in the MSS. at the end of the former and
at both the beginning and the end of the latter. The few exceptions
are evidently due to an effort at condensation on the part of individual scribes. At the end of the *Mort Artu*, as Brugger observes,
the language implies that Map wrote, also, the *Lancelot*, e. g. Add.
10294: "Si se taist ore maistre gautiers map de lestoire de lancelot."
The ascription occurs, also, sometimes at the conclusion of the *Lan-*

ever, is manifestly a fiction and has been generally rejected by recent scholars.[3] The following considerations prove that it is false: (1) As will appear from our analyses of the romances and from the discussion below, there is no likelihood that even the *Lancelot* is the work of one man, much less three romances so different in power, style, and tone as the *Lancelot, Queste,* and *Mort Artu.* (2) No one has ever claimed for the *Lancelot* an earlier date than the last decade of the twelfth century — generally it is dated later — but even in 1190 Map was a man of about fifty years of age[4] and it is in the highest degree unlikely — especially under mediaeval conditions — that he should have taken to the writing of romances at that time of life. (3) Map himself expressly

---

*celot,* but one cannot say how often, until further collations of that branch have been made. — For MSS. of the Vulgate cycle cp. H. O. Sommer, *Vulgate Version of the Arthurian Romances,* I, pp. XXIII —XXXII. For the *Lancelot* MSS. cp. besides, the *Vorwort* to G. Bräuner's *Der altfranzösische Prosaroman von Lancelot del Lac I Branche. Marburger Beiträge zur romanischen Philologie,* Heft II, and for those of the *Mort Artu,* Bruce's edition of that romance, pp. XII, ff. In the last-named list the following MSS. are omitted: 122, f. fr. (B. N.) — which, like MS. 342, shows an unabridged text for the passage, pp. 102 ff. (Bruce's ed.) — and the Vatican MS. Palat. 1967. For the latter (recently discovered), which contains only the *Mort Artu,* cp. *Romania,* XLVI, 151 (1920). F. Lot has in preparation a special work on the MSS. of the Vulgate cycle.

[3] Cp., for example, Birch-Hirschfeld, *Sage vom Gral,* pp. 227 ff. (Leipzig, 1877), G. Paris, *Manuel,* 62, and Sommer, *Zs. f. rom. Ph.,* XXXII, 336 (1908). As will be seen, however, below, p. 371, note 8, the old idea of Map's connection with the cycle has been revived in a modified form by certain scholars.

[4] For the life of Map, see H. L. D. Ward's *Catalogue of the Romances in the Department of Manuscripts in the British Museum,* I, 734 ff. (1883), and the article on him in the *Dictionary of National Biography.* These are better than the fuller, but antiquated, life by Georg Phillips, *Walter Map: Ein Beitrag zur Geschichte König Heinrichs von England und des Lebens an seinem Hofe, Sitzungsberichte* of the Vienna Academy of Sciences, Philos. = hist. Klasse, X, 319 ff. (1853). Concerning earlier views about W. Map and the *Lancelot,* cp. Graesse, *Lehrbuch einer allgemeinen Literärgeschichte,* Band II, Abtheilung III, pp. 188 ff. Dresden and Leipzig (1842).

states in the oft-quoted words preserved by Giraldus Cambrensis[5]
that he wrote little or nothing. According to Giraldus, Map said
to him: "Multa, magister Giralde, scripsisti, et multum adhuc
scribitis: et nos multa diximus. Vos scripta dedistis et nos verba."
He goes on to say that, although the writings of Giraldus were
of much more importance than his (Map's) words, (i. e. spoken
words), yet, because his words were in the vernacular, which everybody understood, they had brought him greater profit than all
of his friend's Latin.[6]

The implication of this statement of Map's is borne out by
the little that we know of his life and activities, his only authentic
literary production being the *De Nugis Curialium (Courtiers'*
*Triflings)*, which is a collection of tales and anecdotes loosely
thrown together. In his own time his reputation was that of
a wit and satirist, and there is no evidence that he possessed even

---

[5] *Hiberniae Expugnatio*, Rolls Series edition of Giraldus's Works,
V, 410 f. (1867).

[6] P. Paris, *Romans de la Table Ronde*, I, 472, tried to get
around the plain meaning of these words by interpreting *scribere* as
writing in Latin, *dicere* as writing in the vernacular, but there is no
such distinction as this elsewhere. Cp. Birch-Hirschfeld, p. 229.
Brugger, too, *op. cit.*, p. 93, note 49, denies any importance to these
words reported by Giraldus; for, as a matter of fact, he says, Map
did write the *De Nugis*, and he may have counted the (supposed)
*Lancelot* romance as just as little worth mentioning as that work.
The two works, however, would certainly be on a different plane, for
the *De Nugis*, as said above, is a mere disconnected collection of
anecdotes and tales and there is no likelihood that Map ever attempted
to make it generally known, seeing that it exists in only one (fifteenth
century) MS. Cp. the recent and best edition of the book by M. R. James
(Oxford, 1914). Indeed, James Hinton, whose study of the *De Nugis*,
viz., "Walter Map's *De Nugis Curialium*, its plan and composition,"
PMLA, XXXII, 81 ff. (1917), is the ablest we have, concludes that
Map left this book in the condition of loose fragments, which were
put together by some one else after his death. So, too, Henry Bradley,
*English Hist. Review*, XXXII, 400 (1917).

It should be remembered, moreover, that many poems, not composed by Map, were fathered upon him. Cp. the volume edited by
Thomas Wright for the Camden Society, *Latin Poems commonly*
*attributed to Walter Map* (London, 1841).

in the prime of his life the power to carry through a work of sustained invention, such as is exhibited in even the shortest of the three romances named above.[7] He was one of the chief men of his age and of Welsh origin, and it was doubtless on these accounts that some scribe or redactor, or possibly even the author of some part of the cycle, endeavored to win the prestige of his name for these pseudo-Celtic stories.[8]

---

[7] Similar is the conclusion of Hinton, *op. cit.* p. 142. J. Bardoux in his Paris thesis, *De Walterio Mappio*, pp. 159 ff. (1900) had argued that Map supplied the material for the romances that are ascribed to him, although he did not write them himself.

[8] Ward, p. 734 of the *Catalogue* cited above, quotes a passage from the *Ipomedon*, ll. 7183 (edition of E. Kölbing and E. Koschwitz, Breslau, 1889), of Hue de Rotelande to prove that Map really composed a romance, which he conjectures to have been a metrical *Lancelot*, of which our Vulgate *Lancelot* is the prose rendering. Hue, who wrote between 1174 and 1191, lived near Hereford, with which place Map was connected all his life, and he presumably knew Map. Shortly after a passage based on the three tournament *motif* in his *Ipomedon*, (the passage ends with l. 6772) Hue excuses himself in a jesting manner for lying and says:

"Sul ne sai pas de mentir lart,
Walter map reset ben sa part."

Now this same three tournament *motif* is found in the prose *Lancelot*, III, 214 ff., and Ward accordingly concludes that Hue, in writing his own passage on this *motif*, had in mind Map's treatment of the same subject in a hypothetical verse original of the prose *Lancelot*. Ward's theory has been taken up enthusiastically by Miss Weston, *Three Days Tournament*, pp. 6 ff. (London, 1902), and in her article on Map in the *Encyclopaedia Britannica* (Eleventh edition) — also, by Brugger, *Zs. f. frz. Spr. u. Litt.* XXIX[1], 90 ff., (1905), both of whom identify this hypothetical verse *Lancelot* with the French original of Ulrich von Zatzikhoven's *Lanzelet*.

Hue's allusion to Map, as we have seen, occurs in a jesting passage, and the most natural interpretation of it would be that he was simply getting off a pleasantry at his friend's expense. Kölbing, p. VI of his edition, suggests that the allusion may be to Map's *De Nugis*. The three days tournament *motif* is so common a one in folk-tales and romances that the instances in the *Ipomedon* and *Lanzelet* need not be directly connected with each other. In any event, we certainly require something more solid than the proximity of this

*motif* and the allusion to Map in the *Ipomedon* (they are really separated by about 460 lines) to justify the hypothesis that Map wrote
the lost French poem which is used at the beginning of the prose
*Lancelot.* Generally speaking, the latter owes precious little to this
lost French original of the *Lanzelet* (cp. RR, X, 54f., note), so that,
even if we accepted Brugger's and Miss Weston's hypothesis, Map's
contribution to the evolution of the cycle would be extremely slight.

H. Suchier, *Zs. f. rom. Ph.*, XVI, 273 (1892) accepts the genuineness of the ascription of the cycle to Map on the ground that
Manessier (Potvin VI, 158), who, in his opinion, wrote between
1214 and 1220 — so shortly after Map's death — had already before him the *Queste* with the same conclusion that we find in our
extant MSS. about the original narrative of the Grail quest being preserved at Salisbury. As a matter of fact, Manessier here does not
mention Map's name, though it stood very probably in his MS. of the
*Queste.* If it did, this would merely prove that the ascription got
into the MSS. very early, not that it was genuine. But the whole
passage in question at the end of the *Queste,* including the ascription
to Map, is, on the face of it, a fraud, for although the fact has been
generally overlooked by Arthurian scholars, there was never any monastery at Salisbury. Cp. Dugdale's *Monasticon Anglicanum* and
Abbot Gasquet's *English Monastic Life,* p. 301 (London, 1904), —
the list of English religious houses.

Suchier's views were adopted by E. Wechssler, *Die Sage vom
heiligen Gral,* pp. 126ff. (Halle, 1898).

Birch-Hirschfeld, *Sage vom Gral,* pp. 234, ff., it should be observed, has called attention to the improbability of Map's always
speaking of himself in the third person, as he is made to do in these
ascriptions which we find in the MSS. of the Vulgate cycle. He suggests that such ascriptions got into the MSS. of that cycle through
the confusion of some Meistre Gautier or other with the Walter, archdeacon of Oxford, who, according to Geoffrey of Monmouth, at the
end of his *Historia,* brought the (fictitious) original of that work "ex
Britannia". But this is not likely.

Of as little value as the passage in Manessier are the oft-quoted
passages (cp. for instance, Birch-Hirschfeld, pp. 230f.) from the pretended Helie de Borron, viz. in the Prologue to *Guiron le Courtois*
and in the Epilogue to the *Bret,* which speak of Map, "qui fu clers
au roy Henri" (Prologue), as the author of "lestoire" (Prologue) or
"lou propre livre" (Epilogue) "de monseigneur Lancelot dou Lac."
There is no ground, however, for believing that this self-styled Helie
de Borron, who certainly was not writing earlier than 1230, knew
any more about the matter than we do. He was simply repeating or

drawing inferences from the ascriptions in MSS. like ours—particularly, MSS. of the *Queste* and *Mort Artu.* This explains sufficiently what C. L. Kingsford in the article on Map in the *Dictionary of National Biography* regards as a confirmation of the correctness of Helie's statement, viz., the fact that he does not speak of Map as archdeacon — the rank which Map held from the year 1197 on — but as a simple clerk, which he was in his earlier life — i. e. at the time when he was most likely to write romances.

The MS. of the *Estoire* printed by Hucher even assigns, III, 504, to Map a share in that romance. Robert wrote it with the "aid" of Map!

## Chapter III.
# The Vulgate Cycle.

Referring our readers to Vol. 2 for analyses of these romances, we shall now examine the successive members or "branches" of the Vulgate cycle in the same order that they occur in our cyclic MSS.

## 1. L'Estoire del Saint Graal.

The *Estoire del Saint Graal* presupposes the *Lancelot* and the *Queste*,[1] and there are apparently allusions in it even to the

---

[1] That the *Queste* was older than the *Estoire* was the opinion of Birch-Hirschfeld, pp. 55 ff., Nutt, pp. 108 ff., and G. Paris, *Manuel*, § 60. See, too, quite recently A. Pauphilet, in his review of Lot's *Lancelot* in *Romania*, XLV, 524 ff. Pauphilet argues convincingly, also, that the *Estoire* and *Queste* are by different authors. The present writer had already expressed the same views, MLN, XXXIV, 397, on both points. Some scholars, however, hold the contrary opinion: viz., on the one hand, Heinzel, pp. 125 ff., who believed, moreover, that the two romances were by different authors, and, on the other, E. Wechssler, *Sage vom heiligen Graal*, p. 126 (Halle, 1898), Miss Weston, *Legend of Sir Lancelot*, p. 139 (London, 1901), Brugger, *Zs. f. frz. Spr. u. Litt.*, XXIX[1], 89, note 45, and 99, note 58 (1905), and Lot, *Lancelot*, pp. 122 ff. (1918), who believe that they have the same author. On these matters see, still further, note 3, below.

If the four scholars last named were right, the numerous allusions in the *Estoire* to the *Queste* would be to a work planned, but not yet executed. Heinzel supposes that such allusions did not belong to the hypothetical first form of the *Estoire* which Nutt, pp. 75, 95, and himself assume. (The redaction of the only extant form of the *Estoire* he places, p. 125, after 1223, because of an allusion in Hucher's text, III, 655, to King Philip Augustus as dead. The allusion, however, may well be a late scribe's addition.) As a matter of fact, apart from the question of the relative dates of the *Estoire* and *Queste*, there are some circumstances that excite suspicion that there did exist such a version. For example, the introduction from Robert of the Bron-Alain Grail-keeper group towards the end of the branch (Sommer, I, 247), when the whole action of the romance up to that point had been carried on by an entirely different set of Grail-keeper characters

*Mort Artu.*[2]   In his *Joseph,* Robert de Boron had given an ac-

— Joseph excepted.  Observe, too, that, according to the extant MSS.
of the *Estoire,* the Grail Winner (Galahad) had no connection by
descent at all with the original Grail-keeper (Joseph of Arimathea).
The latter's direct descendant, according to the romance, is Yvain,
who, of course, nowhere in Arthurian romance has any real connection
with the Grail.  (When Sommer, side-note to p. 281, also, makes
Gawain a direct descendant of Joseph's this is an error).  It is hardly
credible that such was the case in the original authentic text.  On
all this see Bruce, RR, IX, 253f. — Note, also, that according to
the *Estoire* I, 81, the Maimed King, who is to be cured by Galahad's
coming, is destined to be wounded with the (Grail) lance — a conception which harmonizes with *Queste,* VI, 150, where this king, here
called *Pellinor* in some MSS., enters Solomon's ship, despite the warning inscription, draws David's (the Grail) sword, and at the same
moment is pierced through the thighs with a lance.  On the other
hand, in the *Estoire,* I, 290, the Maimed King, here called *Pelleam
(Pellehan),* got his wound (with what weapon is not said) in a "bataille de Rome", the author (as Lot, *Lancelot,* p. 241, has suggested)
having, no doubt, in mind Chrétien's Fisher King, who was thus wounded (ll. 3471ff.).  Lot, *loc. cit.,* sees no difficulty in accepting these
conflicting statements as the blunder of a single author.  I confess
that I find this explanation not so easy.

It may be remarked in passing, that the names, *Pelleam* and
*Pellinor,* are doubtless really the same name, the one springing from
the other by MS. corruption.  See, respectively, Bruce's "Pelles,
Pellinor and Pellean in the Old French Arthurian Romances," MPh,
XVI, 113ff., 337ff. (1918), where Pellinor is taken to be the original
form, and Lot, *Lancelot,* pp. 242ff. (1918), where *Pellehan* (variant
of *Pelleam*) is supposed to be the original.

In regard to the question under discussion it should be observed
that in two of the extant MSS. of the *Estoire* there is an indisputable interpolation, viz., the Grimaud episode, Hucher's edition, III,
311ff.  This failed to fix itself in the general MS. tradition, but it
is possible that some earlier changes or interpolations were more fortunate.  Especially open to suspicion is the prose *fabliau,* I, 171ff.,
concerning a woman's deception of the wise physician, Hippocrates.
Apropos of this episode, Lot himself remarks, p. 382, note 2, that
the text of the *Estoire* shows "traces de remaniement."

[2] Cp. references to this branch in the *Estoire,* I, 226, 280, 283.
To be sure, the Tower of Marvels, I, 226, does not occur in the
*Mort Artu.*

count of the early history of the Grail that is thoroughly imbued
with the spirit of mediaeval Christian legend and doctrine. In
this work, however, neither Lancelot nor his ancestors nor his
posterity had been brought into any sort of connection with the
Grail, as, indeed, they are not mentioned in the whole poem. But
just as in the *Queste* such a connection is established for the quest
of the Grail through the supplanting of Perceval, the original
Grail Winner, by Lancelot's son, Galahad, so for the early history
of the Grail this connection is also established in the *Estoire*
through the linking of the vessel's fate in its earlier wanderings
with that of the ancestors of Lancelot and his son. Now, whether
we accept the theory of some scholars that these intimately connected branches, the *Estoire* and *Queste,* were the work of the
same hand[3] or not, it seems reasonable to suppose that the latter

---

[3] For arguments against identity of authorship, see Birch-Hirschfeld, pp. 58 ff., Nutt, pp. 81, 108 f., and Pauphilet, *op. cit.*, pp. 522 ff.
    Birch-Hirschfeld cites the fullness with which in the *Queste*
matters related in the *Estoire* are recapitulated as tending to prove
that the two were by different hands. It is true that we do have
incidents in the former retold in the latter rather fully (cp. respectively, VI, 24 ff. with I, 21 ff., VI, 54 f. with I, 216, VI, 60 ff. with I,
231 ff.), and, in at least one case, a long passage copied virtually
verbatim (cp. VI, 151, l. 11—161, l. 22 with I, 124, l. 6—137, l. 3).
To a single author, says the German scholar, a mere allusion to the
other romance would have seemed sufficient. One might object to this,
with some plausibility, that, after all, the two romances were separate
works and that the author could not count on both of them being at
the same time in the hands of his readers, so that he may have inserted in the two romances such passages by way of supplying the
necessary thread of connection. In my own opinion, however, these
insertions are much more likely to have been the work of the redactors
of the cycle. It may be remarked, furthermore, that if such redactors
did undertake to interpolate passages of this kind, there is no reason
to doubt that they made other adjustments of the two romances to
each other — more particularly, of the *Queste* to the *Estoire.*
    Birch-Hirschfeld, also, cites supposed contradictions between the
two branches as proving that they were from different hands. These,
it is true, have, for the most part, been reasonably explained away by
Lot, *Lancelot*, pp. 80 ff. Such inconsistencies, however, as the following
seem, to say the least of it, very singular, under the theory of single

was first composed. The great departure in Grail tradition which distinguishes the two romances is the substitution of the chaste Galahad for the unchaste Perceval of Chrétien and his earlier continuators as the Grail Winner. But the ascetic who first hit upon the idea of this substitution would surely have proceeded forthwith to endow his new conception with life — to create his new hero and put him in action — instead of first composing a long romance (the *Estoire*) about this hero's ancestors and their re-

authorship: (1) In the *Estoire*, I, 247, the vacant seat at the Grail table is reserved for Christ or for some one whom he will send to fill it, and Moys (a relative of Josephe's, according to I, 248), who tries to occupy it, is snatched away by fiery hands; in the *Queste*, VI, 55, this seat is said to be reserved for Josephe, and a rebellious relative (unnamed) of his, who tries to occupy it, is swallowed up by the earth. (2) In the *Estoire* (I, 247) the vacant seat is at the Grail table; in the *Queste* (VI, 5, 7) at the Round Table.

In the present writer's opinion, however, Pauphilet, *loc. cit.* has furnished a conclusive argument against the theory of identical authorship, by pointing out essential differences of conception between the two in respect to various passages not noted by Birch-Hirschfeld, including those in the respective romances (I, 40, VI, 190, 578) which reflect the conflicting views in contemporary theology as to the point in the sacramental service when the miracle of transubstantiation took place.

In conclusion, with regard to these questions of identical authorship and relative date, I wish to add the following: If the Bron-Alain group really belonged to the *Estoire* from the beginning — which, to be sure, is very doubtful — and is not a later addition, it would seem that considerable force should be credited to Nutt's argument that, if the *Queste* were later than the *Estoire*, some mention would have been made of this group in it. Again, such an obscure allusion as that to the maiming of the Maimed King by the lance in the *Estoire*, I, 81, seems much more naturally interpreted as an allusion to an incident already related (*Queste*, VI, 150) than to one that the author merely intended to write about. If the latter supposition is true, he took his time about executing his intention; for, leaving out of account the intervening branches, I, 81 and VI, 150 are separated by upwards of 400 quarto pages.

Although generally similar, moreover, in style, the differences noted above, between the two works in this respect should be observed. The *Queste* is compact and austere, the *Estoire* runs easily into the romantic and the sensational.

lation to the early history of the Grail — a romance, indeed, half as long again as that which tells the hero's own story.[4] Just as in the *chansons de geste* the poets naturally began by celebrating the great deeds of their heroes, performed in the full vigor of maturity — the deeds that had given these characters their renown — and only later (the original author, or more frequently, another), if occasion arose, exploited the curiosity which the narration of such feats of arms may have awakened among their hearers or readers by presenting, still further, the story of the *enfances* (achievements of early youth) of the heroes in question, so, doubtless, it was with the Grail. First would come the narrative of the holy vessel, where its quest constituted the highest adventure that could enlist both the bodily and the spiritual energies of the best knights of Arthur's court; in the second line would come the history of its origins and early fortunes. Thus everything in the *Estoire* would be conditional on the conceptions and narrative of the *Queste*. But when the two romances were brought into intimate manuscript union, as members of the Vulgate cycle, such insertions would have to be made in the *Queste* by the *assembleurs* as would harmonize it with the new inventions concerning the early history of the Grail (the *Estoire*). Similar insertions were certainly made in the original *Lancelot* after the

---

[4] Lot, who believes that the *Estoire* and the *Queste* are by the same man and that the *Queste* was the later of the two has the following theory (pp. 122 ff.) concerning the composition of the *Estoire:*

Owing to certain allusions to Perceval as the Grail Winner in the early part of the *Lancelot* (cp. Part IV, below), he conjectures that the author of the Lancelot-Grail *corpus* had written a considerable portion (approximately, a third) of the *Lancelot* before it occurred to him to deprive Perceval of that honor in favor of a new character, Galahad. He then laid aside the *Lancelot*, went back and composed the *Estoire*, returned again to the *Lancelot*, completed it and composed thereafter, in succession, the *Queste* and the *Mort Artu*. For criticism of this theory see Bruce, RR. X, 385 f. and Pauphilet, *Romania*, XLV, 521 f. The enormous length of these romances, besides, should be remembered; but, even in the case of shorter compositions, can anything parallel to the procedure which Lot attributes to his hypothetical author be found anywhere in the world's literature?

composition of the Grail romances of the cycle, so that there is nothing arbitrary in assuming modifications of this kind in the *Queste*.[5]

Looking, however, exclusively at the *Estoire* for the present, the author takes Robert's account of the early history of the Grail as the basis of his romance, but he modifies his source so as to make it conform to the new conceptions throughout, keeping constantly in mind, above all, the new hero (Galahad) and the ascetic ideal which that character embodies. Just as this ascetic ideal, however, required a new champion as the knight of the Grail quest, so it required a new and stricter representative of the church as the guardian and minister of the Grail in its early wanderings in the Orient and in Great Britain. The tone of Robert's poem is profoundly religious, but to an ecclesiastic with strongly orthodox and ascetic views, such as our author evidently held, there was a flaw even in Robert's conception of the first Grail-keeper (Joseph of Arimathea): He did not fulfill the condition of celibacy which was required by the mediaeval church of the ministers of its sacraments (symbolized by the Grail).[6] Accordingly, just as in the *Queste* the Perceval of Chrétien and his continuators has to yield the first place to Galahad, so in the *Estoire* Robert's Joseph has to yield the first place to a new creation, Josephe(s), who fulfilled this necessary condition. Never-

---

[5] I am postulating here, of course, contrary to Lot, that the Lancelot-Grail *corpus* is not the work of one author. For the weaknesses of Lot's theory see Part IV, below, and RR, X, 377 ff. — also, A. Pauphilet, *Romania*, XLV, 521 ff.

[6] This is obviously the reason why the new character, Josephe(s), was created. Similar is the opinion expressed by Lot, *Lancelot*, p. 205. There is no reason, therefore, to imagine with Heinzel, pp. 105 ff., that already in Christian legend, before the composition of the Grail romances, Joseph had been given a son, Josephe, owing, in some way, to a confusion, originally, of the former with the historian, Josephus. So, too, Brugger, who derives the *Estoire* from the *Perlesvaus*, discusses, *Zs. f. frz. Spr. u. Litt.*, XXIX [1], 100 f., the creation of the character, Josephe, as if it were a great problem. It might be, if the *Estoire* really were dependent on the *Perlesvaus*, but on that subject see Part IV, below.

theless, it is to be noted, that in neither case is the previous hero totally discarded; he is merely subordinated to the new one.[7] In the case of the *Estoire,* moreover, the author softens the change by making the new hero the son of the old and by conferring on this son (Josephe) the father's name, only in a slightly variant form.[8]

In the new romance, as in Robert's *Joseph,* the identification of the Grail with a vessel of the Eucharistic service is complete — except that, through an inopportune recognition of the fact that the true meaning of the word, *graal (grail),* was a kind of dish, the author rejects Robert's more harmonious conception and makes this vessel the dish,[9] not the chalice of the Last Supper. Since our Lord, himself, however, had declared that the chalice contained his blood, this circumstance, apart from the natural fitness of that vessel for the purpose, had pointed to it rather than to the dish as the proper receptacle for the blood which flowed from his wounds on the day of his crucifixion. Nevertheless, in other respects, the choice between the two vessels was immaterial, for the ineffable sanctity that pertained to the Grail was due to the holy blood, itself, and not to the containing vessel. Furthermore, it is as a general symbol of the Eucharistic mysteries and doctrines that the Grail is clothed with majesty and power.[10] Consequently, there is nothing inconsistent when we find it side by

---

[7] Even in his subordinate rôle, however, Perceval is represented in the *Queste* as perfectly chaste, to suit the spirit of that romance.

[8] On these names, derived, respectively, from *Joseph* and *Josephus,* cp. *Perlesvaus* section, Part IV, below.

[9] Cp. I, 13, "lescuele en le quele li fiex dieu auoit mangiet. This term, *escuele,* which is applied generally to the Grail in this text (cp. I, 14, 18, 19, *et passim*), often designates a bowl or similar vessel. For example, it was commonly used in the Middle Ages of the receptacle in which beggars received the food that was given to them. On the other hand, it, also, meant sometimes simply *dish,* as in Pseudo-Wauchier's description of the dinner at the Grail castle, Potvin, III, 367.

[10] This general symbolism, no doubt, encouraged vagueness in the description of the Grail.

side with actual individual vessels that are used in the celebration of the mass.[11]

The wanderings of the Grail company in Robert's poem, so obviously modelled after those of the children of Israel in the wilderness, in the book of *Exodus*, suggested the idea of the ark in which our author represents the sacred vessel to have been borne about.[12] But this ark, too, like everything in the narrative, has its symbolical meaning. It is Holy Church which carries in her bosom the fundamental mysteries of the true faith.

For our author, as for Pseudo-Wauchier,[13] and Wauchier,[14] the bleeding lance is the lance with which the side of our Lord was pierced whilst he hung on the cross. The blood, then, which drips from its point, is the blood of the Savior, and it, accordingly, possesses, in a miraculous degree, the power of healing.[15] On the other hand, Chrétien, another of his sources, had ascribed to this same lance a terribly destructive power: the whole kingdom of Logres was one day to be destroyed by it.[16] Consequently, according to our author's conception, it is an instrument of wrath

---

[11] Cp. I, 33, 41. Heinzel, p. 132, cites these passages as proving that, owing to orthodox hesitations, the author of the *Estoire*, after all, did keep the Grail worship separate from the mass. The explanation, however, which I have given in the text is, I believe, the true one. On the other hand, when at the end of the *Queste*, VI, 190, Christ, himself, and not a mortal, conducts the sacramental service, the questers receive "la haute viande" direct from the Grail.

[12] I, 20 f., 30 ff. *et passim*.

[13] Potvin, IV, I, 4 f.

[14] *Ibid.* V. 143 ff.

[15] *Estoire*, I, 80 f. So, too, in *Queste*, VI, 191, the restoration of Nascien's sight, in the first of these passages, with blood that drops from the lance, corresponds exactly to the Longinus legend. Cp. Miss R. J. Peebles, *Legend of Longinus*, pp. 21, 48 ff., 194.

[16] Potvin, II, 252, Baist's ed., ll. 6129 ff. The Montpellier MS. (cp. Potvin, *loc. cit.*), to be sure, leaves out the statement about the destruction which the lance is fated to cause and says "La pes sera par ceste lance," but this is, no doubt, an unauthorized change of the true text. Certainly Pseudo-Wauchier had the commoner reading before him, when he penned ll. 20288 ff., although he attributes there this destructive power to the sword.

as well as of beneficence.[17] By thus combining both of the previous accounts, he is able to enhance greatly the interest of this weapon as a symbol of the two-fold attributes of our Lord — first, his power to heal and save, secondly, his power to inflict vengeance on those who disobey his will. The Bible furnished illustrations enough of both sides of the divine nature, and there was besides, the well-known story of the spear of Achilles[18] to support our author in ascribing to the Grail lance this union of apparently contradictory qualities.

One would imagine from the "dread voice" of the angel in his words of thunder, spoken to Josephe, after the blood from the mystical weapon had healed the latter's wound and restored Nascien's sight,[19] that the lance was destined to play a part of the highest importance in the story. From this time on, the heavenly messenger declares, not a drop of blood will fall from the lance until the Grail adventures shall commence in the land

---

[17] *Op. cit.* p. 192, Miss Peebles has cited from the fifteenth century *Meditation of the Five Wounds* a passage in which the terribleness of the spear is emphasized and, at the same time, the saving power of the blood, which gushed forth from the wound that it made.

Lot, p. 233, has rightly explained these "contradictions" as due to the writer's use of Chrétien and Pseudo-Wauchier, respectively. To my mind, however, he exaggerates their effect on the Grail romances of the Vulgate cycle. To our author (or authors), for the reasons given in the text above, I do not believe that they seemed to be real contradictions.

[18] The lance of Achilles could both wound and heal. Heinzel, p. 131, has suggested the influence of this story. He cites, besides, as parallels, Wolfram's *Parzival*, 490, 13 ff. and *Li Chevaliers as deus Espees*, l. 10692.

[19] I, 80 f. The MS. followed by Sommer is very corrupt at the beginning of the angel's speech — so much so, indeed, that Sommer in his marginal note, interpreting the text of this MS., makes Josephe the speaker and Nascien the hearer. It is really, however, the angel who is speaking to Josephe. Hucher's text, II, 310 ff., is much better, although there are some corruptions here, also, in the case of individual words.

(Great Britain) whither God is to lead Nascien. Then it will bleed again and the marvels which this bleeding is to inaugurate will be so great and awful that all people will be filled with fear. At that time the good knights will undertake feats of earthly chivalry, in order that they may know the marvels of the Grail and the lance. Only one man will ever be struck by the lance — namely, a descendant of Nascien.[20] This person will be a king (the Maimed King) — "the last of the good." He will be pierced through the thighs by the lance and will not be cured until the wonders of the Grail shall have been revealed to him who is to be full of virtues (Galahad) — the last of Nascien's lineage. Just as Nascien was the first to behold these wonders, so the last to do so will be the last of his lineage. Christ has determined to execute vengeance on Nascien and his descendant (the Maimed King), in order that they may testify that, when he was on the cross, his death was sought through the lance by the wicked Jews. As many days as Joseph bore the lance-head in his thigh, over so many years will the Grail adventures extend in the land (Great Britain) whither God will take Nascien.[21]

After all this pother, however, which owes its inspiration, doubtless, to the prophetic speeches of various angels in the *Book of Revelation*, the lance is henceforth dropped from the *Estoire*,

---

[20] This is an error, however, for Galahad was descended from Nascien through his father (Lancelot), not through his mother (member of the Grail family, to which the Maimed King belonged). Cp. I, 293.

[21] As Lot, *Lancelot*, p. 234, has observed, the author here limits to twelve years the flow of blood from the spear, which, according to his source, Pseudo-Wauchier (Potvin, IV, 4), would continue forever. In Lot's opinion, the author made the change, because the idea of the Savior's blood flowing eternally seemed to him an irreverence. It strikes me, however, that the writer's love of symbolism is more likely to have been the cause. Perhaps, after all, he may have forgotten, for the moment, Pseudo-Wauchier's idea on the subject and invented this detail for the nonce. In any event, he forgot the limitation subsequently, for nowhere else in the *Estoire* (or *Queste*) is it implied that the Grail adventures lasted twelve years. A part of Galahad's quest lasted five years (*Queste*, VI, 186f.), but we know nothing more.

save for one casual allusion,[22] and when it reappears in the *Queste,*
it does not fill at all the function which is predicated for it in
the angel's speech. On the contrary, it is not mentioned until
most of the Grail adventures are over and the narrative of the
stroke by which it renders the Maimed King maimed is merely
incidental and of the tamest kind.[23] At the end of the *Queste*
it appears again (p. 189), along with the Grail, in the mass which
the spirit of Josephe holds for the questers, and, on the completion of this service (p. 191), Galahad, in fulfillment of the
angel's prophecy, heals the Maimed King with blood from the
sacred weapon. Finally (p. 198). just after Galahad's decease,
a celestial hand, in the sight of Bohort and Perceval, snatches
both Grail and lance up to heaven, since when, as the author of
the *Queste* leaves us to understand, it, like the Grail, has been
seen no more by mortal eyes.

As we have seen above, "the sword of the strange hangings",
which is found already in Chrétien's *Perceval* (ll. 4668ff.), though
hardly as a Grail relic in this poem, had increased immensely in
importance in the continuations to that work. In the same spirit
the author of the *Estoire* has thrown the greatest lustre about
it (pp. 121f.), so that, at the same time that it duplicates, in a
measure, the functions of the lance, it eclipses here that relic more
than ever in the economy of the Grail story. In the execution
of his design to connect everything in his narrative with Christian
history and doctrine, the writer identifies (pp. 133f.) this sword,
so obscure in its origin, with the sword of David, who was, on

---

[22] I, 107, where, in an allusion to the wound of Joseph by the
lance (p. 77), the weapon is called "la lanche vengeresce." The only
passages in the *Estoire* where the Grail lance is mentioned are I,
32f. (it is here enumerated among the relics that are carried in the
ark with the Grail), 77—81 (wounding and healing of Joseph, restoration of Nascien's sight, and angel's prophecy), 107 (allusion to
pp. 77ff.).

[23] VI, 150. The Maimed King, although usually nameless in
the Vulgate cycle, is here called *Pellinor* in some MSS. Cp. Sommer,
*loc. cit.* This name, however, was most probably introduced late into
the manuscript tradition from the Vulgate *Merlin* continuation. See
Bruce, MPh., XVI, 337ff.

the human side, the greatest of the progenitors of Christ. Through the Dolorous Stroke (p. 290), when King Brulan(s), newly converted to Christianity, slew Lambor, the sainted Grail King, with his sword, it caused a magical blight to fall on the latter's land (Terre Foraine or Logres)[24] and provoked such wars of retaliation against the realm (Gales-Wales) of the former that the two kingdoms came to be known as the Waste Land (Terre Gaste). Thus, as in the case of the bleeding lance, the sword is said to bring on a series of afflictions, which, we may suppose, were not to cease until the coming of Galahad. Here again, however, having imparted to the mysterious weapon the prestige of marvels to come, the author drops the subject and says nothing more of these marvels. As in the case of the lance, the sword does not appear again in the two Grail romances until towards the end of the *Queste* (pp. 161 ff.) — in this instance, when Galahad enters Solomon's ship. Here, as a symbol of the redemption of mankind by the Virgin Mary from the curse which Eve's sin brought upon our race, Perceval's sister replaces with her beautiful hair the cheap hangings of tow which Solomon's wife had attached to the sword and girds the weapon upon Galahad.[25] From that point on, the sword is mentioned incidentally only a few times.

---

[24] According to Pseudo-Wauchier, Potvin, IV, 5, such was the nature of the blight that rested upon the Grail country after the stroke of the Grail sword. Our author is here borrowing from this passage in Pseudo-Wauchier, just as, in making the calamities which afflict Wales the ordinary ones of war, he is borrowing from Chrétien, ll. 4640 ff. (describing the disasters that ensued from the wounding of the Fisher King).

[25] In Chrétien's *Perceval*, ll. 3622 ff., the sword forged by Trebuchet was destined to fail the person who handled it in his need. The author of the *Queste*, VI, 149, had that passage in mind when he makes David's sword break in Nascien's hands (p. 149), because of his unworthiness, although the pure Mordrain is able to unite the pieces again.

David's sword, it should be remarked, is duplicated in the sword with which the seneschal of Argon wounds Joseph in the *Estoire*, I, 256. Galahad joins the pieces of this sword together again in the *Queste*, VI, 188.

Robert de Boron's *Joseph,* as we have already noted, is the
main source of the *Estoire.* To that poem our author owes his
conception of the origin and early history of the Grail and of
its connection with Joseph of Arimathea — also, of Joseph's proselytizing activities and of his wanderings with the Grail and
the Grail company in Eastern lands — finally, of the transference
of the Grail to the West and of the conversion of Britain to
Christianity by Joseph, Josephe and Celidoine.[26] It will be
evident, however, from the analysis of the *Estoire,* given below,
that its author modified, according to his own pleasure, the
materials which were offered to him by his source and that
he, still further, filled out Robert's framework with elements that
were derived from a great variety of extraneous sources. Inasmuch
as Robert, himself, moved so completely in an atmosphere of
Christian legend, it is natural that in the sources of his follower
legendary materials should, next to the *Joseph,* have occupied the
first place. It is very questionable, however, whether our author
had a first-hand knowledge of the apocryphal narratives concerning the careers of the primitive apostles after the ascension of
Christ, such as has been attributed to him.[27] These constituted, of

---

[26] It will be observed that these elements constitute the fundamental framework of the *Estoire.* There are, besides, of course,
other borrowings from the *Joseph.* Among them is the Grail group
— Bron, Alain, etc., — first introduced towards the end of the
*Estoire.* As I have said above, I do not feel quite sure that this
group is not a late addition to the romance.

[27] Heinzel, pp. 136 ff. maintains that (1) the Latin legend of the
*Acts of the Apostles, Simon und Judas,* and (2) the *Passio Matthaei* are sources of the account of the conversion of Evelach and
his kingdom, I, 21 ff., — moreover, that our author had access to
historical narratives (now unascertainable) of the events with which
the above-named legends are connected. For the texts of the legends
just indicated cp. J. A. Fabricius, *Codex Apocryphus Novi Testa-
menti,* I, 608 ff., 636 ff., (2 vols., Hamburg, 1719), respectively. For
the historical narratives referred to, see the parallels from Persian
and Abyssinian history which Heinzel, pp. 137, 139, has assembled.
Brugger, *Zs. f. frz. Spr. u. Litt.,* XXIX [1], 100, accepts Heinzel's views.
So, too, Lot, *Lancelot,* p. 206, who thinks, however, that the author

course, the fountain-head of all legendary narratives in regard to
the conversion of pagan lands to the Christian faith, but the mar-

of the *Estoire* did not follow the two legends closely, but was merely
inspired by them.

Let us take first the *Acts of Simon and Judas*. The resemblances here are of a very general nature. If our author, instead
of conveying Joseph and the Grail directly to Britain decided to ex-
pand Robert's accounts with episodes of that hero's proselytizing activities, the scene of such activities would have to be laid in Western
Asia, since Joseph was still in that part of the world at the close
of Robert's poem.

For the rest, in the legend of Simon and Judas, there is no
battle between the Persian General (Varardach) or his king (Xerxes)
and the invading army, for the latter voluntarily surrenders (p. 615)
before there is any fighting and the only advantage to the apostles
in the premises is through this verification of their prediction as to the
issue of the war, as against that of the magi, to overthrow whom
they came to Persia in the first instance. The models of the *Estoire*
here were, obviously, such legends as those of Constantine the Great
*(Inventio Crucis)* and Clovis (Gregory of Tours, Book II, ch. 30—31),
who were converted to Christianity, because Christ granted them victory in answer to appeals offered in hours of danger. — Again, the
advocates, who, in the Latin legend, are so prominent (pp. 618 ff.) as
instruments of the apostles in humiliating the magi in contests of
eloquence, do not appear at all in the *Estoire*. Indeed, in the latter
there is only one heathen clerk who disputes with the Christians
(Joseph and Josephe), and that only in one scene (pp. 62 f.). — Similarly, there is nothing in the *Estoire* to correspond to the episodes
of the torture of the magi by the serpents which they call forth, of
the deacon who is vindicated by the speech of the one-day-old child,
of the tigers miraculously tamed, of the priests of the temple where
images of both sun and moon are worshipped and of the conflict of
these priests with the apostles. It will be seen, then, that in only
a few cases have the episodes in the legend of Simon and Judas anything
corresponding in the *Estoire*. In a still smaller proportion of cases,
of course, do the far more numerous episodes of the *Estoire* find parallels
in the legend.

The main points of resemblance between the Latin legend and
the *Estoire* are in the power of the missionaries to overcome demons
and expel them from the idols whence they have been accustomed to
deceive the people through false oracles. Cp. the Latin legend, pp. 631 ff.,
and the *Estoire*, pp. 45 ff., 75 ff. But this was a commonplace of

vellous elements in such stories had been so frequently repeated
as to have become a part of the general tradition of mediaeval

saints' lives and even of secular literature. Cp. MPh., X, 575, note I.
Cp., besides *Acta Bartholomaei*, C. Tischendorf: *Acta Apostolorum
Apocrypha*, pp. 243 ff., (Leipzig, 1851), and the life of St. Patrick
by Jocelyn of Furness (twelfth century), *Acta Sanctorum* for March,
II, 552 (idol is overthrown by Patrick's prayer), 555 (the idols fall
and break of themselves, as soon as Patrick approaches the temple).
Examples of this superstition could be cited almost indefinitely.

As far as the *Passio Matthaei*, itself, is concerned, there is
really no resemblance at all here to the *Estoire*. On the other hand,
the historical events in the life of the Ethiopian king and saint, Caleb
Elesbaan (first half of the sixth century), with which, in a disguised
form, this Latin legend is ultimately connected, do offer some resemblance to the story of Mordrain, but the similarity is only a general
one. Besides, Heinzel has produced no evidence that there existed
any account of these events, so distant from our author with respect
to both space and time, to which he might have had access. For the
life of Caleb (the monarch's original name) or Elesbaan (his epithet,
meaning in the Ethiopian language, "the blessed"), as he is more generally called, see the article, *Elesbaan,* in Smith and Wace's *Dictionary
of Christian Biography*. In the *Acta Sanctorum* his life is given
under the date of Oct. 27. Cp. the Bollandist edition, Octobris, vol.
XII, pp. 296 ff. For other details touching his crusade cp. *ibid.*, vol.
X, 694 ff. (in the account of the martyrdom St. Arethas, etc.). The
events in question are as follows: Dhu Nowas, about 523 A. D., over-
threw the rule of Elesbaan in Homeritis (Southern Arabia or Yemen),
then a province of Ethiopia, and massacred the Christians — especially at Negran, where St. Arethas and St. Ruma were among the
victims. Urged by the emperor Justin and the patriarch of Alexandria,
Elesbaan in 525 A. D. led a great expedition to the Yemen, defeated
and slew Dhu Nowas, restored Christianity in the land and returned
to Ethiopia. Pious narratives of these events (cp. *op. cit.*, X, 758)
represent that just after his return from this crusade he abdicated his
throne and entered a monastery, where he died some time later. As
a matter of fact, there was an interval of something like twenty-five
years between his crusade and his abdication and retirement to a
monastic life.

Now, it will be observed that the most important elements of this
situation were familiar to all educated Europeans at the beginning of
the thirteenth century in a form that affected them much more closely
than this story of the royal saint of times already ancient in far

piety. As far as the *Estoire* is concerned, the conversions both of Evelach's land and of Great Britain follow, in essentials, the

off Abyssinia — namely, in the crusades of the period to the Holy Land, especially the Third Crusade (1189—1192). In both cases, of course, the expeditions were undertaken, not for the rescue of imprisoned missionaries, but to recover a land which unbelievers had wrested from Christian rule and, incidentally, to avenge the cruelties which had been inflicted on the followers of Christ. Apart from the requirements of his story, the success of the First Crusade in 1099 might well have justified the author of the *Estoire* in making Mordrain's expedition successful. That he should have added the idealizing touch, by which this monarch, having won his victory, is represented as renouncing earthly glory and adopting a life of religious devotion, would be surely natural in an ecclesiastic of that age.

The similarity which Heinzel sees (p. 139) between the rôles of Elesbaan's sons and those of Mordrain's in the Grimaud episode of the *Estoire* is negligible, apart from its vagueness, for this episode occurs in only two MSS. and is, beyond question, spurious.

The true motive which, above all others, no doubt, has led Heinzel and his followers to imagine that the life of Elesbaan was a source of the *Estoire* is their identification of *Kalafes (Calafres)- Alphasan (Aufassain, Alphesim, Alfesim, Alfasein)*, name of the king of the *Estoire*, I, 286 ff., who became a Christian on being healed of leprosy by Alain, with *Kaleb (Caleb)* — *Elesbaan*, name of the famous monarch of Ethiopia. As a matter of fact, in the extant records he is called either *Caleb* or (more often) *Elesbaan*, never *Caleb Elesbaan*, as far as I have been able to discover. To call the historical Caleb or Elesbaan, *Caleb Alfassam*, as Lot does, pp. 206, note 10, 207, is, of course, unwarranted. But the identity of these names is extremely questionable. There is no real correspondence at all between their second elements, and, besides, as I have observed in Part IV, below, *Alphasan* is, no doubt, derived from *Elisaphan, Exodus*, VI, 22, and *Numbers* III, 30. On the other hand, *Calafres* (the reading of Hucher's text, III, 287) is, doubtless, the correct form of the original heathen name of the king, for that is a mere variant of *Galafres*, which is one of the commonest of all names for heathen kings in the *chansons de geste*, as a glance into E. Langlois's *Table des noms propres dans les chansons de geste* will show. That the *Calafes* of Sommer's text is merely a corruption of *Galafres* is virtually certain, for in Hucher's text the wicked pagan who excites his fellows against Nascien is called, II, 334 *Calafres (Calafer)*, but, II, 336, *Galafres, Galafre*. Sommer's text here I, 87 ff., has *Calafer*.

As is generally agreed, the story of the conversion of Kalafes

natural course of such events in the authentic history of Christianity, under like conditions,[28] and the fables with regard to the intervention of supernatural agencies in such episodes find their parallels in the mediaeval chronicles of Western Europe. In the romance, as in the actual life of the times, the conversion of the king meant inevitably, also, the conversion of his subjects. Accordingly, when the missionaries had gained the permission of the monarch, a great assembly would be held in which they would preach the new doctrine before him.[29] The priests of the prevailing heathen religion would be present — generally, we may conjecture, in a hostile mood[30] — and questions and debates would naturally be features of such occasions.[31] Then, when the king had decided to embrace the new religion, the first act would be the destruction of the temples and idols of the vanquished gods.[32] Moreover, according to the legends of the chroniclers about the time of the missionaries' arrival the monarch might be engaged in a desperate battle with his enemies, and so might be impelled by the urgency of his peril to promise the adoption of the new faith, if the god of its votaries will secure him the victory.[33]

---

Alphasan in the *Estoire* is imitated from the legend of Abgar, King of Edessa, Fabricius, I, 317 f.

[28] For example, in the conversion of England by St. Augustine and other missionaries, as related by Bede, *Historia Ecclesiastica Gentis Anglorum.*

[29] Cp. Bede, Book I, ch. 25—26 (St. Augustine's conversion of Ethelbert, King of Kent) and Book II, ch. 13 (Paulinus's conversion of Edwin, King of Northumberland).

[30] Occasional subsequent lapses into paganism, as in the case of Ethelbert's sons, Bede, II, ch. 5, confirm this natural inference from the conditions. This was not always true, however, if we may accept the accounts of our ecclesiastical chroniclers — e. g. Bede, II, 13, just cited, and Gregory of Tours, II, (conversion of Clovis).

[31] Cp., especially, Bede, II, 13, The romancer, besides, would be influenced by Jesus's disputations with the Pharisees in the Gospels.

[32] In the celebrated passage in Bede, II, 13, it was the converted high priest of the heathen religion who led in the destruction.

[33] Besides the legends of Constantine and Clovis, already cited, cp.. too, the similar story concerning Edwin, King of Northumberland, in Bede, II, 9.

Next in importance among the writer's innovations is the
allegory of Solomon's ship (Holy Church) and the mystical objects which it contains — the bed, the golden crown, the spindles made from the wood of the Tree of Life, and King David's
sword (pp. 120 ff.). The oriental legend of *Solomon and Marcolf*,
according to which the wise king is so often the victim of his
guileful wife, has here been taken as the starting-point of one
of the most remarkable outbursts of the mediaeval imagination,
as bizarre as it is vigorous. Our author, however, did not restrict
himself to Christian or oriental legend.[34] His purpose was that
of story-tellers in all ages — namely, to interest his readers or
hearers — and provided he attained that object, he felt himself
at liberty in his romance to compound with the deepest theological and mystical conceptions of his time stories of piracy,[35]
of *voyages imaginaires*,[36] and even, perhaps, of farce.[37]

The *Estoire del Saint Graal* derives such plan as it possesses,
as well as its most significant conceptions concerning the Grail,
from Robert de Boron's *Joseph*.[38] There already we find, first,
the history of the Grail down to the departure of Joseph of Ari-

---

[34] On the minor sources of the *Estoire*, see particularly Heinzel,
pp. 145 ff. The references, however, vary very much in pertinency.
In MPh., X, 522, the present writer has cited some more exact
parallels to the curious *motif* of Mordrain's cohabitation with the
wooden image of a beautiful woman, I, 83.

[35] I, 89 ff.

[36] Mordrain's and Nascien's experiences, I, 89 ff., 114 ff. The
*Navigatio Sancti Brendani*, whose influence Nutt has detected, also,
in the beginning of our romance, is especially important here.

[37] The Hippocrates *fabliau*, I, 171 ff., the genuineness of which,
however, is not altogether certain. Its sources are given by Heinzel,
pp. 145 f.

[38] Hucher's text, pp. 12 f., as Heinzel, p. 149, remarks, seems
intended to indicate a sort of division into four parts, i. e. accounts
of (1) lineage of the Grail family, (2) account of the Grail (origins?),
(3) *paours*, incidents displaying the powers of the Grail? (4) *mer-
veilles*, adventures of the Grail company? As Lot observes, in *Lancelot*,
a tripartite division was more likely the author's true intention. The
matter, however, is of little importance, as he really does not carry
out the indicated divisions.

mathea from Jerusalem, then, the wanderings of Joseph and the
Grail company in the East, and lastly (merely foreshadowed) the
journey of the Grail and its guardians westward for the conversion of Great Britain. We have just seen with what materials
its author filled out these meagre outlines, but if we except the
tripartite division of the adventures of Mordrain, Nascien, and
Celidoine before their arrival in Britain — another tribute to the
power of the mystical number three (the number of the Christian
Godhead), which is a sort of obsession with the writers of the
Grail romances — there is nothing that evinces any real reflection
in the arrangement of these materials. The author dulls the effect
of his finer conceptions, such as the allegory of Solomon's ship
and its contents, by a deluge of minor incidents that are
both insignificant and extravagant. As a result, we have the
usual formlessness of Arthurian romance in a heightened degree,
owing to the length of the work. Few other productions even of
the Middle Ages illustrate so well the truth of the Greek proverb
that "the half is better than the whole". The climax of in-
competence, however, in respect to form would be reached, if our
author were really responsible for the eleventh-hour introduction
of Robert's Grail family as guardians of the Grail, after characters of his own creation (save Joseph) had been fulfilling that
function through nearly five sixths of the romance. The two sets
of characters are fundamentally irreconcilable and it is difficult
to believe that a writer of any capacity whatever, such as the
author of the *Estoire*, despite all his limitations, was, would have
wantonly spoiled his work in this fashion.[39] It seems much more

---

[39] The bungling of the genealogies excites similar suspicions.
Cp. p. 375, note I, above. The case of the elder Galahad is particularly bad.
The character has no *raison d'être* at all. Lot, *Lancelot*, p. 223,
thinks that an unlucky *penchant* for fanciful etymologies on our author's
part caused his creation and that afterwards our author himself was
embarrassed by this new Galahad. If this is so, the remedy was
easy: All he had to do was to strike out the few passages in which
the character occurred. Heinzel's idea that he was derived from a
preexisting legend (p. 134 f.) is, of course, a purely gratuitous assumption.

likely that some redactor who regretted the loss of the Grail characters of our author's source (the *Joseph*) endeavored to save
them by combining them in this impossible manner with those of
the derivative romance.[40]

The *Estoire* has, of course, its share of the religious symbolism which hangs like a heavy cloud over its companion romance,
the *Queste*, but the application of the allegorical method is much
less constant and rigorous here than in the case of the latter.
Whether its author was identical with the author of the *Queste*
or not, the romance exhibits the common mediaeval delight in
descriptions of fighting in a much greater degree than the *Queste*
and it presses into the service of religion a much greater variety
of romantic incident than is found in the companion[41] work. But
this very variety gives the *Estoire* its rambling character and
there is no one "divine event" at the end of the romance to hold
the author down to a certain concentration in the development
of the action, as is the case with the *Queste*. In accordance with
these characteristics, the romance, though in the same general vein
as the *Queste* and moving within the same range of ideas, as
compared with the latter, leaves an impression of inferior spiritual
earnestness, or fanaticism, if you will.

That both of these romances are the productions of ecclesiastical workshops has never been questioned and is not likely
to be. No one but an ecclesiastic would have possessed in the
same degree such learning in matters pertaining to the Bible, to
ritual, and to dogma, or such mastery of contemporary methods
of allegorical interpretation. It would seem, indeed, that the romance, itself, supplied an indication as to the place of its origin;

---

[40] Lot, *Lancelot,* p. 81, rejects the theory of alteration, here
suggested.

[41] This is, also, apparent from the variety of sources used in this
romance.

[42] On this subject cp. Bruce, "Mordrain, Corbenic and the Grail
Romances," MLN, XXXIV, 385 ff. (Nov., 1919). The name, which
is of Germanic origin, is only found in the extant documents in the
Latinized forms, *Maurdramnus, Maurdrannus, Mordramnus, Mor-
thrannus.* Our meagre records do not state where he was born. The
fact that whilst Maurdramnus was abbot of Corbie, a king, Desiderius

for the name of the heathen king who, strange to say, was born
(according to the romancer) at Meaux in France and who, after his
conversion and zealous service in the cause of Christ, adopted a
religious life and died in a monastery of his own founding, viz.
Mordrain(s), has been discovered nowhere else in mediaeval records save as the name of the abbot who presided over the famous
Benedictine monastery of Corbie in Picardy from 769 to 781,
A. D.[42] It appears obvious that only a monk of Corbie would have
had an interest in conferring on his royal saint the name of an abbot
of this foundation — one, too, who had been dead for upwards
of four centuries.  It accords with this indication that the name
given to the Grail castle ("palais spiriteux") in this romance
and in the *Queste,* viz., Corbenic, coincides with that of Corbeni
(in the Middle Ages, *Corbiniacum*), a town, somewhat southeast
of Laon (so, in the same general region as Corbie), where there
was and had long been a royal palace and at the same time a
Benedictine establishment connected with one of the most famous
and venerable shrines of France (St. Marculf's).  That the name
of the Grail castle in our romances was derived from the name
of this place is hardly open to doubt.[43]

---

of Lombardy, was actually leading a life of religious devotion in the
abbey may have led our romancer to combine the two characters in
Mordrain.  Note, too, that the four hundred years' interval between
the death of Maurdramnus and the composition of the *Queste* may
be responsible for the author's making Mordrain live four hundred
years.  Cp. VI, 62.

[43] For details concerning Corbeni, the palace and shrine, see my
article just cited.

In view of what has been said in the text above it seems needless to discuss A. Wesselofsky's effort, "Zur Frage über die Heimath
der Legende vom heiligen Gral," *Archiv für Slavische Philologie,*
XXIII, 321 ff. (1910), to trace the names in the *Estoire* to extra-
Biblical oriental sources.  His identifications are fantastic to the last
degree.  The same thing is true of Miss M. A. Murray's attempt in the
journal, *Ancient Egypt,* (London and New York), for 1916, Part I,
pp. 1 ff., to establish an Egyptian origin for certain of these names.
Thus she derives Nascien's name from a hypothetical Arabic noun,
*Nâshi'un,* which would mean "one who is growing up." But *Nascien*
is, beyond question, derived from *Naasson* in the genealogy of Christ,
*St. Matthew,* I, 4.  *Ex uno omnia.*

## 2. L'Estoire de Merlin.

As has been stated already, the *Merlin* branch of the Vulgate cycle consists of (1) the prose rendering of Robert de Boron's *Merlin* and (2) a continuation of this prose rendering, which is much longer than the original work.

It is generally agreed that this continuation is the latest in date of any division of the cycle.[44] Its frequent allusions to other branches and its dependence on these same branches in numerous episodes put this beyond doubt.[45]

It will be observed from the analysis given below that the continuation is, for the most part, made up of interminable descriptions of wars between Arthur and his rebellious barons, or between Arthur and the Saxons, or between the rebellious barons and the Saxons. Of more interest than these prolix and monotonous descriptions are the occasional passages that deal with incidents of peace — particularly, those that relate to Arthur's courtship and marriage of Guinevere.[46] After all, however, the Vulgate *Merlin* continuation might well have been left a prey to oblivion, without any loss to the world, were it not for the famous episodes concerning the enchanter's passion for Vivien and her treacherous imprisonment of him through the force of his

---

[44] Cp., e. g. Brugger, *Zs. f. frz. Spr. u. Litt.*, XXIX[1], 109 ff. (1905), Lot, *Lancelot*, p. 7 (1920).

[45] Cp. allusions to the *Lancelot:* the incestuous conception of Mordred, Sommer, II, 129, the veiled prediction (in allegorical form) of Lancelot's career, *ibid.* p. 214, the part played throughout the continuation by Ban (Lancelot's father), pp. 245 ff. (Guinebaut and the magic chessboard), etc.; allusion to the *Estoire*, pp. 221 f. (circumstances of its composition); to the *Queste:* p. 335 (Galahad, the Grail Winner, as the perfect knight); to the *Mort Artu:* p. 265 (Mordred's treason). As is said below, the whole continuation is obviously a sort of introduction to the *Lancelot,* and passages in it that were suggested by the latter might be counted by the scores. — The Pelles of the Vulgate *Merlin* continuation is, of course, derived from the *Lancelot* and *Queste* — only he is here always called "Pelles de Listenois." Cp. MPh., XVI, 126 f. Lot, *Lancelot*, p. 239, note 3, makes a distinction between the two Pelles, but this is unwarranted.

[46] pp. 157 ff., 216 ff.

own magic spell which he had been weak enough to betray to her.[47] An exception, perhaps, might, also, be made in favor of the spirited description of Arthur's combat with the monster cat on the shores of the "Lake of Lausanne".[48]

The continuation which we are discussing was composed as a sort of introduction to the *Lancelot*. There was no obstacle to the assumption that the coronation of Arthur — at which point Robert's *Merlin* ended — and the birth of Lancelot — with which the *Lancelot* began — were separated by a considerable interval, and the author of our continuation availed himself of this circumstance to exploit the general interest in the Arthurian story in his own behalf — doubtless, with some particular patron in view. His work, then, is a pseudo-history of Arthur's reign, down to the birth of Lancelot, and it constitutes, accordingly, an introduction to the *Lancelot*. Merlin continues to play a leading rôle in the events of that reign, but, inasmuch as in the *Lancelot* we hear of him only in the episode,[49] probably interpolated,[50] in which the story of his imprisonment by Vivien is told, our author is under the necessity of accounting for the magician's disappearance, and he does so by adopting and expanding the conceptions of the *Lancelot* episode just alluded to.

In general, the writer's main guide in the composition of his chronicle is Wace's *Brut*,[51] possibly, in an expanded form,[52]

---

[47] Cp. pp. 209 ff., 450 ff.      [48] pp, 441 ff.

[49] Cp. Sommer, III, 19 ff.

[50] Cp. Brugger, *Zs. f. frz. Spr. u. Litt.*, XXX[1], 188. On the supposed source of the interpolation (viz. the hypothetical *Brut* by a certain Martin — of Rochester, according to some MSS. of the Vulgate *Merlin*), cp. *ibid.* pp. 181 ff.

[51] In the *Huth-Merlin*, I, p. XXIV, G. Paris, in speaking of the sources of the Vulgate *Merlin*-continuation, mentions, besides the *Lancelot*, Geoffrey of Monmouth and "le Perceval de Robert" (i. e. the *Didot-Perceval*). But we may safely assume that the romancers always used French paraphrases of Geoffrey — especially, Wace's — rather than the Latin original. — Instead of the *Didot-Perceval*, Paris should have mentioned the *Perlesvaus*, I, 170, 219 ff., whose influence in the passage, II, 316, relating to Kay's murder of Arthur's son, Lohot, seems undeniable.

[52] Namely, the lost original of Layamon, or Brugger's Martin of Rochester, if the latter ever really existed.

but he has also developed suggestions of the *Lancelot*[53] and, doubtless, of still other romances.[54] There are probably, in addition, some episodes of the author's own invention, but it is safe to assume that, if such there be, they are of little significance; for, on the whole, the *Merlin* continuation is decidedly the dullest and least original portion of the whole Vulgate cycle.

## 3. Li Livres de Lancelot.

There is no certain indication of any division or divisions in the text of the *Lancelot*, itself,[55] and we shall see below[56] that,

___

[53] Already at II, 97 — so within nine pages of the beginning of the continuation — Ban and his brother, Bohort, are introduced as allies of Arthur and they are prominent in the action down to the end of the romance. The author took them, of course, from the *Lancelot*. So, too, with the character of Claudas, II, 98, 206f., 279, etc. At II, 214, there is a veiled prediction of Lancelot's career as told in the *Lancelot*; at II, 159, 346, mention is made of Pelles' daughter, and so on. The continuation is dependent on the *Lancelot* in so many episodes that further citations are superfluous. The author, indeed, refers, II, 221, directly to that romance as the one which will relate Lancelot's adventures.

[54] There is a direct reference to the *Estoire del Saint Graal* in the passage, II, 221, where the author introduces the younger Nascien (his own creation) as the kinsman of Celidoine and of the older Nascien. Cp., too, II, 334f., where the references to Joseph, Galahad and Sarras evince a knowledge of both the *Estoire* and the *Queste*. The allusion, II, 385, to the fatal encounter of Arthur and Mordred on Salisbury Plain is, of course, based on the *Mort Artu*, VI, 365ff. The story of Mordred's incestuous birth, II, 129, may have been suggested either by the *Mort Artu*, VI, 325, 349, 377, or the *Lancelot*, V, 284. — *Meraugis de Portlesguez* has supplied the continuation with the character of that name who fights against the Saxons, II, 148, as the *Vengeance de Raguidel* of the same poet has supplied the "vile del gaut destroit," II, 164. On the other hand, the Chastel des Caroles, II, 246, is borrowed from the *Lancelot*, V, 149ff., not from *Meraugis*, ll. 4334ff. (source of the *Lancelot* episode). The reference to the expedition of the Argonauts and to the children of Oedipus, II, 230, are, doubtless, derived from the *Roman de Troie* and *Roman de Thebes*, respectively.

[55] On this subject see, especially, Lot, *Lancelot*, pp. 9ff. There are divisions, to be sure, in the manuscript tradition. Particularly common in this tradition is the division into two parts, the so-called

according to the theory recently advanced by Ferdinand Lot, the whole of the *Lancelot* is really the work of a single author — the same that composed, also, the *Estoire del Saint Graal*, the *Queste del Saint Graal*, and the *Mort Artu*. Having given in another place my reasons, however, for rejecting this theory, in the following pages I shall adopt the view as to the plural authorship of this branch which has been generally held by Arthurian scholars and which I have attempted to justify elsewhere.[57]

There was, of course, no connection, originally, between the stories of Lancelot and the Grail. Chrétien's *Lancelot* contains no allusion to the Grail and his *Perceval* contains no allusion to Lancelot. It was the creator of Galahad who first connected the two. Owing to the considerations which have already been set forth,[58] we cannot accept the *Lancelot* and the *Queste* as works of the same author, yet the dependence of the latter on the former is obvious, and the *Lancelot* was certainly the earlier romance. Galahad, of course, exists purely as the hero of the Grail quest and must therefore have been created by the author of the *Queste*.

---

*Agravain* forming the second part. Lot's explanation of this division, *op. cit.*, pp. 11 f., as due to purely material considerations — to have included the whole romance in one volume would have been intolerable, on account of its bulk — is, doubtless, correct, but a want of harmony in the narrative between the beginning of the *Agravain* and the end of the preceding part still needs to be explained. Cp. RR, X, 63 ff.

Some MSS. (cp. Lot, pp. 13 ff.) assume a tripartite division, viz. 1. *Galehaut* (through Galehaut's death) 2. *Charete (Charrette)*. 3. *Agravain*. This division has been frequently adopted in discussions of the *Lancelot*, and, in the opinion of the present writer, is connected with a real difference of authorship for the parts in question.

The summaries of the preceding narrative given at irregular intervals throughout the *Lancelot* (cp. Lot, p. 15) are, I believe, without significance. They are very likely scribal insertions, intended to serve, in a rudimentary fashion, the purpose of modern tables of contents.

[56] Cp. Part IV.

[57] In "The Composition of the Old French Prose *Lancelot*," RR IX, 241 ff., 353 ff. (1918), X, 48 ff., 97 ff. (1919).

[58] Cp. study just cited.

All references then, to Galahad and Grail matters[59] which we find in the *Lancelot* — and the same thing is true of other branches of the cycle — must have been later additions to the primitive text of this romance. Some of these references are brief, but others involve whole episodes.[60]

Apart from such interpolations, the enormous length of the *Lancelot* and the differences of style in different parts of the romance[61] render it virtually certain that this branch, as it stands in our extant MSS., is not the production of one hand, but represents rather the result of successive continuations and other additions to the original work,[62] just as is the case with the *Conte del Graal* and with the prose *Tristan* in its cyclic form.[63] To be sure, it is not always easy to fix the limits of these various expansions of the original romance. The *Galehaut*,[64] however, has been gene-

---

[59] All references to Grail matters in the *Lancelot* imply that Galahad is the Grail hero. Many of these references are to the *Queste,* but others are to the *Estoire,* in which Galahad, of course, is assumed to be the Grail Winner, as well as in the *Queste.*

[60] See my article, already cited, in RR, IX, and X. We have, for example, Sommer, III, 226, a passing remark that a certain quest for Lancelot was "la plus haute queste qui onques fust apres celi del Graal." On the other hand, we have long episodes like the visits of Gawain, Lancelot, and Bohort to the Grail castle.

[61] Lot, it is true, in his *Lancelot,* pp. 65 ff., disputes that there are such differences. My discussion of the different branches, however, will show, I believe, that he is wrong.

[62] Cp. RR, IX, 241 ff., for a summary of critical opinion to this effect.

[63] Cp. *op. cit.,* pp. 244 ff. There are four continuations to Chrétien's *Perceval (Conte del Graal),* viz. Pseudo-Wauchier, Wauchier, Manessier and Gerbert. Moreover, in the first of these continuations there are, incontestably, interpolations, and not improbably, also, some of minor extent in Wauchier, at least. Besides, we have prefixed to Chrétien's romance in certain MSS. the so-called *Elucidation* and Bliocadrans-prologue. Note, too, the introductory and final episodes of Wolfram's *Parzival,* which, as we have seen, many scholars attribute to the much-discussed Kyot (Guiot). These episodes represent additions to Chrétien's poem. — For the prose *Tristan* cp. E. Löseth, *Le roman en prose de Tristan,* p. XII (Paris, 1890).

[64] This extends from the beginning of the romance down to IV, 155 (death of Galehaut).

rally accepted as a separate division—justly so, we believe, since, despite a multitude of extraneous episodes, it forms a complete narrative, in itself, of Lancelot's love for the queen and his friendship for Galehaut — a narrative, which is, in the main, uniform in spirit and style.[65] Immediately after the *Galehaut* comes the *Charete* section (IV, 155 ff.) — so called, because it begins with a paraphrase of Chrétien's *Lancelot (Conte de la Charete)*. It has been customary to regard this section as extending down to the point where Agravain suddenly appears in the quest for Lancelot (V, 3). A more natural line of division, however, seems to be furnished by the beginning of this same quest (IV, 321). The narrative of this search for Lancelot by Gawain and other knights, which embraces nearly one-third of the whole *Lancelot* (IV, 321— V, 318), was, probably, a separate continuation. There were, still further, two more continuations, it would seem, viz. 1. Brumant's disastrous attempt to occupy the Seat Perilous, Arthur's wars with the Romans and with Claudas, which end with Lancelot's recovery of his patrimony (V, 318—377).[66] 2. The concluding section of the romance, in which, for the first time, Perceval is introduced as one of the characters of the *Lancelot*[67] (V, 377—409). The

---

[65] Among those who have accepted the division of the *Lancelot* into 1. *Galehaut*, 2. *Charete*, 3. *Agravain*, cp. G. Paris, *Huth-Merlin*, I, p. XXXVII, note 2, and G. Gröber, *Grundriss*, Band II, Abteilung I, pp. 996 ff. The latter attributes distinctly each of the divisions to a different author. I believe, however, that the composition of these divisions is not so simple as Gröber imagines — moreover, that the *Galehaut* was written before the *Charete*. The fact that the *Charete* follows rather closely its metrical original (Chrétien's *Lancelot*) doubtless inclined Gröber to date this part of the *Lancelot* before the other parts which are more independent.

[66] On this continuation cp. RR, X, 109 ff. The author probably had before him the whole of the *Lancelot* — substantially as we know it in the extant MSS. — down to p. 318 — also, the *Estoire*, *Queste* and *Mort Artu*. Arthur's wars here were doubtless based on his wars against Lancelot and the Romans in the *Mort Artu*, VI, 317 ff. Cp. RR. IX, 390 ff.

[67] His brother, Agloval had already appeared — for the first time in extant Arthurian romance — at the beginning of the long

number of passages in these last two sections which reveal a knowledge of the *Mort Artu* prove that they were both written after
that branch.[68]

Each of the divisions of the *Lancelot* which I have just indicated, except the last two, appears, however, to have undergone
changes and interpolations of various kinds. For example, there are
reasons for doubting whether the characters, Lionel, Bohort, and
Hector, figured in the original *Galehaut*,[69] and the episodes of
Merlin's magical imprisonment by Vivien (III, 19ff.), of Arthur's
infatuation with the false Guinevere (IV, 10ff.), of Galehaut's
dreams (IV, 19ff.), not to mention others in this same section,
were, most likely, later interpolations. So, too, doubtless, with
the episode of Bohort and Brangoire's daughter in the *Charete*
section (IV, 270ff.), which is, obviously, an imitation of the story
of Galahad's conception in a later part of the *Lancelot* (V, 105ff.).

Of all parts of the romance most subject to interpolation
and expansion was the one (commencing IV, 321) in which the
long quest of Gawain and his companions for Lancelot is narrated

---

quest for *Lancelot*, IV, 321, and had played a considerable rôle in
the subsequent narrative.

Lot, *Lancelot*, p. 207, note 1, derives Agloval's name from *Aglebûl,* a variant for *Aeglippus,* name of a king of Ethiopia in the
*Passio Matthei.* The Ethiopian *Aglebûl* is, itself, derived from *Aglibal,*
the name of one of the gods of Palmyra. Lot arrives at his derivation
as follows: According to his theory, the *Lancelot* and the *Estoire*
are by the same author—but, since this author seems to have drawn
upon Ethiopian history (cp. Heinzel, Grail treatise, pp. 138f.) for names
in the *Estoire,* he may have done so, likewise, in the *Lancelot.*
Granting, however, that the *Lancelot* and the *Estoire* were from the
same hand — which, as we have seen, is extremely doubtful — it
is very improbable that even an ecclesiastic in Northern France at
the beginning of the thirteenth century would have had access to
writings on Ethiopian history. As a matter of fact, this name, *Aglebûl,*
has only become known to European scholars in recent years.

[68] Cp. RR, X, 109ff., 114ff.

[69] Cp. RR, X, 57ff. Lot, *Lancelot*, p. 125, derives Bohort's
name from· that of Beor, a king of Ethiopia in the *Passio Matthei.*
But the name, *Beor,* occurs only once in that text, and the derivation
is not probable. Cp., too, what I have just said in the previous note,

— the part which, in a large measure, coincides with the so-called *Agravain* division of the *Lancelot*. The loose quest form, as it were, invited additions and expansions. It is here that we have inserted the episodes which connect the *Lancelot* with the *Queste*[70] and *Mort Artu*[71] that follow it in the cycle.

Here, however, as in the other divisions of the *Lancelot*, many of the inserted passages are not cyclic either in aim or in effect. They are of the same general character as other adventures in Arthurian romance and were composed by the continuators or expanders of this branch in its earlier form (or forms) simply for the additional entertainment of their readers.

Among the latest interpolations of the *Lancelot* should be reckoned especially a certain number[72] — doubtless, by the same person — which were inserted, it seems, with the object of uniting the *Lancelot* and the *Estoire*. These include probably the brief phrases which, in conformity with the ideas of the *Estoire*, represent Lancelot as descended from the line of David, the holy king of Israel,[73] the motive for imputing this descent to our hero,

---

[70] Especially, the visits to Corbenic (Grail Castle) of Gawain, IV, 339 ff., Lancelot, V, 105 ff. (which includes, of course, the account of how Galahad was begotten), and Bohort, V, 139 ff., 294 ff.

[71] Cp. V, 215 ff. (Lancelot, treacherously imprisoned by Morgan, paints on the walls of his chamber the picture of his intrigue with Guinevere, which convinces Arthur in the *Mort Artu*, VI, 236 ff., of his wife's adultery), 284 f. (a priest tells Mordred of his — Mordred's — incestuous birth and predicts that he and his father, Arthur, will slay each other — a prediction which is fulfilled in the *Mort Artu*, VI, 377). Other parts of the *Agravain* are, probably, also from the pen of the author of the *Mort Artu*, but, unlike the ones just cited, they have no cyclic significance. Cp. RR, X, 99 ff., 105 ff.

[72] III, 3, 13, 88, 140, IV, 174 ff. 321 f., 324 ff., V, 231 ff. 243 ff., 249, 277 ff. The passages, IV, 321 f., 324 ff., indeed, are reproduced bodily from the *Estoire*, only with somewhat abbreviated text. The distribution of these interpolations seems to show that they were first made after the *Lancelot* had been expanded down to V, 318. On the whole subject see more fully RR, X, 120 f.

[73] III, 13, 88 (Lionel and Bohort, whose ancestry was the same as Lancelot's), V, 17, 237. The passage, III, 3, about Lancelot's change of name from *Galahad* to *Lancelot* was, also, written under

in turn, being the desire to derive Galahad, his son, from this same line; for Christ was a descendant of David's, and Galahad typifies Christ.

As regards the sources[74] of the *Lancelot,* it was, no doubt, the fame of Chrétien's *Lancelot (Conte de la Charete)* that led the author of the prose work in its primitive form[75] to make this character the subject of a full biographical romance; for Chrétien, after all, had dealt with but one episode in his career. To be sure, there already existed such a biographical romance relating to Lancelot — namely, the lost French original of the Middle High German *Lanzelet* — but, apart from its literary inferiority, Lancelot and Guinevere were not lovers in that romance; yet it was the story of their intrigue that had rendered the former an object of general interest to contemporary readers. Notwithstanding his adoption of Chrétien's ideas in regard to his hero, as the lover

---

the influence of the *Estoire,* although the subject of his descent from David is not here touched upon. For a discussion of Lancelot's genealogy cp., particularly, Bruce, RR, IX, 250 ff. Lot, *Lancelot,* pp. 218 ff., has, also, discussed the genealogies of Galahad and *Lancelot,* but he makes the serious mistake of failing to recognize that, just as Galahad typifies Christ, his genealogy is equated with Christ's. As we have seen above, the fact that the name of the head of his paternal line, viz. *Nascien,* is taken from the genealogy of Christ (St. Matthew, I) — so, too, with that of his uncle Eliezer puts the matter beyond doubt. Consequently, what the French scholar says in regard to the influence of Abyssinian tradition on this genealogy is beside the mark. The fact that the original Grail Winner, Perceval, was connected with the Grail king on his mother's side is, also, to be reckoned with in the discussion of Galahad's ancestry.

[74] On this subject, cp. P. Märtens, "Zur Lanzelotsage," E. Boehmer's *Romanische Studien,* V, 643 ff. (1880) and, especially, Lot, *Lancelot,* pp. 166 ff. (1918).

It may be observed here, once for all, that the sources of the *Lancelot* are purely literary. There is no ground whatever for believing that our author had access to any oral traditions of the Celts concerning Lancelot or any of the other characters. This view is, also, that of Sommer, I, p. VII and Lot, *op. cit.* p. 182, note 1.

[75] Brugger, *Zs. f. frz. Spr. u. Litt.,* XXXI[3], 276, conjectures that the primitive *Lancelot* was in verse, but there is no evidence to support this conjecture.

of the queen, and, above all, as a lover who exemplified impeccably the rules of the *amour courtois,* the author of the new prose work took, with modifications, from this earlier biographical romance, the account of Lancelot's origin and childhood and of his first departure from his foster-mother's dwelling in search of adventure. In the lost poem, as we see from the German adaptation, it was told how Lancelot was the son of Ban, king of Benoic,[76] and how by an uprising of his subjects the latter was driven out of his kingdom. On his flight, however, Ban dies from his wounds. His wife, who was tending him at the time of his death, had laid the infant Lancelot down under a tree, when she went to her husband's side. Whilst she was thus occupied, a water-fairy carried off the child in a mist to fairy-land (Maiden-land) and there brought him up in ignorance of his name and rank and of everything, indeed, that pertained to knighthood, with the ultimate purpose of obtaining through him, when grown, the deliverance of her son from an enchanter. Accordingly, when he was fifteen years old, the fairy permitted him to ride forth to seek his fortunes, but she would not reveal to him his name or parentage until he had conquered a certain knight, the strongest in the world — the enemy of her son. With these initial incidents all resemblance between the *Lanzelet* and the *Lancelot* virtually ceases.[77]    The

---

[76] Pant, King of Genewis, he is called in the *Lanzelet. Pant,* however, is evidently the same name as Ban, being derived from the oblique form *(Bant)* to a nominative, *Banz* (variant of *Bans*). Moreover, Lot, *Romania,* XXIV, 335 (1895), has pointed out that the German poet's *Genewis* is identical with Chrétien's *Gomeret* (Bans de Gomeret, *Erec,* 1975) and with *Benoic,* all three being alterations of *Gwynedd,* the Welsh name for North Wales. Cp., too, the same scholar's *Lancelot,* p. 147, note 8, where the alternative derivation from Breton *Guenet* (Modern French *Vannes*) is rejected.    On these matters and on Brugger's identification of *Ban* with Scotch *Bain* (accepted by Lot, *Lancelot,* p. 166, note 4, though not by the present writer) see his article in the Morf *Festschrift,* pp. 53 ff. (Halle, 1905) and Bruce, RR, X, 55, note.

[77] P. Märtens, *op. cit.,* pp. 690 ff. lists, it is true, some additional similarities for the part that follows Lancelot's setting forth on his adventures. They are all slight, however, as he, himself, acknowledges, and, in most cases, mere commonplaces of Arthurian romance.    The

reader, however, will have observed that the author of the prose
work has not adopted even these meagre borrowings without alteration, for he has rationalized the fairy into a great lady of the
Middle Ages and explained her lake as a mere illusion. Above
all, in order to relieve his hero's father of the discredit of a domestic rebellion, he represents this father's disasters and unhappy
end as due not to his own tyranny, but to the aggressions of an
unjust foe, King Claudas of the Desert Land,[78] who becomes,

same remark applies substantially to Lot's list, *op. cit.*, pp. 167f. An
exception should, probably be made, however, in the case of the name
of Lancelot's friend, Galehaut, son of the beautiful giantess (cp. Sommer, III, 201, etc.). In the *Lanzelet* (l. 7544) there is a young giant
named *Esealt,* which represents doubtless a distortion of *Galehalt* in
its lost French source.

[78] Identified with the province of Berry in France, III, 3. In
Old French *berrie* meant "desert plain," hence by popular etymology
the province of Berry becomes the "Terre Deserte." This is so already in the *chanson de geste, Girart de Roussillon.* Cp. Lot,
p. 189, note 1. — Claudas's capital was Bohorges (Bourges) and he
was, himself, "hom le roi de Gaule qui ore est apelee Franche." Ban's
kingdom was contiguous to Claudas's — i. e. it was in France. In
the *Lanzelet* it was placed in Great Britain.

Among other speculations as to places and persons that are named
in the beginning of the *Lancelot,* P. Paris, *Romans de la Table
Ronde,* II, 109 ff., suggests (p. 109) that Claudas is identical with
Clovis or his successor, Clothaire I. Brugger, Morf *Festschrift,* p. 57,
note 2 (1905) and *Zs. f. frz. Spr. u. Litt.,* XL[2], pp. 55 ff. (1912)
accepts the identification with Clovis and conjectures that the Claudas
story represents an actual oral tradition concerning Clovis. In his
appendix on Claudas's name, *Lancelot,* pp. 356f., Lot speaks with
some severity of this identification. I agree with him as to the historical tradition. Nevertheless, in certain Tristan MSS. we find a form
very near *Claudas,* viz. *Claudes (Claudex)* as a variant of the name
of the first Christian king of Gaul, where other MSS. have *Clodovex,
Clodeus, Clovis,* etc. Cp. Löseth, *Le roman en prose de Tristan,*
p. 6, note 4, and p. 477. It seems to me, then, that the name *Claudas*
may, after all, be a variant for *Clodeus (Clovis).* If this is so, it
came to the prose *Lancelot,* no doubt, either from the lost *chanson
de geste,* which I have suggested above, or from some chronicle source.

Lot, *loc. cit.,* derives the name from the same Ethiopian source
as *Agloval.* Cp. p. 401, note 67, above. But the objections which I
have raised to that derivation apply, also, to this.

of course, a character of the first importance in the romance.[79] On the death of Ban's brother, the older Bohort, Claudas seizes the kingdom of Gannes (Bohort's realm), also, and thus usurps the patrimony of Lionel and the younger Bohort, as well as of Lancelot.

Next come the episodes concerning the usurper's strife with Bohort's children and with his own rebellious barons. These episodes delay the narrative of Lancelot's career, which, in the *Lanzelet*, develop without interruption after the pattern of the usual biographical romance. They show, however, such vigor and so firm a grasp on reality that a different hand from that which penned the Lancelot *enfances* seems discernible in them. In any event, their similarity to the *chansons de geste* in style and spirit is manifest and it appears highly probable that we have combined here with the original Lancelot theme an adaptation of some lost poem of that species.[80]

Aside from the general influence of Chrétien's *Lancelot*, noted above, specific use is made of this romance in the so-called *Charete* section of the prose *Lancelot*.[81] The basis of this section, indeed, as we have seen, is a free paraphrase of Chrétien's poem.[82] The influence of the same writer's *Perceval* is, likewise, strongly stamped on the Grail interpolations of our romance[83] — especially,

---

[79] Lot, *loc. cit.*, points out, too, how the author of the *Lancelot* annuls the relationship which, according to the *Lanzelet*, subsisted between Lancelot and Arthur, and how he deprives Guinevere of the son, Lohot, who is accredited to her in the *Lanzelet*, ll. 6875 ff., as in some other romances. It would have seemed odious, if Lancelot's adultery had been committed with the wife of a kinswoman, and Guinevere, herself, in this intrigue, would have found a son embarrassing.

[80] On the discussion of these matters see RR, X, 48 ff.

[81] IV, 155 ff.

[82] For discussions of this *Charete* section, its composition, its relations to Chrétien's poem, the significance of the interwoven episodes, cp., respectively, Lot, *Lancelot*, pp. 170 ff. (1918) and Bruce, RR, X, 57 ff. (1918). The former assumes single authorship for this section as for the entire *Lancelot-Graal* corpus, the latter plural authorship.

[83] The influence is partly direct, partly indirect (through the *Queste*). Lot, *op. cit.* pp. 173 f., has enumerated a number of details

on the narrative of Gawain's visit to the Grail castle (Corbenic).[84] Moreover, it is, doubtless, owing to a reminiscence of the *Yvain* (ll. 2804ff.) that, in the prose *Lancelot*, difficulties that arise in Lancelot's love affairs with the queen drive him on various occasions[85] into a frenzy.

The continuations of Chrétien's *Perceval* by Pseudo-Wauchier and Wauchier de Denain, respectively, are, likewise, among the undoubted sources of the *Lancelot*. The self-playing chessmen of the Forest Perdue (III, 151f.) are borrowed from Wauchier (ll. 22442ff.).[86] That the band of questers in Gawain's long search for Lancelot should have been fixed at forty (IV, 321) appears to betray, also, the influence of the same writer, (l. 31421), and similarly with the luminous apparition of the Grail in the forest (V, 392), — far from its habitual shrine in the Grail castle, — through which the wounds of Perceval and Hector are healed.[87] In this last case, it is true, the conception may have reached our romance through the *Queste* (VI, 42), as an intermediary.[88]

---

in other parts of the *Lancelot* which he thinks were derived from Chrétien's *Perceval*, the sending of vanquished knights by the hero to Arthur or Guinevere, the characterization of Kay, numerous proper names, etc. In many cases, however, it is impossible to say whether the derivation is direct.

[84] IV, 339 ff. Here, as in Chrétien's *Perceval*, ll. 3047 ff., the lord of the Grail castle is an unnamed maimed king; moreover, as in Chrétien's poem, ll. 3182 ff., the Grail is borne in by a girl. Contrast with this Lancelot's visit, V, 105 ff., where the lord of the Grail castle is called Pelles and is not maimed.

[85] III, 414, IV, 155 (cp. p. 151), V, 381.

[86] For the affiliation of the various versions of this *motif* cp. RR, IX, 375f. In the Dutch *Walewein* (edited by W. J. A. Jonckbloet, Leiden, 1846), which G. Paris, *Histoire littéraire de la France*, XXX, 82ff., has analyzed, under the title of *Gavain et l'échiquier*, there is a marvellous chessboard, but no self-playing chessmen attached to it. For this *motif*, however, see the Dutch *Lancelot*, Book II, ll. 18391ff., which derives it from the prose *Lancelot*, III, 151f.

[87] Cp. *Conte del Graal*, ll. 34407ff.

[88] Lot, *Lancelot*, pp. 175f., cites some additional points of influence which appear to me more doubtful — especially, those that relate to style. The fact that the prose *Lancelot* (as it stands in our MSS.)

From Pseudo-Wauchier (ll. 15892 ff.) is derived the incident (III, 272), when Arthur wounds himself at the table whilst he is leaning on a knife in melancholy revery over the failure of his knights to undertake the promised quest for Lancelot.[89] So, too, with the whole conception of Gawain's visit to the Grail Castle. Furthermore, it was because of the example of Pseudo-Wauchier and Wauchier that in the *Lancelot* there is only one king[90] at Corbenic (the Grail Castle) and that, except in the episode of Gawain's visit, just referred to, this king is unmaimed. The idea that the blight which rested on the Grail land and which only the predestined Grail knight could remove was due to the dolorous stroke of a mysterious sword is drawn by the author of Lancelot's visit to Corbenic directly from the *Estoire*,[91] but it was ultimately derived from Pseudo-Wauchier,[92] and, doubtless, the author of the episode in question was familiar with it, also, in its original form.[93]

With the exception of the compositions of Chrétien, Pseudo-Wauchier and Wauchier, no romance, perhaps, has supplied more important materials for episodes of the *Lancelot* than Raoul de

combines passages of a mystical import with others bordering on license he attributes to the example of Wauchier. — Lot is probably right, pp. 180 f., in ascribing also to imitation of Wauchier some points in which the *Lancelot* might seem to be imitating *Li Biaus Descouneus.*

[89] On this incident cp., more fully, RR, X, 54, note 119.

[90] Cp. IV, 339 ff. (Gawain's visit), V. 105 ff. (Lancelot's), 139 ff., 294 ff. (Bohort's two visits).

[91] The *Estoire* is explicitly cited, V, 110, as the source.

[92] ll, 20288 ff.

[93] Lot, *Lancelot*, pp. 177 ff., cites a few other points, which are less certain. He lays stress, especially, on the indebtedness of the *Lancelot*, IV, 156, and the *Queste*, VI, 6, to Pseudo-Wauchier, ll. 12610 ff., for the well-known *motif* according to which Arthur would not sit down to table on feast-days, until some adventure was announced. Pseudo-Wauchier may well be the source here, since the authors of the two passages in question undeniably show elsewhere a knowledge of his work, but Lot overlooks the fact that this *motif* is, also, found in Chrétien's *Perceval*, ll. 2784 ff., whence Pseudo-Wauchier, doubtless, derives it.

Houdenc's *Meraugis de Portlesguez*.[94] From this source (ll. 3663ff., 4331ff.) comes the famous incident of the enchanted carols in the Forest Perdue (V, 123f., 148ff.), to which for a time even Lancelot succumbs, but the spell of which he ultimately undoes, as the best knight in the world. So, too, with the vows of the knights at Brangoire's court to perform various fantastic exploits for the sake of their ladies (IV, 266),[95] and the adventures of Yvain and Bohort which begin with the exaction of a kiss from the former by a hideous woman (V, 127).[96]

The reading of the authors of the *Lancelot*, however, was, of course, not confined to Arthurian romance,[97] and it is accordingly not strange if we, also, find here and there traces of the influence of the other forms of literature that were then most in vogue —

---

[94] The best study of the relations of the two romances is G. Huet's "Le *Lancelot* en prose et *Meraugis de Portlesguez*", *Romania*, XLI, 518ff. (1912). In the opinion of the present writer he proves that the *Lancelot* is the borrower. Brugger, *Zs. f. frz. Spr. u. Litt.*, XXVIII [1], 59, note 107 (1905), was inclined to the contrary view.

[95] Lot, *Lancelot*, p. 186, speaks of this episode as inspired by the "gabs" (boasts), of Charlemagne and his knights in the *Pelerinage de Charlemagne*. Huet, *op. cit.*, p. 531, had already shown, however, that the *Meraugis*, ll. 1777ff., was the source.

[96] Cp. *Meraugis*, ll. 1447—2632 and ll. 4445ff. Huet, *op. cit.*, pp. 524ff., has analyzed and discussed the relation of these episodes to *Lancelot*, V, 127ff.

[97] In addition to the romances which I have noted above, Lot, *Lancelot*, pp. 182ff., counts among the sources of the *Lancelot* the Mort Arthur section of the *Didot-Perceval* (J. L. Weston's *Legend of Sir Perceval*, II, 82ff.). In the RR, IX, 390f., however, I have tried to prove that the episodes in question — Arthur's wars against Claudas and the Romans, V, 335ff. — are really based on the account of his wars with Lancelot and the Romans in the *Mort Artu*, VI, 317ff., supplemented by Wace, ll. 10341ff. These episodes of the *Mort Artu*, in turn, were developed indisputably from the lost French original of Layamon's *Brut*. Cp. RR, IV, 452ff. In any event, Wace, alone, would have sufficed as the basis of these *Lancelot* episodes. — On the relation of *Lancelot*, V, 335ff., to the political situation in the early thirteenth century, Lot, p. 185, note 2, has some interesting remarks. He is probably right when he maintains that Frollo is here made a German because of French hostility to the

saints' lives,[98] *chansons de geste*,[99] romances of antiquity.[100] In a passage which is manifestly from the hand of a cleric — namely, the one concerning the interpretation of Galehaut's allegorical dream (IV, 23) — there is even a reminiscence of a philosophical treatise,[101] Alexander of Neckham's *De Naturis Rerum* (ch. 74). The passage in this work, it is true, which caught our cleric's attention contained not the record of a scientific observation, but one of the fictitious vaticinations of the Arthurian enchanter and prophet, Merlin — in this case, with regard to the destined migration of wisdom from Oxford to Ireland.

Taking the *Lancelot*, as it is preserved to us in our extant manuscripts, it is unquestionably one of the most rambling productions in European literature. Coherence had never been a virtue even of the metrical romances, but, after all, if we exclude the *Conte del Graal* (Chrétien's *Perceval* and its continuations), they had, at least, been compositions of moderate length, whereas in the *Lancelot*, as stated above, we have, with one or two exceptions,[102] the longest work of fiction in the whole history of European

German Empire at that time, but it is not necessary to assume that the battle of Bouvines (1214) had already been fought.

Some episodes of the *Lancelot* are, doubtless, derived from Arthurian and other romances, now lost. P. Paris, RTR, IV, 208, note 1, conjectured that this was the case with the episode of Gawain's imprisonment by Caradoc in the Dolorous Tower, IV, 85 ff. It seems quite likely, too, that Agloval (Perceval's brother) was drawn from some lost metrical romance. These matters, however, are purely speculative, so that there is no profit in lingering over them.

[98] Lot, p. 186, sees in the episode of the mad Lancelot, living unrecognized and contemned at Corbenic, an imitation of the legend of St. Alexis.

[99] *Ibid.* Lot cites *Girart de Roussillon* among the sources.

[100] The story of Aeneas which Lancelot, V, 217, saw painted on the wall at Morgan's palace is more likely to have been derived from the French romance *Eneas* than from Vergil. So, too, with the name of the enchantress, Camille, III, 406. The name *Serses (Cerses)* = *Xerxes*, V, 144, is doubtless taken from the *Roman de Troie*, ll. 6854, *et passim*.

[101] This is pointed out by Lot, p. 186, note 8.

[102] French romances of the seventeenth century.

fiction, and, in varying degrees, we encounter in every part of
the romance the same desultory combination of incoherent elements.
To unify and at the same time to impart an air of verisimilitude
to the narrative, an apparently coherent system of dating the movements of the hero, such as one might find in the chronicle of
an actual historical personage, is adopted — especially in the
*Galehaut* section. Nevertheless, the effect, of this device is feeble
and its very existence passed unobserved until recently.[103] On the
other hand, the principle, which is applied, more or less, everywhere in the *Lancelot* of interlacing the various episodes is obvious enough.[104] An episode is interrupted, to be resumed later on
in the midst of another episode, whose further development is
thus postponed — to be resumed, perhaps, in its turn, in the midst
of still a third episode. The structural unity, however, which results from this second device, is purely mechanical, since the interwoven episodes, for the most part, have no organic connection with
one another and the essential incoherence of the narrative elements is still patent. The device becomes, then, most frequently,
a mere trick to pique the curiosity of the reader by breaking off
abruptly the adventures of one character and turning to those of
another at a point where the former appear to be approaching a
*dénouement*. There is never any trouble about prolonging the
narrative, for, under these conditions, the author has no scruples
in regard to sudden transitions or the introduction of new characters. Above all, the quest *motif*, which Chrétien had employed,[105] was always at hand to give a new start to the flagging story,
and nothing else is so much responsible for the inordinate length
of our romance as the frequent application of this *motif*, with
its inevitable temptations to accumulate to an indefinite extent
disconnected adventures. A number of knights set forth in search

---

[103] Cp. Lot, *Lancelot,* ch. III. He calculates (p. 35) that the
action from Lancelot's arrival at Arthur's court to the end of Sommer's
first volume covers three years and four months.

[104] Cp. Lot, *ibid.* ch. II. The inference as to the single authorship of the *Lancelot,* however, which the French scholar draws from
this device is disputable. Cp. Bruce, RR, X, 380 f.

[105] Cp., particularly, the quest for Guinevere in his *Lancelot*.

of the hero, say; after a while they separate, and each of the
original company has his own series of combats and other"moving
accidents by flood and field" — in most cases, entirely independent
of the rest. Obviously, under such circumstances, the bulk of the
narrative depends merely on the writer's whim as to the number of
questers he will put on the hero's track and the number of adventures he will allow any individual quester to achieve. There is
no organic plan to be interfered with.

Altogether, the only true unity which the *Lancelot* possesses
is a certain unity of spirit which pervades the whole, as it pervades the Arthurian romances, in general, this spirit being of
a kind to foster an idealistic attitude of mind, and through the
exhibition of examples of knightly valor and honor and noble
conduct, to stimulate the reader to the attainment of high standards of physical and moral excellence.[106] From the modern point
of view, to be sure, in one domain of morals there are serious
limitations to the ideals of conduct which are expressed by the
romance — namely, in that of the sexual relations; for, in the
*Lancelot*, as in the metrical romances, love is practically always
illicit and often adulterous. The hero's passion for the queen,
which furnishes the *raison d'être* of the work is, of course, adulterous, and the divine champion of religion and chastity (Galahad)
is himself the fruit of an irregular and transient union. Needless
to say that Arthur is no better than his spouse, as is shown by
his affairs with Camille and the false Guinevere.[107] These instances are the most conspicuous, but many others occur in the
course of the narrative. The immorality of the underlying conceptions concerning the relations of the sexes is hidden, to some
degree, in the case of the love-story of Lancelot and Guinevere

---

[106] Cp. the excellent remarks on this subject by Gröber in his
*Grundriss*, Band II, Abt. I, p. 998. He is speaking of the prose-
romances, in general, but his description applies with especial force
to the *Lancelot*. For an important study of the relations of the
prose *Lancelot (Charete* section*)* and Chrétien's poem to each other
in respect to spirit, as well as matter, cp. Mme. Lot-Borodine in
F. Lot's *Lancelot*, pp. 383 ff.

[107] III, 410 ff. and IV, 10 ff., respectively.

by the veneer of the contemporary code of courtly love which this affair illustrates, but it appears in its full grossness in such episodes as those of Agravain and the "damoisele roigneuse" (III, 318ff.) and of Guerrehes and the Lady of the Pavilion (V, 31ff.).

Since the merits of the *Lancelot* are not to be found in the skilful disposition or development of the narrative as a whole, we have to seek them in the individual episodes. Even here, however, there are glaring faults enough — especially, the fault of monotony through endless repetitions of the same *motifs*.[108] The number of cases in which the interest of an encounter between two knights, whether in tourney, battle, or single combat, turns on the fact that the adversaries are friends or kinsmen who are unaware of each other's identity[109] must run into the scores. And such episodes do not exhaust the instances in which the *motif* of Lancelot's own incognito is exploited. In the French original of the *Lanzelet* his name had not been disclosed to him until he had distinguished himself by a notable achievement, and this fairy-tale conception is taken over into the prose-romance, despite the general rationalizing tendency of the latter. It is, perhaps, fitting that this hero, who was so long nameless in his youth, should, in his maturer years, so often choose to disguise himself in armor, not his own, although his superiority in feats of arms always betrays his identity in the end.

Apart from these episodes and the innumerable combats which differ hardly at all from each other, many other instances of repetition might be cited — such as the hero's three frenzies,[110]

---

[108] Lot, *Lancelot*, pp. 263ff., gives a partial list of nineteen such cases.

[109] This is, of course, an extension of the wide-spread Sohrab and Rustem *motif* (combat between father and son). A few of the numerous examples of the extension (combats between kinsmen and friends) are given in M. A. Potter's *Sohrab and Rustem*, pp. 208ff. (London, 1902). Cp. too, Bruce, *Mort Artu*, pp. 268f. Occasionally, however, in the Middle Ages, there were actually such encounters, mutual recognition being prevented by the armor. Thus William the Conqueror came near being killed by his son, Robert of Normandy.

[110] III, 414ff., IV, 155, V, 381.

his two imprisonments by Morgan,[111] the carrying off of knights
by giants on two occasions,[112] various rescues of others from captivity,[113] Lancelot's double cohabitation with Pelles' daughter,[114]
etc. In Bohort we have even a character who is the mere replica
of another character — namely, Lancelot — and whose exploits
are all virtually pale reflections of those of his model.[115] The
same thing is true, in some degree, also, of Hector.

The present writer, it is true, believes that the repetitions
with which the narrative in our extant MSS. of the *Lancelot*
is diluted are due, in a large measure, to later expansions of the
primitive romance, but probably at no stage of its existence was
the *Lancelot* entirely free from this weakness. It was the romance, however, in its expanded and cyclic form that has been
read ever since the fourth decade, say, of the thirteenth century,
and in our analysis it is needless, therefore, to concern ourselves
with any earlier hypothetical form, however plausible, in which
it may have existed.

The *Lancelot* is frequently marred, still further, by the trivial
or absurdly fantastic nature of the adventures. Take, for instance,
the very first exploit of the hero after his arrival at Arthur's
court, when he pulls the lance-heads and sword out of the wounded
Trahant's body and swears to avenge him (Trahant) "on all who
liked him less than the man that wounded him".[116] How is it
possible for a modern reader to follow with any interest adventures
based on a pure absurdity like this that possess no charm either
for the reason or the imagination? In a somewhat similar way,
we have preceding the excellent episodes in which Gawain's and
Lancelot's visits to Corbenic are respectively described the pre-

---

[111] IV, 124 ff., V, 215 ff.      [112] IV, 88, V, 88.
[113] III, 167, 425, etc.      [114] V, 110, 379.
[115] For the numerous points of similarity between the two, cp
RR, X, 59 f.
[116] III, 126 ff. In one of the episodes which constitute the sequel
of this vow, Lancelot finds himself compelled to combat a knight who
has just entertained him most hospitably. Bound by his vow, however,
he drowns his host, weeping for the necessity of the act as he commits
it. Cp. III, 199.

posterous incident of the girl who for an undefined sin is condemned to sit in a tub of scalding water.[117]  In a few cases the
extravagant code of courtly love is responsible for the absurdities
in question, as when Lancelot barely escapes drowning at Camelot,
his gaze being fixed so ecstatically on Guinevere that he does
not observe that his horse is taking him into the river.[118]  In the
aimlessness of the combats which make up so much of its narrative, the *Lancelot,* it is true, does not differ from the other Arthurian romances, — only here, owing to the length of the work,
the accumulation of such incidents is immensely greater than anywhere else.

Instances of obtuseness in matters of art being so numerous
throughout our romance, it is, perhaps, not surprising that we
should find the process of euhemerisation applied so frequently
to the highly poetical materials of folk-lore origin which it contains.[119]  As we have seen, even in the beginning of the romance,
the lake of Lancelot's fairy foster-mother is reduced to a mere
illusion.  She and her damsel do still retain some super-natural
powers,[120] but by the end of the work they have been stripped
even of these.[121]  Similarly, access to Sorelois, which is modelled
after Chrétien's Gorre, is no longer by such perilous approaches
as the swordbridge and the underwater bridge, but by ordinary
causeways.[122]  In the episode of Guinevere's visit to the Fairies'
Fountain, even the fairies are explained away as, in reality, simply
beautiful ladies.[123]  It is only the more delicate or extravagant

---

[117] IV, 342 and V, 106.

[118] III, 303.  This incident is developed from Chrétien's *Lancelot,* ll. 3685 ff.

[119] Lot, *Lancelot,* pp. 272 ff., has some very good remarks on
this subject, although he exaggerates somewhat the thoroughness of
the euhemerization.

[120] Cp. III, 55 ff., where Saraide, obeying her mistress's command,
turns Lionel and Bohort into greyhounds.

[121] V, 321 ff.

[122] III, 269 f.

[123] IV, 305.  The words are: "Cele fontaine estoit apelee la
fontaine a fees, pour chou que cil qui en la forest habitoient disoient
quil y auoient veu de trop beles dames, et si ne pooit on riens sauoir

fancies of the popular imagination, however, that we find rejected here and there in the *Lancelot;* for the more palpable forms of enchantment or supernaturalism we meet with everywhere in the romance — in the copper men and marvellous shields of Dolorous Gard,[124] in the terrors of Escalon the Tenebrous,[125] in the spell that rested upon the Valley of False Lovers,[126] in the carols and automatic chessboard of the Lost Forest,[127] etc.

As over against the weaknesses of the *Lancelot* which have been analyzed above, one may point to a great number of episodes, especially, in the *Galehaut* section, totalling in the aggregate some hundreds of pages, which constitute admirable specimens of the narrative art. This is true, for example, of the whole series of episodes that extend from the beginning of the romance down to the hero's arrival at Arthur's court,[128] although they are probably of composite origin. These pages include, *inter alia,* charming pictures of aristocratic boyhood (Lancelot and Lionel),[129] and in the wars of Claudas with his barons,[130] a narrative of feudal strife, unsurpassed in vividness and energy by any other that has come down to us from the Middle Ages. The conquest of Dolorous Gard,[131] though somewhat long drawn out, is, on the whole, an excellent re-telling of a fairy-tale exploit in terms of contemporary life. Similar adaptations of folk-lore *motifs,* effected with a high degree of literary skill, are the episodes of the False Guinevere[132] and of the Valley of the False Lovers.[133] They are brought close to actual life, yet retain much of the wild charm of their origin.

In the later divisions of the romance, also, we have such striking episodes as those of the visits of Gawain and Lancelot to Corbenic, when they first see the Holy Grail,[134] Lancelot's second

---

de lor estre, et por ce disoit on que ce estoient fees." Lot, *Lancelot,* pp. 272f., has called attention to this passage.

[124] III, 144, 150.    [125] IV, 111.

[126] IV, 117ff.    [127] V, 149ff.

[128] III, 125.    [129] III, 33ff., 50ff., 111ff.

[130] III, 60ff.    [131] III, 143ff.

[132] IV, 110ff.    [133] IV, 116ff.

[134] IV, 339ff., V, 105ff.

imprisonment at the hands of Morgan,[135] and the hermit's prediction of Mordred's evil end,[136] all of which are instinct with imaginative vigor.

The elements in the *Lancelot,* however, which have won for it its greatest fame are, of course, the love-story of Lancelot and Guinevere and the story, inspired by classical models, of the friendship of Galehaut and Lancelot. Both suffer, it is true, from the want of concentration, which is the bane of the romance — the main themes are interwoven with all sorts of extraneous episodes — but, after all, the total impression produced in both instances is a memorable one. The part of the love-story which lies within the *Galehaut* section of the work represents the highest reach in literature of the *amour courtois* in its purest and most serious form.[137] This remark applies especially to the scene[138] — immortalized by Dante in the Paolo and Francesca episode of the *Inferno* (V, 127 ff.) — in which Guinevere bestows on her lover the crowning kiss.[139] The picture of the meek submissiveness of the great exemplar of chivalry in the presence of his mistress and of the latter's arch consciousness of her power possesses an old-world charm. Admirable, too, is the episode of the first meeting of the two lovers,[140] with the fine psychological touch by which Guinevere is represented as pretending dissatisfaction with the young aspirant to knighthood, in order that she may hide the really profound impression which he has made upon her.

A deeper note, however, is struck in this love-story in the last division of the romance (the so-called *Agravain*), where the queen's jealousy is aroused[141] by Calles's daughter — the girl who had healed Lancelot in the poisoned spring incident. The author of these pages has his eye fixed upon nature, rather than upon the artificial rules of the *amour courtois,* and so, besides the pas-

---

[135] V, 215 ff.       [136] V, 284 ff.

[137] Chaucer's *Troilus and Criseyde,* although it, too, suffers, from prolixity, is, of course, a greater work of art than the *Lancelot,* but it contains humorous and even ironical elements.

[138] III, 258 ff., but one should read also the preceding passage, 253 ff. (the dialogue of the queen with Galeheut).

[139] III, 263.       [140] III, 125 f.       [141] V, 59 ff.

sages just alluded to, we have such excellent scenes as the one in which the king is led to interpret his wife's illness as purely physical, although it is really caused by her anxiety about Lancelot, or the one in which she feigns cheerfulness, despite the sorrow with which her heart is filled on her lover's account.[142] The variations which are wrought on this theme of Guinevere's jealousy and on an additional new *motif*, viz. that of her intimacy with Lancelot's kinsmen, Bohort and Lionel, impart an individuality to the character in this last division of the romance which it lacked in the earlier divisions.[143]

Altogether, characterization in our romance, as in most works of the Middle Ages, is elementary, but the principal figures, although dim in outline, as compared with the best masterpieces of later ages, have a certain grandeur of their own. This is true not only of Lancelot and Guinevere, but of Galehaut — noble and melancholy, to whom the foreknowledge of his early death involves no pang so bitter as the thought of his separation from his friend — and of Claudas — the most complex character in the romance — a leader of men, astute, avaricious, jealous of power, and full of ruthless energy in the prosecution of his evil ambitions, yet capable of a deep paternal tenderness and of acts of generosity towards the youthful foes whom he has wronged.[144]

---

[142] V, 60 ff. Lot, *Lancelot*, p. 277, calls attention, also, to the fine scene later in the *Lancelot*, V, 193 f. where Guinevere reproaches herself with being the cause of Lancelot's failing in the Grail quest.

[143] These two *motifs* are fundamental in the *Mort Artu*. There are so many similarities between that branch and certain episodes in this part of the *Lancelot* that I believe they are by the same author. For a detailed discussion of the subject cp. RR, X, 97 ff.

[144] In the romance, itself, III, 26 f., this mixture of good and evil qualities is commented on and the respective qualities are enumerated. The passage is a remarkable one and gives us a life-like portrait of Claudas. One gets the impression that some actual personage, so to speak, sat for this picture.

## 4. La Queste del Saint Graal.

As was stated above,[145] the *Queste del Saint Graal* is the
companion-romance to the *Estoire del Saint Graal*, the latter being
the early history of the Holy Grail down through the conversion
of Britain by Joseph and other members of the Grail company,
the former a narrative of the quest for the sacred vessel by certain
knights of Arthur's court in that monarch's reign, some four
hundred years after the conversion.[146] We have seen that in the
*Estoire* references forward to incidents in the *Queste* are frequent.
In a similar manner, in the *Queste*, references backwards to incidents in the *Estoire* are also frequent — indeed, there is one
long passage (about the spindles in Solomon's ship) in the former
that is taken over from the latter with but little change of wording.[147] From the nature of the case, moreover, the main sources
of the two branches were bound to be the same — namely, Chre-
tien's *Perceval* and its first two continuations,[148] besides Robert de
Boron's *Joseph* — since these were the only works on the Grail,
except Chrétien's lost *livre*, that had been composed up to that

---

[145] Cp. p. 374 ff., above. I have discussed there everything pertaining to the mutual relations of the two romances. The *Queste* is
printed, VI, 3—199 in Sommer's *Vulgate Version*.

[146] Cp. *Queste*, VI, 62, where Mordrain, who was so prominent
in the *Estoire* and who dies in the *Queste*, is said to have lived
this number of years.

[147] On this passage, VI, 151—161, and the cross-references between the two branches cp. p. 376, note 3, above.

[148] The continuation of Pseudo-Wauchier is much the most important single source for the *Queste*, barring Robert's *Joseph*, from
which the definitely Christian, mystical, conception of the Grail was
derived. In MLN, XXX, pp. 395 f., note 29, I have already noted
the indebtedness of the *Queste* to Pseudo-Wauchier in the following
points: 1. The Fisher King (Pelles) is not maimed, (VI, 5, 98, 114).
2. The Grail is brought into the hall supernaturally, and not by
attendants (VI, 13). 3. The dolorous stroke which causes the blight
of the land, (VI, 146 f.). 4. The importance ascribed to the joining
of the sword, (VI, 187 f.). 5. The chapel and the bodyless hand
(VI, 108).

Perceval's sister is doubtless derived direct from Wauchier, her
inventor. On this character in the *Queste* cp., especially, Madame

time.[149] The minor sources, however, though of the same general character, are less varied in the case of the *Queste*[150] than in the case of the *Estoire*.

We need hardly repeat here[151] that the purpose of the author of the *Queste*, in supplanting Perceval, the earlier Grail Winner, with his new creation, Galahad, was to make the Grail knight an incarnation of his own rigid ideals of asceticism. No person who failed to fulfill the requirements of these ideals seemed to him

---

Lot-Borodine in Lot's *Lancelot*, pp. 432 ff. Madame Lot regards her as a reincarnation of the Virgin Mary.

As to these borrowings, see, still further, RR, IX, 367, note 77. On the character, Pelles, who originated probably with the author of the *Queste*, cp. Bruce, "Pelles, Pellinor, and Pellean in the Old French Arthurian Romances", MPh., XVI, 116 ff. For notes on Chrétien as a source of the *Queste*, cp. Lot, *Lancelot*, pp. 192 f.

[149] I have combated below, Part IV, the hypothesis that the *Perlesvaus* was earlier than the *Estoire* or the *Queste*. Similarly, with regard to the hypothesis that the *Didot-Perceval* was a source of these romances, cp. *ibid.*, below. Lot, *Lancelot*, p. 190, on the other hand, goes so far as to declare that the *Didot-Perceval* (the extant MSS. of which include a brief *Mort Arthur*) suggested the idea of writing the *Queste* and *Mort Artu* of the Vulgate cycle.

[150] When Galahad draws the sword from the stone after Gawain and Perceval had failed, VI, 10, this is imitated from Robert de Boron, II, 83, in which Arthur is the hero of a similar incident. — The incident of the grateful lion, VI, 69, is taken, doubtless, from Chrétien's *Yvain*, ll. 3341 ff. — The bestiaries (e. g. Hugo of St. Victor's) and saints' lives (St. Eustace, etc.) had already made the stag as a symbol of Christ familiar to the Middle Ages, and from the time of the patristic writers the four evangelists had been identified with the man, the eagle, the lion and the ox of *Ezechiel*, I, 10. Cp., on these subjects, Alfred Maury, *Croyances et Légendes du Moyen Age*, pp. 257 ff., 279 ff. (Paris, 1896). These, then, are the sources of Galahad's adventure in the forest, VI, 166, which, in turn, is, no doubt, the source of *Estoire*, I, 257 ff. and *Lancelot*, V, 249. — The episode of the dead girl (Perceval's sister) whom Lancelot finds in a ship with a scroll in her hand that tells her history, VI, 175, is imitated from *Historia Apollonii Regis Tyri*, ch. 25—26. (edited by A. Riese, Leipzig, 1893) — the story of the hero's daughter. Cp. Bruce, *Mort Artu*, pp. 280 f.

[151] Cp. p. 379, above.

fitted to win the vessel which symbolized the most sacred mysteries of the Christian religion. Chastity, however, was the essential basis of asceticism, and Perceval, as the writer found him in Chrétien (ll. 2030 ff.) and Wauchier (ll. 25017 ff.), was not chaste. On the other hand, it had, of course, been an implication of Robert's *Joseph* that in the sequel to that poem, which was probably never written, his Grail hero (whether Perceval or another) would satisfy this condition, and in the invention of Galahad, the author of the *Queste* was doubtless merely putting into effect Robert's conception. The same condition is likewise applied to Perceval and Bohort, the other members of the trinity of questers,[152] who share with Galahad the mystic vision of the Grail, but who, in proportion to their lapses from the ideal perfection of chastity,[153] are inferior to him in the marks of divine favor.

It may well be that the contemporary order of Knights Templars, also, offered suggestions for the new character,[154] since he, like the Templars, is a monk-knight — ascetic yet militant. But Galahad is even more than that, for he moves on a semi-divine plane and typifies Christ himself; indeed, he is merely Christ in armor.[155]

---

[152] This number was adopted to correspond to the number of the Christian godhead.

[153] Perceval is represented as chaste in act (cp. VI, 58), but not in intention (cp. VI. 78). No mention is made of his lapses from virtue that had been recounted in Chrétien and Wauchier. — Bohort, it is said, (VI, 119), was unchaste only once, viz. in the affair with Brangoire's daughter (IV, 270 ff.) and then through the influence of magic.

[154] The influence of this order on the description of the Grail Knights in Wolfram's *Parzival*, Book XVI, ll. 171, 201, *et passim* is, of course, beyond dispute. Alfred Nutt saw its influence, also, in the characters of Mordrain and Nascien in the *Estoire* and *Queste*. Cp. his pamphlet, *The Legends of the Holy Grail*, pp. 48 f.: *Popular Studies in Mythology, Romance and Folklore*, No. 14 (London, 1902). Galahad, however, embodies the Templar ideal much more perfectly than these two.

[155] In the *Queste*, VI, 57, Galahad at the Round Table is compared to Christ at the table of the Last Supper. Resemblances of Galahad to Christ, have been noted, besides, by Heinzel, *Gralromane*

In one important respect, the *Queste* is very superior to the
branches of the Vulgate cycle which we have so far considered —

---

p. 142, and Wechssler, *Sage vom Heiligen Gral*, p. 117. See, too,
Brugger, *Zs. f. frz. Spr. u. Litt.*, XXIX[1] 97 and Lot's *Lancelot*,
p. 432. The present writer, moreover, has shown in his article "Galahad, Nascien and Some Other Names in the Grail Romances", MLN,
XXXIII, 129 ff. (1918), that *Nascien*, the name of the head of Galahad's paternal line, and *Eliezer*, the name of his uncle, are both
drawn from the genealogy of Christ, *St. Matthew*, I, and *St. Luke*,
III, where they appear respectively as *Naasson* and *Eliazer*. — The
identity of Galahad and Christ was so obvious that the story of the
conception of the former in the *Lancelot*, V, 105 ff., is, substantially,
a sort of parody of the story of the conception of the latter. Cp.
Bruce, RR, IX, 368 ff. (1918). Each is begotten of a virgin for the
express purpose of becoming a savior of the people. In Robert de
Boron's *Merlin*, II, 4 ff., the story of Christ's conception had already
been parodied in the account of how the Devil begot Merlin upon a
virgin, with the idea of raising up an Antichrist. God, however, frus-
trated his purpose. It is possible that this passage in Robert suggested the parody of Galahad's conception.

Malory and Tennyson have standardized *Galahad* as the name
of the Grail Winner, but in the MSS. of the Old French romances
the usual form is *Galaad,* which in the Latin Bible (Vulgate) is the
equivalent of the *Gilead* of our Authorized Version. *Galaad (Gilead)* occurs most frequently as the name of a district in the Bible,
but it, also, occurs as the name of three different persons: (1) a great-
grandson of Joseph's. Cp. *Numbers*, XXVI, 29, XXVII, 1, *et passim*.
(2) Jephthah's father, *Judges*, XI, 1, 2. (3) chief of a family of
Gad, I, *Chronicles*, V. 14. None of the three, however, are really
prominent and there can be little doubt that the assonance with
*Gales* really determined our author in choosing this name. Perceval
had been of Gales (Wales) — hence the author of the *Queste*, who
needed a biblical name for his religious hero and, at the same time,
wanted to keep up the connection with Gales, selected *Galahad*. This
view is confirmed by the statement in the *Estoire*, I, 282, that Gales
was named after Galahad. The reverse, of course, was the truth.
Possibly the name of the famous friend of Galahad's father, viz:
*Galehaut,* may have had some influence, too, for that seemed also
connected etymologically with Gales. — On the matters here discussed
see my article in MLN, just cited. Heinzel, *Gralromane*, pp. 134 f.,
imagined that the name was taken from the first of the three Bible
Galahads, because, he, too, had an ancestor named Joseph. Lot, *Lan-*

namely, in unity of plan. The plan here again takes the form of a quest, — the form which had already been employed so often in the *Lancelot*, — but, in the present instance, the effect of the device is not weakened by repetition: the whole book is made up of a single quest, in which the participants and adventures are relatively few. Moreover, the object of this quest is not to recover an absent companion of the Round Table, but to obtain possession of the mysterious symbol of our highest spiritual aspirations: in other words, the quest, in this case, is a quest for the ideal. Throughout, everything is centred on the attainment of the ideal object. The knights leave Arthur's court in search of it and those who had been predestined by divine grace to achieve it meet at the end in the enjoyment of the deepest spiritual satisfaction that the heart of man can know. Thus, by giving a new direction to a threadbare device, the writer, despite many shortcomings, has turned it into an instrument for expressing the mystical spirit of the Middle Ages with a power that is hardly equalled elsewhere. Certainly no other expression of that spirit has captured the imagination of subsequent ages so widely or so enduringly.

Notwithstanding this unique achievement, our author has, by no means, rid the quest form of its inherent weakness. The adventures of the individual knights are still as disconnected as ever. Furthermore, in a considerable proportion of cases, these adventures are the old familiar commonplaces of Arthurian romance,[156]

---

*celot*, p. 120 (including notes) thinks that Galahad was selected because of some mystic meaning and cites *Genesis*, XXXI, 47, where as a place-name, it is interpreted as "acervus testimonii". The authors of the Grail romances, however, did not seek very far in such matters. For example, the name of the heavenly city, Sarras, is obtained by cutting off -*in* from *Sarrasin*, the name of the people (Saracens) among whom it was situated. Cp. *Estoire* I, 21. — On Rhys's impossible derivation of the name, *Galahad*, from the Celtic, *Arthurian Legend*, pp. 166 ff., cp. MLN. XXXIII, 132, note 5, — On Christ as a knight in mediaeval conceptions cp. Lot, *op. cit.*, p. 449.

[156] e. g. VI, 100 (Lancelot joins the black knights in a tourney, because he sees that their side is the weaker), 124 (Bohort champions a disinherited damsel), 140 (Galahad joins the weaker side in a tourney), etc.

and in still other cases they are as vapid as any in the *Lancelot*. The writer, it is true, endeavors to invest them with a religious significance by attaching to the narrative of each adventure an allegorical interpretation, just as was done in the contemporary exegesis of the Scriptures. The method, however, is unconvincing, and there is no trouble about discerning through the attempted disguise the essential triviality of the incidents in question. The only advantage of the method, in such cases, is that its regular and rigorous application helps to impart a certain unity to the succession of isolated episodes.

In characterization the *Queste* falls much below the *Lancelot*. In fact, only in the case of Galahad and Gawain is there anything that even distantly approaches individualization in the romance. For the purpose of exalting the ascetic ideal, as contrasted with the prevailing ideal of worldly chivalry, the author emphasizes the sinfulness of Gawain, the chief type of the latter. According to the first hermit who receives the confession of this character, he is so hardened in sin that the good man gives up the effort to convert him because of its uselessness.[157] According to Nascien, he is lacking in charity, truth, and abstinence.[158] Moreover, he is represented as the slayer of the noble Baudemagu, and others.[159] Nevertheless, it is mainly in the reproofs of the confessional that Gawain's portrait is painted in these dark colors, and, in general, his character is much the same as elsewhere, only the outlines are fainter.

Galahad, of course, represents the antipodes of the Gawain of this romance as depicted by the confessors of that "flower of courtesy". After all, however, he, too, is not a living figure, but,

----

[157] VI, 40.          [158] VI, 115.

[159] Cp. VI, 37, 109, 184. The actual slaying of Baudemagu is not related in our MSS. of the *Queste,* though it is referred to at p. 184. It must have stood, however, in the original version. Very likely identical with the original version is the account of the affair in MS. 112, Part III, fol. 97, col. 1, which the present writer out some years ago, *Mort Artu,* p. 266. References are made to it, too, in the unpublished part of the Portuguese *Demanda,* Huth 1, 273f. (cp. Bruce, *loc. cit.,* including notes and *Mort Artu,* VI, 204.)

in the main, a mere puppet of the ascetic imagination. There is a certain impressiveness about his first appearance at Arthur's court — his occupation, as by right, of the Perilous Seat and his drawing from the stone the sword which even the greatest champions had failed to draw and which, indeed, was reserved exclusively for his use in the prosecution of the Grail quest. For a long time after that, however, the adventures which he achieves do not differ from the ordinary adventures of Arthurian romance, except in the fact that they are explained in an allegorical sense, and he, himself, does not develop any individual traits. Only in the final scenes of the romance is the character again lifted out of the common run of Arthurian knights — first, at the Grail castle, by the ecstacy of his aspirations for union with the divine spirit, and, later, through the sanctity of his death and the marvels that attend it.

There are other religious elements in the *Queste,* however, besides those which have just been indicated — such, for example, as Solomon's ship with the five staves, the Maimed King (Mordrain), whom only Galahad can heal,[160] Perceval's sister — "a thing enskied and sainted" — the allegorical stag and lions. Everywhere, moreover, as we have already seen, even the most commonplace incidents are interpreted in terms of religious allegory, so that the work has been well described as a "forest of allegories".[161] The air of the enchanted forests of Arthurian romance thus becomes heavy with symbolism. A religious fanatic has entered them and put them under the spell which was already binding and cramping the minds of the Middle Ages in every other line of effort.[162]

---

[160] These first two belong, of course, to the *Estoire,* also.

[161] Cp. A. Pauphilet, *Romania,* XXXVI, 605.

[162] If we take the Grail romances as they stand—leaving aside the problems of their evolution — the most penetrating appreciation of the two Grail heroes, Perceval and Galahad, that we have is Mme. Lot-Borodine's, "Les deux conquérants du Graal, Perceval et Galaad", *Romania,* XLVII, 41 ff. (1921). I regret that the same writer's *Trois essais sur la Queste du Saint Graal* (Paris, 1921) did not reach me until this book had gone to press.

## 5. La Mort Artu. [163]

The most widely known of all the traditions concerning Arthur
was the one that related to his last battle, the mortal wound which
he received in that conflict, and his subsequent translation to Avalon, the Celtic Elysium. This tradition, as we have seen, had
been made famous especially by Geoffrey of Monmouth's *Historia*
and its derivatives, not to mention the same writer's *Vita Merlini*,
the circulation of which, however, seems to have been limited.
The very fact that this phase of the Arthurian story had already
received such frequent treatment was, no doubt, in part, responsible for the comparatively late appearance of a prose romance
on the subject. Besides, the Grail theme, which, owing to its
religious character, exercised an irresistible attraction for the
Middle Ages, was now absorbing the main energies of the Arthurian romancers, whether their chosen vehicle of expression was
verse or prose. In any event, there is no ground for doubting that
the Vulgate *Mort Artu* was the first prose-romance on the Death-
of-Arthur theme[164] and that it was composed later than the *Queste,*
to say nothing of the *Lancelot,* its dependence upon which is
manifest on nearly every page.[165] As regards the second of these

---

[163] The text has been printed by J. D. Bruce, *Mort Artu* (Halle a. S.,
1910), and by Sommer, VI, 203—391 (1913) in his *Vulgate Version.*

[164] Miss Weston, *Legend of Sir Perceval,* II, 336 and Lot,
*Lancelot,* 193, both of whom regard the *Didot-Perceval* as a prose-
rendering of a lost poem by Robert de Boron, take the Mort Arthur
section of that romance as the model for the Vulgate *Mort Artu.*
Neither, however, is able to point to any specific borrowings of the
latter from the former, so that their assumption of a general influence,
one may fairly say, is entirely unsupported by any evidence. As has
been observed, pp. 30 f., above, the previous Death-of-Arthur narrative,
which constituted the source of the Vulgate branch, was Layamon's
lost French original.

[165] The passages in the *Mort Artu* which show the influence
of the *Lancelot,* are so numerous that it would be supererogatory to
give a list of them. The main ones, with the corresponding passages
in the *Lancelot,* are already recorded in notes to my edition of the
*Mort Artu* — e. g. those that relate to the quests for Lancelot,
his incognito participation in tournaments, the unrequited love which

points, it should be observed that in the *Mort Artu*, apart from its opening paragraphs, which connect it explicitly with the *Queste*,[166] there are several other allusions to that branch.[167] Moreover, in the beautiful passage (VI, 256f.), which describes how a boat bearing the dead body of the Maid of Ascalot (Escalot)[168] drifted down the river to Camelot and how a letter in the hand of the dead girl laid the blame of her death upon Lancelot, who had not requited her love, we have an indisputable imitation of the episode in the *Queste* (VI, 175) of Perceval's sister, whose dead body, as discovered by Lancelot in Solomon's ship, bore, likewise, in its hand, a scroll relating the manner of her life and death. So, too, with Lancelot's retirement into a hermitage at the end of the present romance (VI, 386ff.) which is modeled

---

maidens cherish for him, his rescue of the queen from burning, his stronghold of Joyous Gard, etc. As I have stated above, p. 418, note 143, the connection between the *Mort Artu* and the last division of the *Lancelot,* viz. the so-called *Agravain,* is particularly close — indeed, some episodes in the latter, in all likelihood, are by the author of the *Mort Artu.* Such episodes were doubtless inserted in that division, to prepare for corresponding episodes in the *Mort Artu.*

[166] Miss Weston, *Legend of Sir Lancelot,* pp. 137 (note), 145, 184, *Folk-Lore,* XX, 497f. and Sommer, VI, 204, note 10, maintain that these opening pages of the *Mort Artu* originally formed a part of the *Queste.* For a refutation of this assumption see Bruce, RR, III, 173ff., IV, 458ff.

[167] Galahad is named, Sommer, VI, 219, 390, Bruce, pp. 24, 262. We have, besides, mention of the Perilous Seat of the *Queste,* Sommer, VI, 293 (souurain lieu) = Bruce, p. 125 (Sieges Perilleus) and of the Sword of the Strange Hangings Sommer, VI, 379 = Bruce, p. 247. The former appears already in Robert's *Merlin,* II, 56f., but it is called there the "Empty Seat", not the "Perilous Seat." The above-mentioned sword is also found in Chrétien and his continuators, as we have seen. Inasmuch, however, as other passages show that our author knew the *Queste,* doubtless this allusion, too, is drawn from that romance.

[168] As suggested by J. Rhys, *Studies in the Arthurian Legend,* p. 393, *Ascalot* is, no doubt, derived from *Alclut,* the old Welsh name of the Rock of Dumbarton in the Clyde. On this name and its variants see, still further, Bruce, *Mort Artu,* pp. 269f.

on Perceval's similar retirement after Galahad's death at the end
of the *Queste* (VI, 198).[169]

On the other hand, in the *Queste*, there is not a single reference of any kind[170] to the *Mort Artu*. The former romance, indeed, gives us no reason to suppose that the downfall of the Round
Table had been connected with the love-affair of Lancelot and
Guinevere at the time that it was written. The confession of
Lancelot to the hermit afforded the best opportunity possible for
some allusion to the tragical consequences which the sin of the
lovers was to entail — an opportunity which the author of the
*Queste* with his craze for sermonizing would surely have availed
himself of — but there is no such allusion. The reason is plain:
That conception was the invention of the author of the *Mort Artu*
and the *Mort Artu* was not yet written.

In view of these circumstances, there is obviously no reason
for adopting the view, which has been expressed by some scholars,[171] that the *Mort Artu* is of earlier date than the *Queste*.

The author of the *Mort Artu*, at the beginning of his romance,[172] links it with the *Queste*, but his interests were secular, —

---

[169] The two agree even in detail: Lancelot has a companion
(Hector) in his hermitage, just as Perceval had one (Bohort). When
Perceval dies, he is buried in Galahad's tomb; so is Lancelot in
Galehot's.

[170] In my article, "The Development of the Mort Arthur Theme
in Mediaeval Romance," RR, IV, 403 ff (1913), I have discussed,
pp. 458 ff., the relative dates of the *Queste* and *Mort Artu*. The
next three sentences are taken from that discussion, pp. 461 f.

[171] This is implied in Miss Weston's *Legend of Sir Lancelot*,
p. 145 (1901) and *Folk-Lore*, XX, 497 f. Cp., too, Brugger, *Zs. f.
frz. Spr. u. Litt.*, XXIX[1], 95 (1905), XXXVI[2], 207 (1910). In
the article mentioned in the previous note I have endeavored to show
that the views of these two scholars as to the *Mort Artu's* being
a compilation or the result of successive accretions to an original
nucleus are without foundation. If we except Geoffrey and his derivatives (including the Mort Arthur section of the *Didot-Perceval*)
every version of the Death-of-Arthur theme in existence is derived
from the Vulgate *Mort Artu*. This is clear from the above-mentioned
investigation.

[172] Bruce's edition, pp. 1—3, Sommer's edition, VI, 203—205.

not religious, — and in spiritual kinship he stood far closer to the authors of the *Lancelot* than to the fanatic who penned the *Queste*. Nevertheless, apart from the direct allusions to this latter romance which his work contains,[173] he was otherwise profoundly indebted to it; for the *Queste* had stressed the sinfulness of Lancelot's adulterous relations with the queen,[174] and it was, no doubt this circumstance that suggested to our author the happy invention of making the passion of the guilty pair, which had been glorified in the *Lancelot*, the cause of the downfall of Arthur and the Round Table.

As a work of art, the *Mort Artu* is superior, at every point, to the preceding branches of the cycle; in this respect, it outweighs all the rest put together. In the first place, it is the only one of the branches that is marked by a genuine constructive skill. The narrative of the love affair of Lancelot and Guinevere and its fatal consequences is developed continuously throughout the romance with virtually no interruption from digressions;[175] for even the episodes of the Maid of Ascalot[176] and of the poisoned fruit[177] which might appear at first sight to retard the action, in reality, reinforce it, since Guinevere's jealousy, in the one instance, and Lancelot's rescue of her, in the other, strengthen the lovers' passion, so as to render the tragical issue all the more inevitable. With similar skill the *motif* of Lancelot's encounters, incognito, with Gawain and his (Lancelot's) kinsmen in the lists,

---

[173] See above, p. 427, including note.

[174] Cp. VI, 45 ff. (Lancelot's confession to the hermit).

[175] There are, perhaps, two exceptions; 1. VI, 358 f. the lord of Beloe kills his wife out of jealousy of the dead Gawain. 2. VI, 347 ff. the Roman wars. The first seems an inopportune invention of our author; the second was traditional.

[176] VI, 208 ff.

[177] VI, 248 ff. A Scotch knight wishes to kill Gawain and at the table hands Guinevere some poisoned fruit with the idea that she will pass it on to Gawain, not knowing that it is poisoned. She, happens to give it, however, to the brother of Mador de la Porte, who dies from eating it. Mador accuses her of having poisoned his brother on purpose and she would have been burned as a punishment but for Lancelot's rescuing her.

though repeated so often already in the *Lancelot,* is made effective here through the superior concentration of the narrative and from the fact that the combats in question are so intimately connected with the story of the unhappy Maid of Ascalot, and hence with the development of the vital theme of the queen's jealousy. From the point where this jealousy is quenched by Lancelot's rescue of the victim from the stake and the lovers are surprised in the queen's chamber, the action unfolds itself, without a break, through the successive stages of the flight of the detected pair to Joyous Gard, Arthur's siege of that stronghold, the intervention of the Pope and the consequent reconciliation of the king and his consort, Lancelot's return to his native land, Arthur's reluctant renewal of the war against Lancelot in the latter's dominions, Mordred's treason and the king's return to Logres, Guinevere's retirement to a nunnery, the final battle on Salisbury Plains,[178] involving Mordred's death, the annihilation of the

---

[178] In Geoffrey's *Historia,* XI, 1—2, and its derivatives we have three battles between Arthur and Mordred. Cp. Bruce, *Mort Artu* pp. 291 ff. It was one of the numerous marks of our author's constructive skill that he reduces these three to one. Moreover, he places the last battle on Salisbury Plains, whereas according to the Geoffreyan tradition, it was fought in Cornwall. Only in the *Didot Perceval* (Miss Weston's edition. p. 111) was it fought in Ireland, the author of that romance desiring to bring it nearer to the supposed site of Avalon, whither the wounded king was to be taken. Cp. Lot, *Lancelot,* p. 195, note 1. Lot, *ibid.* pp. 194 ff. (including notes) suggests that the author of the Vulgate *Mort Artu* put the last battle on Salisbury Plains, under the influence of Goeffrey, VI, 15, or Wace, ll. 7409 ff. — more likely the latter — because Geoffrey implies and Wace expressly declares that the treacherous massacre of the British princes by Hengist, the Saxon chieftan, took place on these plains. It is hardly open to doubt, however, that our author really derived this idea from Robert de Boron's *Merlin,* Sommer, II, 49 ff., where Arthur's father, Uther, is already represented as defeating the Saxons on Salisbury Plains in a battle of which the prophet, Merlin, had said (II, 50): "puis que sainte crestiente fu establie en ceste ille not mais si grant bataille ne naura en nos tans com ceste sera." It was evidently with this prediction of Merlin's concerning the earlier battle in mind that he, also, inserted in his work a prophetic inscription

knights of the Round Table, and the fatal wounding of Arthur, which is followed by his translation to Avalon and his mysterious burial at the Vaire Capiele.[179] Among the heroines of the imagination, only Guinevere and Helen of Troy, by the enchantment of their beauty, have provoked such storms of passion or called down upon the nations such overwhelming catastrophes. For modern tastes, the description of the last battle is, perhaps, too much prolonged. Nevertheless, the total impression of these final chapters of Arthur's eventful history is, unmistakably, one of tragic sublimity.[180] The significance of the stupendous disaster seems to pass beyond the limits of an individual tragedy, and the ruin of the legendary monarch and his hosts becomes full of profound suggestion as to the general lot of man and the transitoriness of all earthly glory. In the sequel, too, of the translation to Avalon we have a corresponding expression in adequate imaginative form of the infinite longings of the human heart for some far-off supernatural abode where we shall be permitted to enjoy eternally the felicity that is denied us in this world.

So much for the superiority of the *Mort Artu* in respect to construction. Perhaps, even more important, however, is the fact that its author does not aim at engaging or holding the reader's attention by cheap supernaturalism or by the puerile extravagance of his hero's exploits or by appeals to the prevalent taste for the

---

by the same sage in regard to Arthur's final battle (VI, 362 f.) and at a corresponding point — namely, just before the description of the battle, itself. In both cases, moreover, the enemies of the British king perish to the last man. Cp. respectively, II, 51 and VI, 377.

[179] The present writer has already pointed out, *Revue Celtique*, XXXIII, 432 (1912), and RR, IV, 454, (1913), that the author here awkwardly combines the old popular tradition concerning the wounded Arthur's being borne to Avalon with the new idea, first started by the monks of Glastonbury in 1191, that he was buried in Glastonbury abbey.

[180] Brugger, *Zs. f. frz. Spr. u. Litt.*, XXIX, ¹ 95 (1905), speaks of the "erhabene Tragik" of the *Mort Artu*, as well as of its other beauties. E. Freymond, *Deutsche Literaturzeitung* for May 3, 1913, has rightly declared it to be one of the most important prose-works of Old French literature.

artificial fashions of courtly love. The potency of his narrative rests rather on permanent elements of human interest — on the variety and, in the climax, the grandeur of its action, on its delineation of powerful passions of different kinds, on its dramatic interplay of character with character. We have, consequently, a subtler psychology displayed in the invention of situations and in the portrayal of the actors in the story than is observable in the other branches of the cycle, save, possibly, in a few of the earliest[181] and latest episodes[182] of the *Lancelot*. Take, for instance, the scene[183] just before Gawain learns of the death of his brothers, Agravain, Guerrehes, and Gaheries, in combat, with Lancelot and his companions. The first two and Mordred had surrounded Lancelot and Guinevere at an assignation. Lancelot escapes, but Guinevere is about to be burnt for adultery, when Lancelot comes to her rescue. Gawain's brothers, except Mordred, are all killed in the affray, but Gawain, himself, is absent, for he had refused to be present at the burning of the queen. He comes forth at last, and, as he goes to the king's palace, he sees all the people silent and plunged in grief, as he believes, for the queen, but it is really on account of his brothers, and so, ignorant of the cause of their sorrow, he passes down the street with the sad and sympathetic gaze of the throng fixed upon him. There is a Homeric strength and simplicity about the unknown French writer's treatment of this fine situation.

The same qualities which excite our admiration in the handling of a situation such as that which has been just described, reveal themselves naturally, also, in the author's delineation of character. We do not expect to find a thirteenth century romancer penetrating to the obscurest recesses of the human soul, like the best masters of fiction in the present age of science. Indeed, the

---

[181] More particularly, the Claudas episodes.

[182] The episodes in which the *motifs* are Guinevere's jealousy and her chequered friendship with Lancelot's kinsmen. I have already given reasons (p. 418, note 143, above) for my belief that these episodes are by the author of the *Mort Artu*.

[183] Bruce, pp. 116 ff., Sommer, VI, 286 ff.

men and women that moved about him in the actual life of the
time were framed on simpler lines than has been the case under
the more complex conditions of recent centuries. Measured, however, by the standards of characterization in the mediaeval romances, the *Mort Artu* shows, in this respect, also, a remarkable
advance on its predecessors. Through a combination of traits and
incidents, such as her jealous agitation with regard to Lancelot,[184]
her troubled relations with Bohort on that account,[185] her self-
reproaches at having driven her lover from court,[186] the compassion
which she inspires in the poisoned fruit affair, when she is about
to be executed on an unjust charge,[187] the character of Guinevere
here takes on a distinct individuality. Similarly, Gawain, who,
in previous Arthurian tradition, had figured merely as a general
embodiment of chivalrous valor and courtesy, is brought down
to earth by the indignant pity on Guinevere's account which causes
him to absent himself from her intended execution,[188] by his prophetic
anticipation of the evils that will flow from his brother
Agravain's disclosures to Arthur of Lancelot's intrigue with the
queen, and his vain protests against these disclosures,[189] and by
his implacable wrath against the friend whom he had loved best
(Lancelot),[190] when, through no fault of his own, this friend and
his kinsmen become the slayers of the headstrong Agravain and
the other brothers who had rejected his (Gawain's) advice. Still
other instances of effective characterization in the romance might
be cited; it will suffice, however, to name that of the Maid of

---

[184] Bruce, pp. 26 ff., Sommer, VI, 221 ff. This and the two
following *motifs* are already found in the *Agravain* (last division of
the *Lancelot*), in passages, however, which, I believe, are by the author
of the *Mort Artu*.

[185] Bruce, pp. 29 ff., 57 ff., 86 ff., Sommer, VI, 223 ff., 244 ff.,
264 ff.

[186] Bruce, pp. 77 f., Sommer, VI, 258 f.

[187] Bruce, pp. 63 ff., Sommer, VI, 248 ff.

[188] Bruce, p. 107, Sommer, VI, 279. This, to be sure, is imitated
from *Lancelot*, IV, 59, or Beroul's *Tristan* (ed. Muret), pp. 34 ff.

[189] Bruce, pp. 92 f., Sommer, VI, 269 f.

[190] Bruce, pp. 155 ff., Sommer, VI, 316 ff.

Ascalot, whose character is drawn with such a tender pathos and grace that her story [191] constitutes one of the most memorable pictures of unrewarded love in the history of fiction. Especially, the final scene [192] in this story, already referred to above, in which Arthur and Gawain discover the dead body of the girl, with the accusing letter in its hand, in the boat that drifts down to Camelot, is one of the passages in mediaeval literature that touch the very acme of romance.

We have already commented on the sparing use of the supernatural which is made by our author. Indeed, it is only in the concluding phase of his story that he draws at all on this source of romantic interest. He had inherited from his verse-chronicle original [193] the age-hallowed legend or myth as to Arthur's translation to the Other-world isle, after he has been wounded in his last battle. Our author has not only adopted this splendid conception, but he has enhanced its grandeur and heightened the imaginative coloring of the whole final catastrophe by the employment of still other supernatural *motifs*, which are in harmony with it, viz: 1. the dream in which a day or two before the battle Arthur is warned by the spirit of the dead Gawain to call Lancelot to his aid, [194] 2. Arthur's vision of the Wheel of Fortune, [195] 3. Merlin's prophetic inscription in regard to the king's death in the impending battle, [196] 4. the marvel which attended Gifflet's (Girflet's), return of Excalibur to the lake [197] — the arm clad in

---

[191] Bruce, pp. 8 ff., Sommer, VI, 208 ff.

[192] Bruce, pp. 74 ff., Sommer, VI, 256 f.

[193] On this matter see pp. 30 f. above.

[194] Bruce, pp. 218 f., Sommer, VI, 360.

[195] Bruce, pp. 220 f., Sommer, VI, 361.

[196] Bruce, p. 222, Sommer, VI, 362 f.

[197] Bruce, pp. 248 f., Sommer, VI, 380. On this incident Cp. Bruce, *Mort Artu*, pp. 297 f. According to Geoffrey, Book IX, ch. 4, Excalibur (Caliburnus) was made in Avalon. See, too, Wace, l, 9516. The account in the *Huth-Merlin*, I, 195 ff., as to how Arthur got Excalibur from this same lake is evidently a mere invention of the author, suggested by the present passage. No parallel to the incident has ever been adduced save one from the Persian *Remembrancer of*

samite rising from the water, seizing and brandishing the sword
and then drawing it under — an incident which immediately
precedes the king's embarkation in the ship of his sister, Morgain,
and her fairy companions. Thus we see that, whereas in the earlier
portion of the branch, the story moves within the bounds of the
actual, passing at most at one or two points into the realm of
high romance, in the later portion — that is to say, from the
time that Arthur begins his march to Salisbury Plains,[198] which
are to be the scene of his ruin, up to the end — its whole atmosphere is filled with signs and wonders, as befitted the mythical
catastrophe.

The mention of our author's handling of the ever-memorable
tradition concerning the end of Arthur and all his glory brings
us to a consideration of the sources of his romance. In accordance
with his superior genius, we shall find him combining and reshap-
ing his materials with even greater freedom than his predecessors
had done. Having determined to connect the downfall of Arthur
and the Round Table with the adultery of Lancelot and the queen,
it was necessary for him to develop the story of this affair through
a variety of incidents which would show how the ever-growing
passion of the lovers drew them and with them, Arthur and his
knights, irresistibly towards the tragical issue. But a story of

---

*the Saints* (twelfth century), pointed out by R. A. Nicholson in the
*Athenaeum* for April 6, 1901, p. 434. Here the object thrown into
the water (the river Oxus, not a lake) consists of some writings of
"the Shaikh". An open chest which God sent by a fish to preserve
them appears. The incident is not connected with the hero's death,
and, it is safe to say, stands in no historical relation to the one in
the *Mort Artu*. The fact that there is no similar story in the extant
Celtic records and that, apparently, the incident was not contained in
our author's verse-chronicle source for this part of his romance—for it
is not found in Layamon — tells against the theory of Celtic origin,
which generally prevails. I am more inclined to believe that it was
invented by our author and I expect to discuss it in a separate article
from this point of view.

[198] Bruce, p. 218, Sommer, VI, 360. The fact that only Arthur
and two of his knights survive the conflict of the two hosts approaches,
also, the supernatural. This accords, in essentials, with Welsh tra-

overpowering passion, although its consequences involved no general
disaster, lay ready to the writer's hand in the *Tristan* romances,
and his mind would turn for a model all the more naturally to
these romances, inasmuch as the story of Lancelot and Guinevere had been, from the beginning, a mere adaptation of that of
Tristan and Iseult. As a matter of fact, the narrative of the
*amours* of Lancelot and the queen in the *Mort Artu* down through
the former's surrender of the latter to her husband after the siege
of Joyous Gard[199] is based primarily on the story of the earlier
lovers. We have the same *motifs:* 1. of the informer who is an
enemy of the hero and who, despite previous failure, finally brings
about the detection of the guilty couple,[200] 2. of the hero's rescue

---

dition. Cp. *Kulhwch* and *Olwen*, Loth's *Mabinogion*[2], I, 270, and
the triad, *ibid.* II, 290. Gifflet and Lucan nearly always appear together
in the romances, and they were the last to be with Arthur, no doubt,
because they were officers of his household. For a full discussion of
all these matters cp. Bruce, *Mort Artu*, pp. 294 ff.

    According to W. J. Gruffydd, "The Mabinogion", *Transactions of
the Honorable Society of Cymmrodorion,* Session, 1912—13, p. 38,
the writer of *Kulhwch and Olwen,* in declaring that only three men
escaped from Arthur's last battle, was imitating two earlier Welsh
accounts of battles, viz. Catraeth and Arfderydd, in regard to both
of which a similar statement is made. For Catraeth see Skene, *Four
Ancient Books of Wales,* I, 382. The triad referred to above is
late, and, although it does not agree entirely with *Kulhwch and
Olwen,* it may very well have been written under the influence of the
passage in that tale.

    [199] Bruce, p. 148, Sommer, VI, 310 f.

    [200] Cp. the editions of the romance which we have been citing,
respectively, pp. 4, 96 ff., and VI, 205 f., 272 ff. In his *Über die verschiedenen Redaktionen des Robert von Borron zugeschriebenen
Graal-Lancelot Cyklus,* p. 36 (Halle, 1895), E. Wechssler assumes
that our romance, in its original form, began with the second of these
attempts of Agravain to incite the king against Lancelot and the queen,
but he has won no adherents to his hypothesis and it is supported
by no evidence. Cp. on the subject, IV, 461, note 93.

    For passages in the *Tristan* romances corresponding to those in
the *Mort Artu,* just cited cp. particularly, Thomas's *Tristan,* ed.
Bédier, I, 175 ff., where Mariadoc's rôle is like Agravain's. There are,
of course, differences of details between the romances. The influence

of the heroine from the penalty of her adultery, viz. burning at
the stake,[201] and the subsequent flight of the lovers, 3. of the
hero's return of the heroine to her husband on condition that her
offence shall be pardoned and that he himself shall leave the
kingdom, the act of returning the unfaithful wife being accompanied in each case by the lover's denunciations of her accusers
and false asseverations as to her chastity.[202] The author, however, has interwoven these *Tristan motifs* inextricably with others
that are drawn from the prose *Lancelot* [203] — in a considerable
measure, to be sure, from parts of the *Lancelot* which were pro-

---

of Béroul's *Tristan,* ed. Muret, pp. 19 ff., seems evident, also, in the
circumstances of the disclosure.

[201] Cp. *op. cit.,* pp. 108 ff. and VI, 280 ff. Cp. Béroul's *Tristan,*
ed. Muret, pp. 34 ff. On burning as the penalty for adultery in women,
which is so common in the romances, cp. Bruce, *Mort Artu,* pp. 282 f.,
where references to the literature of the subject are also given. In
regard to the usual statements that there was no such custom in the
actual life of the Middle Ages, it is there pointed out that in the
laws of the Christian kingdom of Jerusalem, *Assises de Jerusalem*
(ed. Beugnot), I, 176, provision was made that, if a knight champions
the cause of a woman in any matter "et se son champion est vencu
elle sera arce et il deit estre pendu, que de quelque carelle que se
seit". This would come near covering the case of Guinevere. It
should be observed, moreover, that convicted adulteresses were actually
burned under the old Jewish law — Cp. *Genesis,* XXXVIII, 24 and
*Leviticus,* XXI, 9 — so that the romancers may well have derived
the idea from that source.

[202] Cp. *op. cit.,* p. 148 and VI, 310 f. with Béroul's *Tristan*
(ed. Muret), pp. 89 f. Béroul here is undoubtedly the source of our
romance. It is worth observing, however, that already in the *Vita
Gildae* the monks of Glastonbury induce Arthur to take his wife back,
after Melwas's abduction.

[203] Especially the episode of the False Guinevere, Sommer, IV,
10 ff., in which, likewise, Lancelot, pp. 59 ff. rescues the queen. We
have there, also, pp. 72 f., an intervention of the Pope in Arthur's
marital affairs. With much plausibility E. Freymond, *Zs. f. rom. Ph.,*
XVI, 97, note, (1892), argues that this incident was suggested by Pope
Innocent III's intervention in the matrimonial dissensions of Philip
Augustus and his wife, Ingeborg, during the last years of the twelfth
century. Cp., too, Bruce, *Mort Artu,* pp. 284 f.

bably of his own composition.[204] Moreover, as has been intimated above, he has enriched the interest of his romance and inten-
sified the impression of the strength of the lovers' passion by
the insertion of two more episodes, derived from still other sources—
namely, the episodes, respectively, of the Maid of Ascalot and of
the poisoned fruit. The suggestion of the immortal Maid came,
it is true, from Iseult of Brittany[205] in the *Tristan* poems, but
the beautiful conclusion of her story — the boat with the dead
body borne down stream until it reaches Arthur's palace — is
an indubitable imitation of the similar passage concerning Perceval's sister in the *Queste.*[206] On the other hand, the incident of
the poisoned fruit has its source in one of two *chansons de geste,*
*Gaydon* or *Parise la Duchesse,* in both of which we find heroines
whose lives are imperilled by mistaken accusations of the same
kind.[207]

Just as the *Tristan* poems constituted the main basis for the
narrative of the *Mort Artu* down to the point where Lancelot

---

[204] On these passages (in the so-called *Agravain*) cp. p. 402
note 71, above.

[205] Cp. Bruce, *Mort Artu,* pp. 270f. By an oversight in this
note on the Maid of Ascalot and in the headlines to the text, pp. 7ff.,
I have called the Maid „Elaine (Elayne)". We do not find that name
given her, however, before Malory. As is remarked in this note, the
character seems to owe something, also, to that of Pelles' daughter
(Galahad's mother) in the *Lancelot.* I was misled by P. Paris, III,
17 *et passim,* into supposing that the latter character was, likewise,
called "Helene", which is, of course, identical with "Elaine". Sommer,
too, erroneously gives her this name in the Index and marginal notes
to his *Vulgate Version.* Nevertheless, she did not actually acquire
it until later and through a scribal blunder which I have explained,
MPh., XVI, 340, note 1.

[206] Cp. p. 420, note 150, above.

[207] Cp. Bruce, *Mort Artu,* pp. 274ff. Miss L. A. Paton, *MLN,*
for June, 1903, p. 164, note 101, and Brugger, *Zs. f. frz. Spr. u.
Litt.,* XXX², 225, note 114 (1906) regard the poisoned fruit as the
Otherworld apples of folklore in rationalized form. Neither scholar,
however, was aware of these *chanson de geste* sources. Besides, in
the note just cited, I have called attention to recent actual instances
of poisoning by means of apples.

returns to his own dominions, after surrendering Guinevere to her husband, so the main framework of his subsequent narrative was supplied the author by Wace — not the Wace of our manuscripts, but the expanded version of that poet's *Brut*, which, though lost in its original French form, has been preserved in Layamon's English paraphrase.[208] With even greater boldness than in the first part of his work, however, the writer has here reshaped the materials of his source, so as to fit them to his new design of connecting the adulterous relations of Lancelot and the queen with the destruction of Arthur and the Round Table. Thus, in his romance Lancelot usurps the rôle of Mordred as Guinevere's lover.[209] Furthermore, he fills the place of Frollo,[210] Arthur's enemy, before his death, and of Constantine, the same monarch's avenger, after his death.[211] This double rôle suits the conception of Lancelot which runs all through the *Mort Artu*. Having wronged Arthur through his guilty passion for Guinevere, he becomes, against his will, the king's enemy. On the other hand, he has never faltered in his personal loyalty, and so, being the greatest of Arthur's knights, he is the proper avenger of his sovereign.

---

[208] On this subject cp. pp. 30 ff., above.

[209] This and the following four sentences are taken, with some slight changes of wording, from pp. 452 f. of the present writer's article, "The Development of the Mort Arthur Theme in Mediaeval Romance", RR, IV, (1913). In the section of that article, pp. 451 ff., entitled "The Verse-Chronicle Source of the Vulgate *Mort Artu*", there is a full discussion of the relation of our romance to this lost source.

[210] Cp. Geoffrey's *Historia* IX, 11, Wace, ll. 10158 ff., Layamon, ll. 23393 ff. All three represent Frollo (Frolle, etc.) as a Roman, by birth, who ruled France as a vassal of the Roman emperor and was slain by Arthur in the latter's invasion of France. In the *Lancelot*, V, 374, and *Mort Artu*, VI, 346, however, he is a German prince whom Arthur kills in France. He is an ally, moreover, of the Romans — hence, according to the *Mort Artu*, the Roman emperor began his war against Arthur. Otherwise, Lancelot, in the present romance, has annexed the part which Frollo plays in the Geoffreyan tradition.

[211] Constantine was the son of Cador, Duke (or Earl) of Cornwall. On embarking for Avalon, Arthur named him as his successor and he defeated and slew Mordred's sons. Cp. Geoffrey, XI, 2—4, Wace, ll. 13601 ff., Layamon, ll. 28590 ff., 28652 ff.

With this substitution of Lancelot for the char̈ʇters just named, the old narrative of Geoffrey and the metrical chronicles gains immeasurably in dramatic force, and every incident in it is given new life. Arthur's continental war[212] is no longer inspired by a mere idle lust of conquest. Though ready to condone the wrongs which he himself has suffered, he is driven, contrary to his better judgment, into this disastrous conflict with the best beloved of his followers by Gawain, who, in his eagerness to avenge his own brothers' death, pursues unrelentingly his lifelong friend and companion-in-arms. Again, under the new circumstances, Gawain's death is no longer simply one of the ordinary chances of war, but the penalty which he pays for his inexorable spirit of vengeance.[213] Similarly, in the new form of the story, Arthur's avenger is not merely a relative (Constantine), whose chief aim is to secure his own succession to the throne, but the friend whose affection for his dead lord remains undiminished, in spite of the hostilities with which the latter had, in his last days, continued to visit him. Even Guinevere profits by these changes; for the object of the passion which has caused her to violate her marriage vows is not the false and treacherous Mordred, as in the Geoffreyan tradition, but a man who was the lodestar of chivalry in his age. Thus, in the climax of the action, she appears as a fugitive from the traitor's embraces, not as his partner in crime.

It should be observed, moreover, that this climax, as, indeed, the whole story of Arthur's ruin, is invested with a greater tragic intensity through the author's original conception (not inherited

---

[212] Geoffrey, IX, 11, X, 2, Wace, ll. 10146 ff., 11452 ff., Layamon, ll. 23397 ff., 25465 ff., distinguish two expeditions of Arthur to the continent — the first against Frollo, the ally of Rome, the second against the Romans, who are led by their emperor. In the *Lancelot,* V, 336, 370, the order of the expeditions is reversed and Arthur does not go with the first. In the *Mort Artu* we have the war with the Romans repeated, but Frollo is mentioned only once, VI, 346, and then as dead.

[213] The wound which he received from Lancelot was ultimately the cause of his death. This was the invention of the author of the *Mort Artu,* like the whole story of the conflict between the two characters.

from his predecessors) of the traitor who was the cause of that
ruin as being Arthur's own son — the child of an unwitting act
of incest which he had committed with his sister. Thus, as in
the legend of Oedipus, the sin of the father, though unconsciously
perpetrated, brings with it the blind and terrible retribution of
the Fates.[214]

We have already discussed above[215] our author's sources for
the concluding episodes of Arthur's career and his treatment of
the same — also, his awkward attempt at combining the ancient
tradition as to the fate of the king, after he received his fatal
wound, with the late fabrication of the monks of Glastonbury to

---

[214] G. Paris, *Huth-Merlin,* I, p. XLI (including note 3), thought
that the idea of Mordred's incestuous birth was imitated from the story
(Plutarch's *Brutus,* ch. 5) that Caesar was Brutus's father. He suggests, also, the possible influence of the mediaeval legend of Pope Gregory. On the other hand, Lot, *Lancelot,* p. 444, believes that the
story of Roland's being the child of Charlemagne and his sister (Cp.,
for example, G. Paris's edition of the *Vie de Saint Gilles,* pp. LXIV ff.,
LXXV f. in the publications of the Société des Anciens Textes Français)
is the source. The conception is, however, probably derived from the
legend of Pope Gregory, which was much the most widely diffused
of all the numerous tales of incest in the Middle Ages. Moreover,
other Arthurian romances show contamination· with this legend, which
is not the case with the Brutus or Roland stories. Such romances
are the Latin romances, *De Ortu Waluuanii* (thirteenth century) and
its cognates. Cp. my edition of this and the *Meriadoc* romance,
pp. XXXV ff. Still another is the *Chevalier à la Manche.* The Middle
English romance, *The Awntyrs of Arthur at the Terne Wathelyne,*
also, uses a legend concerning Gregory, but not the one which told
of his incestuous birth.

G. Paris, *loc. cit.* states that this conception, as applied to Mordred,
first appeared in the *Lancelot,* V, 284 f. That passage, however, was
certainly written with reference to the *Mort Artu,* (VI, 325, 349,
377) and I believe was interpolated by the author of the latter. Cp. the
present writer, RR, IX, 382 ff., on this question. The detailed account
of Mordred's conception in the Vulgate *Merlin* II, 128 ff., was, of
course, inspired by the passages just cited from the *Lancelot* and
the *Mort Artu.*

J. Rhys's contention, *Arthurian Legend,* pp. 21 ff. that the story
is of Celtic origin is unsupported by any evidence.

[215] Cp. pp. 439 f., above.

the effect that the monarch was entombed in their abbey.[216] There was an epic grandeur about the great tradition which the writer was here handling, but the tradition was not Christian in origin. On the other hand, to a mediaeval author, however secularly inclined, it would have seemed unfitting to end the story of such high and serious matters on a non-religious note, and so, apart from the touches of Christianization which he has imparted to the last scenes of Arthur's life, he makes the passion-tost Lancelot and his surviving kinsmen, like so many other knights of the Middle Ages, both real and fictitious, seek a final calm in religious devotion and a hermitage.[217]

---

[216] Cp. p. 431, note 179 above.

[217] As I have already observed, the author was here influenced especially by the *Queste*, VI, 198, where Perceval, after the conclusion of the Grail quest, retired to a hermitage, accompanied by Bohort. Among the heroes of mediaeval romance who have ended their lives in a similar manner, Guillaume d'Orange, Robert le Diable and Guy of Warwick are conspicuous. On the whole subject cp. T. Walker, *Die altfranzösischen Dichtungen vom Helden im Kloster.* Tübingen, 1910.

The main sources of the *Mort Artu,* as we have seen, are the *Tristan* poems, the *Lancelot,* and Layamon's lost French original. I have, also, noted Robert's *Merlin,* the *Queste* and the two *chansons de geste* (one or the other, or possibly both), *Gaydon* and *Parise la Duchesse,* as minor sources of the branch. I do not think that it is necessary to assume with Lot, *Lancelot,* pp. 194, 201, note 2, that our author drew directly from Geoffrey's *Historia* or *Vita Merlini.* The features of these works in question, I doubt not, reached our author through his lost verse-chronicle source.

As far as Chrétien (whose works must have been known to him) is concerned, I agree with Lot, p. 199, that the *Lancelot* and *Perceval* of that poet have had no perceptible influence on the *Mort Artu.* His *Erec,* ll. 6865ff., however, suggested, I believe, the crowning of Bohort and Lionel, VI, 377. Possibly, as Lot suggests, p. 201, note 2, it may have influenced, too, his conception of Avalon, although, personally, I question this. The same scholar has also suggested, pp. 199ff., the influence of Pseudo-Wauchier and Wauchier in certain matters — correctly, I believe, save in respect to the episode of the Maid of Ascalot's dead body and the boat, which, according to Lot, he derived from Pseudo-Wauchier, ll. 20857ff. The immediate original of the *Mort Artu,* here, however, seems plainly the *Queste,* as I have observed above.

## Chapter IV.

# Variant Versions of Parts of the Vulgate Cycle.[1]

We have so far discussed the successive members of the Vulgate cycle, as they have descended to us in the numerous MSS. of what we may call, roughly speaking, the *textus receptus* of the five branches. Before we leave the subject, however, it should be stated that, after the completion of the Vulgate cycle, various attempts were made to substitute new narratives for different parts of the cycle. Thus, leaving aside variants of more limited extent, we have:

1. The so-called *Livre d'Artus*[2] of the unique thirteenth century MS. 337 (fonds français, Bibliothèque Nationale)[3] — a long *Merlin*-continuation which was intended to supplant the usual Vulgate version. The marked variation from the Vulgate commences just after the episode in which Guinevere excites Morgan's enmity

---

[1] As will be seen later on, in the opinion of the present writer, the whole pseudo-Robert de Boron cycle is derived directly from the Vulgate, but, inasmuch as that is a separate cycle, which will be discussed below, I do not include its various branches in the present list of variants.

[2] P. Paris, RTR, II, 392ff., was the first to use the term, *livre d'Artus*, as an equivalent of "*Merlin*-continuation." Latterly, however, there has been a tendency to apply it only to the particular *Merlin*-continuation which is preserved in MS. 337. When Sommer in his edition of Malory III, 176, says that the last three branches of the Vulgate cycle combined are sometimes called the "*Livre d'Artus*," this is an error. He has misled W. H. Schofield, *English Literature from the Norman Conquest to Chaucer*, p. 236. (London and New York, 1906).

[3] The MS. is defective at the beginning and at the end. It belongs to the last quarter of the thirteenth century.

by disclosing the latter's intrigue with young Guionmar.[4] From that point on, this version constitutes an entirely different romance—one, too, which, in spite of its enormous length and many repetitions of well-known *motifs*, is, on the whole, of very su-

---

[4] E. Freymond, *Zs. f. frz. Spr. u. Litt.* XVII[1], 21 ff., calls the narrative through this episode (Vulgate *Merlin*, II, 339, l. 4), Part I, and the remainder, Part II. In the *Zs. f. rom. Ph.*, XVI, 103, moreover, he ascribes (rightly, no doubt) the two parts to different authors, on the following grounds: (1) they contradict each other in some points, (2) Part II cites its sources often, as Part I does not, (3) Part I is pseudo-historical, Part II an *Abenteuerroman*. These two articles of Freymond's "Zum Livre d'Artus," *Zs. f. rom. Ph.*, XVI. 90 ff. (1892) and "Beiträge zur Kenntnis der altfranzösischen Artusromane in Prosa," *Zs. f. frz. Spr. u. Litt.*, XVII[1], l. ff. (1895), are the best studies of the romance. The second of them contains a minute analysis of it, which has been rendered superfluous, however, for Part II (the really important division of the MS.) by Sommer's publication (1913) of the text of that Part as vol. VII of his *Vulgate Version of the Arthurian Romances*. (For an elaborate review of this volume from the textual point of view cp. Miss L. M. Gay, MPh., XIV, 430 ff.) The first of Freymond's articles is devoted especially to the sources of the romance, and there are, also, supplementary notes on this subject in the second one. It appears from these studies that the author of Part II knew all the members of the Vulgate cycle. There is evidence to the same effect with regard to the author of Part I, save in the case of the *Estoire del Saint Graal*. Among the sources of Part II is, also, *Meraugis de Portlesguez*. Cp. Friedwagner's edition of the latter, p. LXXXVIII. The citation of Walter Map as an authority, pp. 69, 127, *et passim* is, of course, imitated from the Vulgate cycle. Freymond, in his second article, p. 116, note 2, observes that the work shows no knowledge of the prose *Tristan*. Nevertheless, one of its two Pellinors — the one who is Perceval's father — was probably derived from that romance. Cp. Bruce, MPh., XVI, 343 ff. (1918), where Sommer's charge of confusion (p. 243, note 1) in the romance with regard to the two Pellinors is also shown to be erroneous. The importance of the *Livre d'Artus* of MS. 337, as a source for early Arthurian traditions, is much exaggerated by Freymond. Its sources are purely literary, and none of them possess any particular value. Noteworthy are the versions which it contains, respectively, of the Medusa-saga (Laide Semblance) pp. 150 ff., and of the pseudo-Gospel of Nicodemus, pp. 247 ff.

perior interest to the version which it is intended to supplant. The former, as we have seen, is a dry pseudo-chronicle — the latter, whilst retaining some chronicle elements (especially, in the earlier part), such as narratives of Arthur's personal prowess and of his wars against the Saxons, is, in the main, like all the later developments of Arthurian romance in prose, a veritable maze of duels, rescues of ladies from violence and of knights from captivity, lovers' assignations, related in a most licentious spirit[5] — an illicit love-affair, moreover, being placed in one instance in naive juxtaposition to a version of the most hallowed of Christian legends, viz. the Harrowing of Hell[6] — and so on.

2. Just as the *Livre d'Artus* of MS. 337 was intended to take the place of the Vulgate *Merlin*-continuation, pp. 339—466 (end), so we have variants for considerable stretches of the narrative of the *Lancelot*, which were intended to supplant the usual text of that branch. They are as follows: (a) the redaction, still unprinted, which exists in a number of MSS. and which corresponds to Sommer, IV, 3—204 — i. e. to the part of the *Lancelot*

---

[5] E. g. pp. 67, 109, 191, 197, 276.

In his brochure, *The Structure of Le Livre d'Artus and its Function in the Evolution of the Arthurian Prose Romances* (London and Paris, 1914), Sommer, adopting an erroneous suggestion of P. Paris. RTR, II, 397, argues that the present romance is derived from a lost one which was also the source of the Vulgate *Merlin* (continuation) and which even antedated the *Lancelot*. The argument, however, is mainly based on differences between the text of the Vulgate *Merlin* which he (Sommer) has published (as Vol. 2 of his *Vulgate Version*) and that of the *Livre d'Artus* of MS. 337. These differences lead him to the theory af a common source for the two. But the probabilities are that the author had before him a fuller text of the Vulgate *Merlin* than that which Sommer has printed. Moreover, — and this is the most important point — Sommer is demanding such a conformity between branches of the cycle as the romancers never concerned themselves about. On the lateness of the present romance, as compared with the Vulgate *Merlin*, see Brugger, *Zs. f. frz. Spr. u. Litt.*, XXVIII[1], 57f. There is no ground whatever for Sommer's hypothesis (prefatory note to his edition and above-mentioned brochure) that this romance was once part of a lost cycle.

[6] Cp. pp. 247ff. and 261ff., respectively.

which extends from the departure of Lancelot and Galehaut for
Sorelois, after the death of the sorceress, Camille, to Lancelot's
arrival in the capital of Gorre to fight Meleagant and deliver
Guinevere.[7] Since not even an analysis of this redaction has been
published, we have no means of passing judgment on its value or
significance. (b) Another and much briefer account[8] of the greater
part of the same incidents, corresponding to Sommer, II, 5—185 —
i. e., from the false Guinevere's appearance in person before Arthur
to the abduction of Gawain by Karados of the Dolorous Tower.
(c) A variant redaction[9] of the adventures of Bohort, Lionel,
Hector and Gawain in the long quest for Lancelot which begins
Sommer, IV, 321. Both the second and third of these variant
versions are abbreviated and, in the opinion of the present writer,
without importance. (d) A greatly shortened version of *Lancelot*,
V, 105—409 — i. e. from Lancelot's arrival at Corbenic, where
he is destined to beget Galahad, to the end of the branch — which
is preserved in the MS. of the prose *Tristan*, Add. 5474 (B. M.).[10]

---

[7] In the prefatory note to his Vol. IV, Sommer speaks of this
redaction, but tells us nothing of its contents. Until it has been
printed and studied, no one can say whether it is earlier or later
than the text of this part of the *Lancelot* which he has printed.

[8] Printed as an appendix in Sommer IV, 365—394. It is
found in only three MSS., one of which is fragmentary. One of the
three MSS., however, is MS. 768 (Bibl. Nat.), which is, on the whole,
probably the best single MS. of the *Lancelot*. Lot, *Lancelot*,
pp. 359 ff., compares it, incident by incident, with the usual text and
concludes that it is an earlier draft by the same author as the latter.
One cannot point, however, to anything similar to this suggested
procedure anywhere else in the Vulgate cycle and Lot's argument
is unconvincing. The version is, no doubt, one of the numerous later
redactions of the *textus receptus*.

[9] Printed as an appendix by Sommer V, 413—474. It is
preserved only in Harley MS. 6342 (British Museum).

[10] It runs from fol. 144a to 162a of that MS. and has been
printed, along with the episodes that immediately precede and follow
it, by Sommer in his articles entitled "Galahad and Perceval", MPh.,
V, 55 ff., 181 ff. (1907), 291 ff. (1908). The text begins *ibid.* p. 60,
l. 18 and ends p. 337, l. 27. It occupies altogether 58 pages
in MPh., V. For information concerning the occurrence of this

Its author gives us here a variant version of the episodes in the *Lancelot* that relate to the two great Grail heroes, Galahad and Perceval, omitting everything else. This narrative of the lives of the two characters down to the point where they enter upon the Grail quest was planned to serve as an introduction to the *Queste,* itself, which is here regularly incorporated into the MSS. of the prose *Tristan.* The writer does not depart from his original in any essential[11] and the text is, in the opinion of the present writer, wholly without distinction.[12]

---

intercalation in the *Tristan* MSS., generally, see Wechssler, *Über die verschiedenen Redaktionen des Robert von Borron zugeschriebenen Graal-Lancelot-Cyklus,* pp. 18 ff. (Halle, 1895).

[11] The points of difference noted by Wechssler, *op. cit.,* p. 19, have manifestly no importance — e. g. the fact that Perceval shares in the long quest for Lancelot from the beginning. So, too, with the inclusion of Tristan among Arthur's knights in Malory's Book XI, ch. 7. His French original was an interpolation in a *Tristan* MS., so, it is not strange, if Tristan should have been added to Arthur's knights.

[12] Its greatest interest, perhaps, lies in the fact that it represents, with some differences and in a somewhat abbreviated form, the original of Malory's Books XI and XII. On the subject cp. Sommer's edition of Malory, III, 276 ff., 286 ff., where the variant version, however, is given the inappropriate name of *Suite de Lancelot.* This version is so obviously a mere abstract (with unessential variations) of the Vulgate *Lancelot,* V, 105—409, that we need not discuss Sommer's theory, MPh., V, 308 ff., about its supposed connection with a purely hypothetical cycle. One may say somewhat the same thing of the view expressed by Wechssler, *loc. cit.,* and by Brugger, *Zs. f. frz. Spr. u. Litt.* XXXIV ¹, 109 ff. (1909), to the effect that the text is a fragment of their hypothetical lost *Lancelot* of the pseudo-Robert cycle of the prose-romances. But there is no need of evoking an imaginary source, when we have an extant source (the Vulgate *Lancelot*) that fills every requirement. The fact cited by Wechssler, p. 20, viz., that the episode of Tristan's parting with Iseult when he goes to Arthur's court for the Grail quest— which precedes the inserted account of the early lives of the two Grail knights, — merely repeats something that had already been told, (Löseth, p. 260), is of no importance in the premises, for, however we may interpret this repetition, the dependence of the Galahad-Perceval episodes on the Vulgate *Lancelot* is manifest. My own suggestion as to the most probable

3. Variant redactions[13] of the Vulgate *Mort Artu* are preserved
in the following works: (a) Malory's Books, XVIII, XX, and
XXI.[14] From this version, which includes the whole romance,
Tennyson drew his knowledge of the last phase of the story of
Arthur. Especially noteworthy in Malory's version is the fine
episode, Book XXI, Ch. IX, of Lancelot's last interview with
Guinevere (in her nunnery, after the downfall of Arthur and the
Round Table), in which the two lovers express their resolve to
abjure the world and henceforth lead lives of religious devotion.
(b). The Italian prose compilation, *Tavola Ritonda*[15] (thirteenth
century) contains, *inter alia,* an inferior adaptation of the com-
prete romance, based, no doubt, on some lost French redaction
of the Vulgate. (c) The Middle English stanzaic *Le Morte Arthur,*[16] composed near the end of the fourteenth century, which

---

explanation of the repetition in question would be that the interpolator
who composed these episodes for the purpose stated in the text above,
wishing to indicate that they belonged just after the episodes of
Tristan's parting with Iseult and encounter with Palamedes, prefaced
his interpolation with a version of these last-named incidents. His
interpolation was then inserted into the MSS., but owing to the negli-
gence of the scribes, the repetition which the insertion brought about
was left standing. For similar repetitions and unevennesses in the
Vulgate cycle, from similar causes, cp. RR, IV, 465 f. (including notes).

[13] Only versions (b) and (d) show any wide departures from the
narrative of the Vulgate text. Nevertheless, they all differ enough
from the Vulgate to be counted as separate redactions.

[14] For detailed comparisons of these books with the Old French
Vulgate cp. Sommer's edition of Malory III, 220 ff., 249 ff., Bruce,
"The Middle English Metrical Romance Le Morte Arthur (Harleian
MS. 2252): Its Sources and Its Relation to Sir Thomas Malory's Morte
Darthur", *Anglia,* XXIII, 67 ff. (1900), and "The Development of the
Mort Arthur Theme in Mediaeval Romance", RR, IV (1913) — espe-
cially, pp. 407 ff. It results from the two last-named studies that
Malory and the Middle English *Le Morte Arthur* (Harleian MS. 2252),
ll. 1672—3969, go back to a lost common source, which was, in
its turn, a mere redaction of the Vulgate *Mort Artu.*

[15] Edited by F. Polidori (Bologna, 1864—5). The Mort Arthur
section will be found Part I, pp. 524—545.

[16] Last edited (with full critical apparatus), in 1903, by Bruce,
for the Early English Text Society, Extra Series, No. 88. The

agrees with Malory in LL. 1672—3969 — i. e. from the scene in which Arthur comes upon Agravain and his brothers discussing Lancelot's intrigue with Guinevere down to the end,[17] but in what precedes offers a unique version of the incidents in this part of the story.[18] (d) *Li Chantari di Lancellotto*,[19] an Italian poem (probably from the first half of the fifteenth century), adapted with considerable changes from the Vulgate *Mort Artu* and strongly contaminated with elements from the prose *Tristan*. This poem, which is of very poor quality, gives, also, a complete version of the Mort Arthur incidents.[20]

---

alliterative *Morte Arthure* (see p. 27, above) seems to have no connection with the prose romances.

[17] Bruce, p. 92, Sommer, VI, 269.

[18] For the proof of this, see my article in *Anglia*, XXIII, cited above — more especially, pp. 75 ff., 87 ff.

[19] The best edition is that of Walter De Gray Birch (London, 1874). It is written in *ottava rima*. For a detailed analysis and comparison of its narrative with that of the Vulgate cp. Bruce, RR, IV, 436 ff. It is not unlikely that this poem was based on some earlier Italian prose version of the Vulgate, rather than directly on the Vulgate, itself.

[20] For foreign versions of the Vulgate *Mort Artu* which do not constitute separate redactions cp. my edition of that romance, pp. XXIII ff.

# Chapter V.
# Date of the Vulgate Cycle.

We have seen that the ascription of the last three branches of the Vulgate cycle to Walter Map, which is so common in the manuscript tradition, is a fabrication, and that, consequently, we cannot accept it as affording any genuine evidence touching the date of the cycle. Nevertheless, we have in the well-known passage of Helinandus's chronicle, quoted above,[1] a sufficient indication with regard to the downward limit of date of at least one member of the series — viz. the *Estoire del Saint Graal (Grand St. Graal)* — and hence, inferentially, of others. Since at the end of that chronicle the author speaks of King John of England as still reigning, it is indisputable that this work — and hence the *Estoire,* to which it alludes — was composed before 1216, the year of John's death.[2] But, if the view of the evolution of

---

[1] Cp. p. 254, above.

[2] That this was the true *terminus ad quem* for the dating of Helinandus's chronicle was first pointed out in the Introduction, p. XXV, note, to the edition (1905) of that author's *Vers de la Mort* by F. Wulff and E. Walberg (Société des Anciens Textes Français). In my article, *Arthuriana,* RR, III, (1912) — particularly, pp. 185 ff. — I called attention to the importance of this discovery for the dating of the Vulgate cycle.

In the passage cited above, Helinandus uses the following words: "Hanc historiam latine scriptam invenire non potui, sed tantum gallice scripta habetur a quibusdam proceribus, nec facile, ut aiunt, tota inveniri potest." Now, Brugger, *Zs. f. frz. Spr. u. Litt.,* XXIX[1], 108 and XXXVI[2], 208, has interpreted these words as referring not merely to the *Estoire,* but to the whole Grail cycle of the prose-romances. As will be seen from the next sentence, one may grant the correctness of this interpretation — only with the restrictions that the *Merlin*-continuation was not yet a part of the cycle and that the *Lancelot* had not yet attained its full enormous length.

In his elaborate and, in many respects, valuable discussion of the

the Vulgate cycle which is developed below[3] is correct, only one of its branches, the *Merlin*-continuation, was composed later than the *Estoire*. We may, therefore, affirm with certainty that by 1216 the whole cycle, with the exception of this continuation, was

date of the Vulgate cycle, *Lancelot*, pp. 126 ff., Lot unfortunately overlooked Wulff and Walberg's discovery, which renders his dating of the composition of the cycle (p. 140), viz. 1221—1225 (inclusive) impossible.

It is worth recording that in a private communication, which I received from Professor Wolfgang Golther early in 1920, he expressed the conviction that the whole passage about the Grail in Helinandus is merely a late thirteenth century interpolation. He acknowledges, however, that he is unable to produce any "unmittelbare Beweise" in support of this view, and, so long as that is the case, it seems better to accept the passage as genuine.

The fact that Manessier and Gerbert in their continuations to Chrétien's *Perceval* use the Vulgate cycle is of no value for fixing the *terminus ad quem* of the date of the cycle, since the exact dates of these writers are unknown. Manessier wrote some time between 1211 and 1244. That is all we know. Gerbert wrote probably about 1225. For a fuller consideration of these matters cp. pp. 290 ff., above.

The earliest MS. of any part of the cycle — viz. the first division of MS. 768 (Bibl. Nat.), which contains the first part of the *Lancelot* — dates from the middle of the thirteenth century. Cp. Lot, *Lancelot*, p. 135. The earliest dated MS. of any part of the cycle, — MS. 342 (Bibl. Nat.), which contains the last part of the *Lancelot*, *Queste* and *Mort Artu* — belongs to 1274.

Interesting, though of little value for the dating of the cycle, is the earliest known allusion to the prose *Lancelot* — first pointed out by P. Meyer, *Romania*, VI, 494 ff. (1877) — viz. in a thirteenth century MS. (British Museum, Add. 21212, fol. 4) of the prologue to a French version (now lost, if it ever existed) of the *Philippis* of Guillaume le Breton. The *Lancelot* is there referred to as "li livres Lancelot Ou il n'a de rime un seul mot." According to this prologue, the version of the *Philippis* was executed at the instance of Gile de Flagi, of whom the last mention we have dates from 1236. Meyer was inclined to ascribe the allusion to the end of the twenties of the century, but, obviously, this is pure conjecture. It may have been penned even after 1236, for no one knows when Gile de Flagi actually died.

[3] Cp. p. 455, below.

in existence. To be sure, the *Lancelot* of that date was, most likely, of considerably less bulk than the huge work of our extant MSS.

In determining the upward limit of date for the cycle, we have, at least, one important fact to guide us — namely, that the *Mort Artu* was composed after the pretended exhumation of Arthur and Guinevere at Glastonbury in 1191, for in this branch we have obviously combined with the old Celtic tradition of the wounded Arthur's journey to Avalon the new invention which the monks of Glastonbury first put into circulation in that year to the effect that the great king and his consort were really buried in the local abbey.[4] It does not, however, seem reasonable to suppose that the author of the *Mort Artu* would have made so serious a concession to this invention, unless it had already gained a pretty widespread credence at the time that he composed his romance, and for that a period of at least ten years would be required; indeed, an even longer time would seem more likely. In view of these circumstances, it appears safe to conjecture that the composition of the *Mort Artu* fell somewhere in the neighborhood of the year 1205. But this romance presupposes the existence of the *Lancelot* (in some form or other) and the *Queste*, so that the composition of these latter romances would fall in the closing years of the twelfth century (doubtless, the last decade).[5] On

---

[4] Cp. p. 264, above.

[5] All sorts of efforts have been made to establish the *terminus a quo* of different members of the cycle—especially, by means of the sources. But in not a single instance can we fix definitely the date of these sources themselves. In connection with this question, it should be observed that Lot, *Lancelot*, p. 134, is wrong in limiting the beginning of Wauchier's literary activity to 1206. Brugger, *Zs. f. frz. Spr. u. Litt.*, XXXVI[2], 45 ff. (1910) had already proved convincingly that this limitation (which originated with P. Meyer, *Hist. litt. de la France*, XXXIII, 291) was unwarranted and that his *Perceval*-continuation, indeed, may possibly have been written as far back as the eighties of the twelfth century. Moreover, most students who make a distinction between Wauchier and Pseudo-Wauchier — and it is the latter on which the authors of the *Lancelot* and *Queste* have drawn particularly — will agree that whatever may be the date of Wauchier, Pseudo-Wauchier's date is still earlier.

It is not necessary to discuss again in this connection such

the other hand, the *Estoire del Saint Graal*, which, as we have seen, was certainly in existence by 1216, contains allusions to the *Mort Artu*[6] — consequently, we may place the composition of this branch with a considerable degree of confidence between 1205 and 1216. Finally, the *Merlin*-continuation of the cycle, which was written to connect the *Estoire* and the *Lancelot*, was, of course, later than either, and, if we may judge by its allusions to the *Perlesvaus*, later even than that romance. The most probable date, then, for this latest division of the cycle would be a few years before 1230.

---

fundamental sources of the Vulgate cycle as Chrétien's *Perceval* (not to mention his other works) or the French original of Ulrich's *Lanzelet*, since the dates of these sources are too indefinite to help us materially in our present inquiry. If the dates, however, of these romances, respectively, which we have argued for above are accepted, we should have the eighties of the twelfth century as the *terminus a quo* for the *Lancelot* — the earliest member of the cycle. The same conclusion is fortified with regard to the cycle, in general, by our dating of Robert's *Joseph* (a source of the *Estoire* and *Queste*) and *Merlin* (used in the Vulgate *Merlin* and *Mort Artu*).

The *Tristan* romances, which are drawn upon so freely in the *Mort Artu*, are relatively too early to add anything to the evidence in the case. The *chansons de geste*, *Gaydon* and *Parise la Duchesse*, which are apparently sources (one or the other, or both) of the poisoned fruit incident in this branch were written not later than the first part of the thirteenth century, but the extant form of *Gaydon* is probably not the earliest, and both poems may really be productions of the latter part of the twelfth. For a detailed examination of the evidence, cp. Bruce, *Mort Artu*, pp. XXIX ff.

The date of Raoul d'Houdenc's *Meraugis de Portlesguez* (a source of the *Lancelot* and *Merlin*) falls in the latter part of the twelfth or first part of the thirteenth century — no one can say which. Cp. Friedwagner's edition, pp. LXIII, f. (Halle, 1897).

Lot, *Lancelot*, p. 165, — observes that the raising of the host (cp. *Queste*, VI, 189) is first mentioned in the statutes of Eudes de Sully, bishop of Paris, 1196—1208. But the practise was certainly earlier. See the eleventh century example from St. Gall, given by Karl Young, *The Dramatic Associations of the Easter Sepulchre*, pp. 30 f. (Madison, Wisconsin, 1920).

Following the authorities on mediaeval armour who state, apparently with one accord, that horse-armour was first introduced in the beginning of the thirteenth century, the present writer in his edition of the *Mort Artu*, pp. XXXIIf. used this supposed fact as affording an approximate *terminus a quo* for the romance. He has since discovered, however, mention of elaborate horse-armour being worn as early as 1187 by followers of Count Baldwin of Flanders. Cp. A. Cartellieri, *Philipp II. August, König von Frankreich,* I, 255 f. (3 vols., Leipzig and Paris, 1899—1910).

⁶ One might, of course, query whether these allusions to the *Mort Artu* in the *Estoire* may not be late insertions — especially, since there are other grounds for suspecting that the original text of the *Estoire* underwent subsequent changes and additions. Cp. p. 371 note 1 above and RR, IX, 380. As long, however, as no cogent reasons are offered for regarding the allusions in question as late interpolations, we may accept them as belonging to the original *Estoire*.

The *Mort Artu* plainly presupposes the *Queste,* but is, itself, referred to in the *Estoire* (if the above-mentioned allusions are not late additions to the *Estoire*). This then would confirm the conclusion which we reached pp. 428ff., above, that the last-named romance was composed after the *Queste.*

# Chapter VI.
# Development of the Vulgate Cycle.

It will be observed from the above discussions that according to general agreement,[1] the *Lancelot* (in a shorter and earlier form) was the oldest romance in the Vulgate cycle and that the other branches postulate its existence. The evidence which we have presented as to the priority of the *Queste* over the remaining branches of the cycle prove that it was composed next to the *Lancelot*. Then followed the *Mort Artu,* which is dependent on the *Queste,* but is referred to in the *Estoire* — next expansions and extensions of the original *Lancelot* that connect it with the *Queste* and *Mort Artu,*[2] and after that, the *Estoire*. That the *Merlin*[3] was the last of the branches to be composed has never been disputed.

If the scheme of relative dates which is set forth in this summary is correct, it is manifest that the cyclic character of the five great romances with which we are dealing does not spring from the fact that they were composed in execution of a pre-conceived design, whether on the part of a single author or of more than one author, working in collaboration,[4] but rather from

---

[1] Lot constitutes a partial exception to this statement, inasmuch as he supposes (pp. 122 f.) that, after the author of the *Lancelot* had written a large part of that romance, he turned aside, in order to compose the *Estoire,* and only resumed his work on the *Lancelot* after he had completed the *Estoire*. Cp. p. 378, note 4, above.

[2] The passages here referred to occur especially in the later portions of the *Lancelot,* beginning with Gawain's visit to the Grail castle. They are particularly numerous in the so-called *Agravain* division of the *Lancelot*. On these subjects cp. pp. 402, note 71, above.

[3] Strictly speaking, the Vulgate *Merlin*-continuation, which its author combined with the old prose-rendering of Robert's *Merlin* to make up the Vulgate *Merlin*. On its relative date, cp. p. 395, above.

[4] These are the theories of Lot and Brugger, respectively, and will be discussed below. Brugger propounded his first.

the romancers' practise of attaching their inventions concerning any particular phase of Arthurian tradition to those of their predecessors concerning some other phase of that tradition.[5] In a period, then, when the sense of literary property was non-existent and the sense of personal authorship not very strong, such a practise was entirely natural, and the result was the creation of the vast composite cycle before us. We face, then, virtually, the same conditions that have called into existence the other great cyclic works of the past — for example, the Greek cyclic poems concerning the siege of Troy or the cycle of Guillaume d'Orange among the Old French *chansons de geste*.[6] An incitement to the composition of a connected series of romances on the Arthurian theme was supplied by Robert de Boron's *Joseph-Merlin* and its proposed sequels, but how little Robert's series really influenced the Vulgate cycle as a model is patent from the fact that the author of the *Queste* of this cycle threw overboard that poet's Grail hero and attached his work to a romance (the *Lancelot*) to which there is nothing even remotely corresponding in Robert's series. By this act an element that was totally alien to the *Joseph-*

---

[5] The cyclic connection is, largely, of a general kind, and, in the case of the *Lancelot*, especially, the connecting episodes are most often cyclic in effect, not in aim. Cp. Bruce, RR, X, 121.

[6] Cp. RR, IV, 463f. The interval that separated the composition of the various members of the Vulgate cycle was not so long as in the case of the other cyclic works mentioned above. — The romances that make up the Guillaume d'Orange cycle are also combined in some cyclic MSS. — e. g. MS. 24369 (fonds français, Bibl. Nat.), which contains 17 romances of the total of 24 extant and the Boulogne MS. which contains 11. The latter MS. ends with the words, *Explicit li Roumans de Guillaume d'Orange,* on which Bédier, *Legendes Épiques*[2], I, 8, remarks: "cette rubrique nous est temoin que les hommes du XIIIe et du XIVe siecle, lisant nos chansons, croyaient lire un seul roman." The romances in such a collection, however, were, of course, by different authors. Gröber, *Grundriss,* II, 997f. tried to trace the history of the development of the Arthurian Vulgate cycle by an examination of the grouping of the romances in the extant MSS, but these MSS. are too late to throw any light on this subject and Gröber's effort is a failure.

*Merlin,* etc., in every way, became incorporated into the history of the Grail. Moreover, if Robert's cycle had, in any strict sense, furnished the model of a pre-conceived plan for the Vulgate cycle, the execution of this plan would, of course, have begun with the composition of the *Estoire* (which corresponds to Robert's *Joseph*), but, to say nothing of the priority of the *Lancelot,* the whole weight of evidence goes to show that the *Estoire* is later than the *Queste,* and even than the *Mort Artu.*

The cyclic character of the romances, it should be said in conclusion, was finally still further strengthened by the occasional cross-references which were inserted in the different branches by individual scribes or by *assembleurs.* It was the latter — themselves, doubtless, scribes — who started the manuscript tradition of our extant MSS. by bringing copies of these romances together and editing them in a very rudimentary fashion.[7]

----

[7] Brief anticipatory cross-references in any one branch to later members of the cycle must have got into the manuscript tradition in this manner — occasionally, also, somewhat longer interpolations of considerable importance — e. g. the interpolations in the *Lancelot* which are based on the Vulgate and MS. 337 *Merlin*-continuations and *Perlesvaus,* respectively. Cp. RR, X, 393f. The passages, remarked on above, pp. 402f., which serve to connect the *Lancelot* with the *Estoire* probably belong to a somewhat earlier stage in the development of the *Lancelot.* How artless an interpolator could be is shown by the instance in the *Lancelot,* III, 117, where King Pelles is spoken of as dead although his whole share in the story falls later in the romance. Of course, this interpolator was writing with the complete romance before him. Another speaks unequivocally, III, 429, of the *Lancelot* being "adjusted" to the Grail story. — It seems likely that the insertions in the *Lancelot* and *Queste* of passages taken virtually verbatim from the *Estoire* (cp. p. 376, note 3, and p. 402, note 72, above), was the work of *assembleurs.* So, too, with the recapitulation, here and there in the *Lancelot,* of preceding adventures. On the general conditions under which our extant manuscript tradition was established, cp. Bruce, MPh., XVI, 113 ff.

## Chapter VII.

# The Pseudo-Robert de Boron cycle of the Prose Romances.

The second of the prose cycles, as far as it has been preserved, is ascribed in the MSS. to Robert de Boron.[1] This ascription, however, is unquestionably false,[2] and we, therefore, retain the manuscript designation only in the modified form which will be noted above and which has latterly become general.

The feature of this second cycle which distinguishes it essentially from the Vulgate (Walter Map) cycle is the fact that in the former the characters of the Tristan story play a part, which is not the case with the latter. These characters, Tristan, Marc, Iseult, etc., have evidently been introduced into the cycle from the prose *Tristan*.[3]

Of the Pseudo-Robert cycle mere fragments have survived. Curiously it seems to have been more popular abroad than in the country of its origin (France), so that for important portions of the cycle we have only versions in foreign languages — especially Portuguese and Spanish — the French originals having been lost. In fact, the very existence of this cycle was first pointed out by G. Paris in 1886.[4] From indications in the *Huth-Merlin* — i. e.

---

[1] For the passages concerned, cp. G. Paris, *Huth-Merlin*, pp. XXVIIf.

[2] Everything shows this — its dependence on the Galahad *Queste*, the difference of style, the character of the incidents — secular and often fantastic, etc. Cp., especially, A. Pauphilet, *Romania*, XXXVI, 591 ff.

[3] The prose *Tristan*, in its earlier forms, is undoubtedly anterior to the Pseudo-Robert cycle. We treat the latter first, however, — immediately after the discussion of the Vulgate — because of its close connection with the Vulgate.

[4] Cp. his Introduction to the *Huth-Merlin* — particularly, pp. 1 ff. This Introduction, although it needs correction in some important

the (somewhat abbreviated) *Merlin* branch of this cycle — he was able to infer the existence of other members of the cycle and to suggest what would probably prove to be their distinctive characteristics — suggestions that have been amply confirmed by subsequent discoveries.

Notwithstanding the view to the contrary held by G. Paris, Wechssler, and others,[5] the Pseudo-Robert cycle is, indisputably, a mere derivative of the Vulgate cycle — a new attempt to give vitality to the Arthurian theme in its prose forms, by a recasting of the older cycle. Originally, no doubt, the cycle was conceived of as consisting, like the Vulgate, of the following divisions: 1. *Estoire* (or *Livre*) *del Saint Graal*, 2. *Merlin* (prose-rendering of Robert's *Merlin*), 3. *Merlin*-continuation, 4. *Lancelot*, 5. *Queste del Saint Graal*, 6. *Mort Arthur*. Not all of the six divisions, however, were re-written for the new cycle.

1. The first of these branches has not come down to us — very likely, because it differed so slightly, if at all, from the Vulgate *Estoire* that the few copyists who ever occupied themselves with the Pseudo-Robert cycle[6] rarely considered it worth

---

points, laid the foundation for all subsequent investigation with regard to the formation of the prose cycles. Valuable, too, is Edward Wechssler's Habilitationschrift, *Über die verschiedenen Redaktionen des Robert de Boron zugeschriebenen Graal-Lancelot-Cyklus* (Halle, 1895).

In his discussion of the Pseudo-Robert cycle, *Zs. f. frz. Spr. u. Litt.*, XXIX[1], 114ff. (1905), Brugger accepts Wechssler's results, in the main, but, *inter alia*, regards the cycle as cast in the form of a trilogy from the beginning.

At present, much the most informative work on the Pseudo-Robert cycle is E[lla] Vettermann's above-mentioned treatise — especially pp. 89ff., 299ff. We have here an excellent critical exposition of the various theories concerning the origin and constitution of the cycle. The author, herself, adopts Wechssler's theory.

[5] E. g., Brugger.

[6] The fact that only fragments of this cycle have survived in the original French shows that it was never widely diffused.

Wechssler, p. 14, conjectured that the *Estoire* of the cycle might be preserved in the Portuguese form in a certain Torre do Tombo (Lisbon) MS. (he is referring to MS. Alcobaça 643 of that library), but it seems from Otto Klob, "Beiträge zur Spanischen

their while to transcribe for the new series a romance that was already so widely diffused in the Vulgate form.[7]  In the MS.

---

und Portugiesischen Graal - Litteratur," *Zs. f. rom. Ph.*, XXVI, 169 ff. (1902), that the Portuguese text in question — misleadingly entitled *Liuro de josep abaramatia* — is a mere translation of the Vulgate *Estoire*, executed in 1313 and preserved here in a sixteenth century transcription.  Klob, pp. 185 ff., describes, also, a Spanish *Libro de josep abarimatia* in MS. 2. G. 5 of the Royal Library at Madrid which shows a few variations in the narrative, as compared with Furnivall's edition of the Vulgate *Estoire*, but none that would warrant the inference that it represents a lost (French) Pseudo-Robert *Estoire*.  An edition of this Spanish text by Karl Pietsch and W. A. Nitze, along with a greatly abridged *Merlin (La Estoria de Merlin)* and *Lançarote (Lancelot)* of the same MS., was announced some years ago by the *Gesellschaft ·für Romanische Literatur*, but has not yet appeared.  Pietsch, however, in "MS. 2—G—5 of the Palace Library at Madrid," MPh., XI, 1 ff. (1913), has studied the relations of the Arthurian texts in this MS. to *El Baladro del Sabio Merlin con sus Profecias* (Burgos, 1498) and the Spanish *Demandas* of 1515 (Toledo) and 1535 (Sevilla), both editions of the *Demanda*, in his opinion (p. 4) being derived from a *Merlin y demanda del Santo Grial* (Sevilla, 1500), of which, however, no copy is now known to be extant.  He thinks (p. 14) that the *Baladro*, the lost text last-named and the texts contained in MS. 2—G—5 all go back to a common hypothetical Spanish source.  As regards the *Baladro*, Pietsch is undoubtedly wrong, for this text is certainly nothing but an incomplete Spanish version of the lost *Conte del Brait*.  For a criticism of Pietsch cp. Brugger, *Archiv f. d. Studium der neueren Spr.*, Vol. 133, pp. 229, (1920).  For a study by Pietsch of the language, partly non-Castilian, of these texts cp. his "On the language of thc Spanish Grail fragments," MPh., XIII, 369 ff. (1915), 625 ff. (1916).  Cp., too, his "Madrid Manuscript of the Spanish Grail Fragments," XVIII, 147 ff., (1920), 591 ff., (1921).

    Lastly, C. Michaelis de Vasconcellos, Gröber's *Grundriss*, Band II, 2 te Abt., pp. 214 f. (1894), seems to regard as the first division of the Grail cycle to which the Portuguese *Demanda* belongs — i. e. of what we call the Pseudo-Robert cycle — the Portuguese *Estoria do Emperador Vespasiano* (also called *Livro da Destruicão de Jerusalem*). This book exists both in MS. and in an early print (1496).  The account of the work which she gives, however, does not sustain her conjecture.

    [7] The explanation here proposed seems more plausible than that

(Huth-MS.) which contains a larger proportion, perhaps, of the original Pseudo-Robert than any other extant, the prose rendering of Robert's *Joseph* has been substituted for the original *Estoire*,[8] but from no point of view was the substitution justifiable, for not only did it destroy the artificial symmetry in regard to the length of the branches, which, as we shall see, had been established in the manuscript tradition by this time, but Robert's *Joseph* does not harmonize at all in its narrative with a Galahad-*Queste*, such as constituted the *Queste* branch of the Pseudo-Robert cycle.[9]

2. The *Merlin*[10] is the prose rendering of Robert's *Merlin* — the same that was incorporated into the Vulgate cycle.

3. A large part, although not the whole, of the *Merlin*-con-

---

which is implied in Wechssler's Habilitationschrift, p. 16, viz., that the *Estoire (Livre del Graal)* was too ascetic for the new cycle. As is well known, the Vulgate *Queste* is much more ascetic, yet it was recast for this cycle. Moreover, Robert's *Joseph*, which takes the place of the *Estoire* in the Huth MS., is likewise more purely ascetic than the *Estoire*.

[8] Heinzel in his Grail treatise (pp. 167 f.) first pointed this out. Allusions in the *Queste* division of the cycle (Spanish and Portuguese *Demandas*), as he observed, are to an *Estoire*, not to Robert's *Joseph*. On this subject cp. also, Wechssler, *op. cit.*, pp. 8 f. There is no evidence that the *Estoire* which the author of these allusions had in mind was anything but the Vulgate version of that branch, and I do not believe that any other ever existed.

[9] Besides the prose-rendering of Robert's *Joseph*, which did not really belong to the Pseudo-Robert cycle, the Huth-MS. contains only Robert's *Merlin* (the prose version) and the *Merlin*-continuation of the cycle just named, though incomplete. According to Wechssler, the *Merlin*-continuation of this MS. belongs to the hypothetical form of Pseudo-Robert which he calls "Kürzung C", which, in turn, rests on his hypothetical „Kürzung B". The statement at the end of the Huth-MS. II, 254, that the *Merlin*-continuation ends here shows that the scribe or redactor of the MS. purposely left out the episodes preserved in MS. 112.

[10] It ends at the bottom of p. 146 of. Vol. I in the edition of the *Huth-Merlin* by G. Paris and J. Ulrich (2 vols., Paris, 1886).

tinuation of the cycle is preserved in the Huth MS.[11] and in the Spanish *Demanda*,[12] respectively. An additional fragment is preserved in MS. 112 (Bibl. Nat.)[13] and in Malory's *Morte Darthur*.[14]

---

[11] Begins *Huth-Merlin*, 1, 147 (top of page). For a history and description of this MS., which is now Add. 38117 of the British Museum, see G. Paris, *Huth-Merlin*, I, pp. Iff., and Vettermann, pp. 85 ff.

[12] *La Demanda del Sancto Grial* (Toledo, 1515, of which only a part is preserved — in the British Museum copy — and Seville, 1535). This work (edition of 1535) has been reprinted in the *Nueva Biblioteca de Autores Españoles bajo la direccion des Excmo. Sr. D. Marcelino Menendez y Pelayo*, in the volume entitled *Libros de Caballerias, Primera Parte, Ciclo arturico-ciclo carolingio, por Adolfo Bonilla y San Martin*, Madrid, 1907. In this reprint the editor has given an unauthorized title, *El Baladro del Sabio Merlin*, to the part of the book, pp. 3—162, which contains the Spanish version of the Pseudo-Robert *Merlin*-continuation. The original sixteenth century print which he is editing designates it clearly at the beginning as *El Primero Libro de la Demanda del Sancto Grial*. Hence we shall speak of this Book as *Demanda I* and of the Second Book, which contains the Spanish version of the Pseudo-Robert *Queste* and *Mort Arthur*, as *Demanda II*.

Besides the prose-rendering of Robert's *Merlin*, *Demanda I* contains a large part of the Pseudo-Robert *Merlin*-continuation, interpolated with fragments of prophecies by Merlin and of the lost *Conte del Brait* in Spanish dress. For a table of the correspondences in detail, cp. Vettermann, pp. 124f. Sommer has described, *Romania*, XXXVI, 369ff., the early prints of the Spanish *Demanda I*, and *ibid.* pp. 383ff., has compared it with the *Huth-Merlin*. Vettermann's minute comparative study of the Balen tale in the two texts (pp. 144ff.), however, gives a more exact idea of the nature of their relations to each other.

[13] According to Wechssler, Habilitationschrift, p. 13, this fragment supplies the part of the Pseudo-Robert *Merlin*-continuation which was missing from the Huth MS. — consequently the two combined give us this continuation complete, as it stood in his Redaction B. Moreover, he has compared, pp. 29ff., this fragment with the very condensed version of the same incidents in Malory, Book IV, ch. 20—28. The fragment has since been published by Sommer: *Die Abenteuer Gawains, Ywains, und Le Morholts mit den drei Jungfrauen, nach HS. 112: Beiheft 47 zur Zs. f. rom. Ph.*, (Halle a. S., 1913).

[14] Book I ch. 19—28 and Books II, III and IV. Sommer,

The divergence between the Vulgate and Pseudo-Robert cycles is greatest in their *Merlin*-continuations. From the time of Chrétien on, the predominant tendency of Arthurian romance had been to express itself in forms of purely fanciful adventure. But the *Merlin*-continuation of the Vulgate, as we have seen, was a pseudo-chronicle, and thus accorded very imperfectly with the spirit of the *Lancelot,* which came immediately after it in the series. It occurred, therefore, to the author of the corresponding division of the pseudo-Robert cycle,[15] who, in any event, was in search of novelty, that there was room for a *Merlin*-continuation which would be more in harmony with the ultra-romantic character of the *Lancelot,* and it was, doubtless, to this feeling that the new *Merlin*-continuation owes its existence. Besides, the author of the prose *Tristan,* with whose work the author of Pseudo-Robert was thoroughly familiar, had already set the example of handling the characters and incidents of the Vulgate with great freedom.[16]

Like the Vulgate continuation, the corresponding division of

---

in his edition of Malory, III, 58ff., compares Malory in detail with the corresponding parts of the *Huth-Merlin,* throughout. When his study was published (1891), it was not known (cp. III, 145) that the (approximate) source of Malory, Book IV, ch. 20—28, had been preserved in MS. 112.

[16] Was the author of the *Merlin*-continuation, also, the author of the *Queste* of this cycle? G. Paris, Introduction to the *Huth-Merlin,* p. LXII, thought not, but this idea was connected with his theory of the development of the prose cycles, which, as I have tried to prove below, Part IV, was unsound. We know that the Pseudo-Robert *Merlin* is merely the old prose version of Robert's *Merlin,* adopted without change — moreover, that the Pseudo-Robert *Mort Arthur,* save in omissions, does not differ greatly from the Vulgate. Now, if, as I surmise, no substantially new *Estoire (Grand St. Graal)* or *Lancelot* was composed for this cycle, one man could easily have rewritten the remaining parts-viz. the *Merlin*-continuation and the *Queste.*

[16] It is possible, too, that the *Merlin*-continuation of the Vulgate, being a comparatively late composition, did not possess as yet the authority of the other branches of that cycle. Nevertheless, as a part of the great Vulgate cycle, it was able to maintain itself against the other *Merlin*-continuations — viz. those of the Pseudo-Robert cycle and MS. 337 — though it is hardly superior to either in literary value.

Pseudo-Robert was planned to fill out the gap between the coronation of Arthur, with which Robert de Boron's *Merlin* had terminated, and the appearance of Lancelot on the stage. Merlin, however, is even more prominent in the narrative of Pseudo-Robert than in that of the Vulgate, so that the former is somewhat more closely connected with Robert's *Merlin* than the latter. On the other hand, references in it to the *Lancelot*, though fairly numerous, are less so than in the case of the Vulgate.

We shall not invite the reader to follow us through the labyrinth of fantastic adventures which make up the Pseudo-Robert *Merlin* continuation.[17] They are of the same general kind as the adventures of the *Lancelot*, by which they were manifestly inspired. The earlier portion of the work, in which Arthur, Merlin, Loth, Pellinor (Perceval's father, according to this romance) and Balaain are the principal characters, is the best; the incidents of the later portion, such as the adventures of Accalon, Yvain, Gawain, and Le Morhout, though, also, related with ease and fluency, are of less significance.[18] It is characteristic of the author that he should begin his continuation [19] with the most sensational, perhaps, of all the *motifs* that are to be found in the Vulgate, namely, the story of Mordred's incestuous birth. With this he has combined in a modified form the biblical *motif* of Herod's slaughter of the innocent children; for, warned by Merlin's prophecy that a child who is to be born on the next May-day will be the cause of the undoing of Arthur and his kingdom,[20] the king has all the children in his dominions who are born at that time set afloat in a pilot-less vessel.[21]

---

[17] There is a good analysis of it in its Huth MS. form in the edition of the *Huth-Merlin*, by G. Paris and J. Ulrich, *II*, 285 ff.

[18] It was in this part of Pseudo-Robert (Sommer's *Beiheft* 47, pp. 25 ff.), however, that we first find the story which Tennyson has made familiar under the name of *Pelleas and Ettarre*, his source, of course, being Malory IV, 22—24. Malory, however, uses an altered version of Pseudo-Robert, which ends differently. *Arcade* is the original form of the heroine's name, *Pellias* of the hero's. The latter name is doubtless a corruption of *Pellean(s)*.

[19] *Huth-Merlin*, I, 147 ff.        [20] *Ibid.* I, 158 ff.

[21] I, 207 ff.

This vessel, however, was not destroyed, as Arthur intended, but drifts to the castle of Amalvi in the land of King Oriant (father of Le Lait Hardi), and the children are saved. But already in the assembling of the children, Mordred, the fatal infant of Merlin's prophecy — the fruit of Arthur's own unwitting incest with his sister — had escaped the king's net; for the ship which was bearing him to Camelot was wrecked and all on board perished, save the child, who was picked up on the seashore by a fisherman and later adopted by the father of Sagremor.[22]

Just after the account of Mordred's conception, comes what is perhaps the most extravagant of all Arthurian fancies — namely, that of *la beste glatissante* (the barking beast)[23] — borrowed from the prose *Tristan*.[24] The hideous creature, which has a whole cry of dogs in its belly, has been pursued in vain by Pellinor for a year.[25] The achievement of this quest, however, is to be one of the Grail adventures, and, as Merlin informs Arthur,[26] none but the virgin knight, Perceval (Pellinor's son), will be able to tell the king the true story of the strange beast.

We have, still further, in the romance many other folktale *motifs* — armor that renders invisible,[27] lances thrust by invisible hands,[28] blood-baths to cure leprosy,[29] etc. A precious piece of mediaevalism, especially, is the story[30] as to how the goddess,

---

[22] I, 204 ff. The story of the infant Mordred is due to contamination with the legend of Pope Gregory. Cp. Bruce's edition of the *Historia Meriadoci and De Ortu Waluuanii,* pp. XXXVII ff. (1913).

[23] I, 149 f.

[24] Löseth, pp. 55 ff. According to certain *Tristan* MSS. (cp. Löseth, pp. 57 ff.) the beast has a stag's feet, the thighs and tail of a lion, a leopard's body and a serpent's head, and its cry was equal to that of a hundred dogs. In the *Huth-Merlin* I, 149, 160, *et passim,* the term applied to the creature is "diverse". In Malory, chapter-headings to ch. 19 and 20 of Book I, it is called "the questing beest," and at the end of ch. 19 this writer says that Pellinor first, and, after Pellinor's death, Palamedes pursued it. This fabulous monster figures also in Gerbert's continuation of Chrétien's *Perceval,* Potvin VI, 219 ff., and in the *Perlesvaus,* pp. 187 ff.

[25] I, 151.    [26] I, 160.    [27] II, 24.    [28] II, 9.

[29] II, 16 f.    [30] II, 145 ff.    [31] I, 195 ff.

Diana, having found a new lover, gets rid of the old one (Faunus) by enticing him into a sarcophagus, on the plea of giving him a medicinal bath, and then filling it with boiling lead. As a complement to the famous incident in the Vulgate *Mort Artu* of Gifflet's casting Excalibur into the lake, at the wounded monarch's behest, our author describes,[31] from his own invention, how Arthur, in the first instance, received the sword from this same lake — only by a cheap effort at originality he imputes to the scabbard the supernatural excellence that had traditionally belonged to the weapon, itself.

Much the most felicitous episode of the present romance, however, is that of Balaain and Balaan[32] — the two brothers who,

---

[32] II, 47 ff. Already from I, 215 (where he acquired an additional sword that Arthur and his knights had failed to loose from the waist of a damsel of the Lady of Avalon) on, Balaain had played a prominent part in the romance as "le chevalier as deus espees" (I, 233 *et passim)* — a title which he owes most likely to the *Lancelot,* IV, 323 ff., where this is the epithet of Eliezer (Galahad's maternal uncle), although we find it applied to other knights elsewhere in Arthurian romance, e. g. in the prose *Tristan* (Löseth), pp. 21 ff., to Palamedes, p. 395, to Samaliel, in the metrical romance *Chevalier as deus Espees* to Meriadeuc. Cp., besides, Heinzel's Grail treatise, p. 17 (including note). Above all, it was he who had given King Pellehan of the Grail castle the dolorous stroke (II, 27 f. — wanting in the Huth MS., but supplied by the editors from Malory, Book II, ch. 15—16) with the marvellous lance, whereby a magical blight descended upon the kingdom of Listinois (II, 30) or Logres (II, 7), so that it was henceforth designated "li roiames de terre gastee et li roiames de terre forainne." It was this disastrous stroke that sealed Balaain's own fate (II, 7 f.). In PMLA, XXV, 42 ff. (1910), A. C. L. Brown has tried to establish a Celtic origin for this episode, by citing supposed Irish parallels to it. For a refutation of his argument, however, cp. Brugger, *Zs. f. frz. Spr. u. Litt.,* XXXVI[2], 190 (1910) and, especially, Vetterman, pp. 290 ff. (1918). *Gallan, Garlan* (name of Balaain's adversary), which Brown (p. 43, note 8) identifies with *Weland* (name of the famous smith of Germanic legend), is, of course, simply a corrupt form of *Varlan (Brulant* etc.) of the Vulgate *Estoire,* I, 290. Balaan's name was, doubtless, taken from that of the British nobleman who was converted to Christianity by Pharain in the Vulgate *Estoire,* I, 268. That personage was named *Balaan (Balan),* and, like the

not recognizing each other, engaged in a combat that proved fatal
to both. Only after both had suffered mortal wounds. did mutual
recognition take place. The incident, of course, was not new, but
a variant of a folk-tale *motif* of immemorial antiquity, best known
in its Persian form of *Sohrab and Rustem.* The episode, however, had the good fortune to belong to the part of the Pseudo-
Robert *Merlin*-continuation which Malory adopted for his *Morte
Darthur,* and it was in the latter place[33] that it attracted the attention of two of the greatest English poets of the nineteenth century — Tennyson and Swinburne. Both, accordingly, clothed the
old story in new poetical forms.[34] In neither case, to be sure,
does the result represent the best art of the author.

hero of the present episode, was from North Britain. The name was
very probably chosen by our author for his hero, because in sound it
was similar to that of the old deliverer of the dolorous stroke
— *Varlan (Brulant* etc.) in the *Estoire,* I, 290, the heathen king
whom he wishes to supplant. Vetterman, pp. 196 ff., has discussed at
length possible original Celtic connections of the name — e. g., with
Belinos, a Celtic god, with Belinus, a British prince in Geoffrey of
Monmouth's History, Book III, ch. 1—10, who, for a time carried on
a feud with his brother, Brennius, etc. Only Geoffrey (or his translator, Wace), however, really need be taken into consideration, and
even this connection is doubtful; for one can point easily to parallels
in Arthurian romance for every individual element in Balaain's story,
and the combination of these elements was, of course, our romancer's
work. The name of the British nobleman which I mentioned above,
as furnishing the true source of the name of the hero of the present
episode, occurs only once in the *Estoire,* and the names of persons
and places in MSS. of the mediaeval romances were so subject to
mutilation that no one can possibly affirm that the form, *Balaan
(Balan),* which we find in this single passage, is not, itself, merely
a scribal corruption. Consequently, all discussion of its origin is,
from the start, pretty well doomed to futility.

The name of the hero's brother, *Balaain,* is, of course, merely
an intentional variant of *Balaan.* In a similar manner, we have
*Huth-Merlin* I, 120, two sisters made out of Morgan le Fay. Upon
one of them is conferred the nominative form of that enchantress's
name, viz. *Morgue(s),* upon the other the objective form, *Morgain.*

[33] Malory, II, 18—19.

[34] Tennyson's *Balin and Balan* (1885), Swinburne's *The Tale
of Balen* (1896).

4. There is no reason to believe that a re-cast *Lancelot* ever
formed a part of the Pseudo-Robert cycle.[35] This cycle presupposes
merely the Vulgate form of that branch.

---

[35] To be sure, Wechssler, Habilitationschrift, pp. 18 ff. and Brugger,
*Zs. f. frz. Spr. u. Litt.*, XXXIV[1], 109 ff., express the contrary opinion,
and, as has been said above, (p. 447, note 12), accept as fragments of a lost
Pseudo-Robert *Lancelot* certain episodes that are found in some MSS.
of the prose *Tristan:* 1. the episodes relating to Galahad's birth and
upbringing which Sommer has edited (along with their prose *Tristan*
setting) from the early fourteenth century MS. Add. 5474 (British
Museum), under the title of "Galahad and Perceval". MPh., V, 55 ff.,
181 ff. (1907), 291 ff. (1908). 2. the tourney at Louvezerp (analyzed
by Löseth, pp. 271 ff.). No. 1 forms, also, the approximate original
of Malory's Books XI and XII. It is closely dependent on the corresponding part of the Vulgate.

Brugger, *op. cit.*, p. 109, note 13, has suggested that an interpolation in the *Tristan* MS. 12599 (B. N.) — end of thirteenth
century — is also drawn from the hypothetical Pseudo-Robert. Cp.
Löseth, pp. 206 ff., for this interpolation. The sweeping inference,
however, which the above-named scholars have drawn from these
episodes — viz. that Pseudo-Robert originally comprised a *Lancelot* —
is obviously unjustified and has already been rejected by Sommer, the
discoverer of the main one (No. 1). See *Beiheft* 47, pp. XIX f. For
a refutation of this view, cp. p. 447 note 12, above. Besides, there are no
allusions in that cycle that require such a supposition, and it is evident
from the words of the *Huth-Merlin* II, 57, although they are probably due
to a redactor and not to the original author, that the unexampled
length of the *Lancelot* prevented the rewriting of that branch. There
it is said; "et cel anelet li [= Lancelot] avoit doune la damoisele
del lac, si coume la grant hystore de Lancelot le devise [cp. Sommer,
III, 123], cele meisme ystoire qui doit estre departie de mon livre, ne
mie pour chou qu il [error for *qu'ele*] n'i apartiegne et que elle n'en
soit traite, mais pour chou qu'il couvient que les trois parties de mon
livre soient ingaus, l'une aussi grant coume l'autre, et se je ajoustaisse
cele grant ystore, la moi[ene] partie de mon livre fust au tresble plus
grant que les autres deus. Pour chou me couvient il laissier celle
grant ystoire qui devise les oevres de Lancelot et la naissance [Gala-
had] et voel deviser les neuf lignies des nascions [error for *de Nascien*,
Cp. Sommer I, 203], tout ensi coume il apartient a la haute escriture
del saint graal, ne n'i conterai ja chose que je ne doie, ains dirai
mains asses que je ne truis escrit en l'ystoire dou latin."
(G. Paris, *Huth-M.*, p. LIV, suggested the necessary emendations,

5. Only fragments of the *Queste* of the present cycle in the original French have come down to us.[36] The whole branch, however, has been preserved in a pretty close translation in the Portuguese *Demanda*[37] and, much more condensed, in the Spanish *De-*

which I have inserted in brackets in this quotation. — Furthermore, the pretence here that the cycle was translated from the Latin is simply the common fiction of mediaeval romancers, and, in this case, is borrowed from the Vulgate. — Note, too, that, when the author of the passage speaks of the *Lancelot* as being drawn from "mon livre," he merely refers to the fact that the *Lancelot* is the natural immediate sequel of the *Merlin*-continuation in the series.)

Finally, with regard to the question at issue — it is impossible to maintain that an author or redactor could not interpolate or recast individual episodes in any one branch of a cycle, unless he was redacting the whole cycle. We know positively that arbitrary variants of episodes in the *Lancelot,* ranging from a few lines up to 204 quarto pages (cp. pp. 443 ff., above), were composed, without any thought on the part of their authors of recasting the whole cycle. Now, similar variants to the *Lancelot,* doubtless, continued to be written after Pseudo-Robert was composed, in which case they might well show the influence of the new cycle. Then, too, it is quite possible that interpolators of the *Tristan* MSS. may have, themselves, composed such episodes under the influence of this same cycle.

[36] Namely, 1. in MS. 343 (Bibl. Nat.) fols. 61 a—104, col. d. For this MS., cp., especially, Sommer, *Romania,* XXXVI, 563, note 1, and extracts from it, *ibid.* pp. 570, 573 ff. — likewise, *ibid.,* 591 ff., A. Pauphilet's article, "La Queste du Saint Graal du MS. Bibl. Nat. Fr. 343." 2. in MS. 112 (Bibl. Nat.) fols. 84 d—128 b, 146 d—152 c, 179 d—180 c. Cp. Wechssler's Habilitationschrift, p. 55. 3. in certain MSS. of the prose *Tristan* (version commune). Cp. Löseth, Preface, Sections VI and IX.

[37] Preserved in the unique fifteenth century MS. 2594 of what was formerly the Imperial Library at Vienna. Karl von Reinhardtstoettner edited about one fourth of it (Cp. Wechssler, p. 13, note 2), under the title: *A Historia dos Cavalleiros da Mesa Redonda e da Demanda do Santo Graall* (Berlin, 1887). The remainder is still (March, 1921) unedited, although an edition of the complete text by E. Wechssler and A. Klein has figured now for some years in the list of prospective publications of the Gesellschaft für Romanische Literatur (Dresden). At present the best information available concerning the contents of the unpublished portion of the Portuguese *Demanda* is to be found in *Romania,* XXXVI, 543 ff. (1907), where Sommer gives

*manda.*[38]

The rambling and fantastic adventures of the *Lancelot,* as we have seen above,[39] embodied the ideal of romance for the author of the Pseudo-Robert cycle, and it was this fact that prompted him to substitute his new *Merlin*-continuation for that of the Vulgate. Inasmuch as the latter was a mediocre composition and the new continuation was superior to it in fluency and liveliness of style, there was, in some respects, a profit to the reader in the substitution. It was a different matter, however, when, under the influence of this ideal the same writer undertook to transform a work of high seriousness and, despite all drawbacks, of unmistakable power, like the *Queste,* into a romance of commonplace adventure. It betrays the shallowness of the author's own nature that he should have ever conceived of such an enterprise. The result is the debased version of this branch which we have in the above-mentioned forms.[40]

---

us the results of his systematic comparison of this text with the Spanish *Demanda* (pp. 163 ff., of Bonilla's edition) and the Vulgate. In general, the Portuguese text represents the original French more fully and accurately than the Spanish does, but the latter preserves some passages omitted in the former. It has not yet been determined whether the two translations were derived independently from the French.

That the Portuguese *Demanda* represents the Pseudo-Robert *Queste* is indisputable, although Heinzel, p. 164, has pointed out some matters in which it contradicts the *Merlin*-continuation of that cycle. *(Huth-Merlin.)* Pauphilet, pp. 594 f. — very properly, no doubt — lays such inconsistencies to the account of the literary activities of the scribes. Not infrequently, however, in such cases in mediaeval romance the author is, himself, to blame.

[38] See p. 462, note 12, above. Either because of injudicious condensation or because the translator had before him a defective MS. of the original, there are serious omissions in both the *Queste* and *Mort Arthur* of the Spanish *Demanda* — so serious, indeed, as to obscure some times the real meaning of the narrative. For the former cp., for example, Sommer, *Romania,* XXXVI, 557 f., 563 and for the latter, Bruce. RR, IV, 429 f.

[39] Cp. p. 463.

[40] For an excellent criticism of the Pseudo-Robert *Queste,* cp. A. Pauphilet, *Romania,* XXXVI, 598 ff.

In this redaction of the *Queste*, indeed, except for the beginning and the latter part of the story, where the author follows, in the main, his original, the Vulgate *Queste* — in the
episodes of Galahad's arrival at court[41] and occupation of the
Perilous Seat, of his obtaining his sword and shield for the Grail
quest, and, again, near the end, in the mystical healing of Pellan,[42]
the banquet in the Perilous Palace, and the other incidents that
mark the conclusion of that quest — the Grail theme disappears
almost entirely from view, and Galahad, as already in the prose
*Tristan*, differs from the other knights merely in being the hardest
hitter of them all. Only once or twice in the intervening narrative
are we reminded of the Grail and the Grail castle, and, even in
these instances, the "Spiritual Palace" of the Vulgate has lost
all genuine title to its name; as, for instance, when Galahad arrives
there, as he might arrive at any other hospitable abode, and,
after a brief entertainment by his grandfather, Pelles, passes on.[43]
Lancelot's visit, to be sure, is more elaborately described,[44] but
it, too, lacks the solemnity of the Vulgate *Queste*. The romancer
has still further cheapened the conception of the Grail and its
castle by establishing in the latter a sorcerer — whose power,
however, is in abeyance, as long as Galahad is present.[45] For the
rest, the episodes with which he has made up the bulk of the work
are of the same type as the most threadbare and extravagant ones
that we encounter in the *Lancelot* — quests, combats, rapes, etc.
For the sake of novelty, and with the example of the prose *Tristan*,

---

[41] Portuguese *Demanda*, pp. 10ff., Spanish, pp. 168ff.

[42] Printed by Sommer from MS. 343, in its original French form
in *Romania*, XXXVI, 573ff. For the remainder of the text see
Sommer's analysis *ibid.*, pp. 579ff.

[43] Cp. Spanish *Demanda*, pp. 238f. It is true that he does not
enter the castle itself at this time.

[44] Cp. *op. cit.*, pp. 280ff.

[45] *Op. cit.*, 238f., 290ff. The sorcerer, called *Atanabos* in
the Spanish text and *Thanabus* in MS. 343 (cp. *Romania*, XXXVI,
604), is, of course, the Nectanabus of the Alexander legend. The incident is, doubtless, borrowed from the similar one in the prose *Tristan*,
p. 356.

doubtless, also, in mind, he adds to the Grail questers Arthurian knights who had never figured in that rôle before. e. g. Erec[46] and Meraugis de Portlesguez.[47] Above all, he introduces Tristan betimes[48] into the company of the Grail questers, — Tristan whose life was inseparable from his illicit *amours* — and, somewhat later, other characters of the prose *Tristan* — Marc[49] (Mark) and Palamedes.[50] The latter — at first, a pagan, but afterwards baptized — has succeeded Pellinor as the pursuer of the barking (or questing) beast.[51]

The profoundly religious spirit of the Vulgate *Queste*, we observe, then, has vanished from this imitation, and we find ourselves confronted with what is essentially a romance of secular adventure. The inferiority of the new production is mitigated only by the author's gusto in his own work and by a certain vivacity which results therefrom.

6. For reasons which will be stated later on, the *Mort Arthur* of this cycle was hardly treated as a separate branch, but rather as a mere epilogue to the *Queste*. Only a fragment of it is preserved in the original French — viz., in MS. 340 (Bibl. Nat.).[52]

The Portuguese[53] and Spanish[54] *Demandas,* however, contain it virtually entire in translation.

---

[46] Portuguese *Demanda,* pp. 9ff., Spanish, 167f., 210ff., 228.

[47] Spanish *Demanda,* pp. 210ff.

[48] *Ibid.,* p. 168. This had been done in the prose *Tristan.*

[49] *Ibid.,* p. 248.

[50] *Ibid.,* pp. 296ff. (where he is killed by Lancelot), p. 301 (where he, not Pellinor — as in the *Huth-Merlin* — is said to have slain the *bestia ladradora* or *beste glatissante*).

[51] Cp. previous note and the Portuguese *Demanda,* pp. 83f., 86f.

[52] Cp. Löseth, p. 409.

[53] In his "Dois episodios da Demanda do Santo Graal," *Rivista Lusitana,* VI, 332ff. (1910), Otto Klob has printed a small portion of the Portuguese *Mort Arthur* (corresponding to the Spanish *Demanda* ch. 421—437), beginning with Arthur's victory over the Romans. Otherwise, the text still remains unpublished. For a collation with the Spanish see Sommer, *Romania,* XXXVI, 584ff. (1907).

[54] This text is printed in Bonilla's edition of the Spanish *Demanda,* pp. 313ff. It begins in the middle of ch. 391 of that work with the

As compared with its original, the Vulgate, this version shows great condensation, but otherwise no striking differences, save at the end. At this point, however, we have a curious addition — evidently written under the influence of the prose *Tristan* — as follows:[55]

After Lancelot has been buried and Bohort has settled in the hermitage (where Lancelot had ended his days) along with the archbishop and Blioberis, Meraugis de Portlesgeuz joins them there. By this time Tristan and Iseult had been dead for some years and Marc is very old. Nevertheless, having heard of Lancelot's death, he hopes to conquer Logres. Accordingly, he invades it, lays everything waste, including Joyous Gard[56] and Lancelot's tomb, and burns the bones of Lancelot and Galehaut. He, also, destroys most of Camelot and with it the Round Table. Next he goes to the hermitage in order to kill the four companions there. He does kill the archbishop, but is, himself, killed by Paulart, a knight of Ban's lineage. Marc's men dare not put his body in consecrated ground, so they inter him before the hermitage. Few of them, in fact, knew how he had died.

There is something terrible about this conception of the end of the glory of Arthur and his knights. It is as if a beast were trampling under foot some of the fairest creations of the human imagination.

It is not likely that the Pseudo-Robert cycle, from its in-

---

words: "Dize el cuento que un dia se apartaron los. v. hermanos en una camara del rey" (Bruce's edition of the *Mort Artu,* p. 92 l. 13, Sommer's, VI, 269, l. 15). Agravain is about to stir up Arthur against Lancelot a second time on account of the latter's intrigue with the queen. In the Spanish text the beginning of the *Mort Arthur* is not indicated by a new chapter to show that a new division of the story has commenced. For a detailed comparison of the Spanish with the French original, cp. Bruce, RR, IV, 429 ff.

[55] I follow here Löseth's analysis (p. 409) of this conclusion as it is preserved in the original French in MS. 340. The Spanish version shows some insignificant differences. Cp. Bruce, *loc. cit.*

[56] Already in Arthur's life-time, Spanish *Demanda,* pp. 248 ff. (Queste section), Marc had invaded Logres and ravaged Joyous Gard.

ception, was cast in the form of a trilogy,[57] yet in all the extant

---

[57] This is explicitly stated in the *Huth-Merlin*, I, 280 and II, 287, with reference to the form of the cycle which that MS. represents. The Portuguese *Demanda*, likewise, refers more than once to the tripartite division. Cp. Heinzel, pp. 163f. and Sommer, *Romania*, XXXVI, 570. So, too, the fragment of the original French text preserved in MS. 343. Cp. Wechssler, p. 60.

The passages in the *Huth-Merlin* were, of course, observed by G. Paris, when he edited that text, and on the basis of the indications which they contained he pointed out (Introduction, p. LXI) that the third member of the trilogy, which at that time was not known to exist, must have embraced not merely a *Queste,* but a *Mort Arthur* with *Tristan* contaminations. The publication of a part of the Portuguese *Demanda* by von Reinhardstoettner in the following year (1887) confirmed Paris's conjecture and he himself fully recognized this fact in his review of the work just named, *Romania*, XVI, 582ff. (1887). There followed, however, much discussion as to the original form of the trilogy and how its individual members were constituted. First, Heinzel, Grail treatise, pp. 162ff. (1892), proved that in its original form the Pseudo-Robert cycle began with an *Estoire (Grand St. Graal)*, not a *Joseph.* Moreover, he surmised — erroneously, no doubt, — that it contained the *Conte del Brait,* besides all the branches represented in the Vulgate. Next came Wechssler with his Habilitationschrift (1895) in which he regards Pseudo-Robert as made up originally of six branches, like the Vulgate (counting the prose *Merlin* and its continuation as separate). He tries to prove, however, that subsequently the cycle underwent two successive redactions in each of which it was shortened. These redactions — both cast in the form of trilogies — he calls respectively "Kürzung B" and "Kürzung C". In the first the *Lancelot,* according to his theory, was left out, in the latter the *Estoire,* also. The *Huth-Merlin,* according to Wechssler, represents the Merlin continuation of both these redactions — except that it omits the episodes at the end (preserved in MS. 112), which belonged to Redaction B — and the Portuguese *Demanda* the *Queste-Mort Arthur* (last third) of B. If the *Queste-Mort Arthur* of C was ever actually written, as Wechssler, p. 9, supposes, this division must have been condensed to half its original bulk, for, being the last third of the trilogy, it could only have had one half the length of the first two thirds (*Merlin* continuation of the Huth MS.) and that would have been only one half the length of the last third of B (the Portuguese *Demanda*). There is no extant text, however, even of a fragmentary kind, that corresponds to this description, and we are, therefore, com-

fragments of the cycle, such is assumed to be its structure. Now, in endeavoring to account for this particular form which the work eventually received in the manuscript tradition, it is to be observed, first of all, that its author plainly designed to make the new cycle shorter than the old (the Vulgate). On this account, although accepting the *Lancelot,* in a general way, as belonging to the same cycle of romances,[58] he did not actually include it in his series. Furthermore, in carrying out his plan of shortening the whole, his own predilections evidently suggested to him that he could best sacrifice the *Mort Artu.*[59] The Grail branches proper

pletely in the dark as to whether any such was ever composed.

Since the publication of Wechssler's Habilitationschrift Sommer has, in different places, argued that there was only one redaction of the Pseudo-Robert trilogy and that this was made up as follows: 1. *Estoire, Merlin,* (where the *Merlin,* however, was not the usual prose version of Robert's poem, but the modification of that version in the Spanish *Demanda,* I, described above, p. 462, note 12). 2. *Merlin*-continuation. 3. *Queste-Mort Arthur.* For Sommer's (very confused) expositions of this theory, see his "The Queste of the Holy Grail, forming the Third Part of the Trilogy indicated in the Suite du Merlin Huth-MS." *Romania,* XXXVI, 369 ff., 543 ff. (1907), "Galahad and Perceval" MPh. V, 291 ff. (1908), "Zur Kritik der altfranzösischen Artus-Romane in Prosa," *Zs. f. rom. Ph.,* XXXII, 327 ff. (1908), and, most completely, in Beiheft 47 to the last-named journal, pp. XIV ff. (1913). The grouping for 1 and 2 suggested by Sommer is improbable in itself, and has been well refuted by Vetterman, pp. 135 f. For a criticism to the same effect of Sommer's first articles on the subject see Brugger, *Zs. f. frz. Spr. u. Litt.,* XXXIV[1], 99 ff. (1909).

Wechssler's theory concerning the development of the Pseudo-Robert cycle seems nearest the truth — only the following restriction is to be observed: He bases his hypothesis that his Redaction B represented a shortening of an earlier original form (A) of the cycle on the idea that certain prose *Tristan* MSS. preserve fragments of a Pseudo-Robert *Lancelot* and that such MSS. and Malory preserve, also, some episodes of the Pseudo-Robert *Merlin* in an earlier form. But we have pointed out above that there is nothing that compels conviction in these suppositions. Nevertheless, there do seem to have been two successive abridgments of the original cycle. See, pp. 476 ff. below. These abridgments involved, however, merely condensation and omissions but substantially no rewriting of the parts.

[58] Cp. the passage from the *Huth-Merlin,* II, 57, quoted, above, p. 468, note 35.

of the cycle, viz. *Estoire* and *Queste,* of course, had to be represented in the new cycle; so these two branches were retained — only the latter was thoroughly recast. Similarly, the writer decided to retain the *Merlin* branch with its continuation, but supplanted the continuation of the Vulgate with a new version that accorded with his own taste for combats and extravagant adventures in the style of the *Lancelot.*

Next, as regards the *Mort Artu,* this branch, likewise, was essential to the cycle, yet, in its Vulgate form, it was too close to actual life to lend itself to modifications in the same fantastic sense as the *Merlin*-continuation. Consequently, when the writer rewrote this branch, in order to adapt it to the new cycle, he chose to abridge it to a greater extent than any of the other parts that were rewritten. Moreover, he treated it as if it were virtually a part of the *Queste* — a mere epilogue to it. The cycle, as thus developed, fell naturally into three divisions of approximately equal lengths: 1. *Estoire,* 2. *Merlin* + continuation, 3. *Queste* + *Mort Artu.*[60] Doubtless, not long after the completion of the cycle in its original form, however, the *Conte del Brait*[61] was composed. Now, this work was, in a large measure, a compilation from the *Merlin*-continuation of Pseudo-Robert — consequently, it occurred to some scribe, who was preparing a somewhat abbreviated transcription[62] of the cycle that, in executing his plan of abridgment, he could leave out of his copy of the above-mentioned continuation passages that had already been taken up into the *Conte del Brait* and simply refer the reader to that work for these epi-

---

[59] Besides, this text was easy to shorten; for the situation at VI, 269 (Sommer's edition of the Vulgate), was virtually the same as at the beginning of the romance: In both Agravain was instilling suspicions into the king's mind as to his wife's relations with Lancelot. Hence Pseudo-Robert omitted everything down to VI, 269.

[60] The present writer, as stated above, does not believe that the *Lancelot* ever constituted an integral part of the Pseudo-Robert cycle; hence, this conception of the original grouping of its members differs from the conceptions of Wechssler and Brugger, respectively.

[61] With regard to this work, cp. pp. 480 ff., below.

[62] Wechssler's Redaktion B.

sodes.[63] It occurred to him, also, as it would seem, that by such omissions and, no doubt, by other abbreviations here and there of less significance, he could make the three groups into which, as stated above, the cycle naturally fell, not merely approximately equal in length, but strictly so.[64] Thus, under the influence of a whim, he established an artificial symmetry between the three parts of the cycle.[65]

We have, it is true, no definite statements in the extant fragments of this first abbreviating redaction of Pseudo-Robert as to the exact constitution of the three separate divisions of which it consisted. Such statements we possess only in the case of a second shortened redaction[66] of the cycle which is represented in a fragmentary form by the Huth MS. But the lines of division between the members of the cycle there indicated[67] are indubitably

---

[63] See, especially, the statements *Huth-M.*, II, 57f.[1], 172f., 198 and in MS. 112, II, f. 49b. (Wechssler, p. 43, note). On the first of these statements cp. Wechssler, pp. 39f. and on the relations of Pseudo-Robert to the *Conte del Brait*, *ibid.* pp. 37ff. His refusal, however — implied, also, in this passage — to accept Pseudo-Robert as a derivative of the Vulgate is futile. — In the *Huth-M.* passages the writer first (pp. 57f.) appeals to Helie to write up the adventures which he himself, omits, — then (pp. 172f.) pretends that Helie is doing it. — next (p. 198) that he has done it. All this is plainly mere fiction.

[64] Cp. the passages in the Portuguese *Demanda* and MS. 343 mentioned p. 474, note 57, above.

There was doubtless, after all, the difference of a few pages between the length of the several parts.

[65] The number, three, as the number of the Christian Trinity, is, of course, a sort of obsession throughout the Grail romances. It hardly seems probable, however, that the same idea is responsible for the threefold division of Pseudo-Robert.

[66] Wechssler's Redaction C. It was based upon Redaction B.

[67] *Huth-M.*, 1, 280, with which II, 254 (last sentence) should, also, be compared.. In the first of these passages, after the statement that "mon signeur de Borron" divided the history into three equal parts, it is said: "Et la premiere partie fenist il au commenchement de ceste queste (i. e. the quest which an unknown knight, just slain by an invisible foe had pursued, and which Balaain at this point, I, 280, takes up), et la seconde el commenchement dou graal (i. e. at the beginning of the *Queste* branch), et la tierche fenist il apries la mort

different from the true original ones; for allusions in the fragments of the original cycle that have survived prove, beyond question, as has been stated, that in its unaltered form this cycle began
with an *Estoire*. For the same reason, however, that, in the first
instance, prompted the omission of the *Lancelot* from the new
series — namely, its bulk — in this second redaction (archetype
of the Huth MS.), the *Estoire* was also discarded. Moreover, the
redactor amputates, so to speak, a whole series of episodes at the
end of the *Merlin*-continuation which he found in the first abridged redaction of the cycle. Notwithstanding these omissions, he
still retained the principle of a tripartite division for the shortened
cycle, although such a division was now wholly without justification and its adoption had the awkward result of making the
first of the three parts end in the middle of the *Merlin*-continuation.[68]

From the specific statement in the Huth MS. as to the equal
lengths of the three parts and the bounds of each,[69] it is clear,
furthermore, that the prose *Joseph* which we find in that MS.
did not figure in the reckoning of the originator of this new
tripartite division, and we must attribute its addition to the series
to the scribe of the Huth MS., itself, who not unnaturally missed
an account of the early history of the Holy Grail, but, in trying
to make good this deficiency, unluckily chose a version of that
history which did not agree with the narrative of the other members
of the new cycle.[70]

---

de Lanscelot, a chelui point meisme quil devise de la mort le roi
March (i. e. at the end of the *Mort Arthur* branch).

The writer, whoever he was, goes on to say that he makes this
statement at the end of the first of the three divisions, in order to
prevent the corruption of "l'estoire dou graal" by any future "translatours".

We find, also, *ibid.*, II, 57 (quoted above), a general reference
to the fact that the work is divided into three equal parts.

[68] At p. 280 of the *Huth-Merlin*, Vol. I.

[69] Cp. p. 474, note 57, above.

[70] There is really no reason why one should not call the Huth
MS. "Redaktion D" — for, by introducing the *Joseph* into the cycle,

he, too, gives it a new form — an inconsistent one, to be sure.

The main sources of the Pseudo-Robert cycle, it should be said, in conclusion, are the Vulgate cycle and the prose *Tristan*. Minor sources, probably, are Chrétien's *Perceval* and its continuations, *Meraugis de Portlesguez*, and *Li Chevaliers as Deus Esprees.* Cp. Brugger, *Zs. f. frz. Spr. u. Litt.*, XXXVI², 190, and Vettermann, pp. 255 ff., 259 ff., 278 ff.

We have no clue to the identity of the author of the cycle. It was obviously the first redactor of the shortened cycle, not the author of this cycle in its original form, that speaks, *Huth-Merlin*, II, 57, of the author of the *Conte del Brait* as "mon signeur Helye, qui a este mes compains a armes et en joveneche et en viellece." Besides, one cannot even feel certain that this statement is not a fiction. — G. Paris, *op. cit.*, p. LXIX, dates the work from 1225 or 1230, which is, surely, too early. Being dependent on the prose *Tristan*, it was, of course, later than that work in its earlier form — i. e. later than 1230, say. On the other hand, it is itself used in the cyclic form of the prose *Tristan*. Consequently, its date lies somewhere (approximately) between the early thirties of the thirteenth century and 1250. most likely, in the second half of this period.

## Chapter VIII.

## Li Contes del Brait Merlin.

A work of the above name, as we have seen, is repeatedly referred to in the fragmentary manuscript tradition of the Pseudo-Robert cycle,[1] and its author is called *maistre*,[2] or (more properly, no doubt), *messire*,[3] *Helies (Helyes)*. It would seem to have consisted largely of the usual prose-renderings of Robert's *Merlin*, plus excerpts from the Pseudo-Robert *Merlin*-continuation in its original form[4] — namely, those portions that related specifically to Merlin and to Baudemagus (the oldest of Arthur's knights). The work takes its title from the shriek which Merlin uttered (it was his last) when he discovered that by the deception of Vivien he was imprisoned forever in his tomb.[5] This cry was so loud and so horrible that it was heard through the length and breadth of Logres and gave rise to many marvels. Although no fragments, even, of this romance are known to exist in the original French,

---

[1] Cp. *Huth-Merlin*, II, 57f., 172f., 198 and Wechssler, pp. 42f., notes, (from MS. 112) and p. 60 (from MS. 343). So, too, in the Portuguese and Spanish *Demandas*, fol. 179 and ch. 355 (*Queste* section), respectively, (quoted by Sommer, *Romania*, XXXVI, 570). For its relation to Pseudo-Robert, cp. p. 476. In references to the work, *Brait* is often misspelt *Bret*. Through some error, the prose *Tristan* is called "li livres dou *Bret*." Cp. Löseth, p. 405.

[2] *Huth-Merlin*, II, 198.

[3] MS. 112. Cp. Wechssler p. 51. *Maistre* would imply that the author was a professional scholar, *messir* that he was a knight. G. Paris, *Huth-Merlin*, I, pp. XXXIf., has offered various suggestions as to the identity of Helie, but none of them are certain.

Cp. G. Paris, *Huth-M.*, pp. LXXIIff. The best discussion of the subject is Wechssler's, pp. 37ff. See, too, a good summary, Vettermann, p. 97.

[5] *Huth-Merlin*, II, 198, and I, p. LXXXV (from the Spanish *Baladro*).

the major part of it has been, doubtless, preserved in a Spanish
version entitled *El Baladro del Sabio Merlin,*[6] and an examination
of such information concerning the contents of the Spanish work
as is now available seems to show that the author of the *Conte del
Brait,* although he compiled his romance, in the main, from the
sources mentioned above, in the case of the Pseudo-Robert *Merlin*-
continuation did not confine himself merely to reproducing the
text of his original—rather he redacted, apparently, the excerpts
which he made from that continuation and added inventions of

---

[6] Printed at Burgos in 1498. It was composed, probably, early
in the fifteenth century. A copy in the possession of the Marquis of
Pidal at Madrid — cp. G. Paris, *Huth-M.,* p. LXXII, — is the only one
extant, as far as is known. G. Paris, *op. cit.,* pp. LXXXI ff. has printed
a few extracts from it — also, the chapter headings. Our knowledge
of its contents is still limited to these meagre materials, since the book
has never been reprinted. Portions of the *Conte del Brait* appear
also to have been preserved in the Spanish *Demanda* I. For a list
of the specific passages, involved cp. Vettermann, pp. 124 f. In the *Zs.
f. frz. Spr. u. Litt.,* XXIX [1], pp. 121 ff., Brugger has discussed the
fragmentary Spanish forms of the *Conte del Brait.*

G. Paris, *op. cit.,* I, pp. LXXII ff., did not regard the Spanish
*Baladro* as a translation of the *Conte del Brait,* but as a compilation
from the Pseudo-Robert *Merlin*-continuation and the *Conte Del Brait*
combined to which the name of the latter was given. Apart from the
arguments for a contrary view which Wechssler, pp. 37 ff., has advanced, it is to be observed that there is every reason to believe that
the *Conte del Brait* was subsequent to the *Merlin*-continuation, just
mentioned, in its original form, and dependent on it. One can understand why the redactor of the new cycle, who was giving such a form
to his *Merlin*-continuation as to bring it into close conformity with
the spirit of the *Lancelot,* should take over the character of Baudemagus from the latter into his own work and associate him closely
with Merlin, but in the case of an independent romance, such as Paris
supposes the *Conte del Brait* to have been, no such reason would
have existed. Baudemagus played such a large rôle in the lost French
romance that in the Pseudo-Robert *Merlin* — continuation of MS. 112
(Cp. Wechssler, p. 43, note) the redactor declares that a certain incident is omitted from his own work and told in the *Conte del Brait*
"por ce quelle appartient a la vie Baudemagus." This accords entirely
with what we know of the Spanish *Baladro.*

his own, as in the case of the wonders that attended Merlin's last cry of despair. Until the Spanish *Baladro,* however, has been published, it is impossible to characterize more fully, even at second hand, the *Conte del Brait.* In the meanwhile, there is no reason to believe that this romance differed materially either in the nature of its contents or in literary quality from the Pseudo-Robert cycle.[7]

---

[7] In referring the reader to the *Conte del Brait* for matters which he himself omits, the redactor of the shortened form of the cycle represented by the *Huth-Merlin* speaks *ibid.,* II, 58, of that work as "une petite branke qui apartient a mon livre" and declares that he only omits it (i. e. from his redaction of Pseudo-Robert), because it would make his "livre" too large. Similarly, *op. cit.* II, 172f. It is obvious, however, that the *Conte del Brait* was, in reality, composed as a separate work.

# Chapter IX.

## The Prose Tristan.

Superior even to the prose *Lancelot* in popularity, in the Middle Ages, if we may judge by the number of MSS. in which it has been preserved, was the prose *Tristan*[1] — a romance of

---

[1] The prose *Tristan* has not been reprinted since the sixteenth century. MSS. of the romance are very numerous, the earliest dated one (and probably as early as any), viz., 750, Bibl. Nat., bearing the date, 1278. In the Bibliothèque Nationale alone there are twenty-four that contain the whole romance or parts of it; in the British Museum, six. For the enumeration and description of all prose *Tristan* MSS. — and of the early prints of the romance, also, — cp. E. Löseth's *Le roman en prose de Tristan, le roman de Palamède, et la compilation de Rusticien de Pise: analyse critique d'après les manuscrits de Paris*, pp. IIIff., Paris, 1890 (no. 82 in the Bibliothèque de l'École des Hautes Etudes: Section dés Sciences historiques et philologiques), and his *Le Tristan et le Palamède des manuscrits français du British Museum*, Christiania 1905 (Videnskabs-Selskabets Skrifter. II, Hist.-Filos. Klasse, 1905, No. 4). In my discussion of the romance I shall refer to the first of these publications — which is the leading authority on everything pertaining to the prose *Tristan* — simply as "Löseth".

Following are the early prints of the romance: 2 vols. Rouen (Jehan le Bourgoys) 1489; 2 vols. Paris (A. Verard) in two undated editions, which probably belong to 1496 and 1603, respectively; 2 vols. Paris (Michel Le Noir) 1514 and 1520; Paris (Denis Janot), undated, but probably 1533. There were, moreover, three (Paris) editions of Jean Maugin's modernisation of the romance, entitled *Le Premier Livre du Nouveau Tristan*. They are dated, respectively, 1554, 1567, 1586, and the successive publishers were veuve Maurice de la Porte, Gabriel Buon and Nicolas Bonfons. On these early prints, besides Löseth's preface, cp. Ernst Schürhoff: *Über den Tristan-Roman des Jean Maugin*, Halle diss. 1909.

For Danish, Russian, Italian, German and Spanish translations and derivatives of the prose *Tristan*, cp. Löseth, pp. IVf. and Golther's

similar design as the former and of equal prolixity. We have seen that the Lancelot-Guinevere romance was, in origin, merely a re-adaptation by Chrétien of the legend of Tristan and Iseult, to which he himself had already devoted a poem. In their prose forms, however, the relations of the romances of these famous couples, respectively, are exactly reversed, for the prose *Tristan* in plainly modelled after the prose *Lancelot*.[2] This means that the old Celtic story of lawless and irresistible passion, with all the primitive elements, both of poetry and of barbarism, which had continued to cling to it even in the hands of the French metri-

*Tristan und Isolde,* pp. 127ff., 133ff. For the Spanish derivatives see, especially, Part IV, below. The prose *Tristan* constitutes the main basis of the (prose) *La Tavola Ritonda o L'Istoria di Tristano,* edited by F. L. Polidori, 2 vols. (Bologna, 1864—1865), which belongs probably to the end of the thirteenth century.

The German "volksbuch", *Die Histori von herren Tristan und der schoenen Isalden von Irlande,* Augsburg (Anton Sorg), 1484, has been edited latterly (Jena, 1912) by R. Benz. He has taken into consideration, also, the later fifteenth century issues of this book. There are no MSS. or early prints of the prose *Tristan* on this side of the ocean, so that the present writer, although he has read through the 1520 print, uses for reference Löseth's admirable analysis of the romance. The only portions of it that are generally accessible in the original text are those which Bédier has printed in his edition of Thomas's *Tristan,* II, 321—395. A brief, but good, analysis of the romance — with especial reference to those elements of the narrative that connect it with the earlier metrical versions is given by W. Golther, *Tristan und Isolde,* pp. 114—126 (Leipzig, 1907). Cp., too, Dunlop-Wilson, *History of Fiction,* I, 196ff.

[2] Brugger's assertion, *Zs. f. frz. Spr. u. Litt.,* XXIX[1], 135, that the prose *Tristan* and the Vulgate cycle (or his hypothetical earlier redactions of the latter) were originally independent of each other is erroneous. Even in its simpler form the *Tristan* shows the influence of the latter — especially, the *Lancelot* branch — throughout. Gröber, *Grundriss,* Band II, Abt. I, p. 1007, fully recognizes this. Cp., too, the second of Löseth's publications cited in the previous note, pp. 34ff. Lancelot's prominence in the *Tristan* is, of course, entirely due to the prose *Lancelot,* and the former has, also, borrowed from the latter many of its subordinate characters.

cal romancers, was now to be diluted with innumerable episodes that reflected the occupations, tastes, and ideals of French lords and ladies in the first half of the thirteenth century — endless descriptions of jousts and tournaments, knight-errant adventures, love-affairs conducted in the fashion of a highly organized society, with letters and poems *(lais)* addressed by the lover to his mistress [3] — and so on.

As with the prose *Lancelot,* so with the prose *Tristan* — the romance in its original form has not come down to modern times.[4] The extant MSS. often differ greatly from each other, but two versions, especially, of the original are distinguishable among them: [5] 1. an earlier and better version, which is relatively short and simple, 2. a longer and later one, which is sometimes called "the common version", since it exists in much the largest number of MSS., and sometimes "the cyclic version", since the MSS. of this version regularly connect the romance with the Vulgate by a reference to the *Mort Artu* or even (in some MSS.) by the incorporation of that romance[6] and, still further, by the incorporation of the greater part of the *Queste* branch, in a mixture of its Vulgate and Pseudo-Robert forms.[7] The first of these ver-

---

[3] Such letters and poems are wanting in the *Lancelot.*

[4] Cp. Löseth, p. XXIV.

[5] *Op. cit.,* pp. XIIff. Löseth here describes the *Tristan* of the extant MSS. as consisting merely of "des fragments juxtaposés de rédactions differentes." These MSS. make no division within the romance, itself, but, for convenience' sake, scholars have been accustomed to divide it into two parts. In the better version, according to Löseth, Part I ends with Daras's liberation of his prisoners, Tristan, Palamede and Dinadan (§ 183), in the common version with the Cornishmen's defeat of the Saxons (§ 279). Cp. *op. cit.,* p. V, note 1.

[6] Cp. Section XVI of Löseth's preface. The reference to the *Mort Artu* occurs pp. 110f. The romancer there remarks that Mordred will be the cause of Arthur's death, "comme nous deviserons vers la fin de nostre livre."

[7] Cp. Löseth's preface, p. XII, note 1, and p. XVI — also, sections 383 a — 394 a and 398 a of his analysis. Influenced, most likely, by G. Paris, who regarded the Pseudo-Robert *Queste* as earlier than the Vulgate, Löseth, p. XVI, observes that the former was, no doubt, the first to be intercalated in the *Tristan* MSS. But Paris's

sions is attributed to a *missire* Luce, knight and lord of the castle of Gaut[8] (Gant, Gat, Gast, etc.) near Salisbury, the second to a *missire* Helie (Helyes, Helys, etc.) de Boron (Berron, etc.), who claims to be a friend and relative of Robert de Boron.[9] In both versions we have the usual fraudulent declaration that the romance is translated from a Latin original.

Besides, Luce, in a prologue, apologizes, as a native of England, for the quality of his French, whilst Helie pretends to be

view is certainly erroneous — so the reverse of Löseth's remark is probably true. Cp., still further, on this subject Wechssler's Habilitationsschrift, pp. 16 ff., 60 ff.

According to Löseth, p. XII, only Part II of the earlier version is preserved in our MSS.

[8] In all modern discussions of the prose *Tristan*, this name appears as „Luce(s) de Gast" — presumably, because Count Tressan's (eighteenth century) analysis first gave this form of the name currency. But, to judge by Löseth's two publications, mentioned above, and by the description of the *Tristan* MSS. in the British Museum in Ward's *Catalogue*, I, 356 ff., the form, *Gast*, does not occur a single time in all the MSS. of the Bibliothèque Nationale and British Museum. Under these circumstances, I do not believe that we are justified in clinging to the traditional form of the name just mentioned. Of the great variety of forms *(Gant, Cant, Gail, Cal*, etc.) in which the name is found in our MSS., *Gaut* seems most likely to have been the original form. Except *Gant* (doubtless, a corruption of *Gaut*), it occurs oftener than any other, and from it and its equivalent, *Galt* — both of which are common in Old French, as representatives of Germanic *wald* = *wood* — the other variant forms are easily explained. I have, consequently, adopted it in the text above.

For the ascription of the *Tristan*, in its original form, to this Luce, cp. the passages listed in Löseth's Index under *Luce de Gast* — also, Ward's *Catalogue*, I, 357 f., 363, 365 .

[9] For this claim and the other details concerning the pretended Helie de Boron (Borron) which I am here giving, see the Epilogue to the prose *Tristan* in Löseth, pp. 402 ff. Cp. *ibid.* p. 402, note 4, for earlier modern works in which this epilogue had been printed. This epilogue is plainly connected with the prologue to *Palamedes* and doubtless, derived from it. One can easily study the two together in Hucher, *Le Saint Graal*, I, where they are printed, respectively, pp. 35 ff. (note), and pp 156 ff. Cp. too, G. Paris, *Huth-Merlin*, I, pp. XXXIII ff.

a member of the distinguished family of Barres in Northern France [10] — "lords of Outres in Romenie, which is now called France". The latter asserts, moreover, that his king (of what country he does not specify),[11] being much pleased with his present work (the *Tristan*), had commanded him to write another book "which would contain all the matter that was wanting in this book." This task, he avers, he will take up "as soon as the great cold of the present winter is past and we are in the sweet season called spring", when he will have become rested from his five years' arduous labors on the *Tristan*. The new book, too, is to be translated from the Latin, but the author intends also to draw upon Master Walter Map's *Lancelot*, the great books of Robert de Boron (doubtless, the Pseudo-Robert cycle) and the book of Luce de Gaut (i. e. the prose *Tristan* in its earlier form). The name of this second author, or, rather redactor — Helie de Boron — is certainly fictitious,[12] and the same thing is doubtless true of "Luce de (du) Gaut (Gast, etc.)" — the pretended name of the author of the first version. We know, therefore, nothing with regard to the real author of either version of the romance; with regard to its date, however, we can hardly go wrong in accepting the decade, 1226—1235, as the period in which it —

---

[10] On this family see Hucher, *Le Saint Graal*, I, 37 ff. This author's attempt to connect himself with it, like all other evidence, tends to prove that he was a Frenchman.

[11] Some MSS. (*cp.* Löseth, p. 405) call the king, Henry (one even Henry d'Engleterre), but this is very likely imitated from the Vulgate cycle (end of the *Queste* or beginning of the *Mort Artu*).

[12] G. Paris, *Huth-Merlin*, I, pp. XXXIIIff., had given good reasons for believing that the attribution of the second version of the *Tristan* to this pretended Helie de Boron was imitated from the prologue to *Palamedes (Guiron le Courtois)*, which was anterior to this version, although posterior to the first. The name, in the first instance, no doubt, was attached to the *Conte del Brait (Bret)*. Cp. p. 480, note 1, above. Pseudo-Helie confounded this last-named work, it seems, with the earlier version of the *Tristan,* and hence refers to the latter wrongly as "li Bret" or „le livre du Bret". Cp. Löseth, p. 1 and p. 405, respectively.

in its original form — was composed.[13]

The great innovation which the author of the prose *Tristan* introduces into the tradition of his hero is that he completes the Arthurization of the latter's story and makes him, in the course of the romance, a knight of the Round Table,[14] like Gawain, Lancelot, and the rest. In the hands of this new author, Tristan retains from the earlier tradition his especial skill in music and song and his old astuteness in evading detection in his secret intrigue with Iseult, but, otherwise, he is hardly distinguished either

---

[13] The earliest dated MS. of the romance (MS. 750, Bibl. Nat.) bears the date, 1278, as we have stated, and since that MS. (MS. 750, Bibl. Nat.) happens to belong to the second version, we know that even this later version was in existence by the aforesaid date. As regards the original romance, we know that it was composed before 1240, for *Palamedes*, which is dependent on it, was in existence by that year. See chapter XI. The *Tristan*, itself, then, could hardly have been composed later than 1235. On the other hand, the Vulgate *Merlin*-continuation appears to be one of its sources.

An interesting early borrowing from our romance will be found in Brunetto Latini's *Tresor*, p. 488 (Chabaille's edition, 1863) — composed between, 1260 and 1269. The author here adopts a description of Iseult in the prose *Tristan* as a model of style.

The only evidence in regard to the *terminus a quo* of our romance is that which is supplied by the fact of its dependence on the Vulgate cycle. Except for its *Merlin*-continuation, as we have seen (p. 453), the Vulgate was completed, in all likelihood, early in the second decade of the thirteenth century. Hence the *Tristan*, in its original form, must have been subsequent, say, to 1215. Indeed, if the character of Pellinor in the *Tristan* is taken from the *Merlin*-continuation of the Vulgate, as seems certain (cp. Bruce, MPh., XVI, 337 ff.), we should have to advance the composition of the former to 1230 or somewhat later, for the continuation in question, as said above, can hardly be earlier than 1225.

On the basis of its falling between the *Lancelot* and *Palamedes*, Löseth, p. XXIV, dates our romance between 1215 and 1230. Bédier, similarly, in his edition of Thomas's *Tristan*, II, 309, dates it about 1230. I should, myself, be inclined to date it in the early thirties of the thirteenth century.

[14] Löseth, p. 149. He had already, however, been associated with Arthur's knights in various ways.

in character or accomplishments from his companion-in-arms, Lancelot. Like the latter, he spends his time largely in going from tournament to tournament — whether in Cornwall or Logres  — and, in all the situations of life, he displays the usual knightly qualities of courtesy and generosity, to say nothing of valor. Similarly, he excels in fencing and chess-playing and in the other accomplishments that were prized most highly in aristocratic circles of the thirteenth century. In one respect, doubtless, he resembles the actual members of those circles more closely than was the case with Lancelot: as a lover, his fidelity was not above reproach.[15] Finally, like the other knights who were preeminent at Arthur's court, he is made a participant in the Grail quest,[16] although his disqualifications for success in an enterprise to achieve which chastity was an indispensable condition, were even more obvious than Lancelot's.

The prose *Tristan* follows the tradition of the primitive (lost) metrical romance[17] concerning its hero, and it derives from this tradition, of course, the primary conception of the adulterous passion of Tristan and Iseult, including even the parts that are played by the minor characters in the drama, Bringvain and Andret (Audret); but the individual episodes which our author inherited from his source are so lost in the flood of new and, for the most part, inferior inventions, that they hardly constitute any longer the most prominent element in the story. They occur naturally in those portions of the romance in which Cornwall is the scene

---

[15] Cp., especially, his intrigue with Segurade's wife, Löseth, p. 25. In the romance Iseult, too, has other lovers, besides Tristan, viz. Palamedes and Kahedin, but she grants her favors only to Tristan.

[16] Löseth, pp. 283 ff.

[17] Cp. Brédier's statement in his edition of Thomas's *Tristan*, II, 309. He takes the primitive romance as the immediate source of the prose. It was formerly customary to assume that the prose *Tristan* was based on Chrétien's lost *Tristan* poem. Cp. G. Paris, *Manuel*, p. 101, Löseth, p. XXV, and G. Gröber, *Grundriss*, Band II, Abt. I, p. 1007. At a later period, however, Paris, as we have seen (p. 155, note 5, above), denied that Chrétien ever wrote a *Tristan* romance in any proper sense. On this question see *loc. cit.* above and Foerster's Chrétien *Wörterbuch*, Introduction, pp. 47 ff.

of action, and they cover more especially the period of the hero's youth up to the point where the narrative of the lovers is linked up with that of Lancelot and Guinevere.[18] At this point these episodes are dropped and only resumed, when Tristan returns from Logres to Marc's court for a while [19] and again runs the gauntlet of detection in his continued *amours* with the queen. After this the influence of the source ceases, for in the prose romance even the death of the hero is differently managed, Tristan being here the victim of Marc's treachery, who, in a fit of jealousy, thrusts a poisoned spear through his nephew, as the latter was singing a lay to Iseult in her apartment.[20] The character of Marc, we may observe, is blackened throughout the prose romance. Here he is false and treacherous, a tyrant and a coward. The author's object, of course, in this degradation of the wronged husband was to lessen the opprobrium of his hero's adultery, but the tragic situation was, surely, much finer in the old story, where even the nephew committing the wrong could not dispute the essentially noble and generous character of the king and could plead no excuse for dishonoring him, save the force of a passion which was as irresistible as Fate.

It was not only, however, with respect to the character of Marc that our author exercises the usual privilege of the romancers in altering or modifying his originals. Thus the birth of the hero, as well as his death, is differently related in the prose romance,[21] as compared with the *Tristan* poems. In the former, the hero's father, Meliadus, King of Leonois, is held captive by a fairy mistress in her tower, in the midst of a forest, and, through his captor's magical powers, loses all memory of his wife. This wife, however, who is pregnant, goes in search of him in this same forest, and, having learned there from Merlin,[22] who is disguised as a forester, that she will never see her husband again,

---

[18] Löseth, p. 46.          [19] *Ibid.*, pp. 172 ff.          [20] Pp. 383 ff.

[21] Pp. 16 f.

[22] Merlin here plays somewhat the same part towards the child, Tristan, that he does towards young Arthur in Robert de Boron's *Merlin*. Our author is, of course, imitating Robert.

she gives birth to a son in the forest and dies, after having conferred the name of *Tristan* on the child, because of the sorrowful
circumstances under which he was born. Two kinsmen of Meliadus,
who now arrive on the scene, are about to kill the infant, in order
that they, themselves, may get possession of the kingdom, but
a damsel of the dead queen persuades them to renounce the pro-
ject on the condition that she will hide the child so effectively
that he will never be heard of again. Merlin, however, is the
means of saving the child from this fate and of the liberation of
Meliadus. Moreover, it is on his advice that Tristan is committed
to the tutelage of Gouvernal.

Space fails us to note the romancer's numerous alterations
of his source — some of them even more audacious than the one
which I have just cited. We can only remark that he is especially
fond of changing the traditional order of incidents and of giving
the old *motifs* new connections in the story. For example, the
incident of the evening rendezvous at which Tristan and Iseult,
having detected Marc in the tree above them, give their conversation such a turn as to deceive him, is postponed to a later point
in the narrative,[23] and the *motif* of the tell-tale blood-stains from
Tristan's wound on the bed-clothing of his mistress is no longer
connected with Iseult of Cornwall, but with the wife of Segurade.[24]
Moreover, the rationalizing tendency is even stronger in this romance than in the *Lancelot*. Consequently, the fairy-tale voyages
of the hero in the poetical tradition are stripped of their marvellous
quality and even the philtre becomes virtually superfluous in the
development of the lovers' passion.[25]

Among the noteworthy additions to the story are to be num-
bered many new episodes and many new characters. The latter
are drawn mainly from the Vulgate cycle — especially, the *Lancelot*
and the *Queste* — e. g. Lancelot, Hector, Perceval, Galahad —
who here, however, is thoroughly secularized and does not differ
in any essential from the other knights — Sagremor, etc. Nevertheless, two of the new characters, who fill rôles of considerable
importance in the romance — viz. Lamorat, Perceval's brother,

---

[23] Pp. 186 ff.      [24] P. 25.      [25] Pp. 29 f.

and Palamedes — were invented by its author. The second of these characters sprang, doubtless, in the first instance from that of the lying seneschal in the old poem, who endeavored to deprive Tristan of his credit for the slaying of the dragon near Dublin, but our author, though still representing him as a lover of Iseult's, has converted him into a model of generosity and courtesy, even towards his successful rival (Tristan), so that he is one of the most sympathetic figures in the romance. The creation of Lamorat was, doubtless, due to the writer's desire to interweave his hero's story more closely with that of Perceval.

In the way of incident the most original additions are the series of episodes at the beginning of the romance that make up the history of Tristan's ancestors. Like Lancelot, Tristan here is represented as of the lineage of King David and Joseph of Arimathea.[26] Especially striking in this preliminary narrative is the story of the hero's grandmother, Chelinde, with its strange medley of *motifs*, drawn from widely separated sources[27] — *Athis and Prophilias* (the mediaeval romance of ideal friendship), the legend of Oedipus (the great tragic tale of incest), some fairy-tale of a giant who proposes riddles to his captives with life as the stake, the oriental *conte* of the much-married princess. It is the last-named element, in particular, that constitutes the backbone of Chelinde's weirdly scandalous history, and we have here in its earliest preserved form the tale which Boccaccio[28] has im-

---

[26] On the subject of Lancelot's ancestry see Bruce, RR, IX, 250 ff. The name of Tristan's grandfather, Sadoc, — here represented as a great-nephew of Joseph of Arimathea's — is, as I have pointed out, *Historia Meriadoci and De Ortu Waluuanii*, p. XXIIf., note 1 (Göttingen and Baltimore, 1913), taken from the genealogy of Christ, *St. Matthew*, I, 14. The author confounds Joseph, husband of the Virgin Mary, with Joseph of Arimathea, as happens elsewhere, also, in the romances.

[27] For an analysis of the story of Chelinde and a discussion of its sources cp., especially, Bruce, "A Boccaccio Analogue in the Old French Prose Tristan," RR, I, 384 ff. (1910).

[28] *Decameron*, II, 7. The heroine is here named Alatiel. The *Tristan* and Boccaccio, as I have shown in the article just cited, go back to a common source of oriental origin.

mortalized by his inimitable vivacity and cynical humor, concerning the daughter of the Sultan of Babylon who is betrothed to a pagan monarch, but on the voyage to his country, where the wedding is to be celebrated, through a series of misadventures, falls successively into the possession of a number of different men, with each of whom she is compelled to cohabit. According to the *Tristan*, she never reaches her original destination, but in Bocaccio she finally turns up there, after having passed through the hands of nine lovers, one after the other, and is able to satisfy her credulous husband with respect to the delay in her arrival by the assertion that she had been spending the time in a nunnery.

Genuine mediaeval traits of these Chelinde episodes are the following, viz. that some of the heroine's lovers get their names from the Latin Bible [29] and that St. Augustine, the missionary, here takes the place of Tiresias in the Oedipus legend as the prophet who discloses the terrible truth with regard to the incestuous union of the mother (Chelinde) and her son (Apollo).[30]

It is not always easy to establish what portions of the *Tristan*, as it is preserved in our MSS., belonged to the romance in its original form. There is no question, however, that from the beginning its author aimed at enhancing the appeal of his work by interweaving the fortunes of his hero and heroine with those of the specifically Arthurian characters from whom they had hitherto stood apart. The first connection of this nature which he creates is the one with Lancelot and Guinevere, when Iseult of Cornwall, at the time of her lover's marriage to Iseult of Brittany, wrote in despair to Guinevere, asking her advice (p. 46), and received a consolatory answer. Naturally, Lancelot, the ideal exemplar of the *amour courtois*, disapproved of this act of infidelity on the

---

[29] Sadoc, as we have just seen, from *St. Matthew*, I, 14; his brother, Nabusardan (Nabuzardan) from IV *Liber Regum*, XXV, 8, 11, 20 (Nebuchadnezzar's captain of the guard) and elsewhere in the Old Testament. Cp. Bruce, MLN, XXXIII, 136 (1918). *Gonosor*, name of the king of Ireland in the story (Löseth, p. 13), is, probably, also, a mere corruption of *Nabugodonosor*, the name of Nebuchadnezzar in the Latin Bible.

[30] Löseth, pp. 11f.

part of Tristan, and his censure on the subject was reported to the latter. They are on opposite sides in the tournament at the Chateau des Pucelles (p. 107), but they do not come into conflict with one another until their subsequent combat at the Perron Merlin (p. 147). On this latter occasion, however, each inspires his adversary with such an admiration for his valor that they cease fighting and begin a contest in courtesy with one another which leads to the cementing of a firm friendship between them. Lancelot, accordingly, introduces Tristan at Arthur's court (p. 148), and later, when Tristan and Iseult have fled from Cornwall together, he puts Joyous Gard at their disposal as a refuge (p. 258). Strange to say, however, the two queens do not meet in the romance.[31]

In a similar spirit, the author of our romance draws Perceval into the story of Tristan, by making the former duplicate Lancelot's feat[32] of freeing the latter from captivity (p. 245). All three, of course, are, subsequently, participants in the Grail quest, through which, still further, as we have seen, Tristan is brought into relations with Galahad.

Like the *Lancelot*, on which it is modelled, the *Tristan* has no plot such as we require in a modern work of fiction. Its form is simply that of a rambling biographical romance of the type which Chrétien had made popular — expanded, however, to an enormous extent, as we have seen, after the fashion of the prose romances. On the other hand, the style of the *Tristan* has been highly commended by the best judges both of the Middle Ages[33] and of Modern Times,[34] and, in this respect, it stands, doubtless, in the front rank of the mediaeval prose romances.[35]

---

[31] P. 260, Guinevere expresses a desire to visit her at Joyous Gard, but that is all.

[32] P. 217.

[33] Cp. the passage from Brunetto Latini's *Tresor*, cited, p. 488, note 13, above.

[34] Cp. G. Paris, *Manuel*, p. 111. It was this quality, doubtless, that rendered the romance such a favorite with Ariosto, if we may judge by the frequent use of it which he made in the *Orlando Furioso*.

[35] The main sources of the prose *Tristan*, as we have seen, are